GORDON COLLEGE
Graduate Division
of Education

SUPERVISION
HUMAN PERSPECTIVES

SUPERVISION

HUMAN PERSPECTIVES

FOURTH EDITION

Thomas J. Sergiovanni
Trinity University

Robert J. Starratt
Fordham University

McGRAW-HILL BOOK COMPANY

New York   St. Louis   San Francisco   Auckland   Bogotá   Caracas
Colorado Springs   Hamburg   Lisbon   London   Madrid   Mexico
Milan   Montreal   New Delhi   Oklahoma City   Panama   Paris
San Juan   São Paulo   Singapore   Sydney   Tokyo   Toronto

This book was set in Times Roman by the College Composition Unit
in cooperation with Bi-Comp, Inc.
The editors were Phillip A. Butcher and John M. Morriss;
the cover was designed by Rafael Hernandez;
the production supervisor was Leroy A. Young.
Project supervision was done by The Total Book.
R. R. Donnelley & Sons Company was printer and binder.

SUPERVISION
Human Perspectives

1 2 3 4 5 6 7 8 9 0   DOCDOC   8 9 3 2 1 0 9 8

ISBN   0-07-056313-6

Library of Congress Cataloging-in-Publication Data

Sergiovanni, Thomas J.
    Supervision: human perspectives.

    1. School supervision.   2. School management and
organization.   I. Starratt, Robert J.   II. Title.
LB2806.4.S47   1988   371.2'013   87-26045
ISBN 0-07-056313-6

ABOUT THE AUTHORS

THOMAS J. SERGIOVANNI is presently Lillian Radford Professor of Education at Trinity University. He received his Ed.D. from the University of Rochester, in joint study in educational administration and business administration. An active teacher, writer, and editor, he brings to the text his extensive experience teaching and writing about educational and business administration. He has published numerous articles in professional journals, prepared abundant papers for professional associations, and many books.

ROBERT J. STARRATT, Professor of Educational Administration, Graduate School of Education at Fordham University, is also an accomplished author and educator. He received his Ed.D. from the University of Illinois, specializing in administration and curriculum theory. Like Dr. Sergiovanni, Dr. Starratt has published extensively, including papers for professional associations, articles in major educational journals, as well as numerous presentations. He is actively involved in research involving leadership theory and the process of change.

CONTENTS

5 Faculty and School Culture 102

6 Teacher Motivation and Supervisory Effectiveness 128

FOREWORD

When a textbook is issued in a fourth edition, several related signals are being sent to the profession, and especially to those being newly introduced to the content the textbook covers. One signal is that the authors have established a solid reputation through their previous published work, which has enjoyed at least reasonable success as reflected in sales, adoptions, reviews, and reader response. Another is that the field is so dynamic that revision and updating of the prior editions seems to be needed. Implicit in these messages is that the authors have a special and respected perspective within that field, as well as a clear and inclusive view of the scholarship and research that continually provides new information and insights to be taken into account. Readers therefore can safely assume that ownership of the latest version of a leading work will be an excellent investment.

Having written forewords for the previous editions, I have a long and deep perspective to guide me in commentary on the present volume. Furthermore, I have had the privilege of associating with both authors, especially Sergiovanni, over several decades. Although the field of supervision has been transformed from a minor to a major branch of educational thought and activity in less than ten years, it remains one whose adherents and leaders are relatively few in number. Only twenty or so textbooks compete for the market in graduate courses, and fewer than one hundred professors (and other specialists) contribute regularly to books, articles, and other publications devoted primarily to the theory and practice of instructional supervision. Almost certainly those numbers will soon increase as the field prospers, but in the 1980s it has been possible for supervision specialists to interact with each other and to collaborate in ways that have profited not only themselves but the work that we define as "supervision."

Within the community of such specialists, none enjoys more professional respect than Sergiovanni, and the Sergiovanni-Starratt conceptualization of supervision is widely accepted as a towering contribution. Those of us who have used the textbooks with our graduate classes find that students, although sometimes awed (even overwhelmed) by the depth and breadth of the material, invariably conclude by the end of the term that they have been thoroughly informed, intellectually challenged, and professionally enriched by the text material. I think it worth noting additionally that some students, while preparing for comprehensive master's or doctoral examinations in educational leadership, have found the Sergiovanni-Starratt volume to be a treasure chest of scholarly reference material. The next generation of such students, I am happy now to report, will find the fourth edition to be even more helpful.

The human resource-development theme, articulated more thoroughly in each successive edition, may well be the most significant emphasis that can be given to material about supervision. The resounding message contained in all of the "best-seller" books about corporate management and leadership (to cite just a few: Naisbitt, Peters and Waterman, Ouchi, Iacocca, Drucker, Kanter, Geneen and Toffler) is that people in organizations can perform miracles when empowered to use their full resources on tasks they have helped to define. Few if any of the "hot" ideas in these popular volumes are really new to educational leaders, but greater public awareness and acceptance of them has helped to create a climate more favorable to staff development in school systems, of which supervision is a major component. It therefore seems probable that leaders will find it possible to implement many of the concepts and strategies to which this edition introduces them—more so than many have been the case in 1971, 1979, or 1983 when the previous editions appeared.

The book embraces nineteen chapters divided into four parts: Human Resources Supervision (Chapters 1 through 6), Human Resources Supervision and Leadership (7 through 9), Human Resources and Educational Leadership (10–13) and A Human Resources Approach to Staff Development, Clinical Supervision, and Teacher Evaluation (14–19). There is good balance in the four sections. My advice to the reader would be to turn first to the introductory material that precedes chapters 1, 7, 10, and 14, in order to get a sense of how the chapters are intended to fit together as a whole. Pursuing further the strategy of overview, it might be useful to consult the "summary" pages of the first eighteen chapters, in order to see how the authors have placed and arranged the intellectual building blocks for their argument that supervision is an exciting lifelong vocation of extraordinary importance not only to teachers and schools, but to society itself.

From their Preface we learn that the authors acknowledge a steady progression over some sixteen years in their awareness of, and advocacy for, a human resources perspective. They note, in my view too modestly, that while still drawing upon a rapidly maturing literature they have this time introduced more of their own theories and speculations. In particular, they have expanded upon the meaning of leadership within the field of education; they have introduced provocative analogies; they have challenged educators to stop being embarrassed when talking about and acting upon values; and they have given new dimension to questions of defining and measuring teacher effectiveness. The authors have also talked more than before about the school *culture,* and how to help develop a healthy, productive culture.

Especially in Chapter 5, they introduce the intriguing notion that school cultures can probably be "domesticated," i.e., committed to quality teaching and learning rather than seeking to protect existing norms and domains. In a very impressive Chapter 9, dealing with supervision as moral action, the authors examine the underside of supervision and propose a "politics of the possible" as supervisors do what they can to transform people and communities in pursuit of the end values of justice, freedom, and community. This is an uplifting chapter that raises questions not often examined at a public level.

It would be my guess that if a fifth edition should ever be ventured, the authors will pursue even further such important questions as moral leadership, empowering teachers, nurturance of school culture, and facilitating work groups. Meanwhile, the thoughts presented here on these topics are fresh as well as useful.

Experienced administrators and supervisors whose course work in supervision predates 1983 or thereabouts would find in this volume a great deal of reinforcement for the good practices they employ, as well as a great many thoughts and suggestions that could inspire them to a surer and more efficacious approach to their daily work with teachers. All of us who are veteran supervisors have much to learn from this book. Further, we will envy those whose supervisory careers are only now on the launchpad, and who (guided by this excellent volume) can approach that privileged role with a far better sense than we could have had, of what good supervision can be.

Robert H. Anderson
University of South Florida, Tampa

PREFACE

Completing a book used to have a certain finality to it. One could place it in a prominent part of one's book collection and get on with other projects. If an author wished to change a position he held in that book in a subsequent publication, that would be an easy matter of a footnote reference. This book, however, has refused to be finished. We used to say that the third edition of the book was the book we should have written the first time. Yet in the space of five short years, enough has changed so that we felt obliged to engage in yet another major overhaul of the work.

Anyone familiar with the first editions would recognize in this new edition both continuity and change. The first edition focused on "human perspectives" in supervision, linking human concerns which emerged from research on organizational dynamics with human concerns as found in instructional and curriculum literature. In that first edition we asserted, "Humanizing education, with its focus on self actualization of youngsters, can be achieved only in a humanizing organization which focuses on the self actualization of teachers and other educational professionals." The second edition unfolded similarly, giving attention to the supervisor's human concerns in organizational leadership, educational leadership, and instructional leadership. The theme of human resource development, articulated in the second edition, was carried forward in more sophisticated and expansive treatments in the third edition as we gave more attention to values and to substantive components of supervisory leadership.

In this, the fourth edition, we develop the human resource theme more extensively than in previous editions. In the past, we had been more content to summarize the work of others and to marshal research evidence to support the thrust of human resource development as the most productive or effective form of supervision. In this edition we have continued to update the reader with the most promising approaches in the literature but have also introduced more of our own original thinking. Hence, while adopting, for example, Donald Schön's category of "the reflective practitioner," we have given that term some additional meaning through various analogies such as mindscapes and clockworks and teaching as surfing. Likewise, in the chapters on leadership, we have summarized many of the latest theories but have also proposed our own theory and added a chapter on a concern that appears only on the horizon in the literature: "moral action." In this regard, the present edition may be unique in its effort not only to recapitulate recent research and theory but also to break new ground.

Despite substantial revisions, the book retains many features of earlier editions. From a supervisory point of view, the school is still seen as encompassing three interdependent subsystems—organizational, educational, and instructional. The supervisor's unique role is that of linking pin for all three subsystems. The book continues to rely heavily on theoretical foundations. Our focus on the human forces us to focus on meaning—cultural meanings, rational meanings, political meanings, technical meanings. This involves sacrificing, perhaps, discussions of some job entry competencies needed by supervisors in favor of building long-term perspectives of what supervision is and can be. Our interest is in a career-long view of supervision.

We are indebted to reviewers and other colleagues who over the last seventeen years helped us with the four editions of this book and wish to add to those the following individuals who reviewed this edition: Jeanne C. Baxter, Northeastern Illinois University; Lee Goldsberry, University of Southern Maine; E. John Kleinert, University of Miami; and Frank J. Lineberry, Nut Swamp School-Middletown. We are grateful to them and only wish we were wise enough to accept all the advice we received.

Thomas J. Sergiovanni
Robert J. Starratt

SUPERVISION
HUMAN PERSPECTIVES

PART ONE

ONE

HUMAN RESOURCES
SUPERVISION

INTRODUCTION: THE NATURE OF SUPERVISION

In previous editions we characterized supervision as a dormant activity. Supervisors were hired in schools, university courses were offered in the subject, but much of what took place under the name of supervision was ritualistic. A good deal of the supervisor's time was spent on administrative matters. Teacher-evaluation systems tended to be perfunctory. Overall a certain complacency characterized the role and function of supervision.

The third edition noticed that a mild renaissance of interest in supervision and supervisory activities was in the making. At the national level the Association for Supervision and Curriculum Development had begun to place stronger emphasis on supervision. The literature in the field was expanding and improving in quality. With respect to classroom supervision, for example, clinical strategies and artistic strategies began to emerge and to compete successfully with more traditional approaches to teacher evaluation. Publications focusing on problems and issues in supervision began to emerge as among the most popular offered by the Association for Supervision and Curriculum Development. Supervisory topics were appearing more frequently on the programs of this organization's national conference and series of National Curriculum Study Institutes. The founding of the Conference of Professors of Instructional Supervision in 1976 was clearly evidence that scholars studying problems of supervision were increasing in numbers, interested in identifying themselves and in establishing better communication networks and developing more systematic approaches to research and development.

SUPERVISION TODAY

Today supervision is clearly the "in thing" in American schooling. What was once a mild renaissance has turned into a revolution. Supervision ranks high on the agendas of both state policymakers and local school administrators. Since 1983, for example, many states have provided mandates for increased supervision. These mandates range from required "training" in the techniques of supervision and evaluation for principals and supervisors to the provision of comprehensive and standardized state systems of supervision and evaluation. One of the prime contributors to this interest is the body of research associated with the school-effectiveness movement. This research noted that "effective schools" were characterized by principals and other supervisors who exercised strong instructional leadership.

Instructional leadership is the hot topic in thousands of seminars and workshops provided for administrators and supervisors by states, professional associations, local school districts, and individual entrepreneurs. Some states have even gone so far as to mandate that all principals and supervisors go through state-approved and -sponsored instructional leadership training programs as a condition of their continued employment and as part of a licensing system to certify them as teacher evaluators.

The academic side of the professional educational community is experiencing a similar flurry of interest in supervision. In 1985, the Association for Supervision and Curriculum Development established the scholarly journal, *The Journal of Curriculum and Supervision*. By the end of the first year of its existence this journal's subscription rate placed it among the most popular of all professional journals in education. Scholarly articles on supervision and evaluation began to appear more frequently in such established journals as *Curriculum Inquiry* and *Educational Evaluation and Policy Analysis*. *The Journal of Personnel Evaluation in Education* was established in 1986. The prestigious American Educational Research Association established a special-interest group in instructional supervision in 1983. This marked the beginning of a concentrated and continuous appearance of sessions devoted to supervision at the annual meeting of this association.

These events place supervision at a critical point in its history. It is clear that supervision is emerging as a key role and function in the operation of schools. In many schools this development is already fact. At issue is the form and substance of this new emergence and interest, how its influence will be felt by teachers, and what its effects will be on teaching and learning. Will this "new supervision," for example, provide support for teachers and enhance their roles as key professional decision makers in the practice of teaching and learning? Or will this new supervision result in increased regulation and control of teachers and teaching? If the latter future is our fate, what are the consequences of supervision for teacher professionalism and for teaching and learning? In sum, the increased importance attributed to supervision is both attractive and euphoric for those interested in this field. But whether this new emphasis will develop into promises fulfilled or promises broken will depend, we believe, on the form that supervision takes.

THEORIES OF PRACTICE

Supervisors and other busy professionals typically do not characterize their work as being informed by theory. Instead they talk about how they rely on what works, hunches about what works, the principles that they can derive from these hunches and the new practice insights and ideas which evolve from this very practical view of their work. What at first glance seems not to be theoretical, however, turns out to be theoretical. In fact, it is very difficult to engage in teaching or supervisory practice without being theoretical. When professionals say they are not being theoretical, they mean they are not manifestly aware of the theoretical assumptions and basis of their actions and behaviors. Much of the theory which guides professional practice is implicit and informal.

Van Miller, one of the pioneers in administrative theory, often spoke of the practical art of using theory. He noted that it was difficult to administer and supervise without using theory.[1] Practices typically do not lead to other practices without some help. When practice does lead to practice directly, the relationship can be depicted as follows:

practices → practice

This is a monkey-see-monkey-do operation. One's practices are rooted in custom. When something new is proposed, the supervisor asks, "Where else is it being done?" and "How does one do it?"

Very few supervisory or teaching practices evolve so simply from other practices. Instead professionals think about what they are doing and form hunches. The relationship between hunch and practice can be depicted as follows:

practices → hunch → practices

The addition of hunch shows that one is thinking about his or her practice.

Hunches, however, do not appear out of thin air. They are shaped by insights which are derived from one's broader experience with events and activities similar to the problem under consideration as well as one's assumptions and beliefs. Insights, assumptions, and beliefs are informal and implicit theories. As supervisors are engaged in the practice of supervision they think about their practices and develop hunches which guide subsequent practices. With experience, hunches become more formalized and codified into operating principles. Practice based on operating principles is more advanced than practice based on hunches.

---

[1] This discussion of practices, hunches, theories, and principles follows closely Van Miller, "The Practical Art of Using Theory," *The School Executive*, vol. 70, no. 1, pp. 60–63, 1958.

The relationship among hunches, principles, and practice can be depicted as follows:

practices → hunches → principles → practices

Here one uses experience to select the most appropriate hunch. This represents a degree of codification which results in the development of operating principles to guide subsequent professional practice.

Operating principles stand and fall on the basis of trial and error. Further, principles become more elegant as one's hunches become more refined. One's readings, interactions with other professionals, and practical experience in assessing operating principles provide the basis for the development of theories of action. When theories of action emerge to connect hunches and principles, professional behavior is more deliberate and manifest. The supervisor is conscious of the theoretical basis of professional practice, can articulate this basis, and can continuously revise this theory of action as a result of practice. How theory fits into this chain of events is depicted as follows:

practices → hunches → theories of action → principles → practices

With theory, the professional reaches a new step in professional decision making and practice. Theory provides the professional with a more rational view of the situation, serves as a guide to the selection of principles, and provides a basis for evolving improved practices in light of improvements in one's theoretical outlook.

In sum, rarely does teaching or supervisory practice emerge from other practices. Instead, hunches are at play and operating principles emerge which provide a basis for one's decisions and behaviors. Typically hunches and operating principles are implicit and when they are explicit they are not thought about systematically. As professional practice matures, hunches and principles emerge as theories of action which provide a more rational basis for practice. The question for most supervisors and teachers, then, is not whether they are being theoretical or not but what are the theories (the implicit hunches and operating principles) which help shape the way they see their professional worlds and provide the basis for professional decisions and practice.

IMAGES OF SUPERVISION

Different theories of supervision and teaching compete with each other for the attention of professionals. Present supervisor practices in schools, for example, are largely based on one or a combination of three general supervisory theories. The question is which of the three theories best matches the hunches and operating principles which govern the way you think about teaching and supervision and are likely to provide the basis for your behavior as a supervisor?

One way in which these implicit theories can be made explicit is by evaluating the decisions that you make or the ways in which you size up supervisory situations. For example, place yourself in the role of school supervisor in Metro City. A year ago another school in Metro City was selected by the superintendent and central office staff to become a model school. This school would incorporate a new educational system featuring standard goals and teaching objectives across grade levels and a highly structured and tightly paced curriculum linked to the objectives. The curriculum included new textbooks and workbooks for all the major subject areas as well as carefully thought out assignments and activities designed to provide students with needed practice. Daily and weekly lesson plans were provided to make things easier for teachers and to ensure that students received the same instruction and assignments. Criterion-referenced weekly, 6-week, and semester tests were included in the package. The system provided as well for test scores to be evaluated by grade level and by each class within grade level every 6 weeks to monitor student progress. Teachers were formed into quality-control committees or quality circles to discuss the scores and in instances of low scores to come up with ways in which the system might be better implemented. The administration was particularly proud of this quality-circle concept, for it wanted teacher participation. The administration felt that teachers needed only to become familiar with the materials and that by following directions carefully and relying on their own ingenuity in presenting instruction they would teach successfully. The central office had high hope for the success of this new initiative and saw it as a model for export to other schools in the district.

To help things along, the principal received extensive training in the new curriculum and in staff supervision. Further, a new supervisor who had a thorough understanding of the new curriculum, the testing procedures, the daily and weekly lesson plans, and the needed teaching to make things work was assigned to the school. Both principal and supervisor provided instructional leadership by monitoring teaching carefully to ensure compliance with the new system on the one hand and by providing help to teachers who were having difficulty in complying on the other. Prior to the beginning of the school year teachers were provided with a carefully planned and implemented one-week training program, receiving one week's salary for their participation. Schools ran on a half-day schedule for the first week, thus allowing additional training and debugging. The training seemed to be successful, for by the end of September teachers developed an acceptable level of understanding and competence in using the system.

Before the introduction of the new educational system the teachers and principal of this school enjoyed a reputation for being a closely knit faculty with high morale. This situation began to change shortly after the new system was introduced. Teachers begin to complain. They did not like the new curriculum, feeling that frequently it did not fit what they thought was important to teach. They complained of pressure from the tests. They found themselves teaching lessons and adopting teaching strategies that they did not like. They expressed displeasure too with the overall climate in the school, describing it as increasingly impersonal with respect to students and competitive with respect to colleagues. Discontent among teachers grew as the semester continued. Things really began to sour when it became apparent that student performance did not measure up to the high expectations of the administration. By spring break the administration reached the disappointing conclusion that student performance had been better the previous year. They were puzzled as to why such a well-thought-out and carefully implemented educational system was not working in this school. Shortly after the spring break the principal became disillusioned enough to request a transfer. The supervisor was equally discouraged.

With the departure of the principal imminent, the superintendent has asked you and two other supervisors to review matters at the school in an effort to determine the source of the supervision problems and to arrive at a solution to these problems. Each has been asked to work independently to develop solutions and to bring their ideas to the meeting which is to take place shortly. Below are descriptions of how three supervisors size up the problems at this school and the solutions that they are likely to propose. Each of the supervisors is working from an implicit theory of how the world of schooling, and perhaps even the world itself, works. Which of the three descriptions best matches your own view of the situation and your opinion as to how the situation might be remedied?

Supervisor A

You feel that the present problems in the redesigned school are obviously attributable to the people who work there. If the teachers have not yet adapted to the new curriculum and its procedures, they probably are incapable of functioning in a school committed to school improvement. It is also possible that the principal and the new supervisor are not the experts they were assumed to be and are therefore to blame for inadequate monitoring of the system and for their inability to provide the teachers with the proper help and supervision needed so that they might use the system better.

If you had had your way from the beginning, you would have staffed the school with new teachers. A systemwide search would have been conducted to find the kinds of teachers who would best fit such a system: those who would carefully follow the pattern of teaching and working which the system requires. In introducing the new system at the school, you believe that too much emphasis was placed on helping existing teachers to develop a conceptual understanding of the new procedures. This resulted in too many questions, too much confusion, doubts, and other problems. All teachers needed to know was how they fit into the system and what their jobs were. Clearer directions and expectations combined with close monitoring would have provided the needed controls to make the system work.

You believe that the curriculum, lesson plans, materials, tests, and other parts of the educational package introduced into the school are the best available. Although you know that it is possible for snafus to occur and that no educational system can be designed perfectly, you attribute the failure in this case to the unwillingness and inability of the teachers to do what they're supposed to do. Therefore, during the upcoming meeting you plan to make it clear that the problem is not the new educational system but the teachers who are using it. The answer is not to change the system but to train better and more closely monitor the teachers or to find teachers who are willing to use the system in the way in which it is intended.

Supervisor B

You're convinced that the source of the problems at the redesigned school is the lack of emphasis on human relations. Throughout the year the teachers and other employees have been complaining. As you suspected from the outset, the teachers were not consulted about the type of curriculum or the procedures that should be used, just as they were excluded from the decision-making process that led to the development of this model of the school of the future. You believe that teachers want to feel that they have a say in the matters which influence them. They want to be remembered and noticed, to be considered important. The formula for success is simple and straightforward. When these conditions do not exist, morale sinks. When teachers are satisfied and morale is high, on the other hand, they are more cooperative and their performance improves.

The teachers state that the new curriculum and teaching procedures were too cumbersome and rigid and thus made it impossible for them to work comfortably. As you have always said, when the school fulfills its responsibility to teachers' needs, everything else falls into place and school goals are met automatically. After all, the teachers were happy before the redesigning process and student performance was then considerably higher than it is now. Under the new system they have to cope not only with a reduction in the amount of teamwork that previously had promoted morale and satisfaction but also with new supervisors who were hired or trained because of their technical skills instead of their human skills. During the upcoming meeting you plan to point out top management's error in judgment.

Supervisor C

In your opinion the problems in the redesigned school are attributable to one source: a failure to provide teachers with opportunities to fulfill their individual needs and their natural desire to do competent work. You form this opinion on the basis of what you have learned about teachers in general as well as those at this troubled school. The teachers in this school, like those in your own school, are mature adults who want to do their best for the school; they enjoy their work and supervise themselves when completing it. Indeed, their performance record and their level of job satisfaction before the redesigning process prove that to be the case. The formula for success is simple and straightforward. Give people responsibility and authority to make decisions about how they are to work, and they respond with increased motivation. Provide them with opportunities to be successful in accomplishing their goals and their performance improves. The best strategy is to practice tight and loose connectedness. Teachers respond to expectations, need broad goals, like to be part of a vision of accomplishment, and *want* to be held accountable to those values if trusted and given the discretion to make the implementing decisions that make sense to them. In this school not enough attention was given to deciding together what the school was about and too much attention was given to what people are supposed to do.

In its plans to redesign the school top administration has overlooked these facts and has chosen to treat employees like children. A new supervisor was brought in to monitor the work of teachers and a new educational system was programmed to keep track of their comings and goings. The teachers were expected to meet new organizational goals for increased student performance while their needs for autonomy, self-direction, and a sense of fulfillment were ignored. Under the circumstances, a drop in performance was inevitable. You feel strongly that the present school attitude toward teachers is counterproductive, and you plan to make your feelings known during the upcoming meeting.

SCIENTIFIC MANAGEMENT, HUMAN RELATIONS, AND NEOSCIENTIFIC MANAGEMENT SUPERVISION

Many of the supervisory practices found in schools today and many of the policies emerging from state governments and local school boards which influence these practices are based on one or a combination of three general theories of supervision—traditional scientific management, human relations, and neoscientific management. In our view, none of the three theories of supervision is adequate to provide a model for school supervision. Reasons for their inadequacy range from scientific limitations on the one hand to lack of fit with the realities of school supervision on the other. In the next section we propose human resources supervision as a theoretical approach and model of practice which is more sound from a scientific point of view and more accurate in its fit to practice.

Traditional scientific management emerges from the thinking and work of Frederick Taylor and his followers during the early 1900s. Many of the ideas that shaped this theory stem from his experience and research in America's steel industries. For example, he analyzed the loading of pig iron onto railroad cars at the Bethlehem steel plant. Noting certain inefficiencies, he devised techniques for increasing the workers' productivity. His techniques were "scientific" in the sense that they were based on careful observation and task analysis. He determined, for example, that the equipment the workers were using was inadequate to the task. He substituted standardized shovels and other work equipment which were designed specifically for the tasks to be done. He then instructed workers to do exactly as they were told and only as they were told. By closely adhering to his methods and by using the equipment he provided, the workers were able to increase their average loading per day from 12 to 47 tons. Taylor felt that the secret to scientific management was a compliant worker who did not think too much but instead followed directions exactly.[2]

Traditional scientific management represented a classic autocratic philosophy of supervision within which workers were viewed as appendages of management and as such were hired to carry out prespecified duties in accordance with the wishes of management. These ideas carry over to school supervision when teachers are viewed as implementers of highly refined curriculum and teaching systems and where close supervision is practiced to ensure that they are teaching in the way in which they are supposed to and that they are carefully following approved guidelines and teaching protocols. Control, accountability, and efficiency are emphasized in scientific management within an atmosphere of clear-cut manager-subordinate relationships. Though vestiges of this brand of supervision can still be found in schools, by and large traditional scientific management is not currently in favor. Its basic premises and precepts, however, are still thought to be attractive by many policymakers, administrators, and supervisors. Despite this attractiveness, traditional scientific management's operational emphasis on domination, inspection, and control seems not to fit the times.

Human relations supervision had its origins in the democratic administration movement which emerged during the 1930s. Elton Mayo, a social philosopher and professor at Harvard University, is often considered to be the father of human relations supervision. He held views that were in opposition to those of Taylor. He believed that the productivity of workers could be increased by involving them in the decision-making process. His classic research study at the Western Electric Hawthorne plant during the 1920s gave testimony to these ideas.[3] Ultimately human relations supervision was a successful challenger to traditional scientific management. When it was applied to schooling, teachers were to be viewed as "whole persons" in their own right rather than as packages of needed energy, skills, and aptitudes to be used by administrators and supervisors. The early human relations studies pointed out that the social needs of teachers were very important. Supervisors needed to work to create a feeling of satisfaction among teachers by showing interest in them as people.

[2] See, for example, Frederick Taylor, *The Principles of Scientific Management,* New York: Harper & Row, 1911. Reprinted by Harper & Row in 1945; Raymond Callahan, *Education and the Cult of Efficiency,* Chicago: University of Chicago Press, 1962.

[3] See, for example, Elton Mayo, *The Human Problems of an Industrial Civilization,* New York: Macmillan, 1933; F. J. Roethlisberger and W. J. Dickson, *Management and the Worker,* Cambridge: Harvard University Press, 1949.

It was assumed that a satisfied staff would work harder and would be easier to work with, to lead, and to control. Participation was to be an important supervisory method and its objective was to make teachers *feel* that they were useful and important to the school. "Personal feelings" and "comfortable relationships" were the watchwords of human relations.

Human relations supervision is still widely advocated and practiced today, though its support has diminished. Human relations promised much but delivered little. Its problems rested partly with misunderstandings as to how this approach should work and partly with faulty theoretical notions inherent in the approach itself. The movement actually resulted in widespread neglect of teachers. Participatory supervision became permissive supervision which in practice was laissez-faire supervision. Further, the focus of human relations supervision was and still is an emphasis on "winning friends" in an attempt to influence people. To many, "winning friends" was a slick tactic that made the movement seem manipulative and inauthentic, even dishonest. Though this approach developed a considerable following during the thirties, forties, and fifties, it became clear that increases in school productivity would not be achieved merely by assuring the happiness of teachers.

We are experiencing in schooling a renewed interest in scientific management thinking, though its shape and form in practice have changed considerably from the more traditional form. This *neoscientific* management is in a large part a reaction against human relations supervision with its neglect of the teacher in the classroom and its lack of attention to accountability. Neoscientific management shares with traditional management an interest in control, accountability, and efficiency, but the means by which it achieves these ends is far more impersonal. For example, there is a renewed interest in closely monitoring what it is that teachers do, the subject matter they cover, and the teaching methods that they use. But checking daily lesson plans and visiting classes daily to *inspect* teaching often breeds resentment and results in tension between teachers and supervisors. A more impersonal way to control what it is that teachers do is to introduce standardized criterion-referenced testing and to make public the scores by class and school. Since it is accepted that what gets measured gets taught, tests serve as an impersonal method of controlling the teacher's work. Within neoscientific management the task dimension, concern for job, and concern for highly specified performance objectives, all lacking in human relations supervision, are strongly emphasized. Critics feel that this emphasis is so strong that the human dimension suffers. Neoscientific management relies heavily on externally imposed authority and as a result often lacks acceptance from teachers.

Human relations supervision and the two versions of scientific management share a lack of faith and trust in the teacher's ability and willingness to display as much interest in the welfare of the school and its programs as that presumed by administrators, supervisors, and the public. Within traditional scientific management teachers are heavily supervised in a face-to-face setting in an effort to ensure that good teaching will take place. In human relations supervision teachers are provided with conditions which enhance their morale and are involved in efforts to increase their job satisfaction so that they might be more pliable in the hands of management, thus ensuring that good teaching will take place. In neoscientific management impersonal, technical, and rational control mechanisms substitute for face-to-face close supervision. Here it is assumed that if visible standards of performance, objectives, or competencies can be identified, the work of teachers can be controlled by holding them accountable to these standards, thus ensuring better teaching.

Sometimes neoscientific management and human relations are combined into one theory of action. For example, the work of teachers may be programmed by an impersonal system of regulation and control but day-to-day supervision might emphasize pleasant and cordial relationships, building teachers up (telling them, for example, how important they are), encouraging positive attitudes, and rewarding teachers who conform.

HUMAN RESOURCES SUPERVISION

In 1967, the Association for Supervision and Curriculum Development's Commission on Supervision Theory concluded its 4-year study with a report entitled *Supervision: Perspectives and Propositions*.[4] In this report William Lucio discussed scientific management and human relations views of supervision and spoke of a third view—that of the revisionists—which sought to combine emphasis on both tasks and human concerns into a new theory. Standard bearers of the revisionists were Douglas McGregor, Warren Bennis, Chris Argyris, and Rensis Likert.[5]

Beginning with the second edition of this book, the concepts and practices associated with this new theory have been referred to as human resources supervision.[6] The distinction between human resources and human relations is critical, for human resources is more than just another variety of human relations. Human resources represents a higher regard for human need, potential, and satisfaction. Argyris captured the new emphasis succinctly as follows:

> We're interested in developing neither an overpowering manipulative organization nor organizations that will "keep people happy." Happiness, morale, and satisfaction are not going to be highly relevant guides in our discussion. Individual competence,

[4] William Lucio (ed.), *Supervision: Perspectives and Propositions*, Washington, D.C.: Association for Supervision and Curriculum Development, 1967.

[5] Douglas McGregor, *The Human Side of Enterprise*, New York: McGraw-Hill, 1960; Warren Bennis, "Revisionist Theory of Leadership," *Harvard Business Review*, vol. 39, no. 2, pp. 26–38, 1961; Chris Argyris, *Personality and Organization*, New York: Harper & Row, 1957; and Rensis Likert, *New Patterns of Management*, New York: McGraw-Hill, 1961.

[6] This distinction was first made by Raymond Miles, "Human Relations or Human Resources?" *Harvard Business Review*, vol. 43, no. 4, pp. 148–163, 1965; and by Mason Haire, Edwin Ghiselli, and Lyman Porter, *Managerial Thinking: An International Study*, New York: Wiley, 1966.

commitment, self-responsibility, fully functioning individuals, and active, viable, vital organizations will be the kinds of criteria that we will keep foremost in our minds.[7]

Leadership within this new kind of supervision would be neither directive nor patronizing but instead would be supportive:

> The leader and other processes of the organization must be such as to ensure a maximum probability that in all interactions and in all relationships within the organization, each member, in light of his background, values, desires, and expectations, will view the experience as supportive and one which builds and maintains his sense of personal worth and importance.[8]

Douglas McGregor, pointing out that every managerial act rests on a theory, would provide a new theory more conducive to this new human resources management. Theory Y, as he called it, would be based on optimistic assumptions about the nature of humankind and would provide a more powerful basis for motivating workers than the older Theory X.

> Theory X leads naturally to an emphasis on the tactics of control—to procedures and techniques for telling people what to do, for determining whether they are doing it, and for administering rewards and punishments. Since an underlying assumption is that people must be made to do what is necessary for the success of the enterprise, attention is naturally directed to the techniques of direction and control.
> Theory Y, on the other hand, leads to a preoccupation with the *nature of relationships,* with the creation of an environment which will encourage commitment to organizational objectives and which will provide opportunities for the maximum exercise of initiative, ingenuity, and self-direction in achieving them.[9]

In schools, conditions created by human resources management would result in a better life for teachers and more productive schooling. Satisfaction and achievement were to be linked in a new and more expansive way. Instead of focusing on creating happy teachers as a means to gain productive cooperation, the new managerial emphasis would be on creating the conditions of successful work as a means of increasing one's satisfaction and self-esteem. As Frederick Herzberg described the new emphasis:

> To feel that one has grown depends on achievement of tasks that have meaning to the individual, and since the hygiene factors do not relate to the task, they are powerless to give such meaning to the individual. Growth is dependent on some achievements but achievement requires a task. The motivators are task factors and thus are necessary for growth; they provide the psychological stimulation by which the individual can be activated toward his self-realization needs.[10]

---

[7] Chris Argyris, *Integrating the Individual and the Organization,* New York: Wiley, 1964, p. 4.
[8] Rensis Likert, *New Patterns of Management,* New York: McGraw-Hill, 1961, p. 103.
[9] Douglas McGregor, *The Human Side of Enterprise,* New York: McGraw-Hill, 1960, p. 132.
[10] Frederick Herzberg, *Work and the Nature of Man,* New York: World Publishing Co., 1966, p. 78.

HUMAN RELATIONS AND HUMAN RESOURCES
SUPERVISION COMPARED

Neoscientific management and scientific management are really the same theory, though each has a slightly different look in practice. Human relations and human resources supervision, however, are two distinct theories. For example, though both are concerned with teacher satisfaction, human relations views satisfaction as a means to a smoother and more effective school. It is believed that satisfied workers are happier workers and thus easier to work with, more cooperative, and more likely to be compliant. Supervisors find it easier to get what they want from teachers when human relationships are tended to. Consider, for example, the practice of shared decision making. In human relations supervision this technique is used because it is believed it will lead to increased teacher satisfaction. This relationship is depicted as follows:

The human relations supervisor
↓

adopts shared → to increase → which in turn increases
decision-making teacher school
practices satisfaction effectiveness

The rationale behind this strategy is that teachers want to *feel* important and involved. This feeling in turn promotes in teachers a better attitude toward the school and therefore they become easier to manage and more effective in their work.

Within human resources supervision, by contrast, satisfaction is viewed as a desirable *end* toward which teachers work. Satisfaction, according to this view, results from successful accomplishment of important and meaningful work, and this accomplishment is the key component to building school success. The human resources supervisor, therefore, adopts shared decision-making practices because of their potential to increase school success. The supervisor assumes that better decisions will be made, that teacher ownership and commitment to these decisions will be increased, and that the likelihood of success at work will increase. These relationships are depicted as follows:

The human resources supervisor
↓

adopts shared → to increase → which in turn increases
decision-making school teacher
practices effectiveness satisfaction

The theories of supervision are illustrated by the perspectives of the three supervisors described earlier.

Scientific management and neoscientific management comprise the theory of action which governs the thinking and practice of supervisor A. This supervisor supports a highly structured and finely tuned teaching and learning system characterized by close connections among objectives, curriculum, teaching methods, and testing. Supervisor A believes that if teachers do what they are supposed to the system will produce the results that are intended.

Human relations comprises the theory of action to which supervisor B gives allegiance. Supervisor B is concerned with the teaching system's insensitivity to teachers' needs. Further, teachers were not consulted about the system to be implemented and thus feel left out. The answer to this supervisor is to back off and try again, this time getting teachers involved and making compromises in the proposed change which get in the way of teachers' social interaction and other needs. With the right human relations strategy, supervisor B believes, any school-improvement initiative will be successful. It is just a matter of how you work with people.

Supervisor C comes closest to operating from within the human resources perspective. This supervisor believes that successful teaching and school improvement occurs when teacher motivation and commitment are high. Being in charge of one's work life and being held accountable to shared values and broad goals contribute to motivation and commitment. Authentic participation in decision making and providing responsibility are viewed as key supervisory strategies by supervisor C.

Each of the supervisory model sketches provided is an oversimplification, and probably none is exclusively adequate. Successful supervision is shaped by the circumstances and situations which the supervisor faces, and at different times different models may be appropriate. Still, it matters greatly which of the general theories of supervision one accepts as her or his overarching framework.

SUPERVISION II

In this fourth edition human resources remains our overarching framework. But this edition provides a more comprehensive and expansive view of human resources. A new emphasis on the importance of school culture and increased attention given to leadership and supervisory concepts and strategies which enhance meaning and significance are examples of this more expanded view. Indeed the maturing of human resources thinking suggests to us that a new supervision is on the horizon. This supervision, Supervision II, is based on a better understanding of the world of professional practice, new theoretical and research perspectives on motivation to work, a more rational view of teaching and evaluation, and encouraging insights into improving the quality of schooling. Though traditional supervision, Supervision I, remains firmly entrenched, it is being successfully challenged.

CHAPTER 1

PERSPECTIVES FOR SUPERVISION

Many of the issues associated with supervision over the years remain unchanged. Other issues are relatively new and still others are beginning to emerge. The purpose of this chapter is to provide an overview of persistent, new, and emerging issues and concerns in supervision. Confusion in role definition still plagues the field, and uncertainty exists in determining who are supervisors, what are the key components of their jobs, how much authority they should have, and what their relationship to administrators and teachers should be. Further at issue is whether supervision should be viewed as a special role or as a process component of several roles. Elementary school supervisor or assistant principal for instruction might be examples of specialized supervisory roles. The principal, on the other hand, is a general administrator whose role includes supervisory responsibilities and functions.

Purposes of supervision and the basic principles for guiding practice are still debated, though one often wonders just how different are recent statements when compared with classical writings. Another issue is whether the emphasis in theory and practice should be on what supervisors and teachers do and how they behave or on the *meanings* of these actions as perceived by others. This is an old debate which in recent years has been renewed with considerable intensity, particularly with reference to how models of supervision and evaluation of teachers are to be understood and used in practice. Differences of opinion exist with respect to how supervisors should be viewed within the school's hierarchical structure. Are they line or staff? Helpers or evaluators? Monitors of instruction or facilitators? Research which seeks to map the real world of supervision by providing detailed descriptions of what supervisors and teachers actually do and how they spend time has revealed a discrepancy between the world of "is" and the world of "ought."

This raises important questions about the adequacy of textbook prescriptions and about the fit between theoretical models derived from research and the realities of practice. In addition to these issues, or perhaps as a result, new conceptions of supervisors are on the horizon. These conceptions frequently challenge older views. These are the issues which are discussed in this chapter as we seek to provide a perspective. The issues are delineated in greater detail in subsequent chapters.

THE ROLE-PROCESS DEBATE

Reaching agreement on which roles and positions in schools are supervisory is not easy as one observes today's scene. In many larger school districts specialists are employed as supervisors and are solely responsible for working with teachers on matters of curriculum and teaching. In some high schools chairpersons function as supervisors in this way. Often assistant principals are employed who have responsibilities that focus specifically on curriculum and teaching. These are clear examples of supervisory roles. But what about the director of instruction, assistant superintendent for instruction, curriculum coordinator, and similar positions? Incumbents of such positions are less directly involved with teaching and deal less directly with matters of curriculum and classroom supervision. Nonetheless these roles are also considered to be supervisory even though incumbents function more generally and less clinically in providing supervision.

It is less clear whether principals and others with broader responsibilities should be considered as supervisors or as administrators. In reality many schools and school districts are too small to employ supervisors in a specialized sense and if supervision is to take place at all it must become part of the responsibilities of these more general administrative roles. This is more likely to be true in states such as Texas and Illinois where over 1000 school districts exist and less likely to be true in some of the southeastern states where school districts are larger and fewer.

In sum, supervision is often viewed on the one hand as a process component of a variety of roles and on the other as a useful label to categorize a group of specialized school roles whose primary function is to be directly involved in the improvement of teaching and learning. Instead of categorizing roles, it may be more useful to distinguish between modes of behavior that can be described as supervisory and others that cannot. Deciding on what constitutes supervisory behavior helps us to realize the scope and breadth of supervision. Below are several statements that help to clarify the concept of supervision. In the actual work of schools the distinctions are less clear.

1 Viewing supervision as a process is in some respects more meaningful than viewing supervision as a role or the supervisor as a particular role incumbent.

When supervision is viewed as a process, all personnel who practice supervision in schools (superintendents, principals, librarians, staff personnel, department or division chairpersons, classroom teachers, and others, including nonprofessional personnel) are supervisors at one time or another.

2 Supervision is a process used by those in schools who have responsibility for one or another aspect of the school's goals and who *depend directly upon others* to help them achieve these goals.

A crucial aspect that differentiates supervisory behavior from other forms of organizational behavior is *action to achieve goals through other people*. A principal who works to improve the effectiveness of the educational program for students by helping teachers become more effective in the classroom is behaving in a supervisory way. A critical aspect of this relationship is that the principal is dependent upon the teacher in attempting to increase program effectiveness.

3 Since behavior is a significant part of the supervisory process, for understanding the process as a whole it is often useful to focus on this aspect of supervision. Thus supervisory behavior is a key construct in this book and, as such, forms an important basis for analyzing other aspects of the supervisory process and their relationship to supervisory effectiveness.

THE PHONETICS AND SEMANTICS OF SUPERVISION

Supervision and its complement teaching can be viewed and understood both phonetically and semantically.[1] Tending to supervisory behaviors and accounting for what the supervisor does, when, how, and under what circumstances, comprises a phonetic view. It does not matter whether the supervisor is involved in leading, coaching, managing, evaluating, administering, or teaching. If the emphasis in these activities is on "the looks and sounds" of behavior, on the form or shape that this behavior takes as opposed to what the behavior means, the view is phonetic.

Identical behaviors can have different meanings as contexts change and as different people are involved. A supervisor, for example, may walk through the classrooms of several teachers on a regular basis, making it a practice to comment to teachers about what is happening and to share their impressions. Some teachers may consider this behavior inspectorial or controlling and view the supervisor as one who is closely monitoring what teachers do. Other teachers may consider this same behavior symbolic of the interest and support which the supervisor provides to teachers. In this case, supervisory behavior is interpreted as being caring and helpful. At one level, the phonetic, the behavior is the same for both supervisors. At another level, semantic, the behavior results in different meanings. When concerned with different interpretations and meanings, one is tending to the semantic aspects of supervision.

---

[1] Thomas J. Sergiovanni, "We Need a TRUE Profession!" *Educational Leadership,* vol. 44, no. 8, 1987.

Much of the literature in supervision and teaching is phonetic. Great interest is shown in describing the supervisor's job, prescribing leadership styles, and charting teaching behaviors. A complete picture and understanding of supervision and teaching, however, requires that the phonetic view be linked to the semantic. Carrying this reading metaphor a step further, in this book we are interested in the "syntax" of supervision and teaching. Much like the grammatical linking of words as elements to word groups and phrases as symbols, our intent is to link supervisory behavior and the various supervisory and teaching models of practice upon which it is based to the meanings such behavior holds for different people and different contexts. Throughout our discussion it will be helpful to keep in mind this phonetic and semantic distinction.

CHARACTERISTICS OF SUPERVISORY ROLES

Supervisors work primarily in the area of instructional improvement. Organizational demands require most personnel in schools to be involved in some aspects of administrative behavior, but for those who work in the area of instructional improvement, supervisory behavior will tend to predominate. Supervisory roles can be further differentiated from the more administrative roles by such characteristics as (1) heavy reliance on expertness as an educational program leader and instructional leader, (2) the necessity of living in two worlds and of speaking two languages, and (3) limits imposed on their authority.

Supervisors in education, as in other fields ranging from medicine to industry, are expected to be experts in the technical system of their organizations. A high school principal who functions primarily as an administrator-manager can get along quite well with only a conversational acquaintance with classroom organizational patterns, problems, and prospects, but a high school principal or a department chairperson who functions as a supervisor needs a more detailed perspective to be successful. Supervisors are expected to be experts in educational and instructional matters. As educational and instructional leaders, their work exhibits a high concern for:

Curriculum and teaching objectives
Educational program content, coordination, and scope
Alternatives and options
Curriculum and teaching innovations
The structure of knowledge in the major disciplines and content areas
Grouping and scheduling patterns
Lesson and unit planning
Evaluating and selecting learning materials
Patterns of teacher and student classroom influence
Developing and evaluating educational encounters
Teaching styles, methods, and procedures

Classroom learning climates
Teacher, student, and program evaluation

A second characteristic differentiating supervisory from other roles is the necessity of living in two worlds and of speaking two languages—the language of teachers and the language of administrators. Teachers and administrators operate from different perspectives, each of which often makes one unintelligible to the other. True, most administrators have been teachers previously, but having been cast into a different arena and subjected to different pressures, they often have difficulty in understanding the problems teachers face. Teachers, on the other hand, view the school from a limited, often unrealistic, perspective. Their perspective is frequently accompanied by an unsympathetic view of the administrator and his or her role. Supervisors are forced to live in both worlds and to mediate difficulties in communication and perspective between the two worlds without alienating either—no small order!

A third characteristic involves limitations placed on the supervisor's authority. Supervisors are often considered "staff" rather than "line" officers, though admittedly the difference between the two is more muddled than clear. As such they must rely more heavily on functional authority derived from their expert knowledge about matters of teaching and learning and on personal leadership qualities as sources of authority rather than more formal sources of authority derived from their position in the hierarchy or their access to rewards and punishments. Even supervisors in line positions such as school principals find that they are more effective in matters of teaching and learning when they behave as staff. They develop a collegial perspective and rely on expert authority and their ability to provide facilitative leadership rather than managerial or bureaucratic authority. The basis of supervisory power and the limits of supervisory authority will be discussed more fully in Chapter 3.

THE SUPERVISOR IN THE HIERARCHY

Just what is the supervisor's place in the hierarchy of the school? Keith Davis identifies five different views of the supervisor's role.[2] The views afford the supervisor a place in the hierarchy ranging from critical to marginal. The viewpoints are illustrated in Figure 1-1. Note that a sixth view, "monitor of instruction," is added to Davis's list.

The *person-in-the-middle* view of the supervisor is characterized by a process of mediating between the two opposing worlds of teachers and administrators. Here administrators are seen as emphasizing task-oriented leadership and a variety of quality-control mechanisms in efforts to push teacher and school closer to achieving objectives and increasing production. Teachers as human beings, however, are seeking a more relaxed, trusting, and congenial atmosphere within which to work—one that is secure from tension

[2] Keith Davis, *Human Behavior at Work: Human Relations and Organizational Behavior,* 4th ed., New York: McGraw-Hill, 1972, pp. 120–123.

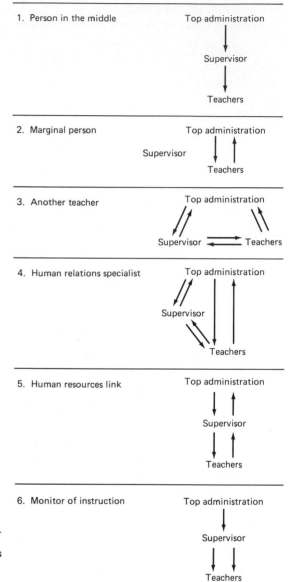

FIGURE 1-1
Viewpoints on the supervisor's role. (*Adapted from Keith Davis,* Human Behavior at Work: Human Relations and Organizational Behavior, *4th ed., New York: McGraw-Hill, 1972.*)

and responsive to their needs. Supervisors are caught in the middle, struggling valiantly to reconcile what may well be impossible differences. In this sense, supervisors are seen as buffers, or persons in the middle.

As a *marginal person,* the supervisor is also in the middle but is excluded from or on the margin of important decisions affecting the school. Here the supervisor is not accepted by either group and is ignored for the most part by both groups. As a result the marginal-person supervisor often spends more time as a curriculum administrator, as a materials procurer, or engaged in some other impersonal activity associated with desk work.

The *another-teacher* view of supervision is characterized by affording supervisors low authority and status and by permitting them only minimum discretion. Supervisors, in this view, are often considered liaison persons upon whom administrators rely to get the word down to teachers. Housekeeping chores and maintenance activities, rather than leadership responsibilities, occupy the attention of this type of supervisor. Many secondary school chairpersons, for example, can be characterized as supervisors of this sort.

As a *human relations specialist* the supervisor is considered a staff specialist charged with the caring for, and maintaining of, the human side of the school enterprise. The need for such a specialist is based on the assumption that in any organization job demands and human demands are in conflict. Teachers have needs and feelings and are subject to frustration, disappointment, and other maladies that can endanger morale. According to this view, poor morale is not good for the school and should be avoided. The supervisor's job as human relations specialist is to get along with teachers, be sympathetic to their problems, and otherwise tend to their idiosyncrasies in an attempt to gain their cooperation and compliance to administrative directives.

As a *human resources link,* the supervisor is a key member of the school's leadership team. Here the supervisor is a critical link between the school's organizational and management subsystem and its educational-instructional subsystem. This is indeed an in-the-middle view, but here the supervisor serves an integrating rather than a buffering role. It is assumed that though educational programs and instruction exist within an organized setting, organization and management exist to serve educational programs and instruction. That being the case, the integrating role of the supervisor is considered critical in the administrative hierarchy, and he or she assumes a key role in school district decision making. The reasons why the school exists constitute the supervisor's primary area of responsibility.

In recent years a new supervisory role has emerged, *monitor of instruction.* This role has been shaped by interpretations of the school effectiveness-teaching literature which suggests a relationship between effectiveness *as defined by this literature* and close monitoring of teachers and teaching by supervisors (typically the school principal). In such schools a tight alignment often exists between specific and standardized objectives and the curriculum, the curriculum and specific teaching methods and protocols, teaching and testing. As monitor of instruction the supervisor is responsible for ensuring that teachers are teaching to the objectives and using the proper teaching protocols most likely to result in achievement of these objectives. In addition to direct and frequent observation of teachers emphasis is placed on periodic and systematic testing of students. Though the purpose of such testing is typically formative, summative judgments are unavoidable. The analysis of these tests is used to evaluate the effectiveness of teachers and teaching *and* to make corrections in the teaching system so that it is more in line with the achievement of the stated objectives. The monitor of instruction role places the supervisor in a strong position with regard to hierarchy and authority over teachers. This strong hierarchical position is represented in Figure 1-1 by the two arrows between supervisor and teachers. Instead of being "caught in the middle" of the school's bureaucratic and professional faces or of trying to integrate these two dimensions, the supervisor as monitor of instruction works to directly influence and indeed program the work of teachers and teaching according to an established system.

A NORMATIVE VIEW OF SUPERVISION

Normative views are concerned with what ought to be done, with prescribing actions designed to produce the best solutions. For example, when one writes a book on the topic of supervision, invariably the intent is to improve the field. Authors want to make things better, and professional books usually prescribe best ways of operating or propose a series of propositions hopefully designed to improve matters. A normative view of supervision is depicted in Figure 1-2. Here it is assumed that choices are made by supervisors to maximize certain desirable values and objectives. The supervisor, being faithful to certain value statements and committed to certain objectives, uses the resources available to him or her to achieve goals in accordance with a maximum cost-benefit exchange. To this end, the supervisor performs certain processes such as planning, organizing, leading, helping, supporting, developing, and evaluating.

FIGURE 1-2
A normative view of supervision. (*Adapted from T. J. Sergiovanni, M. Burlingame, F. S. Coombs, and P. W. Thurston,* Educational Governance and Administration, *p. 315. ©1980. Adapted by permission of Prentice-Hall, Englewood Cliffs, N.J.*)

Following the decision-rule "Choices are made to maximize values and objectives," a supervisor should behave as follows:

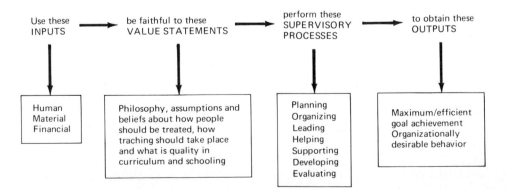

Use these INPUTS	be faithful to these VALUE STATEMENTS	perform these SUPERVISORY PROCESSES	to obtain these OUTPUTS
Human Material Financial	Philosophy, assumptions and beliefs about how people should be treated, how traching should take place and what is quality in curriculum and schooling	Planning Organizing Leading Helping Supporting Developing Evaluating	Maximum/efficient goal achievement Organizationally desirable behavior

Normative theories have a number of advantages. They specify what should be done. They challenge individuals who are involved with the school to place highest priority on moral rather than instrumental values, on what is most effective rather than on some lesser condition. They help to set goals, to reach agreement on future directions, and to develop plans for future action. And they set the standard for improving present levels of supervision. Despite these important advantages, normative theories fail to capture the world and work of supervision as it really is. By contrast, descriptive theories are concerned with what is, with accurately describing the activities and events they represent.

A DESCRIPTIVE VIEW OF SUPERVISION

A key difference between normative and descriptive theories is that in the latter it is assumed that choices are made to satisfy constraints rather than to maximize objectives. As is depicted in Figure 1-3, the supervisor is conscious of and interested in value statements and goals important to his or her school and desires to perform supervisory processes in an ideal way, but this desire is mediated by such realities of organizational life as politics, the pressure for conflict resolution, the constraints of bureaucracy, limits on rationality, and the distribution of power and authority. Satisfactory goal achievement and self-serving behavior tend to be more accurate descriptions of outcomes as supervisors seek to satisfy these constraints.

Accounts of gaps between normative and descriptive views of supervision are not necessarily cause for alarm. Presently, abundance and richness characterize the normative literature but not the descriptive literature. The

FIGURE 1-3
A descriptive view of supervision. *(From T. J. Sergiovanni, M. Burlingame, F. S. Coombs, and P. W. Thurston,* Educational Governance and Administration, *p. 317. ©1980. Adapted by permission of Prentice-Hall, Englewood Cliffs, N.J.)*

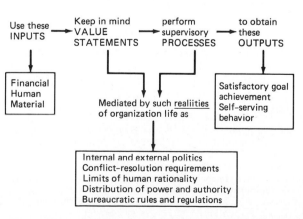

need exists, therefore, for researchers to focus more talent and attention on mapping and describing the real world and work of supervision.[3]

A number of studies have been conducted that attempt to develop accurate descriptions of supervisory reality. One such study was commissioned by the Association for Supervision and Curriculum Development and conducted by the ASCD Working Group on Roles and Responsibilities of Supervisors chaired by A. W. Sturges.[4] The report of this group covers a number of topics but focuses its attention on discrepancies between the real and ideal in supervision. One study summarized was concerned with the amount of supervision actually experienced by teachers in Tennessee. The researchers, Lovell and Phelps,[5] note that 83 percent of the teachers in Tennessee reported no observations of their teaching by a supervisor during the 1974–75 academic year. When observations were held, more than two-thirds of the teachers reported that they were not scheduled in advance, were not preceded by a conference, or were not requested. Further, one-half of this group reported that no follow-up conference took place. Contrast these findings with views presented in this book and in other books on the topic of supervision that prescribe what supervisors should be doing.

In recent years Tennessee has been a front-runner in instituting school reform intended to improve the quality of work life in teaching, the quality of teaching and learning for students, and the attractiveness of teaching as a profession. The Tennessee career ladder plan, for example, is an example of such a reform. Prescriptively it was assumed that a career ladder combined with merit pay would provide an incentive to teachers and would improve teaching quality. One result of the Tennessee career ladder has been to provide teachers with the supervision and evaluation missing in the Lovell and Phelps study conducted in 1974–1975. These days Tennessee teachers are very carefully and closely supervised. While the final vote on this ambitious career ladder plan has not been taken, many indications exist that in the real world of schooling in Tennessee the plan has resulted in a number of unanticipated and negative consequences—consequences which could be interpreted as decreasing the quality of work life in teaching, the quality of teaching and learning, and the attractiveness of the teaching profession. A 1984 survey of Tennessee teachers conducted by the Tennessee Education Association, for example, revealed that 76 percent of the respondents agreed with the view that the career ladder program had a negative effect on teacher morale; 92 percent disagreed

[3]Blumberg's book gives more attention than most to the descriptive world of supervision. See Arthur Blumberg, *Supervisors and Teachers: A Private Cold War,* Berkeley, Calif.: McCutchan, 1974.

[4]A.W. Sturges, R.J. Krajewski, J.T. Lovell, E. McNeill, and M.G. Ness, "The Roles and Responsibilities of Instructional Supervisors," *Report of the ASCD Working Group on the Roles and Responsibilities of Supervisors,* Alexandria, Va.: Association for Curriculum and Development, October 1978.

[5]John T. Lovell and Margaret S. Phelps, "Supervision in Tennessee: A Study of Perceptions of Teachers, Principals and Supervisors," Tennessee Association for Supervision and Curriculum Development, July 1976, reported in Sturges et al., op. cit., p. 35. See also *Educational Leadership,* vol. 35, pp. 226–228, 1977, for a summary of this study.

with the view that the career ladder program was a significant positive factor in keeping them in the profession; 91 percent disagreed with the view that young teachers would be more attracted to teaching because of the career ladder plan; and 64 percent agreed with the view that the documentation required under the career ladder process distracted from instructional and preparation time.[6] A 1986 study of Tennessee teachers reported that 40 percent of the respondents indicated they would leave the profession within the next 7 years. This study found that the quality of work life for teachers in Tennessee could hardly be considered to be favorable.[7] It seems apparent that in Tennessee prescriptive and descriptive views of the career ladder and the effectiveness of accompanying supervisory systems are at odds with each other.

In summarizing the report of the ASCD working group Sturges notes the following inconsistencies between normative and descriptive view of supervision:

Nature and Objectives of the Instructional Supervisor

Intended. The instructional supervisor should assist in the improvement of instruction. This includes (1) direct psychological and technical support, service and help to teachers; (2) curriculum development, coordination and evaluation of instruction; (3) development and evaluation of educational goals; (4) professional development of personnel; (5) evaluation of personnel performance; and (6) the evaluation of educational outcomes. The maintenance and continuing support of ongoing programs and people are included, as well as the teachers' desire for supportive and non-threatening services that are directly related to the improvement of teachers' classroom performance.

Actual. Teachers perceive some instructional supervisors as primarily concerned with administrative responsibilities. Some individuals with primary administrative or management responsibilities (e.g., principals, assistant superintendents for curriculum and/or instruction) employ their supervisory responsibilities to assist them in accomplishing tasks that may be indirectly related to the improvement of instruction at the classroom level.

Conflict. Teachers want direct assistance to improve instruction; some educators with supervisory responsibilities combine both administrative and supervisory responsibilities to meet more global goals than at the specific classroom levels.

The Activities of the Instructional Supervisor

Intended. The instructional supervisor should provide direct assistance to the classroom teacher for the improvement of instruction and the improved learning by children. This assistance can include instructional materials, demonstration teaching, and the acquisition of appropriate facilities and equipment. Evaluation of teaching performance is to provide specific assistance toward the improvement of teaching.

[6]Tennessee Education Association, "Where Does Tennessee Rank?" *Tennessee Teacher,* vol. 53, no. 7, p. 13, March 1986.

[7]Susan J. Rosenholtz, Otto C. Bassler, and Kathleen V. Hoover-Dempsey, "I Quit," *Tennessee Teacher,* vol 53, no. 7, pp. 9–14, March 1986.

Actual. Some teachers do not perceive the instructional supervisor as devoting enough time to the improvement of instruction in the individual classrooms. Administrative responsibilities that require the instructional supervisor to spend time at the central office rather than with specific teachers are perceived as restricting direct assistance by the instructional supervisor. The conflict resulting from the line versus staff responsibilities of instructional supervisors is illustrated by criticisms by some teachers of the lack of classroom visits and the limited direct assistance by the instructional supervisor.

Conflict. Teachers want assistance at the classroom level. Those educators with mixed assignments of instructional supervision and administration/management do not provide the type of assistance desired by teachers.

The Organizational Structure for Instructional Supervision

Intended. The instructional supervisor should be as close as possible to the teachers being assisted. This can include the housing of a supervisor in the building where the teachers are to be assisted.

Actual. Instructional supervisors are frequently assigned to work with teachers in several buildings; instructional supervisors often have offices at a central location in the school district.

Conflict. Teachers want more direct and immediate access to assistance from instructional supervisors that are familiar with the environment of specific classrooms. Other types of instructional supervisors (e.g., principals) have a role conflict of administrator versus the direct and extensive instructional assistance desired by teachers.

The Preparation of Instructional Supervisors

Intended. To meet the aspirations that teachers hold for instructional supervisors, appropriate preparation would include coursework, practical and field experiences to help supervisors accurately analyze existing classroom conditions and make appropriate recommendations for improving the learning environment of children.

Actual. Less than half the states offer certification for instructional supervisors; very few specify a minimum number of hours in supervision, a few require an internship. Among those states requiring certification, there is a wide range between the lowest and highest number of hours in supervision that are required.

Conflict. There seems to be little agreement between what teachers want instructional supervisors to do, and the ways in which they are being prepared by universities.[8]

THE NATURE OF SUPERVISORY WORK

The publication in 1973 of Henry Mintzberg's book, *The Nature of Managerial Work,*[9] sparked a great deal of interest in descriptive studies of administration and supervision. Instead of attributing roles to administrators, Mintzberg

---

[8]Sturges et al., op. cit., pp. 67–70.
[9]Henry Mintzberg, *The Nature of Managerial Work,* New York: Harper & Row, 1973.

sought to infer real roles based on what administrators actually did. This is an inductive approach that relies on continued, detailed, and systematic study of administrative actions. Using diaries and engaging in direct observation over an extended period, Mintzberg studied five executives, including a school super-intendent. Mintzberg was able to identify 10 administrative roles that reflected the actual activities observed. The roles were then grouped into three major categories as follows:

Interpersonal	
Figurehead	Symbolic head; obliged to perform a number of routine duties of a legal or social nature.
Leader	Responsible for the motivation and actions of subordinates; responsible for staffing, training, and associated duties.
Liaison	Maintains self-developed network of contacts and informers who provide favors and information.
Informational	
Monitor	Seeks and receives wide variety of special information (much of it current) to develop thorough understanding of organization and environment, emerges as nerve center of internal and external information of the organization.
Disseminator	Transmits information received from outsiders or from other subordinates to members of the organization; some information factual, some involving interpretation and integration of diverse value positions of organizational influences.
Spokesperson	Transmits information to outsiders on organization's plans, policies, actions, results, etc.; serves as expert on organization's industry.
Decisional	
Entrepreneur	Searches organization and its environment for opportunities and initiates "improvement projects" to bring about change; supervises design of certain projects as well.
Disturbance handler	Responsible for corrective action when organization faces important, unexpected disturbances.
Resource allocator	Responsible for the allocation of organizational resources of all kinds—in effect the making or approving of all significant organizational decisions.
Negotiator	Responsible for representing the organization at major negotiations.*

*Mintzberg, *The Nature of Managerial Work,* Table 2 (pp. 92–93). Copyright © 1973 by Henry Mintzberg. Reprinted by permission of Harper & Row, Publisher.

Replication of Mintzberg's work in other areas, including education, has shown that the 10 roles and three categories are stable. That is, they seem to categorize the nature of managerial work in a variety of fields. Sullivan tested the Mintzberg framework with supervisors.[10] She limited her study to "system level supervisors" in a metropolitan area. Following Mintzberg's methods, she recorded 14,753 minutes of actual supervisory behavior and used this as a basis for her analysis. Are Mintzberg's categories stable when applied to supervisors in education? Sullivan was able to classify 98 percent of all the supervisory activity actually recorded into this framework; thus the answer, based on her study, is yes.

In sorting out the activities of supervisors across the 10 roles Sullivan found that 30 percent of the activities could be classified as resource allocator, 19 percent as monitor, and 16 percent as disseminator. By contrast, the three interpersonal roles of figurehead, liaison, and leader accounted for only 10, 9, and 8 percent, respectively. On the basis of this distribution, she concluded that the supervisors in her study were primarily insiders concerned with internal operations.

Normative views of supervision tend to elevate the interpersonal roles over others, with the greatest emphasis given to leadership. It is assumed that these roles have the most to do with quality in supervision. Information roles are often emphasized and the supervisor is seen as a key communications link between teachers and administrators, among teachers, and between teachers and developments that occur outside the school. Less important in the literature are the decisional roles. Typically these roles are associated with more administrative positions. Sullivan found almost the opposite configuration when she categorized supervisory activities into the role categories. Informational roles, for example, accounted for 30 percent of the activities, decision-making roles for 33 percent, and interpersonal roles for only 27 percent.

One problem with the Mintzberg approach is the tendency to treat all activities equally—to disregard their proportionate impact on quality and effectiveness. The leadership act and other interpersonal encounters, for example, get the same weight as reading a memo or filing a report. If one were to weight role activities according to the categories with the assumption that some role categories are more important than others, a more qualitative assessment could be made of what supervisors do.

ACCOMMODATING DISCREPANCIES

No wonder supervisors become cynical when they read the literature on supervision with its typical normative bias. After all, some conclude, if you want to survive out there you have to accommodate yourself to the real world. A temptation exists to abandon standards and ideals and to play the game as it is. On the other hand, one wonders if games without meaning and purpose are

[10]Cheryl Granade Sullivan, "The Work of the Instructional Supervisor: A Functional Analysis," Ph.D. dissertation, Atlanta, Ga.: Emory University, Division of Educational Studies, 1980.

worth playing at all. Obviously, the normative side of the enterprise cannot be ignored, But still, there is no hope of improving things if we remain naive about existing practices and conditions in supervision. The two go hand in hand. Descriptive views provide accurate images of the world of supervision and normative views provide standards toward which we strive. One task of this book is to help to bring the views closer together with a minimum of sacrifice to the normative view.

PURPOSES OF SUPERVISION

William Burton and Leo Brueckner, two pioneers in the area of supervision whose classic 1955 book, *Supervision: A Social Process,* seems remarkably contemporary, identified supervisory operating principles and purposes which still provide the basis for today's writings and much of the prescriptions for supervisory behavior which are generated by these writings. The principles are provided below.

PRINCIPLES GOVERNING THE OPERATION OF SUPERVISION

1 Administration is *ordinarily* concerned with providing material facilities and with operation in general.
2 Supervision is *ordinarily* concerned with improving the setting for learning in particular.
3 Administration and supervision considered *functionally* cannot be separated or set off from each other. The two are coordinate, correlative, complementary, mutually shared functions in the operation of educational systems. The provision of any and all conditions favorable to learning is the common purpose of both.
4 Good supervision is based on philosophy and science.
  a Supervision will be sensitive to ultimate aims and values, to policies, with special reference to their adequacy.
  b Supervision will be sensitive to "factness" and to law, with special reference to their accuracy.
  c Supervision will be sensitive to the emergent, evolutionary nature of the universe and of democratic society in particular, hence should be permeated with the experimental attitude, and engage constantly in reevaluation of aims and values, of policies, of materials and methods.
5 Good supervision is (in the United States) based upon the democratic philosophy.
  a Supervision will respect personality and individual differences between personalities, will seek to provide opportunities for the best expression of each unique personality.
  b Supervision will be based upon the assumption that educational workers

are capable of growth. It will accept idiosyncrasies, reluctance to cooperate, and antagonism as human characteristics, just as it accepts reasonableness, cooperation, and energetic activity. The former are challenges; the latter, assets.

c Supervision will endeavor to develop in all a democratic conscience, that is, recognition that democracy includes important obligations as well as rights.

d Supervision will provide full opportunity for the cooperative formulation of policies and plans, will welcome and utilize free expression and contributions from all.

e Supervision will stimulate initiative, self-reliance, and individual responsibility on the part of all persons in the discharge of their duties.

f Supervision will substitute leadership for authority. Authority will be recognized as the authority of the situation and of the facts within the situation. Personal authority if necessary will be derived from group planning.

g Supervision will work toward cooperatively determined functional groupings of the staff, with flexible regrouping as necessary; will invite specialists when advisable.

6 Good supervision will employ scientific methods and attitudes insofar as those methods and attitudes are applicable to the dynamic social processes of education; will utilize and adapt to specific situations and scientific findings concerning the learner, the learning processes, the nature and development of personality; will cooperate occasionally in pure research.

7 Good supervision, in situations where the precise controlled methods of science are not applicable, will employ processes of dynamic problem solving in studying, improving, and evaluating its products and processes. Supervision either by scientific methods or through orderly thought processes will constantly derive and use data and conclusions which are more objective, more precise, more sufficient, more impartial, more expertly secured, and more systematically organized than are the data and conclusions of uncontrolled opinion.

8 Good supervision will be creative and not prescriptive.

a Supervision will determine procedures in the light of the needs of each supervisory teaching-learning situation.

b Supervision will provide opportunity for the exercise of orginality and for the development of unique contributions, of creative self-expression; will seek latent talent.

c Supervision will deliberately shape and manipulate the environment.

9 Good supervision proceeds by means of an orderly, cooperatively planned and executed series of activities.

10 Good supervision will be judged by the results it secures.

11 Good supervision is becoming professional. That is, it is increasingly seeking to evaluate its personnel, procedures, and results; it is moving toward standards and toward self-supervision.

PRINCIPLES GOVERNING THE PURPOSES OF SUPERVISION

1 The ultimate purpose of supervision is the promotion of pupil growth and hence eventually the improvement of society.
2 A second general purpose of supervision is to supply leadership in securing continuity and constant readaptation in the educational program over a period of years; from level to level within the system; and from one area of learning experience and content to another.
3 The immediate purpose of supervision is cooperatively to develop favorable settings for teaching and learning.
   a Supervision, through all means available, will seek improved methods of teaching and learning.
   b Supervision will create a physical, social, and psychological climate or environment favorable to learning.
   c Supervision will coordinate and integrate all educational efforts and materials and will supply continuity.[11]

The underlying theme for Burton and Brueckner was for supervisors to provide both technical and personal help to teachers in an effort to increase their understanding and improve their teaching practice. This effort, in turn, would support the *ultimate* purpose of supervision which in their view was "the promotion of pupil growth and hence eventually the improvement of society." Burton and Brueckner and most of the writers who followed brought to their work a human relations perspective which incorporated some features of human resources thinking. Critics of this view then and now are concerned that human relations approaches do not give sufficient attention to accountability. They point out that accountability is part of any professional endeavor and this concern is rightly a part of supervision—a view with which we agree.

To the questions then "What is supervision for? Who is to be served? Why evaluate?" we would respond that supervision and evaluation have many purposes. These include ensuring that minimum standards are being met, and that teachers are being faithful to the school's overall purposes and educational platform as well as helping teachers grow as persons and professionals. Grouped into categories, they are as follows:

1 *Supervision for quality control.* Principals and other supervisors are responsible for monitoring teaching and learning in their schools and do so by visiting classes, touring the school, talking with people, and getting to know students.

2 *Supervision for professional development.* As in Burton and Brueckner's theory, principals and other supervisors help teachers to grow and to

---

[11]William H. Burton and Leo J. Brueckner, *Supervision: A Social Process,* 3d ed., New York: Appleton-Century-Crofts, 1955, pp. 85, 88. Reprinted by permission of Appleton-Century-Crofts, Division of Meredith Corporation.

develop in their understanding of teaching and classroom life, in improving basic teaching skills, and in expanding their knowledge and use of teaching repertoires.

3 *Supervision for teacher motivation.* Often overlooked is the third purpose of supervision—the building and nurturing of motivation and commitment to teaching, to the school's overall purposes, and to the school's defining educational platform.[12]

Quality supervisory practice and effective supervisory systems account for each of these purposes. Indeed a supervisory system based on only one of these purposes is not likely to be successful over time. Focusing only on quality control invites problems from teachers and must be balanced with needed expansive qualities. At the same time, professional development and increased motivation and commitment are too important to overlook. Indeed one cannot have quality schooling without them. Nonetheless a supervisory system concerned *solely* with providing support and help to teachers (and thus, by omission, neglecting teaching inadequacies and instances where overriding purposes and defining platforms are ignored) is also inadequate. Though quality control and teacher improvement are the basic purposes which should drive any system of supervision and evaluation, teacher motivation and commitment may, in the long run, be the most powerful ingredient in building quality schooling. Overwhelming evidence exists which suggests that "knowledge of results" is an important ingredient in increasing a person's motivation to work and in building commitment and loyalty to one's job.[13]

SUPERVISION, SYMBOLISM, AND CULTURE BUILDING

Supervision in practice has always been more inclusive than quality control and professional development. Good supervisors have always used formal supervisory settings and occasions as *opportunities* to build motivation and commitment on the one hand and to engage in culture building on behalf of school quality on the other. Indeed for many supervisors this informal aspect of supervision is their reason for being. Coining a phrase borrowed from studies of highly successful enterprises in the private sector, good supervisors practice "supervision by walking around" and the "management of attention." They are highly visible in visiting classes, talking with teachers about their work, and interacting with students. As informal activities, supervision by walking around and the management of attention become routinized and accepted ways of operating in the school. They become, in fact, normal and accepted characteristics of the school's culture. These strategies are the means the supervisor uses to communicate to teachers what is important. In a sense supervisors "anoint"

---

[12] Thomas J. Sergiovanni, *The Principalship—A Reflective Practice Perspective*, Boston: Allyn and Bacon, 1987, p. 153.
[13] See, for example, J. R. Hackman and Greg Oldham, "Motivation through the Design of Work: Test of a Theory," *Organizational Behavior and Human Performance*, vol. 16, no. 2, pp. 250–279.

teaching and learning as "sacred" dimensions of the school's culture and work by "witnessing" these acts. The strategies serve as well to communicate to teachers how important they are to the success of the school. As a result, teachers come to view their work as being more meaningful and significant, experience empowerment and a greater sense of efficacy. Motivation and commitment to work increases, leading to increases in teaching quality and student achievement.[14] In this sense supervision becomes more than something technical and interpersonal. It is a symbolic act.

SUPERVISION I AND SUPERVISION II

Since the publication of the third edition of this book human resources supervision has become better understood and its practices have expanded considerably. In this edition it is useful to make a distinction between a new supervision now emerging, Supervision II, and more traditional conceptions of supervision, Supervision I.

Among the basic assumptions underlying Supervision I is the view that the world of schooling is tightly structured and connected. Ideally, teachers, curriculum, teaching methods, supervisor and evaluation systems, schedules, and events are all *linked* together in an orderly fashion much like the gears and pins which comprise the mechanical workings of a clock.[15] Within this view the aim of supervision is to get control over the main gear and pins. Once this is accomplished, all the other parts will work predictably and in unison. Supervisors who hold this view of teaching and schooling are likely to focus their attention on management controls and other supervisory strategies and techniques in an attempt to regulate the various parts.

Supervision II, by contrast, is based on a view of teaching and schooling which is quite different. Teachers, curriculum, students, teaching, strategies, schedules, and events all exist but are disconnected from each other. They are, in a sense, cogs and pins which are spinning independently in a clockworks gone awry. This is a view well documented by such organizational theorists as Cohen, March, and Olsen[16] and Weick[17] as well as by recent commentaries of how schools work and the nature of teaching.[18] This is also the view described

---

[14] Patricia T. Ashton and Rodman B. Webb, *Making a Difference—Teachers' Sense of Efficacy and Student Achievement,* New York: Longman, 1986.

[15] Thomas J. Sergiovanni, "The Theoretical Basis for Cultural Leadership," in Linda Sheive and Marian B. Schoenheit (eds.), *Leadership: Examining the Elusive,* 1987 Yearbook of the Association for Supervision and Curriculum Development, Alexandria, Va.: The Association, pp. 116–129. This chapter contrasts clockworks I, a tightly connected view of how enterprises operate, with clockwork II, a loosely connected view, and discusses implications for each view on leadership.

[16] Michael D. Cohen, James G. March, and Johan Olsen, "A Garbage Can Model of Organizational Choice," *Administrative Science Quarterly,* 1972, vol. 17, no. 1, pp. 1–25.

[17] Karl Weick, "Educational Organizations as Loosely Coupled Systems," *Administrative Science Quarterly,* 1976, vol. 21, no. 2, pp. 1–19.

[18] See, for example, William A. Firestone and Bruce L. Wilson, "Using Bureaucratic and Cultural Linkages to Improve Instruction: The Principal's Contribution," *Educational Administration Quarterly,* 1985, vol. 21, no. 2, pp. 7–30; Thomas J. Sergiovanni, "Landscapes, Mindscapes and Reflective Practice in Supervision," *Journal of Curriculum and Supervision,* 1984, vol. 1, no. 1, pp. 5–17.

in a recent Association for Supervision and Curriculum Development book *Productive School Systems in a Nonrational World.*[19] Supervisors who hold this view are less likely to rely on management controls and similar supervisory strategies in an effort to regulate the various parts. Both groups of supervisors share a common commitment to the importance of schools having goals and the importance of coordinating the activities of teachers and others in some systematic way in achieving those goals. But they are likely to pursue these aspirations quite differently. In Supervision II, supervisors rely far less on management controls and more on *bonding* people together by developing norms which are derived from a shared vision of what is important. In other words, these supervisors are more likely to view the problem of coordination as a cultural rather than management one.[20]

The key to Supervision II is a new and enlarged vision of teacher motivation and commitment. Traditional conceptions of motivation rely very heavily on charting and categorizing needs, identifying various job factors which correspond to these needs, and manipulating these factors in some kind of an investment and exchange system. Give to teachers those job factors and conditions which are important to them (which respond to their needs) and they in turn will provide the school with the things that it considers to be important. Motivation in Supervision I invariably leads to calculated involvement. Supervision II, by contrast, is less concerned with instrumental motivational theories and more concerned with the meanings that teachers and others derive from their work experiences, the values that they hold, and their connectedness to a shared vision of what the school is about.

The dimensions of Supervision I and Supervision II will be elaborated on in greater detail in the chapters which follow. At this point it is important to recognize that while a conceptual distinction between Supervision I and Supervision II is drawn the two emphases represent two distinct continua. Thus, the idea is not to emphasize one at the expense of the other but to provide a balance of emphasis on both dimensions. A well-thought-out curriculum, for example, combined with a professional development program designed to provide teachers with understandings and skills in using teaching models is as much a part of Supervision II as of Supervision I. In Supervision I, however, the emphasis is on placing this curriculum and its teaching models in a position that is *superordinate* to teachers. Teachers are expected to implement these curriculum and teaching protocols according to the provided specifications. Supervision, in this case, serves to monitor the work of teachers to ensure their compliance with the system and its protocols. Teachers, therefore, are *subordinate* to this work system.[21]

---

[19] Jerry L. Patterson, Stewart C. Purkey, and Jackson V. Parker, *Productive School Systems in a Nonrational World,* Alexandria, Va.: Association for Supervision and Curriculum Development, 1986.
[20] See, for example, Sergiovanni, "The Theoretical Basis for Cultural Leadership," op. cit., and Firestone and Wilson, op. cit.
[21] Sergiovanni, "We Need a TRUE Profession!" op. cit.

Supervision I: A bureaucratic view of teaching and supervision: Teachers are subordinate to the system

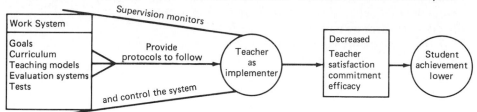

Supervision II: A professional view of teaching and supervision: Teachers are superordinate to the system

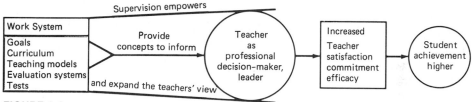

FIGURE 1-4
Supervisions I and II: The characteristics and effects of bureaucratic and professional views of teaching.

There is a striking similarity between the basic tenets and operating principles of Supervision I and scientific management discussed in the Introduction. Only when practiced today, scientific management is combined with human relations. As teachers implement the prescribed system they are provided with positive reinforcement, told how important they are, and encouraged to have a "positive attitude" about the whole thing. Human relations is the "spoonful of sugar" intended to make scientific management supervision "go down" better with teachers.

In Supervision II the same curriculum and teaching models are provided but *for use by* teachers. The models exist less to tell teachers what to do and more to help teachers make better decisions about their professional practice. Teachers, therefore, are *superordinate to this work system.*[22] The place of teachers within the work system is critical for determining whether teaching is to be considered bureaucratic or professional.

Views of teaching and their link to Supervisions I and II are depicted in Figure 1-4. In Supervision I the work system is dominant and supervision is controlling. The predicted result is less teacher satisfaction, commitment, and efficacy and declines in student achievement. Supervision II, by contrast, places the work system in a subordinate position to the teachers as decision maker with positive results in student achievement. Links between bureaucratic and professional systems and teacher satisfaction, commitment, and

[22] Ibid.

efficacy are well established in the literature.[23] Recent studies now provide compelling evidence that teacher satisfaction, commitment, and efficacy are linked to student achievement.[24]

If the distinctions between Supervisions I and II seem a bit distant at the moment, they will become clearer in later chapters. By the book's conclusion, Supervision II will have become ingrained into one's professional fiber. When put into practice, Supervision II holds the greatest promise for promoting professional values in teaching and for improving teaching and learning.

SUMMARY

This chapter presented perspectives on supervision. Supervision, it was pointed out, can be viewed as a process component of a variety of administrative and supervisory roles or as a label to categorize roles the primary responsibility of which is the improvement of instruction.

Supervisory roles were characterized by three distinguishing features: (1) heavy reliance on expertness as an educational program and instructional leader, (2) the necessity to live in two worlds and to speak two languages, and (3) limits imposed on their authority. Six viewpoints of supervisory roles within the administrative hierarchy were then described. They include the person in the middle, marginal person, another teacher, human relations specialist, human resources link, and monitor of instruction. The human resources link perspective was then proposed as the most effective model for supervision.

Normative and descriptive views of supervision were then discussed. Normative views specify what should be done and describe a more ideal world of supervision. They are useful in setting standards and for helping to select targets and goals toward which supervisors strive. Descriptive views focus specifically on the real world of supervision and provide descriptions of actual behaviors and events.

Principles governing the operation of supervision and the purposes of supervision were then discussed from a historical perspective. Supervisory purposes were grouped into three categories: supervision for quality control, for professional development, for teacher motivation. Pointing out that supervision in practice has always been more inclusive than quality control and professional development, a discussion of symbolism and cultural building in supervision was provided. A distinction was then made between Supervision I and Supervision II. Supervision I is the view that the world of schooling is tightly structured and connected. Within this view the aim of supervision is to get control over this tightly connected system. Supervision II, by contrast, is

[23] See, for example, Thomas J. Sergiovanni, "Factors Which Affect Satisfaction and Dissatisfaction in Teaching," *Journal of Educational Administration,* vol. 5, no. 2, pp. 66–82, 1967. Margaret C. Pastor and David A. Erlandson, "A Study of Higher Order Need Strength and Job Satisfaction in Secondary Public School Teachers," *Journal of Educational Administration,* vol. 20, no. 2, pp. 172–183, 1982.
[24] Patricia T. Ashton and Rodman B. Webb, *Making a Difference—Teachers' Sense of Efficacy and Student Achievement,* New York: Longman, 1986.

based on a view of teaching and supervision that is quite different. Teachers, curriculum, students, teaching, strategies, schedules, and events that comprise the process of schooling all exist but are disconnected from each other. Supervisors who hold this view are less likely to rely on management controls and similar supervisory strategies in an effort to regulate the various parts. Instead they are likely to practice a form of supervision that relies heavily on developing norms derived from a shared vision of what is important. Contrasts were then drawn between how teacher motivation is understood and practiced within each of the views. Views were then linked to scientific management, human relations, and human resources.

STUDY GUIDE

Recall the concepts, ideas, and meanings associated with each of the following phrases and terms included in this chapter. Can you discuss each of them with a colleague and apply them to the supervisory context of your school? If you cannot, review them in the text and record the page number for future reference.

1 Bureaucratic and professional view of teaching
2 Descriptive view of supervision
3 Distinguishing characteristics of supervisory roles
4 Human relations specialist
5 Human resources link
6 Monitor of instruction
7 Normative view of supervision
8 Person in the middle
9 Phonetics and semantics of supervision
10 Purposes of supervision
11 Supervision I
12 Supervision II
13 Supervisory roles and processes
14 Syntax of supervision
15 Symbolism and culture building in supervision

EXERCISES

1 Who are the persons in your school or district that are considered primarily as supervisors? How is their work distinguished primarily as administrators?
2 Review persons in your school or district in both supervisory and administrative roles. Develop a chart listing the role, the type of supervisory activities demonstrated in the role, and the percentage of time spent on each supervisory activity in a typical week. Base your estimates of percentage on the total time spent in all activities (administrative and supervisory) for each role.
3 Identify a supervisor with whom you work. Take a recent 2-week period and review how this person seemed to use his or her time. Write a brief job description for this

supervisor based on what he or she actually does. As part of this description identify primary job objectives and major responsibilities and tasks.

4 Describe the "ideal" supervisor as seen by the average teacher in your school or district. How does this description measure up to your analysis of supervisory roles in 2 and 3 above? How does this description measure up to your view of the "ideal" supervisor?

5 Using Figure 1-4 as a guide, interview three teachers with whom you have an open-candid relationship. To what extent do these teachers view the supervision they now receive as approximating Supervision I? Supervision II?

THEORETICAL FRAMEWORK FOR HUMAN RESOURCES SUPERVISION

Among professionals, "theory" does not enjoy high standing. Indeed many professionals label anything that is not practical theory or, more accurately, "just theory." Theory to them is a handy way to sort out and dismiss speculations and ideas which are not sensitive to the complex, fast-paced, and messy world in which they must live. Supervisors, for example, are particularly impatient with theories which purport to tell them what to do or theories that are proposed and marked as the "one best way" to practice. Theorists, meanwhile, are puzzled as to why professionals react the way they do toward theory. They take the high ground and point out that all professions are based on a body of knowledge which is research-based and theoretically sound. Thus they express disappointment and dismay when professionals view their theoretical models and research arrays as being remote and ill-fitting to practice.

Our sympathies are with the professionals' view of theory.[1] They have a right to expect more from theory and research than has been the case to date. Part of the problem is that theorists and researchers have been laboratory-oriented rather than school-oriented as they inquire into problems of teaching and learning, leadership and supervision. They collect data from schools about school problems but typically rely heavily on survey techniques and other methods which provide "thin" rather than "thick" views of reality. Many studies of leadership-effectiveness behaviors and teaching-effectiveness behaviors are examples. Such studies tend to emphasize "brute" data rather than "sense" data. Brute refers to the raw material of an idea or behavior—how

[1] Thomas J. Sergiovanni, "Landscapes, Mindscapes and Reflective Practice in Supervision," *Journal of Curriculum and Supervision,* vol. 1, no. 1, pp. 5–17, 1985.

something looks. When brute data are interpreted or understood given their context, purposes, and perception of others, they become sensible or sense data.[2] When brute data are emphasized, the result is descriptions of overt leadership or teaching behaviors which seem to be correlated with certain effectiveness indicators. The meaning of such behaviors to different individuals and in different settings is often overlooked. Much leadership and teaching research assumes the situations that professionals face are standard rather than changing, simple rather than complex, and amenable to specificity and definition rather than being vague in definition and tacitly known. From the researcher's view of things the idea is to establish fixed and true relationships between and among various dimensions of reality. But because of the complexity of the real world, truth remains elusive.

HOW PROFESSIONALS VIEW THEORY

Professionals, on the other hand, are interested in theoretical findings and research arrays that help them think about their problems rather than findings and arrays which purport to be true relationships that lead to specific practice prescriptions. What is considered to be rational to the theorists is often considered to be rationalistic to the professional. "The rationalistic tradition is distinguished by its narrow focus on certain aspects of rationality which...often leads to attitudes and activities that are not rational in a broader perspective."[3] The real "culprits," however, may not be the theorists and researchers but the educational synthesizers and model builders. The synthesizers and model builders are less concerned with creating new knowledge, focusing instead on integrating and developing knowledge into broader forms and arrays which can be more directly applied to practice. The arena for their work is the institute or workshop which seeks to *train* supervisors and teachers in a particular way. The "Hunter" Model of Teaching, the Direct Instruction Model, Fiedler's Leadership Model, and the Job Characteristics Model of Motivation developed by Hackman and Oldham[4] are examples of such efforts. The models are all research-based and theoretically derived. When proposed and indeed marketed as truth and prescribed to supervisors and teachers as a one best way to practice, they are likely to be ill-fitting to the realities of practice. But when the models are proposed as ways that encourage supervisors and teachers to think about practice and that provide frames for understanding the problems professionals face, they can be very useful. The models

[2] Charles Taylor, "Interpretation and the Sciences of Man," *The Review of Metaphysics,* vol. 25, no. 1, pp. 3–51, 1971.
[3] Terry Winograd and Fernando Flores, *Understanding Computers and Cognition,* Norwood, N.J.: Ablex Publishing Corp., 1986, p. 8.
[4] Madeline Hunter, "Knowing, Teaching and Supervising," in Philip L Hosford (ed.), *Using What We Know about Teaching,* Alexandria, Va.: Association for Supervision and Curriculum Development, 1984; Fred E. Fiedler, *A Theory of Leadership Effectiveness,* New York: McGraw-Hill, 1967; J. R. Hackman and Greg Oldham, "Motivation through the Design of Work: Test of a Theory," *Organizational Behavior and Human Performance,* vol. 16, no. 2, pp. 250–279, 1976.

are not true with respect to telling the professional what to do but are useful for informing the professional's judgment, guiding the decision-making process, and making professional practice more rational.

Supervision and teaching practice are best informed when theoretical designs, research arrays, and practice models are viewed metaphorically as designs to enlighten and illuminate rather than to prescribe and direct practice. It is in this tradition that a theory of supervisory behavior is proposed in this chapter. The theory will be largely instrumental and thus is more a part of Supervision I. In Chapter 8 the nature and usefulness of theory in supervision from a more substantive perspective in the tradition of Supervision II is proposed.[5] The emphasis in that chapter will be less on supervisory behaviors and their instrumental links to certain effectiveness indicators and more on how the actions of people and the events of school life relate to sense making and the building of meaning and significance. Taken together the theoretical perspectives underlying Supervision I and Supervision II will not tell supervisors what to do but can provide supervisors with a sound and useful basis for sorting out their world, making informed decisions, and practicing in a way which promotes quality schooling.

EVERYBODY USES THEORY

In the Introduction to Part One we referred to the practices, hunches, principles, and practices chain which comprised the practical art of using theory as proposed by Miller.[6] In that discussion it was pointed out that despite protestations to the contrary all supervisory actions are theoretically based. The question for supervisors and teachers, we proposed, is not whether they are being theoretical or not, but what are the theories (the implicit hunches and operating principles) which help shape the way they see their professional worlds and which provide the basis for professional decisions and practice. There are two levels of action at work as teachers and supervisors practice: stated theories of action and theories in use. Chris Argyris and Donald Schön describe the theories as follows:

> When someone is asked how he would behave under certain circumstances, the answer he usually gives is his espoused theory of action for that situation. This is the theory of action to which he gives allegiance, and which, upon request, he communicates to others. However, the theory that actually governs his action is his theory in use. This theory may or may not be compatible with his espoused theory; furthermore, the individual may or may not be aware of the incompatibility of the two theories.[7]

[5] Supervisions I and II are described and contrasted in Chapter 1.
[6] Van Miller, "The Practical Art of Using Theory," *The School Executive,* vol. 70, no. 1, pp. 60–63, 1958.
[7] Chris Argyris and Donald A. Schön, *Theory in Practice: Increasing Professional Effectiveness,* San Francisco: Josey-Bass, 1974.

When theorists and researchers emphasize too much the phonetic side of teaching (focusing on observable teaching behaviors and on adapting rationalistic approaches to supervision and evaluation), they may be focusing on the wrong theory of action. Teaching reality is often a result of one's theory in use rather than one's stated theory. Theories in use are typically not known to holders and if known are known only tacitly or implicitly.

It is difficult to identify theories in use by asking a teacher or supervisor what she or he believes or intends. Instead theories in use are inferred from one's actions and behaviors. Illuminating theories in use in teaching, for example, require that much more attention be given to developing better representations of teaching (data displays, pictures of reality, case studies, videotapes, artifact collections) than to charting and checking, assessing and score-crediting observable teacher behaviors. Throughout this process the teacher needs to play a key role in constructing these representations and in coming to grips with what the representations of teaching mean. The idea is to examine this teaching reality in light of the teacher's stated theory of action. When confronted with discrepancies between the two theories, one typically seeks a resolution and frequently this resolution results in a change in behavior. Dialogue and conferencing are key in this process. Teaching theories in use are best revealed and understood when the focus of supervision and evaluation shifts from an emphasis on the teacher and his or her behaviors to describing and understanding the teaching that is taking place. Using a metaphor from baseball, as useful as a box score may be, it cannot substitute for a vivid description of the ball game, complete with accounts by the players themselves. These issues and the uses and misuses of theory as it relates specifically to the supervision and evaluation of teaching are discussed further in Chapters 14, 15, and 16.

We are now stating the ground rules by which the following discussion of theory as it relates to the leadership and organizational dimensions of supervisory behavior needs to be understood. First, the purpose of the discussion is not to provide a set of principles considered to be true and thus applied uniformly by supervisors. Instead, the discussion is meant to help frame and expand the ways in which supervisors think about their practice and to provide them with constructs and concepts which can help them make better decisions about this practice. Second, by engaging in this discussion of theory it is hoped that supervisors will examine the ideas presented in light of the assumptions and beliefs that they hold and which comprise their theory in use. Keep in mind that the emphasis here is on the instrumental aspects of supervisory behavior. In later chapters more substantive aspects are considered.

A FRAMEWORK FOR UNDERSTANDING
THEORY AND SUPERVISION

Supervisors bring to their professional practice assumptions and beliefs which provide them with biases, understandings, and frames of reference. These biases, understandings, and frames of reference are formed and shaped by prior professional experience, educational encounters, political and religious views, principles gleaned from one's upbringing, educational philosophy and convictions, and even one's personality characteristics and needs. Together these biases, understandings, and frames of reference provide the basis for a supervisor's educational and management platform. Often implicit, this platform serves two important purposes. On the one hand it is the means by which the supervisor can sort out the professional problems he or she faces and make sense of a complex world of practice. On the other hand educational and management platforms provide the rationale for making sensible the decisions one makes in practice. These decisions affect the people with whom the supervisor must work in various ways. If a supervisor decides on a highly authoritarian and directive approach to supervision, teachers will be affected in one way. If the supervisor uses shared decision making, teachers are affected in another way, and so on. These reactions to the supervisor's behavior, in turn, have a telling effect on the level and quality of performance which teachers provide to the school. This chain of events is the heart of the supervisory theory we propose.

The theory identifies and describes three sets of variables. One set is the *action variables*.[8] The action variables are what supervisors start out with. They include the assumptions, values, and beliefs which determine the leadership style and pattern and the priorities of supervisors and the kinds of decisions they are likely to make. Different assumptions, values, and beliefs result in different supervisory actions. With regard to school structure, for example, how supervisors view and use rules and regulations, the decision-making traditions and procedures they establish, and the patterns of authority they develop and enforce are examples of action variables.

Reactions of teachers and others influenced by the action variables make up the second set of variables referred to as *mediating*. Teachers, for example, might be either inspired, indifferent, or discouraged as a result of being influenced by certain action variables. The third set, the *effectiveness* variables, represent the "output" that results from school efforts and activities. The effectiveness variables are estimates and measures of how well the school is doing. These are the key components of the theory we propose.[9]

The following list of action, mediating, and effectiveness variables is not conclusive or exhaustive but represents examples that fall into each of the three categories. In each case the emphasis is on teachers and other adults but the categories and the theory itself can be applied to students as well.

[8] In the first three editions of this book action variables were referred to as initiating.
[9] See, for example, Rensis Likert, *New Patterns of Management*, New York: McGraw-Hill, 1961; Rensis Likert, *The Human Organization, Its Management and Value*, New York: McGraw-Hill, 1967.

WHAT THE SUPERVISOR BRINGS AND DOES
(ACTION VARIABLES)

1 The assumptions and beliefs that supervisors hold about themselves, teachers, students, and others at work in the school.
2 The management and leadership behavior patterns which supervisors consistently display.
3 The sources of authority and power which supervisors use in working with teachers and students.
4 The nature of goals and directions for the school and the means used to determine these goals.
5 The ways in which supervisors seek to motivate teachers.
6 The supervisor's view of change and the ways in which the supervisor works to bring about change.
7 How problems are identified and decisions made.
8 The emphasis the supervisor gives to the following in providing a management structure to the school:
   a Formalization (the extent to which the supervisor emphasizes rules and regulations).
   b Stratification (the importance the supervisor places on status systems and the rights of those in superordinate positions).
   c Centralization (the extent to which the supervisor emphasizes shared decision making, as opposed to hierarchical decision making).
   d School productivity (the emphasis the supervisor gives to the numbers). The number of learning objectives, the number of students served, the amount of time spent, the number of months gained, the numbers associated with test scores could be considered as examples. School productivity should not be confused with more qualitative conceptions of how well the school is doing.
   e Efficiency (the extent to which the supervisor emphasizes quantity of output at least cost). Large classes and lecture methods, for example, are more efficient means to cover text material than small classes. Providing options to students is less efficient than providing standardized learning experiences. A standard evaluation system and uniform staff development activities provide for a more efficient supervisory system.
   f Adaptability (the emphasis the supervisor gives to being responsive to changing needs and requirements of students, advances in educational technology and pedagogy, and changes in the community). The extent to which the supervisor encourages teachers to be innovative and adaptive in the organization of their classrooms and in their teaching practices.
   g Complexity (the extent to which the supervisor relies on the personal and professional expertness of teachers and respects the status of teachers as specialists and professionals).

h Job satisfaction (the emphasis the supervisor gives to providing teachers and others with opportunities to experience intrinsic satisfaction at work).

HOW TEACHERS REACT (MEDIATING VARIABLES)

1 Attitudes that teachers and other staff members have toward their jobs and toward their supervisors, peers, and students.
2 The extent to which the staff is committed to school goals and purposes.
3 The extent to which teachers have confidence and trust in themselves, fellow teachers, and their supervisors.
4 The extent to which teachers feel that they have control over their immediate work environment and can meaningfully influence the larger school environment.
5 The extent to which a system for communication exists at all levels of the school enterprise and in all directions.
6 The extent to which teachers collaborate with each other and help each other.
7 Levels of performance goals held by teachers and other staff members.
8 Levels of group loyalty and group commitment that exist in the school.

HOW SCHOOLS ARE INFLUENCED
(EFFECTIVENESS VARIABLES)

1 Performance levels of teachers and other staff members.
2 Performance levels of students as measured by traditional tests.
3 Performance levels of students as assessed by other means.
4 Personal growth levels of teachers and students.
5 Absence and dropout rates of students.
6 Absence and turnover rates of teachers.
7 Quality of school-community relations.
8 Quality of teacher-supervisor relations.
9 Levels of intrinsic satisfaction for teachers.
10 Levels of morale for teachers.

HOW THE VARIABLES ARE CONNECTED

Traditionally the relationship between action variables and effectiveness variables has been conceived as being direct. Supervisory actions and behaviors were assumed to directly affect school outcomes. By planning, organizing, goal setting, controlling, supervising, directing, and instructing, supervisors worked to improve the performance levels of teachers and students and achieve as well other dimensions which comprise the school effectiveness variables. What was important in this approach was the development of the right management systems and rational controls which would program the work of teachers and others in a predetermined way. In some respects the idea was to override the idiosyncrasies of people at work. Neglecting the mediating variables and working directly from action to effectiveness variables is a form of bureaucratic supervision.

Patterns of supervision associated with human resources, on the other hand, are based on the premise that consistent and long-term achievement of school success is dependent upon the motivation and commitment of teachers and other school workers. Thus in human resources supervision the mediating variables are considered to be very important. They comprise the human organization of schools and include the quality of communications, group loyalty, levels of job satisfaction, and commitment to task. It is assumed that if the mediating variables are influenced in this direction the school is more likely to show positive results in the effectiveness variables.

Bureaucratic supervision is characterized by little mutual confidence and trust among supervisors and teachers, direct supervision, high control, centralized decision making, detailed rules and regulations and work operating procedures, top-down communications, the routinization of work, and regulation by inspection. Human resources supervision, by contrast, reflects a commitment to the development of teachers and other workers and is characterized by trust, supportive relationships, goal clarity and commitment, autonomy with responsibility, group decision making, authority more closely linked with ability, teamwork, social interaction, and controls linked to agreed-upon goals and purposes.

The key to understanding the theory is to differentiate between long- and short-term effectiveness. Often working directly from action to effectiveness variables is more effective in the short run than working to effect changes in the mediating variables. But over time this strategy can result in a serious erosion of the school's human organization. Consider, for example, the now classic Morse and Reimer study[10] which examined the effectiveness (the productivity and well-being of the human organization) of employees subjected to two different styles of supervision. Group One, subjected to a bureaucratic style of supervision, outdistanced Group Two (participatory style) in production. But Group One showed a commensurate decline in the quality of its human organization. This research suggests that over the short run bureaucratic supervision is indeed more effective than participatory. But over time the erosion of the human organization took its toll in worker performance. Group Two gradually began to outperform Group One. In commenting on this phenomenon, Rensis Likert noted that "the attitudes, loyalties, and motivation which improved the most in the participatory program and deteriorated the most in the hierarchical controlled program are those which these studies have consistently shown to be most clearly related *in the long run* to employee

[10] Nancy Morse and E. Reimer, "The Experimental Change of a Major Organizational Variable," *Journal of Abnormal and Social Psychology*, vol. 52, no. 1, pp. 120–129, 1956.

motivation and productivity."[11] It is clear that human resources supervision requires an investment in time by supervisors before appreciable results can be realized. As the "mellowing" process sets in, the school's investment in its human organization is likely to show improvements in each of the effectiveness variables. The variables and their relationship to quality schooling are illustrated in Figure 2-1. If, for example, the supervisor brings to his or her practice a sense of purpose, a plan of operation, high performance goals, and strong management and leadership skills and if the supervisor emphasizes bureaucratic supervision, then the mediating variables will be affected as illustrated with telling negative consequences for the school. If, however, the supervisor emphasizes human resources supervision, the mediating variables are affected more positively and the effectiveness variables associated with quality schooling are likely to have been achieved. Note that in Figure 2-1 the mediating variables are grouped into three categories: Type 1, Type 2, and Type 3 with Types 1 and 3 illustrated. These reactions of teachers to the supervisory system they experience are described below.

MEDIATING VARIABLES: TYPE 1 REACTION

Type 1 reactions of teachers are typically characterized by considerable job dissatisfaction with working conditions, supervision, school policies, and administration. Further, dissatisfaction with job security, with peer and student interpersonal relationships, and with supervisors can be expected. In extreme cases teachers become alienated from their supervisors and from the school itself. Of course, supervisors do not deliberately seek a Type 1 reaction from teachers. Such reactions are usually unanticipated consequences of ignoring the human organization of the school. The Type 1 reaction results, over time, in lower levels of performance for teachers and students; resistance to change, higher turnover, anti-school informal group activity; and formal labor problems for the school. In many respects the teachers described in the Introduction to this book who were subjected to scientific management supervision were providing a Type 1 reaction.

MEDIATING VARIABLES: TYPE 2 REACTION

Human relations supervisory patterns tend to evoke Type 2 responses from teachers. The Type 2 reaction is characterized by a feeling of apathy toward the work of the school and by patterns which emphasize social relationships, high morale, good feelings, and low tension. When this is the case, teachers are relieved from job dissatisfaction but few performance expectations are present and little or no work pressure is eliminated. Further, security is guaranteed. Though teachers may be quite content under these circumstances, they feel no compulsion to exert commitment, energy, and effort beyond that which is minimally required to carry

[11]Likert, *New Patterns of Management,* p. 68.

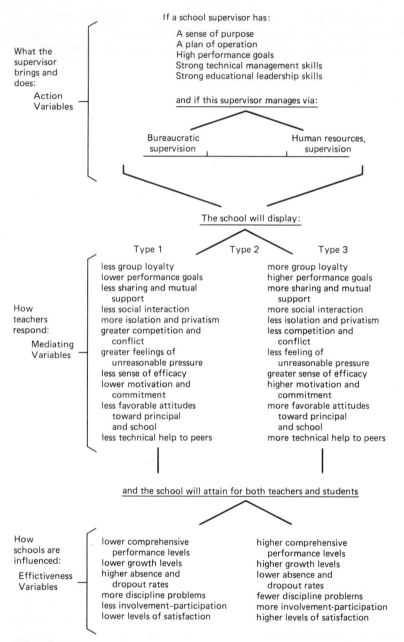

If a school supervisor has:

A sense of purpose
A plan of operation
High performance goals
Strong technical management skills
Strong educational leadership skills

What the supervisor brings and does:
Action Variables

and if this supervisor manages via:

Bureaucratic supervision   Human resources, supervision

The school will display:

Type 1   Type 2   Type 3

How teachers respond:
Mediating Variables

less group loyalty	more group loyalty
lower performance goals	higher performance goals
less sharing and mutual support	more sharing and mutual support
less social interaction	more social interaction
more isolation and privatism	less isolation and privatism
greater competition and conflict	less competition and conflict
greater feelings of unreasonable pressure	less feeling of unreasonable pressure
less sense of efficacy	greater sense of efficacy
lower motivation and commitment	higher motivation and commitment
less favorable attitudes toward principal and school	more favorable attitudes toward principal and school
less technical help to peers	more technical help to peers

and the school will attain for both teachers and students

How schools are influenced:
Effectiveness Variables

lower comprehensive performance levels	higher comprehensive performance levels
lower growth levels	higher growth levels
higher absence and dropout rates	lower absence and dropout rates
more discipline problems	fewer discipline problems
less involvement–participation	more involvement-participation
lower levels of satisfaction	higher levels of satisfaction

FIGURE 2-1
A theoretical framework for human resources supervision. *Summarized from Rensis Likert (1961),* New Patterns of Management, *New York: McGraw-Hill, Rensis Likert, 1967.* The Human Organization: Its Management and Value, *New York: McGraw-Hill; and Thomas J. Sergiovanni (1967),* The Principalship, A Reflective Practice Perspective, *Boston: Allyn and Bacon. Figure 2-1 is an adaptation and extension of Figure 4-10 in Likert, 1967. p. 76.*

on day by day. Little opportunity exists for teachers to grow personally and professionally and to enjoy deep intrinsic satisfaction from their work. Though little that is bad is happening in Type 2 reaction schools there is little that is good. Supervisors who evoke a Type 2 reaction from teachers often fail to distinguish between providing for teacher contentment and engaging with teachers as colleagues in the work of the school.

MEDIATING VARIABLES: TYPE 3 REACTION

Human resources supervisory patterns which emphasize working to achieve the school-effectiveness variables through engaging teachers and encouraging their growth and development evoke responses that are labeled as Type 3. This response is characterized by high commitment to the work of the school, high loyalty to the school, high performance goals, and the desire combined with an opportunity for personal and professional growth. Job satisfaction in this case centers around growth opportunities, achievement, recognition, responsibility, and advancement. The reward system that encourages Type 3 responses depends heavily upon achievement and responsibility.

To this point we have been discussing a broad theoretical framework for the leadership and organizational dimensions of supervisory behavior. Specific theories of leadership, motivation, and organization which fit into this framework will be discussed in later chapters. Important, of course, will be those which hold the greatest promise for eliciting the Type 3 reaction. As the theories are provided, keep in mind that none can be applied specifically as described and none can be applied in all cases. Rather, goodness will be determined by the fit between the proposed theory and the problems and purposes of interest to the supervisor on the one hand, and by the ability of the theory to inform and enhance the supervisor's thinking and guide his or her decisions on the other.

CAUTIONS IN IMPLEMENTING
HUMAN RESOURCES SUPERVISION

The philosophical, theoretical, and research base supporting human resources supervision is well established. In subsequent chapters we point out that this supervision is not only humane and fitting for educational organizations with their "people-intensive" characteristics and distinctly human undertakings but that the view is supported by a formidable body of theory and research and enjoys claims of success from practitioners in many fields. Still one must be cautious in applying human resources supervision. It would be a mistake, we believe, to view the assumptions, concepts, and practices associated with this supervision as being universally applicable. Human beings are much too complex for this sort of blanket prescription.

Consider, for example, the problem of motivating teachers to work and how this problem is addressed in human resources supervision. In Chapter 6 a distinct and powerful view of teacher motivation will be presented. Documentation for this view will be provided on several counts—ethical, theoretical, and empirical. Though the point of view will be applicable to most teachers, many will not respond. One's sets of values and work norms, for example, affect one's orientation toward work. Some teachers will never be properly motivated to work and others will usually be motivated to work regardless of what supervisors do. Indeed, a good rule of thumb is if you want motivated workers hire motivated people. The majority of teachers desire and seek satisfying work and will respond to human resources supervision but many will not and alternative supervisory methods and procedures that suit these teachers will need to be provided. In such cases, patterns of supervision associated with either the bureaucratic or human relations may well be appropriate.

It is important to recognize at the starting gate of this book that human resources supervision is not an elixir to be administered indiscriminately to all. It is, nonetheless, a powerful concept of supervision which we believe can markedly improve the identity, commitment, and performance of most teachers and the quality of teaching and learning in most schools.

As a further note, one should not interpret this caution as a rationalization for abandoning the principles of human resources supervision. Supervisors may well find that the theory does not fit some teachers, but they need to be careful if this number is very large or increases rapidly. The problem may not be with the teachers but with the supervisor and his or her assumptions about teachers.

TACTICAL AND STRATEGIC REQUIREMENTS OF LEADERSHIP

To this point the theoretical framework for human resources supervision has emphasized interpersonal and behavioral dimensions. Relying heavily on social science and management science research these dimensions are linked by relating them to ways in which teachers are influenced and subsequently relating influence patterns to effects on the school and its work.

A question worth asking at this point is whether it is conceivable that a supervisor can master all the social and management science wizardry associated with human resources supervision (and forthcoming in the next several chapters) and thus become an expert in articulating leadership skills, and still not contribute to quality schooling? The answer to this question is yes. Mastering management and leadership skills and other behavioral dimensions of organization is important but is not enough to ensure that supervisors will be able to build school quality. For example, knowing how to arrange and prepare for a group meeting, mastering a contingency theory of leadership, and being able to articulate effectively conflict management techniques may have more to do with keeping a school out of "trouble" than building its excellence. Going beyond satisfactory conditions to excellence requires that supervisors give attention to more substantive aspects of leadership. Mary Parker Follett made this point over fifty years ago:

Let us look further at the essentials of leadership. Of the greatest importance is the ability to grasp a total situation. The chief mistake in thinking of leadership as resting wholly on personality lies probably in the fact that the executive leader is not a leader of men only but of something we are learning to call the total situation. This includes facts, present and potential, aims and purposes and men. Out of a welter of facts, experience, desires, aims, the leader must find the unifying thread. He must see the relationship between all the different factors in a situation.

She continues:

The leader then is one who... can organize the experience of the group and thus get the full power of the group. The leader makes the team. This is preeminently the leadership quality—the ability to organize all the forces there are in an enterprise and make them serve a common purpose. Men with this ability create a group power rather than express a personal power. They penetrate to the subtlest connections of the forces at their command, and make all these forces available and most effectively available for the accomplishment of their purposes.[12]

And finally:

The most successful leader of all is one who sees another picture not yet actualized. He sees the things which belong in his present picture but which are not yet there.... Above all, he should make his co-workers see that it is not *his* purpose which is to be achieved but a common purpose born of the desires and the activities of the group.[13]

A similar differentiation can be made between tactical and strategic requirements of leadership. Quality in leadership requires that balanced attention be given to both tactical and strategic requirements. Unfortunately the emphasis in supervisory leadership today is often on the tactical. Strategy can be defined as the art and science of obtaining and employing support for policies and purposes and for devising the means for accomplishing long-term goals. Tactics, by contrast, involves smaller-scale objectives, decisions, and actions that serve a larger purpose and refers to the methods and means of less magnitude. One of the reasons why tactical aspects of leadership are so strongly emphasized in school supervision and administration is that they reflect the broader management culture of our western society. Such values as efficiency, specificity, rationality, measurability, and objectivity combined with beliefs that good management is tough-minded are part of this culture. Results-oriented management is the slogan, the bottom line is worshiped, and the direct, in-control manager is admired. Leadership theory, in this view, puts the emphasis on the leaders' behavior and on results. The metaphors of the battlefield are often used to remind us that one must be hard-nosed and that the

---

[12] Excerpted by permission of the publisher, from Mary Parker Follett, "The Essentials of Leadership," in Harwood Merrill (ed.), *Classics in Management*, pp. 299–300, © 1960, 1970 AMACOM, a division of American Management Association, New York. All rights reserved.
[13] Mary Parker Follett, *Dynamic Administration*, New York: Harper & Row, 1941, pp. 143–144.

going is tough. Evaluation is quickened to the point and success is determined on the basis of short-term accomplishments.

Missing from this emphasis on tactical concerns in supervisory leadership are holistic values of purpose, goodness, and importance. This point can be illustrated by examining the popularity of the school-effectiveness and teaching-effectiveness research and the use of models derived from this research in practice. In each case the models and their research base are limited and highly focused, emphasizing highly explicit, short-term, and readily measurable indicators of effectiveness (typically elementary school achievement test score gains in reading and mathematics). Given the definition of effectiveness one might ask, can a school be effective but not good? Many experts think so.[14] Questions of effectiveness and goodness are different. Goodness has to do with what is valued. Is, for example, a school which is effective in raising reading and mathematics scores really a good school if science or art are neglected; if students find learning stressful and hurried; if teachers experience burnout; if teaching is mechanical; if high-level thinking and problem-solving skills are neglected; if intellectual experiences are rare; if students wind up being well trained but poorly educated? Coming to grips with goodness requires that supervision and teaching emphasize long-term quality schooling and long-term commitment to the quality of the human organization—strategic concerns.

Tactical and strategic requirements of supervisory leadership are compared in Table 2-1. Proper balance requires that tactical requirements be clearly linked to and dependent upon the strategic. They represent short-term and highly focused managerial expressions that characterize day-by-day leadership activity. Separate from the strategic, they are in themselves devoid of the purposes and meaning needed for quality leadership and quality schooling. When writing a book, however, it is sometimes necessary to deal with one and then the other. Chapters 7 and 8, both dealing with leadership, are examples. Chapter 7 examines leadership from a tactical perspective and Chapter 8 from a strategic perspective.

SUMMARY

This chapter provided a theoretical framework for understanding and practicing human resources supervision. The assertion was made that present conceptions and the dominant models of supervision and teaching are inadequate when literally applied because they do not fit the actual world of practice. It was recommended that professional practice would be better served if the models were used metaphorically to help inform professional judgment rather than as prescriptions for practice.

With this understanding in mind a theory of supervisory behavior was

---

[14] See, for example, Sara Lightfoot, *The Good High School*, New York: Basic Books, 1983; Thomas J. Sergiovanni, *The Principalship, a Reflective Practice Perspective*, Boston: Allyn and Bacon, 1987; and Carl D. Glickman, "Good and/or Effective Schools: What Do We Want?" Undated, mimeo.

TABLE 2-1
TACTICAL AND STRATEGIC REQUIREMENTS OF SUPERVISORY LEADERSHIP

Tactical requirements of leadership	Strategic requirements of leadership
1. Ask what should be done now to achieve objectives. An atomistic or task-specific view is important.	Ask what is good in the long haul. A holistic view is important.
2. Develop a contingency perspective for education supervision, management, and the organization that permits altering arrangements to suit unique short-term circumstances.	Develop an enduring philosophy of education supervision, management, and organization to ensure consistency and to give a proper purpose and meaning to events.
3. Emphasize leadership styles that are carefully and skillfully matched to task requirements.	Emphasize leadership qualities that reflect and nurture this philosophy.
4. Develop operating structures, procedures, and schedules for implementing purposes.	Develop an overall plan or image that provides a frame for implementing purposes.
5. Having a plan is important.	Having a vision is important.
6. Decisions should be governed by stated objectives.	Decisions should be governed by purposes and philosophy.
7. The outputs to be achieved are important. Be concerned with structures and results.	The meaning of events to people is important. Be concerned with processes and substance.
8. The development and articulation of sound techniques are key to success.	Sensitivity to and involvement of people are key to success.
9. Quality control is a result of careful planning and organizing of the work to be done and/or providing continuous evaluation.	Quality control is a state of mind that comes from loyal and committed people who believe in what they are doing.
10. Evaluation should be short-term to determine if specific objectives are being met and to enable the provision of systematic and continuous feedback.	Evaluation should be long-term to determine more adequately the quality of life in the school and to assess effectiveness more holistically.

11. A basic corollary: *Strategic requirements should never be sacrificed in favor of tactical requirements.*

From Thomas J. Sergiovanni, "Ten Principles of Quality Leadership," *Educational Leadership*, vol. 39, no. 5, p. 331, 1982, copyright © 1982 T. J. Sergiovanni.

then provided as a framework for thinking about one's practice. The theory identified three sets of variables: action (what supervisors do), mediating (how teachers react), and effectiveness (how schools are influenced) and discussed their interrelationships as a basis for human resources practice. Cautions in implementing human resources supervision were then discussed. The chapter concluded with an analysis and comparison of the tactical and strategic requirements of leadership.

STUDY GUIDE

Recall the concepts, ideas, and meanings associated with each of the following phrases and terms included in this chapter. Can you discuss each of them with a colleague and apply them to the supervisory context of your school? If you cannot, review them in the text and record the page number for future reference.

1 Action variables
2 Brute data
3 Bureaucratic supervision
4 Educational and management platforms
5 Effectiveness variables
6 Human resources supervision
7 Mediating variables
8 Rational theory
9 Rationalistic theory
10 Sense data
11 Stated theories
12 Tactical and strategic leadership requirements
13 Theories in use
14 Type I, II, and III reactions

EXERCISES

1 Paul Mort is often quoted as having said, "Action without theory is like a rat scurrying through a maze." Another favorite quote of theorists is, "There is nothing as practical as good theory." In your own words, develop a working definition of theory. Give examples of how theory is dependent upon practice.
2 Develop a paragraph or two describing three real or imagined teachers, one whose reactions to organizational life is Type 1, another whose reaction is Type 2, and a third, Type 3. To what extent are these reactions related to administrative, organizational, and supervisory characteristics as described in the synthesizing theory, and to what extent are these reactions related to other factors? Other factors might include the teacher's interest in teaching, the teacher's personality, or perhaps competing demands from forces outside the school.
3 Using the examples of mediating variables provided in Figure 2-1, how are teachers in your school responding to the supervision they are receiving? What would need to be done to move responses closer to Type 3?
4 Use the paired statements that appear in Table 2-1 to describe the relative emphasis your principal gives to tactical and strategic leadership requirements. Using a total of 10 points for each of the paired statements, allocate points to reflect emphasis. A distribution of 9 and 1 for the first set of paired statements would suggest that only rarely does the principal reflect a concern for the larger picture over the long haul, being preoccupied with more specific and immediate matters.

THE ORGANIZATIONAL CONTEXT: BUREAUCRACY, POWER, POLITICS

Bureaucracy, power, and politics. What do these ideas have to do with supervision? After all, supervisors are concerned with teaching and learning, with helping teachers, and with other matters relating to curriculum and instruction. Had this question been asked, what should these ideas have to do with supervision, the answer might well be "very little." Unfortunately, this is not the case, for the organizational context which defines schools exerts considerable influence on teaching learning decisions and how supervision is practiced.

Supervisors, for example, are often required to use state- or district-mandated effectiveness indicators to evaluate teachers in cases where they think such use is inappropriate. Teachers frequently select learning objectives and teach lessons in response to mandated student testing rather than professional estimates of what students need. Rules and regulations may require that a teacher hold a student back even when that teacher feels promotion makes more sense. A curriculum series considered to be inferior in a literary and intellectual sense is selected over a superior one because it meets district guidelines for noncontroversial materials. Against the teacher's better judgment special-education students are labeled as being in a special category in order to comply with federal funding requirements. An administrator may be responsible for evaluating teachers even though she or he may know less than a supervisor or other teachers. A group of teachers succeeds in "stonewalling" a school-improvement effort it recognizes as being good for students because it will result in their being more vulnerable to evaluation by administrators. The facts of the real world are that bureaucracy, power, and politics are everywhere and must be dealt with as supervisors practice.

In this chapter we examine bureaucratic characteristics of schools and how the values underlying these characteristics often conflict with professional values. Much of the work of supervision occurs at the tension point between the conflicting values of bureaucracy and professionalism. The characteristics of bureaucratic and professional organization are described and contrasted and attention is given to the delicate task of balancing one against the other in a fashion which provides for managerial stability on the one hand and best teaching practice on the other. Questions of authority and power are considered and the basis for supervisory power is examined. And finally we examine the supervisor's role as a manager of conflict. We begin by examining the school as a complex organization.

THE SCHOOL AS A COMPLEX ORGANIZATION

We live in an organized world. To quote from a recent book on organizations: "Children are born into the physical confines of large medical organizations—hospitals—spend much of their growing years in even larger organizations—schools—and graduate, most of them, into the employ of even larger businesses or government organizations. Many of our large high schools are as populous as small towns, universities are veritable cities, and multinational corporations are virtual nation states."[1]

Romantic vestiges of the little red schoolhouse still exist in America, but most schools, like most other organizations, have experienced phenomenal growth in size, areas serviced, and professional complexity. The emergence and spread of the large high school, for example, has progressed to the point where this unit dominates American secondary education. The operation of the large high school is usually characterized by sophisticated management techniques, scientific staff utilization, computerized scheduling, diverse program offerings, and a variety of student services. Elementary schools share many of these features, though on a smaller scale.

Modern organizations are characterized by a high degree of specialization as well as by size. They too have their share of experts who claim monopolies over certain aspects of the management system (directors, vice-principals, division heads for instructional units, student personnel administrators, finance experts, and so on) and "technical" system (subject-matter specialists, hardware experts, early-childhood-disadvantaged-compensatory-education specialists, and school psychologists, for example).[2] Numerous new positions and functional roles have appeared in the last two decades in American education that have made schools more complex. For example, in states and school

---

[1] H. Randolf Bobbitt, Jr., Robert Breinholt, Dobert Doktor, and James McNaul, *Organizational Behavior: Understanding and Predicting*, Englewood Cliffs, N.J.: Prentice-Hall, 1974, p. 1.

[2] The terms "management systems" and "technical systems" are used, after Parsons, to differentiate between the administrative side of school life and the teaching and learning side. See Talcott Parsons, "Some Ingredients of a General Theory of Organization," in Andrew W. Halpin (ed.), *Administrative Theory in Education*, Chicago: University of Chicago, Midwest Administration Center, 1958.

districts with centrally mandated uniform teacher-evaluation systems specialists have emerged who do little else but evaluate teachers. Often this complexity in managerial structure and proliferation of specialized roles results in increased bureaucracy.

BUREAUCRATIC ELEMENTS AND TENDENCIES IN SCHOOLS

What does the word "bureaucracy" mean to you? Chances are, this word conjures up negative feelings and reactions from most Americans. The antibureaucracy bias often limits rational discussion of the positive and negative bureaucratic characteristics of schools. We perhaps contribute to this bias by designating schools as either bureaucratically oriented or professionally oriented. For the purposes of this discussion, the bureaucratic designation for schools is used in a negative sense, in that human resources supervision will tend not to thrive there. The professional designation for schools is used in a positive sense to indicate an ideal environment for supervision. Yet underlying these perspectives, the authors recognize that schools are actually on a continuum extending from more bureaucratic to less bureaucratic.

The person responsible for developing the concept of the ideal bureaucracy, with its accompanying characteristics, was Max Weber. He believed that "the decisive reason for the advance of bureaucratic organization has always been its purely technical superiority over other forms of organization."[3] Weber's ideal bureaucracy is characterized as follows: (1) a division of labor and specific allocation of responsibility; (2) reliance on fairly exact hierarchical levels of graded authority; (3) administrative thought and action based on written policies, rules, and regulations; (4) an impersonal, universalistic bureaucratic environment for all inhabitants; and (5) the development and longevity of administrative careers.[4]

The extent to which schools follow the bureaucratic model varies, of course, from school to school but all schools exhibit some bureaucratic tendencies.[5] Consider, for example, Abbott's listing of the following characteristics of bureaucracy applied to schools.

1 The school organization has clearly been influenced by the need for specialization and the division of tasks. The division of the school into elementary and secondary units; the establishment of science, mathematics, music, and other departments within a school; the introduction of guidance programs and psychological services; and, indeed, the separation of the administrative function from the teaching function all represent responses to this need.

[3] Max Weber, "Bureaucracy," in Hans Gerth and C. Wright Mills (eds.), *From Max Weber,* New York: Oxford, 1946, p. 214.

[4] Max Weber, *Theory of Social and Economic Organization,* A. M. Henderson and T. Parsons (trans.), New York: Oxford, 1947, pp. 333–336.

[5] Any list of items that characterize or describe the "ideal type" bureaucracy is limited in that no organization fits the description exactly. In this sense no organization is a bureaucracy but most organizations approximate bureaucracy in various degrees.

2 The school organization has developed a clearly defined and rigid hierarchy of authority. Although the term "hierarchy" is seldom used in the lexicon of the educational administrator, the practices to which it refers are prevalent. The typical organization chart is intended specifically to clarify lines of authority and channels of communication. Even in the absence of such a chart, school employees have a clear conception of the nature of the hierarchy in their school systems. In fact, rigid adherence to hierarchical principles has been stressed to the point that failure to adhere to recognized lines of authority is viewed as the epitome of immoral organizational behavior.

3 The school organization has leaned heavily upon the use of general rules to control the behavior of members of the organization and to develop standards which would assure reasonable uniformity in the performance of tasks. Whether they have taken the form of policy manuals, rules and regulations, staff handbooks, or some other type of document, general rules have been used extensively to provide for the orderly induction of new employees into the organization and to eliminate capricious behavior on the part of all school personnel, including administrators and members of boards of education.

4 Despite frequent proclamations regarding togetherness and democracy, the school organization has made extensive application of Weber's principle of impersonality in organizational relationships. Authority has been established on the basis of rational considerations rather than on the basis of charismatic qualities or traditional imperatives; interpersonal interactions have tended to be functionally specific rather than functionally diffuse; and official relationships have been governed largely by universalistic, as contrasted with particularistic, considerations. Thus, by operating in a spirit of "formalistic impersonality," the typical school system has succeeded, in part, in separating organizational rights and obligations from the private lives of individual employees.

5 Employment in the educational organizations has been based upon technical competence and has constituted for most members a professional career. Promotions have been determined by seniority and by achievement, tenure has been provided, and fixed compensation and retirement benefits have been assured.[6]

DYSFUNCTIONS OF BUREAUCRACY

Certain goals, objectives, and educational activities can best be pursued within a bureaucratic setting. But others suffer somewhat because of this setting. Are the benefits worth the cost? Can the costs be lived with? Are the benefits of long-term value? Are some costs so high that benefits need to be forsaken? These are important questions for supervisors to consider.

[6] Max G. Abbott, "Hierarchical Impediments to Innovation in Educational Organizations," in M. G. Abbott and John Lovell (eds.), *Change Perspectives in Educational Administration*, Auburn, Ala.: Auburn University School of Education, 1965, pp. 44–45.

The benefits of bureaucracy are in the orderliness and efficiency that it brings to the school. Its costs are in deterministic and programming character-istics which often result in rigid and impersonal organizational structures. The basic dimensions of bureaucracy seem less offensive than the excessive application of its underlying assumptions of rationality by many administrators and supervisors. Bureaucracy assumes, for example, that the clockworks metaphor for organizing discussed in Chapter 1 fits the real world of schooling. Do these rational assumptions fit the real world? Cyert and March,[7] March and Simon,[8] and Thompson,[9] for example, point out that organizations may not be as rational in operation as they seem on paper. They provide a view of the real world of school organization, which resembles the workings of a clock gone awry.

Decision making is often used to illustrate this point. Administrators, supervisors, and teachers tend not to "seek the best needle in the haystack" when they search for solutions to problems but to use the first one which will work. Given time limits and other constraints, a supervisor settles on a workable approach in helping a teacher rather than the best possible approach. Instead of planning the best possible lesson, a teacher plans and teaches a lesson based on the easy availability of materials, being satisfied that this lesson will reach given objectives. After all, the teacher reasons, I have over 1,500 other lessons to teach these kids this year and one has to be practical. In this sense experts conclude that schools tend to seek not maximizing solutions to their problems, but rather solutions that they can accept as satisfying current needs. *Organizations are notoriously "satisficing" as they follow their own impulses.* Thus the bureaucratic image of rational organization and decision making seems not to approximate reality.

Many critics of excessive bureaucracy point out that the features of this model of organizing discourage organizational learning and interfere with the problem-solving capacities of workers.[10] The problem is particularly serious in schools where learning and problem solving are at the very heart of teaching and supervisory practice. For example, the characteristics of bureaucracy are ideally suited for facilitating the making of uniform and reliable decisions which match predetermined rules and requirements, for monitoring the system to ensure that this process continues, and for making corrections that are needed. This ability of the school to detect and correct errors given certain specifications is referred to (using a computer meta-phor) as "single-loop" learning. "Double-loop" learning, by contrast, adds to this cycle an additional step which questions the *assumption* on a regular basis. If the assumptions do not make sense given the circumstances at

---

[7] Richard M. Cyert and James G. March, *A Behavioral Theory of the Firm*, Englewood Cliffs, N.J.: Prentice-Hall, 1963.

[8] James G. March and Herbert A. Simon, *Organizations*, New York: Wiley, 1958.

[9] James Thompson, *Organizations in Action*, New York: McGraw-Hill, 1968.

[10] See, for example, Chris Argyris and Donald A. Schon, *Organizational Learning: A Theory of Action Perspective*, Reading, Mass.: Addison-Wesley, 1978.

hand, the cycle is broken and problem solving is required to create a new, more appropriate cycle. This double-loop learning, so characteristic of practice in all the professions, is discouraged by bureaucratic designs. Single- and double-loop learning are depicted in Figure 3-1.

PROFESSIONAL ELEMENTS AND TENDENCIES IN SCHOOLS

Although schools contain many bureaucratic characteristics, they possess some distinguishing characteristics common to professional organizations as well. Professionally oriented organizations differ from other organizations in the nature of their authority and power systems. They are characterized by the development and application of a pluralistic power structure that is (1) spread out throughout the organization; (2) based on the ability and competence of people; (3) dynamic, in the sense that power shifts from person to person as circumstances change; (4) interdependent, in that usually coalitions of individuals are needed to marshal sufficient competence to command authority at a given time; and (5) functional, in that power tends not to keep well in storage

FIGURE 3-1
Single- and double-loop learning in schools.

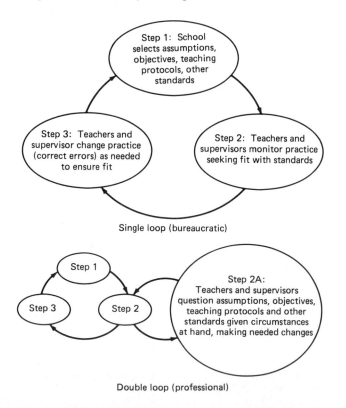

but needs to be constantly examined for "goodness of fit" in terms of one's competence and the task at hand. In this sense, the professional organization tends to rely on task-oriented rather than people-oriented power bases, on expert rather than formal authority.

Professionals enjoy more power than ordinary workers because of their special training and of images most have of professional work. Professionally oriented workers, for example, can be characterized as having (1) considerable advanced formal preparation; (2) skills not readily available in others, including other professionals; (3) a commitment to their profession, discipline, or area that often assumes priority over a commitment to their place of employment; (4) a belief that autonomy is necessary for them to practice best; (5) an overriding belief in service to the public and in a concept of best practice defined by what is best for "clients"; and (6) an interests34in a reward system that emphasizes growth and development, achievement, and responsibility but does not ignore bread-and-butter items such as security and salary.

From this list of characteristics one might assert that not all teachers can be described as professionals, but many can. When this is the case, we have professionally oriented teachers who are expected to practice in schools that are often bureaucratically oriented in design and operation. This predicament provides the basis for much of the conflict which exists between teachers and supervisors and the setting for many difficulties supervisors and administrators face in trying to provide helpful leadership to teachers.

BUREAUCRATIC AND PROFESSIONALLY ORIENTED SCHOOLS

Schools can be described as fairly complex organizations that contain both bureaucratic and professional characteristics. But schools vary in the extent to which one or another of these characteristics is emphasized. Some schools, for example, are organized in ways which discourage the articulation of professional values and the nature of professional work. Other schools are organized in a fashion which encourages these characteristics. The basic structural features of schools, from an organizational point of view, and how various school functions are shaped and prescribed are keys in determining the extent to which a school might be characterized as more professional or more bureaucratic. To illustrate this point, a theory of organization proposed by Jerald Hage will be described.[11] His theory, called the axiomatic theory of organizations, illustrates these relationships very effectively. He assumes that all organizations have structures and functions. Emphasizing some structures contributes more to certain functions than to others. Further, when some structures are emphasized, other structures are de-emphasized. Knowing the relationship between and among these various structures and functions can provide supervisors and administrators with powerful understandings and tools for action. They can structure in ways that enhance

---

[11] This discussion is based on Jerald Hage, "An Axiomatic Theory of Organization," *Administrative Science Quarterly*, vol. 10, no. 3, pp. 289–320, 1965.

bureaucratic or professional values and goals. For example, structurally schools are concerned with degrees of centralization, formalization, stratification, and complexity. These are the organizational means schools use to achieve their ends. The ends comprise four school functions. Functionally schools are concerned with the emphasis they give to production, efficiency, adaptiveness, and satisfaction. The structural and functional characteristics of schools can be described as follows:

THE SCHOOL'S STRUCTURAL-FUNCTIONAL SYSTEM

Structure-School Organizational Means

Complexity. This refers to how specialized the school is organizationally and administratively as well as to the degree of professional and technical specialization which exists in the teaching staff. Complexity is concerned with *specialization in people,* not in jobs or tasks. For example, the heart surgeon is a person specialist, the assembly-line worker is a task specialist. Normally, the teacher who is an expert on constitutional government is a person specialist, but normally the teacher who teaches nothing but sophomore American history is a task specialist. The more professional the staff, the more complex the organization. The more complex the organization, the more influence professionals have in decisions relating to their work.

Centralization. The extent to which levels of decision making correspond to predetermined hierarchical arrangements or organizational charts determines the school's centralization tendencies. When responsibility and authority for important decision making is dispersed throughout the school, we have low centralization. When important decision making is primarily the prerogative of the central office or principal, we have high centralization. Schools can be characterized by low centralization with regard to adults (teachers heavily involved) but high centralization with regard to students (students not involved).

Formalization. This refers to the extent to which a school relies on standardized rules and regulations or standard operating procedures in order to increase uniformity in decision making and similarity in behavior. High formalization is related to high centralization because it programs the decision making of teachers, students, and often administrators, and funnels upward any situations which are varied and cannot be accounted for by the rules or by standard operating procedures.

Stratification. This refers to the amount of status differences which exist between and among hierarchical levels in the school. As status differences increase, that is, as rights and privileges of people at one level increase over those at other levels, stratification increases.

Function-School Ends

Production. Within the theory production refers to school outputs which can be counted and easily measured. The number of students graduated, the number of courses offered, the number of Carnegie units accumulated, the number of pages read or problems completed are examples of production. *Production does not refer to quality.* Thus according to the theory, when schools are more concerned with the quality of services they render to students, and work to improve this quality as opposed to increasing the *number* of services rendered or the *number* of clients served, they are de-emphasizing production.

Efficiency. This refers to costs per unit of output. Costs include not only money, but utilization of staff, time, materials, and space as well. A teacher-student ratio of 35 to 1 is more efficient than one of 25 to 1.

Adaptiveness. This refers to the school's ability to respond and its emphasis on responding to changing professional and societal environments. An adaptive school is one which utilizes the most advanced professional and technical knowledge and know-how and whose educational program adjusts to changing student needs.

Satisfaction. This refers to the extent the school focuses on the worth of its human organization as a school goal. Need fulfillment and professional and personal growth and development of teaching staff are considered legitimate and important goals which are ranked with student learning, growth, and development.

In applying the principles from Hage's theory, the eight structural-functional characteristics of schools can be related to each other in fairly predictable ways. For example, as a school increases its emphasis on *centralized* control and decision making, it is likely to become more *formalized* and its *stratification* system is likely to become more pronounced. At the same time, its emphasis on *complexity,* or person autonomy and specialization, will decrease. Higher centralization, formalization, and stratification and lower complexity are very likely to increase the school's *production* and *efficiency* levels, but the school will become less responsive and *adaptive* and people will become less *satisfied.*

The basic propositions as proposed by Hage are as follows:

The higher the centralization, the higher the production.
The higher the formalization, the higher the efficiency.
The higher the centralization, the higher the formalization.
The higher the stratification, the lower the job satisfaction.
The higher the stratification, the higher the production.
The higher the stratification, the lower the adaptiveness.
The higher the complexity, the lower the centralization.[12]

Perhaps the easiest way to understand the relationship between and among the eight organizational dimensions is to view them as being in two groups—one more characteristic of bureaucratically oriented schools and the other of professionally oriented schools. The groupings are illustrated below. The group associated with bureaucratically oriented schools is composed of centraliza-

[12] Ibid., pp. 297–299.

tion, formalization, stratification, production, and efficiency. The professional group is composed of complexity, adaptability, and satisfaction.

Bureaucratically Oriented Schools			
L	complexity	L	adaptiveness
H	centralization	H	production
H	formalization	H	efficiency
H	stratification	L	job satisfaction
Professionally Oriented Schools			
H	complexity	H	adaptiveness
L	centralization	L	production
L	formalization	L	efficiency
L	stratification	H	job satisfaction

L = lower, H = higher.

Note that in each case when one of the characteristics designated higher (H) is increased, others designated H also increase but those designated lower (L) decrease. Increasing the emphasis on centralized decision making, as in our earlier example, results in higher formalization, production, and efficiency but lower complexity, adaptiveness, and job satisfaction. In this context bureaucratic values flourish and professional values suffer. By the same token, professional values can be enhanced by recognizing the expertness of teachers and empowering them (H complexity). When this is the case the school becomes more adaptive and teachers derive more satisfaction from their work. Though work *quality* may improve, school production (as defined by this theory) and efficiency are likely to suffer and centralization, formalization, and stratification will be less apparent in the school's organization structure.

According to the theory, it is possible to shift the emphasis from bureaucratic to professional or the other way by manipulating various aspects of the school's structural-functional system. It is even possible, and often desirable, to create *different* organizational systems for different purposes. A bureaucratic system might be emphasized for the school's management-oriented concerns (i.e., record keeping, paperwork, scheduling, ordering books and supplies) and a professional system for more direct teaching and learning concerns (i.e., classroom organization, curriculum, teaching, staff development).

BUREAUCRATIC AND PROFESSIONAL CONFLICT

Despite the fact that supervisors and other administrators might become quite skilled at walking the line of tension between the school's bureaucratic and professional faces, conflict is unavoidable. It seems inevitable that occasions will occur when professional and bureaucratic values confront each other and choices need to be made as to which of the two will prevail. Corwin believes that this conflict is institutionalized in the ways in which schools are organized and run. He observes, for example, that administrators typically hold bureaucratic expectations for teachers and students while teachers typically hold professional expectations. He compares these different sets of expectations in Table 3-1.

In an analysis of school conflict identified through research based on this comparison, Corwin makes the following observation:

> Approximately forty-five percent of all the incidents involved teachers in opposition to members of the administration; about one-fifth of these disputes were "open" discussions involving direct confrontations of parties in an argument or "heated" discussions (as judged by content analysis), or "major incidents" including a third party in addition to those teachers and administrators initially involved; this is a larger number of

TABLE 3-1

CONTRASTS IN THE BUREAUCRATIC- AND PROFESSIONAL-EMPLOYEE PRINCIPLES OF ORGANIZATION

Organizational characteristics	Bureaucratic-employee expectations	Professional-employee expectations
Standardization		
Routine of work	Stress on uniformity of clients' problems	Stress on uniqueness of clients' problems
Continuity of procedure	Stress on records and files	Stress on research and change
Specificity of rules	Rules stated as universals; and specific	Rules stated as alternatives; and diffuse
Specialization		
Basis of division of labor	Stress on efficiency of techniques; task orientation	Stress on achievement of goals; client orientation
Basis of skill	Skill based primarily on practice	Skill based primarily on monopoly of knowledge
Authority		
Responsibility for decision making	Decisions concerning application of rules to routine problems	Decisions concerning policy in professional matters and unique problems
Basis of authority	Rules sanctioned by the public	Rules sanctioned by legally sanctioned professions
	Loyalty to the organization and to superiors	Loyalty to professional associations and clients
	Authority from office (position)	Authority from personal competence

From Ronald Corwin, "Professional Persons in Public Organizations," *Educational Administration Quarterly*, vol. 1, no. 3, p. 7, autumn 1965.

open conflicts than reported among teachers themselves. About one-half of all incidents involved *groups* of teachers (teachers' organizations in seven percent of the cases).

Twenty-four percent of all conflict incidents fell in the categories of classroom control, curriculum management, and authority in the school; these incidents embraced such issues as the use of proper teaching techniques and procedures, changing the curriculum and selection of textbooks. About half of these involved administrators. Of the 159 incidents that were in the open, about one-fourth were with the administration over these issues of authority.[13]

The higher the professional orientation of teachers, according to Corwin's findings, the higher the rates of conflict. He concludes, "The weight of evidence from this very limited sample suggests that there is a consistent pattern of conflict between teachers and administrators over the control of work, and that professionalization is a militant process."[14] The dilemma for the supervisor is, of course, reconciling for himself or herself the increasing bureaucratization and professionalism that Corwin and others see as two simultaneous but conflicting thrusts for schools.

Another dimension of bureaucratic and professional conflict is that which occurs when one has to choose between ability authority, and hierarchical authority. The two kinds of authority are frequently contesting each other. In studying this problem, Victor Thompson spoke about the ability-authority gap which he believed characterizes modern organizations.[15] He pointed out that there is an increasing gap between those in schools and other organizations who have the right to decide and those who have the ability to do. In the ideal type of bureaucratic organization, it is assumed that those who have authority also have ability. In the real world, however, this is not the case. When schools honor authority over ability they are reflecting their bureaucratic face. When they honor ability over hierarchical authority they are reflecting their professional face. Of course it is easy to say, when writing a book, that ability-authority ought to prevail over hierarchical. But this is not always possible and indeed in some instances may not even be desirable. Principals, for example, are expected by the public to "run" their schools and supervisors to evaluate teachers whether or not they are most qualified to do so.

DEFINING POWER AND AUTHORITY

Power is one of those words that makes some people nervous. Supervisors, for example, typically do not like to view themselves as power holders and brokers and are reluctant to admit that they seek and need power in order to practice successfully. The reality is that without power little can happen in the school. It is, metaphorically, a form of organizational energy which fuels the decision-making

---

[13] Ronald Corwin, "Professional Persons in Public Organizations," *Educational Administration Quarterly*, vol. 1, no. 3, p. 12, 1965.
[14] Ibid., p. 15.
[15] Victor A. Thompson, *Modern Organization*, New York: Alfred Knopf, 1961.

process—providing for both stability and change. Schools, like other organizations, require a reasonable amount of order and conformity. They represent organized ways in which to accomplish certain ends. Thus directions are given, actions coordinated, suggestions made, activities assigned, meetings held, standards set, programs adapted, performance appraised, resources distributed, and plans developed within an organized structure in a systematic attempt to effect the school's purposes. Each of these tasks and functions requires exchanges in influence in order to obtain the compliance of one person to the wishes of another.

In this section the authority and the bases of social power available to supervisors and others are discussed. Though authority typically rests in the hands of a few, the bases of social power are more widely distributed and are accessible to many. Competing sources of authority and accessibility to bases of power often lead to competing claims of influence and to conflict between and among individuals. Therefore, attention is also given to the development of conflict-management techniques. Power and authority are concepts often difficult to separate in practice, but useful differences exist between the two that can help in understanding their respective origins, expressions, and effects. Authority is the right to act or to require others to act on behalf of school purposes. Weber defines authority as the willing compliance of people based on the belief that it is legitimate for the designated leader to impose his or her will on subordinates.[16] The most common view of authority is that it is related to one's position and the inherent rights associated with that position.[17]

Power, on the other hand, refers to anyone's ability to influence the decision-making process. This ability comes sometimes from authority associated with one's formal position in the hierarchy of the school but at other times from other sources. Indeed, often those with little authority exert considerable influence (power) on the decisions. In many supervisory roles authority is weak. Chairpersons, curriculum coordinators, resource persons, and instructional supervisors might be examples. Contrast the authority found in these staff-type roles with that of superintendent for instruction, principal, general superintendent, and other line positions.[18] Lacking sufficient organizationally derived authority, supervisors are often required to look elsewhere in order to generate enough influence to affect educational decisions.

Since influence is a natural and important aspect of life in schools,

[16] Max Weber, *The Theory of Social and Economic Organization,* Talcott Parsons (ed.), A. M. Henderson and T. Parsons (trans.), Glencoe, Ill.: Free Press, 1947.

[17] Chester Barnard provides a contrasting view of authority. In his "acceptance theory" he assumes that authority comes from below rather than above. Authority in itself does not exist but is based on the willingness of subordinates to accept. Without acceptance, in his view, no authority exists. See, for example, Chester Barnard, *The Function of the Executive,* Cambridge, Mass.: Harvard University Press, 1938.

[18] Traditionally a distinction has been made between *line* and *staff* positions. Line authority is straightforward and consists of a direct superordinate-subordinate relationship between individuals. Staff authority is more complex and is designed to support line authority by advising administrators and teachers and by providing special services at the request of either administrators or teachers. Operationally the distinction is more muddled, as our discussion of social power and authority will reveal.

supervisors need to understand the nature of authority—its many origins, form, operational feasibility, and acceptance. As schools have matured into complex professional organizations, newer forms of authority have emerged to challenge traditional authority sources.

WEBER'S AUTHORITY TYPES

Max Weber[19] distinguishes among three types of authority as follows:

> *Traditional.* This authority base is legitimized by the belief in the sanctity of tradition. A given person or caste of people, usually on the basis of heredity, is preordained to rule over the others. The divine right of kings is a classical example of traditional authority. In contemporary organizations, the management caste treasures and passes on traditional prerogatives which other employees are perceived not to have. This is particularly visible in patriarchal family businesses and in paternalistic schools.
>
> *Charismatic.* This authority base rests on a profession of faith which considers the pronouncements of a given leader to be inspired by supernatural powers. Disciples willingly follow the charismatic leader as they become converted to and champions of his cause. In contemporary organizations, the innovator, the champion of new educational and social movements, may be able to tap the charismatic power base. Charismatic movements eventually evolve into traditional or bureaucratic management systems.
>
> *Legal.* This authority base is legitimized by a formalistic belief in the supremacy of norms and laws. In legal systems, compliance occurs as a result of a body of impersonal and universal principles and rules rather than of loyalty to the traditional or charismatic leader. Legal authority forms the basis for the ideal bureaucratic organization.

The Weber formulation provides a background for most scholarly discussions of organizational authority and power. In recent years a fourth source of organizational authority has emerged—one based on professional norms and skill. Professional authority is similar to legal authority in that both are legitimized by codes, rules, and norms. This similarity is a major cause of conflict between the two. In our discussion of bureaucratic and professional conflict we pointed out that school norms and rules often conflict with professional. Consider, for example, the guidance counselor who feels it unethical or harmful to disclose test scores to parents but who is required to do so by the school code or by administrative rules.

THE SOURCES OF SUPERVISORY POWER

It seems useful to consider authority as a broad basis for action not directed at any one individual. Power, on the other hand, at least in an administrative sense, is directed at obtaining individual or group compliance to superiors in the organization.[20]

---

[19] Max Weber, op. cit.

[20] This definition is not limited to compliance between and among superordinates and subordinates. Teacher A may have a powerful influence on teacher B and thus be assured of teacher B's reliable compliance, yet both are officially at the same hierarchical level.

French and Raven identify and describe five bases for the social power that person O can exert over person P:

(a)reward power, based on P's perception that O has the ability to mediate rewards for him; (b) coercive power, based on P's perception that O has the ability to mediate punishments for him; (c) legitimate power, based on the perception by P that O has a legitimate right to prescribe behavior for him; (d) referent power, based on P's identification with O; (e) expert power, based on the perception that O has some special knowledge or expertness.[21]

Reward power is typically emphasized in benevolent or paternalistic schools. Rewards need to be acceptable to teachers or to be desired by them. Pay increases, recognition, special favors, better schools, favorable work assignments and schedules, better equipment, and so on are among the reward incentives available to administrators and supervisors. *Coercive* power is the ability to impose sanctions on teachers. Coercive power systems are the reverse of reward. They often go hand in hand. For example, the department budgets of chairpersons who comply with the wishes of the principal are increased, but if they challenge the wishes of the principal, budgets are cut.

Expert power is the ability to obtain compliance on the basis of professional knowledge, information, and skills. Administrators and supervisors who are able to command the admiration and respect of others operate from a referent power base. This power source is often a result of expert power—that is, we respect and admire an individual's competence. *Referent* power is nevertheless conceptually independent of expert power. Many supervisors gain the support of others because they are admired as people. Their leadership styles, interpersonal skills, and other personality characteristics often help to win this admiration.

Legitimate power refers to administrative prerogatives of command and the ability to influence as a right of one's office. When the new teacher meets the superintendent at the September orientation tea, be assured that the new teacher understands fully the concept of legitimate power. It is legitimate for the principal to decide certain things because that is what principals are supposed to do. Rules and regulations exist and the supervisor has a responsibility to enforce them.

BASES OF SUPERVISORY POWER, SATISFACTION, AND PERFORMANCE

In an attempt to answer the question "Why do people comply with the requests of supervisors, and how are these reasons related to organizational effectiveness and individual satisfaction?" Bachman, Bowers, and Marcus[22] examined

---

[21] J. R. P. French, Jr., and B. Raven, "The Bases of Social Power," in D. Cartwright and A. F. Zander (eds.), *Group Dynamics: Research and Theory*, 2d ed., Evanston, Ill.: Row, Peterson, 1960, p. 612. In more recent work Raven speaks of a sixth source of social power he calls *informational power*. See, for example, Raven, "Social Influence and Power," in I. D. Steiner and M. Fishbein (eds.), *Current Studies in Social Psychology*, New York: Holt, 1965, pp. 371–382.

[22] Jerald D. Bachman et al., "Bases of Supervisory Power: A Comparative Study in Five

the bases of supervisory power in five organizational settings. The investigators asked subordinates why they complied with their supervisor's wishes. Additional measurements were obtained for worker satisfaction and, in three of the organizations, for worker performance. Table 3-2 shows the mean ratings of bases of power for each of the five organizations on each of the five power variables. Note that power variables are adapted from French and Raven.

The investigators observe that the most important reason for complying with the wishes of superiors was response to legitimate power and expert power. Referent and reward power were cited less often, with coercive power the least likely reason for compliance. This trend seems more pronounced for organizations described as professional—the branch office, the college, and the insurance agency. Public schools would be expected to respond similarly.

Correlations between the five bases of supervisory power and measures of satisfaction with the supervisor or with the job appear in Table 3-3. This table shows that expert power and referent power seem to provide the strongest and most consistent positive correlation with worker satisfaction. Coercive power, particularly for the educational organizations studied, draws the most negative correlation with satisfaction. The investigators summarize their findings as follows:

This summary of data obtained in five organizational studies has provided a number of fairly consistent findings. (1) Legitimate power was rated one of the two most important bases of power; however, it did not seem a consistent factor in organiza-

TABLE 3-2
MEAN RATINGS OF BASES OF POWER*

	Organizational settings				
	1	2	3	4	5
Bases of power	Branch offices	Colleges	Insurance agencies	Production work units	Utility company work groups
Legitimate	4.1	3.6	3.3	3.4	4.7
Expert	3.5	4.1	3.8	3.4	3.0
Referent	2.9	3.5	2.5	2.7	2.1
Reward	2.7	2.3	2.8	2.8	2.7
Coercive	1.9	1.6	1.8	2.3	2.5

*All ratings have been adjusted so that a value of 5.0 represents the highest possible rating and 1.0 represents the lowest possible rating. Respondents in organizational settings 1, 2, and 5 used a ranking procedure; those in settings 3 and 4 used a procedure that permitted independent ratings of the five bases of power.
    Source: Jerald D. Bachman et al., "Bases of Supervisory Power: A Comparative Study in Five Organizational Settings," in A. S. Tannenbaum (ed.), *Control in Organizations,* New York: McGraw-Hill, 1968, p. 234.

Organizational Settings," in Arnold S. Tannenbaum (ed.), *Control in Organizations,* New York: McGraw-Hill, 1968, p. 229.

TABLE 3-3

CORRELATIONS WITH SATISFACTION MEASURES

	Organizational settings				
	1	2	3	4	5
Bases of power	Branch offices (N = 36)	Colleges (N = 12)	Insurance agencies (N = 40)	Production work units (N = 40)	Utility company work groups (N = 20)
Legitimate	−.57*	−.52	.04	.40†	−.35
Expert	.69*	.75*	.88*	.67*	.30
Referent	.75*	.67†	.43†	.57*	.11
Reward	−.57*	−.80*	.48*	.27	−.12
Coercive	−.31	−.70†	−.52*	.01	−.23

* *p* .01, two-tailed.
† *p* .05, two-tailed.
Source: Jerald D. Bachman et al., "Bases of Supervisory Power: A Comparative Study in Five Organizational Settings," in A. S. Tannenbaum (ed.), *Control in Organizations,* New York: McGraw-Hill, 1968, p. 235.

tional effectiveness, nor was it related significantly to total amount of control. (2) Expert power was the other very prominent basis of power, and it was strongly and consistently co-related with satisfaction and performance. Of the five bases, expert power was most positively related to total amount of control. (3) Referent power was of intermediate importance as a reason for complying with a supervisor's wishes, but in most cases it was positively correlated with criteria of organizational effectiveness. In two sites it was significantly and positively related to total amount of control. (4) Reward power was also of intermediate importance; in this case the correlations with organizational effectiveness and with total control were not consistent. (5) Coercive power was clearly the least prominent reason for compliance; moreover, this basis of power was often negatively related to criteria of effectiveness and in two cases negatively related to total amount of control.[23]

In another study using the French and Raven formulation, Bachman, Smith, and Slesinger[24] examined the relationship among bases for social power and satisfaction and performance in a professional sales office. Correlations among worker perception of office-manager power, office mean-performance scores, and office mean-satisfaction scores are provided in Table 3-4. This table again suggests that referent power and expert power yield higher positive and significant correlations with performance and satisfaction, while reward, coercive, and legitimate power bases yield some significant but all negative correlations with performance and satisfaction. The investigators conclude the following:

[23] Ibid, p. 236.
[24] Jerald D. Bachman et al., "Control, Performance, and Satisfaction: An Analysis of Structural and Individual Effects," in Arnold S. Tannenbaum, op. cit., p. 213.

TABLE 3-4
POWER, PERFORMANCE, AND SATISFACTION

Bases of manager's power	Mean standardized performance	Mean satisfaction with manager
Referent	.40*	.75*
Expert	.36*	.69*
Reward	−.55†	−.51†
Coercive	−.31	−.71†
Legitimate	−.17	−.57†

Note: Sell entries are product-moment correlation.
* *p* .05, two-tailed.
† *p* .01, two-tailed.
Source: Bachman et al., "Control, Performance, and Satisfaction: An Analysis of Structural and Individual Effects," in A.S. Tannenbaum (ed.), *Control in Organizations*, New York : McGraw-Hill, 1968, p. 213.

Total control, performance, and satisfaction with the office manager were all relatively high for the office manager whose leadership was perceived as resting largely upon his skill and expertise (expert power) and upon his personal attractiveness (referent power). Conversely, the less effective office manager was one who appeared to rely more heavily upon the use of rewards and sanctions (reward power and coercive power) and upon the formal authority of his position (legitimate power) as a formal description of his role might indicate. At the level of interoffice comparison, this overall relationship was substantial and highly consistent.[25]

In examining the relationship between influence and satisfaction in secondary schools, Hornstein and his associates conclude:

These data, which are in full accord with the findings of previous studies, suggest that the effects of superior-subordinate relations in school systems are very much like those of various industrial, sales, and voluntary organizations. Teachers report greatest satisfaction with their principal and school system when they perceive that they and their principals are mutually influential, especially when their principal's power to influence emanates from their perceiving him as an expert. Moreover, this same principal-teacher relationship is associated with a perception of higher student satisfaction.[26]

They also note that teachers' perceptions of the principal's use of coercive power were highly related to their dissatisfaction with the principal and the school and with their perceptions of students' dissatisfaction with teachers.

In a Canadian study that investigated sources of power used by elementary school principals and their relationship to teachers' perceptions of satisfaction and performance, Balderson notes:

Schools with principals whose power was perceived to rest on relevant expertise

---

[25] Bachman et al., op. cit., p. 225.
[26] Harvey A. Hornstein et al., "Influence and Satisfaction in Organizations: A Replication," *Sociology of Education*, vol. 41, no. 4, p. 389, fall 1968.

received *high* scores for teacher morale, teacher satisfaction with principal's performance, and the degree to which the principal favored (1) teacher doing an effective job
helping students learn, (2) teacher experimenting with new ideas and techniques, and (3)
teacher suggesting ideas to improve the school. In addition these schools also received
high scores for the degree to which teachers feel their principals are open to their ideas
and the degree to which they feel their principals have delegated enough authority to
teachers to enable them to do their work. Without exception, those schools with
principals who were perceived to exercise coercion in attempting to influence teachers
revealed the lowest scores on these measures.[27]

Studies of this sort make it difficult to determine cause and effect, but the
relationship between expert authority and other factors associated with school
effectiveness seems clear. Balderson concludes that "if we also note that
supervisors are involved in the task of achieving better instruction by working
through others, that is teachers, it seems evident from these data that the
effectiveness of supervisory practice will be enhanced by the adoption of
practices based on expertise,"[28] a view entirely consistent with human resources supervision.

It seems apparent that supervisory behavior that relies on functional
authority and on expert and referent power bases will have positive effects on
the human organization of the school.

THE EMPOWERMENT ISSUE

Some researchers have discovered a link between the extent to which all
members of an organization, regardless of rank, experience empowerment and
effectiveness.[29] This line of inquiry suggests that the total feeling of empowerment experienced by principals, supervisors, and teachers may be more
important than the relative distribution among them. These studies plot
perceptions of empowerment for individuals at various hierarchical levels as
shown in Figure 3-2, where sloped lines indicate the distribution of power.

Note that in School B administrators, supervisors, and teachers perceive that
they have approximately the same amount of empowerment. This slope suggests
a high degree of equality. By contrast the slope for School A shows that
comparatively, administrators enjoy substantially more power than do supervisors
and teachers. Tannenbaum and his colleagues would conclude that though the
slope itself is important, what is more important is the size of the *area* beneath the
slope line. Thus though things may be a bit more unequal in School A the total
amount of power available is higher and thus everyone has more control, with
more positive consequences for both morale and productivity.[30]

[27] James H. Balderson, "Principal Power Bases: Some Observations," *The Canadian Administrator,* vol. 14, no. 7, pp. 3–4, 1975.
[28] Ibid., p. 5.
[29] See, for example, Arnold Tannenbaum, *Control in Organizations,* New York: McGraw-Hill,
1968, and Tannenbaum and R. A. Cooke, "Organizational Control: A Review of Studies Using the
Control Graph Method," in *Organizations Alike and Unlike,* London: Routledge and Kegan Paul, 1979.
[30] Arnold Tannenbaum, *Control in Organizations,* New York: McGraw-Hill, 1968.

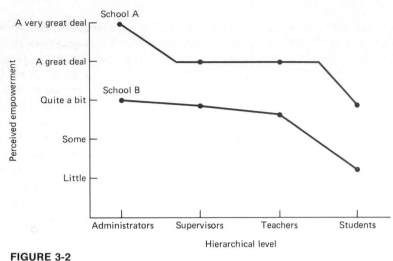

FIGURE 3-2

MORAL AND CALCULATED INVOLVEMENT

There is a relationship between the kind of power used in order to obtain compliance and the kind of involvement one gets in return. If, for example, extrinsic rewards are used as the primary means to get compliance, involvement becomes calculative. That is, you get the person to do what it is that he or she is supposed to do. But their commitment is contingent upon a reward continuing to be available. A school district that adopts a merit pay system that takes into account the extent to which teachers give extra effort, meet students after school, and take students on Saturday field trips might very well find that should monies not be available to continue the merit system, teachers are likely to stop doing these things. When one is involved in a calculated way in her or his work, that person is conscious of what constitutes a "fair day's work for a fair day's pay." On the other hand, when one is morally involved in work one engages in the activity because of intrinsic reasons. A teacher might feel that spending time with youngsters after school and taking youngsters on Saturday field trips is something that you are *supposed to do* because that's what teaching is about. To them, good teaching requires this kind of extra effort.

The organizational theorist Amitai Etzioni has examined the relationship between how one achieves compliance and the subsequent nature and degree of involvement of a person at work. In addition, the nature of compliance and involvement is linked to type of organizational goals. Together, these dimensions comprise his compliance theory.[31] His is an important theory, for it suggests that overemphasis on certain methods of obtaining compliance might well be short-sighted in the long run. For example, students who read books or engage in other learning activities primarily to get good grades may not engage in these activities

[31] Amitai Etzioni, *A Comparative Analysis of Complex Organizations*, New York: Free Press, 1961.

when grades are no longer available. In Etzioni's view a number of strategies, power bases, and authority systems may be appropriate depending upon the nature of goals to be achieved and the tasks that constitute action toward the goals. He identifies four dimensions which are interrelated in his theory: the method of compliance or the power strategy, goals, the degree of subsequent involvement, and tasks. These dimensions are summarized in Table 3-5.

One interpretation of Etzioni's theory is that the appropriateness of a given compliance strategy will depend largely on the nature of the goal being pursued. If, for example, the goal is order and the task is a routine one, the most efficient compliance strategy is coercive. Yet before one chooses this strategy one must be prepared to pay the price of alienation which is likely to occur among workers. If it is worth the price to accomplish the goal, the coercive strategy may well make sense.

The goals of schools are generally considered to be predominantly cultural and the tasks of teachers and students are largely expressive in that they define, legitimize, and strengthen commitment to the cultural goals. These goals require, according to this theory, normative compliance strategies and these strategies, in turn, result in moral commitment. Normative compliance strategies are those which rely on the sense one sees in an activity and a degree of commitment to engage in that activity because the activity itself is worthwhile, useful, or otherwise considered to be good. At one time or another order, economics, and cultural goals all make sense in schools and thus each of their corresponding expressions of power is appropriate. But for schools a proper balance among the three would emphasize cultural over the other two. Much of the interest in understanding schools metaphorically as cultures and in providing "cultural" leadership is based on dimensions of Etzioni's theory. Supervision II, for example, views the world of schooling as being somewhat loosely connected, making difficult the achievement of coordination by using traditional management techniques. Instead, Supervision II relies heavily on moral authority to build commitment, on the development of shared norms to achieve coordination. This theme will be explored in greater detail in Chapters 5, 8, and 9.

TABLE 3-5
THE COMPONENTS AND CHARACTERISTICS OF ETZIONI'S
COMPLIANCE THEORY*

Component	Type A	Type B	Type C
Goal	Order	Economic	Cultural
Power	Coercive	Utilitarian	Normative
Involvement	Alienative	Calculative	Moral
Task	Routine	Instrumental	Expressive

* *Order goals* are oriented toward control of actors in the organization. *Economic goals* refer to increasing or maintaining output at favorable cost to the organization. *Cultural goals* refer to the socializing, institutionalizing, preserving, extending, and applying of value systems and life systems.

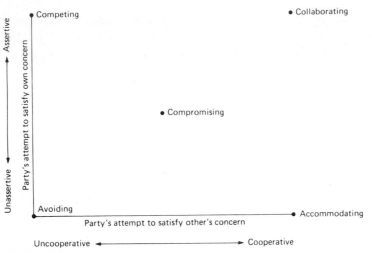

FIGURE 3-3
Conflict-handling modes, plotted according to party's attempt to satisfy own and other's concern. (*Reproduced by special permission from David W. Jamieson and Kenneth W. Thomas, "Power and Conflict in the Student Teacher Relationships," Journal of Applied Behavioral Science, vol. 10, no. 3, p. 326, 1974.*)

CONFLICT-HANDLING STYLES

Conflict must be controlled if it is to be used productively, and this leads to the supervisor's ability to manage conflict and to cultivate conflict-handling styles.

Following Blake and Mouton,[32] David Jamieson and Kenneth Thomas view conflict-handling styles as consisting of two critical dimensions. One dimension is concerned with the extent to which an individual attempts to satisfy the interest of the other party or partner in the conflict.[33] This is the *cooperative* dimension. A person's concern here can be described on a conceptual continuum ranging from uncooperative to cooperative. The second dimension focuses on the extent to which an individual emphasizes the satisfaction of his or her own concerns. This is the *assertiveness* dimension. A person's concern here can be described on a conceptual continuum ranging from unassertive to assertive. As illustrated in Figure 3-3, five specific conflict-handling styles, competing, accommodating, avoiding, collaborating, and compromising, can be identified from combinations of the two dimensions.

Each of the styles is based on certain assumptions and is characterized by distinctive actions. Styles characterized as competing are based on assump-

[32] Robert Blake and Jane Mouton, *The Managerial Grid*, Houston: Gulf, 1964. See also Blake and Mouton, "The Fifth Achievement," *Journal of Applied Behavioral Science*, vol. 6, no. 4, pp. 413–426, 1970; and Blake, Mouton, and Herbert Shepard, *Managing Intergroup Conflict in Industry*, Houston: Gulf, 1964.
[33] David W. Jamieson and Kenneth W. Thomas, "Power and Conflict in the Student-Teacher Relationship," *Journal of Applied Behavioral Science*, vol. 10, no. 3, pp. 321–336, 1974.

tions that differences between people are natural and can be expected, that some people have knowledge and others do not, and that some issues are right and others wrong. Therefore, the supervisor owes it to herself or himself to prevail in conflicts with others whose opinions and knowledge and goals are in doubt. Further, persuasion and force are acceptable tools in resolving conflict. Competing supervisors engage in a win-lose strategy and are quite willing to endanger some relationships and to sacrifice others in order to have their personal goals realized.

Accommodating supervisors, by contrast, feel that differences drive people apart and that good relationships cannot be ignored. The slogan of accommodating supervisors is, "To differ is to reject." Conflict requires that such supervisors sacrifice their personal convictions and goals in order to accommodate those of others and, if necessary, ignore differences in order to preserve harmony. Accommodating supervisors strive to maintain relationships at any cost.

Compromising supervisors feel that at times some parties (themselves included) are obliged to set aside their own views in the interest of the majority, and that people should be allowed to express their views but should not be allowed to block progress. Compromising supervisors will change course and alter plans if necessary but maintain enough consensus to keep moving, in the belief that motion is more important than destination and therefore that decisions should be made and purpose and direction compromised in order to maintain the consensus needed to keep moving.

Collaborating supervisors believe that differences are natural and healthy and view them as neither good nor bad. Conflict requires honest confrontation and objective problem solving. Such supervisors do not see an inherent difference in their personal goals and aspirations for the school and the view of others and are hopeful that both views can be integrated into some common good.

Avoiding supervisors see no virtue in conflict and do not personally face up to it. If avoiding supervisors cannot handle conflict in some impersonal manner (relying on rules and precedents, for example), they are likely simply to withdraw from the situation.

It is difficult to decide which of the conflict-handling styles is best. Often different situations require different styles. *Constant* use of the accommodating, avoiding, or competing styles, however, is not likely to be very effective. Still, when the issues are important enough for one's view to prevail, or the situation is such that the other party is not sufficiently knowledgeable, the competitive style may be necessary. Sometimes the task or issues at stake are not important and much can be gained by emphasizing relationships, and here the accommodating style might be best. In sum, any of the conflict-handling styles might be appropriate in different circumstances.

Thomas provides some general guidelines for deciding when to use one or another of the styles.[34] He suggests that the competing style might be used

---

[34]Kenneth W. Thomas, "Toward Multi-dimensional Values in Teaching: The Example of Conflict Behaviors," *Academy of Management Review*, vol. 2, no. 3, pp. 484–490, 1977.

when quick, decisive action is needed; when unpopular actions need implementing; on vital issues when you are convinced you are right; against people who are taking advantage of noncompetitive situations and behavior. The collaborative style might be used when it is important to find a team solution because conflicting concerns are too important to be compromised; when learning is the objective; when commitment to a solution is important; or to improve relationships among competing groups. The compromising style might be used when conflicting goals are important but not worth the disruption of choosing between them; when those who hold different views are equally powerful; to arrive at a temporary settlement or solution to a complex problem; to get the job done under severe time constraints; as a backup when collaboration or competition seem not to be working. The avoiding style might be used when an issue is trivial in comparison with other issues; when possible disruptions clearly outweigh the benefits of getting the problem solved; when it is important to let tension be relaxed or people cool off; when gathering information may be more important than making a decision; when others can handle the conflict better than you can. The accommodating style might be used when you realize your position is wrong or it is important to allow another position to be heard or it is important for you to show how reasonable you are; when the issue at stake is more important to other people than to yourself; to build credibility today which may help you to resolve issues in the future; to minimize your losses when you are clearly losing in the long run; when harmony and stability are particularly important; when in your judgment accommodation will allow others to profit from their mistakes.

SUMMARY

A purpose of this chapter was to introduce those who supervise to the broader environment within which supervision takes place. The school was described as a complex organization that shares many characteristics of bureaucracy and professionalism. One hazard of viewing the school as a bureaucracy is to attribute to it degrees of rationality that do not match with reality. It was pointed out that schools are more accurately characterized as "satisficing" than as "maximizing" organizations, but this "satisficing" tendency does not prevent people from valuing and striving for excellence. Indeed, basic to the human resources view is the belief in the human capacity for setting goals, for striving for greater achievement even though people are subjected to "satisficing" limitations.

Professional elements and tendencies in schools were described and contrasted with bureaucratic by viewing the school as a structural-functional system. Supervisors and teachers live at the tension point between the school's bureaucratic and professional face, and conflict between bureaucratic and professional values is common.

Power and authority were then discussed as two key concepts in understanding organizational life. Authority is the right to act or to require others to act on behalf of school purposes. Authority is related to one's position and the inherent rights associated with that position. Power, on the other hand, refers to anyone's ability to influence the decision-making process regardless of his or her position. Sometimes power is associated with one's authority but other times it is not.

Weber's authority types and the sources of power proposed by French and Raven were then discussed and linked to satisfaction and levels of performance of teachers. Though discussions of power tend to emphasize differences that exist in the amount of power among people at various levels of the hierarchy, it was pointed out that more important to organizational school effectiveness is the total amount of power available in the school regardless of rank. In one school, for example, teachers and principals might enjoy equal power in a relative sense but in a total sense neither may have very much power. In another school, though relative differences might exist between administrators and teachers in favor of administrators if both groups are empowered things are likely to be better. The association between use of power and level of identity of organizational members was than discussed in terms of Etzioni's compliance theory. The chapter concluded with a discussion of five conflict-handling styles available to supervisors. These include competition, accommodation, compromise, collaboration, and avoidance.

STUDY GUIDE

Recall the concepts, ideas, and meanings associated with each of the following phrases and terms included in this chapter. Can you discuss each of them with a colleague and apply them to the supervisory context of your school? If you cannot, review them in the text and record the page number for future reference.

1 Authority
2 Axiomatic theory of organizations
3 Bureaucratic dysfunction
4 Bureaucratic-professional conflict
5 Bureaucratic school characteristics
6 Bureaucratically oriented schools
7 Calculated involvement
8 Conflict-handling style
9 "Double-loop" learning
10 Empowerment slope line
11 Etzioni's compliance theory
12 Moral involvement
13 Power
14 Professional authority
15 Professional school characteristics
16 Professionally oriented schools

17 "Satisficing" and "maximizing"
18 Sources of power
19 Structural-functional system
20 Weber's authority type

EXERCISES

1 This chapter emphasizes the negative aspects of bureaucracy in schools. But bureaucracy provides us with benefits too. Consider, for example, an inexperienced teacher in conference with parents who are influential in the community (perhaps the local banker and spouse, a former teacher). How can the school as an organization with bureaucratic characteristics help provide this teacher with authority?

2 Prepare a one-page "case study" involving supervisors in a situation that illustrates conflict between bureaucratic and professional values. Prepare a second case study involving teachers.

3 "People tend to seek not the best needle in a haystack, but rather one that satisfies the reason for their search." This metaphor was used to suggest the "satisficing" rather than maximizing nature of decision making in schools. Carefully observe one or two administrators or supervisors for a week. Describe the extent to which decisions they make are "satisficing."

4 In a typical elementary school setting the cast of characters might include teachers, students, custodians, principal-supervisor, parents, secretaries, and superintendent. What authority does each of these groups have over classroom decisions? How does this authority differ from the actual influence patterns (power) you observe?

5 Which of the descriptions of conflict-handling modes best fits the way you operate (or are likely to operate)?

BUILDING A CLIMATE FOR SUPERVISION

Before we begin this discussion of school climate and its implications for supervision, let us examine the dimensions of climate of groups and organizations with which we are familiar. Take a moment to recall the one group or organization of which you were a member or that you know about that seemed best to encourage members to learn, solve problems, and take reasonable chances. Now recall the one group or organization that most hindered learning, problem solving, and moderate risk taking of members. If you did not choose a school or school group in your analysis, try repeating the exercise limiting yourself to schools. Briefly describe the organizations or groups recalled. Who were the members? What was to be accomplished? How did the people work together? How did the people treat one another? What were the leaders like? Using the questionnaire depicted in Exhibit 4-1, evaluate each of the organizations or groups recalled. Start first with the most effective learning organizations or groups. Circle the number for each category that best describes this organization. Now evaluate the less effective organization or group using check marks to indicate responses. Compare your circled and checked responses.

By describing organizations and groups that help and hinder learning and then evaluating them, you have been describing and measuring dimensions of organizational climate. The seven item categories shown in Exhibit 4-1 are composed of several dimensions that social psychologists have found to be important in determining whether a climate is open (supportive) or closed (hindering). To obtain an overall climate score, total the score values given for each of the seven items. Remember to reverse the score given to item 1, conformity, for in this case low scores suggest a supportive climate. The higher the score, the more open or supportive the group or organization is. Now, using

Introduction

For each of the seven organization climate dimensions described below place an (A) above the number that indicates your assessment of the organization's current position on that dimension and an (I) above the number that indicates your choice of where the organization should ideally be on this dimension.

1 **Conformity** The feeling that there are many externally imposed constraints in the organization; the degree to which members feel that there are many rules, procedures, policies, and practices to which they have to conform rather than being able to do their work as they see fit.

Conformity is not charac-   1 2 3 4 5 6 7 8 9 10   Conformity is very characteristic of this organization   teristic of this organization

2 **Responsibility** Members of the organization are given personal responsibility to achieve their part of the organization's goals; the degree to which members feel that they can make decisions and solve problems without checking with superiors each step fo the way.

No responsibility is given   1 2 3 4 5 6 7 8 9 10   There is great emphasis on
in the organization.   personal responsibility in the
                                                                     organization.

3 **Standards** The emphasis the organization places on quality performance and outstanding production including the degree to which the member feels the organization is setting challenging goals for itself and communicating these goal commitments to members.

Standards are very low   1 2 3 4 5 6 7 8 9 10   High challenging standards
or nonexistent in the   are set in the organization.
organization.

4 **Rewards** The degree to which members feel that they are being recognized and rewarded for good work rather than being ignored, criticized, or punished when something goes wrong.

Members are ignored,   1 2 3 4 5 6 7 8 9 10   Members are recognized and
punished, or criticized.   rewarded positively.

5. **Organization clarity** The feeling among members that things are well-organized and goals are clearly defined rather than being disorderly, confused, or chaotic.

The organization is dis-   1 2 3 4 5 6 7 8 9 10   The organization is well-
orderly, confused, and   organized with clearly
chaotic.   defined goals.

6 **Warmth and support** The feeling that friendliness is a valued norm in the organization; that members trust one another and offer support to one another. The feeling that good relationships prevail in the work environment.

There is no warmth and   1 2 3 4 5 6 7 8 9 10   Warmth and support are
support in the organization   very characteristic of the
                                                                    organization.

7 **Leadership** The willingness of organization members to accept leadership and direction from qualified others. As needs for leadership arise, members feel free to take leadership roles and are rewarded for successful leadership. Leadership is based on expertise. The organization is not dominated by, or dependent on, one or two individuals.

Leadership is not rewarded;   1 2 3 4 5 6 7 8 9 10   Members accept and reward
members are dominated or   leadership based on expertise.
dependent and resist
leadership attempts.

EXHIBIT 4-1
Organizational climate questionnaire. *(From David A. Kolb, Erwin M. Rubin, and James M. McIntyre,* Organizational Psychology: An Experiential Approach, *3d ed., 1979, pp. 193–194. Reprinted by permission of Prentice-Hall, Englewood Cliffs, N.J.)*

the item categories and scores, describe again the helpful and hindering organizations or groups you recall. You are now describing organizational climate in the language of social psychologists.

WHAT IS ORGANIZATIONAL CLIMATE?

Since the climate of the school is a matter of impression, it is often difficult to define with precision. Climate might be viewed on the one hand as the enduring characteristics that describe a particular school, distinguish it from other schools, and influence the behavior of teachers and students, and on the other hand as the "feel" that teachers and students have for that school. Litwin and Stringer, for example, define climate as: "The perceived subjective effects of the formal system, the informal 'style' of managers, and other important environmental factors on the attitudes, beliefs, values, and motivation of people who work in a particular organization."[1]

According to this view, climate represents a composite of mediating variables that intervene between the structure of an organization and the style and other characteristics of leaders, and teacher performance and satisfaction.

A measure of school climate, for example, can provide a pretty good indication of the condition of a school's set of mediating variables. This measure can be used to evaluate the action variables on the one hand and to predict school-effectiveness variables on the other.

THE IMPORTANCE OF CLIMATE

The metaphor barometer aptly describes school climate. Climate provides a reading of how things are going in the school on the one hand and a basis for predicting school consequences and outcomes on the other. Such a barometer represents an important tool, therefore, for evaluating present conditions, planning new directions, and monitoring progress toward new directions. Indeed school climate is a key dimension of human resources supervision as described in previous editions of this book. Newer understandings of human resources supervision (Supervision II) also rely on school climate as an important dimension for understanding school culture. The concept of school culture will be discussed in Chapter 5.

Despite the importance of climate, supervisors often fail to give it adequate attention. They prefer, instead, to devote full attention to what they feel really matters—the school program, teaching, and student learning. Despite the importance of these educational concerns, supervisors will have a difficult time providing the needed leadership without a sufficiently supportive climate within which to work. A healthy school climate, for example, frees supervisors and teachers to work more fully on educational matters. Further, pushing for

[1] George H. Litwin and Robert A. Stringer, Jr., *Motivation and Organizational Climate*, Boston: Harvard University, Division of Research, Graduate School of Business Administration, 1968, p. 5.

more effective teaching and schooling without giving attention to climate is often perceived by teachers as being authoritarian, and this perception can limit the leadership initiatives of supervisors. Emphasizing school climate, on the other hand, not only allows the supervisor to take a direct lead in matters of teaching and learning but draws out the leadership talents of others as well. Leadership becomes a process rather than a set of prerogatives associated with the supervisor's role.

THE SUPERVISOR AND SCHOOL CLIMATE

An important link exists between the school's organizational structure and teacher attitudes and behavior. George and Bishop, for example, found that the formal structural characteristics of schools they studied had an important influence on the ways in which teachers perceive the school's climate. Teachers were more likely to view the climates of bureaucratically oriented schools as closed and constricting. Professionally oriented schools, by contrast, were viewed as being more trusting and open and as producing less anxiety in teachers.[2]

In addition to structure, supervisors are interested in the link which exists between leadership assumptions, characteristics, and behavior and school climate. Research reveals that this link is strong. Halpin, for example, found that the behavior of elementary school principals (the extent to which they were seen as aloof, emphasizing production and close supervision, setting an example through their own hard work, and showing consideration) was quite influential in setting a climate tone for their schools.[3]

In a more direct investigation of leadership behavior and organizational climate, Litwin and Stringer found that by varying the leadership style in each of three simulated organizations they were able to create different climates, each with distinct implications for member performance and satisfaction.[4] In organization A, for example, the leader strongly emphasized structure, status, assigned roles, position authority, vertical communications, and a punitive system of rules and regulations. This organization resembled the scientific management or bureaucratic view. In organization B, by contrast, the leader emphasized an informal, loose structure and promoted shared decision making, teamwork, and friendliness. This organization was fashioned pretty much in accordance with human relations ideas. Organization C was also characterized by interpersonal support and cooperation, but in this case the leader provided an added emphasis on quality performance and encouraged creativity among workers. Organization C approximates the human resources model.

---

[2] J. George and L. Bishop, "Relationship of Organizational Structure and Teacher Personality Characteristics to Organizational Climate," *Administrative Science Quarterly*, vol. 16, pp. 467–476, 1971.

[3] Andrew W. Halpin and Donald B. Croft, *Organizational Climate of Schools*, Chicago: University of Chicago, Midwest Administration Center, 1963.

[4] Litwin and Stringer, op. cit.

TABLE 4-1
LEADERSHIP, CLIMATE, AND EFFECTIVENESS: LITWIN AND STRINGER

Leadership	Climate	Effectiveness
Organization A	Closed	Performance low
Bureaucratic leadership		Satisfaction low
Organization B	Warm	Performance low
Human relations leadership	Supportive	Satisfaction very high
	Friendly	Innovation high
Organization C	Supportive	Performance very high
Human resources leadership	Goal-oriented	Satisfaction high
		Innovation very high

Members in organization A viewed the climate as punitive and nonsupportive and as offering little chance for individual initiative. They viewed their leader as being aloof, and interpersonal conflict was common within this organization despite efforts by the leader to suppress it. Members of group B viewed their climate as being warm, cooperative, participatory, tension-free, and friendly. Finally, members of organization C viewed their climate as being somewhat cooperative and loosely structured but bounded by norms of responsibility, personal initiative, and risk taking. Though they found membership in the organization rewarding, it was characterized by moderate conflict.

Each of the climates was, in turn, associated with quite different outcomes for the three organizations. Job satisfaction and performance were low in organization A. Performance was also low in organization B, but in this case innovation was moderately high and satisfaction was very high. Organization C, by contrast, was characterized by very high performance and innovation and high satisfaction. These relationships are summarized in Table 4-1.

ORGANIZATIONAL CLIMATE AND SCHOOLS

The works of Matthew Miles[5] and of Andrew Halpin and Don Croft[6] are examples of two well-known constructs for conceptualizing organizational climate for schools.

Halpin views schools as being on a conceptual climate continuum that extends from open to closed.[7] This framework is not unlike that which

---

[5] Matthew Miles, "Planned Change and Organizational Health: Figure and Ground," *Change Processes in the Public Schools,* Eugene, Ore.: The University of Oregon, Center for the Advanced Study of Educational Administration, 1965, pp. 11–34.

[6] Halpin and Croft, op. cit. For a condensed version see Halpin's *Theory and Research in Administration,* New York: Macmillan, 1967, pp. 131–249.

[7] The Halpin climate "continuum," as measured by the Organizational Climate Description Questionnaire, moves from open, through autonomous, controlled, familiar, and paternal, to closed.

considers individual personalities as being on a continuum from open-mindedness to closed-mindedness. At a very simple level, organizational climate refers to the feeling that exists in a given school and the variability in this feeling as one moves from school to school. Halpin, in describing climate, notes that "as one moves to other schools, one finds that each has a 'personality' of its own. It is this 'personality' that we describe here as the 'organizational climate' of the school. Analogously, personality is to the individual what organizational climate is to the organization."[8]

The Organizational Climate Description Questionnaire (OCDQ) was developed by Halpin and Croft as a means to measure and chart the difference in "feel" that characterizes individual schools. The instrument examines eight dimensions of organizational climate, four of which focus on teacher behavior (disengagement, hindrance, esprit, and intimacy) and four on the behavior of the principal (aloofness, production emphasis, thrust, and consideration).

With respect to teachers, disengagement refers to the psychological distance teachers feel from the school and from other teachers. This condition results in going through the motions rather than being committed to one's work. Hindrance refers to all the nonteaching tasks (paperwork, hall monitoring, committee work, busy work) that teachers are required to do but find burdensome. As a result they view the principal who emphasizes these tasks as getting in the way or hindering their effectiveness as teachers. Esprit refers to the general feeling of morale, togetherness, and common commitment that teachers share as a result of the work they do and the relationships they have. Intimacy refers to the closeness of social relationships that exist among the faculty.

With respect to principals, aloofness refers to the psychological distance the principal maintains from the faculty. Principals who are more formal and more inclined to go by the book appear more aloof to teachers. Production emphasis refers to the amount of monitoring or close supervision the principal does and the extent to which teachers feel pressure for results. Principals with high production emphasis emphasize checking and controlling to ensure that teachers conform to administrative and supervisory directives. Thrust refers to the extent to which the principal models a commitment to work goals and models as well as strong effort and persistence in meeting these goals. As Halpin points out, "Thrust behavior is not marked by close supervision but by the principal's attempt to motivate teachers through the example which he personally sets."[9] Consideration is reflected in the concern the principal shows for teachers as persons. The four teacher dimensions and four principal dimensions are shown below. Note that an intensity scale is provided to illustrate the strength of influence of each of the behaviors on openness and closedness in school organizational climate.

[8] Halpin, *Theory and Research in Administration*, New York: Macmillan, 1967, p. 131.
[9] Ibid., p. 151.

	Intensity scale	
	Open climate	**Closed climate**
Teachers		
1. Disengagement	−	+ +
2. Hindrance	−	+
3. Esprit	+ +	− −
4. Intimacy	+	+
Principal		
5. Aloofness	−	+
6. Production emphasis	−	+
7. Thrust	+ +	−
8. Consideration	+	−

+ +Very high emphasis
+High
−Low
− −Very low

Each of the eight dimensions of climate is represented in the instrument as a subtest.[10] Various combinations of emphasis on each of the subtests, as perceived by the teachers responding to the instrument, reveal for the school a climate-similarity score that determines the relative position of the school on the open-to-closed continuum. The school with an open climate, for example, is characterized by low disengagement, low hindrance, very high esprit, high intimacy, low aloofness, low production emphasis, very high thrust, and high consideration. The closed school exhibits very high disengagement, high hindrance, very low esprit, high intimacy, high aloofness, high production emphasis, low thrust, and low consideration. Open- and closed-school climates are described by Halpin as follows:

The Open Climate depicts a situation in which the members enjoy extremely high *Esprit*. The teachers work well together without bickering and griping (low disengagement). They are not burdened by mountains of busy work or by routine reports; the principal's policies facilitate the teachers' accomplishment of their tasks (low hindrance). On the whole, the group members enjoy friendly relations of intimacy. The teachers obtain considerable job satisfaction, and are sufficiently motivated to overcome difficulties and frustration. They possess the incentive to work things out and to keep the organization "moving." Furthermore, the teachers are proud to be associated with their school.[11]

The Closed Climate marks a situation in which the group members obtain little

[10] Ibid., p. 150. The dimension that seems to have the strongest relationship to open climate is esprit.
[11] Ibid., pp. 174–175.

satisfaction in respect to their task-achievement or social-needs. In short, the principal is ineffective in directing the activities of the teachers; at the same time, he is not inclined to look out for their personal welfare. This climate is the most closed and the least genuine climate that we have identified.[12]

The values associated with human resources supervision suggest that the work of the school needs to be accomplished within the framework of open climates. Attention to climate is particularly crucial in that the classroom door does not provide a sufficient buffer to protect the classroom from the prevailing school climate. Closed climates in organizations tend to breed closed learning climates. Open climates in organizations tend to breed open learning climates. A significant direction for leadership-supervisory behavior is moving toward the development and maintenance of the climate most conducive to dynamic instructional leadership.

THE REVISED ORGANIZATIONAL CLIMATE DESCRIPTION QUESTIONNAIRE

A major breakthrough in understanding the concept of school climate and in measuring its dimensions is represented by the work of Wayne Hoy and his associates at Rutgers University in revising the OCDQ.[13] Two new climate forms have been developed; the OCDQ-RE for elementary schools and the OCDQ-RS for secondary schools. The RE form identifies three dimensions of principal behavior—supportive, directive, and restrictive—and three dimensions of teachers' behavior—collegial, intimate, disengaged—patterns of which provide for different school climates. These six dimensions of the OCDQ-RE are described in Table 4-2.

Supportive principal behavior reflects a concern and support for teachers and includes use of constructive criticism, the provision of compliments, and listening to and accepting teachers' suggestions. Directive principal behavior, by contrast, describes a rigid system of close supervision within which the principal monitors virtually everything that teachers do, rules the school with an "iron fist," and inspects lesson plans on a regular basis. Restrictive behaviors are similar to the hindrance behaviors in the original OCDQ and are characterized by burdening teachers with busy work, excessive routine duties

---

[12] Ibid., p. 180. We should caution at this time that OCDQ was developed for use with elementary schools. Some controversy seems to exist over whether the instrument can be used in other school settings, but the instrument tends not to be valid for large secondary schools and perhaps (in our opinion) even for large elementary schools. As schools increase in size and/or complexity, the referent-point principals should perhaps be changed to someone closer to the teachers. See J. Foster Watkins, "The OCDQ—An Application for Some Implications," *Educational Administration Quarterly*, vol. 4, pp. 46–60, spring 1968. See also Fred D. Carver and T. Sergiovanni, "Some Notes on the OCDQ," *Journal of Educational Administration*, vol. 7, no. 1, May 1969.

[13] W. Hoy and S. Clover, "Elementary School Climate: A Revision of the OCDQ," *Educational Administration Quarterly*, vol. 22, no. 1, p. 101, 1986. Copyright ©1986 by the University Council for Education Administration. Reprinted by permission of Sage Publications, Inc.; and Cecil G. Miskel, *Educational Administration Theory, Research and Practice*, 3d ed., New York: Random House, 1987. Hoy's research associates at Rutgers included Robert Kottkamp, Sharon Clover, John Feldman, and John Mulhern.

TABLE 4-2
THE SIX DIMENSIONS OF THE OCDQ-RE

Principal's Behavior

1. *Supportive* behavior reflects a basic concern for teachers. The principal listens and is open to teacher suggestions. Praise is given genuinely and frequently, and criticism is handled constructively. Supportive principals respect the professional competence of their staffs and exhibit both a personal and a professional interest in each teacher.

2. *Directive* behavior is rigid, close supervision. Principals maintain close and constant control over all teacher and school activities, down to the smallest details.

3. *Restrictive* behavior hinders rather than facilitates teacher work. The principal burdens teachers with paperwork, committee requirements, routine duties, and other demands that interfere with their teaching responsibilities.

Teachers' Behavior

4. *Collegial* behavior supports open and professional interactions among teachers. Teachers are proud of their school, enjoy working with their colleagues, and are enthusiastic, accepting, and mutually respectful of the professional competence of their colleagues.

5. *Intimate* behavior reflects a cohesive and strong network of social support among the faculty. Teachers know each other well, are close personal friends, socialize together regularly, and provide strong support for each other.

6. *Disengaged* behavior refers to a lack of meaning and focus to professional activities. Teachers are simply putting in time and are nonproductive in group efforts or team building; they have no common goal orientation. Their behavior is often negative and critical of their colleagues and the organization.

W. Hoy and S. Clover, "Elementary School Climate: A Revision of the OCDQ." *Educational Administration Quarterly,* vol. 22, no. 1, p. 101, 1986. Copyright © 1986 by the University Council for Education Administration. Reprinted by permission of Sage Publications, Inc.

that interfere with the job of teaching, too much paperwork, and too many committee requirements.

On the part of teachers, collegial behavior is that which is helpful and supportive, respects the professional competence of colleagues, and is characterized by teachers accomplishing their work with "vim, vigor, and pleasure." Intimate teacher behaviors are characterized by teachers socializing with each other, forming close friendships, and having parties for each other. When disengaged, teachers view faculty meetings as being useless, bicker and argue among themselves, and ramble when they talk.

An important departure in this new work with OCDQ is the ways in which various climates are depicted. Instead of climates being viewed as on a continuum, four climates are identified, two of which are somewhat functional and the remaining two dysfunctional. The functional climates are open and engaged. Open school climates are characterized by cooperation and respect within and among the faculty and by a great deal of support from principals. The engaged climate, by contrast, is lacking in principalship support. As Hoy and Miskel describe this climate, "The engaged climate is marked, on one hand, by ineffective attempts of the principal to control, and on the other, by high

TABLE 4-3
CLIMATE DIMENSION PATTERNS

Climate dimension	Open	Engaged	Disengaged	Closed
Supportive	High	Low	High	Low
Directive	Low	High	Low	High
Restrictive	Low	High	Low	High
Collegial	High	High	Low	Low
Intimate	High	High	Low	Low
Disengaged	Low	Low	High	High

From Wayne K. Hoy and Cecil G. Miskel, *Educational Administration Theory, Research and Practice,* 3d ed., New York: Random House, 1987, p. 233.

professional performance of teachers. The principal is rigid and autocratic (high directiveness) and respects neither the professional competence nor the personal needs of the faculty (low supportiveness). Moreover, the principal hinders the teachers with burdensome activities and busy work (high restrictiveness)."[14] Nonetheless within the engaged climate teachers are able to ignore or otherwise overcome these dysfunctional principal behaviors and conduct themselves as professionals. They respect each other and provide support for each other and they are proud of themselves and their work.

Closed climates, as might be expected, represent the opposite of open climates and are characterized by teachers and principals who simply go through the motions of schooling with little commitment and mutual support.

The disengaged climate is the flip side of the engaged. Here the principal provides the necessary support and avoids being directive and restrictive but teachers are, nonetheless, highly disengaged and display low levels of collegiality and intimacy. In Hoy and Miskel's words, "Nonetheless, the faculty is unwilling to accept the principal. At worst, the faculty actively works to immobilize and sabotage the principal's leadership attempts; at best, the faculty simply ignores the principal. Teachers not only do not like the principal but they neither like nor respect each other as friends (low intimacy) or as professionals (low collegial relations)."[15] The dimension patterns for the four climates are illustrated in Table 4-3.

The RS form of the OCDQ differs from the RE form in that five climate dimensions are identified. Two of the dimensions describe the principal's behavior and three teacher behaviors. The five dimensions are included in Table 4-4. Restrictive principal behaviors found in the RE form are not included in the RS form. Among teacher behaviors, frustrated and engaged appear as substitutes for collegial and disengaged. Engaged teachers help and support each other, spend time after school with students who have

[14] Hoy and Miskel, op. cit., p. 233.
[15] Ibid.

TABLE 4-4
DIMENSIONS OF THE OCDQ-RS

Principal's Behavior

Supportive principal behavior is characterized by efforts to motivate teachers by using constructive criticism and setting an example through hard work. At the same time, the principal is helpful and genuinely concerned about the personal and professional welfare of teachers.

Directive principal behavior is rigid and domineering supervision. The principal maintains close and constant control over all teachers and school activities down to the smallest details.

Teachers' Behavior

Engaged teacher behavior is reflected by high faculty morale. Teachers are proud of their school, enjoy working with each other, and are supportive of their colleagues. Teachers are not only concerned about each other, they are committed to their students. They are friendly with students, trust students, and are optimistic about the ability of students to succeed.

Frustrated teacher behavior refers to a general pattern of interference from both administrators and colleagues that distracts from the basic task of teaching. Routine duties, administrative paperwork, and assigned nonteaching duties are excessive; moreover, teachers irritate, annoy, and interrupt each other.

Intimate teacher behavior reflects a strong and cohesive network of social relationships among the faculty. Teachers know each other well, are close personal friends, and regularly socialize together.

From Wayne K. Hoy and Cecil G. Miskel, *Educational Administration Theory, Research and Practice*, 3d ed., New York: Random House, 1987, p. 235.

problems, and are proud of their schools. Frustrated teachers report that the mannerisms of teachers at the school are annoying, administrative paper-work is burdensome, and nonteaching duties are excessive.

The Rutgers research team finds that the original conception of schools being on a continuum from open to closed generally fits the secondary schools studied. Open school climates are characterized by high support and engagement scores on the one hand and low directive and frustrated scores on the other. Intimacy seemed not to bear very much on whether schools were more open or closed.

Hoy and Miskel are confident that the revised version of the OCDQ, like the original, are linked to the emotional tone of schools in predictable ways. They note, for example, that students in schools with open climates, as measured by the original OCDQ, are less alienated than those in closed; open schools have stronger principals who are more confident, secure, cheerful, sociable, and resourceful than closed; and teachers who work with principals in open schools express greater confidence in their own and the school's effectiveness.[16] That is, they experience heightened feelings of efficacy. Efficacy, in turn, is linked to student achievement.[17] And finally principals in more open school climates have more loyal and satisfied teachers.

[16] Ibid., p. 236.
[17] Patricia T. Ashton and Rodman B. Webb, *Making a Difference: Teachers' Sense of Efficacy and Student Achievement*, New York: Longdon, Inc., 1986.

ORGANIZATIONAL HEALTH: A SUPERVISORY GOAL

A concept similar to climate but broader in its approach to understanding the flavor, attitude, sentiment, and orientation of a given school is suggested by the metaphor organizational health. Miles describes the "healthy" school as one that exhibits reasonably clear and reasonably accepted goals (goal focus); communication that is relatively distortion-free vertically, horizontally, and across boundary lines (communication adequacy); equitable distribution of influence to all levels of the organization (optimal power equalization); and effective and efficient use of inputs, both human and material (resource utilization). The healthy school reflects a sense of togetherness that bonds people together (cohesiveness), a feeling of well-being among the staff (morale), self-renewing properties (innovativeness), and an active response to its environment (autonomy and adaptation). Finally, the healthy school maintains and strengthens its problem-solving capabilities (problem-solving adequacies).

Each of the 10 dimensions of health is described in detail below. They form a major share of the content that composes the process of supervision. From Miles, they are:

1 *Goal focus*. In a healthy organization, the goal (or more usually goals) of the system would be reasonably clear to the system members, and reasonably well accepted by them. This clarity and acceptance, however, should be seen as a necessary but insufficient condition for organizational health. The goals must also be *achievable* with existing or available resources, and be *appropriate*—more or less congruent with the demands of the environment.[18]

2 *Communication adequacy*. Since organizations are not simultaneous face-to-face systems like small groups, the movement of information within them becomes crucial. This dimension of organizational health implies that there is relatively distortion-free communication "vertically," "horizontally," and across the boundary of the system to and from the surrounding environment. That is, information travels reasonably well—just as the healthy person "knows himself" with a minimum level of repression, distortion, etc. In the healthy organization, there is good and prompt sensing of internal strains; there are enough data about problems of the system to ensure that a good diagnosis of system difficulties can be made. People have the information they need, and have gotten it without exerting undue efforts, such as those involved in moseying up to the superintendent's secretary, reading the local newspaper, or calling excessive numbers of special meetings.

3 *Optimal power equalization*. In a healthy organization the distribution of influence is relatively equitable. Subordinates (if there is a formal authority chart) can influence upward, and even more important—as Likert has demonstrated—they perceive that their boss can do likewise with *his* boss. In such an organization, intergroup struggles for power would not be bitter, though intergroup conflict (as in every human system known) would undoubtedly be present. The basic

---

[18] Miles, op. cit., pp. 18–21.

stance of persons in such an organization, as they look up, sideways, and down, is that of collaboration rather than explicit or implicit coercion.

4 *Resource utilization.* We say of a healthy person, such as a second-grader, that he is "working up to his potential." To put this another way, the classroom system is evoking a contribution from him at an appropriate and goal-directed level of tension. At the organization level, "health" would imply that the system's inputs, particularly the personnel, are used effectively. The overall coordination is such that people are neither overloaded nor idling. There is a minimal sense of strain, generally speaking (in the sense that trying to do something with a weak or inappropriate structure puts strain on that structure). In the healthy organization, people may be working very hard indeed, but they feel that they are not working against themselves, or against the organization. The fit between people's own dispositions and the role demands of the system is good. Beyond this, people feel reasonably "self-actualized"; they not only "feel good" in their jobs, but they have a genuine sense of learning, growing, and developing as persons in the process of making their organizational contribution.

5 *Cohesiveness.* We think of a healthy person as one who has a clear sense of identity; he knows who he is, underneath all the specific goals he sets for himself. Beyond this, he *likes himself*; his stance toward life does not require self-derogation, even when there are aspects of his behavior which are unlovely or ineffective. By analogy at the organization level, system health would imply that the organization knows "who it is." Its members feel attracted to membership in the organization. They want to stay with it, be influenced by it, and exert their own influence in the collaborative style suggested above.

6 *Morale.* The implied notion is one of well-being or satisfaction. Satisfaction is not enough for health, of course; a person may report feelings of well-being and satisfaction in his life, while successfully denying deep-lying hostilities, anxieties, and conflicts. Yet it still seems useful to evoke, at the organization level, the idea of morale: a summated set of individual sentiments, centering around feelings of well-being, satisfaction, and pleasure, as opposed to feelings of discomfort, unwished-for strain, and dissatisfaction.

7 *Innovativeness.* A healthy system would tend to invent new procedures, move toward new goals, produce new kinds of products, diversify itself, and become more rather than less differentiated over time. In a sense, such a system could be said to grow, develop, and change, rather than remaining routinized and standard.

8 *Autonomy.* The healthy person acts "from his own center outward." Seen in a training or therapy group, for example, such a person appears nearly free of the need to submit dependently to authority figures, *and* from the need to rebel and destroy symbolic fathers of any kind. A healthy organization, similarly, would not respond passively to demands from the outside, feeling itself the tool of the environment, and it would not respond destructively or rebelliously to perceived demands either. It would tend to have a kind of independence from the environment, in the same sense that the healthy person, while he has transactions with others, does not treat their responses as *determinative* of his own behavior.

9 *Adaptation.* The notions of automony and innovativeness are both connected with the idea that a healthy person, group, or organization is in realistic, effective contact with the surroundings. When environmental demands and organization resources do not match, a problem-solving, restructuring approach evolves in which *both* the environment and the organization become different in some respect. More adequate, continued coping of the organization, as a result of changes in the local system, the relevant portions of the environment, or more usually both, occurs. And such a system has sufficient stability and stress tolerance to manage the difficulties which occur during the adaptation process.

10 *Problem-solving adequacy.* Finally, any healthy organism—even one as theoretically impervious to fallibility as a computer—*always* has problems, strains, difficulties, and instances of ineffective coping. The issue is not the presence or absence of problems, therefore, but the *manner* in which the person, group, or organization copes with problems. Argyris has suggested that in an effective system, problems are solved with minimal energy; they stay solved; and the problem-solving mechanisms used are not weakened, but maintained or strengthened. An adequate organization, then, has well-developed structures and procedures for sensing the existence of problems, for inventing possible solutions, for deciding on the solutions, for implementing them, and for evaluating their effectiveness.

Each of the dimensions of organizational health for any school operates in a system of dynamic interaction characterized by a high degree of interdependence. Clear goal focus, for example, depends upon the extent to which the school communicates its goals and permits inhabitants to modify and rearrange them. At another level, a high degree of organizational health encourages school adaptiveness, while school adaptiveness contributes to, and is essential to, organizational health.

Each of the dimensions of school health is characterized by a high degree of interdependence. Clear goal focus, for example, depends upon the extent to which the school communicates its goals and permits inhabitants to modify and rearrange them.

THE SYSTEM 4 CLIMATE: AN INTEGRATED APPROACH TO SCHOOL SUPERVISION

In 1961 *New Patterns of Management*[19] by Rensis Likert appeared as part of the general literature in supervision. The book made a significant and wide-

[19] Rensis Likert, *New Patterns of Management,* New York: McGraw-Hill, 1961. In the early chapters of *New Patterns of Management,* Professor Likert summarizes, synthesizes, and articulates hundreds of studies performed through the institute that have relevance to supervision. In the remaining chapters, Likert uses this mass of findings to develop and support a theory of supervision based on three fundamental principles: (1) the principle of supportive relationship, (2)

spread impact on noneducational settings and a small but nevertheless significant inroad in the literature and in the practice of educational supervision. The significance of this book to educational supervision is that it offered an integrated, research-based system of supervision applicable to schools. This system is based on the development of highly effective work groups whose members are committed to the goals of the school and who work toward these goals as a means to professional growth and development and personal self-fulfillment. These groups are linked together in an overlapping pattern that permits them to function, on the one hand, as relatively small and cohesive primary groups and, on the other hand, as dynamic contributors to, and influencers of, the total school enterprise.

A highly effective school work group is described as one that: (1) members perceive as supportive and that builds and maintains their sense of personal worth, (2) has high performance goals that are consistent with those of the school and/or the profession, (3) uses group decision making, and (4) is linked to other school groups through multiple and overlapping group structures.

From these ideas Likert was able to develop a theory of supervision that relies heavily on the concept of climate as a mediating variable between what supervisors and administrators do and organizational effectiveness. The theory was described in Likert's 1967 book entitled *The Human Organization: Its Management and Value*.[20] Here Likert proposed four different climates known as management systems 1, 2, 3, and 4. The profile of organizational characteristics is the instrument used by Likert to measure the extent to which each of the climates is reflected in an organization or group. Such characteristics as leadership processes (from nonsupportive to supportive), motivational forces (low to high), communication processes (weak and inaccurate to strong and accurate), interaction and influence processes (cold and formal to warm and informal), decision-making processes (hierarchical to shared), goal-setting processes (hierarchical to shared), control processes (hierarchical to shared), and the nature of performance goals (low to high) are measured by the profile. Subscales and selected items from the profiles are shown in Table 4-5.

Respondents generally perceive high-performing groups or organizations as scoring toward the right end of the scale on each of the organizational variables and low-performing groups or organizations as scoring toward the left. Likert reports research that supports these perceptions and notes that as organizations move toward System 4, they are more productive, are characterized by high-performing work groups, have lower costs, have more favorable attitudes, and display improved labor-management relationships, with System 4 organizations achieving excellent records in each of these dimensions. The converse seems to be true for organizations displaying management systems that lie well

the principle of group decision making and group supervision, and (3) the principle of high-performance goals for individuals, groups, and the organization.

[20] Rensis Likert, *The Human Organization: Its Management and Value,* New York: McGraw-Hill, 1967.

TABLE 4-5
SUBSCALES AND SAMPLE ITEMS FROM PROFILE OF ORGANIZATIONAL CHARACTERISTICS

Organizational variable	System 1 (Exploitive-authoritarian)	System 2 (Benevolent-authoritarian)	System 3 (Consultative)	System 4 (Participative)
1. Leadership processes used *a.* Extent to which superiors have confidence and trust in *subordinates*	Have no confidence and trust in subordinates	Have condescending confidence and trust, such as master has in servant	Substantial but not complete confidence and trust; still wishes to keep control of decisions	Complete confidence and trust in all matters
2. Character of motivational forces *a.* Underlying motives tapped	Physical security, economic needs, and some use of the desire for status	Economic needs and moderate use of ego motives, e.g., desire for status, affiliation, and achievement	Economic needs and considerable use of ego and other major motives, e.g., desire for new experiences	Full use of economic, ego, and other major motives, as, for example, motivational forces arising from group goals
3. Character or communication process *f.* Psychological closeness of superiors to subordinates. (How well does superior know and understand problems faced by subordinates).	Has no knowledge or understanding of problems of subordinates	Has some knowledge and understanding of problems of subordinates	Knows and understands problems of subordinates quite well	Knows and understands problems of subordinates very well
4. Character of interaction-influence process *a.* Amount and character of interaction	Little interaction and always with fear and distrust	Little interaction and usually with some condescension by superiors; fear and caution by subordinates	Moderate interaction, often with fair amount of confidence and trust	Extensive, friendly interaction with high degree of confidence and trust
5. Character of decision-making process *f.* To what extent are subordinates involved in decisions related to their work?	Not at all	Never involved in decisions; occasionally consulted	Usually are consulted but ordinarily not involved in the decision making	Are involved fully in all decisions related to their work

TABLE 4-5 (Continued)
SUBSCALES AND SAMPLE ITEMS FROM PROFILE OF ORGANIZATIONAL CHARACTERISTICS

Organizational variable	System 1 (Exploitive-authoritarian)	System 2 (Benevolent-authoritarian)	System 3 (Consultative)	System 4 (Participative)
6. Character of goal setting or ordering b. To what extent do the different hierarchical levels tend to strive for high performance goals?	High goals pressed by top, generally resisted by subordinates	High goals sought by top and often resisted moderately by subordinates	High goals sought by higher levels but with occasional resistance by lower levels	High goals sought by all levels, with lower levels sometimes pressing for higher goals than top levels
7. Character of control processes a. At what hierarchical levels in organization does major or primary concern exist with regard to the performance of the cnotrol function?	At the very top only	Primarily or largely at the top	Primarily at the top but some shared feeling of responsibility felt at middle and to a lesser extent at lower levels	Concern for performance of control functions likely to be felt throughout organization
8. Performance goals and training a. Level of performance goals which superiors seek to have organization achieve	Seek average goals	Seek high goals	Seek very high goals	Seek to achieve extremely high goals

toward System 1. We would, of course, expect similar responses from educators and similar findings in educational organizations.

LIKERT'S MANAGEMENT SYSTEMS

Each of the management systems described in Table 4-5 is comprised of characteristics and tendencies which are interdependent. It is not likely, for example, that a school can be described as possessing some characteristics of System 1, others of System 2, and still others of System 4. Typically, a pattern of response emerges that types the school into one or another system category. In explaining this phenomenon Likert observes: "The communication processes of System 1 are compatible with all other aspects of System 1 but are not compatible with any aspect of System 3 or System 4. The same is true of the decision-making processes and the compensation plans. *The management system of an organization must have compatible component parts if it is to function effectively.*"[21]

[21] Ibid., p. 123.

Systems 1 and 2

System 1 is referred to as exploitive-authoritarian and System 2 as benevolent-authoritarian. Differences between the two exist, but they are close enough to be described together. Supervisors (principals, teachers, and others) who adopt System 1 or System 2 perspectives rely on high-control methods and hierarchical pressures and authority. They hold Theory X assumptions[22] regarding subordinates, domination, regulation, and distortion of communication channels, and use programmed, delimited, and centralized decision making as they work to achieve school goals.

Systems 1 and 2 supervisors can expect from subordinates less group loyalty, lower performance goals, less cooperation, more conflict, less teamwork and mutual assistance among peers, more feeling of unreasonable pressure, less favorable attitudes toward supervisors and the school, and lower motivational potential for performance.[23] This response from the human organization of the school takes its toll in poor performance on each of the school-success variables.

Systems 3 and 4

System 3 is described as consultative, while System 4 is labeled participative. System 3 is somewhat descriptive of supervisory practice, which characterizes schools well on their way toward developing a true professional organization. It is a transitional management system that is often characterized as being "better than before" but still clings to many of the features of the earlier type of management.

Administrators, teachers, and others who adopt System 4 rely on the principle of supportive relationships, group methods of supervision, Theory Y assumptions,[24] self-control methods, ability authority, and other principles associated with human resources supervision. Teachers react to this perspective by displaying greater group loyalty, high performance goals, greater cooperation, more teamwork and sharing, less feeling of unreasonable pressure, more favorable attitudes toward the supervisor and the school, and high levels of motivation for performance.[25] The result is increases in the dimensions of school success. System 4 is an ideal difficult to achieve in practice. Therefore, it may be more useful in actual situations to speak of *tendencies toward System 4* rather than actually meeting this goal.

CLIMATE AND LEARNING

Both the climate and health metaphors for thinking about schooling help us to focus attention on the school's interpersonal work life dimensions as they affect teachers, the administrative and supervisory actions which influence these

---

[22] Theory X will be discussed further in Chapter 7. Theory X is a view of management based on negative assumptions about people and autocratic principles of leadership.

[23] Likert, op. cit., p. 75.

[24] Theory Y will be discussed further in Chapter 7. Theory Y is a view of management based on positive assumptions about people and empowerment principles of leadership.

[25] Likert, op. cit., p. 76.

dimensions, and the consequences of different teacher reaction patterns for ineffective teaching and schooling. One important related line of inquiry has been able to link the assumptions that teachers and administrators hold for *students* to many of these same climate dimensions. This research uses the Pupil Control Ideology Scale (PCI) developed by Willower and his associates.[26] This scale measures the assumptions and attitudes of teachers and supervisors toward students on a continuum from custodial to humanistic. "Custodial schools" tend to be rigidly controlled and concerned with maintenance and order. Students do not participate in decision making and are expected to accept decisions without question. Further they are viewed as being irresponsible, undisciplined, untrustworthy, and trouble-prone. Strong emphasis is given to controlling students through the development and articulation of punitive methods. "Humanistic schools," on the other hand, resemble a community that includes students as fuller members and seeks their cooperation and interaction. Self-discipline is emphasized and learning is considered to be promoted and enhanced by obtaining student identity and commitment. In schools with humanistic climates teachers are more likely to cooperate with one another as they work together, to have higher morale, and to enjoy a sense of task achievement. Social interaction among teachers is also high. In custodial schools these characteristics are not found and students are likely to be more alienated. Teachers are more likely to view the school as a battlefield. In comparing climates of schools as measured by the OCDQ and by the PCI, Hoy and Appleberry found that schools with more custodial climates had significantly greater disengagement, less esprit, more aloofness, and less thrust than those with humanistic climates.[27]

Many of the recent studies of highly successful schools point out the importance of climate. In a study of 12 inner-London secondary schools, Rutter, Maughan, Mortimer, and Ouston found that important differences in climate existed between those schools which were more or less effective.[28] Effectiveness in this case was defined as higher scores on national examinations, better behavior, and better attendance. In the more effective schools teachers worked harder and had better attitudes toward learning, spent more time in actual teaching, relied more heavily on praising students, and were better able to involve students as active learners. Studies of highly successful schools that emphasize ethnographic techniques and the importance of culture reach similar conclusions.[29]

[26] Donald J. Willower, Terry I. Eidell, and Wayne K. Hoy, *The School and Pupil Control Ideology*, Pennsylvania State University Studies no. 24, State College, Pa.: Pennsylvania State University, 1967.

[27] Wayne K. Hoy and James B. Appleberry, "Teacher-Principal Relationships in 'Humanistic' and 'Custodial' Elementary Schools," *Journal of Experimental Education*, vol. 39, no. 2, pp. 27–31, 1970.

[28] Michael Rutter, Barbara Maughan, Peter Mortimer, and Janet Ouston, *Fifteen Thousand Hours: Secondary Schools and Their Effects on Children*, Cambridge, Mass.: Harvard University Press, 1979.

[29] See, for example, Joan Lipsitz, *Successful Schools for Young Adolescents*, New Brunswick, N.J.: Transaction Books, 1984; Sara Lightfoot, *The Good High School*, New York: Basic Books, 1983.

SUMMARY

In this chapter the importance of school climate to supervisory effectiveness was discussed. Climate was viewed as a combination of the enduring characteristics that describe a particular school and distinguish it from other schools and the feeling teachers and students have for that school. Climate represents a composite of the mediating variables that intervene between what supervisors do (the action variables) and school effectiveness. It was pointed out that although supervisors may have difficulty in influencing climate through the school's structure and function they can exert direct influence through the leadership they provide. Bureaucratic leadership, for example, tends to be associated with relatively closed climates and low performance and satisfaction. Human relations leadership tends to be associated with a warm, supportive, and friendly climate and with comparatively lower performance though satisfaction tends to be high. Human resources leadership tends to be associated with supportive, goal-oriented climates characterized by high performance, satisfaction, and innovation. Views of organizational climate as conceptualized by Halpin and Croft, Hoy and Miskel, and Miles were then presented as examples of ways of thinking about climate. Items from Likert's profile of organizational characteristics were then presented as one method for charting and monitoring school climate. This presentation was accompanied by a discussion of four organizational climates, Systems 1, 2, 3, and 4. System 4 was then discussed as the ideal toward which human resources supervisors work. Finally a discussion of the relationship between climate and learning was presented.

STUDY GUIDE

Recall the concepts, ideas, and meanings associated with each of the following phrases and terms included in this chapter. Can you discuss each of them with a colleague and apply them to the supervisory content of your school? If you cannot, review them in the text and record the page number for future reference.

1 Climate
2 Closed climate
3 Custodial climate
4 Disengaged climate
5 Engaged climate
6 Humanistic climate
7 Leadership climate
8 Likert's management systems
9 Open climate
10 Organizational climate description questionnaire
11 Organizational health
12 Pupil control ideology scale

EXERCISES

1 Describe the climate of your school using the seven dimensions of organizational climate included in Exhibit 4-1. Provide specific examples or describe specific critical incidents that illustrate each climate dimension.
2 Have a group of teachers from the same school fill out the sample profile of organizational characteristics provided in Table 4-5, indicating for each item the way their school actually is (real) and the way they would perfer it to be (ideal). Average responses, and develop a real and ideal profile for that school. How might such a profile be used as a planning device for the supervisor?
3 Compare organizational climate as conceptualized and personalized by Halpin, Miles, Hoy, and Miskel, and Likert. How are these views similar and how are they different? Using these views, develop a 10-item questionnaire that you believe summarizes the most important dimensions of organizational climate.

FACULTY AND SCHOOL CULTURE

Supervisors are committed to school improvement, and the overriding purpose of supervision is to provide for more effective teaching and learning. Easy to say but tough to do, especially when one accepts the reality that schools are surprisingly disconnected, loosely structured, or in the jargon of social science "loosely coupled."[1] As a result of this disconnectedness supervisors cannot assume that because an idea is mandated it will find its way into the day-by-day teaching practices of teachers. States and school districts which have adopted uniform and elaborately detailed evaluation systems that require teachers to demonstrate a list of behaviors, for example, cannot be sure whether teachers are merely "showboating" or whether the behaviors are indeed part of the teachers' daily repertoire. Basic to human resources supervision is acceptance of the reality that little gets done in the school without the cooperation and commitment of teachers. Models of management, leadership, and supervision that ignore this reality will not work over the long run. In Chapter 4 school climate was discussed as one important dimension in getting the cooperation and commitment needed to make things work in schools. In this chapter we examine more closely the faculty as a work group, the concept of school culture, and implications of both for building cooperation and commitment.

THE CONCEPT OF CULTURE

It does not take a newcomer to a school very long to figure out what the ground rules are if one wants to get along; what the real priorities of the school are; the

[1] Karl E. Weick, "Educational Organizations as Loosely Coupled Systems," *Administrative Science Quarterly,* vol. 21, pp. 1–19, 1976.

do's and don'ts; the array of behavior codes that govern how students are to be treated; how cooperative teachers can be with administrators and indeed what is and is not acceptable talk in the teachers' lounge. Some schools even have elaborate, albeit implicit, codes and rules that define what is a "fair day's work for a fair day's pay." Many stories are told about work-restrictive norms that evolve in the workplace and how workers must adhere to these norms if they are to get along with their colleagues.

A school principal related the following story to us which illustrates his experiences with work-restrictive norms. Like many teachers early in their careers, this principal took summer employment at a local paper mill. He joined a force of other summer workers who replaced regular workers while on vacation. One evening he was assigned to the midnight shift with another summer employee. Together they operated a machine that layered wood sheets in the formation of plywood. Shortly after beginning work, a new task for both, they noticed a plaque located near the machine that honored the two workers who held the production record for this layering process. As the two caught on to how the job was to be done, they began to realize that this record was beatable. Not only did they beat the record but they exceeded the number of sheets produced by about 50 percent. This news was not received very warmly by the regular workers and indeed our two "eager beaver" summer helpers received a "visit" from worker representatives the very next day. Informal norms had developed at the mill that defined for employees exactly what was a fair day's work for a fair day's pay, and violations of the norm would not be tolerated.

In every organization there are observable behavioral regularities that are defined by the rules of the game for getting along. These rules are norms that define for people what is right and correct to do, what is acceptable, and what is expected. Norms are expressions of certain values and beliefs held by members of the work group. When trying to understand how norms emerge and work the metaphor culture can be helpful. Though some readers might want to debate whether schools have cultures or are cultures, to us the issue is less the reality of culture and more what can be learned by *thinking about* schools as cultures. The metaphor school culture helps direct our attention to the symbols, behavior regularities, ceremonies, and even myths that communicate to people the underlying values and beliefs that are shared by members of the organization. The concept of culture is very important, for its dimensions are much more likely to govern what it is that people think and do than is the official management system. Teachers, as suggested earlier, are much more likely to teach in ways that reflect the shared assumptions and beliefs of the faculty as a whole than they are in ways that administrators want, supervisors say, or teacher-evaluation instruments program.

The noted sociologist Edward A. Shils uses the concept of "central zone" to illustrate many of the characteristics of culture. He believes that all societies and organizations within society have central zones that provide a sense of order and stability and a source for the development of norms that give meaning and significance to the lives of people:

> The central, or the central zone, is a phenomenon of the realm of values and beliefs. It is the center of the order of symbols and values and beliefs, which govern the society.... The central zone partakes of the nature of the sacred. In this sense every society has an official "religion."... The center is also a phenomenon of the realm of action. It is a structure of activities, of roles and persons, within the network of institutions. It is in these roles that the values and beliefs which are central are embodied and propounded.[2]

As repositories of values these centers are sources of identity for individuals and groups and the means by which their work lives become meaningful. Centers provide a sense of purpose to seemingly ordinary events and bring worth and dignity to human activities within the organization. Centers will evolve naturally in schools in response to human needs. But if left unattended they evolve in the form of "wild" cultures. As wild cultures they may or may not be compatible with the school's goals; may or may not be supportive of improved teaching and learning; may or may not be growth-oriented; may or may not be good for students. Is it possible for supervisors, principals, and teachers to come to grips with the system of shared values and beliefs which defines for them their way of life? Is it possible, in other words, for "domesticated" school cultures to emerge that are committed to quality teaching and learning? The evidence suggests that the answer is yes.

LEVELS OF CULTURE

It is important for supervisors to try to understand just what is the existing culture in the schools in which they work. The values, beliefs, and norms which loom large in providing the parameters within which teachers will work are just too powerful to be ignored. Further, given the assertion that little can be accomplished without the cooperation and commitment of teachers and the reality that cultural dimensions are key in influencing the actions that they take, cultural leadership becomes an inescapable part of supervision. Providing cultural leadership on behalf of school improvement is the theme of Chapters 8 and 9. But before a supervisor can provide cultural leadership she or he needs to come to grips with the existing culture.

It is useful to think about dimensions of school culture as existing at at least four levels.[3] The most tangible and observable level is represented by the *artifacts* of culture as manifested in what people say, how people behave, and how things look. Verbal artifacts include the language systems that are used, stories that are told, and examples that are used to illustrate certain important points. Behavioral artifacts are manifested in the ceremonies and rituals and other symbolic practices of the school.

[2] Edward A. Shils, "Centre and Periphery," in *The Logic of Personal Knowledge: Essays Presented to Michael Polanyi,"* London: Routledge and Kegan Paul, 1961, p. 119.

[3] See, for example, Nancy Morse and E. Reimer, "The Experimental Change of a Major Organizational Variable," *Journal of Abnormal and Social Psychology,* vol. 52, no. 1, pp. 120–129, 1956.

The next level at which school culture can be understood is the *perspectives* of people. Perspectives refer to the shared rules and norms to which people respond, the commonness which exists among solutions to similar problems, how people define the situations they face, and what are boundaries of acceptable and unacceptable behavior.

The third level is that of *values*. Values provide the basis for people to judge or evaluate the situations they face, the worth of actions and activities, their priorities, and the behaviors of people with whom they work. In domesticated school cultures, the values are arranged in a fashion which represents the covenant that teachers share. This convenant might be in the form of an educational or management platform and statements of school philosophy. Platforms and philosophy are discussed in more detail in Chapter 10.

The fourth level is that of *assumptions*. Assumptions are more abstract than each of the other levels because they are typically tacit or implicit.

IDENTIFYING THE CULTURE OF YOUR SCHOOL

The four levels of culture provide a framework for analyzing the school's history and tradition, patterns of beliefs, norms, and behaviors. They are, for example, very much in evidence in the questions provided below to help supervisors identify and describe important aspects of the culture of their schools.

The School's History. How does the school's past live in the present? What traditions are carried on? What stories are told and retold? What events in the school's history are overlooked or forgotten? Do heroes and heroines among students and teachers exist whose idiosyncrasies and exploits are remembered? In what ways are the school's traditions and historical incidents modified through reinterpretation over the years? Can you recall, for example, a historical event that has evolved from fact to myth?

Beliefs. What are the assumptions and understandings that are shared by teachers and others, though they may not be stated explicitly? These may relate to how the school is structured, how teaching takes place, the roles of teachers and students, discipline, the relationship of parents to the school. Perhaps these assumptions and understandings are written somewhere in the form of a philosophy or other statement.

Values. What are the things that your school prizes? That is, when teachers and principals talk about the school, what are the major and recurring value themes underlying what they say?

Norms and Standards. What are the oughts, shoulds, do's, and don'ts that govern the behavior of teachers, supervisors, and principals? Norms and standards can be identified by examining what behaviors get rewarded and what behaviors get punished in the school.

Patterns of Behavior. What are the accepted and recurring ways of doing things, the patterns of behavior, the habits and rituals that prevail in the school?

These dimensions comprise a chain of events within which the school's history and its tradition influence beliefs, beliefs influence values, values influence norms and standards, and finally norms influence patterns of behavior. Corwith Hansen suggests that teachers be asked the following questions in seeking to identify the culture of a school.[4] Describe your work day both in and outside of the school. On what do you spend your time and energy? Given that most students forget what they learn, what do you hope your students will retain over time from your classes? Think of students you are typically attracted to—those that you admire, respect, or enjoy. What common characteristics do these students have? What does it take for a teacher to be successful in your school or in your department? What advice would you give new teachers? What do you remember about past faculty members and students in your school or department? If you were to draw a picture or take a photo or make a collage that represented some aspect of your school, what would it look like? How are students rewarded? How are teachers rewarded? What might a new teacher do that would immediately signal to others that he or she was not going to be successful? "The School Culture Inventory: Identifying Guiding Beliefs" appears as Exhibit 5-1. This inventory is designed to help faculties tackle the task of identifying their culture by examining their school's belief structure.

From this discussion of school culture one might reasonably conclude that the concepts of culture and climate are similar. But still they are unique in many ways. In Chapter 4 we discussed the pupil control ideology scale and its use in identifying custodial and humanistic schools. These schools differed with respect to the assumptions and beliefs that teachers made about students, discipline, and control. In many respects the PCI conception of climate is concerned with aspects of school culture. Further, as was pointed out, a relationship seems to exist between dimensions of climate as defined by the OCDQ and climate-culture as defined by the PCI, suggesting that the two concepts share commonalities. Further, dimensions of culture can be inferred from school climate. It is clear that schools characterized by System 4 or human resources climates are driven by values, assumptions, and beliefs that are quite different from those of schools characterized by System 1 or bureaucratic school climates. Still, the climate metaphor leads us to think about the interpersonal life in schools. Culture leads us deeper into the life of the school, into the tacit world of beliefs and norms, into the realm of meaning and significance.

UNDERSTANDING THE FACULTY AS A WORK GROUP

The clusters of faculty which comprise the school's various work groups and the faculty as a whole are the setting within which the dimensions of culture are initially shaped and subsequently influence what teachers think and how they behave. The work group, therefore, is where the action is for supervisors and

---

[4] Corwith Hansen, "Department Culture in a High-Performing Secondary School," unpublished dissertation, Columbia University, 1986.

Exhibit 5-1 School Culture Inventory: Identifying Guiding Beliefs

Before a school's culture can be understood, evaluated, or changed, it needs first to be described. The list of questions which comprise this inventory can help faculties describe the culture of their school. The questions are patterned generally after those which appear in Jerry Patterson, Stuart C. Purkey, and Jackson Parker's, *Productive School Systems for a Nonrational World.*[*] Though presented in the form of an inventory, the questions will have the most meaning when discussed by faculty. When individual and group ratings are obtained from teachers they should be supplemented by examples. To help acquaint you with the inventory items, try evaluating a school with which you are familiar using the following scale:

(*A*lways, *M*ost of the time, *P*art of the time, *N*ever)

School Purposes

To what extent does the school:

1	Communicate a set of purposes that provide a sense of direction and a basis for evaluating?	A M P N
2	Value the importance of teachers and students understanding the purposes?	A M P N
3	Want decisions to be made which reflect purposes?	A M P N

Empowerment

To what extent does the school:

4	Value empowering teachers to make decisions that are sensible given circumstances they face?	A M P N
5	Link empowerment to purpose by requiring that decisions reflect the school shared values?	A M P N
6	Believe that teachers, supervisors, and administrators should have equal access to information and resources?	A M P N
7	Believe power to be an expanding entity which increases when shared?	A M P N

Decision Making

To what extent does the school:

8	Believe that decisions should be made as close to the point of implementation as possible?	A M P N

[*]Jerry Patterson, Stuart Purkey, and Jackson Parker, "Guiding Beliefs of Our School District," *Productive School Systems for a Nonrational World,* Arlington, Va.: Association for Supervision and Curriculum Development, 1986, pp. 50–51. Reprinted with permission of the Association for Supervision and Curriculum Development and Jerry Patterson, Stuart Purkey, and Jackson Parker. Copyright © 1986 by the Association for Supervision and Curriculum Development. All rights reserved.

Exhibit 5-1 School Culture Inventory: Identifying Guiding Beliefs *Continued*

9   Believe that value decisions should be made by those directly affected by them?   A   M   P   N

10   Believe that decisions should be made by those who are most expert, given the circumstances or problem being considered, regardless of hierarchical level?   A   M   P   N

Sense of Community

To what extent does the school:

11   Value a "we" spirit and feeling of ownership in the school?   A   M   P   N

12   Consider teachers and other employees as shareholders and stakeholders in the school?   A   M   P   N

13   Demonstrate commitment to helping and developing school members?   A   M   P   N

Trust

To what extent does the school:

14   Believe that given the opportunity teachers will want to do what is best for the school?   A   M   P   N

15   Have confidence in the ability of teachers to make wise decisions?   A   M   P   N

Quality

To what extent does the school:

16   Value high standards and expectations for teachers and students?   A   M   P   N

17   Believe in a "can do" attitude in teachers and students?   A   M   P   N

18   Value an atmosphere of sharing and encouraging within which school members "stretch and grow."   A   M   P   N

Recognition

To what extent does the school:

19   Value recognizing teachers and students for taking chances in seeking new and better ideas?   A   M   P   N

20   Value recognizing the achievements and accomplishments of teachers and students?   A   M   P   N

Exhibit 5-1 School Culture Inventory: Identifying Guiding Beliefs *Continued*

Caring

To what extent does the school:

21	Value the well-being and personal concerns of all school members?	A	M	P	N
22	Take a personal interest in the work concerns and career development of teachers?	A	M	P	N

Integrity

To what extent does the school:

23	Value honesty in words and actions?	A	M	P	N
24	Adopt a single standard of norms and expectations for teachers, students, and other school members?	A	M	P	N
25	Value consistency?	A	M	P	N
26	Demonstrate commitment to highest personal and ethical convictions?	A	M	P	N

Diversity

To what extent does the school:

27	Value differences in individual philosophy and personality?	A	M	P	N
28	Value differences in teaching style?	A	M	P	N
29	Value flexibility in teaching and learning approaches in response to student differences?	A	M	P	N
30	Link diversity in style and method to common school purposes and values?	A	M	P	N

comprises the context within which they must work in efforts to improve schooling. This is the reality of supervision. Person-to-person patterns of supervision which now dominate are not as effective as group patterns. They ignore the power of both climate and culture in influencing teachers. Further, person-to-person patterns encourage privatism and isolation among teachers. Many experts believe these conditions must be changed if schools are to be improved significantly.[5] And finally, person-to-person patterns of supervision resemble a system of inspection that typically evokes negative responses from teachers.

[5] S. J. Rosenholtz and S. J. Kyle, "Teacher Isolation: Barrier to Professionalism," *American Educator*, vol. 8, pp. 10–15, 1984.

HOW EFFECTIVE IS YOUR FACULTY AS A WORK GROUP?

How can supervisors judge the extent to which faculty groups are working effectively? One answer is by examining the outcomes or products of the group. What is the group supposed to be accomplishing and to what extent is it accomplishing these aims? If outcomes are being accomplished, the group is judged to be *efficient*. The problem with viewing effectiveness in this way is that efficiency is only one necessary component. The other component is growth. Any effective group is concerned not only with accomplishing its immediate tasks but with improving its ability to accomplish even more difficult and varied tasks tomorrow. Efficiency criteria are typically bound by short-term time frames and focus on small-scale objectives. Effectiveness, on the other hand, is concerned with the long-term ability of a group to accomplish its goals and objectives while increasing its capacity for growth and development. Many studies have shown that giving prime attention to efficiency and neglecting effectiveness may result in short-term increases in productivity, but over time the work group loses its productive edge and becomes less productive.[6] In sum, the relationship between effective supervision and group effectiveness is becoming increasingly important as supervisors work more and more within the context of groups. Examples of such work include peer-collegial supervision, clinical supervision, team-oriented staff-development programs and curriculum-development projects and team, family, or group teaching. W. J. Reddin considers the eight functional characteristics listed below as critical dimensions of group effectiveness.

1 The amount of enthusiasm and commitment that exists for group goals and purposes.
2 The quantity and quality of member contributions to the group.
3 The quality of listening by members to one another.
4 The amount of creativity exhibited in problem solving.
5 Ways in which conflict and disagreements are handled within the group.
6 The quality and nature of leadership that exists.
7 The methods and means of making decisions.
8 The ways in which the group evaluates its performance.[7]

Take a moment to address the present effectiveness of a group for which you have responsibility or of which you are a member. (If you are presently taking a university course and have recently engaged in a class project requiring group effort, you might want to use this setting for your evaluation.) Recall the actual members of the group and how they typically work together. Now bring to mind a specific assignment or set of tasks on which the group has actually worked. Use this special occasion as the basis of your analysis.

---

[6] See, for example, Rensis Likert, *The Human Organization*, New York: McGraw-Hill, 1967; and Rensis Likert, *New Patterns of Management*, New York: McGraw-Hill, 1961.
[7] Team Style Diagnostic Test, Fredericton, New Brunswick: Managerial Effectiveness, Ltd., by W. J. Reddin and used with his permission.

You are now ready to assess the group using the eight critical dimensions provided earlier. You will be using a modification and abbreviation of the Team Analysis Key (Exhibit 5-2), a part of the Team Style Diagnostic Test developed by Reddin.[8] This modification allows you to evaluate a group on the basis of Reddin's eight critical dimensions but utilizes only one set of item descriptors concerning only the criterion goals and purposes. (The complete Reddin materials provide a separate set of items for each of the eight criteria of group effectiveness.) To the left of Exhibit 5-2 is listed the critical dimension of goals and purposes. To the right appear eight alternative descriptions of group functioning. Select the three descriptors that best indicate how your group functioned on the occasion being evaluated. Now assign 10 points across the three descriptors to indicate their relative accuracy in describing the group. Use any possible combination (8-1-1, 2-6-2, 3-3-4, 0-10-0, 1-3-6, etc.) proving that 10 points are distributed.

You are now ready to assess the group using the other seven critical dimensions: member contributions, quality of listening, creativity in problem solving, management of conflict, leadership quality, decision making, and evaluation of performance. To assist in your assessment first examine the item descriptors Reddin provides for goals and purposes and identify key words or phrases in each. Item A, for example, suggests "lack of interest" and Item B suggests "harmony." The array of key words and phrases for Items A through H are as follows:

A	B	C	D	E	F	G	H
Lack of interest	Har-mony	Arguing	Lack of focus	Proce-dural orienta-tion	Devel-opment orienta-tion	On task	Team work

Use these item descriptors to evaluate your group on each of the remaining seven dimensions scoring in the same fashion as you did for goals and purposes. Imagine the items and descriptors being arranged in the form of a grid. Total your scores in each column by summing the values given for each category A through H. Keep in mind that this adaptation of the Team Analysis Key is designed to provide only a rough evaluation of group functioning and more importantly is *intended to raise the issue of group effectiveness and its characteristics.* A more functional evaluation would necessitate using the entire Team Style Diagnostic Test package and the complete Team Analysis Key. We will return to the Team Analysis Key and explain your scores for A through H later in this chapter. Let's now examine some of the characteristics of groups at work.

---

[8] Copyright by W. J. Reddin and used with his permission.

↓ START HERE	A	B	C	D
PURPOSE (READ ACROSS) ——→	( ) There was little interest in getting the job done.	( ) There was more interest in harmony than in getting the job done.	( ) There seemed more interest in argument than in getting the job done.	( ) There was little consistent focus on the problem.
NEXT SEVEN ITEMS				
INDIVIDUAL TOTAL	( )	( )	( )	( )

WHAT IS A GROUP AND WHY DO TEACHERS JOIN GROUPS?

What constitutes a group and why do teachers seek membership in groups? Cattell describes a group as "an aggregate of organisms in which the existence of all is utilized for satisfaction of the needs of each."[9] Bass defines a group as a collection of persons which is mutually reinforcing.[10] Groups are characterized by the extent to which participants find group membership rewarding. In return for some form of need satisfaction, group members are expected to provide the group with loyalty, effort, and interest. An awareness of the relationship between rewards and investments is fundamental to understanding faculty work groups. Participants will tend to become margin group members or to withdraw from the group when they perceive that the rewards they receive become out of proportion to their contributions to the group. Further, some individuals abandon group membership when the group is no longer potent enough to provide the kind of need satisfaction that they require. This relationship is not a balanced one. Investors must perceive that the rewards they earn as a result of their active membership exceed their investment in the group.[11] As illustrated in Figure 5-1, investors need to get more out of group membership than they put into the relationship. This critical principle seems to defy the laws of logical mathematics but psychological rewards do not follow such laws.

Many school groups might be better characterized as collections of individuals rather than as a group. Though strictly speaking a collection of teachers

---

[9] Raymond Cattell, "New Concepts of Measuring Leadership in Terms of Group Syntality," *Human Relations*, vol. 4, pp. 161–184, 1951.

[10] Bernard Bass, *Leadership, Psychology and Organizational Behavior*, New York: Harper & Row, 1960, chap. 3.

[11] Homans refers to this phenomenon as the "theory of distributive justice." See, for example, Leonard Sayles and George Strauss, *Human Behavior in Organizations*, Englewood Cliffs, N.J.: Prentice-Hall, 1966, p. 99. The theory works in either direction—the group ceases its reward-granting behavior when it no longer values or requires the commitment of individuals, and individuals cease their commitment when rewards, in their view, are not sufficient to warrant their commitment.

E	F	G	H	TOTALS
( )	( )	( )	( )	
There was much attention to following procedures and established patterns.	There was much attention to the development of a team.	There was a clear-cut attempt to stay directly with the problem.	There was an enthusiastic team attempt to look at the problem as broadly and deeply as possible.	= 10
				= 10
				= 80

may qualify as a physical group if they are in the same area of the building or as a department or grade-level group if they all teach in the same academic level or area, they do not qualify as a psychological group. In a psychological group, members share common purposes, interact with one another, perceive themselves to be a group, and obtain satisfaction of their needs as a result of group membership.

When a department or unit gets together, one can only be sure that a physical group is assembled. If only some of the teachers share common goals, interact with one another, share a group identity, and get needs met as a result of membership, then we have a psychological group within a physical group. Psychological groups are concerned with both "body and spirit"—physical groups are concerned only with body. Perhaps the deciding factor for most teachers as to whether they are merely physical members or are psychological members of a group is whether their needs are met as

FIGURE 5-1
The investment exchange. Active group membership ceases (or becomes marginal) when investments in the group are equal to or exceed returns for members.

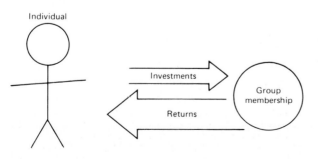

a result of group membership. Teachers will tend to become marginal group members or withdraw from the group when rewards cease or when rewards are not worth the contributions they are currently making to the group. *In return for rewards teachers are expected to provide the group with loyalty, effort, and interest.*

The development of a unit into a psychological group is a first step, but in itself it is not enough. Psychological groups are not necessarily effective work groups. Consider, for example, a group of teachers who share a common purpose, *the maintenance of things the way they are*; who interact regularly, *to discredit attempts to change their school*; who identify as a group, *the regulars*; and who find group membership comforting and satisfying, *sort of a mutual protection society.* This group indeed qualifies as a psychological group but probably does not qualify as an effective work group. The culture which characterizes this group, for example, might be characterized as "wild" rather than "domesticated" with respect to school goals.

A physical group is a collection of individuals. A psychological group is a collection of individuals who share common purposes, interact with one another, perceive themselves to be a group, and find group membership rewarding. Psychological groups have strong and binding cultures that influence what teachers think and do. Effective work groups are always psychological groups, but psychological groups are not always effective work groups. In an effective work group the purposes that members share are consistent with school objectives, and interaction between and among members is usually concerned with job-defined tasks, purposes, and activities. There is high identity with and commitment to school objectives, and task effectiveness is high. Effective work groups have cultures which support and enhance the work of the school.

PROPOSITIONS ABOUT GROUP FUNCTIONING

Let us consider several general propositions and assumptions that are basic to understanding how groups function.

1 Groups exist because they have to exist. Group life is a natural form of social organization for human beings. We influence groups and are influenced by groups throughout our lives. In the long run, more harm is done when schools work to frustrate and discourage group activity (among teachers *and* students) than when schools allow groups free expression.

2 Groups are neutral. In and of themselves, groups are neither good nor bad. School groups can be powerful forces that work to achieve school goals also. They can be equally powerful in working against school goals. For example, a teaching faculty with high morale may obtain satisfaction by working to frustrate school goals—and perhaps by discrediting the principal in the bargain—or by working to enhance school goals. Indeed, many student groups receive satisfaction in their dedication to frustrate the school's operation, while others are equally satisfied working for or with the school.

3 Groups have unique "personalities" that are conceptually similar to individual personalities. This group personality stems from and is composed of characteristics that individuals bring to the group. Thus, two school faculties or two departments with similar goals differ markedly because their membership differs.

4 As part of the group's personality, a group culture emerges that includes norms of behavior and a value system or belief pattern that are unique to the group. This belief pattern provides the cement that holds the group together and that regulates group behavior. This belief pattern can be referred to as the group's *dynamic center*. A zone of freedom exists that permits individuals to stray somewhat from the dynamic center but still maintain group membership (see Figure 5-2).When group members move beyond the zone of freedom, they cross the group's boundary and forfeit membership. The closer a group member is to this dynamic center, the more influential that person will be. Figure 5-3 illustrates various positions of group membership and levels of agreement in relation to the group's dynamic center. One who holds marginal membership in a group can improve his or her position by adopting more of the group's culture, thus moving closer to the dynamic center, or by moving the dynamic center of the group closer to himself or herself. This second strategy is difficult in that those who are removed from the dynamic center are often perceived by other group members as having little influence.

5 When individuals assume roles as group members, they behave differently than when they operate as free agents. Groups influence people. As a result of this influence, people behave differently—they react to group pressure. This phenomenon is suggested by Heron when he contrasts the actions and demands of workers as groups with their desires as individuals:

> The opinion polls almost always show that the most prominent desires of the individual employee relate to the most important thing in the world—*himself*, his

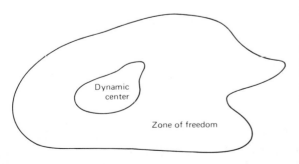

FIGURE 5-2
The group and its boundaries. (*From Harold Wilson et al., "The Group and Its Leaders," unpublished manuscript, Columbus: Ohio State University, Center for Educational Administration, Department of Education, 1963.*)

Dynamic center

Zone of freedom

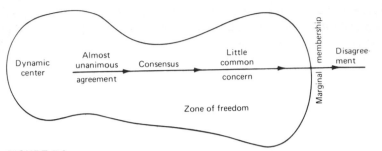

FIGURE 5-3
Group membership and movement. (*Harold Wilson et al., "The Group and Its Leaders," unpublished manuscript, Columbus: Ohio State University, Center for Educational Administration, Department of Education, 1963.*)

personality, his recognition, his security, and his progress. He wants recognition, for his skills, his suggestions, his attention and energy, his performance and production.

But when he gets together with his fellow workers—who want exactly the same things—they agree almost unanimously to demand standard wage rates for all workers on the same job, the prohibition of piecework and incentives, and uniform increases in all wage rates.

He wants fair treatment, as an individual, in job assignments and promotions. He resents favoritism or any process of selection which seems to overlook his abilities and gives the foreman job to someone less competent. He wants to be rewarded for his merit.

But in united action with his fellow workers he will demand that in promotions, layoffs, or rehirings, the principles of seniority shall strictly apply. He will stand on this demand with almost emotional devotion.[12]

Group pressures result in group conformity. Conformity in turn stifles creativity and individual expression. Therefore, as this argument develops, groups have negative and frustrating effects on individuality. Indeed, groups do have enormous potential for applying normative pressure to individuals. Further, these pressures often require some "conformity" from group members. Conformity, however, if viewed moderately, is the strength in groups that supervisors should seek. Conformity is not inherently bad. Indeed, a group norm may be one of creative expression by its members. Thus members conform by expressing their individuality. This position is effectively argued by Cartwright and Lippitt by making a distinction between conformity and uniformity.

It is important, first, to make a distinction between conformity and uniformity. A group might have a value that everyone should be as different from everyone else as possible. Conformity to this value, then, would result not in uniformity of behavior but in nonuniformity. Such a situation often arises in therapy groups or training groups where it is possible to establish norms which place a high value upon "being different" and upon tolerating deviant behavior. Conformity to this value is presumably greater the more cohesive the group and the more it is seen as relevant to the group's objectives.[13]

---

[12] Alexander Heron, *Why Men Work*, Stanford, Calif.: Stanford University Press, 1948, p. 20.
[13] Dorwin Cartwright and Ronald Lippitt, "Group Dynamics and the Individual," *International Journal of Psychotherapy*, vol. 7, no. 1, p. 95, 1957.

6 Goals held *for* the group but not *by* the group tend to be rejected by the group. The zone of freedom for a group is similar to the concept of self for individuals. A behavioral change for individuals is best accompanied by broadening one's concept of self to include the change. Groups change by broadening zones of freedom to include new alternatives. Even the most forceful leadership is frustrated if it overlooks this important concept.

CHARACTERISTICS OF EFFECTIVE WORK GROUPS

The research of Rensis Likert and his colleagues at the Institute for Social Research, University of Michigan, on the dimensions and nature of work group effectiveness is considered to be pioneering. Work groups maximize their effectiveness, according to Likert, when they are characterized as follows:

1 The members are skilled in all the various leadership and membership roles and functions required for interaction between leaders and members and between members and other members.

2 The group has been in existence sufficiently long to have developed a well-established, relaxed working relationship among all its members.

3 The members of the group are attracted to it and are loyal to its members, including the leader.

4 The members and leaders have a high degree of confidence and trust in each other.

5 The values and goals of the group are a satisfactory integration and expression of the relevant values and needs of its members. They have helped shape these values and goals and are satisfied with them.

6 Insofar as members of the group are performing linking functions, they endeavor to have the values and goals of the groups which they link in harmony with one another.

7 The more important a value seems to the group, the greater the likelihood that the individual member will accept it.

8 The members of the group are highly motivated to abide by the major values and to achieve the important goals of the group.

9 All the interaction, problem-solving, decision-making activities of the group occur in a supportive atmosphere.

10 The group is eager to help each member develop to his or her full potential. It sees, for example, that relevant technical knowledge and training in interpersonal and group skills are made available to each member.

11 Each member accepts willingly and without resentment the goals and expectations that he or she and the group establish for themselves.

12 When necessary or advisable, members of the group will give other members the help they need to accomplish successfully the goals set for them. Reciprocal help is a characteristic of highly effective groups.

13 The supportive atmosphere of the highly effective group stimulates creativity. The group does not demand narrow conformity as do the work groups under authoritarian leaders.

14 There is strong motivation on the part of each member to communicate fully and frankly to the group all the information which is relevant and of value to the group's activity.

15 There is high motivation in the group to use the communication process so that it best serves the interests and goals of the group.

16 Just as there is high motivation to communicate, there is correspondingly strong motivation to receive communications.

17 In the highly effective group there are strong motivations to try to influence other members as well as to be receptive to influence from them.[14]

Consistent with the assertion that group members abide by the norms and rules of the group in return for rewards and conditions they value it seems useful to differentiate between two major sources of rewards. One reward source is the mutual satisfaction, or reinforcement, that individuals get from interacting with other individuals. The more satisfaction for group members as a result of this interaction, the higher the interaction effectiveness of the group. Interaction effectiveness is an important characteristic of a psychological group. Another source of rewards for group members comes from actual implementation of the group's purposes. The more satisfaction for group members as a result of doing the task, the higher the task effectiveness of the group. Task effectiveness and interaction effectiveness lead to group effectiveness. The more satisfaction for group members as a result of interaction effectiveness and task effectiveness, the higher the group effectiveness.[15]

THE COMPONENTS OF GROUP EFFECTIVENESS

Interaction effectiveness refers to the quality of group sentiment that exists for a given group. It includes such concepts as morale, cohesiveness, and communication ease. Bass suggests that this dimension of group effectiveness can be assessed by (1) the amount of harmony present and the absence of conflict, (2) the amount of satisfaction for members as a result of interaction, and (3) the perceived congruence between actual and expected relations among group members.[16]

Interaction effectiveness is facilitated by a number of variables, each having the strength to increase the potential for group members to interact. For example, collections of individuals about the same age, with similar educa-

---

[14] Abridged from Rensis Likert, *New Patterns of Management,* New York: McGraw-Hill, 1961, p. 166. Likert's list is much more illustrative and comprehensive.

[15] The notion of group effectiveness containing a task dimension is borrowed from Bernard Bass. Bass feels that *either* dimension or both dimensions may result in group effectiveness. Our view is that *both* dimensions are necessary for group effectiveness. Bernard Bass, *Leadership Psychology and Organizational Behavior,* New York: Harper & Row, 1960, chap. 3. This discussion follows that which appears in Thomas Sergiovanni, "Group Effectiveness: Human Relations Is Not Enough," *Illinois Elementary Principal,* pp. 15–17, September 1967.

[16] Bass, op. cit., p. 46.

tional backgrounds, and with similar interests will tend to have high interaction potential. The more homogeneous the group, the higher the interaction potential of the group. Exposure to contact, size, and pressures to participate are other variables affecting interaction potential.[17] Perhaps the most indicative factor of interaction potential is mutual predictability among group members. That is, a given group member is able to predict what other group members will do. The higher the mutual predictability among group members, the higher the interaction level of the group.

Consider, for example, a group of special teachers in an elementary school. One would suppose that this group, being somewhat homogeneous, manageable in size, having frequent interaction opportunities, and possessing common sentiments of educational philosophy and school organization, would enjoy high interaction effectiveness. It is more difficult, however, to predict whether this group—or any other school group, for that matter—will use its energies, its power, its pressures, and its unique reward system on behalf of the school's purposes. Perhaps this group of special teachers will harness its energies to provide the very best services that it can to the school. Or perhaps this same group may decide that it is more rewarding to be a thorn in the supervisor's side. Another possibility is that this group may simply enjoy its unique informal reward system at the expense of doing no more than a minimum job, if it does a job at all.[18]

The direction and orientation of a school group hinge on another aspect of group effectiveness, the accomplishment of task. *Task effectiveness* refers to activity that promotes, defines, clarifies, pursues, and accomplishes relevant school goals. It is described in terms of the rewards that group members get from doing or completing a task. Challenging work; responsibility; intrinsic satisfaction; autonomy; feelings of success, achievement, and competence; recognition for task efforts; bolstering of self- and group esteem; and individual and group status are words and phrases that best describe the flavor of the reward system that characterizes task effectiveness.

A group whose primary reward system rests with task effectiveness will have at its disposal an arsenal of weapons to encourage, motivate, and perhaps even pressure group members to work on behalf of the school and its purposes. On the other hand, a group deprived of this reward system may divert its efforts from work-centered activities and tend to concentrate on seeking satisfaction solely from the interaction-effectiveness domain. The group, not the job, becomes the focus of attention. Group norms that conflict with the purposes of the school may be established. Conformity to the group and its norms becomes necessary if one wishes to benefit from the group's reward system. This conformity may require that teachers not exert more than a minimum effort in their jobs.[19]

[17] See James G. March and Herbert A. Simon, *Organizations,* New York: Wiley, 1958, pp. 68–71, for an interesting and comprehensive discussion of factors that affect frequency of interaction.

[18] Dubin discusses subversive, cooperative, and neutral groups in his analysis of informal organization. Robert Dubin, *Human Relations in Administration,* 2d ed., Englewood Cliffs, N.J.: Prentice-Hall, 1961, pp. 84–87.

[19] The rate-buster phenomenom and the sanctions that follow have been well documented in industry. We suspect that the analogy works for education, too. For example, elementary school

Interaction effectiveness and task effectiveness are not at opposite ends of a continuum. The effective group is highly successful in its task endeavors and uses its interaction potential on behalf of the task. Such a group would tend to reap rewards (acceptance, affiliation, belonging, and security, for example) while at the same time deriving satisfaction from getting a job done.

FUNCTIONAL ROLES OF GROUP MEMBERS

The question of leadership is one that cannot be avoided for long in an examination of groups. Traditionally, the group leader is considered the key determiner of a group's effectiveness. Good leaders, according to this view, are those who point direction for group activity, clarify goals, make relevancy judgments as they guide group discussion, keep people on the track, are the agenda watchdogs, push for full participation, and force decisions. Good leaders get things done! Their tools are their official role as supervisors and administrators, an acceptable agenda, group know-how, and guided discussion.

Human resources supervision suggests that designated group leaders (teachers, chairpersons, supervisors, consultants, principals, and so on) come to conceive of their role primarily as one of providing service rather than direction to the group. For example, while traditional supervisory patterns require that the leader get things done (presumably by using the group and its resources), human resources supervisors work to help the group accomplish its tasks. Within this context, leaders do not attempt to solve the group's problems but focus on the group solving its problems; they do not seek to move the group forward but to help the group as it moves forward. But somebody must get the group going, must initiate discussion, define problems and goals, evaluate, summarize, monitor, provide information, and the like. Indeed, the group will not accomplish its goals without these and other leadership roles being fulfilled. Human resources supervisors are concerned with these roles but hold no monopoly on them. *Leadership functions are considered to be the responsibility of the entire group—not just of the designated leader.* The discussion that follows focuses on leadership and other group roles that are needed in effective groups rather than on who should assume what role. Roles are best assumed by those most capable of assuming them.

Group roles are often classified into three broad categories depending upon whether they support group task effectiveness, support group interaction effectiveness, or exist solely for the satisfaction of group members. The first category, group task roles, includes roles that facilitate and coordinate the selection and definition of a common group problem and help in solving this problem. The second category, group-binding or group-maintenance roles, includes roles that are oriented to the functioning of the group as a group. The

teachers often mentioned that too much effort, too many displays, noticeable project work, elaborate bulletin boards, taking work home, and other signs of rate busting frequently result in informal and formal sanctions from the group.

third category, individual roles, includes roles directed not primarily toward the group or the task but toward the individual participant.

Following Kenneth Benne and Paul Sheats, the roles are described below.[20]

Group task roles	Group maintenance roles	Individual roles
Initiator-contributor	Encourager	Aggressor
Information seeker	Harmonizer	Blocker
Opinion seeker	Compromiser	Recognition seeker
Information giver	Gatekeeper	Self-confessor
Opinion giver	Standard setter	Playboy
Elaborator	Group observer	Nominator
Coordinator	Follower	Help seeker
Orientator		Special interest
Evaluator-critic		Pleader
Energizer		
Procedural technician		
Recorder		

Groups need to work for balance among the three types of roles. Surely task roles depend upon maintenance roles, and maintenance roles are legitimized and become purposeful as a result of task roles. A mature group permits its members to occasionally assume individual roles. Sustained behavior of this type by one or another group member, however, creates problems for the group. Use the three groups of roles provided to evaluate a meeting at your school. You might, for example, construct a grid comprised of the three groups of roles as one dimension and the names of group members as the other. Each time a person speaks, place a check mark in the appropriate grid cell. Do certain individuals limit their participation to single role sets? What roles are played the most and least? Are critical roles missing? Can you figure out what is really on a member's mind when she or he assumes one of the individual roles?

COOPERATION AND COMPETITION AMONG GROUPS

As supervision takes on more of a group character, the issues of cooperation and competition become very important. What happens, for example, when one group of teachers involved in clinical supervision finds itself in competition

---

[20] Kenneth D. Benne and Paul Sheats, "Functional Roles of Group Members," *The Journal of Social Issues,* vol. 4, no. 2, pp. 43–46, 1948.

with another group involved in another approach to supervision? Or what happens when one teaching team committed to approach A finds itself in competition with another team committed to approach B? Often such rivalry is nothing more than good-natured fun that has positive effects for everyone. But if genuine competition emerges (if one group perceives itself as the winner and the other the loser), serious problems quickly follow.

The effects of competition within and between groups is a thoroughly researched area. In summarizing a number of studies Schein describes the effects as follows:[21]

A What happens *within* each competing group?
  1 Each group becomes more closely knit and elicits greater loyalty from its members; members close ranks and bury some of their internal differences.
  2 Group climates change from informal, casual, playful, to work- and task-oriented; concern for members' psychological welfare declines while concern for task accomplishment increases.
  3 Leadership patterns tend to change from more democratic to more autocratic; the group becomes more willing to tolerate autocratic leadership.
  4 Each group becomes more highly structured and organized.
  5 Each group demands more loyalty and conformity from its members in order for it to be able to present a "solid front."
B What happens *between* the competing groups?
  1 Each group begins to see the other groups as the enemy.
  2 Each group begins to experience distortions of perception. It tends to perceive only the best parts of itself, denying its weaknesses, and tends to perceive only the worst parts of other groups, denying their strengths; each group is likely to develop a negative stereotype of the other.
  3 Hostility toward the other group increases while interaction and communication with the other group decreases; thus it becomes easier to maintain negative stereotypes and more difficult to correct perceptual distortions.
  4 If the groups are forced into interaction, each group is likely to listen more closely to its own representative and not to listen to the representatives of the other group, except to find fault with the presentation; in other words, group members tend to listen only to that which supports their own position and stereotypes.

Intergroup competition has some beneficial effects *within* groups. The sense of battle builds cohesiveness and provides an incentive to focus on tasks. But as one group becomes more effective as a result of competition, the faculty as

[21] Edgar H. Schein, *Organizational Psychology,* © 1965, pp. 81, 82. Reprinted by permission of Prentice-Hall, Englewood Cliffs, N.J.

a whole becomes less effective and the result is a less effective school overall. In battle, for every winner there is a loser. The consequences of winning and losing as a result of competition are described by Schein as follows:

C What happens to the *winner*?
    1 The winner retains cohesion and may become even more cohesive.
    2 The winner tends to release tension, lose its fighting spirit, become complacent, casual, and playful.
    3 The winner tends toward high intergroup cooperation and concern for members' needs, and low concern for work and task accomplishment.
    4 The winner tends to be complacent and feel that winning has confirmed the positive stereotype of itself and the negative stereotype of the enemy.
D What happens to the *loser*?
    1 If the situation permits, there is a strong tendency for the loser to deny or distort the reality of losing; instead the loser will find psychological escapes such as "the supervisor was biased," "the principal really didn't understand our solution," "the rules of the game were not clearly explained to us."
    2 If loss is accepted, the losing group tends to splinter, unresolved conflicts come to the surface, fights break out, all in an effort to find the cause for the loss.
    3 The losing group is more tense, ready to work harder, and desperate to find someone or something to blame: the leader, the person who decided against them, the rules of the game.
    4 The loser tends toward low intergroup cooperation, low concern for members' needs, and high concern for recouping by working harder.
    5 The loser tends to learn a lot about itself as a group because positive stereotypes of itself and negative stereotypes of the other group are upset by the loss, forcing a reevaluation of perceptions; as a consequence, the loser is likely to reorganize and become more cohesive and effective, once the loss has been accepted more realistically.

The positive effects of intergroup competition may outweigh the negative on some occasions and in the short run. But as a long-term strategy intergroup cooperation makes more sense. Intergroup cooperation requires that supervisors see themselves as a cadre of individuals committed to team leadership rather than as isolated local supervisors concerned exclusively with the self-interests of their particular group. The supervisor's commitment, in other words, is to educational leadership that is targeted at the school as a whole. In this effort, greater emphasis needs to be given to total school effectiveness and how a group contributes to it. Groups should be rewarded on the basis of their contributions to the total school effort rather than only on their own effectiveness. Opportunities for interaction and communication should be provided to enable groups to discuss intergroup problems with the aim that the groups will be better coordinated. Opportunities for rotation of members among groups should be provided to stimulate mutual understanding and empathy.

SIZING UP YOUR GROUP

Earlier in this chapter we suggested that a group could be evaluated by examining eight critical items:

1 The amount of enthusiasm and commitment that exists for group goals and purposes
2 The quantity and quality of member contribution to the group
3 The quality of listening by members to one another
4 The amount of creativity exhibited in problem solving
5 Ways in which conflicts and disagreements are handled within the group
6 The quality and nature of leadership that exists
7 The methods and means of making decisions
8 The ways in which the group evaluates its performance

Using an adaptation and abbreviation of Reddin's Team Analysis Key, you were asked to evaluate a group with which you were familiar on each of the eight dimensions. You totaled each of columns A through H to obtain eight scores. Each of the scores represents a particular mode of group functioning. Score A, for example, describes the group in *flight*. The group functional modes are described below and identified by the appropriate letter:

A The group in *flight* is a group that displays little energy in getting the job done. Conflict is kept at a minimum because of the energy it requires. Creativity and contributions are low, and leadership appears to be absent. Usually the decision is, in effect, not a decision but a rewording of the problem as it originally existed. There is rarely any effort made to evaluate or improve group performance. When a group operates in this way, the supervisor usually functions as a *deserter*.

B The *dependent* group is a group whose byword is harmony. More attention is paid to avoiding conflict than to discussing problems. Most of the contributions are ones with which everyone can be expected to agree, and creative ideas are blocked when they are seen as possible criticisms of members or the group as a whole. Disagreements, even when obviously functional, are avoided. Leadership sometimes evolves, but it is usually friendly and weak. Evaluation of the group's efforts is usually in the form of compliments. When a group operates in this way, the supervisor usually functions as a *missionary*.

C The *fight* is a group characterized by conflict and argument. The conflict is not functional, as contribution and creativity are usually blocked by arguments of group members. Leadership is dominated by one or two individuals, often those with the loudest voices. Disagreements between individuals sometimes become personal rather than based on the issues.

Evaluation of the group's efforts usually amounts to attacks on group members. When a group operates in this way, the supervisor usually functions as an *autocrat*.

D The *mixed* group is a group that attempts to compromise between getting the task done and sparing people's feelings. The result is less effective. The group lacks focus on problems. Its members' comments are often irrelevant, and attempts at leadership usually fail. Disagreement exists but serves no useful purpose. Leadership is often absent when it is needed and often present when it is not needed. Evaluation is weak. When a group operates in this way, the supervisor usually functions as a *compromiser*.

E The *procedural* group is a group that follows procedures and established patterns. Creativity and contributions, although forthcoming within defined procedures, are sound. Members listen politely, and disagreement is handled in a formal manner. Leadership is routine; evaluation usually amounts to a comparison of the group's effort to the efforts of other groups. Evaluation is, however, functional. When a group operates in this way, the supervisor usually functions as a *bureaucrat*.

F The *creative* group is a group that focuses primarily on developing its members and its ideals. Much attention is paid to the minority opinion and to attempts to incorporate the ideas of all members in the decision. Disagreement, although rare, is looked into closely, so that benefit is derived from it. Evaluation of the group's effort is usually aimed at improving group creativity. When a group operates in this way, the supervisor usually functions as a *developer*.

G The *productive* group is a task-oriented group whose primary concern is the immediate task. Contributions come from those who push for their own ideas. Disagreement occurs frequently but is usually useful. Discussions about productivity may be dominated by a few members, but their leadership is beneficial. Evaluation is usually focused on making the group more efficient. When a group operates in this way, the supervisor usually functions as a *benevolent autocrat*.

H The *problem-solving* group is a group that attempts to examine problems as broadly and deeply as possible and thus reach an optimal solution to which all are committed. Due consideration is given to both the task at hand and the feelings of group members. Ideas are of high quality and are highly relevant to the task. When a group operates in this way, the supervisor usually functions as an *executive*.

Some groups may operate closely to one of Reddin's descriptions most of the time, but probably most groups shift operating styles occasionally on certain issues. The problem-solving, productive, creative, and procedural groups are indeed very different in operating styles, but nevertheless each is effective in its own way. On the other hand, the mixed, fight, dependent, and flight groups, although different in operating styles, are each relatively ineffective. The contingency variables associated with choice of leadership styles that will be presented in Chapter 7 can help supervisors to select a team mode and group operating style most consistent with the problems, tasks, and circumstances facing the group at a given time.

SUMMARY

This chapter examines and applies the concept of culture to schools. Thinking about schools as cultures helps supervisors to understand in a new way how they operate and to develop supervisory strategies and behavior that move beyond traditional management. Culture was described as the observed behavioral regularities that describe the rules of the game for people. These rules are the norms that define what is right and correct to do, what is expected, and what is accepted. Schools, for example, were described as containing central zones that served as repositories of values and sources of identity for individuals and groups and provide the means by which their work lives became meaningful. Four levels of culture were then discussed: artifacts, perspectives, values, and assumptions. These levels provide a framework for analyzing the school's history and tradition, patterns of belief, norms, and behavior.

The cultural perspective then provided a framework for understanding the faculty as a work group. Within this discussion it was pointed out that groups are a natural, necessary, and important part of the organizational life in schools. Group supervision was offered as an alternative to person-to-person supervision as a means to work more effectively with people to achieve school purposes. Three types of groups were identified: physical, psychological, and effective work groups. Physical groups were defined as collections of individuals. Psychological groups were defined as collections of individuals who share common goals and interact with one another, viewing themselves as a group and obtaining satisfaction from group membership. Effective work groups were defined as psychological groups whose common purposes were consistent with those of the school.

Several propositions about group functioning were then discussed and the characteristics of an effective work group, as proposed by Likert, were presented as ideal standards for group supervision. Two key components of group effectiveness, interaction effectiveness and task effectiveness, were identified and the factors contributing to the establishment of these components in supervision were discussed. A listing of critical group task maintenance and self roles was then provided. A discussion of cooperation and competition among groups followed. Critical to this discussion was an analysis of the costs and benefits of group competition. The chapter concluded with guidelines for sizing up a group and determining its effectiveness.

STUDY GUIDE

Recall the concepts, ideas, and meanings associated with each of the following phrases and terms included in this chapter. Can you discuss each of them with a colleague and apply them to the supervisory context of your school? If you cannot, review them in the text and record the page number for future reference.

1 Central zone
2 Culture
3 Culture defined
4 Cultural metaphor
5 "Domesticated"
6 Effective work group
7 Group maintenance roles
8 Group supervision
9 Group task roles
10 Individual roles
11 Interaction effectiveness
12 Leadership function
13 Levels of culture
14 Likert characteristics
15 Loosely coupled
16 Person-to-person supervision
17 Psychological group
18 Sizing up the group
19 Task effectiveness
20 "Wild" culture

EXERCISES

1 Using the format of a short story or novel, describe the culture of a school you know using the "level of culture" question provided in the text. The cast of characters in your plot should be set in the school's historical tradition. Their words, actions, and behaviors should reflect the school's prevailing beliefs and values, norms, and standards.
2 How would you describe the group life in your department, unit, or school? How would your group measure up to the characteristics of group effectiveness suggested by Likert?
3 In sizing up your group, in what ways do you find it to share characteristics and features of the eight group types suggested by Reddin? Which of the four effective group types best fits your own leadership inclinations?
4 What are the consequences for a supervisor who recognizes natural group tendencies in schools but who views them as undesirable and therefore works to subvert or discourage group activity?

TEACHER MOTIVATION AND SUPERVISORY EFFECTIVENESS

Supervisors often ask why some teachers seem to work so hard and why others, by comparison, are relatively indifferent to their work or even seem dedicated to doing as little as possible. This question typically leads to speculations as to what supervisors can do to influence levels of commitment and the actual performance of teachers. The area of work motivation has been well researched, and a number of theories have been developed that can help supervisors understand why commitment levels of teachers vary and decide what to do to improve work performance.

Since the publication of *A Nation at Risk*[1] in 1983 a rash of studies and reports have been issued cataloging the ills of schooling in America and recommending reforms. Most of the early reports viewed teachers as the problem to be fixed as we move on the road to school improvement. The emphasis was on testing competencies of teachers, controlling what teachers teach, evaluating teaching behaviors, and providing incentive pay (under the guise of elaborate career ladder schemes) for improved performance. The states took the lead in mandating these reforms. Studies of schooling by Ernest Boyer,[2] Theodore Sizer,[3] and John Goodlad,[4] which appeared at about the same time stood in sharp contrast to the recommendations that fueled these

---

[1] National Commission on Excellence in Education, *A Nation at Risk*, Washington, D.C.: Government Printing Office, 1983.

[2] Ernest Boyer, *High School: A Report on Secondary Education in America*, New York: Harper & Row, 1983.

[3] Theodore R. Sizer, *Horace's Compromise: The Dilemma of the American High School*, Boston: Houghton Mifflin, 1984.

[4] John Goodlad, *A Place Called School*, New York: McGraw-Hill, 1984.

early reform initiatives. These authors suggested that long-term improvement of schooling would require viewing teachers as part of the solution and would give prime emphasis to the enhancement of teaching itself as the lynchpin to successful reform. The latter reports were initially overshadowed by the former. But within three years of the publication of *A Nation at Risk* school-improvement themes shifted from an emphasis on reforming teachers to reforming teaching as a profession; from working on teachers to working with teachers; from structuring and programming what teachers do as a means to ensure quality to improving the quality of work life in teaching itself. In July 1986, for example, the Education Commission of the States issued a report on new directions for school improvement entitled "What Next? More Leverage for Teachers."[5] In prefacing the report, Bernard Gifford stated:

> If we are going to make a dent in the problems we face in public education, we are going to have to find ways of permitting talented teachers to play a much larger role. We need to find ways of giving talented people, first rate professionals, extra leverage.[6]

At about the same time the Carnegie Forum for the Advancement of Teaching and the Holmes Group, a confederation of research-oriented universities interested in reforming teacher education, issued reports calling for a similar shift from fixing teachers to fixing the system within which teachers work. Summarizing this shift, the Education Commission of the States called for a major restructuring of the schools. The suggested characteristics of this restructuring appear in Table 6-1. Note the emphasis the commission gives to empowerment, encouraging local initiative, and upgrading both the stature and responsibility of teachers, supervisors, and principals. Teacher motivation and commitment, teacher efficacy, the quality of work life in teaching, intrinsic job satisfaction—all themes written about in books on supervision, taught in university classrooms, and practiced by forward-looking supervisors are now part of our nation's school reform agenda. Teacher motivation and commitment, in other words, is not only a good idea but a matter of national school policy.

BUREAUCRATIC AND PROFESSIONAL WORK

Despite what is known about motivation, regressive school policies and administrative practices can be found resulting in job dissatisfaction, lack of work motivation, and even alienation among teachers. It seems as though for every sound policy mandated by a state and for every promising practice found in the schools there are regressive counterparts. How can such contrasts between exemplars and regressive practices be explained? Key is the view that many policymakers and administrators have of teachers and teaching.

---

[5] Josyln Green, editor, "What Next? More Leverage for Teachers," Denver: Education Commission of the States, 1986.
[6] Ibid.

TABLE 6-1
EDUCATION COMMISSION OF THE STATES: RESTRUCTURING THE SCHOOLS

Restructuring schools means integrating what is known about effective schools, effective school leadership, how changes take place, and supportive school policy environments. The process will require whole new policies, new ways of doing business, and new ways of delivering educational services.

Some of the recent reports suggest these characteristics of restructured schools:

- There is a focus on student development—including academic, social, and psychological growth. Schools will be "human centered."

- The curriculum is personalized, tailored to student needs, and frequently delivered one-on-one.

- There exists a strong parent-school partnership, and the school serves as an active coordinator of community services needed by students and their families.

- Schools organized for improvement require extensive leadership—much of which must come from teachers. Decisions are made closer to the classroom.

- Management is shared by a corps of principals and teacher leaders.

- Qualities that are seen as hallmarks of productivity in business—mutual help, exchange of ideas, cooperative work to develop better practices, encouragement of risk taking—are fostered in schools.

- Shared aims, common priorities, favorable expectations of students, and consistent approaches to discipline create a collegial and productive school climate.

- Different teachers play different roles—as mentors, for example, or as teacher-leaders.

- Students are more responsible for their own learning. Through active learning, they strengthen higher-order thinking skills, develop creativity, and practice problem solving in all curricular areas.

- Principals are selected on the basis of their skills and rewarded on the basis of their performance.

- School personnel have greater control over hiring, more discretion over school expenditures, and greater responsibility for making decisions.

From Education Commission of the States, "Restructuring the Schools States Take on the Challenge," *Education Week,* vol. 6, no. 12, p. 19.

Some practices are based on a view of teachers as trusted and responsible professionals capable of accepting responsibility, providing individual initiative, being committed to school excellence, and concerned with professional growth and development. Other more regressive practices stem from a view of teachers as workers not to be trusted, incapable of self-discipline, and lacking in commitment to their work. Teachers, in this view, are best regulated and controlled by an elaborate work system which specifies what must be done and ensures that it is done. When this is the case, the work of teachers becomes increasingly bureaucratic. Bureaucratic and professional work are different. Though both bureaucrats and professionals are part of a rationally conceived work system, bureaucrats are *subordinate* to this system. They are responsible for implementing the system according to the provided specifications, and supervision is designed to monitor this process. The emphasis is on doing things right. Professionals, by contrast, are *superordinate* to their work system. They use the system in ways that make sense to them as they practice. Supervision for professionals, while no less demanding, is helpful and facilitating in its orientation. In professional work the emphasis is on doing right things and doing them well.

ORIGIN AND PAWN FEELINGS AND BEHAVIORS

Studies of successful schools reveal that teachers are committed, harder workers, more loyal to the school, and more satisfied with their jobs. The research on motivation to work reveals that these highly motivating conditions are present when teachers:

Find their work lives to be meaningful, purposeful, sensible, and significant and when they view the work itself as being worthwhile and important.

Have reasonable control over their work activities and affairs and are able to exert reasonable influence over work events and circumstances.

Experience personal responsibility for the work and are personally accountable for outcomes.[7]

When teachers experience meaningfulness, control, and personal responsibility at work, they are functioning more as "origins" than as "pawns." An origin believes that one's behavior is determined by his or her own choosing. A pawn, by contrast, believes that one's behavior is determined by external forces beyond his or her control.[8] Origins have strong feelings of personal causation. They believe that they can affect events and circumstances which exist in their environment. Pawns, by contrast, believe that forces beyond their control determine what it is that they will do. Pawn feelings, according to DeCharms, provide people with a strong sense of powerlessness and ineffectiveness.[9] Many experts such as DeCharms believe that persons strive to be effective in influencing and altering events and situations that comprise their environment. They strive to be causal agents, to be origins of their own behavior. And when this is not the case they experience frustration, powerlessness, and often alienation.

The bureaucratic view of teachers, teaching and pawn feelings is illustrated in the following example provided by Ashton and Webb as a result of their research on teacher efficacy:

---

[7] See, for example, Frederick Herzberg, Bernard Mausner, and Barbara Snyderman, *The Motivation to Work*, New York: Wiley, 1959; J. R. Hackman and G. Oldham, "Motivation through Design of Work: Test of a Theory," *Organizational Behavior and Human Performance*, vol. 16, pp. 250–279, 1976; and Thomas J. Peters and Robert H. Waterman, *In Search of Excellence*, New York: Harper & Row, 1982.

[8] Richard DeCharms, *Personal Causation: The Internal Affective Determinants of Behavior*, New York: Academic Press, 1968.

[9] Ibid.

Teachers in most schools reported that the administration treats them disrespectful-ly. They considered themselves to be professionals and were offended when they were treated like bureaucratic functionaries or naughty children. For example, on a teacher work day after students had been dismissed for summer vacation, the faculty at one school were grading exams, turning in grades, and straightening up their classrooms. Frequently during the day the principal used the public address system to remind his staff that "no one was to leave the school" until grades had been turned in and an administrator had checked the classrooms for cleanliness. Teachers were warned that a vice principal would come to each room and check everything, including the desk drawers and file cabinets, to make sure they were cleaned out. A teacher turned to a member of the research team and said in exasperation: "I've taught at a lot of schools, and nobody has never looked into my desk drawers, never! I feel it's rather an intrusion. They're saying I'm not professional. The biggest [problem at this school] is that we're being treated unprofessionally. We're talked down to. We're asked our opinion, but we know that it isn't going to make any difference. We all get talked down to at faculty meetings. If a teacher has done something wrong, then [the administration] should tell him. But the whole faculty shouldn't have to be lectured to."[10]

Contrast this example with one of professionalism provided by Sara Lightfoot as she describes Highland Park High School in her book *The Good High School*:

> In Highland Park, teachers seem to be nurtured by what many refer to as "a sense of professionalism" that combines relatively high status in the community, autonomy and respect, creature comforts, and an association with a school of fine reputation ...teachers were most thankful for being recognized as intellectuals whose respon-sibility it was to define and shape the curriculum....There were few directions sent down from above and many teachers spoke of the rejuvenating quality of intellectual discovery that their autonomy permitted. In the best cases, students could witness the teacher's intellectual adventure and could become part of the improvisational effort.
>
> Second, Highland Park teachers were given the freedom to express their own personal style in their work. Benson (the principal) believed that staff homogeneity was deadly, so he encouraged individuality among teachers and permitted idiosyn-crasies to flourish. Even those teachers whose style and behavior was somewhat controversial received his protection.[11]

Lightfoot continues her description as follows:

> Benson interpreted teacher nurturance, therefore, as providing autonomy, pro-tection, and support for individuality among them. Similar themes were present at Brookline [another high school studied by Lightfoot] where teachers were regarded as intellectuals, where diversity among them was encouraged, and where they were asked to take a responsible role in the authority structure of the school. Only in

---

[10] Patricia T. Ashton and Rodman B. Webb, *Making a Difference Teachers' Sense of Efficacy and Student Achievement,* New York: Longman, 1986, p. 49.

[11] Sara Lawrence Lightfoot, *The Good High School Portraits of Character and Culture,* New York: Basic Books, 1983, p. 336.

Brookline was there an even stronger emphasis on teachers as "academics" and a great admiration for teaching as a craft. When teachers talked about their work, they would frequently refer to the intellectual puzzles they were trying to unravel or their search for the appropriate pedagogical strategies that would meet the diverse needs of students.[12]

The glimpses provided by Lightfoot deal with issues well beyond that of motivation and commitment, but it is clear that the view of teaching in Highland Park and Brookline is one of professionalism.

TEACHERS' EFFICACY AND STUDENT ACHIEVEMENT

One of the consequences of experiencing personal causation, of being an origin rather than a pawn, is that one's sense of efficacy is enhanced. An efficacious teacher believes that she or he has the power and ability to produce a desired effect. Efficacy has to do with personal effectiveness, a feeling that one can control events and produce outcomes. Low efficacy deprives teachers of their motivation, damages their professional self-esteem, and results in low job satisfaction. Recent research links sense of efficacy not only with motivation and commitment to work but with student achievement.[13]

In early studies of teachers' sense of efficacy Armor and colleagues[14] and Berman and colleagues[15] defined efficacy as the extent to which teachers believe they have the capacity to affect student performance. These researchers measured efficacy by asking the following questions:

1 When it comes right down to it, a teacher really can't do much because most of a student's motivation and performance depends his or her home environment.

2 If I really try hard, I can get through to even the most difficult or unmotivated students.[16]

The first question assesses the extent to which the teacher believes that students can learn and the second the teacher's belief in his or her ability to teach. In their study of teachers' sense of efficacy and student achievement, Ashton and Webb found that efficacy was related to such teacher behaviors as being warm, accepting, and responsive to students; acceptance of student initiatives; and giving attention to all the students' individual needs. Efficacy

---

[12] Ibid.

[13] Ashton and Webb, op. cit.

[14] D. Armor, P. Conry-Oseguera, M. Cox, N. King, L. McDonnell, A. Pascal, E. Pauly, and G. Zellman, *Analysis of the School Preferred Reading Program in Selected Los Angeles Minority Schools* (Report R-2007-LAUSD), Santa Monica, Calif.: The Rand Corporation, 1976 (ERIC Document Reproduction Service No. ED 130 243).

[15] P. Berman, M. McLaughlin, G. Bass, E. Pauly, and G. Zellman, *Federal Programs Supporting Educational Change*, vol. 7: *Factors Affecting Implementation and Continuation*, Santa Monica, Calif.: The Rand Corporation, 1977 (ERIC Document Reproduction Service No. ED 140 432).

[16] Ibid., pp. 136–137.

was also related to such student behaviors as student enthusiasm and student initiation of interaction with teachers. And finally, *teachers' sense of efficacy was related to student achievement*. The subjects of their research were high school teachers of mathematics and communications, and student achievement was measured by metropolitan mathematics and language basic skills tests. Ashton and Webb's model of the relationship between teachers' sense of efficacy and student achievement is illustrated in Figure 6-1.

The factors contributing to teachers' sense of efficacy and to enhance the motivation and commitment are depicted in Figure 6-2. Many of the factors were discussed in earlier chapters and others will be discussed later in this chapter. Key are such school factors as a supportive school climate, the presence of collegial values and shared decision making, and a school culture which provides a sense of purpose and defines for teachers a shared covenant. These in turn provide for cooperative relationships, high social identity, high personal causation, origin feelings, high responsibility for work outcomes, and a shared commitment to common goals. Teachers view their work as being meaningful and significant, have a sense of pride and self-esteem, and have high standards and expectations. Given these conditions, teachers experience a greater sense of efficacy as well as enhanced motivation and commitment. Figures 6-1 and 6-2 provide glimpses of how the story of teacher motivation to

FIGURE 6-1
The Ashton and Webb study: Relation between teachers' sense of efficacy, teaching and learning behaviors, and student achievement.

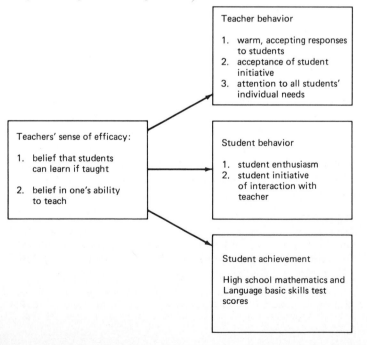

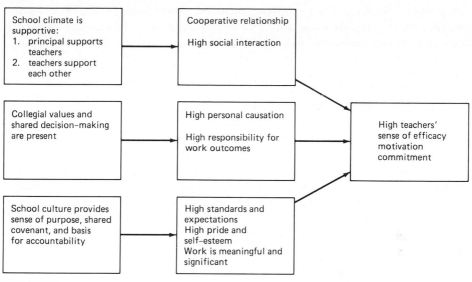

FIGURE 6-2
Factors contributing to teachers' sense of efficacy, motivation, and commitment.

work ends. To understand the relationships presented it is important to go back to the beginning and examine some basic assumptions that provide the theoretical basis for understanding work motivation.

SOME BASIC ASSUMPTIONS

Before we begin our discussion, however, it is important to provide some cautions. Researchers and theorists have vested interests in their ideas, and thus in their enthusiasm often seem to suggest that the theories they develop apply to everyone, in the same way, all the time. Indeed, one criticism that can be made about the various theories of motivation is that they assume workers to be very much alike. Hence, though the theorists present different ways of looking at people at work, they assume that particular needs and wants are universal. Another criticism is that they assume that all situations are similar and that motivational strategies, such as shared decision making, are therefore applicable in all situations. These assumptions lead to the conclusion that a "one best way" exists to motivate everyone.[17] A sounder perspective is to assume that motivation theories are modes of analysis that can help us to understand issues and to develop practices but that they cannot provide universal prescriptions applicable to everyone and in every situation. In this spirit, we will try to point out what the various theories can and cannot do and

[17] For a discussion of this problem see, for example, David A. Nadler and Edward E. Lawler III, "Motivation: A Diagnostic Approach," in J. R. Hackman and E. E. Lawler III (eds.), *Perspectives on Behavior and Organizations,* New York: McGraw-Hill, 1977.

where they do and do not apply. Our intent, therefore, is not to prescribe practice but to provide some useful thinking frames and practice models which can help inform one's professional judgment.

HUMAN MOTIVATION AND TEACHERS

Let us begin our inquiry into human motivation by examining needs of people at work. A common-sense approach to identifying human needs would undoubtedly reveal a list of factors such as air, water, shelter, food, protection, love, acceptance, importance, success, recognition, and control. This approach provides a random and undifferentiated list, and a significant effort is required to condense it into guidelines for supervisory behavior. Abraham Maslow, the distinguished psychologist, proposed a theory of human motivation that integrates the common-sense approach with human needs. His theory can help form an operational basis for supervisory behavior.

THE MASLOW THEORY

Maslow's theory differs from other motivational formulations in that it does not consider an individual's motivation on a one-to-one basis or as a series of independent drives. Each of the human needs is examined in relation to others, and they are classified and arranged into a hierarchy of prepotency. Thus before need B can be satisfied, one must first satisfy need A, and so on.

> Human needs arrange themselves in hierarchies of prepotency. That is to say, the appearance of one need usually rests on the prior satisfaction of another, more prepotent need. Man is a perpetually wanting animal. Also no need or drive can be treated as if it were isolated or discrete; every drive is related to the state of satisfaction or dissatisfaction of other drives.[18]

Maslow proposed a hierarchy of needs consisting of five levels. Specific need dimensions that compose each of the five levels are bound together by similarities in description, but, more importantly, by similarities in potency potential. Essentially, the most prepotent need occupies, and to a certain extent monopolizes, an individual's attention, while less prepotent needs are minimized. When a need is fairly well satisfied, the next prepotent need emerges and tends to dominate the individual's attention, while less prepotent needs are minimized. When a need is fairly well satisfied, the next prepotent need emerges and tends to dominate the individual's conscious life. Gratified needs, according to this theory, are not active motivators of behavior. Douglas McGregor describes each of the five Maslow levels and the prepotency feature of the theory simply and concisely as follows:[19]

---

[18] Abraham H. Maslow, "A Preface to Motivation Theory," *Psychosomatic Medicine*, vol. 5, p. 85, 1953. See especially his *Motivation and Personality*, New York: Harper & Row, 1954.
[19] Douglas McGregor, *The Human Side of Enterprise*, New York: McGraw-Hill, 1960, pp. 36–39.

Physiological Needs

Man is a wanting animal—as soon as one of his needs is satisfied, another appears in its place. This process is unending. It continues from birth to death.

Man's needs are organized in a series of levels—a hierarchy of importance. At the lowest level, but pre-eminent in importance when they are thwarted, are his *physiological needs*. Man lives for bread alone, when there is no bread. Unless the circumstances are unusual, his needs for love, for status, for recognition are inoperative when his stomach has been empty for a while. But when he eats regularly and adequately, hunger ceases to be an important motivation. The same is true of the other physiological needs of man—for rest, exercise, shelter, protection from the elements.

A satisfied need is not a motivator of behavior! This is a fact of profound significance that is regularly ignored in the conventional approach to the management of people. Consider your own need for air: Except as you are deprived of it, it has no appreciable motivating effect upon your behavior.

Safety Needs

When the physiological needs are reasonably satisfied, needs at the next higher level begin to dominate man's behavior—to motivate him. These are called *safety needs*. They are needs for protection against danger, threat, deprivation. Some people mistakenly refer to these as needs for security. However, unless man is in a dependent relationship where he fears arbitrary deprivation, he does not demand security. The need is for the "fairest possible break." When he is confident of this, he is more than willing to take risks. But when he feels threatened or dependent, his greatest need is for guarantees, for protection, for security.

The fact needs little emphasis that, since every industrial employee is in a dependent relationship, safety needs may assume considerable importance. Arbitrary management actions, behavior which arouses uncertainty with respect to continued employment or which reflects favoritism or discrimination, unpredictable administration of policy—these can be powerful motivators of the safety needs in the employment relationship at *every level,* from worker to vice president.

Social Needs

When man's physiological needs are satisfied and he is no longer fearful about his physical welfare, his *social needs* become important motivators of his behavior—needs for belonging, for association, for acceptance by his fellows, for giving and receiving friendship and love.

Management knows today of the existence of these needs, but it often assumes quite wrongly that they represent a threat to the organization. Many studies have demonstrated that the tightly knit, cohesive work group may, under proper conditions, be far more effective than an equal number of separate individuals in achieving organizational goals.

Yet management, fearing group hostility to its own objectives, often goes to considerable length to control and direct human efforts in ways that are inimical to the natural "groupiness" of human beings. When man's social needs—and perhaps his safety needs, too—are thus thwarted, he behaves in ways which tend to defeat organizational objectives. He becomes resistant, antagonistic, uncooperative. But this behavior is a consequence, not a cause.

Ego Needs

Above the social needs—in the sense that they do not become motivators until lower levels are reasonably satisfied—are the needs of greatest significance to management and to man himself. They are the *egoistic needs,* and they are of two kinds:

1 Those needs that relate to one's self-esteem—needs for self-confidence, for independence, for achievement, for competence, for knowledge.
2 Those needs that relate to one's reputation—needs for status, for recognition, for appreciation, for the deserved respect of one's fellows.

Unlike the lower needs, these are rarely satisfied; man seeks indefinitely for more satisfaction of these needs once they have become important to him. But they do not appear in any significant way until physiological, safety, and social [needs] are all reasonably satisfied.

The typical industrial organization offers few opportunities for the satisfaction of these egoistic needs to people at lower levels in the hierarchy. The conventional methods of organizing work, particularly in mass-production industries, give little heed to these aspects of human motivation. If the practices of scientific management were deliberately calculated to thwart these needs, they could hardly accomplish this purpose better than they do.

Self-fulfillment Needs

Finally—a capstone, as it were, on the hierarchy of man's needs—there are what we may call the needs for *self-fulfillment*. These are the needs for realizing one's own potentialities, for continued self-development, for being creative in the broadest sense of that term.

It is clear that the conditions of modern life give only limited opportunity for these relatively weak needs to obtain expression. The deprivation most people experience with respect to other lower-level needs diverts their energies into the struggle to satisfy those needs, and the needs for self-fulfillment remain dormant.

Although McGregor's analysis forces the needs into specific steps, Maslow considered all of them as being somewhat interdependent and, in fact, overlapping. It is nevertheless useful, at least conceptually, to consider human needs as being arranged into fairly delimited prepotency levels.

THE IMPORTANCE OF AUTONOMY

Some controversy exists as to whether needs that are at the lower levels of the hierarchy are ever activated enough to be considered work motivators.

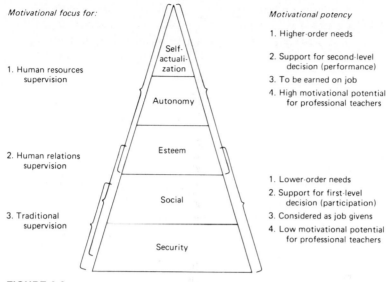

FIGURE 6-3
The hierarchy of needs: A motivational focus for supervision.

Porter,[20] for example, in adopting the Maslow hierarchy of needs for his research, eliminated physiological needs from the list. Presumably, Porter feels that in our society this category lacks the prepotency to motivate behavior for most people. He substitutes instead a category of needs labeled "autonomy." The Porter modification seems to have particular relevance to education, for while physiological needs have tended to depreciate in importance,[21] teachers and students have expressed a demand for control over their work environment and, indeed, over their destiny. The need for autonomy that many educational participants express is based on the principle of self-government, self-control, and self-determination. Teachers, in particular, display formidable credentials in terms of professional expertness as justification for expression of this need.

In Figure 6-3 Porter's revision of the Maslow categories is used to illustrate the hierarchical relationships that constitute the theory of human needs.

THE PARTICIPATION AND PERFORMANCE INVESTMENTS

A basic principle in motivation theory is that people invest themselves in work in order to obtain desired returns or rewards.[22] Examples of that investment are

---

[20] Lyman Porter, "Attitudes in Management: Perceived Deficiencies in Need Fulfillment as a Function of Job Level," *Journal of Applied Psychology,* vol. 46, p. 375, 1962.

[21] Basic provision for needs at this level seems largely guaranteed in our society.

[22] This discussion of participation and performance investments follows closely that which appears in T. J. Sergiovanni and David Elliott, *Educational and Organizational Leadership in Elementary Schools,* Englewood Cliffs, N.J.: Prentice-Hall, 1975, p. 138. See also T. J. Sergiovanni, "New Evidence on Teacher Morale," *North Central Association Quarterly,* vol. 42, no. 3, pp. 259–266, 1968.

time, physical energy, mental energy, creativity, knowledge, skill, enthusiasm, and effort. Returns or rewards can take a variety of tangible and intangible forms, including money, respect, comfort, a sense of accomplishment, social acceptance, and security. It is useful to categorize expressions of investment in work as being of two types: first, a *participation* investment and second, a *performance* investment.

The participation investment includes all that is necessary for the teacher to obtain and maintain satisfactory membership in the school. Meeting classes, preparing lesson plans, obtaining satisfactory to good evaluations from supervisors, following school rules and regulations, attending required meetings, bearing her or his fair share of committee responsibility, projecting an appropriate image to the public—in short, giving a fair day's work for a fair day's pay. Teachers not willing to make the participatory investment are considered to be unacceptable. On the other hand, one cannot command teachers to give more of themselves—to go beyond the participatory investment. In return for the participatory investment, teachers are provided with such benefits as salary, retirement provisions, fair supervision, good human relations, and security. This is the traditional legal work relationship between employer and employee. No great institution in our society and no great achievements have resulted from merely the traditional legal work relationship. Greatness has always been a result of employers' and employees' exceeding the limits of this relationship.

The performance investment exceeds the limits of the traditional work relationship. Here, teachers give more than one can "reasonably expect," and in return are provided with rewards that permit them to enjoy deep satisfaction with their work and themselves. It is important to distinguish between the kinds of return or rewards that evoke each of these investments. One does not exceed the limits of the traditional legal work relationship for more rewards of the same kind. Supervisors and administrators cannot buy this second investment with more money, privileges, easier and better working conditions, and improved human relationships. These are important incentives, as we shall see, but their potency is limited.

Though the Maslow hierarchy contains five need levels, it is helpful to visualize needs as falling into two categories: those described as lower-order (security, social, and, to some extent, esteem), and those described as higher-order (esteem, autonomy, and self-fulfillment). The lower-order needs are those which are available to teachers as they make the participation investment in schools. The school exchanges money, benefits, position, friendship, protection, interpersonal gratification, and the like, for satisfactory participation of teachers.

The higher-order needs are those whose fulfillment is exchanged for service that teachers give to the school and its clients as a result of the performance investment. Teachers tend not to be concerned with the pursuit of higher-order needs without consistent and considerable satisfaction of the lower-order needs. Since meaningful satisfaction of the esteem, autonomy, and self-fulfillment variety is intimately connected to performance, teachers will need to earn rewards of this kind through efforts toward the achievement of school goals. Supervisors who rely on reward structures characteristic of the higher-order needs are tapping potent motivational levels in teachers.

The motivational base for human resources supervision consists of needs of each of the five levels but focuses on those that we describe as higher-order. The limited motivational basis for traditional and, to some extent, human relations supervision is totally inadequate for providing personal and professional growth opportunities that professionally oriented teachers seek. These relationships are summarized in Figure 6-3.

COMPETENCE AND ACHIEVEMENT: PROFESSIONAL MOTIVES

Maslow's theory provides an integrated view of interdependent need structures, but some scholars have tended to focus on one need, often to the exclusion of other needs. Two such efforts seem to have particular relevance to understanding teaching. One effort explores the competence motive—the desire for mastery—and the other, the achievement motive—the desire for success. The first effort, developed and popularized by Robert White,[23] presumes that people wish to understand and control their environment and wish to be active participants in this environment. This need is traced by White to early infancy and childhood experiences and is observed in the seemingly random and endless searching, feeling, tinkering, exploring, and investigating that characterize this age. White claims that the years 6 to 9 are critical ones in developing this motive. If early experiences prove successful, people are likely to continue developing and extending their competence motives. As adults, they behave in ways that permit them to test and reconfirm the adequacy of their competence. The competence test recurs as successes are compiled, and each new test is usually at a level that is more challenging than that of a person's previous success.[24]

Many teachers have lost the capacity to strive for competence largely because of a history of failure. They are less ready to try something new or to undertake a more difficult assignment, for fear of additional failure. Schools benefit by developing and encouraging the competence motive, since teachers and other professional workers typically express a desire for job mastery and professional growth. A useful exercise for readers is to identify those aspects of the curriculum, the classroom management system, and the school management system that prohibit, delimit, or otherwise frustrate the opportunity for teachers and students to develop, express, and confirm the competence motive. When this motive is reinforced in teachers, personal satisfaction for the human organization and high-quality performance for the human school can be expected.

---

[23] Robert W. White, "Motivation Reconsidered: The Concept of Competence," *Psychology Review,* vol. 66, no. 5, pp. 297–333, 1958.
[24] As people perceive themselves as becoming increasingly competent, they evoke the self-fulfilling prophecy.

The second need, the achievement motive, is one studied intensively by David C. McClelland.[25] In commenting on McClelland's work, Gellerman describes a person who is "blessed" or "afflicted" with high need for achievement as follows:

> He tries harder and demands more of himself, especially when the chips are down. Consequently, he accomplishes more. We find, for example, that college students who have a strong achievement drive will usually get better grades than equally bright students with weaker needs for achievement. Executives "on their way up" in their companies are usually driven by stronger achievement needs than those who do not rise so quickly. The stronger the achievement drive, the greater the probability that the individual will demand more of himself.
>
> *Perhaps the most fascinating aspect of the achievement motive is that it seems to make accomplishment an end in itself.* If anything, it is the person who has little achievement motivation who expects a tangible reward for greater effort. While the achievement-motivated person does not spurn tangible rewards and even has a rather unexpected use for them, they are not really essential to him, either. He takes a special joy in winning, in competing successfully with a difficult standard; this means more to him than money or a public pat on the back. He is not an altruist: He simply finds enough delight in doing difficult things that he does not need to be bribed to do them.[26]

Teachers with a strong need for achievement have much to contribute to school effectiveness. They display an entrepreneurial behavior pattern that McClelland describes as being characterized by (1) moderate risk taking as a function of skill rather than chance, (2) energetic or novel instrumental activity, (3) individual responsibility and accountability for behavior, (4) the need for knowledge of results, and (5) anticipation of future possibilities.[27] As one would expect, teachers with a strong need for achievement demand a great deal from the school. They need opportunities to display the behavior manifestations that McClelland describes above and resist attempts to limit this behavior. Often if achievement needs cannot be expressed in the school, an individual seeks expression (1) organizationally in a "negative" fashion, (2) extraorganizationally in teacher associations and unions, or (3) in noneducational organizations and institutions. Teachers with a strong need for achievement can often be troublesome for many administrators and supervisors, but they have the potential to give fully and in a spirit of excellence to the school and its efforts. Competence and achievement are motives related to the concept of efficacy. When the motives are allowed to be expressed in schools, sense of efficacy is heightened.

Motivation-Hygiene Theory

An examination of human needs and important work motives such as achievement, competence, power, and affiliation provides supervisors with important

[25] David C. McClelland et al., *The Achievement Motive,* New York: Appleton-Century-Crofts, 1953; also, David C. McClelland, *The Achieving Society,* Princeton, N.J.: Van Nostrand, 1961.
[26] Saul Gellerman, *Motivation and Productivity,* New York: American Management Associations, 1963, p. 124.
[27] McClelland, *The Achieving Society,* p. 207.

concepts. In this section a more operational approach to motivation-commitment is presented in the form of the motivation-hygiene theory as proposed originally by Frederick Herzberg and his associates.[28]

All the paragraphs that appear below are descriptions of important features of the motivation-hygiene theory. They are stated first, in an attempt to sketch out the nature, scope, and potency of the theory. Their description is followed by an analysis of theoretical and research findings that provide the origins of the theory.

1 There are certain conditions in work that teachers expect to enjoy. If these conditions are present in sufficient quantity, teachers will perform adequately, but only adequately. If these conditions are not present in sufficient quantity, teachers will be dissatisfied and work performance will suffer.

2 The conditions in work which teachers expect as part of the traditional legal work relationship are called *hygienic factors*. Their absence results in teacher dissatisfaction and poor performance. Their presence maintains the traditional legal work relationship but does not motivate performance. Hygienic factors are associated with the participation investment in work.

3 The factors which contribute to teachers' exceeding the traditional work relationship are called *motivators*. The absence of motivators does not result in dissatisfaction and does not endanger the traditional work relationship. Motivational factors are associated with the performance investment in work.

4 Motivational factors and hygienic factors are different. Motivation to work does not result from increasing hygienic factors.

5 Hygienic factors are associated with the conditions of work and are extrinsic in nature. Examples are money, benefits, fair supervision, and a feeling of belonging. Motivational factors are associated with work itself and are intrinsic in nature. Examples are recognition, achievement, and increased responsibility.

6 Hygienic factors are important, for their neglect creates problems in the work environment. These problems can result in dissatisfaction and lowered performance. Taking care of the hygienic factors prevents trouble, but these factors are not potent enough to motivate people to work, to evoke the performance decision.

---

[28] Frederick Herzberg, Bernard Mausner, and Barbara Snyderman, op. cit.; Frederick Herzberg, *Work and the Nature of Man,* New York: World Publishing, 1966. This discussion follows closely Sergiovanni and Elliott, op. cit., pp. 139–148. See also T. J. Sergiovanni and Fred D. Carver, *The New School Executive: A Theory of Administration,* 2d ed., New York: Harper & Row, 1980, chaps. 5–8. The motivation-hygiene theory is not without its critics. See, for example, M. D. Dunnelle, J. P. Campbell, and M. D. Hakel, "Factors Contributing to Job Satisfaction and Job Dissatisfaction in Six Occupational Groups," *Organizational Behavior and Human Performance,* vol. 2, pp. 143–174, 1967. For support, see D. A. Whitsett and E. K. Winslow, "An Analysis of Studies Critical to the Motivation-Hygiene Theory," *Personnel Psychology,* vol. 20, no. 4, pp. 391–415, 1967. Our review of motivation-hygiene studies leads us to conclude that the theory is indeed appropriate for white-collar and professionally oriented workers but less appropriate for other workers.

7 Hygienic factors meet the human need to avoid unpleasantness and hardship. Motivational factors serve the uniquely human need for psychological growth.

8 Satisfaction at work is not a motivator of performance per se, but results from quality performance. Administrators and supervisors should not use satisfaction as a method of motivating teachers, but satisfaction should be thought of as a goal that teachers seek, one that is best obtained through meaningful work.

9 Administrators and supervisors who use job satisfaction to motivate teachers are practicing human relations. This has not been proven to be an effective approach. Human relations emphasize the hygienic factors.

10 Administrators and supervisors who consider job satisfaction as a goal that teachers seek through accomplishing meaningful work and who focus on enhancing the meaningful view of work and the ability of teachers to accomplish this work are practicing human resources supervision. This has been proven to be an effective approach. Human resources development emphasizes the motivational factors.

11 True, not all teachers can be expected to respond to the motivation-hygiene theory, but most can.

In summary, the theory stipulates that teachers at work have two distinct sets of needs. One set of needs is best met by hygienic factors. In exchange for these factors, one is prepared to make the participatory investment—to give a fair day's work. If hygienic factors are neglected, dissatisfaction occurs, and one's performance on the job decreases to a level below the acceptable. Another set of needs is best met by the motivational factors that are not automatically part of the job but that can be built into most jobs, particularly those found in elementary schools. In return for the motivational factors, one is prepared to make the performance investment, to exceed the limits of the traditional legal work relationship. If the motivational factors are neglected, one does not become dissatisfied, but one's performance does not exceed that typically described as a fair day's work for a fair day's pay.

The Motivation-Hygiene Factors

Hygienic factors are those largely extrinsic in nature and associated with our lower-order needs, and motivational factors are those largely intrinsic in nature and associated with our higher-order needs. Now let us examine the factors themselves.

Motivation-hygiene theory results from the research of Frederick Herzberg.[29] The model for his research is an interview method whereby workers are asked to describe job events associated with satisfaction and dissatisfaction at work. Further, the effects of these feelings and events on one's performance at work are examined. Dozens of studies have been

---

[29]Herzberg et al., *The Motivation to Work,* New York: Wiley, 1959.

conducted using this approach with a variety of workers, from scientists to assembly-line workers, in a number of countries.[30]

In the majority of cases, studies reveal that traditional linear notions regarding satisfaction and dissatisfaction at work are in need of modification. Traditionally, it has been assumed that if a cause of dissatisfaction is identified, elimination of this cause results in job satisfaction and motivated workers. Teachers unhappy with school policies, the kind of supervision they are getting, money matters, and class scheduling will move to a state of satisfaction and motivation if these deficiencies are remedied. Motivation-hygiene studies by and large show that this is not the case. Remedying the deficiencies that cause dissatisfaction brings a person up to a level of minimum performance that includes the absence of dissatisfaction. Satisfaction and motivation are the results of a separate set of factors. The factors associated with satisfaction, but not dissatisfaction, are called motivators because of their ability to stimulate performance. The factors associated with dissatisfaction, but not satisfaction, are called hygienic because of their ability to cause trouble if neglected.[31]

> The Motivation-Hygiene theory of job attitudes began with a depth interview study of over 200 engineers and accountants representing Pittsburgh industry. These interviews probed sequences of events in the work lives of the respondents to determine the factors that were involved in their feeling exceptionally happy and conversely exceptionally unhappy with their jobs. From a review and an analysis of previous publications in the general area of job attitudes, a two-factor hypothesis was formulated to guide the original investigation. This hypothesis suggested that the factors involved in producing job satisfaction were separate and distinct from the factors that led to job dissatisfaction. Since separate factors needed to be considered depending on whether job satisfaction or job dissatisfaction was involved, it followed that these two feelings were not the obverse of each other. The opposite of job satisfaction would not be job dissatisfaction, but rather *no* job satisfaction; and similarly the opposite of job dissatisfaction is *no* job dissatisfaction—not job satisfaction. The statement of the concept is awkward and may appear at first to be a semantic ruse, but there is more than a play with words when it comes to understanding the behavior of people on jobs. The fact that job satisfaction is made up of two unipolar traits is not a unique occurrence. The difficulty of establishing a zero point in psychology with the procedural necessity of using instead a bench mark (mean of a population) from which to start our measurement has led to the conception that psychological traits are bipolar. Empirical investigations, however, have cast some shadows on the assumptions of bipolarity; one timely example is a study of conformity and nonconformity, where they are shown not to be opposites, but rather two separate unipolar traits.

The factors Herzberg associates with motivation and hygiene are shown in Table 6-2. The findings of his original study are illustrated in Figure 6-4. Factors

---

[30] See, for example, Frederick Herzberg, *Work and the Nature of Man,* New York: World Publishing, 1966.

[31] Frederick Herzberg, "The Motivation-Hygiene Concepts and Problems of Manpower," *Personnel Administration,* vol. 27, no. 1, p. 3, 1964.

TABLE 6-2
THE MOTIVATION AND HYGIENE FACTORS*

Motivation (found in the work itself)	Hygiene (found in the environment of work)
Achievement	Salary
Recognition	Possibility of growth
Work itself	Interpersonal relations (subordinates)
Responsibility	Interpersonal relations (superiors)
Advancement	Interpersonal relations (pers)
	Supervision—technical
	Company policy and administration
	Working conditions
	Personal life
	Status
	Job security

*The facts were identified and reported by Herzberg in F. Herzberg et al., *The Motivation to Work*, New York: Wiley, 1959.

to the right of the zero line contribute predominantly to satisfaction, and factors to the left of this line contribute predominantly to dissatisfaction. The longer the line associated with a factor, the more often respondents cited this factor as contributing to job feelings. The greater the width of the line—in the diagram a box—the longer the duration of the attitude. Thus while respondents cited achievement more often than responsibility as a source of positive feelings about a job, when responsibility was cited, the feeling lasted longer than in the case of achievement.

Achievement, recognition, work itself, responsibility, and advancement are the factors identified by Herzberg as contributing primarily to satisfaction. Their absence tends not to lead to dissatisfaction. These are the motivators—the rewards that one seeks in return for the performance investment.

Policy and administration, supervision, salary, interpersonal relationships, and working conditions are the factors that Herzberg identifies as contributing primarily to dissatisfaction. These are the hygienic factors—conditions that workers expect in return for a fair day's work.

In the separate teacher study illustrated in Table 6-3 achievement and recognition were identified as the most potent motivators.[32] Responsibility, although a significant motivator, appeared in only 7 percent of the events associated with satisfaction. We do not take advantage of the motivational possibilities of responsibility in education—this factor is relatively standard-

[32] Thomas J. Sergiovanni, "Factors Which Affect Satisfaction and Dissatisfaction of Teachers," *The Journal of Educational Administration*, vol. 5, no. 1, pp. 66–82, 1967.

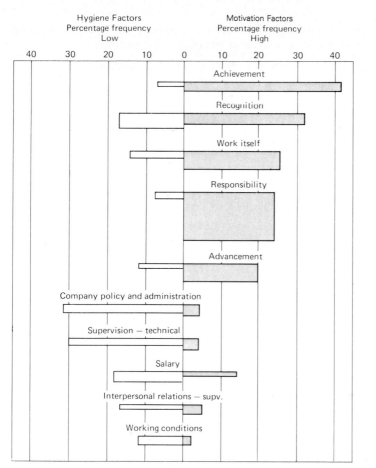

| Hygiene Factors Percentage frequency Low | | | | | Motivation Factors Percentage frequency High | | | |

FIGURE 6-4
Comparison of hygiene and motivation factors. (*From Frederick Herzberg ets36al., The Motivation to Work, New York: Wiley, 1959.*)

ized for teachers, in that responsibility does not vary much from one teacher to another. Work itself did not appear significantly more often as a contributor to satisfaction. Apparently, elements of the job of teaching as we currently know it are inherently less than satisfying. Among these are routine housekeeping, attendance, milk money, paperwork, study hall, lunch duty, and the like. The negative aspects of police, clerk, and custodial roles seem to neutralize professional teaching and guidance roles for these professionals. Poor interpersonal relations with students; inadequate, incompetent, insensitive, and close supervision; unfair, rigid, and inflexible school policies and administrative practices; poor interpersonal relations with other teachers and with parents; and incidents in their personal lives were the job factors found to contribute significantly to teachers' dissatisfaction.

TABLE 6-3
PERCENTAGES FOR THE FREQUENCY WITH WHICH JOB FACTORS CONTRIBUTED TO
HIGH ATTITUDES AS COMPARED WITH LOW ATTITUDES FOR TEACHERS

Job factors	Percentage of highs $NR = 142$	Percentage of lows $NR = 142$	P
1. Achievement	30*	9	.01
2. Recognition	28*	2	.001
3. Work itself	11	8	
4. Responsibility	7*	1	.05
5. Advancement	0	1	
6. Salary	2	3	
7. Possibility of growth	6	2	
8. Interpersonal relations (subordinates)	7	20*	.01
9. Interpersonal relations (superiors)	3	4	
10. Interpersonal relations (peers)	1	15*	.001
11. Supervision—technical	1	10*	.01
12. School policy and administration	2	13*	.01
13. Working conditions	2	6	
14. Personal life	0	5*	.05
15. Status	0	0	
16. Security	0	1	

$N = 72$ teachers; NR = number of responses.
*Significant factor.

Herzberg found in his original study with accountants and engineers[33] that, although recognition and achievement were mentioned most often as motivators, the duration of good feelings associated with these rewards was very short. Work and advancement seemed to have medium effects, but good feelings associated with responsibility lasted more than twice as long as those associated with work and advancement, and more than three times as long as those from achievement and recognition. Negative feelings associated with neglected hygienic factors were generally of short duration.

Teachers as Individuals

The motivation-hygiene theory provides simplified answers to rather complex questions. This is a bold theory that provides broad and general guidelines to administrators and supervisors interested in evoking the performance invest-

[33] Herzberg et al., *The Motivation to Work*, New York: Wiley, 1959.

ment from teachers.[34] Its boldness and its broad propositions require intelligent caution in the application of the theory to practice. For example, while the theory suggests that by and large only the satisfiers motivate, it would be wrong to conclude that some people are not motivated by the dissatisfiers. Some individuals are indeed motivated by the dissatisfiers, but under ordinary circumstances it is not natural to be so motivated. The implication is that healthy individuals respond to the motivation-hygiene dynamic, while those less healthy do not. Further, healthy individuals who are deprived of work satisfactions on the job will seek these satisfactions elsewhere—at home through family membership, hobbies, community activity, sports, and the like. Attention to these aspects of life is important to all of us, but the world of work seems the more natural place for professional workers to find satisfaction for their needs of esteem, competence, achievement, autonomy, and self-fulfillment.

Teachers who seem more interested in hygienic factors than motivational factors can be categorized as follows: (1) those who have the potential for motivation seeking but are frustrated by insensitive and closed administrative, supervisory, and organizational policies and practices; (2) those who have the potential for motivation seeking, but who decide to channel this potential into other areas of their lives; and (3) those who do not have the potential for motivation seeking on or off the job. Those in the second and third groups use their jobs as a means to achieve goals not related to the school.

The second group includes many teachers whose goals are buying a second car or a vacation house, supplementing their spouse's income to achieve a higher standard of living, putting their spouse or children through college, and so on. Men in this group often use the teaching occupation as a means to step into another job, such as coaching, counseling, or administration.

The third group includes individuals who seem fixated at lower need levels. In a sense, they could be described as obsessed with avoiding unpleasantness and discomfort to the point that they have not developed the ability to seek satisfaction through the motivators and at higher need levels. Many psychologists regard this obsession as a symptom of poor mental health; if this is the case, then selection procedures should be devised to identify and filter out teachers of this type. Tenured teachers of this type will need to be heavily supervised.

Teachers who have the potential for motivation seeking, but elect to seek satisfactions of this kind outside of the school are by and large good teachers who give honest labor in exchange for what they hope to gain from the school. Extraordinary performance is lacking among them, however, for such teachers do not have a strong commitment to the school and its purposes. Teachers of this kind will be with us for a long time, but they cannot be depended upon to

---

[34] This discussion of teachers as individuals follows closely Sergiovanni and Elliott, op. cit., p. 147. See also T. J. Sergiovanni, "Human Resources Supervision," in Sergiovanni (ed.), *Professional Supervision for Professional Teachers,* Washington, D.C.: Association for Supervision and Curriculum Development, 1975, pp. 19–21.

FIGURE 6-5
An expanded model of expectancy theory.

substantially upgrade the nation's schools or to display much interest in becoming full partners in the school enterprise unless they can become attracted to the motivational factors. Teachers who are interested primarily in hygienic factors but have potential for being influenced by the motivation factors can make significant contributions to the school's work if supervised kindly, but firmly and competently, or when combined with motivation seekers in schools with differentiated roles and responsibilities for teachers. Hygienically oriented teachers who have the potential for motivation seeking but are frustrated by the school and its administration are unfortunate casualties. When we deny teachers opportunities to channel motivation expressions they desire, we not only waste valuable human resources, but deny youngsters important opportunities for growth in their schooling. In general, hygienically oriented teachers think of their jobs too much in terms of salary, working conditions, supervision, status, job security, school policies and administration, and social relationships.

EXPECTANCY THEORY OF MOTIVATION

Another approach to motivation, Vroom's expectancy theory,[35] takes into account differences in the desires and needs of others, does not prescribe a one best motivational strategy but shares some features of the motivation-hygiene theory. Vroom's is a contingency theory in that he views motivation as a response in a person's needs to a specific goal that person seeks. Performance on the job, in his view, is a means by which the person can achieve a personal goal. This view is consistent with human resources supervision in that it assumes that performance is a means to satisfaction rather than satisfaction being viewed as a means to performance. Since personal goals for individuals are likely to vary, no one set of motivational factors is identified. The basic components of expectancy theory are illustrated in Figure 6-5.

[35]Victor H. Vroom, *Work and Motivation*, New York: Wiley, 1964. See also Vroom, "Organizational Choice: A Study of Pre- and Post-Decision Processes," *Organizational Behavior and Human Performance*, vol. 1, pp. 212–225, 1966; and J. Galbraith and L. Cummings, "An Empirical Investigation of the Motivational Determinants of Task Performance: Interactive Effects between Instrumentality—Valence and Motivation—Ability," *Organizational Behavior and Human Performance*, vol. 2, pp. 237–257, 1967, for studies that substantiate aspects of Vroom's theory.

Basically, individual motivation is viewed as a function of a person's perception that his or her increased performance will result in certain rewards that will help him or her attain personal goals. If a teacher's goal is to be more influential in educational decision making (to attain more expert power), motivation will depend upon that teacher's perception that increased performance (volunteering for difficult curriculum work and doing a good job of it) will lead to appropriate rewards (winning the professional respect of colleagues) that will enable the teacher to achieve this goal. By the same token, another individual with personal goals of group acceptance may not be motivated to volunteer for additional work, and if assigned work, may not be motivated to perform in an extraordinary way unless that behavior is associated with group acceptance.

Since personal goals differ, rewards that appeal to some teachers may not appeal to others. It is therefore necessary, on the one hand, to individualize rewards to match personal goals that are consistent with those of the school and, on the other hand, to help build greater consistency between personal and school goals. Further, the relationship between individual performance, organizational rewards, and personal goals is not always clear to teachers, and clarification of their parts by supervisors may be necessary.

In further developing the expectancy approach Nadler and Lawler provide three concepts as key building blocks of the theory:

1 *Performance-outcome expectancy*. Every behavior has associated with it, in an individual's mind, certain outcomes (rewards or punishments). In other words, the individual believes or expects that if he or she behaves in a certain way, he or she will get certain things.

2 *Valence*. Each outcome has a "valence" (value, worth, attractiveness) to a specific individual. Outcomes have difference valences for different individuals. This comes about because valences result from individual needs and perceptions, which differ because they in turn reflect other factors in the individual's life.

For example, some individuals may value an opportunity for promotion or advancement because of their needs for achievement or power. Others may not want to be promoted and leave their current work group because of needs for affiliation. Similarly, a fringe benefit such as a pension plan may have great valence for an older worker but little valence for a young employee on his or her first job.

3 *Effort-performance expectancy*. Each behavior also has associated with it, in the individual's mind, a certain expectancy or probability of success. This expectancy represents the individual's perception of how hard it will be to achieve such behavior and the probability of his or her successful achievement of that behavior.[36]

---

[36] David A. Nadler and Edward E. Lawler III, op. cit., p. 28.

Nadler and Lawler conclude that, in general, a person will be motivated to behave in a certain way when she or he believes that this behavior will lead to a specific outcome, when the outcome has a positive value, or when he or she feels able to perform at the desired level (Will I be able to do what is required if I try? If I am able to perform appropriately, what will happen? Why do I want to try? That is, how important to me are the likely outcomes?). Nadler and Lawler would add effort and ability to the basic expectancy model. Their expanded view is shown in Figure 6-5. Nadler and Lawler provide the following suggestions to supervisors wanting to use the expectancy theory in practice:[37]

1 Figure out what outcomes (personal goals) each teacher values. Don't assume that everyone wants the same thing. Responsibility, for example, is considered to be an important motivation factor in the motivation-hygiene theory but some teachers may prefer a more easy-going and less stressful environment which permits them to enjoy personal relationships on the job. The same strategy may be used by a supervisor (team teaching or family grouping, for example), but the desired outcomes for teachers may be different. Teacher A might be interested in the team approach because it provides for desirable social interaction; while Teacher B shares a similar interest in the team approach because of desires for increased responsibility.

2 Determine the kind of outcomes you desire. Supervisors need to have some image of the good life; some set of standards which specify what they are trying to accomplish. This image and standard provide the basis for determining the direction of motivational efforts.

3 Make sure that desired outcomes and desired ways of behaving for teachers are within their reach. Realistic objectives which reflect ability and disposition levels of teachers are important. Remember, if a new way of behaving requires too much perceived effort or is not likely to be seen as within reach, teachers will not be motivated.

4 Pay attention to how tasks, jobs, and roles are designed. (One source of desired outcome is the work itself. The expectancy theory model supports much of the job enrichment literature in saying that by designing jobs which enable people to get their needs fulfilled, organizations can bring about higher levels of motivation.)

We will consider this point further when we explore the concept of job enrichment and its implications for supervisory effectiveness in the next section. In sum, expectancy theory recognizes that people at work have different abilities, needs, goals, and aspirations. This implies that supervisors need to take a more individualized perspective in motivating teachers and need to develop flexible strategies that permit choices. Finally, note that in expectancy theory job satisfaction is derived from performance. Similarly, in motivation-hygiene theory intrinsic satisfaction is derived from performing the work itself. Satisfaction from achievement, recognition, and responsibility is

---

[37] Ibid., pp. 30–32.

earned as a result of accomplished work. This thinking (improved performance leads to satisfaction) is an important improvement over human relations theories (which tend to assume that job satisfaction itself is linked to improved performance) and is essential to the human resources approach to supervision.

THE PROBLEM WITH CALCULATED INVOLVEMENT

To this point the emphasis in the motivation theories discussed has been on the wants and needs of teachers and how these might be provided for as part of an exchange with the school. Teachers want and need to be recognized as accomplished professionals. When they contribute to the success of the school, volunteer services, teach well, help others, come up with good ideas and so on, they are rewarded by being recognized. Teachers seek approval from supervisors and colleagues and want to belong to the faculty work group. When they adopt the values of the group and meet their basic job commitments to the school they enjoy such acceptance. After rereading the above statements several times, many will rightly become uncomfortable with the basic tenets of need-oriented motivation concepts. Taken literally need theories provide a highly instrumental view of teachers at work and result in calculated involvement from teachers. Put another way, need theories suggest that the key to motivation is to "strike a bargain" with teachers. Each of the parties involved in this bargain (school and faculty; supervisor and teacher) barters with the other—exchanging one thing for another.

To understand motivation as bartering recall our discussion of Etzioni's compliance theory which appeared in Chapter 3. In the Type B organization discussed, compliance or involvement of workers is obtained by exchanging valued behaviors for valued rewards. The consequences of this highly instrumental bargain is calculated involvement by workers. When this is the case in schools teachers (and students too) become acutely aware of what constitutes a fair day's work for a fair day's pay. Should they perceive that the rewards available are declining or are not worth contributions (this is the calculation) they are likely to adjust contributions downward in some proportion that makes sense to them.

Emphasizing instrumental views of motivation, therefore, has its risks. Often what might normally be considered as the right thing to do or the professional thing to do in teaching is now viewed instrumentally as one's contribution in exchange for a valued reward. Merit pay and similar schemes often take this instrumental turn. Paying teachers extra for things that they are supposed to do as part of their professional commitment is an example of such an exchange. If this additional pay is no longer available (as is often the case in difficult economic times) teachers may no longer be willing to do what previously was something that they did because they were "supposed to." Calculated involvement is exactly what schools get from students when instrumental motivation theories are used excessively. When the attitude is "I give you good grades if you do what I want" we need to wonder whether students will continue to do the correct thing in the absence of calculated rewards.

As part of his compliance theory, Etzioni also described a Type C organization within which involvement of workers was obtained by using norms. Normative authority emerges from sets of agreements which exist with regard to what is proper and acceptable behavior. In Type C schools, when teachers take extra time with students who are having difficulty, they are merely responding to some sense of what is professionally expected of teachers. Normative authority is a key characteristic of the concept of school culture discussed in Chapter 5. When schools and supervisors rely on normative authority in obtaining compliance from teachers they are likely to find that teachers are morally involved in work. When one is involved in a calculated way with work, the relationship is tenuous. Moral involvement, on the other hand, bonds together the teacher with his or her teaching. Motivation and commitment are by-products of one's sense of obligation to professional and group norms and the meaning and significance that one derives from the work itself.

A different emphasis in motivation theory is one of the characteristics which differentiates Supervision I from II. Supervision I relies heavily on needs theories and on bartering conceptions of motivation and commitment. Supervision II, by contrast, emphasizes more norms, meaning, and significance. The spirit of motivation concepts within Supervision II is depicted in Figure 6-2. In the sections below motivation models associated with Supervision II are summarized.

JOB ENRICHMENT AND QUALITY OF WORK LIFE IN TEACHING

Supervisors have long known that how the work of teaching is organized, the structures provided within which teachers must function, and the resulting meanings that teachers attached to their work are important. In recent years this thinking has been formalized and developed into the concept of job enrichment. One very promising avenue of research on job enrichment and its link to motivation and commitment is that of Hackman and Oldham.[38] These scholars have developed a theory of job enrichment that has been successfully applied in practice. In a very real sense, the concept of job enrichment draws upon all of the other theories of motivation presented and shows how they might actually be implemented in practice.

Hackman and Oldham have identified three psychological states they believe are critical in determining a person's motivation for and satisfaction with a job:

> *Experienced meaningfulness.* The individual must perceive his or her work as worthwhile or important by some system of values held.

[38] J. R. Hackman and G. Oldham, op. cit.

Experienced responsibility. The individual must believe that he or she personally is accountable for the outcomes of efforts.

Knowledge of results. The individual must be able to determine, on some fairly regular basis, whether or not the outcomes of his or her work are satisfactory.[39]

Hackman and Oldham maintain that when the three states are present in an individual, she or he feels good and performs well. Further, the presence of good feelings at any one time prompts the person to continue to perform well in an effort to earn more of these feelings in the future. Thus the three psychological states are the basis of "internal motivation." Internal motivation is important to supervisors, for we seem to have less and less to give of an external nature (money, benefits, etc.).

Five job characteristics have been identified that evoke these psychological states. Three of the characteristics—skill variety, task identity, and task significance—cumulatively determine *meaningfulness.* Autonomy, a fourth job characteristic, is associated with feelings of responsibility. Feedback, a final job characteristic proposed by Hackman and Oldham, is associated with *knowledge of results.*

The job enrichment model suggests that in teaching, jobs that require different activities in carrying out the work and the use of a variety of teacher talents and skills (skill variety); require that teachers engage in holistic or complete and identifiable tasks (task identity); are viewed by teachers as having a substantial and significant impact on the lives or work of other people (task significance); provide substantial freedom, independence, and direction to individual teachers in scheduling work and in deciding classroom organizational and instructional procedures (autonomy); and provide teachers with direct and clear information about the effects of their performance (feedback) are likely to evoke the psychological states of meaningfulness, responsibility, and knowledge of results. These in turn will result in high work motivation, high-quality performance, high job satisfaction, and low absenteeism among teachers.

This job enrichment model is depicted in Figure 6-6. Note that in addition to job dimensions, psychological states, and outcomes, an "implementing concepts" panel is provided. These are the suggestions the researchers offer to supervisors interested in building more of the job dimensions into work. As one can see, teaching has advantages over other fields of work in that many of these implementing concepts are already in evidence and the others can be easily introduced. The implementing concepts are translated into the language of teaching below.

The principle of "combining tasks" suggests that fractionalized aspects of teaching should be put together in larger, more holistic, modules. Comprehensive curriculum development strategies, interdisciplinary approaches, and

[39] J. R. Hackman, G. Oldham, R. Johnson, and K. Purdy, "A New Strategy for Job Enrichment," *California Management Review,* vol. 17, no. 4, p. 57.

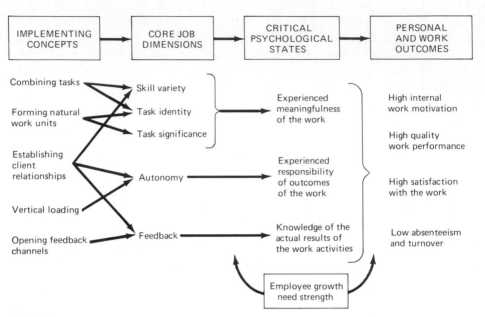

FIGURE 6-6
Job-enrichment concepts and practices. (*From J. R. Hackman, G. Oldham, R. Johnson, and K. Purdy, "A New Strategy for Job Enrichment," © 1975 by The Regents of the University of California. Reprinted from California Management Review, vol. XVII, no. 4, p. 64, by permission of the Regents.*)

team-group teaching modes all contribute to the combining of teaching and curriculum tasks. Combining tasks increases not only skill variety but one's identification with the work as well.

Establishing "client relationships" is easy in that generally teachers and students already work in close contact with each other. Nevertheless, some patterns of organization and teaching encourage a more impersonal relationship between teachers and students than would seem desirable. Missing as well is a closer relationship with parents. Face-to-face contact with students and parents provides a natural avenue for obtaining feedback and encourages the development and use of a variety of skills.

Forming "natural work units" has some interesting implications for supervision and teaching. The intent here is to increase one's sense of ownership and continuing responsibility for identifiable aspects of the work. The self-contained elementary school classroom comes closer to this concept than does the departmentalized and quick-moving secondary teaching schedule. But even in this setting, the building of teaching teams that plan and work together and whose members share a common responsibility with students is often lacking.

"Vertical loading" suggests strategies that bring together teaching and planning. Providing teachers with more control over schedules, work methods, evaluation, and even the training of less experienced teachers might be examples of vertical loading. One might include as well giving teachers some budgetary control that allows them discretion in allocating available funds.

"Opening feedback channels" is another way of saying that the more supervisors are able to let teachers know how well they are doing, the more highly motivated they will be. Indeed, motivation and satisfaction are neglected benefits of teacher-evaluation strategies designed to provide teachers with helpful feedback. We have in mind here such strategies as clinical supervision, peer supervision, target setting, and other similar formats. A better approach still in providing teachers with feedback is to create ways in which feedback occurs naturally from teachers' day-to-day activities and from working closely with colleagues.

Job enrichment theory suggests that virtually every decision supervisors make about school and classroom organization, curriculum development and implementation, materials selection, and teaching itself has implications for building motivation and commitment of teachers.

In the summary model of teacher motivation and student achievement provided in Figure 6-7, note that need theories of motivation and theories of motivation which emphasize enriching the quality of work life in teaching are added to factors contributing to teachers' sense of efficacy. Figure 6-7 is an extension of Figure 6-2. Combined with a school climate that is supportive, collegial values and shared decision making, and a strong school culture the theories of motivation contribute to a heightened sense of teacher efficacy and enhanced teacher motivation and commitment. These conditions, in turn, are linked to improvements in student achievement. When teachers experience success in teaching they enjoy greater job satisfaction and the motivation cycle depicted is reinforced. The philosophical, theoretical, and empirical evidence in support of this model is too overwhelming for it to be ignored. The model should, we believe, provide the basic frame of reference for the development of motivation policies and for guiding motivation practices.

A FINAL CAUTION

We began this chapter by suggesting that no one best way exists to motivate everyone and in every instance. This principle applies as well to the concept of job enrichment. Note, for example, in Figure 6-6 the boxed statement "employee growth need strength." Need strength refers to the extent people will seek personal accomplishment, are interested in learning and self-development, and want to be stimulated and challenged. Workers whose growth need strength is not high will not respond favorably to enriched jobs and will complain of being pushed too far. Most teachers have some potential for high-growth need strength, but for many the spark has become dim and may now even be nonexistent. Often this loss of need strength is not the individual's fault but results from previous experiences with organizations. What should one do in this case? We believe that supervisors still should provide teachers with enrichment opportunities in the hope that the need-strength spark may be rekindled. For the rare few who will not and are not able to respond, job

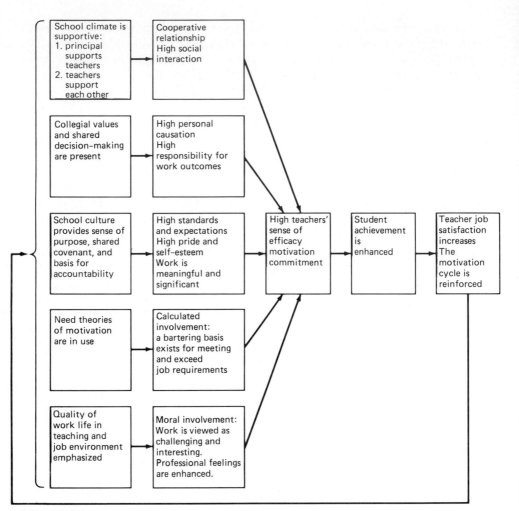

FIGURE 6-7
A summary model of teacher motivation and student achievement.

enrichment strategies will not be appropriate. It would be better, in these cases, to rely more heavily on lower-order needs and hygiene factors. For these teachers, motivation strategies based on one of the human relations or traditional supervision approaches might be appropriate. Thankfully the number of teachers who need to be placed in this discouraging category is small.

SUMMARY

This chapter was concerned with teacher motivation, supervisory effectiveness, and quality schooling. The highly motivated teacher is a high-priority concern of supervision because quality education is largely dependent upon the presence of competent administrators, teachers, and students who are internally committed and motivated to work. Pointing out that often school policies and practices hinder motivation by being based on a regressive view of teachers and teaching, a distinction was made between bureaucratic and professional work. In teaching conceived as bureaucratic work, teachers are regulated and controlled by an elaborate work system which specifies what must be done and which provides assurances that this will be done. Though bureaucrats and professionals are both part of a rationally conceived work system, bureaucrats are subordinate to this system. They are responsible for implementing the system according to specific specifications, and the role of supervision is to monitor this process. Professionals, by contrast, are superordinate to their work system. They use the system in ways that make sense to them as they practice. Supervision for professionals is designed to facilitate their work.

The links between teacher efficacy and student achievement were then discussed and the factors contributing to increased efficacy were provided as the framework for considering the topic of teacher motivation. Maslow's theory of human motivation was then discussed. Needs were classified into a hierarchy of prepotency with lower-order needs identified as security, social, and aspects of esteem and higher-order needs as esteem, autonomy, and self-fulfillment. In addition two professional needs, achievement and competence, were also considered. Teachers were described as being faced with two levels of decision in their jobs—a participation-level decision and a performance-level decision. The participation-level decision was described as a decision to continue in the traditional legal work relationship that exists between employer and employee, and the performance-level decision as a commitment to exceed this relationship. The motivation-hygiene theory as developed by Herzberg was then described as a means to identify motivating factors associated with the performance decisions and hygiene factors associated with the participatory decisions.

A discussion of motivation-hygiene theory concluded with the caveat that though by and large only the motivation factors motivate it would be wrong to conclude that some people are not motivated by the hygiene factors. Vroom's expectancy theory of motivation was then described as being a theory that is able to account for individual differences. Vroom's is a contingency theory in that motivation is considered to be a function of a person's perception that his or her increased performance will result in certain rewards that will help in attaining personal goals. Noting that the theories discussed to this point led to calculated involvement resulting from the bartering of supervisory wants for teacher needs Etzioni's compliance theory was reviewed and moral involvement was discussed as an alternative. The chapter concluded with the consideration of job enrichment research with implications for practice and supervision.

STUDY GUIDE

Recall the concepts, ideas, and meanings associated with each of the following phrases and terms included in this chapter. Can you discuss each of them with a colleague and apply them to the supervisory context of your school? If you cannot, review them in the text and record the page numbers for future reference.

1 Achievement motive
2 Autonomy
3 Bureaucratic work
4 Calculated involvement
5 Competence motive
6 Efficacy
7 Expectancy theory
8 Hygiene factors
9 Job enrichment
10 Maslow's theory of motivation
11 Moral involvement
12 Motivation factors
13 Motivation-hygiene theory
14 Origin
15 Participation investment
16 Pawn
17 Performance investment
18 Professional work

EXERCISES

1 Describe one or two teachers whom you know who are making only the participation decision at school. Contrast this with teachers who are making the performance decision.
2 What cautions should you keep in mind in developing motivational strategies based on Herzberg's motivation-hygiene theory?
3 Which of the three supervisory motives is most important to you? List examples of your behavior that correspond to each of the motives?
4 List 10 characteristics of the job of teaching that can be improved or "enriched." Use the job enrichment model provided in Figure 6-6 as a guide.
5 Using A, B, C, and D, grade your school on each of the dimensions that appear in the 10 boxes to the left of Figure 6-7. Is there a relationship between the grades you give and teachers' sense of efficacy, motivational levels, and commitment levels?

TWO

HUMAN RESOURCES
SUPERVISION AND
LEADERSHIP

In Part One we emphasized that human resources supervision involved enabling and empowering relationships between supervisors and teachers. Beyond the face-to-face dynamic between supervisors and teachers, we emphasized that the organizational context, the climate, the culture, and the structuring of motivational factors into the teaching job itself all had to promote the development of the teachers' effectiveness with children. In Part Two we will analyze human resources supervision from the perspectives of leadership.

This section of the book represents a significant departure from earlier editions, although intimations of the shift could be found in the distinction between strategic and tactical requirements of leadership in Chapter 11 of the third edition. Theories and studies of leadership had tended until recently to be dominated by a rather dogmatic view of social science which was thoroughly grounded in empiricism and positivism.[1] This view rejected all social theories, including theories of leadership, which were not based on observable behavior and carefully crafted empirical research methodology which would yield quantifiable data. These views of social science were based on the paradigms of the natural sciences, even though there were almost as many views of empirical social science as there were social scientists. Nonetheless, social scientists had been waiting for a giant of the stature of Isaac Newton to come along and unify all the disparate views into a single universal paradigm. This

---

[1] For a review of this shift in social science, cf. Bruce Jennings, "Interpretive Social Science and Policy Analysis," in Daniel Callahan and Bruce Jennings (eds.), *Ethics, The Social Sciences and Policy Analysis*, New York: Plenum Press, 1983, pp. 3–35.

hope has been blown away in the last 20 years by the news filtering out from the community of natural scientists that the supposed objectivity of their own paradigms and laws was illusory, that, in fact, they were tainted by subjective bias, imaginative fantasy, and political and self-serving interests. For social scientists awaiting their Newton, there came the painful awareness that they were "not only waiting for a train that won't arrive, they're in the wrong station altogether."[2]

Emerging trends in social science have tended to emphasize the meaningfulness of human action, the purposefulness of practical reasoning carried out by the persons under study.[3] This perspective presents the human beings under study "as acting subjects rather than as behaving objects."[4]

We can find this shift, which has been taking place in the social sciences, reflected in the recent research and theory on leadership. There has been a shift away from concepts such as "role," "behavior," "systems," to "intention," "meaning," "purpose," "moral action," "sense of mission." We also find some of the assumptions about the cultural, political, and economic context of leadership being challenged by women, minorities, critical theorists, and others.

Clearly, the last word on leadership from these new perspectives has not been spoken. Yet there is enough shape to the recent literature to begin to introduce it to those who would be supervisors. A hitherto unspoken premise behind earlier formulations of human resources supervision has been that this form of supervision requires more than technical and superficial political competence. It requires a commitment to making the school a human environment which actively promotes high human ideals, which treats human beings as though they were capable, in some form, of greatness. Given the less than edifying state of affairs in many schools and school systems, to propose those ideals obviously calls for genuine leadership on the part of supervisors. Hence, it is appropriate that we take up that topic in greater depth at this point in history.

Chapter 7 reviews some of the now more familiar theories of leadership, which we label instrumental leadership theory. That is to say, those theories tend to be driven more by what Weber labeled functional rationality. Chapter 8 introduces the more recent contributions to the research and theory on leadership and draws out implications for supervisory practice. As Chapter 8 unfolds, the reader should begin to appreciate an underlying framework that could be said to pervade this whole book. Chapter 9 flows naturally from its predecessor and attempts to explore human resource supervision as fundamentally moral action. This exploration uncovers some of the basic values which should inform supervisory practice.

This part of the book, then, lays the groundwork for what will follow. Parts

---

[2] Anthony Giddens, *New Rules of Sociological Method,* New York: Basic Books, 1976, p. 13.

[3] For a general discussion of this approach, see Richard Bernstein, *The Restructuring of Social and Political Theory,* New York: Harcourt Brace Jovanovich, 1976.

[4] Jennings, op. cit., p. 9.

Three and Four call for supervisors to go beyond a superficial form of practice, to a reflective practice which embraces the challenge of leadership. This, in turn, leads to supervisors holding out a view of education to teachers which will invite greater leadership activity on the part of the teachers. Armed with a clearer sense of the large mission of the school, they can explore ways to make that mission a reality.

LEADERSHIP BEHAVIOR AND SUPERVISORY EFFECTIVENESS

In this chapter, leadership refers to the supervisor's ability to influence an individual or group toward the achievement of goals. The ways in which supervisors use leadership to influence vary. Sometimes supervisors develop a specific set of leadership tactics that involves behaving in a certain way or using a particular approach to decision making. This is the type of leadership on which we will concentrate in Chapter 7. We are concerned with the supervisor's involvement in the deliberate tactical planning of influence and in subsequent leadership behavior designed to influence. This ability to influence can be enhanced by learning about and increasing one's own leadership style skills. This is the orientation to leadership associated with Supervision I. It is doubtful that supervisors can provide the leadership needed for quality schooling and ignore this important orientation. It is equally doubtful that successful leadership will emerge by concentrating *only* on this orientation.

Groups are influenced and goals are achieved by more indirect and subtle supervisory actions as well. For example, sometimes what is appropriate in leadership is not how the supervisor behaves but what he or she stands for and the ability to communicate these values to teachers. Sometimes what is important are the values and intents that teachers infer from what supervisors actually do and say. Of issue as well is the nature of goals and objectives and the direction of supervisory influence. It is, for example, possible that a supervisor with highly developed leadership skills can actually promote the "wrong" goals or influence teachers in the "wrong" direction. More qualitative aspects of leadership will be considered in Chapter 8, where we provide a substantive theory of leadership, the leadership more associated with Supervision II. In this chapter let us focus primarily on Leadership I, specifically on the social and management skills, concepts, and theories that can help improve a supervisor's leadership style skills.

The following questions are considered in this chapter: What assumptions do supervisors and others make about human nature and, particularly, the behavior of teachers at work? How do these assumptions affect the supervisor's behavior? What are the effects of this behavior on teachers? Are they, for example, more committed and able to work more effectively as a result? Or are they frustrated, dissatisfied, and unable to work effectively? Human resources supervision is concerned with the worth, growth, and development of the human organization, for it is upon this growth that the success of the school enterprise depends. Thus the issue of supervisory assumptions and resulting leadership behavior is very important to the theme of this book.

MANAGEMENT PHILOSOPHY AND SUPERVISORY ASSUMPTIONS

Typically how supervisors lead makes sense to them. How do supervisors come to establish styles of supervision? Styles are partly the result of management philosophies and of supervisory assumptions that have been accumulated and learned over the years.

Assumptions affect how teachers behave in classrooms too. Teachers, for example, whose classrooms are characterized as "open" have learned to consider students differently from their counterparts with "controlled" classrooms. These teachers have different management philosophies and different conceptions of their roles and the roles of their students. This is true, too, for principals who operate open, as opposed to closed, schools.

Teachers often respond to the supervisor's assumptions and expectations in such a way that they prove him or her correct. This simply reinforces that supervisor's use of a given supervisory style. Understanding this self-fulfilling prophecy is crucial to understanding the relationship between management philosophy and supervisory behavior. Rensis Likert's study of supervisors of highly effective work groups, for example, strongly suggests that workers generally respond positively to the supervisor's high evaluation and confidence in them and work harder to justify the supervisor's expectations.[1] In the next section we present and discuss Douglas McGregor's comparison of two ideal-type management philosophies, Theories X and Y, along with supervisory assumptions that emerge from these philosophies.

THEORY X AND SCHOOLS

McGregor's language may seem more descriptive of nonschool environments,

---

[1] Rensis Likert, *New Patterns of Management,* New York: McGraw-Hill, 1961. The discussion which follows is based largely on Douglas McGregor, *The Human Side of Enterprise,* New York: McGraw-Hill, 1960. See also Warren G. Bennis and Edgar H. Schein (eds.), *Leadership and Motivation: Essays of Douglas McGregor,* Cambridge, Mass.: M.I.T., 1966.

but his ideas have wide application to schools. The basic assumptions and propositions of his theory are provided below.

Management Propositions—Theory X

1 Management is responsible for organizing the elements of productive enterprise—money, materials, equipment, people—in the interest of economic [educational] ends.

2 With respect to people, this is a process of directing their efforts, motivating them, controlling their actions, modifying their behavior to fit the needs of the organization.

3 Without this active intervention by management, people would be passive—rewarded, punished, controlled—their activities must be directed. This is management's task in managing subordinate managers or workers. We often sum it up by saying that management consists of getting things done through other people.

Supervisory Assumptions—Theory X

Behind this conventional theory are several additional beliefs—less explicit but widespread:

4 Average people are by nature indolent—they work as little as possible.

5 They lack ambition, dislike responsibility, prefer to be led.

6 They are inherently self-centered, indifferent to organizational needs.

7 They are by nature resistant to change.

8 They are gullible, not very bright, ready dupes of the charlatan and demagogue.[2]

One can find many instances in schools when the assumptions of Theory X do indeed seem to be true. Teachers, for example, seem to work only minimally and then only under close supervision. Few instances of teacher initiative can be found. Instead they seem to be defensive and preoccupied with merely holding on. McGregor argued that when such conditions exist the problem may be less with workers and more with the assumptions which their administrators and supervisors hold for them. Sensing negative assumptions and expectations, teachers can be expected to respond to them. This is an example of the self-fulfilling prophecy referred to earlier. Fundamental to Theory X is a philosophy of direction and control. This philosophy is administered in a variety of forms and rests upon a theory of motivation that is inadequate for

[2] These assumptions are quoted from McGregor's essay, "The Human Side of Enterprise," which appears in Bennis and Schein, op. cit., p. 5. The essay first appeared in *Adventure in Thought and Action,* Proceedings of the Fifth Anniversary Convocation of the School of Industrial Management, M.I.T., April 9, 1957. We added the word "education" to item 1 in McGregor's list. The article has been reprinted in *The Management Review,* vol. 46, no. 11, pp. 22–28, 1951.

most adults, particularly professional adults, and indeed is quickly outgrown by students. The case for this assertion was made in Chapter 6 dealing with teachers' sense of efficacy, motivation, and commitment.[3]

The behavior typically associated with Theory X assumptions is labeled by Argyris as Pattern A.[4] Pattern A takes two forms: hard and soft. The hard version is a no-nonsense approach characterized by strong leadership, tight controls, and close supervision by teachers. The soft approach relies heavily on buying, persuading, or winning people through good (albeit superficial) human relations and benevolent paternalism to obtain compliance and acceptance of direction from superiors. The emphasis in both soft and hard versions of Pattern A is on manipulating, controlling, and managing people. The assumptions supervisors hold remain the same regardless of whether the hard or soft approach is used.

There are many problems with Theory X and Pattern A as management systems in the school. As basic philosophies, Theory X and Pattern A seem inconsistent with the hopes of teachers, administrators, and supervisors who are interested in raising the quality of life for young people in schools, and they are not compatible with human resources supervision.

THEORY Y AND SCHOOLS

An alternative management philosophy based on more adequate assumptions of human nature is needed for schools to meet their professional growth commitment to teachers and to improve the intellectual, social, and emotional welfare of their young clients. This optimistic philosophy is called Theory Y after McGregor. Its main components are outlined below:

Philosophy and Assumptions—Theory Y

1 Management is responsible for organizing the elements of productive enterprise—money, materials, equipment, people—in the interest of economic [educational] ends.

2 People are *not* by nature passive or resistant to organizational needs. They have become so as a result of experience in organizations.

3 The motivation, the potential for development, the capacity for assuming responsibility, the readiness to direct behaviors toward organizational goals are all present in people. Management does not put them there. It is a responsibility of management to make it possible for people to recognize and develop these human characteristics for themselves.

4 The essential task of management is to arrange organizational conditions

---

[3] The motivational assumptions that are the bases for Theories X and Y are discussed in chapter 6. See A. H. Maslow, *Motivation and Personality,* New York: Harper & Row, 1954.

[4] Chris Argyris, *Management and Organizational Development,* New York: McGraw-Hill, 1971, pp. 1–26.

and methods of operation so that people can achieve their own goals *best* by directing *their* own efforts toward organizational objectives.[5]

Pattern B is the label that Argyris gives to behavior associated with Theory Y assumptions. Basic to Pattern B is building identification and commitment to worthwhile objectives in the work context and building mutual trust and respect. Success in work is assumed to be dependent on whether meaningful satisfaction for individuals is achieved and whether authentic relationships and the exchange of valid information are present. "More trust, concern for feelings, and internal commitment; more openness to, and experimenting with, new ideas and feelings *in such ways that others could do the same,* were recommended if valid information was to be produced and internal commitment to decisions generated."[6]

The differences between Theory X assumptions and behavior of the hard, or tough, variety and Theory Y assumptions and behavior are readily observable and understood. Theory X *soft* and Theory Y, however, are often deceptively similar. Theory X soft is consistent with human relations practices and Theory Y with human resources practices. These approaches are contrasted in Table 7-1.

INFANCY MANAGEMENT ASSUMPTIONS

A more pessimistic analysis of negative assumptions inherent in many management practices is offered by Argyris.[7] He notes that the ordinary worker (in the school's case teachers and students) is often considered to have little substantial ability for self-direction and self-discipline. Further, individuals largely prefer to be told what to do rather than to think for themselves, and when they do have ideas, they are generally naive or unrealistic. Gellerman, in interpreting the Argyris position, makes the following comments:

> Most organizations, especially at the lower levels, are geared for men who make a very childlike adjustment to life: They leave very little leeway for choosing, for using discretion, or for adapting rules to fit circumstances. Most employees are expected to do just as they are told and leave the thinking to the foreman, whose capacity for doing so is a perennially moot point among the people he supervises. In any case millions of grown men are required to spend forty hours a week suppressing their brainpower in order to maintain a system that is not nearly as efficient as it looks.[8]

[5] McGregor in Bennis and Schein, op. cit., p. 15. Again we add the word "educational" to item 1.

[6] Argyris, op. cit., p. 18. Argyris does not recommend that people be completely open and trusting but that they be open to an extent that permits others to be open. He argues that trust and openness exist only in interpersonal relationships and, therefore, the question is, "How open is the relationship between person A and person B?" In Argyris's words, "To say what you believe is to be honest; to say what you believe in such a way that the other can do the same is to be authentic."

[7] This discussion is based largely on Chris Argyris, *Personality and Organization,* New York: Harper & Row, 1957. See also "Individual Actualization in Complex Organizations," *Mental Hygiene,* vol. 44, no. 2, pp. 226–237, April 1960; and *Integrating the Individual and Education,* New York: Wiley, 1964.

[8] Saul Gellerman, *Motivation and Productivity,* New York: American Management Association, 1963, p. 73.

TABLE 7-1
SUPERVISORY ASSUMPTIONS

Theory X soft human relations model	Theory Y human resources model
Attitudes toward people	
1. People in our culture, teachers and students among them, share a common set of needs—to belong, to be liked, to be respected.	1. In addition to sharing common needs for belonging and respect, most people in our culture, teachers and students among them, desire to contribute effectively and creatively to the accomplishment of worthwhile objectives.
2. While teachers and students desire individual recognition, they more importantly want to *feel* useful to the school and to their own work group.	2. The majority of teachers and students are capable of exercising far more initiative, responsibility, and creativity than their present jobs or work circumstances require or allow.
3. They tend to cooperate willingly and comply with school goals if these important needs are fulfilled.	3. These capabilities represent untapped resources that are presently being wasted.
Kind and amount of participation	
1. The supervisor's basic task (or in reference to students, the teacher's basic task) is to make each worker believe that he or she is a useful and important part of the team.	1. The supervisor's basic task (or in reference to students, the teacher's basic task) is to create an environment in which subordinates can contribute their full range of talents to the accomplishment of school goals. He or she works to uncover the creative resources of subordinates.
2. The supervisor is willing to explain his or her decisions and to discuss subordinates' objections to the plans. On routine mattters, he or she encourages subordinates in planning and in decision making. In reference to students, the teacher behaves similarly.	2. The supervisor allows and encourages teachers to participate in important as well as routine decisions. In fact, the more important a decision is to the school, the greater the supervisor's efforts to tap faculty resources. In reference to students, the teacher behaves similarly.
3. Within narrow limits, the faculty or individual teachers who make up the faculty should be allowed to exercise self-direction and self-control in carrying out plans. A similar relationship exists for teachers and students.	3. Supervisors work continually to expand the areas over which teachers exercise self-direction and self-control as they develop and demonstrate greater insight and ability. A similar relationship exists for teachers and students.
Expectations	
1. Sharing information with teachers and involving them in school decision making will help satisfy their basic needs for belonging and for individual recognition.	1. The overall quality of decision making and performance will improve as supervisors and teachers make use of the full range of experience, insight, and creative ability that exists in their schools.

TABLE 7-1
SUPERVISORY ASSUMPTIONS *Continued*

Expectations	
2. Satisfying these needs will improve faculty and student morale and will reduce resistance to formal authority.	2. Teachers will exercise responsible self-direction and self-control in the accomplishment of worthwhile objectives that they understand and have helped establish.
3. High faculty and student morale and reduced resistance to formal authority may lead to improved school performance. It will at least reduce friction and make the supervisor's job easier.	3. Faculty satisfaction and student satisfaction will increase as a by-product of improved performance and the opportunity to contribute creatively to this improvement.

*Source:*Adapted from Raymond E. Miles, "Human Relations or Human Resources?" *Harvard Business Review*, vol. 43, no. 4, pp. 148–163, 1965, esp. exhibits I and II.

The Argyris position is essentially that the human personality is not given sufficient opportunity to mature in most formal organizations. Schools in general do offer relatively more opportunities for personal growth than most other organizations. Yet proportionally—that is, when one considers that schools are essentially human organizations—*our record on this matter is less than impressive.*

In noting the distinction between the mature and immature personality, Argyris lists seven processes that normally occur as the infant grows into the young adult, as the young adult grows into full adulthood, and as the adult increases his or her capabilities and effectiveness over the course of his or her lifetime. The seven dimensions and directions of human growth follows:[9]

First, healthy human beings tend to develop from a state of passivity as infants to a state of activity as adults. They move from being stimulated, motivated, or disciplined to relying on self-initiative and self-determination. As they mature, they rely less on supervision (teacher's, principal's, or parent's) to control them. Given clear expectations and the opportunity to develop commitment, mature adults act on their own.

Second, they move from a state of dependence upon others in infancy to an adult state of relative independence, and finally to interdependence. They are able to stand on their own feet and yet to acknowledge healthy dependencies. As part of this development, they internalize a set of values, which become the bases of their behavior.

Third, they tend to develop from being capable of behaving in only a few ways as infants to being capable of behaving in many different ways as adults. They actually prefer to vary their style and do not care for fixed or rigid job

[9] Our discussion of the seven directions and dimensions of the mature personality follows closely that which appears in Argyris, "Individual Actualization in Complex Organizations," op. cit., pp. 226–227.

assignments. They prefer to develop their own means to achieve ends rather than to be limited by the *best* way as defined by the organization.

Fourth, they tend to develop from having unpredictable, shallow, casual interests of short duration as infants to having deeper interests as adults. The mature personality is characterized by responding to an endless series of challenges, and reward comes from doing something for its own sake. Adults need a work environment that is challenging to skill and creativity.

Fifth, healthy human beings tend to develop from having a short-term perspective as infants—one in which the present largely determines their behavior—to a much larger time perspective as adults—one in which behavior is affected by past events and future hopes.

Sixth, they tend to develop from being in a subordinate position in the family and society as infants to aspiring to occupy an equal and/or superordinate position in reference to their peers. They are willing to accept leadership from others if they perceive it as legitimate, but they find being "bossed" offensive.

Seventh, they tend to develop from a lack of awareness of self as infants to an awareness of, and control over, self as adults. They are sensitive about their concepts of self and aware of their individuality. They therefore experience with displeasure attempts to lessen their self-worth. They cannot be expected to simply do the work that is put before them. They need to experience ego involvement in their work.

School assumptions that require teachers and students to behave in ways that tend toward the infancy end of the Argyris continuum usually have negative consequences for the human organization and ultimately retard school effectiveness. Such assumptions are reflected administratively in the formal organizational structures of the school in directive leadership and in managerial control through budget, incentive systems, inspection, and review procedures. Argyris describes the effects of "infancy" managerial assumptions as follows:

> Healthy human beings (in our culture) tend to find dependence, subordination and submissiveness frustrating. They would prefer to be relatively independent, to be active, to use many of their deeper abilities; and they aspire to positions equal with or higher than their peers. Frustration leads to regression, aggression, and tension. These in turn lead to conflict (the individual prefers to leave but fears doing so). Moreoever, it can be shown that under these conditions, the individual will tend to experience psychological failure and short-time perspective.[10]

Our focus in this discussion has been on adults in school organizations, but the analogy is perhaps more important in its application to students. Argyris has captured the function of American schools—to move youngsters from infancy to maturity, intellectually, socially, and emotionally. Let us examine some of the alternatives that teachers on the one hand and students on the other have in adapting to school environments that frustrate mature development.[11]

---

[10] Ibid.

[11] The list that follows is an adaptation of one which appears in Argyris, "Individual Actualization in Complex Organizations," op. cit., p. 227.

For teachers	For students
1. Leave the school. Absence and turnover	1. Same.
2. Climb the organizational ladder into administration and supervision.	2. Submit and "play ball" with the system.
3. Become defensive, daydream, become aggressive, nurture grievances, regress, project, feel low self-worth	3. Same.
4. Become apathetic, disinterested, non-ego-involved in the school and its goals.	4. Same.
5. Create informal groups for mutual protection from the organization.	5. Same.
6. Formalize into militant associations and unions.	6. Go underground or dissent in newspapers, organized demonstrations, student unions.
7. Deemphasize in their own minds the importance of self-growth and creativity and emphasize the importance of money and other material rewards.	7. Deemphasize intrinsic learning goals and other values and emphasize grades, credits, and the like, to beat the system.
8. Accept the above-described ways of behaving as being proper for their lives outside the organization.	8. The depressing aspect of this cycle of events is that youngsters may accept socialization into the value system of infancy management and thus reinforce and perpetuate the system for another generation.

Some writers maintain that what Argyris criticizes so vehemently is exactly what workers in organizations want. Dubin, for example, argues:

> The fact of the matter is this. Work for probably a majority of workers, and even extending into the ranks of management, may represent an institutional setting that is not a central life interest for its participants. The consequence of this is that while participating in work, a general attitude of apathy and indifference prevails. The response to the demands of the institution is to satisfy the minimum expectations of required behavior without reacting affectively to these demands.[12]

Of course not everyone is capable of mature behavior or is able to respond to Theory Y assumptions, but what Dubin fails to add is that this reaction is learned as a result of one's experience with organizations. People are not *inherently* removed from organizational life.

[12] Robert Dubin, "Person and Organization," in William Greenwood (ed.), *Management and Organizational Behavior Theories,* Cincinnati: South-Western Publishing Co., 1965, p. 487. See also George Strauss, "Some Notes on Power-Equalization," in Harold J. Leavitt (ed.), *The Social Science of Organizations,* Englewood Cliffs, N.J.: Prentice-Hall, 1963, pp. 45–59.

MISTAKES IN IMPLEMENTING THEORY Y

It is important to point out that Theory Y is not a universal theory of how to administer and supervise. A common misunderstanding is that Pattern B behavior, the behavior most closely associated with Theory Y, should be used at all times in all cases and that it elicits a uniformly positive reaction from subordinates. What is not understood is that Theory Y refers to the *inherent potential* and *capacity* of people rather than their present condition or their disposition at a given point in time.

Consider the example of motivation:

Motivation in teachers depends upon a complex set of factors and conditions, many of which are well beyond the control of the school and the supervisor. One's set of values and work norms, for example, affects one's orientation toward his or her job. Some teachers will never be properly motivated to work and others will usually be motivated to work regardless of what supervisors do. Indeed a good rule of thumb is, if you want motivated teachers, hire motivated people if you can. Wisdom aside, we still face the problem of increasing the identity, commitment, and performance of large numbers of teachers already tenured on the job. The majority of teachers desire and seek satisfying work and will respond to human resources supervision. But many will not and alternate supervisory methods and procedures that suit these teachers will need to be provided. Human resources supervision is not an elixir to be administered indiscriminately to all. But it is a powerful conception of supervision which by using the concepts of motivation and job enrichment can markedly improve the identity, commitment, and performance of most teachers and the effectiveness of schools.[13]

Pattern A behavior, the behavior most associated with Theory X, is not in itself inconsistent with Theory Y. Supervisors need to behave in a variety of ways, sometimes in a rather direct fashion, other times in a supportive or considerate fashion, and at still other times in a manner described as participative or team building. No one best approach applicable to all situations exists, but rather the effectiveness of an approach is dependent upon its suitability to the situation at hand. But the approach or style suited to the particular situation at hand is different from one's overriding assumptions and the beliefs upon which one's behavior is based. In human organizations such as schools it is clear that leadership styles and other behavioral patterns, though they may vary depending upon the situation, are generated from within the broad perspectives of Theory Y.

DETERMINANTS OF SUPERVISORY PATTERNS

This chapter is concerned with the values, assumptions, and management philosophies that are a part of the supervisor's concept of self. As these

[13] Thomas J. Sergiovanni, "Human Resources Supervision," in T. J. Sergiovanni (ed.), *Professional Supervision for Professional Teachers,* Washington, D.C.: Association for Supervision and Curriculum Development, 1975, p. 30. Human resources supervision follows closely the premises of Theory Y. See also Edgar Schein, "The Hawthorne Studies Revisited: A Defense of Theory Y," in Eugene Cass and Frederick Zimmer (eds.), *Man and Work in Society,* New York: Van Nostrand, 1975, pp. 78–94.

dimensions are internalized, they largely determine dominant supervisory behavior patterns. Other forces, however, such as those that exist within the client and those that exist in the environment, contribute to selecting appropriate supervisory style. These forces are delineated and described in the following sections.[14]

Forces in the Supervisor

When supervisors face a problem, their approach, behavior, or style is largely affected by each of the following internalized forces:

1 *Value system.* How strongly does a supervisor feel that individuals should have a share in making the decisions that affect them? Or, how convinced is the supervisor that the official who is paid to assume responsibility should personally carry the burden of decision making? The behavior of the supervisor will also be influenced by the relative importance that he or she attaches to organizational efficiency, personal growth of subordinates, and company profits.

2 *Confidence in subordinates.* Managers differ greatly in the amount of trust they have in other people generally, and this carries over to the particular employees they supervise at a given time. In viewing their particular group of subordinates, managers are likely to consider their knowledge and competence with respect to the problem. A central question managers might ask themselves is, "Who is best qualified to deal with this problem?" Often managers may, justifiably or not, have more confidence in their own capabilities than in those of their subordinates.

3 *Leadership inclinations.* There are some managers who seem to function more comfortably and naturally as highly directive leaders. Resolving problems and issuing orders come easily to them. Other managers seem to operate more comfortably in a team role where they are continually sharing many of their functions with their subordinates.

4 *Feelings of security in an uncertain situation.* The manager who releases control over the decision-making process thereby reduces the predictability of the outcome. Some managers have a greater need than others for predictability and stability in their environment. This "tolerance for ambiguity" is being viewed increasingly by psychologists as a key variable in a person's manner of dealing with problems.[15]

---

[14] This discussion follows Robert Tannenbaum and Warren Schmidt, "How to Choose a Leadership Pattern," *Harvard Business Review,* vol. 36, no. 2, pp. 95–101, 1958. Tannenbaum identifies three forces that managers should consider in deciding how to manage: (1) forces in the manager, (2) forces in the subordinates, and (3) forces in the situation. See also Tannenbaum and Fred Massarick, "Participation by Subordinates in the Managerial Decision-Making Process," *Canadian Journal of Economics and Political Science,* vol. 16, pp. 408–418, August 1950.

[15] Tannenbaum and Schmidt, op. cit. The label "manager" tends to have negative connotations to many school people, but the descriptions are equally appropriate if one substitutes the term "school supervisor" for "manager."

Such an impressive list of internalized forces may provoke feelings of helplessness in supervisors, but each of these dimensions can be altered and modified. A first step toward this end is awareness and understanding. As supervisors come to understand the nature of the values, prejudices, and management styles that have become a part of their conscious or unconscious selves, they are in a better position to evaluate and change their present approach to supervision.

Forces in the Supervisory Environment

The organizational forces that we have described in Chapters 3, 4, and 5 are major influences on supervisory style. The organizational style of the school, the school's normative culture, its role expectations, its belief pattern, and its authority and power systems serve as boundaries that often delimit choice of supervisory action. Further, the nature of the problem, the consequences of the task, and the character of the goal are additional determinants of appropriate supervisory behavior. A teacher, for example, may be required by default to consult with students when class activities are varied and complex, but such consultation is little more than perfunctory when activities are routine and simple.

Forces in Others

The extent to which school supervisors may permit their respective clients to exercise more freedom and control over their own destiny and that of the school depends largely on the following conditions:

1 Whether the subordinates have relatively high needs for independence. (As we all know, people differ greatly in the amount of direction that they desire.)

2 Whether the subordinates have a readiness to assume responsibility for decision making. (Some see additional responsibility as a tribute to their ability; others see it as "passing the buck.")

3 Whether they have a relatively high tolerance for ambiguity. (Some employees prefer to have clear-cut directives given to them; others prefer a wider area of freedom.)

4 Whether they are interested in the problem and feel that it is important.

5 Whether they understand and identify with the goals of the organization.

6 Whether they have the necessary knowledge and experience to deal with the problem.

7 Whether they have learned to expect to share in decision making. (Persons who have come to expect strong leadership and are then suddenly confronted with the request to share more fully in decision making are often upset by this new experience. On the other hand, persons who have enjoyed a considerable amount of freedom resent the boss who begins to make all the decisions alone.)[16]

Indeed the choice of one supervisory pattern over another is partly a function of forces in the client to be supervised, but this rationale should not provide a convenient "out" for those whose dominant supervisory patterns fall outside the range of human resources supervision.

Human resources supervision recognizes that forces in the client may require the supervisor to behave in a variety of ways. Highly dependent teachers may well need paternalistic supervisory environments, and uncommitted students will require closely controlled supervisory environments. Human resources supervisors, however, are not resigned to these patterns in that they do not accept dependency in teachers as being natural or inherent. Dependency of teachers and lack of commitment of students are perceived as symptoms of client immaturity and/or perhaps supervisory immaturity and organizational immaturity. With this perception, the human resources supervisor works to diminish client dependency and to increase client commitment, for in the synthesizing theory these are important means to affect the school-effectiveness variables positively.

We shall now discuss and explore different supervisory leadership behavior patterns and examine their effects on the human organization that constitutes the school.

THE DIMENSIONS OF LEADERSHIP

The research tradition dealing with leadership style in educational and non-educational settings has identified two key dimensions of leadership. These dimensions have been given a variety of labels. Subtle differences may exist in the labels, but by and large experts agree that leadership style is defined by the extent to which the leader seems to shows concern for, focuses on, or seems oriented toward getting work done or accomplishing tasks and the extent to which the leader seems to show concern for, focuses on, or seems oriented toward the needs or feelings of people and his or her relationships with them.

In this discussion we will use the phrases "task-oriented" (TO) to refer to tendencies the leader shows for work and "relations-oriented" (RO) for the leader's tendency to show concern for people in displaying leadership behavior. Each of these dimensions of leadership style is illustrated conceptually in Figure 7-1.

The horizontal marginal axis line (abscissa) that forms the base of the grid represents the extent to which the leader's behavior shows a concern for task accomplishment (TO), with high concern to the right and low concern to the left. You might estimate the extent to which your leadership style shows concern for task accomplishment by checking one of the numbers (1 to 9) on this line. The vertical marginal axis line (ordinate) that forms the left side of the

---

[16] Ibid.

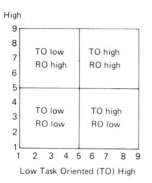

FIGURE 7-1
The leadership grid. (*From T. J. Sergiovanni and David Elliot, Educational and Organizational Leadership in Elementary Schools, Englewood Cliffs, N.J.: Prentice-Hall, 1975.*)

grid represents the extent to which the leader's behavior shows a concern for people and relationships (RO), with the top representing high concern and the bottom low concern. Again, estimate the extent to which you show concern for people and relationships in expressing leadership by checking one of the numbers on this line. To find your location in the grid based on the estimates you have made, simply find the point where lines drawn from each of the numbers you checked would intersect. For example, if you checked a 7 on the TO line and 6 on the RO line, your position on the grid would be indicated by the *x* that appears on the grid.

THE MANAGERIAL GRID

A more descriptive attempt to conceptualize the task dimension and the people dimension of supervisory behavior has resulted in a formulation referred to as the *managerial grid*.[17] The grid focuses on five ideal-type theories of supervisory behavior, each based on the two dimensions that we have identified and discussed as crucial variables found in organizations: (1) task and (2) people. Blake and Mouton, the proposers of the grid formulation, show the relationship between the two variables and present the five ideal-type combinations of style in Figure 7-2.

Notice that the horizontal axis, concern for production, is similar to the task-oriented construct, and that the vertical axis, concern for people, is similar to the relationship-oriented construct. By locating degree of intensity for each of these two dimensions (from 1 to 9), we can see that the grid has potential for generating 81 different styles.

When asked to describe ideal leadership behavior in principals, teachers tend to express a preference for the integrated style that combines both TO and RO.[18] This preference seems to hold even though teachers may vary in terms

[17] Robert Blake and Jane Mouton, *The Managerial Grid*, Houston: Gulf, 1964.

[18] This generalization of *ideal* style results from the Leadership Behavior Description Questionnaire research tradition of Ralph Stogdill and Andrew Halpin. The Leadership Behavior Description Questionnaire was developed by the Personnel Research Board at Ohio State University and Administration Center, 1959. See also "The Leader Behavior and Leadership

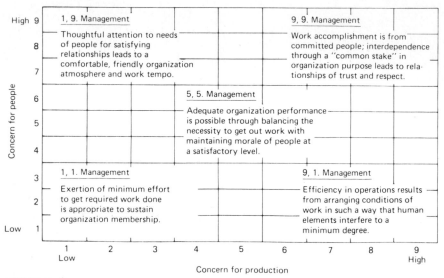

FIGURE 7-2
The managerial grid. (*From Robert Blake and Jane Mouton,* The Managerial Grid, *Houston: Gulf, 1964.*)

of personality or need orientations. This observation lends support to the optimistic assumptions that make up the McGregor-Argyris management philosophy. That is, teachers seem able to describe ideal leadership behavior as emphasizing task—the organizational and structural aspects of the school—as well as providing for individual needs, regardless of their own personality shortcomings or strengths. Human resources supervision maintains that providing for needs of mature teachers is dependent upon efforts toward achieving school goals: the two dimensions then are viewed as interdependent, since goal achievement over time is dependent upon provision for teacher need, and teacher need over time is dependent upon the achievement of school goals.

REDDIN'S 3-D THEORY OF LEADERSHIP

The managerial grid is considered to be a normative theory of leadership in the sense that it prescribes the 9.9 image of leadership as the one best style. In this section we describe a more descriptive theory (Reddin's 3-D theory), which shares many of the features of the managerial grid but assumes that no one best style exists.[19] Reddin views leadership style as consisting of a task and relationship emphasis similar to that illustrated previously in the quadrants of Figure 7-1.[20]

Ideology of Educational Administrators and Aircraft Commanders," *Harvard Educational Review,* vol. 25, pp. 18–32, winter 1955.
    [19] W. J. Reddin, *Managerial Effectiveness,* New York: McGraw-Hill, 1970.
    [20] This discussion follows that which appears in T. J. Sergiovanni, *Handbook for Effective Department Leadership: Concepts and Practices in Today's Secondary Schools,* Boston: Allyn

High	Related	Integrated
	To listen	To interact
	To accept	To motivate
	To trust	To integrate
	To advise	To participate
	To encourage	To innovate
RO		
	To examine	To organize
	To measure	To initiate
	To administer	To direct
	To control	To complete
	To maintain	To evaluate
	Separated	Dedicated
Low ———————— TO ————→ High		

FIGURE 7-3
Basic style behavior indicators. (*From W. J. Reddin, Managerial Effectiveness, New York: McGraw-Hill, 1970.*)

The lower-right-hand quadrant (TO high and RO low) represents a style of supervision that is characterized by a good deal of drive and emphasis on work and little overt concern for the relationship dimension. This is called the *dedicated* leadership style and is characterized by an emphasis on organizing, initiating, directing, completing, and evaluating the work of others.

The upper-left-hand quadrant (TO low and RO high) represents a style of supervision that emphasizes concern for people and little overt concern for the task dimension. This is called the *related* leadership style and is characterized by an emphasis on listening, accepting, trusting, advising, and encouraging.

The upper-right-hand quadrant (TO high and RO high) represents a combination approach to supervision, whereby people concerns are expressed through emphasizing meaningful work, and work concerns are emphasized by bringing together and stimulating committed groups of individuals. This is called the *integrated* leadership style and is characterized by an emphasis on interaction, motivation, integration, participation, and innovation.

The lower-left-hand quadrant (TO low and RO low) represents a style of supervision that expresses very little concern for either dimension. In a sense the leader removes himself or herself from both task and people. This is called the *separated* leadership style and is characterized by an emphasis on examining, measuring, administering, controlling, and maintaining.

The behavior indicators that Reddin suggests are associated with each of the four basic leadership styles shown in grid 4 in Figure 7-3.

Reddin proposes that the effectiveness of a given leadership style can be understood only within the context of the leadership situation. He assumes that related, integrated, separated, and dedicated are four basic styles only, each with an effective and an ineffective equivalent depending upon the situation in

and Bacon, 1977, p. 141. See also Sergiovanni, "Leader Behavior and Organizational Effectiveness," *Notre Dame Journal of Education*, vol. 4, no. 1, 1973; and Sergiovanni and Elliott, *Educational and Organizational Leadership in Elementary Schools*, Englewood Cliffs, N.J.: Prentice-Hall, 1975, pp. 98–116.

which it is used. These effective and ineffective equivalents result in eight operational leadership styles, as shown in Figures 7-4 and 7-5.

In Reddin's terms the basic *integrated* styles when displayed in an inappropriate setting might lead to *compromise* but when displayed in an appropriate setting lead to *executive* effectiveness. As *executives,* supervisors are seen as good motivators who set high standards, who treat teachers as individuals, and who prefer team approaches in operating their units. As *compromisers,* supervisors are seen as poor decision makers who allow pressures in the situation to influence them too much.

The basic *related* style expressed inappropriately may be perceived as *missionary* behavior, but when the situation is ripe for this style, *development* of people takes place. As *developers,* supervisors are seen as being primarily concerned with developing teachers as individuals and professionals. As *missionaries,* supervisors are seen as being primarily interested in harmony.

If supervisors behave in a *separated* way given appropriate conditions, they are displaying an appropriate *bureaucratic* response, but if their involvement in task or people or both is needed but not forthcoming, they are seen as *deserters.* As *bureaucrats,* supervisors are seen as being primarily interested in rules and procedures for their own sake and as wanting to maintain and control the situation by their use, and they are viewed as being conscientious. As *deserters,* supervisors are seen as being uninvolved and passive.

Dedicated supervisors who are inspirational and driving forces given appropriate circumstances are seen as *benevolent autocrats,* but when this style is displayed in inappropriate situations, they are viewed as interfering,

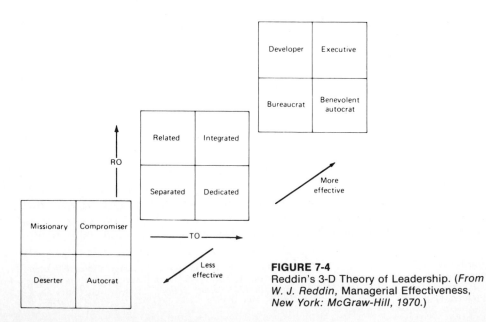

FIGURE 7-4
Reddin's 3-D Theory of Leadership. (*From W. J. Reddin,* Managerial Effectiveness, *New York: McGraw-Hill, 1970.*)

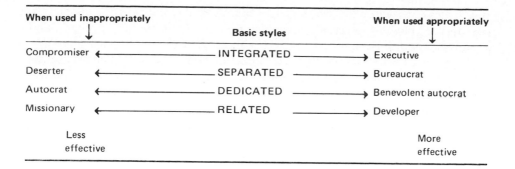

When used inappropriately	Basic styles	When used appropriately
↓		↓
Compromiser ←	INTEGRATED →	Executive
Deserter ←	SEPARATED →	Bureaucrat
Autocrat ←	DEDICATED →	Benevolent autocrat
Missionary ←	RELATED →	Developer
Less effective		More effective

FIGURE 7-5
Effective and ineffective expression of leadership style. (*From W. J. Reddin,* Managerial Effectiveness, *New York: McGraw-Hill, 1970, p. 40.*)

dominant, and *repressive autocrats*. In the first instance supervisors are seen as people who know what they want and know how to get it without causing resentment. In the second instance they are seen as people who have no confidence in others, as unpleasant, and as being interested only in the immediate job.

At first glance the theory seems complex and the labels chosen by Reddin confusing and on occasion inappropriate. But the language system is worth deciphering, for the concepts and ideas basic to the theory are powerful and important. A key to this theory is the notion that the *same* style expressed in different situations may be effective or ineffective. For example, a supervisor who uses the integrated style with a teacher who is in need of personal support may be seen as *compromising* the personal dimension by not giving exclusive attention to the needs of the individual. This same supervisor who relies exclusively on support and understanding when a teacher is searching for a task solution to a problem may be seen as a *missionary* lacking in forceful leadership. This related style, however, would have been perceived as being most effective in the first instance.

UNDERSTANDING SITUATIONAL LEADERSHIP VARIABLES

The situational determinants of leadership style effectiveness are difficult to identify and formally catalog. Nevertheless, some useful generalizations can be made about situational variables and their relationship to leadership style. With a little practice one's ability to match appropriate style to situation can be improved considerably.

Generally speaking, we can assume that educational settings and particularly leadership situations in schools will only occasionally call for separated and dedicated styles, for in each of these cases the human dimension is neglected. This generalization is consistent with the human resources model for supervision. Occasions will exist when styles that show low concern for people are appropriate, but the focus of leadership *in general* will be in the related and integrated quadrants.

A number of exceptions to this generalization come to mind. In each case the job demands are such that the dedicated style, which emphasizes task but not people, will probably be most effective. One exception deals with routine situations where goals and objectives are simple, clear, and uncontroversial, and where the paths to reach the goal are few in number and clearly marked. Another exception relates to situations where very favorable leader-member relationships exist. Here, members trust the leader and are willing to follow him or her. A third exception relates to situations characterized by excessive interpersonal tension, confusion, and stress. Short-term success in these situations can be accomplished through use of the dedicated style. The leader's formal position in the school hierarchy is another important condition. When too much positional or hierarchical distance exists between leader and members, it is often less stressful for everyone if the leader uses a more directive or task-oriented style. Other important considerations that influence choice of style include time constraints and competency and motivational levels of teachers. These and other variables one must consider in matching style to situation are discussed in the sections that follow.

CONTINGENCY LEADERSHIP THEORY (FIEDLER)

A new theory of leadership effectiveness has emerged from some 15 years of research conducted at the University of Illinois through its Group Effectiveness Laboratory and from work done at the University of Washington since 1970. This theory, developed by Fred Fiedler and his associates,[21] stems from a research tradition primarily associated with that of small-group psychology. The theory suggests that both task-oriented and relationship-oriented leaders are able to perform effectively in a group given conditions appropriate to and supportive of their leadership style. Further, the theory accepts the style of the leader as a given, and therefore recommends that the arrangement of tasks and situations accommodate leader styles rather than that styles change to fit situations.[22] Fiedler would suggest, for example, that the supervisor who is

[21] See Fred E. Fiedler, *A Theory of Leadership Effectiveness*, New York: McGraw-Hill, 1967, for a comprehensive treatment of this theory. More popular versions of the theory are found in Fiedler's "Engineering the Job to Fit the Manager," *Harvard Business Review*, vol. 43, no. 5, pp. 115–122, September 1965; "Style or Circumstance: The Leadership Enigma," *Psychology Today*, vol. 2, no. 10, pp. 38–43, March 1969; and Fiedler and Martin Chemers, *Leadership and Effective Management*, Glenview, Ill.: Scott, Foresman, 1974. These references form the basis of the following discussion.

[22] Leadership styles are measured by an instrument that yields a Least Preferred Co-Worker (LPC) score for respondents. Using an Osgood Semantic Differential format, respondents are asked to describe their least preferred co-worker on each of 16 dimensions. Those who describe this worker in a relatively positive sense are typed as relationship-oriented while those who describe him or her in a negative sense are typed as task-oriented. Fiedler presents impressive evidence supporting this method in chapter 3 of his book, *A Theory of Leadership Effectiveness*.

effective on a one-to-one basis with teachers because of the increased status this arrangement provides but is ineffective working with teachers as a group (group situations often decrease status differences between designated leaders and followers) should arrange for a pattern of supervision that favors the first situation and avoids the second.

The task-oriented leader in Fiedler's research corresponds to the dedicated-leadership designation of Reddin's theory, and the relationship-oriented leader to the related designation. Fiedler does not examine the separated and integrated styles.

Fiedler's extensive research strongly indicates that task-oriented leaders perform best in group situations that are either very favorable or very unfavorable to the leader. Relationship-oriented leaders, on the other hand, perform best in group situations that are intermediate in favorableness. Favorableness is defined by the degree to which the situation enables the leader to exert influence over the group.

Three major situational variables seem to determine whether a given situation is favorable or unfavorable to the leader. In order of importance they are listed as follows: (1) leader-member relations, which in our case refers to the extent teachers accept, admire, like, and are willing to follow individual supervisors because of the kind of people they are and the relationship they have developed with the teachers; (2) task structure, which in our case refers to the extent the work of the unit or person being supervised is structured, how clearly the objectives are defined, and how limited the processes available for achieving these objectives are; (3) position power, which in our case refers to the amount of formal authority and status the supervisor has.

Fiedler's Contingency Model

A simplified version of Fiedler's contingency model is presented in Figure 7-6.[23] This figure shows the effectiveness of relationship-oriented leadership versus task-oriented leadership for group situations characterized by different combinations of leader-member personal relationships, task structure, and leader position power.

Eight group situations are identified and categorized according to whether they are high or low on each of the three critical dimensions that determine the favorableness of a given style. The group situations are arranged in declining order of the leader's influence, with Cell 1 providing the leader with the most influence and Cell 8 the least influence. The leader, for example, who is well liked by group members, who is working in structured tasks, and who has a great deal of authority can exert strong influence on the group, while the

---

[23] The contingency model is constructed by plotting correlations of leadership style against the taxonomy of group situations. The approximate median correlations between leader LPC score and group performance plotted for each group situation (Cells 1 to 8 in Figure 7-1) are $-.55$, $-.60$, $-.30$, $.43$, $.40$; none available for Cell 6, $.3$, and -5.0 (Fiedler, *A Theory of Leadership Effectiveness*, p. 146).

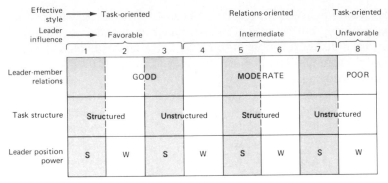

FIGURE 7-6
Fiedler's contingency theory of leadership.

opposite, the leader who is not liked, who has an unstructured assignment, and who comes with little authority has difficulty in exerting influence.

The contingency model suggests that task-oriented leaders perform best in situations that provide them with substantial influence *and* in situations that provide them with very little influence. Relationship-oriented leaders, on the other hand, are most effective in mixed situations that afford them moderate influence over the group. Leadership contexts 1 to 3, for example, provide the leader with the most favorable opportunities to influence the group, and Fiedler finds that task-oriented leadership is the most effective style. Leadership context 8 provides the leader with the least amount of influence on group members, and again the task-oriented or directive style is found to be effective. The remaining four contexts, according to the contingency leadership theory, seem best suited to the relationship-oriented style.

When supervisors have the respect and good wishes of teachers and a great deal of formal authority to back them up, exerting influence is easy. Personal relationships with teachers are such that teachers are more willing to follow. In addition position power is such that teachers more readily yield to the supervisor the right to lead. Combine these with a structured task, as in context 1, which tends not to call for much participation anyway, and we have the perfect setting for more task-oriented or dedicated leadership. Contexts 2 and 3 are not quite as favorable as 1 but possess enough of the same ingredient to permit easy influence.

Contexts 4 to 7, on the other hand, each require the supervisor to earn the right to lead, to win the loyalty and commitment of teachers, or, as in contexts 4 and 7, where tasks are unstructured, to depend upon the knowledge and abilities of others in order to be effective. In each case related and integrated styles are found to be more effective. Context 8 is so unfavorable that, at least for a short period of time, the more directive task style is recommended. As the supervisor works to improve the situation so that it approximates context 4, his or her style needs to change accordingly.

THE HERSEY AND BLANCHARD MODEL

Hersey and Blanchard's model of contingency leadership is a useful and well-known construct for understanding and guiding supervisory leadership. Relying on the traditional four-quadrant format, they suggest that the best leadership style is the one that matches the maturity level of followers. The essentials of their theory are shown in Figure 7-7. When the maturity level of followers is very low, they recommend that the supervisor use a direct and structured style characterized by high-task orientation and low-relationship orientation. As the maturity level increases in a particular individual, changes as individuals and groups change, or changes for an individual as the situation changes, supervisors should use a more integrated blend of task and relationship in their styles. A more participatory approach to leadership characterized by high-relationship orientation is recommended as maturity in followers continues to increase. And finally, for very mature followers who possess a great

FIGURE 7-7
The Hersey and Blanchard model emphasizing maturity.

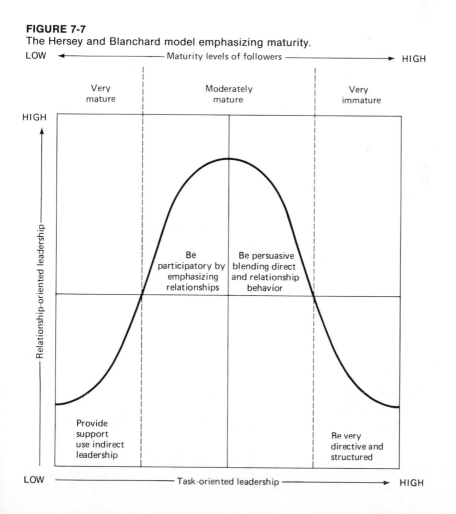

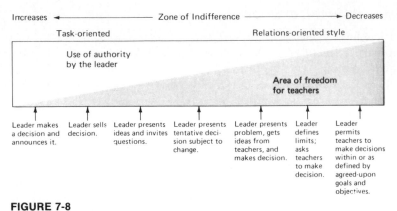

FIGURE 7-8
The zone of indifference. (*Adapted from Robert Tannenbaum and Warren Schmidt, "How to Choose a Leadership Pattern,"* Harvard Business Review, *vol. 36, no. 2, 1957.*)

deal of self-responsibility or a great deal of knowledge about a particular event, a less directive and unobtrusive style is recommended. In the language of Hersey and Blanchard, the emphasis in leadership shifts from telling to selling, participating, and delegating as maturity in followers increases. They define maturity as "the capacity to set high but attainable goals (achievement motivation), willingness and ability to take responsibility, and education and/or experience of an individual or a group."[24] The Hersey and Blanchard theory has great appeal because it is easy to learn and makes intuitive sense.

THE ZONE OF INDIFFERENCE

Not all teachers have a uniform desire to participate in the decision-making processes of the school nor for that matter do all teachers wish to be involved in the same things. When the context of decision making is of little or no concern to a teacher (that is, when it is in his or her zone of indifference), a more task-oriented approach from the leader would be appropriate.[25] Teachers, for example, are not likely to be terribly interested in many of the purely administrative or technical aspects of operating a particular unit and would probably be pleased by a supervisor who can regulate them in a dedicated but unobtrusive way. Teachers often resent being involved in events and activities they consider to be unimportant. As one's zone of indifference with reference to a particular issue decreases, however, one's desire to be involved increases, and this necessitates use of the more related and integrated styles. These relationships are shown in Figure 7-8.

A broad range of styles exists between the two extremes of task orientation and

---

[24] Paul Hersey and Kenneth H. Blanchard, *Management of Organizational Behavior: Utilizing Human Resources,* 3d ed., Englewood Cliffs, N.J.: Prentice-Hall, 1977, p. 161.

[25] This discussion follows Sergiovanni and D. Elliott, *Organizational and Educational Leadership in Elementary Schools,* Englewood Cliffs, N.J.: Prentice-Hall, 1975, pp. 108–109.

relationship orientation. It is difficult to conceptualize leadership on the task and relationship continuum only. For example, as one moves to the extreme right on Figure 7-8 to where the supervisor defines limits and asks teachers to make decisions and to where the supervisor permits teachers to function within limits defined by agreed-upon goals and objectives, concern for task and concern for people are both present. These are the essential character- istics of the integrated style. Nevertheless, it seems appropriate to gener- alize that as the substance of decision making moves closer to the classroom activities of teachers and as proposed changes in operation and procedure require attitudinal and behavioral changes from the teachers, the zone of indifference is likely to decrease. Teachers will be more concerned with the issues at hand and will want to be involved. In such cases, leadership styles that include a general component of relationship orientation (the related and integrated styles) are most likely to be effective. Moreoever, the relation- ship between styles of supervision and the level of teachers' interest holds for the relationship between styles of supervision and the competency, maturity, and commitment levels of teachers. The more competent teachers are, given a particular set of problems or tasks, the more appropriate are related and integrated styles. The less competent teachers are, given a set of problems and tasks, the more appropriate is the dedicated style.

CONTINGENCY LEADERSHIP THEORY (VROOM)

One important characteristic of leadership style is the emphasis, or lack of emphasis, given to the participation of subordinates in decision making. Dedicated and separated styles tend not to emphasize participation. Related and integrated styles, on the other hand, tend to emphasize participation.

Victor Vroom's theory of leadership focuses on this one important dimen- sion of leader behavior, the degree to which the supervisor should encourage participation of teachers in decision making.[26] In a typology similar to that proposed by Tannenbaum and Schmidt[27] as adapted in Figure 7-8 Vroom identifies five decision styles, or processes, that might be available for use by supervisors. This is a contingency approach in the sense that no one decision- making process is best under all circumstances and that the effectiveness of one's choice is dependent upon properties of the situation at hand. The decision styles are described as follows:

1 The supervisor solves the problem or makes the decision using information available at the time. This is an approach consistent with the dedicated style.

[26] See, for example, Victor Vroom, "A New Look at Managerial Decision-Making," *Organizational Dynamics,* vol. 1, 1973; Vroom and P. W. Yetton, "A Normative Model for Leadership Styles," in H. J. Leavitt and L. Pondy (eds.), *Readings in Managerial Psychology,* 2d ed., Chicago: University of Chicago Press, 1973; and Vroom, "Leadership Revisited," in Eugene Carr and Frederick Zimmer (eds.), *Man and Work in Society,* New York: Van Nostrand, 1975, pp. 220–234.

[27] Robert Tannenbaum and Warren Schmidt, "How to Choose a Leadership Pattern," *Harvard Business Review,* vol. 36, no. 2, pp. 95–101, 1957.

2 The supervisor obtains necessary information from teacher(s), then decides on the solution to the problem. The supervisor may or may not tell teachers much about the problem when obtaining information from them. The role of teachers in this case is in providing information—rather than generating or evaluating solutions. This approach combines aspects of the dedicated and separated leadership styles.

3 The supervisor shares the problems with relevant teachers individually, obtaining their ideas and suggestions without bringing them together as a group. Then the supervisor, at times being influenced by their advice and at other times not, makes the decision. This approach combines aspects of the dedicated and related leadership styles.

4 The supervisor shares the problem with teachers as a group, obtaining ideas and suggestions, and then makes the decision, which may or may not reflect the influence of teachers. The approach combines aspects of the integrated and dedicated leadership styles.

5 The supervisor shares the problem with teachers as a group. Together they generate and evaluate alternatives and attempt to reach agreement on a solution. The supervisor does not try to pressure the group to adopt his or her solution and is willing to accept and implement any solution that has the support of the group. This approach combines aspects of the related and integrated leadership styles.[28]

The supervisor determines which decision style is best for a particular situation on the basis of answers to seven critical questions, each of which defines and helps diagnose aspects of the problem at hand. Depending upon how the critical questions are answered, the supervisor is able to determine the best decision styles for this situation. This process, along with the critical questions, is illustrated in the form of a decision tree in Figure 7-9.

Letters A through H representing the eight critical questions are arranged along the top of Figure 7-9 in a fashion that elicits "yes" or "no" responses. To use the model, start with the box on the left-hand side of the diagram and ask question A. The answer, either "yes" or "no," determines the path to take on the decision tree. Continue to the right until you encounter a second box. Answer the question associated with that box and continue the process until a terminal node is reached. At that node you will find a number designating a range of feasible decision styles. This number and the range of decision styles are listed below the decision tree and correspond to the five decision styles discussed previously.

As an example, assume that in starting with square 1 to the left of the model, the answer to question A is "no." The supervisor would then follow the "no" branch of the decision tree to square 2 and respond to question D. A "yes" response to this question leads to square 3 and question E. A "no"

---

[28] Adapted from Vroom, "Leadership Revisited," in Carr and Zimmer (eds.), op. cit., p. 225.

Critical questions: A. Is there a quality requirement such that one solution is likely to be more rational than another?
B. Do I have sufficient info to make a high quality decision?
C. Is the problem structured?
D. Is acceptance of decision by subordinates critical to effective implementation?
E. If I were to make the decision by myself, is it reasonably certain that it would be accepted by my subordinates?
F. Do subordinates share the organizational goals to be attained in solving this problem?
G. Is conflict among subordinates likely in preferred soltuions? (This question is irrelevant to individual problems.)
H. Do subordinates have sufficient info to make a high·quality decision?

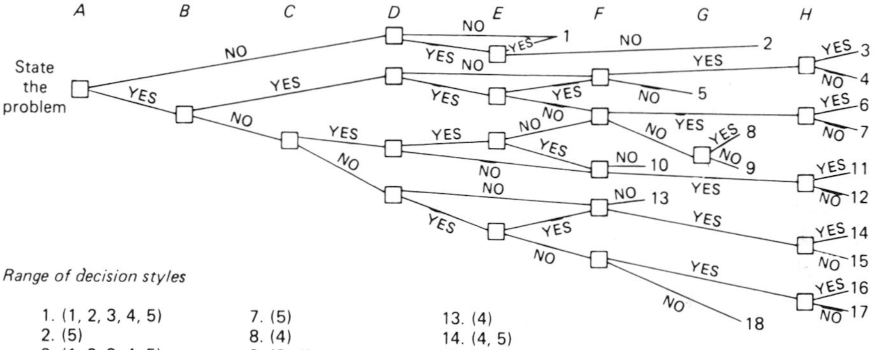

Range of decision styles

1. (1, 2, 3, 4, 5)
2. (5)
3. (1, 2, 3, 4, 5)
4. (1, 2, 3, 4, 5)
5. (1, 2, 3, 4)
6. (5)

7. (5)
8. (4)
9. (3, 4)
10. (2, 3, 4)
11. (2, 3, 4, 5)
12. (2, 3, 4, 5)

13. (4)
14. (4, 5)
15. (4, 5)
16. (5)
17. (5)
18. (4)

FIGURE 7-9
Vroom: Decision process flow chart. (*Adapted from Victor Vroom and Arthur Jago, "Decision-Making as a Social Process: Normative and Descriptive Models of Leadership Behavior," Technical Report No. 5, Organizational Effectiveness Research Programs, Office of Naval Research, N0014-67-A-0097-0027, A, 1974.*)

response to this question leads to a terminal node to the far right of the diagram. Here the supervisor finds the number 2, which prescribes the appropriate decision style range. Consulting the lower portion of Figure 7-10, we find that the number 2 suggests *only* decision style 5, which urges the supervisor to share the problem with the group and seek a consensus solution. Beginning again at square 1 to the far left of the model, we find that a "yes" answer to question A leads to square 2 under question B and so on, until the process has continued through the decision tree to another terminal node.

Notice that in a number of cases several decision styles are listed. Vroom suggests that though the listed styles represent the feasible range of options available, the supervisor must still select one decision style for implementation. Each of the styles is arranged in *ascending* order of time required for implementation and *descending* order in terms of potential for *development* of teachers. Decision style 1 is most efficient in time but promises the least in developing teachers. By contrast, decision style 5 is most costly in time but has the most potential for developing teachers. Vroom suggests that one should select the decision style furthest to the left (closest to 1) from among

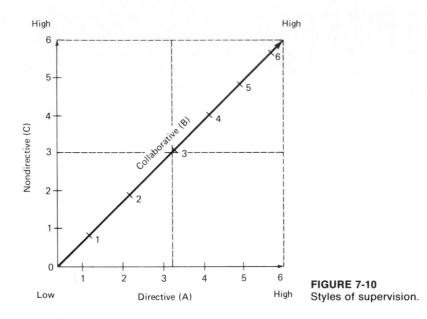

FIGURE 7-10
Styles of supervision.

those identified as feasible on the decision tree when time is scarce and furthest to the right (closest to 5) when time is plentiful.

In the case of schools where the development of human resources is particularly critical, the prudent supervisor will make every effort to choose decision styles closest to 5—that is, those with the greatest potential for developing teachers.

DEVELOPMENTAL SUPERVISION

Listed below are three groups of words: A, B, and C. They characterize ways in which a supervisor might work with teachers in improving instruction. Think about how you as a supervisor work with teachers in this capacity. If you are not a supervisor, think about the extent to which each of the three groups of words suggests how you might behave:

A	B	C
1. Telling	Presenting	Listening
2. Directing	Clarifying	Encouraging
3. Demonstrating	Listening	Clarifying
4. Standardizing	Problem solving	Presenting
5. Reinforcing	Negotiating	Problem solving

Rate *each group* of words on a 6-point scale with 6 as the high to reflect the extent to which each group describes your supervisory style.[29]

Glickman has proposed a useful model of leadership called Developmental Supervision, which is designed specifically for application to the context of supervising teachers to improve instruction.[30] He identifies three basic leadership orientations: directive, collaborative, and nondirective. The words in group A describe the directive style, those in group B the collaborative, and those in group C the nondirective. Figure 7-10 depicts the three styles of supervision superimposed on the traditional four-quadrant leadership grid. Use this figure to plot your A, B, and C scores. Note that high nondirective scores suggest a relationship style, high directive scores a task style, and high collaborative scores a team style.

Glickman proposes a contingency theory based on the premise that each of the styles of supervision might be appropriate or not given characteristics of the specific situation at hand. He suggests that two major characteristics be considered: commitment levels of teachers and abstract levels of teachers' thinking. Commitment is an essential ingredient in the concept of maturity as proposed by Hersey and Blanchard. Commitment can be conceived of as a continuum from low to high.

Abstract thinking refers to "a teacher's ability to stand back from his or her classroom, to clarify his or her own instructions (management, discipline, record keeping, organization, and student attitudes), determine alternative solutions to these problems and then to plan a course of action...."[31] Teachers high in the quality of abstract thinking are able to function more independently and with greater flexibility and complexity and are able to tolerate more ambiguity. In a fashion somewhat similar to the Hersey and Blanchard[32] leadership model, Glickman proposes a contingency model as follows:

1 Use more directive supervision when teacher levels of commitment and abstraction are low.

2 Use more collaborative supervision when teacher levels of commitment are low but levels of abstraction are high or when levels of abstraction are low and levels of commitment are high.

3 Use more indirect supervision when teacher levels of commitment and abstraction are both high.

Note that as teachers become more "mature" on the two dimensions proposed by Glickman, the emphasis shifts from more control to less control by the supervisor.

---

[29] Only a general indication of supervisory style can be obtained from this rating procedure. The descriptions are based on the Supervisory Beliefs Inventory developed by Carl D. Glickman and Roy T. Tamashiro. See Carl D. Glickman, *Developmental Supervision*, Alexandria, Va.: Association for Supervision and Curriculum Development, 1981, pp. 12–14.

[30] Ibid.

[31] Ibid., p. 44.

[32] Hersey and Blanchard, op. cit.

JOB DEMANDS AND LEADERSHIP EFFECTIVENESS

An additional set of concerns for supervisors interested in selecting leadership strategies in a manner consistent with contingency theory is the unique characteristics that define the job or task at hand. Job demands vary as objectives and tasks change or as attention shifts from one set of problems or objectives to another. In one situation, for example, the supervisor might be more expert than teachers, and in another case, they may be more expert than the supervisor.

Reddin suggests that as a general guide, if the problem and objectives currently in focus result in the following job demands and conditions, then the related style will probably be the most effective:[33]

- Teachers have high expertness or unusual technical skills.
- Teacher identification and commitment are necessary for success.
- The job is arranged in a way that teachers can largely decide how tasks will be accomplished.
- It is difficult to evaluate performance outcomes precisely.
- Teachers need to be creative and inventive in their work.

If the situation is such that the following job demands and conditions are present, then the separated style will probably be the most effective:

- The teacher's job is programmed in a routine fashion and requires the following of established procedures, curriculum formats, teaching strategies.
- The teacher's job is easy to perform and easy to regulate.
- Automatic feedback is provided so that the teacher can readily note her or his progress.
- Intellectual privacy and thinking are much more important than the teacher being actively involved in something.

If the situation is such that the following job demands and conditions are present, then the integrated style will probably be most effective:

- Teachers need to interact with each other in order to complete their tasks.
- Teachers are interdependent; the success of one depends upon the help of others, and vice versa.
- Successful completion of tasks requires that the supervisor must interact with teachers as a group.
- Several solutions are possible, and the number of solutions proposed and evaluated is improved by interaction among group members.
- Teachers can set their own pace as the group pursues its task.

---

[33] Charting job demands and relating them to leadership styles is an integral part of Reddin, *Managerial Effectiveness,* New York: McGraw-Hill, 1970, pp. 69–88. This section follows T. J. Sergiovanni, *Handbook for Effective Department Leadership in the Secondary Schools: Concepts and Practices,* Boston: Allyn and Bacon, 1977, pp. 151–152.

If the situation is such that the following job demands and conditions are present, then the dedicated style will probably be most effective:

- The supervisor knows more about the task or problems at hand than the teachers do.
- Numerous unplanned and unanticipated events are likely to occur which require attention from the supervisor.
- Teachers need to be given direction frequently in order for them to complete their task.
- The teacher's performance is readily measurable, and corrective actions by the supervisor are visible and can be easily evaluated.

NOTES ON CONTINGENCY THEORY

Contingency theories of leadership appear at the same time complex and accessible. On the one hand they portray leadership effectiveness in a fashion that causes one to grasp for the security of styles and modes that are familiar. On the other hand their sophistication carries promises of success far beyond that which one might realistically expect. Contingency theories are an improvement over "one best style" theories. They are indeed complex but can be learned and used by most supervisors. They do promise much and therefore may well disappoint many users. On balance we believe that mastery and use of contingency theories can help improve effectiveness, particularly if supervisors keep in mind that the phenomena of leadership still remain somewhat of a mystery and that to date all theories are at best partial explanations, unable to account for all the forces impinging upon leader effectiveness.

One consequence of focusing on the behavioral aspects of leadership and on developing leadership strategies is that the substance of leadership decisions may get slighted. The leadership skills associated with Supervision I are important, but they cannot guarantee genuine leadership if the leader does not have a clear sense of purpose and direction. This qualitative view of leadership, key to understanding Supervision II, is the topic of the next chapter.

SUMMARY

In this chapter leadership refers to the supervisor's ability to influence an individual or group toward the achievement of goals. This ability to influence can be enhanced by learning about and increasing one's own leadership style skills. Recognizing that what is appropriate in leadership may be less a function of how the supervisor behaves than of what he or she stands for, the importance of leadership style skills still cannnot be ignored. The link between management philosophy, supervisory assumptions, and resulting leadership behavior was then discussed. The assumptions basic to Theory X soft (human relations) were compared with those of Theory Y (human resources). It was pointed out that though Theory Y seems more clearly appropriate to human organizations such as schools this appropriateness does not preclude the use of a number of leadership approaches.

Forces in the supervisor, in the environment, and in subordinates were discussed as additional factors impinging upon choice of style. The leadership theories of Blake and Mouton (the managerial grid) and W. J. Reddin (3-D theory) were then discussed. Both theories are concerned with the task and relationship emphasis of the supervisor. Each describes basic styles of leadership as comprising a mix of emphases. In 3-D theory, it was suggested that though four basic styles (dedicated, related, integrated, and separated) could be identified no one best style is appropriate for all cases. Using Fiedler's contingency theory of leadership, the related and dedicated styles were selected for further examination. Leadership situations were defined by three critical variables—the quality of leader-member relationships, the extent to which the group task is structured or unstructured, and the position power of the leader. These variables were then used to identify situations for leadership and corresponding appropriate leadership styles. The popular Hersey and Blanchard model of leadership emphasizing maturity was then summarized.

The zone of indifference of teachers was also discussed as a further consideration in choosing an appropriate style. Vroom's contingency theory of leadership was offered as one approach that focuses on an aspect of leadership behavior of particular importance, the degree to which the leaders should encourage participation in decision making. Five decision styles were described, each effective in some situations but not in others. Vroom provides a methodology that uses a decision tree along which a subject is guided by answers to seven critical questions for determining which decision style is most appropriate to the situation at hand. Glickman's developmental supervisory model, a contingency model designed specifically for the context of supervision, was then briefly summarized. The chapter concluded with a discussion of the various job demands that need to be accounted for as leaders think about style issues and of cautions in using contingency theories as a framework for understanding leadership. In that discussion it was pointed out that focusing on the behavioral aspects of leadership and on developing leadership strategies without concern for the substance of leadership decisions was shortsighted. A discussion of the more qualitative aspects of leadership that concerned itself with visions or beliefs of leaders, consciousness of the dramatic possibilities for leadership, and philosophical and moral questions was promised for subsequent chapters.

STUDY GUIDE

Recall the concepts, ideas, and meanings associated with each of the following phrases and terms included in this chapter. Can you discuss each of them with a colleague and apply them to the supervisory context of your school? If you cannot, review them in the text and record the page numbers for future reference.

1 Contingency theory
2 Developmental supervision
3 Forces in others
4 Forces in the environment
5 Forces in the supervisor
6 Grid numbers
7 Job demands
8 Leadership styles
9 Management assumptions
10 Managerial grid
11 Pattern A
12 Pattern B
13 Self-fulfilling prophecy
14 Theory X
15 Theory X soft
16 Theory Y
17 3-D theory
18 Zone of indifference

EXERCISES

1 Contrast Theory X, Theory X soft, and Theory Y supervisory assumptions. Develop three teacher-evaluation policy statements with implementation guidelines—each based on one of the assumption sets.
2 Though the authors are committed to the values of Theory Y, they suggest that on occasions, *behavior* based on Theories X and X soft is justified. Provide examples suggesting when X or X soft behavior is appropriate.
3 List each of the behavioral indicators contained in Figure 7-3 on a separate sheet of paper, mixing the items so that they are not categorized. Role-play or actually ask teachers to select five of the 20 indicators that they expect supervisors to emphasize. Repeat this procedure with administrators and supervisors. Re-sort the selected indicators into the four grid categories. You should now have three sets of expectations for the supervisor's role. In what ways are these expectations similar and in what ways are they different? Where do differences occur (role conflict), and how might they be resolved?
4 Identify two or three decision-making problems, and analyze each using Vroom's decision tree. How would your analysis differ if you were using Fiedler's contingency theory? Which of the two approaches do you find more useful?
5 The leader's sense of purpose and mission is what elevates the mechanics of leadership (style, contingency theory, and so on) from mere social engineering to a human activity, and indeed this is the note upon which Chapter 7 ends. Where do you stand on the purpose and mission question? What hopes and aspirations do you have as a supervisor? Review your responses to these questions after reading Chapters 8 and 9.

SUBSTANTIVE THEORIES
OF LEADERSHIP

In the previous chapter we reviewed models of leadership which held sway for over thirty years. In distinguishing between these instrumental theories of leadership and what we are labeling in this chapter as substantive theories of leadership, we wish to call attention to the advances made in leadership research and theory in very recent years. Previous theories of leadership tended to be excessively reductionist, in that they reduced leadership to one or to a few variables (decision making; task or relations orientation, etc.).[1] They tended to focus on readily observable, short-term, leader-subordinate relationships, the easier to study empirical aspects of leadership.[2] By and large they tended to be culturally barren and politically naive.

Weber and then Mannheim in their studies of large-scale organizations developed a useful distinction between functional rationality and substantive rationality.[3] Functional rationality refers to the bureaucratic specialization and hierarchicalization of modern organizations. Organizations become organized according to specialized functions. As organizations become divided into more and more subunits, the larger sense of the organization becomes fragmented, thinned out, diminished. Substantive rationality, on the other hand, refers to

---

[1] J. G. Hunt, R. N. Osborn, and C. A. Schriesheim, "Some Neglected Areas of Leadership Research," *Proceedings of the Midwest Academy of Management*, 1978.

[2] M. W. McCall, Jr., *Leaders and Leadership: of Substance and Shadow*, Greensboro, N.C.: Center for Creative Leadership, Technical Report 2, 1977; Bernard M. Bass, *Stogdill's Handbook on Leadership*, New York: The Free Press, 1981, p. 611.

[3] Max Weber, *The Sociology of Religion*, Ephraim Fischoff (trans.), Boston: Beacon Press, 1963; Karl Mannheim, *Man and Society in an Age of Reconstruction*, London: Kegan Paul, Trench and Trubner, 1940. This distinction is aptly elaborated by S. N. Eisenstadt in *Max Weber: On Charisma and Institution Building*, Chicago: The University of Chicago Press, 1968, pp. li–lv.

the larger sense of meaning which the organization as a whole has. As such, the substantive rationality of the organization captures a large and expansive purpose and value.

Seen from this perspective, one could classify the instrumental theories of leadership also as focusing on the functional rationality of leadership. In turning to theories which tend to focus more on the substantive rationality, we wish to highlight the large sense of meaning and purpose which leaders call upon in their guidance of their constituents.

In recent years, several studies and theories of leadership have emerged. It will be helpful to review them briefly and then to incorporate their contributions into a useful framework by which to reflect on supervisory leadership. In so doing, we hope to fulfill a promise made in earlier chapters to enlarge on the emerging picture of Supervision II.

One source of new ideas on leadership comes from looking at organizations and, in particular, at schools as cultures. Sarason studied schools' resistance to change as a phenomenon of school culture.[4] More recently, the work of Deal and Kennedy has described elements of corporate culture with greater precision.[5] Beneath the surface of rationality, technology, and efficiency which most organizations exhibit, one finds a pattern of life where myths, heroes, demons, rituals, and ceremonies exercise a pervasive influence. These make up a tapestry of meaning which we call culture.[6] Within the school's culture, leadership is exercised, not in ways described by scientific management, but by guarding the values of the culture, by articulating those essential meanings of the culture, by promoting those rituals and celebrations which keep the values and principles for which the school stands.[7] As was noted in earlier chapters, schools tend to be loosely coupled organizations when viewed from a management control perspective. What binds the staff of a school together and generates cooperation and high morale is not a close monitoring of many specific details, but a strong adherence to the mission and purpose of schooling, an appreciation of the significance, some would call it the sacredness of teaching. The leader does not prescribe specific remedies for the multiple problems that arise in a school. Rather, the leader encourages the teachers to engage in a search for those solutions, guided by those essential values for which the school and the profession of teaching stand.

Besides cultural leadership, others have used the mission of the school as a focal point. Peter Vaill quotes Philip Selznick's descriptions of two essential functions of the leader as the "definition of institutional mission and role" and

---

[4] Seymour Sarason, *The Culture of School and the Problem of Change,* Boston: Allyn and Bacon, 1971.

[5] Terrence E. Deal and A. Kennedy, *Corporate Cultures,* Reading, Mass.: Jossey Bass, 1982.

[6] Terrence E. Deal, "The Culture of Schools," in Linda T. Sheive and Marian B. Schoenheit (eds.), *Leadership: Examining the Elusive,* Alexandria, Va.: Association for Supervision and Curriculum Development, 1987.

[7] Thomas J. Sergiovanni, "Theoretical Basis for Cultural Leadership," in Sheive and Schoenheit, op. cit.

the "institutional embodiment of purpose."[8] Vaill coins the word "purposing" to describe one of the essential activities of the leader of a high-performing system. By that he means "that continuous stream of actions by an organization's formal leadership which have the effect of inducing clarity, consensus, and commitment regarding the organization's basic purposes."[9] The leader feels strongly about the mission of the organization and hence constantly speaks about it. The leader is very clearly focused on those basic purposes and hence knows how to translate those basic purposes into priorities and into those key elements of the organization that support those basic purposes. Through the leader's dedication to achievement of those purposes no matter the cost, he or she comes to embody the values to which the institution is committed.

The cultural leader embraces the essential values in the culture. The high-performing leader constantly speaks of and exemplifies meanings and values fundamental to the organization. Despite different starting points, Vaill and Deal come to similar essentials of leadership.

In his Pulitzer prize winning book, *Leadership,* James McGregor Burns calls attention to a distinction between transactional and transformational leadership.[10] Transactional leadership frequently involves a *quid pro quo* between the leader and a follower, an exchange of a favor for a vote, a granted request here for a future request there. These transactions are governed by instrumental values or modal values such as fairness, honesty, loyalty, integrity. It is that leadership whereby one sees to it that procedures by which people enter into agreements are clear, above board, and take into account the rights and needs of others. It is the leadership of the administrator who sees to the day-to-day management of the system, listening to the complaints and concerns of various participants, arbitrating disputes fairly, holding people accountable to their job targets, providing necessary resources for the achievement of subunit goals, etc. Transactional leadership deals with people seeking their own individual, independent objectives. It involves a bargaining over the individual interests of people going their own separate ways.

Transformational leadership, on the other hand, involves an exchange among people seeking common aims, uniting them to go beyond their separate interests in the pursuit of higher goals. Transformational leadership is concerned with end values such as freedom, community, equity, justice, brotherhood. It is that leadership which calls people's attention to the basic purpose of the organization, to the relationship between the organization and society. Transforming leadership changes people's attitudes, values, and beliefs from being self-centered to higher, altruistic beliefs, attitudes, and values.

---

[8] Philip Selznick, *Leadership in Administration,* New York: Harper & Row, 1957, quoted in Peter B. Vaill, "The Purposing of High-Performing Systems," in Thomas J. Sergiovanni and John E. Corbally (eds.), *Leadership and Organizational Culture,* Urbana, Ill.: University of Illinois Press, 1984, p. 89.

[9] Vaill, op. cit., p. 91.

[10] James M. Burns, *Leadership,* New York: Harper Torchbooks, 1978.

Because both forms of leadership are guided by values, they may be called a form of moral action. In the next chapter we shall use Burns's distinction to examine supervision as moral action. For now it serves our purpose to note the stress Burns places on values and beliefs. Again, his leadership theory carries echoes of the work of Deal and Vaill.

John Gardner, long known for his thoughtful involvement with public affairs and himself a leader of several organizations, has recently added to his distinguished works several short monographs on leadership.[11] He, too, reaches beyond the narrow empirical categories of earlier theories to elaborate on leadership characteristics culled from his reading of history and from his own experience. He posits six characteristics of leaders, by which they distinguish themselves from the general run of administrators.

1 Leaders think longer-term; they look beyond immediate problems.

2 Leaders look beyond the agency or unit they are leading and grasp its relationship to larger realities of the organization, as well as the external environment.

3 Leaders reach and influence people beyond their own jurisdiction.

4 Leaders emphasize vision, values, and motivation; they intuitively grasp the nonrational and unconscious elements in the leader-constituent interaction.

5 Leaders have political skills to cope with conflicting requirements of multiple constituencies.

6 Leaders never accept the status quo; they always think in terms of renewal.

Warren Bennis and Burt Nanus have brought the term vision into center stage in the discussion of leadership.[12] Around that term they have built a theory of leadership and a program for leadership training. They interviewed 90 people whom their colleagues identified as exceptional leaders, and out of those interviews they culled four major themes. These leaders (1) focused their own attention and the attention of others on a vision; (2) communicated through symbol, rhetoric, and action the meanings embedded in their vision; (3) positioned themselves strategically within the field of competition to maximize their own organization's strengths to embody and communicate the vision; (4) embodied in their own person the quest for the vision through their competence and persistence.

Vision, symbolic meanings, purpose, culture, transformation—all relatively new terms in the literature on leadership. Some educators have been applying the principles proposed in Peters and Waterman's best seller, *In Search of Excellence*. That book contains many similar findings about the role of symbols, culture, and purpose.[13]

[11] John W. Gardner, *The Nature of Leadership: Introductory Considerations,* Leadership Papers/1; *The Tasks of Leadership,* Leadership Papers/2; *The Heart of the Matter,* Leadership Papers/3, Washington, D.C.: The Independent Sector, 1986.

[12] Warren Bennis and Burt Nanus, *Leaders: The Strategies of Taking Charge,* New York: Harper & Row, 1985.

[13] Thomas J. Peters and Robert H. Waterman, *In Search of Excellence,* New York: Harper & Row, 1982.

More recently, Peters has developed many of the ideas contained in the previous book into a theory of leadership.[14] His theory has four main components or areas of attention: customers (or clients), innovation, people (within the organization), and vision. The first three make up a kind of triangle, with vision as the energy and driving force within the space of that triangle. Again, Peters's theory echoes many of the more recent themes about leadership. Although most of this research and background relies on the field of commercial industries, his chapters on school leadership attempt to illustrate his theory by citing the example of three principals whose work was celebrated earlier in Lightfoot's *The Good High School.*[15]

Researchers in Texas studied characteristics of effective and less effective principals and found that vision was an important characteristic of the more effective principals.[16] An ASCD videotape, *The Effective Principal,* proposes five essential features of school principals, one of which is vision.[17] A recent ASCD yearbook carries these themes forward: culture, meaning, mindscape, vision, conscience, significance, purposing.[18]

These new developments in the study of leadership will continue to bring fresh insights. Nevertheless, one is left with the impression that we are still lacking a comprehensive theory of leadership. Such a theory would not only elaborate on the essential elements of leadership but would show the psychological and logical relationships between the elements of leadership in such a way that their organic relationships would be apparent. Vaill attempted this in his exposition of purposing as involving exceptional commitments of time, depth of feeling about purposes, and clarity of focus.[19] While this illuminates the work of the leader, it does not sufficiently explain how that sense of purpose becomes absorbed into institutional structures.[20] The work of Bennis and Nanus, Deal and Kennedy, McGregor, Burns, and Gardner—all brilliant in their own right—appears to leave out one or another element of a more comprehensive view of leadership.

In the remainder of this chapter we wish to present a theory of leadership which contributes to the mosaic of other theories of leadership but explores some elements more fully and develops relationships among other elements that have not been attempted in other theories. As we introduce this theory, it will be helpful to review how theories come to be developed, how, especially, this theory of leadership is built.

---

[14] Tom Peters and Nancy Austin, *A Passion for Excellence: The Leadership Difference,* New York: Warner Books, Inc., 1985.

[15] Sarah Lawrence Lightfoot, *The Good High School: Portraits of Character and Culture,* New York: Basic Books, 1983.

[16] William L. Rutherford, "School Principals as Effective Leaders," *Phi Delta Kappan,* vol. 67, no. 1, pp. 31–34, 1985.

[17] *The Effective Principal,* Alexandria, Va.: Association for Supervision and Curriculum Development, Videotape, 1985.

[18] Sheive and Schoenheit (eds.), op. cit.

[19] Vaill, op. cit., pp. 93–101.

[20] Cf. S. N. Eisenstadt (ed.), *Max Weber: Charisma and Institution Building,* op. cit., for a carefully reasoned exposition of the relationship between leadership and institution building.

LEADERSHIP AS AN ABSTRACTION

When we talk about leadership, we are using an abstraction to label a complex reality made up of many elements in dynamic interaction which surface at various times and in various ways and with various hues and tones in the life of a leader. To talk about leadership, we can point to specific actions a leader has taken and say, "that's an example of leadership." But because the concept "leadership" is so rich and complex, there are many different behaviors of leaders which we can point to as examples of leadership. Because it is an abstraction, it stands above the particular embodiment of it in any particular leader's behavior. As an abstraction we can analyze it by means of other abstractions and refine our understanding of it. We can try to break open the abstraction into component concepts. As we do this we are beginning to create a theory about leadership. We build a construct of these component concepts and show how they are logically and psychologically interdependent. We try to simplify the construct so that it contains only essential elements, but we also try to build a construct rich enough to describe the fullest or most perfect expression of leadership.

This theory of leadership will be such a construct. As such it will try to capture the essential elements of the abstraction we use to label the actions of leaders. Hence, it will leave out those aspects of leadership which might be found in the lives of some leaders but which are not essential to the exercise of leadership. As a theory, moreover, it will try to present leadership in its fullest expression, in the most perfect form. In this sense, the theory presents an "ideal type."[21] As such this ideal type will rarely, if ever, be found in any one leader. On the other hand, this ideal type will enable us to understand what leadership means in its richness and complexity. This understanding will help us evaluate whether and how various people exercise leadership.

THREE ASSUMPTIONS

This theory of leadership makes three important assumptions. The first assumption is that leadership implies a relationship to other people. Sometimes these people are referred to as followers, sometimes as companions, sometimes as colleagues, sometimes as fellow citizens. That relationship involves strong bonds of loyalty, commitment, and a shared sense of humanity. The second assumption is that leadership is exercised over time. Sometimes leadership is exercised in a burst of energy over two or three years and then subsides into activities that consolidate the gains made during these years. In other instances, leadership will mature and reach a sense of completion after 10 or 15 years of relatively routine activity. Leadership, as this theory presents it, cannot be exercised in a single act or event, as though nothing led up to it and nothing was

---

[21] Cf. Sonja M. Hunt, "The Role of Leadership in the Construction of Reality," in Barbara Kellerman (ed.), *Leadership: Multidisciplinary Perspectives,* Englewood Cliffs, N.J.: Prentice-Hall, 1984, p. 160. Cf. also Ernest Becker, *The Structure of Evil,* New York: The Free Press, 1968, pp. 28–32, for an illuminating discussion of the ideal type, as used by Rousseau.

required after the moment. The third assumption is that leadership takes place in relationship to some organization, institution, agency, or community. That is to say, we do not call leadership that activity, however heroic or creative, carried on by a single individual on the fringe of a group. That person may be an inventor, a pioneer, a prophet, a mystic, a genius, but if the activity does not engage other people in the pursuit of some common good, through a common effort, we do not call that the exercise of leadership. In positing leadership as necessarily relating to some social entity like a government or a business or a self-help organization, we include the activity of founding an organization where none had existed before or creating a new organization to replace another.

Implied in this theory of leadership, then, is activity in relationship to other people, exercised over time, and in relationship to some social organization. With these as basic assumptions, we may proceed to a further analysis of leadership.

1 Leadership is rooted in meaning. Leaders act out of deep convictions. These convictions are rooted in meanings, in central human values such as the dignity of human life, the promotion of scientific knowledge, the promotion of health or brotherhood, the need for social justice, or respect for law.[22] Sometimes these meanings carry unhealthy overtones, such as the promotion of one group's welfare at the expense of others. Some political leaders have based their leadership on narrow religious convictions which have led to repressive forms of government. Sometimes those core meanings center around competition, the joy of winning, the prestige of being the best.

More often than not, these core meanings lie deep inside the leader's own culture. The great political leaders have had that ability to probe those basic meanings within a people's history, those central symbols, myths, and concepts that give meaning to ordinary people's lives.[23] The great religious leaders, again, were people who probed beneath the surface and had some profoundly moving experiences in which they rooted their identity and their vision of what was important in life. Whatever the source, leaders tend to center their lives on those values. They dwell inside those core meanings, which become the criteria by which they measure other values, by which they make sense out of the world. Finally, these core meanings make up the foundation of leaders' vision of what they feel called to achieve.

So let that be the first generalization we can propose about leadership: *the inspiration of the leader comes from the leader's contact with meanings, realities, and values that lie beneath the surface of ordinary experience.*

2 Leadership emerges out of a vision. Leaders have a vision of what they and their colleagues can accomplish. While that vision flows out of the core

---

[22] Eisenstadt, op. cit., Vaill, op. cit., and Peters, op. cit., are especially insistent on this point. Cf. also Thomas J. Sergiovanni, "Leadership and Excellence in Schooling," *Educational Leadership*, vol. 41, no. 5, pp. 4–13, 1984.
[23] Cf. Burns, op. cit., passim.

meanings which guide the leader's basic approach to life, it usually has many particular features to it which imply an organizational structure of some kind. By the word vision we do not mean some mystical fantasy. Rather, the leader's vision tends to be a fairly detailed picture of a social unit of some kind, functioning in certain ways which achieve and reflect those core meanings and values at the center of the leader's consciousness. The vision is not something usually given in a flash. Usually it grows over time into something more specific. Sometimes the vision of the leader is based on the vision of a previous leader or on the vision of the founder of the organization. Martin Luther King had his vision of an American society in which black and white could live in brotherhood, a vision based not only on the founding fathers of his own country but also on the teachings of Gandhi and Jesus.

In the case of Horace Mann, one could point to his vision of a democratic society which had melded the various immigrant groups into an enlightened citizenry of one nation by means of a public school system. In the schools, the youth of these various immigrant groups would learn to respect each other's traditions, learn to live in social harmony, and participate together in the building of a free society. His vision in turn fed the vision of countless educators in the public schools who saw themselves as carriers of that sacred mission. John Dewey's writings and teaching helped to form the vision of other educators who went on to become leaders among their colleagues.

The second generalization about leadership is that the *force or compelling power of leadership flows from a shared vision of what a particular social institution might look like or become*. Those who join with the leader share that vision; it motivates them to move beyond the ordinary routine toward something more humanly significant. This element is coupled closely with the next.

3 Leadership emerges out of a dramatic sense. The leader tends to experience life as dramatic. Fed by contact with those central meanings in human life, the leader tends to perceive a drama being played out in human affairs. The leader tends to see the latent possibilities in a variety of circumstances, possibilities for achieving those values which are of central importance. For many people, life tends to go on in a routine; it takes on a predictable, repeatable pattern. There is little drama to the present moment, for it holds no profound possibilities. One day follows the other with a kind of flattened out sameness. The leader, on the contrary, seems driven to capture the significance of the moment. Leaders have about them a sense of excitement for they see the dramatic possibilities for achieving those values they believe so important. Because of the vision of what an organization can become or what it can achieve, a leader sees the ordinary activity of people in the organization as invested with significance, charged with meaning and possibilities.

Some think that leadership emerges only in times of crisis. At normal or ordinary times, people are content to leave well enough alone. When a crisis in the organization occurs, such as a threat of bankruptcy or a threat of a strike, the easy certainties which guide the daily routine lose their force. At times of crises, one is forced back to basics. Hence the leader who offers contact with that deeper or more central level of reality, who can offer a sense of what is real and permanent, who can help one interpret what is going on beyond the level of fear and anxiety, has great appeal.

This insight is quite true. Leadership frequently emerges in a crisis situation. The converse of this is also true; when things appear to be going smoothly, it is very difficult for leadership to emerge; people tend not to accept leadership initiatives when their organization appears to be healthy. However, leadership can be exercised outside of what we would normally call a crisis situation.

Leadership outside of crisis situations flows from the leader's dramatic consciousness. When we go to the theater to see a dramatic production, we experience life within the dramatic context of the stage. On the stage life is condensed and intensified; consequences immediately follow choices. On the stage we see the whole course of a character's life abruptly changed or summed up in one crucial choice. The actors reveal vividly the pain and joy which people cause one another. We identify with the characters. We wrestle with their dilemmas, shudder with their fear, rejoice with their triumphs.

Most of us experience our lives as stretching out over a dull canvas—with small joys and minor disappointments most of the time. Routine dulls the edge of excitement; the bureaucratization of social rituals distances the pain of others. The stage, on the other hand, shows us human life intensely lived. On the stage human actions and gestures appear to be enormously significant. We see that the character's life might have been different if only he had waited one minute longer for his friend, if only...if only....

The true leader enjoys this sense of drama inherent in human life, seeing the significance of what the group is or could be doing. Certainly, when an organization is approaching a crisis, the dramatic consciousness of the leader tends to perceive the crisis well before most others do. And in calmer weather, when the organization is functioning smoothly, the leader can still bring out or heighten the consciousness of the drama of their lives.

The leader of a school sees dramatic possibilities for teachers and students inherent in the everyday activities of the school. On any given day students may achieve a breakthrough in their studies or in some school activity that changes the whole course of their lives. On any given day, a teacher may discover a new way to approach a topic with students or may confront, for the first time, the seeming sterility of his or her life, and decide to do something about it. The leader of the school may also have strong convictions that what happens with the youngsters during the years in school is important for the future of their society. Unless they learn how to live together in some form of harmony, unless they learn how to settle their differences and conflicts in reasonable and nonviolent ways, unless they grapple with issues of the common good and come to appreciate their responsibilities as citizens, the fabric of society will tend to disintegrate. This educational leader will point that out to teachers, indicating that what they do with youngsters is enormously significant.

This leads to a third generalization about leadership: *the leader possesses a* dramatic sense about life and the lives of those in the organization. Leaders tend to perceive their lives as intensely significant, their work as accomplishing something very important, providing society with a service it very much needs.

4 Leadership requires the articulation of a vision and building a covenant. Leaders may have a vision of what their group could do or how their organization could serve its public more effectively, but they have to articulate that vision in ways that capture the imagination and enthusiasm of their fellows. Several considerations enter into this matter of articulation.

Most leaders do not develop their vision in isolation. Much of it comes from listening to other people, listening to their complaints, their sufferings, their dreams, their longings. Much of the vision will begin to be built in conversations with others, bringing their insights and suggestions into a fuller synthesis. While those core ideas and values of leaders provide the synthesizing force to their vision, it will be made up of many particulars derived from observations, reflection, discussion, and debate.

This larger vision which emerges from a collective belief and commitment comprises a set of shared values that forms for the school a binding covenant. This covenant provides a basis for developing norms that guide decisions and actions on the one hand and for making sense and deriving meaning and significance on the other.

Hence, when the leader begins to articulate a vision, the listeners will recognize some of their own ideas, their own dreams, their own points of reference. Yet they will also find themselves called to see those ideas and dreams against a new and larger landscape. What makes the vision of the leader appealing is that it takes the ideas of others, fuses them with a more fundamental meaning and value that is central to human life, and gives them a general, practical shape which the group can operationalize. That vision, however, is more than a mixture of self-interested ideas or subjective perspectives collected from the group. It usually calls the audience to reach beyond themselves and their own self-interest to collaborate in an effort beyond their own horizon, to pursue a cause greater than themselves.

The leader has to communicate a vision both in words and in example. This means using language and symbols which people can understand, but using them in such an original way that the vision can be seen in its freshness. Thus the leader frequently communicates the meaning clearly and engagingly in imagery and metaphor.

After the initial communication of a vision, the leader usually finds that followers will fall back on the old ways of doing or seeing things. Leaders must realize that this pattern will occur not because they reject the vision but mostly because of the force of routine. By repeated efforts leaders will invite them to participate on a continuing basis in the leaders' consciousness, to participate in the universe of meanings and perceptions and values that they, the leaders, inhabit. As the joint appeal of the leader's person and vision attracts followers with deeper fascination they will gradually begin, in fact, to see the world through the leader's eyes. Frequently enough, it is not so much putting on another's mind as it is recognizing that they occasionally see things exactly the way the leader does, but not with the same consistency or intensity of focus.

A leader has to explicate a vision in terms with which followers or an audience are familiar, and yet in ways which will stretch their intelligence and imagination beyond the stereotypes which they currently use to interpret reality. Moreover, the leader must recognize the need for consistent and persistent communication of that vision, for what is involved for followers is a reordering of their habitual ways of seeing and doing things. The leader needs to help them with the transformation or reformation of their perceptual, cognitive, and symbolic frameworks.

One hears a lot about participative decision making and democratic processes in the management literature. Those proponents might object at this point to what might be perceived in their theory as a tendency toward autocratic demagoguery. That is, doesn't this talk about the leader's vision allow for all kinds of charlatans to captivate an audience with irresponsible promises and rhetorical fantasies? Such deceits happen every day, and that is why, in fact, many people are so wary of anyone who comes along with a new vision. The willingness of some to quickly lend their allegiance to any new cause or movement, on the other hand, can become a trap for anyone aspiring to leadership. Such quick allegiance and adulation can create the impression that the leader actually has a power over the lives of followers, and that illusion can lead to other mistakes.

At this point it must be plainly admitted that this element of leadership has its dark and its bright possibilities. On the one hand we can point to the almost pathological willingness of mobs of people to follow a demagogue who offers them a vision of their own glorification. We can also see how these demagogues have used their vision, their cause, to justify any actions, no matter how cruel, as long as it was a step toward their goals. On the other hand, we can point to other leaders who had a vision of humanity's best possibilities and who called others to join in a collaborative effort to achieve at least some of those possibilities.[24] Whether that led to the founding of a nation, of a religious community, of a hospital for incurables, of a chapter of Alcoholics Anonymous, we can point to instances where the vision of the leader or leaders was the key to mobilizing enormous reserves of human energy for the achievement of some noble purpose.

In the case of educational leaders, their vision of what a school might be, or of what learning could mean for students and society, or of what a profound vocation the craft of teaching is—in almost every instance the substance of that vision has already been proposed whether by Plato or Dewey, by Jefferson or Whitehead, by Isocrates or Pestalozzi, and by any number of school boards. In one sense, such a long tradition of statements on the nature and importance of education provides a healthy corrective to any vision of education that is

[24] Cf. Eisenstadt, op. cit., p. xxiv.

narrowly or irresponsibly conceived. What makes the difference for leaders is that, unlike ordinary administrators, they are possessed by the profound awareness of the crucial importance of educating the young, as well as by an intrinsic delight in the blossoming of human potential. The philosophy and objectives statement of the school board, so often a dull and lifeless recital of platitudes, can become infused by the dramatic consciousness of the leader and be transformed into a clarion call to a grand and noble work. To the jaded sensibility of contemporary professionals, that may sound just a bit overblown. But when one listens to leaders articulating their vision, it does in fact sound like a clarion call.

In the matter of articulating the vision of what the school can be for youngsters and for society, the leader will be appealing to a sense of altruism among the faculty. "We can be a significant force for good in the lives of our students." "We can build a great society by nurturing the quest for greatness in our students." "We hold the future in our hands." "We are building a brighter tomorrow." Likewise, we hear other educational leaders say to their constituencies: "We can be the best school in the district or in the region." "We can be the beacon showing other schools the way to truly effective education." "We can be the place where other teachers come to learn how to be great teachers."

Those kinds of appeals, of course, have to be backed up with more specific elements of an overall vision, or they degenerate into jingoism. Nonetheless, we can begin to see how important it is to invite the faculty to exercise their heroism on behalf of society, as they fulfill the noble calling of nurturing the minds, hearts, and multiple human talents of youth.

This theory of leadership simply asserts that every human being is capable of heroism. In proposing a vision of what the faculty can achieve, the leader will invite colleagues to activate that heroic potential, not necessarily by using overblown imagery but by speaking about the marvelous everyday possibilities for growth and insight that are available in and outside the classroom.

In speaking about teachers acting heroically, we are speaking of rather prosaic forms of heroism, such as the teacher who gives up a weekend to go on a wilderness trip with students, or the teacher who faithfully corrects homework every day, or the teacher who works with students after school on material they are having trouble with, or the teacher who takes the time to listen to the fears and frustrations of another teacher going through a difficult time. The school day is filled with examples of this kind of heroism in many schools. In schoolwide awards ceremonies, this kind of commitment can be celebrated by a "Teacher of the Year" or "Teacher for the Month" award.[25]

Leaders must go beyond merely speaking about what the school could be. They must create conditions that enable colleagues to experience some of those possibilities. If that vision includes a deep sense of community among the students, the leader will create opportunities for both students and faculty to communicate in ways that build up trust, that help them to experience

---

[25] Peters gives many examples of the effect of praise and applause, op cit., chap. 15.

reconciliation after a rift, that enable them to take responsibility for maintaining the quality of community life. In these experiences, they will understand the vision of the leader more sharply than by simply listening to words. Therefore, leaders will have to risk some new activities for people in the school in order for them to know experientially what they are talking about as they strive to articulate a vision. Certainly their own behavior should embody those values they seek to promise in their vision, so that people who come into contact with them will recognize the consistency between their words and actions.

Key to the concept of vision is the building of a shared covenant for the school. The very point of leadership is missed should the leader be remiss in expressing and articulating values and dreams. But a vision must reflect, as well, the hopes and dreams, the needs and interests, the beliefs and values of the group. When a vision embodies the collective sharing of ideals, a school convenant is struck that bonds administrators, supervisors, teachers, and students in a common cause. This shared covenant provides the school and its members with a set of norms for guiding action, a sense of purpose and direction and source of meaning and significance. When one unravels and peels away the formal structure and arrangement of successful enterprises one finds that such a covenant exists beneath the surface, and key to this shared covenant is a leader with a vision.

Our fourth generalization about leadership is that *the leader must articulate the vision of what the group can accomplish in ways that capture the imagination and the heroic impulses of colleagues. That articulation must be accompanied by activities in which the group can actually experience what the leader is trying to articulate.*

5 The leader will embody the vision in organizational structures, policies, and procedures. Now we come to one of the crucial aspects of leadership. It is at this point that the leader turns to the long-range program required to bring the vision into reality. Most leaders work within some organizational context. They will inherit an already functioning organization or they will found an organization. In any case, the leader's vision will become operational in and through an organization.[26] Once the group has captured the essence of the leader's vision, they need to be engaged in purposeful activity that will channel their energies in the direction of the vision. That channeling is achieved through the organization.

Every school as an organization has organizational structures. Organizational structures are those ways by which an organization orders and regularizes the energies of its participants in the performance of its tasks. In a factory, the assembly line is a way of ordering the tasks that people perform; it

---

[26] Eisenstadt makes this point very well. Cf. also Thomas J. Sergiovanni, "Leadership and Excellence in Schooling," Stuart Ranson, Robert Hinings, and Royston Greenwood, "The Structuring of Organizational Structures," *Administrative Science Quarterly,* vol. 25, pp. 1–17, March 1980; Edgar H. Schein, *Organizational Culture and Leadership,* San Francisco: Jossey Bass, 1980. Schein proposes a somewhat contrary perspective, namely, that structural changes emerge by trial and error and then become rationalized in the rhetoric of the leader.

structures the work that people do. In a hospital, one can follow patients as they move along a kind of assembly line of health services until released from the hospital. There are those who test the blood, those who x-ray, those who cook the food, those who prescribe medicines, those who admit patients and assign them to various floors, and those who perform operations. There is a uniform pattern to those activities that orders, organizes, and structures the activities of people who work in the hospital.

Moreover, there are procedures that people in the organization at these various stations employ. The nurse has a routine which is followed in administering services to the patient. There are billing procedures that people in the business office follow. There are emergency procedures which all staff follow at certain times.

A school is also made up of organizational structures, policies, and procedures. If one wants to compare a school with a hospital, there are a variety of services that are offered to students—from the time they register for courses at the school to the time they graduate. They are scheduled for classes, assigned to classrooms, buy books, get daily assignments, take tests at certain times, get graded at certain times, are expected to follow certain rules while in the school, etc. The school structures or orders their activity in these ways.

People with professional responsibilities for these services follow certain procedures, as do the students. There are procedures for choosing courses, for doing homework, for behaving in the cafeteria, for signing up for extracurriculars, for reporting to the dean of students after an absence, etc. Unlike some institutions' procedures, however, the school's procedures are supposed to be flexible enough to respond to individual students whose circumstances vary from the norm.

These procedures are frequently governed by policies. A school will have a policy on promotions to higher grades, a policy governing suspensions and expulsions, a policy on participating in athletics with academic deficiencies. These policies tend to support and reinforce basic values which the school stands for. They are supposed to govern making the vision operational.

Leaders understand that the organization of the school carries the real message of what they and the faculty believe about the purposes of schooling. Insofar as that message conflicts with the leader's vision of what the school should be, those organizational structures must be changed to reflect that vision more consistently. Sometimes structures, policies, or procedures which once served useful purposes have become obsolete or dysfunctional owing to changes in the environment and clientele of the school. Leaders must call attention to these and, with a reminder of those large purposes which the structures of the school should be serving, enlist their help in creating new ones.

In bringing the vision into practice, in embedding that vision in organizational structures, policies, and procedures, the leader moves away from his or her own person being the source of inspiration for the group. The daily experience of task achievement and fulfillment by the teachers and students provides the intrinsic reward and motivation. Guided by the organizational structures, policies, and procedures which inform their decisions in the direction of that vision, the group in a sense no longer needs the leader. What the leader stood for tends to become reflected in the group life within the organization.

Leaders, then, must have this profound conviction that their real work is institution building. The generation and articulation of the vision, the gathering of colleagues and companions who want to follow that vision are all preliminary steps to that major undertaking: building an institution which will pursue the accomplishment of the vision. As that gets underway, the leader will have to work painstakingly to see that the organizational structures, policies, and procedures do not become ends in themselves, but rather that they reflect very intentionally and explicitly specific elements of the vision. For example, a school which is built around the vision of a learning community will have different organizational structures, policies, and procedures from those of a school built around rugged individualism.

Sometimes the leader may not possess organizational design and engineering skills. It will be important for him or her to enlist the help of those who do. In the case of a school, this might mean someone who is adept at creating variable and flexible schedules and another who is creative in suggesting various learning environments. More often than not, the leader's intuitive grasp of the implications of the vision will lead him or her to recognize viable expressions of the vision in specific organizational arrangements.

We may then summarize this fifth generalization about leadership: *leadership requires institution building*. Through an organization or institution the necessary resources are brought to bear on the pursuit or achievement of the group's vision. The institution provides for the continuation over an extended period of time of the corporate effort of the group. It routinizes the vision by embodying the vision in structures, policies, and procedures which both reflect the values and meanings in the vision and channel the energies and activities of the group toward the achievement of the vision.

6 Leadership provides mechanisms for the continuous or periodic renewal of the institution. This is frequently the most neglected aspect of leadership. Having succeeded in gathering a group of companions who commit themselves to the achievement or pursuit of a common vision, and having succeeded in reforming or forming an organization that reflects and effects the vision, most leaders rest content (and deservedly so). The temptation is to think that the present organization is the best and permanent embodiment of the vision.

The realities of organizational or institutional life, however, reveal that any institution, no matter how noble and effective, goes through periods of decline, leading for some to extinction, for others to a transformation into something quite other than the original founders intended, for others to a renewal of its original sense of vitality and mission.

First of all, not all aspects of the school life will be formed deductively from blueprints drawn from the vision. Many organizational formats will emerge in the process of tinkering with various organizational arrangements.[27] Intuitions fed by the group's vision will lead them to recognize appropriate organizational structures which might emerge out of trial and error. Likewise, new elements will be added over time as various members of the group bring their own creativity and insight to various organizational tasks. Furthermore, there is no one best and perfect set of organizational structures, policies, and procedures that will perfectly fit a specific vision. Hence, there should always be room for major organizational rearrangements. The crucial consideration is that they should not inhibit the central elements of the vision from being effectively operationalized; on the contrary, they should be justified precisely on the grounds that they better promote the operationalization of the vision.

Another obvious fact about institutional life is that the immediate as well as larger environment of the institution is constantly undergoing flux. New technologies emerge which impact people's life styles (e.g., laser beams). New life styles emerge which impact how people structure their time (e.g., single parent families, working mothers). New cultural forms emerge which alter the way people think about themselves (e.g., the feminist revolution or attitudes that black is beautiful or that handicapped people are deserving of equal employment and educational opportunities). Changes in the environment often require restructuring of the school, along with new policies and procedures. When these occur the question is: do these changes in our structures still reflect the vision of what the school is basically supposed to be?

A third reason for building in self-renewing mechanisms is that structures, policies, and procedures have a way of becoming ends in themselves, rather than serving as means to an end. When they become ends in themselves, they can and usually do become rigid and oppressive. They tend to stifle the creativity and autonomy of people in the organization. Before long, people begin to be treated as means to an end. The institution, not the larger society it was established to serve, becomes the primary value. Clearly a mechanism of self-renewal for any institution has to include a periodic evaluation of organizational structures, policies, and procedures, as well as a constitutional or parliamentary procedure for changing them. Hence, one of the essential characteristics of schools should be that they are, by definition, self-renewing.

Beyond the provision for periodic assessment and restructuring, a self-renewing institution must ensure that the constellation of meanings, values, and purposes—those things that make up and serve as the life blood, the energizers, of the culture of the institution—be exercised in the daily life of the institution. Members of the school community would need to remind themselves of what they stood for through a variety of rituals, celebrations, ceremonies, and daily activities. Some schools display the school motto or coat of arms in conspicuous places around the school. Sports rallies frequently include the school song. Awards ceremonies tend to call attention to cultural values which the school community cherishes, values such as service, creativ-

---

[27] Ranson, Hinings, and Greenwood elaborate on the evolution of organizational structures.

ity, citizenship, and community spirit. Sometimes buttons and hats will carry messages that advertise sentiments and values important to the school. Sometimes teachers will write the school motto on the top of a test or on messages to students and their parents. Some principals use their column in the student newspaper to reinforce central values. Of course, such attempts to highlight values, customs, and traditions can generate cynicism when the school community does not consistently practice them. On the other hand, such efforts do remind the community of the vision they have of themselves and encourage the living out of that vision in action. In the periodic self-assessment, the use and effectiveness of these cultural expressions of the vision should receive special scrutiny.

Hence our final generalization about leadership is this: *the leader provides for the ongoing cultural celebration of the vision on a daily basis, as well as provides for periodic major assessment and renewal.*

In providing this theory of leadership, we attempted to utilize the insights of recent theorists, but put them in a framework that is most amenable to educational leadership. The six elements of this theory of leadership are arranged in a logical order; that is, one element depends on the one before it for its grounding, and one element flows naturally into the next one. Psychologically, the sequence of elements tries to respect the way persons think, feel, and act. The theory is "lean," in that it does not include activities that are often associated with leadership (e.g., decision making, creativity, political bargaining). Those activities frequently do come into play in the practical exercise of leadership, but they are not seen as making up those basic essentials of leadership. Moreover, the six elements we have identified tend to distinguish leaders from managers.[28]

Some would argue that this theory ignores the politics of leadership. Political adroitness is indeed called for in the exercise of leadership, but it is not the point of leadership. The point of leadership is the communal institutionalizing of a vision of human greatness. Just as technical managerial skills will be called into play to effect the institutionalization of the vision, so too will political skills. But political skills are not one of those essential elements of leadership. If one takes away one of the six elements, one knows instinctively that the unity of the construct is destroyed.

On the other hand, we must remember that this theory represents an "ideal type," that is, a picture of leadership in its rich complexity. Rarely, if ever, will we find these six elements fully revealed in any leader. Some will have strengths in some elements, some in other elements. The theory helps us to see where leadership has fallen short in any given case; it also enables us to reach for an agenda that will always call for the best that is in us.

---

[28] One theory of leadership which has not been included in our survey of contemporary writers is that of Christopher Hodgkinson, *The Philosophy of Leadership,* Oxford: Basil Blackwell, 1983. Hodgkinson firmly denies any distinction between administration and leadership. On the other hand, he would very strongly argue for a value perspective on administration.

We are labeling this theory of leadership, "the communal institutionalizing of a vision." Such a label places vision at the center of the enterprise; it also stresses the reciprocal dependence of the leader upon the community and the community upon the leader; finally it emphasizes that the vision must be embedded in an institution so that it will have a permanency and continuity as well as a solidity to its impact on society. Figure 8-1 provides a view of this process as it moves from its mythic roots to its daily operationalization in an institutional setting.

Such a sense of the movement of leadership from a grounding in meaning into the development of a vision and its gradual institutionalization enables us to see leadership as a force that is expressed at four levels, each of which interpenetrates each other.[29] The *cultural-symbolic force of leadership* expresses those essential meanings, values, and purposes of the school. It speaks the vision in imagery, metaphor, symbol; in ritual, songs, celebration; in purposing, correcting, and modeling. The *educational force of leadership* expresses those specifically educational concerns whether they are framed in child development or learning theory terminology, in socialization or citizenship categories, in curriculum design or instructional program frameworks. The *human force of leadership* is expressed in words and actions of caring, trust, empowerment, community building, reconciliation, reaching for ideals, human potential, uniqueness. The *technical force of leadership* is expressed in bringing the vision into reality in and through institutional structures, policies, and programs.

IMPLICATIONS FOR SUPERVISORY PRACTICE

In proposing an emerging model of supervision, Supervision II, we stressed that the various theories, paradigms, and research conclusions which are presented in this book are not meant to be naively applied to practice. Rather, they are to inform the reflections and practice of supervisors as they find them useful in meeting the many demands of their work days. So too, this theory of leadership does not offer a series of prescriptions for supervisors. Rather it may be a help in certain (not all) circumstances, as the supervisor tries to make sense out of his or her own motives and meanings or to understand a procedural problem that is blocking effectiveness with a teacher.

The elements of vision, drama, articulating vision with others, changing institutional procedures to conform to the vision, cultural expressions of the vision—these will illuminate some issues but not others in the everyday life of the school. In some cases they will reinforce practices already in place. In other cases, they will suggest a way of posing a question to a teacher or to another administrator. They will encourage some to reach out for the leadership opportunities their job affords them. They will enable others to collaborate more readily in a team leadership initiative.

[29] Cf. Thomas J. Sergiovanni, "Leadership and Excellence in Schooling," *Educational Leadership*, vol. 41, no. 5, Feb. 1984.

ROOTS OF THE VISION	ARTICULATION OF THE VISION	INSTITUTIONALIZATION OF THE VISION	OPERATIONALIZATION OF THE VISION
Meanings associated with: Human destiny The nature of human person The nature of human society View of the past and of the future Frequently embedded in imagery, metaphor, myth and story	Beliefs about: — the human mind and how one knows — how children develop as full human beings — how children should be socialized — varieties of human learning — moral values — political values — religious values — what kind of future the young will face	Formal Statement of the Mission of the School Cultural purposes Political purposes Academic purposes Moral purposes Economic purposes Social purposes Religious purposes Processes of Communicating the Vision — Thematic purposing — Rituals — Celebrations — Championing — Heroes — Rewards	Formal Organization Policies Programs Procedures — Graduation requirements — Curriculum — Course selection and assignment — Grading criteria — Discipline — Student activities — Staffing — Budget Informal Organization — Community spirit — Style of communications — Tone of relationships — Informal group — Informal curriculum	Woodrow Wilson School a school that opens its doors every day and looks like: People coming and going to — classes — activities — interactions making up a fabric of experience — meanings — patterns — rituals — symbolic action — celebration
MYTH	ASSUMPTIONS, BELIEFS	GOALS, OBJECTIVES	POLICIES, PROGRAMS STRUCTURES	OPERATIONS

FIGURE 8-1
The communal institutionalization of vision.

SUMMARY

In this chapter, we have presented an overview of more recent theories of leadership. We have labeled these theories substantive, because they attempt to get at the substance rather than the form or style of leadership. These theories tend to highlight meaning, purpose, value, and vision. In attempting a synthesis or a more comprehensive theory of leadership, we wished to tie elements of leadership more tightly together and to illustrate from the context of schooling what such elements of leadership might mean. Although an ideal type, this substantive theory of leadership offers a framework for reflective practice for the conscientious supervisor.

STUDY GUIDE

Recall the concepts, ideas, and meanings associated with each of the following phrases and terms included in this chapter. Can you discuss them with a colleague and apply them to the supervisory context of your school? If you cannot, review them in the text and record the page numbers for future reference.

1 Dramatic sense of the leader
2 Communal institutionalizing of a vision
3 Leadership as an abstraction
4 Purposing
5 Transformational leadership
6 Functional rationality

EXERCISES

1 What is involved in the articulation of the vision?
2 Think about your school. What organizational structures block or impede the vision of what the school should be? How would you change those structures to promote the vision?
3 What are the ways your school celebrates those values central to its culture?

SUPERVISION AS
MORAL ACTION

Even ten years ago, it would have seemed embarrassing for professionals and scholars in the field of supervision to talk of supervision as moral action. The literature on supervision had been and continues to be dominated by language and imagery borrowed from the mainstream social sciences of psychology and sociology. Those sciences had attempted to model themselves on the natural sciences in an effort to reproduce similarly objective findings, "value-free" facts and theories, generated by methods that were supposed to screen out subjective impressions, ideological points of views, imaginative speculation, and the like.

Driven by the models of the natural sciences, these social scientists sought to identify quasi-cause-effect relationships that were supposed to ground the intelligibility of phenomena. In this effort social scientists tended to reduce complex social realities such as business organizations, churches, schools, and political parties to a few simple factors. They assumed, for example, that human beings were simple stimulus-response organisms that would tend always to respond uniformly to the same stimulus given the same set of circumstances. By reducing human beings and the interactions between them to matters of stimulus-response and to need-dominated behavior, psychologists and sociologists sought to arrive at fundamental explanations of human behavior that could be traced back to a few, relatively simple variables.

In the last ten years there have been challenges to this positivistic, empiricist, reductionist approach to explaining social systems. More sociologists and social psychologists have begun to include human persons in all their complexity as a central factor in their study of why social systems do or do not work.[1] In these emerging perspectives, the person is seen in a much richer light, as someone questing for meaning and purpose in daily life, as exercising moral agency and seeking for self-fulfillment. Moreover, life in organizations is coming to be seen as far more complex, as involving rational thinking, consideration of social consequences, emotional responses, political influence peddling, ego investment, shifting power alliances, etc.

With this recent shift in mind, we propose in this chapter to consider supervision as moral action. First there will be an explanation of the difference between "behavior" and "action." That will be followed by considering some of those factors which tend to diminish supervision as moral action. That will lead to an examination of those conditions which will enable supervision to become a moral action. Using a distinction from James McGregor Burns's theory of leadership, we will describe supervision both as transactional moral action and also as transformational moral action. The chapter will conclude with a brief commentary on supervision as the politics of the possible.

ACTION VERSUS BEHAVIOR

Although to some it may seem a quibble over words, there is an important distinction to be made between speaking of what human beings do as "behavior" or speaking of it as "action." Behavior is a term used to denote human action seen on the surface. It assumes that it is an activity brought about by some stimulus. It does not imply intentionality on the part of the person behaving. It does not imply free choice, value seeking, or altruism. Neither does it explicitly deny them. It considers merely what is observable, measurable, quantifiable; what fits into an observable pattern of relationships between what preceded and what followed. Behavior is what an organism—cactus, donkey, rose, eagle, London banker, a month-old male baby—does in response to some stimulus or other. That organism is studied under various conditions to see whether the same stimulus is associated with this same response often enough to be statistically significant (not due to random chance or other factors).

Seen in this light, the use of the term "supervisory behavior" usually refers to actions by supervisors that have been associated with positive or negative reactions on the part of teachers or administrators or political authorities, etc. Those associations have been documented by research and evaluation studies as occurring at levels of statistical significance. In the process of defining those associations, the studies employed conceptual simplifications which stripped the activity of its uniqueness and reduced it to a common denominator such as "friendly" or "positive reinforcement" or "directive" or "nondirective" or "authoritarian" or "democratic" or some such univocally chiseled concept. These studies usually claimed a level of objectivity; that is, they were free from the subjective bias of the one doing the study or from any ideological point of view. The study

---

[1] Cf. Bruce J. Jennings' "Interpretive Social Sciences and Policy Analysis," in Daniel Callahan and Bruce Jennings (eds.), *Ethics, The Social Sciences and Policy Analysis,* New York: Plenum Press, 1983, pp. 3–35.

simply reported "factual data," what was "really going on." If others had done the study on the same group using the same methods of research, they would have come up with the same conclusions. If the study were to have greater generalizing ability, however, it would need to be repeated on several other sample populations and be conducted by different people using the same methods of research. An even greater attribution of validity and reliability would be gained if the same findings were generated by several research methods (e.g., by experimental, survey, and in-depth interview methods).

A multiplicity of studies conducted over decades on various aspects of what supervisors do gradually accumulates into a "literature of supervisory behavior." This literature enables us to perceive large patterns of human activity within various social contents. It tells us what "tends to work," what "tends to happen when supervisors behave according to one style rather than another."

On the other hand, these studies are severely limited. Each one of them has begun by limiting itself to studying the relationships among only a few variables. Those variables are usually conceptual constructs arrived at by stripping each individual action of all its uniqueness, and by denying any of the complex and multileveled intentions, motives, feelings which each person brings to the exchange being studied. Only what can be fitted into the conceptual compartments is included.

What is more to the point here, none of these studies raises questions of morality or ethics. Because they are limited to observation of behavior, they exclude questions of "should" or "ought." They simply describe what people tend to do as a result of what is done to them. Even the "what is done to them" is stripped of its symbolic value, that is, what "what is done to them" might mean. We are seldom allowed inside people's minds and feelings. The studies report, primarily, what people do—not what they think about what they do.[2]

The studies are framed from the perspective of "effectiveness." That is to say, they look first to what the goals of the organization are (so many units at such and such a cost, so many cases processed, students' average increases in standardized test scores, etc.). Then they look for those behaviors that bring about those goals and objectives most effectively, that is, at the lowest cost in terms of money, personnel, time, and other resources. "Organizational effectiveness" employs technological rationality, functional rationality, linear logic. Efficiency is the highest value, not loyalty, harmony, honor, beauty, truth. One can run an efficient extermination camp or an efficient monastery. The principles of efficiency are basically the same in either context.

SUPERVISION AS MORAL ACTION

Seen from this perspective, one can return to the literature on "supervisory behavior" and to the research upon which such literature is built and see how

---

[2] Our position has consistently stressed, however, that it is the "mediating variables"—what affects the inside of people, how they feel about themselves and those they work with, how they perceive themselves as making a contribution and using their talents more effectively—which are the critical variables in assessing "outcome variables," namely, how people behave.

it tends to be dominated by these efficiency, functional, reductionist assumptions. The point of highlighting the limitations of these perspectives on supervision is not to deny their usefulness but to indicate the need to balance those perspectives with an appreciation of the rich human qualities of the social context being studied.

Therefore, we will speak of supervision as moral action, rather than as moral behavior. Moral action implies some level of self-initiation, of personal choosing, or a person willing to engage others for a purpose beyond "need fulfillment." In one sense, moral action implies self-fulfillment, but not in some narcissistic concentration on isolated self-gratification. Rather, it is a fulfillment of the self through involvement with and authentic participation in a community's struggle to become more humane, more just, more compassionate, more loving, and yes, more productive, in the sense of making the world a healthier, safer place where the goods of the earth are shared more fairly than they are presently. In a culture still very much dominated by a benign social darwinism and a narrow form of individualism, to propose a morality based on the above values is an embarrassment. They are too soft, too sentimental, too unrealistic, too feminine.

We will take up this objection later when we talk about morality as the "politics of the possible." For now suffice it to say that our view of morality sees moral action as taking place in a context of limits, limits of understanding, limits of maturity, limits of virtue, limits of power. In a sense morality is never a given; it is always something to be negotiated, it is always something only partially achieved. The values we seek are always, in a sense, beyond us. Our actions become moral only as we reach out for what lies beyond those limits and the definition of human possibility which those limits tend to impose.[3]

Supervision as moral action, therefore, can be understood as an effort on the part of supervisors to participate in a community of other moral agents, each of which is struggling to do "the right thing," according to some sense of values, according to some sense of what it means to be or become a human being. Because of their position within the educational community, one of the things supervisors can do, in fact, is to help foster that sense of a moral environment which encourages those in the community to go beyond considerations of efficiency to include other values such as self-fulfillment, community, integrity, and compassion. Supervision as moral action is not a reaction to a stimulus. It involves choosing, taking action, a seeking for values, an intentional promotion of a principle. As such it is dynamic, not reactionary, enriching the environment rather than satisfying some need from the environment.

---

[3] Cf. Bernard Haring, "Justice," *The New Catholic Encyclopedia,* New York: McGraw-Hill, 1967, vol. III, pp. 68–72. Haring states that in order to be just we must go beyond the demands of justice to love because the definition of justice can always be scaled down to suit our self-interest. Alisdair MacIntyre in *After Virtue,* Notre Dame, Ind.: University of Notre Dame, makes a similar point from an epistemological perspective. Cf. Chapter 2.

THE UNDERSIDE OF SUPERVISION

The stories told by teachers of their experiences of "being supervised" are anything but uplifting.[4] Again and again teachers tell of being placed in win-lose situations, of experiencing powerlessness, manipulation, sexual harassment, racial and ethnic stereotyping. At best, their encounters with supervisors lead directly to evaluative judgments based on the skimpiest of evidence. At worst they are destructive of autonomy, self-confidence, and personal integrity. In other words, supervision as practiced by many supervisors is not only nonprofessional, it is unethical and dehumanizing.

The most traditional exercise of supervision is the observation of a teacher in his or her classroom. Again, the purpose of classroom observation is traditionally evaluative. Despite some semblance of clinical supervision, most instances end up with the supervisor making evaluative judgments about the appropriateness and effectiveness of various teaching behaviors. These judgments are usually recorded and placed in the teacher's file. Despite the claims of advocates of effective classroom teaching practices, classroom observations which start out with preconceived formulas for what constitutes good practice tend not to be very helpful.[5] Moreoever, the supervisor's underlying but unspoken assumptions about teaching and learning frequently defeat the supervisory episode right from the start.

Beyond those professional issues, however, there are others which poison supervisors' activity. These have to do with their desire to dominate and control others, with their own insecurities which must be covered over by aggressive and controlling actions and words, with racial, sexual, and ethnic stereotypes which prevent genuine communication and mutual respect. Some older teachers are disdainful of younger supervisors. Some older supervisors are disdainful of younger teachers. A black supervisor raises problems for a white teacher. White supervisors raise problems for black teachers. Women supervising men, men supervising women have to deal with agendas beyond the explicit agenda on the table.

When these underside issues dominate the supervisory episode, they can block any possibility of open, trusting, professional communication. These issues can lead to manipulative words and actions on the part of the supervisor, the teacher, or both. One can seek to control or dominate or intimidate the other. One can go through the motions, playing a superficial role, acting as though everything is perfectly understandable, keeping feelings and honest communication at a safe distance. More often than not, supervisory encounters take place without either teachers or supervisors revealing their true feelings

---

[4] Cf. *Impact*, New York State Association for Supervision and Curriculum Development, vol. 19, no. 1, fall 1983. The whole issue is devoted to dealing with these less than altruistic motives. Arthur Blumberg raises penetrating questions in his treatment of the "cold war" between teachers and supervisors in *Supervisors and Teachers, a Private Cold War*, Berkeley, Calif.: McCutcheon Publishing, 1974.

[5] Cf. Susan Stoldowsky, "Teacher Evaluation: The Limits of Looking," *Educational Researcher*, vol. 13, no. 9, pp. 11–18, November 1984.

toward each other or toward the game they are playing. It is simply an organizational ritual that must be completed to satisfy some political or legal necessity. In those instances, supervision is not moral action. Frequently it is immoral: hypocritical, dishonest, disloyal, vicious, dehumanizing. Sometimes it is immoral simply because it wastes so much time of so many people.

THE MORAL HEURISTICS OF SUPERVISORY PRACTICE

If supervision is to be moral action, it must respect the moral integrity of the supervisor and the supervised. That is to say, the exchange between the supervisor and the supervised must be trusting, open, and flexible so as to allow both persons to speak from their own sense of integrity and to encourage the respect for the other's integrity. In other words, the exchange must begin with the honest discussion of what will be helpful for the teacher and the students. For this to happen, supervisors will need to explore those conditions necessary to establish trust and honesty and open communication, and those conditions necessary to maintain the same. This means that supervisors need to discuss the ground rules ahead of time. This in itself is a kind of moral action, a negotiation of guidelines to be followed so that fairness and honesty can be maintained.

Furthermore, the assumption behind supervision is that it will promote the kind of teaching that benefits children and youth in the classrooms. Teaching itself is a moral action. Supervisors ought to enhance teaching as moral action. Learning is also moral activity. Supervisors ought somehow to enhance that. What happens between teachers and students ought to be guided by high moral purpose and principle. Supervisors must never violate that purpose and principle in seeking to satisfy some administrative necessity. Therefore, at the beginning of each supervisory episode, supervisors need to get agreement on the exchange as essentially a moral action. Without exploring what is necessary to establish and maintain that action precisely as moral, supervisors can easily push the exchange into something dishonest and dehumanizing.

Hence, supervisors will need to explore with the teachers what procedures will be followed, what rights and responsibilities will be defined ahead of time, who controls what, whose needs are being served, what is the purpose behind the exchange, etc. These are the heuristics of moral action, those exploratory discussions on how to keep the exchange moral.

TRANSACTIONAL SUPERVISORY ACTION

James McGregor Burns in his Pulitzer Prize winning book, *Leadership*,[6] introduces a distinction in his analysis of leadership which proves helpful in exploring the moral dimensions of supervisory action. As presented in Chapter 8, Burns distinguishes between action that he calls "transactional" and action

[6] New York: Harper Torchbooks, 1979.

that he calls "transforming."[7] In both instances the action is rooted in values. Transactional leadership normally takes place between individuals and is guided by values which regulate, order, guide the transaction between them. These are "modal" values, those values governing the means someone employs to achieve a given end. These modal values include such values as honesty, fairness, loyalty, and patience.

Transforming leadership involves considerations that go beyond individual interests to the goal of the group or the larger collectivity, and is guided by other values which Burns calls "end" values.[8] Those values include those larger purposes to be served by the action of the parties involved, values such as justice, community, freedom, equality, and the rule of law. In transforming action, people are called to rise above self-interest and the often petty grievances engendered by self-interest to pursue those larger social ends which justify the social organism in the first place.

These categories are helpful because they enable us to analyze supervisory action from two distinct perspectives, both of which constitute essential components of actual supervisory practice and, furthermore, ought to constitute supervisory practice. First and foremost, the values that guide both forms of supervisory action are clearly moral values; that is, they deal with the unequivocal basis for integral human relationships and for the preservation of social organizations as places that hold human beings and the good of human beings as sacred and foremost. These values take us beyond concerns with efficiency (which can easily lead to using human beings as mere means) to the larger purpose of productivity, profit, quantitative organizational growth, expansion of markets, increase of grade scores, etc. The second perspective which these categories introduce is the placing of the moral demands of individual interactions between supervisor and colleagues within the larger moral demands upon the supervisor to see that the organization itself promotes the human good of people within it. The latter perspective requires further elaboration, which the following sections will attempt.

TRANSACTIONAL SUPERVISION

Transactional supervision takes place within an individual supervisory episode and within an organizational context. On an individual basis, that initially will involve what we have called the heuristics of moral action, namely, the exploration of and agreement upon those procedures, ground rules, guidelines which both parties will follow in order to maintain the exchange on a moral plane. Once those are agreed upon, the supervisor and colleague must follow through and maintain those basic values of honesty, fair play, loyalty, etc. That means that both parties will communicate honestly, will not seek to manipulate the other person, will generously pursue the agreed-upon targets of the supervisory episode, and will enter into the evaluation of the outcomes of the

[7] Ibid., chap. 16.
[8] Ibid.

interaction openly. It means that the integrity of each person will be respected and their sense of professional autonomy honored. It also means that the supervisory episode will serve the larger purposes of the school, so that the transaction ultimately benefits the education of the children involved as well as serves some of the instrumental goals of the school, such as the improvement of good order in the school and improved communications between teachers and curriculum directors. In other words, individual supervisory episodes are not to serve simply as therapy sessions for teachers, although they may indeed achieve those purposes. By and large, some larger purpose of the school should be sought, at least indirectly, for that indeed is what supervisors are supposed to engage teachers about. Plainly put, that is why we have supervisors.

Frequently, however, the individual supervisory episode will uncover organizational flaws which inhibit the performances of teachers. Those flaws can take many forms, such as the following: a teacher is assigned to teach a subject for which she is not qualified; a teacher is assigned to five successive periods with no coffee or lunch break; a set of directions for a new program could be read two different ways; the new policy for assigning handicapped children to special education classes may cause twice as many problems as the old policy; inadequate instructional supplies may render a mandated new program impossible to carry out; a change in policies regarding confidentiality between teachers and students may have destroyed a teacher's ability to help troubled youngsters. In the course of the supervisory episode, one or more of these inhibiting organizational deficiencies may come up. It may be apparent that they need to be corrected before the teacher can begin to try out any other growth possibilities.

Frequently there can be a moral value at stake in these cases; that is to say, often the policy was established without consulting the parties involved, and in fact violated someone's human or professional rights or neglected the human factors involved in an attempt to achieve economies of scale.[9] In those instances, the supervisor is in the best position to bring those problems to the attention of those making policy. The supervisor then becomes an agent for improving the transactional context of the organization itself. That is to say, the school as an organization, as a social entity, is a moral agent. Its policies governing teacher and student actions can be fair, honest, participative, or dishonest, unfair, and autocratic. The supervisor frequently has access to and a credibility with senior administrators who have the power and authority to alter decisions which have led to immoral consequences.

Frequently in practice, superiors are afraid to risk their own job security in bringing the organizational flaws to the attention of "higher-ups." But here the supervisor is clearly faced with a moral decision. Not to request a revision of those decisions and policies destroys the very ground of the transactional relationship between the supervisor and teacher. Not to request a revision is to

---

[9] A balanced view of policy-management issues is treated in William L. Boyd, "Policy Analysis, Educational Policy and Management: Through A Glass Darkly," in Norman J. Boyan (ed.), *The Handbook of Research on Educational Administration*, New York: Longman, 1987.

accede to decisions that are unfair, dehumanizing, and unethical and therefore implicate one as an accomplice. On the other hand, the supervisor can argue the case for the teachers and students, showing how the decision could be altered to improve the conditions at issue.

Beyond this kind of reaction to violations of what can be called organizational transactional morality, supervisors can engage in a form of proactive moral action. Frequently, supervisors will learn of new policies that are being formulated well before they are formally promulgated—either at the school building level or the system level. Because of the supervisors' familiarity with the front-line activity of classrooms and school yards and parental involvements in the life of the school, the supervisor can provide adequate critical commentary during the policy formation stage, calling attention to unforeseen consequences of the policy, especially those that will violate the transactional values of the school.

In another scenario, the supervisor may also be in the best position to explain new policies to the teachers, eliciting their opinion on the usefulness or effectiveness of the policy. Depending on relationships with union officials, sometimes supervisors may be in a position to solicit informal responses which then can be communicated to the ones making the policy in order to avoid unnecessary public conflicts with the union.

In all these instances the supervisor serves as an information carrier, bringing information from "below" to those "above" and bringing information from above to those below so that those above can anticipate problems before they occur. In this capacity, the supervisor is a key person, perhaps the primary person who helps the organization observe those transactional values which build an organizational climate of moral action.

TRANSFORMATIONAL SUPERVISION

As was noted above, transformational action involves larger end values such as justice, equality, freedom, community. In a school those large end values might include the following: education of the whole person, education for citizenship, education for excellence, respect for the sacredness of each person, the promotion of a tradition of culture and humane values, the promotion of global perspectives, etc. Transformational action invites the individual and the community to seek these larger, common-good values. It calls attention to the truth that no matter how successful we might be in pursuing narrow self-interests of, for example, higher grade scores, success in academic competition with other countries, success in achieving greater economic purchasing power, human life is simply not worth living without some experience of community, of an order of law that protects the human rights of the weak, of bonds of brotherhood and sisterhood, of the celebration of human heroism.

In a school setting, supervisors have opportunities to engage in at least three kinds of transformational moral actions. One involves a relationship with individual members of the staff which supports that person's efforts at major "transformations" of his or her life. A second involves bringing individual teachers to a greater commitment to the end values of the school such that their day-to-day action with children intentionally attends to those values. The third kind of transforming moral action involves the supervisor's leadership ability to work with a group of other administrators and teachers to bring about a transformation of the school itself. Each of these three forms of transforming moral action requires some elaboration.

INDIVIDUAL TRANSFORMATION

The exchange between a supervisor and a teacher can be relatively superficial or relatively profound. Most of the time, as research shows, the interaction between teachers and administrators and supervisors is very brief and ad hoc.[10] On the other hand, supervisors ought to check out their motives if they find themselves constantly seeking to transform everyone they supervise. Such an attitude may betray an arrogant paternalism which fails to respect the unique gifts of each person. Nevertheless, there will be the occasional moment when a supervisor encounters a person who is going through a crisis of a life-changing dynamic. Sometimes that will involve the break-up of a marriage, the death of a loved one, or a major professional setback. Frequently all that is required or desired is simple acceptance or support. Beyond that, a sympathetic ear, a clarifying question, a rephrasing of what the person is saying can enable the person to name the feeling or problem he or she is grappling with. To be sure, the transforming choices must be made by the individual involved. Sometimes, however, the supervisor can facilitate the insight needed before the choice can be considered.

This kind of responsiveness to a teacher can be termed moral action because the supervisor has moved beyond bureaucratic and technical functions to engage another human being at a deeply human level. That response is guided not only by transactional values of respect and loyalty but by transforming values of freedom and community. That is to say, in many of these crisis situations a person has to confront himself or herself without the customary supports that tended to define that person's life. They have to dig beneath the surface to uncover those rock bottom values by which they can redefine what they want for themselves, by which they can redefine themselves. Sometimes it is only by going through such crises that a teacher can begin to transform his or her life. For someone to stand by with words of support, encouragement, and caring during those moments is indeed moral.

While the examples cited above refer to personal crises a teacher might be facing, those crises frequently have professional consequences. If it is true that teachers express their own personal history in the classroom, whether they are

---

[10] Cf. Van Cleve Morris, et al., *Principals in Action: The Reality of Managing Schools,* Columbus: Charles E. Merrill, 1984.

conscious of doing that or not, then pain, turmoil, personal disorientation is bound to show up in their work with children.

Beyond these personal crises, a supervisor may have a long-term transforming influence on a teacher. The coaching protocols described so well by Bruce Joyce[11] and the collegial heuristics at the heart of Noreen Garman's approach to clinical supervision[12] point to a far-reaching impact on the development of teachers. That development gradually reaches a point where it is fair to say that from point x in time to point y, a teacher has transformed his or her teaching. In these cases, however, the transformation came about only after repeated encouragement, trial and error, struggling with the understanding of what one was trying to do, practice, and gradual mastery of a variety of teaching strategies. The patience and persistence of both supervisor and teacher over several years holds the key to such transformations. In terms of the human consequences for children, supervisors who play a part in such transformations are engaged in moral action.

COMMITMENT TO LARGE EDUCATIONAL VALUES

One of the neglected activities of supervision which the literature on leadership calls attention to is the focus on superordinate values.[13] The leader is one who holds up a vision of what the school can become. The leader engages in "purposing," that is, in frequently recalling those large purposes which the school is supposed to be serving. Within the school culture, someone has to articulate and encourage those end values that stand behind all the functional rationality of the school. Those values need to be represented in symbol, ritual, and celebration.[14]

In Burns's theory of leadership, the transforming leader is one who encourages people to rise above their own self-seeking to work for those "common good" values, those "end values" which represent those ideals by which a community defines its essential humanity. In schools, it is customary for people to compete for scarce resources, whether they be library materials, larger classrooms, brighter students, better class schedules, etc. Moreover,

[11] Bruce R. Joyce, "On Teachers Coaching Teachers," *Educational Leadership*, vol. 13, no. 5, pp. 12–17, February 1987.

[12] Noreen Garman, "Reflection, The Heart of Clinical Supervision: A Modern Rationale for Professional Practice," *Readings: Clinical Supervision as Reflection in Action*, Geelong, Victoria: Deakin University, 1984.

[13] S. N. Eisenstadt, "Charisma and Institution Building: Max Weber and Modern Sociology," *Max Weber: On Charisma and Institution Building*, Chicago and London: The University of Chicago Press, 1968; Peter B. Vaill, "The Purposing of High Performing Systems," in Thomas J. Sergiovanni and John E. Corbally (eds.), *Leadership and Organizational Culture*, Urbana, Ill.: University of Illinois Press, 1984; Warren Bennis and Burt Nanus, *Leaders: The Strategies for Taking Charge*, New York: Harper & Row, 1985; Thomas J. Sergiovanni, "Landscapes, Mindscapes and Reflective Practice in Supervision," *Journal of Curriculum and Supervision*, I.I., fall 1985; Robert J. Starratt, "Excellence in Education and Quality of Leadership," Occasional Paper no. 1, *Southern Tasmania Council of Educational Administration*, Hobart, Tasmania, March 1986.

[14] Allen E. Kennedy and Terrence E. Deal, *Corporate Cultures: The Rites and Rituals of Corporate Life*, Reading, Mass.: Addison-Wesley, 1982; Thomas J. Peters and Robert H. Waterman, *In Search of Excellence*, New York: Harper & Row, 1982.

group affiliations among teachers based on narrow self-interest build up and lead to group rivalry and conflict, for example, when some teachers appear to have greater status and power within the school system. Add to those tensions petty grievances that arise daily: a missed meeting, a favorite parking place usurped by a rival, a misconstrued remark overheard in the faculty room—these easily lead to conflicts, hurts, loss of morale.

If people have a deep ownership of the larger goals of the schools, however, attention to those goals can lead people to lay aside those irritations and to work with a greater sense of teamwork for these goals. The grievances will need to be cleared up whenever that is possible. It will not be possible, on the other hand, that some people will not be assigned last period, or that some teachers are not assigned lunchroom duty, or that some teachers are not assigned to less desirable classrooms. Variations in assignments during and across school years are possible, but at any given time, someone in the school will have a "nose out of joint." Allegiance to these large educational goals, however, draws everyone's perspective away from the small grievances and invites a pride in working toward such goals.

Supervisors who remind themselves and their colleagues of these larger values will be able to draw new energies for the work at hand. Glickman, Hunt, and Garman all point to the importance of teachers being able to think about their work in deeper and broader frameworks.[15] Hackman and Oldham also point to the importance of "task significance" as a basic motivator for enriched job performance.[16] Moreover, these larger values almost always represent high moral values. Teachers who work in response to moral values can transform their work with children so that in the classroom one can see "education of the whole person," "education for citizenship and community building," and "education for global perspectives," taking place. Then, indeed, supervisors who have encouraged that have been involved in moral action.

TRANSFORMING THE SCHOOL OR THE SYSTEM

Finally, we began to see earlier the potential of supervisors who engage in transactional moral action to change an unfair policy and thereby change the school as an organization. It is also possible for supervisors to engage in transforming moral action directed at the school as a moral entity. That is to say, supervisors can encourage administrators in the school to reexamine all their administrative practices in the light of those schoolwide goals that sound so nice when voiced from the podium on graduation day but which are ignored in practice in the daily life of the school.

Instead of constantly tinkering with procedures that violate some transac-

---

[15] Carl D. Glickman, *Developmental Supervision: Alternative Practices for Helping Teachers Improve Instruction,* Alexandria, Va.: Association for Supervision and Curriculum Development, 1981; David E. Hunt, *Between Psychology and Education,* Hinsdale, Ill.: Dryden Press, 1974; Noreen Garman, op. cit.

[16] J. Richard Hackman and Greg R. Oldham, "Motivation through the Design of Work: Test of a Theory," *Organizationl Behavior and Human Performance,* vol. 16, p. 256, 1976.

tional value, supervisors may need to look at how the school practices those large values it espouses in its schoolwide goals or mission statement. Violations of transactional values may stem from a neglect of some of these end values. The need for such an examination may appear after months of many supervisory episodes with teachers where it becomes evident that those large values are totally neglected in classrooms. The evidence may come in various forms: teachers who teach nothing but what will be tested in reading and math standardized tests; teachers who refuse to handle even minor discipline problems and instead send the offenders to "the office"; students whose parents insist that they take only the "hard" subjects in order to increase their chances of admission to a "prestigious" school; administrators who respond to attempted and actual student suicides and rampant drug abuse with bureaucratic procedures which attempt to sanitize the problem; vandalism and high absenteeism; a general sense of student alienation.

Frequently, supervisors spend much more time in classrooms, corridors, and faculty rooms than do other administrators and are therefore in touch with these realities, realities which contradict what the school is supposed to stand for. While they may lack the executive authority to establish the mechanisms necessary to bring the community together to consider those large purposes of schooling, supervisors are nonetheless in a central position of influence to affect such decisions. Because they work with an extensive network of information they are at least in a position to mobilize sentiment and opinion to bring various segments of the community to an expressed concern to pursue those larger purposes of schooling.

This last consideration of transforming moral action—the transformation of a school or a school system—is the weightiest responsibility one could ask a supervisor to assume. It should be undertaken, therefore, only after extended experience within that school or school system, and only when circumstances clearly seem to require it. A supervisor who, after a week in a new school or school system, decides that the whole thing needs transformation, should be suspect. On the other hand, a supervisor who has worked within a system for 15 years and who has helped build coalitions of concerned teachers and administrators and other supervisors who wish to support those large goals of schooling—that supervisor can be said to have participated in transforming the school itself.

THE POLITICS OF THE POSSIBLE

This treatment of supervision as moral action can be viewed as hopelessly idealistic, as out of touch with the realities of schooling. In discussing supervision as moral action, however, it was not our intention to present it as something beyond the reach of every person who serves in a supervisory capacity. Supervision can be moral action, although, perhaps, never untainted by some traces of self-interest or manipulation. The context of schooling is a context of limited rationality, of limited altruism, of limited power, of limited efficiency—as is the context of every organization. Moral action in this context is therefore itself limited. Because it is limited, however, is no reason to deny its importance and its possibility.

In any given example used in the above treatment of supervision as moral action, the exercise of moral action will be limited by the circumstances of that particular episode. Some teachers may never enter into a supervisory exchange with genuine trust. In that case, the supervisor simply does what is possible. In other instances, supervisors will find that their advice to policy makers is neither wanted nor attended to. They can only do what is possible. Perhaps next year will be a more favorable time to seek to change the policy. In any given school, supervisors will find different chemistries among groups of the faculty. Those chemistries will make things either possible or impossible. Because circumstances change every year, new chemistries and hence new possibilities emerge every year. Because the exercise of moral action will not always be possible at any given time does not mean that it should be ruled out altogether. There will always be opportunities for some form of moral action at one level or another. The challenge and the need never go away. What is possible at any given time will always be in flux.

SUMMARY

In this chapter we have attempted to explore the challenges to and opportunities for moral action by supervisors. The practice of supervision has an underside, rarely mentioned in the literature, which poses many moral issues for both teachers and supervisors. The transactions of organizational life in schools also comprise a context for moral action. The most challenging form of moral action involves the quest for those transformations of people and communities in the pursuit of those end values of justice, freedom, and community. Finally, the difficulties of pursuing the moral course of action were alluded to, difficulties which are real enough but not necessarily eternally insurmountable. The very presence of obstacles to moral action frequently underscores the very necessity for moral action so that the obstacles will not come to define the way things have to be.

STUDY GUIDE

Recall the concepts, ideas, and meanings associated with each of the following phrases and terms included in this chapter. Can you discuss each of them with a colleague and apply them to the supervisory context of your school? If you cannot, review them in the text and record the page numbers for future reference.

1 Action versus behavior
2 Moral action
3 The politics of the possible

4 The underside of supervision
5 Transactional supervision
6 The moral heuristics of supervision
7 Reductionist approach to social phenomena

EXERCISES

1 Identify a moral issue in your school system. How do supervisory personnel respond to this moral issue? How should they? Spell out a reasonable plan of action.
2 What is the difference between a professional obligation and a moral obligation to take action? Discuss this with three other members of the class. What are the points of disagreement?
3 Where do the values that undergird moral action come from? Discuss how the class might come to agreement on this question.

PART THREE

HUMAN RESOURCES AND EDUCATIONAL LEADERSHIP

Parts One and Two of this book treat various topics associated with organizational leadership. Those who would be supervisors need to understand that their effectiveness in assisting teachers to become more effective will normally be mediated by the total organizational context of the school. That context is made up of bureaucratic elements, school culture, teacher motivations, climate, formal and informal group dynamics, the school as a social system. Hence, supervisors need to be able to maneuver within that terrain, or swim within that environment, for that determines much if not all of what is possible. Yet supervisors are faced with the challenge of leadership and hence must act for and on the environment.

That environment, moreover, is not any kind of organizational environment. It is a school, a place where formal education takes place. Hence, beyond organizational leadership, supervisors are expected to exert educational leadership. That is to say, supervisors are expected to know a lot about the process and the substance of education as such. They are expected to know, for example, a variety of ways to structure a course (through a historical, a thematic, a problem, or an inquiry pattern of organization). They ought to know about various learning styles and learning blocks which experience and research have uncovered. To be sure, supervisors will not be the only source of educational ideas in the school. Yet they ought to be working from professional understanding of and convictions about what constitutes good educational practice.

What follows in Part Three is a series of chapters that pose critical educational questions for supervisors. The questions posed in these chapters assume that readers have already been exposed to the basics of learning theory, curriculum development, and educational philosophy. Responses to those questions need not be chiseled in stone, but neither should they be so vague, platitudinous, or qualified as to evaporate into thin air at the slightest challenge. The reader should not progress beyond Part Three without articulating some provisional platform, some advocacy position, some general principles of curriculum and instruction, some criteria for program evaluation.

Schools as educational communities are floundering. Outstanding teachers may yet be found in the schools, but they do not work together to form a community of educators whose cumulative impact on student learning would be so much greater than what it is in their present condition of isolation.[1] Someone in the schools needs to ask the larger questions such as "What large and inclusive educational purposes does the curriculum taken as a whole serve?" "Do teachers in this school more or less reflect basic agreements about what is of most value in their work with youngsters?" "Is there a balance within the overall curriculum so that all schoolwide goals receive appropriate attention?" If supervisors attend only to individual teachers and to their mastery of a series of "effective" instructional behaviors, who will answer these questions? Certainly not the testing companies.

Chapter 10 highlights the importance of the supervisor's platform—that constellation of assumptions and beliefs about children and youth, about learning, program development, school climate, and the purposes of schooling. Some sources for the development of a platform are suggested.

Chapter 11 raises the question about the supervisor's advocacy position. Is the supervisor concentrating on the teacher's activities, the actual student learnings, the proposed learning outcomes, or the school system's requirements? The models outlined in this chapter should assist readers in clarifying their underlying advocacy position.

Chapter 12 suggests critical questions supervisory personnel need to ask about curricular programs and the environment of learning. In working with individual teachers, departments, or schoolwide curriculum committees, as well as school administrators, supervisors enjoy unique advantages for creative intervention and advocacy.

In Chapter 13, the question of student and program evaluation occupies center stage. The role of supervisors in assisting in the development of useful forms of student and program evaluation is developed.

---

[1] Cf. Ann Lieberman and Lynn Miller, "The Social Realities of Teaching," *Teachers College Record*, vol. 80, no. 1, 1978.

CHAPTER **10**

THE SUPERVISORS' EDUCATIONAL PLATFORM

Throughout this book we are emphasizing an emerging trend in supervision, what we have labeled Supervision II. This form of supervision attends to what teaching episodes mean to teachers, how students interpret the activity of the teacher, what significance a teacher places on a supervisory intervention, rather than to a prescribed formula of teacher or supervisory behaviors. We are suggesting that the professional's craft, derived from years of trial and error, functions from a base of intuitions which responds to the multiform signals being sent in any given situation. This kind of educator is a "reflective practitioner," one who brings many frames of reference, conceptual blueprints, normative paradigms to bear on a reality that is enormously complex and therefore contains layers of intelligibility.[1]

Besides the technical understandings which emerge from a blend of intuition and conceptual schemata, there is a floor of beliefs, opinions, values, and attitudes which provide a foundation for practice. These beliefs, opinions, values, and attitudes make up what has been called a platform.[2] Just as a political party is supposed to base its decisions and actions on a party platform, so too educators carry on their work, make decisions, and plan instruction based on their educational platform. When a teacher is asked why a child was disciplined in a certain way, he or she will frequently respond with a generalization about how all children should be disciplined. When asked about

[1]Donald A. Schön, *The Reflective Practitioner,* New York: Basic Books, 1983.
[2] Decker Walker, "A Naturalistic Model for Curriculum Development," *School Review,* vol. 80, no. 1, 1971.

the social usefulness of learning a certain lesson, a teacher frequently will frame his or her explanation according to a set of more general beliefs about the socialization of children.

Whether or not a platform position is right or wrong is not the issue here. Knowing *what* the platform position is, knowing the relationship between teaching practices and the platform position, perceiving inconsistencies between platform and practice, appreciating differences between one's own platform and that of another—these are the points of emphasis in this chapter. Both teacher and supervisor need to know what their respective platforms are. They need to examine where they agree and where they differ and whether the differences are so substantial as to interfere with the growth goals of the supervisory episode. They also need to examine whether the teaching practice is sufficiently versatile to fulfill the requirements of the platform position. Finally, in the effort to encourage reflection in practice, teachers and supervisors need to take the time to articulate their platform. Most teachers tend to resist the exercise simply because they are not used to making their platform explicit. They simply act according to the feel of the situation. Yet when they do write out their platform, they experience the satisfaction of naming what they do and why they do it. Greater sense of task identity and task significance strengthens motivation, satisfaction, and commitment to one's work.[3]

What follows are three examples of at least partially developed platforms. They tend to focus on the primary emphasis of the platform. The first example places the central focus of the platform on the individual student and her or his growth in the schooling process. The second example exhibits an emphasis on predetermined learnings. The third example highlights the socialization function of the school.

HUMAN GROWTH PLATFORM

1 The student is unlike input factors in system designs of industrial or military organizations, for instance, a piece of steel that arrives at the "input station" all neatly measured and stable. Steel, wood, and stone do not grow and change during the very time when the production worker is trying to manipulate them. Students do.

2 The school makes a difference in a child's growth, but not *that* much difference. If the school were nonexistent, other influences and experiences would "educate" the child. Besides, human beings are dynamic and constantly growing. The school simply speeds up the growth process and channels it in supposedly beneficial directions, rather than leaving the student to random, trial-and-error growth.

3 Curricular-instructional programs should be designed in conformity to the growth patterns of students. The human growth needs of students should never be subordinated to objectives dictated by the needs of society and the demands

[3] J. Richard Hackman and Greg R. Oldham, "Motivation through the Design of Work: Test of a Theory," *Organizational Behavior and Human Performance,* vol. 16, p. 256, 1976.

of the disciplines. Theoretically, these three concerns—human growth, achievement of disciplined skills and knowledge, and fulfillment of social responsibilities—should not be in conflict. In practice, however, they frequently are in conflict, and the concern for human growth usually is the one to be sacrificed.

4 The educator's primary function is to become obsolete. The job of the educator is to so influence students that the students will gradually but eventually reach the point where they do not need the teacher, where they can pursue their own learning on the basis of their acquired knowledge and skills.

5 *Active* pursuit of knowledge and understanding, an actual dialogue with reality, will produce the most significant and long-lasting types of learning. Whenever possible, therefore, the student must actively search, actively inquire, actively discover, and actively organize and integrate. The teacher's job is to guide and direct this activity toward specified goals.

These five basic assumptions place the individual student at the heart of this platform. In order to clarify this platform, the following diagrams attempt to sketch in broad strokes a picture of this growing human being.

Figure 10-1 attempts a rudimentary, three-dimensional model of growth that emphasizes the individual's gradual increase in freedom to explore his or her world. Initially, the behavior of infants is almost entirely dominated by their biological needs, such as needs for food, warmth, sleep, and basic sensory stimulation. As these needs are regularly taken care of, and as infants become able to provide for these needs themselves, they have more time and energy to seek more complex sensory stimulation and to move away from purely

FIGURE 10-1
Relationship of free activity to behavior controlled by basic needs.

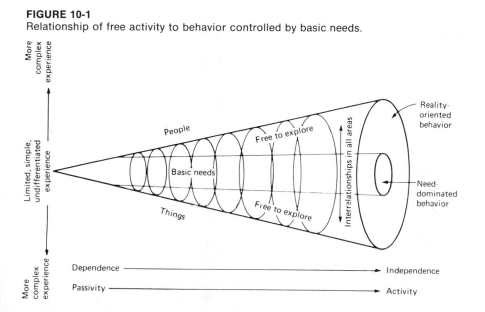

self-centered concerns toward whatever makes up their environment. Their environment, they discover quite early, is made up of people and things. Animals populate their early "people world," but gradually they, too, become part of the nonhuman world. The exploratory behavior of infants is called *reality-oriented behavior* because through it, they move toward discovering things and people in their *own* right and not simply as gratifiers of their physical needs. As they move toward things and people in their own right, infants discover that reality is quite complex—that they have to deal with each situation and each person in different ways at different times.

As individuals mature physically, they discover that they can, and are expected to, manage many of the things that parents and siblings provided in their infancy, such as feeding, washing, dressing, returning toys to the toy closet, and so forth. Moreoever, they are allowed more freedom to explore their environment, first outside their crib and playpen, then outside the house, and eventually outside the neighborhood. This pattern of continued movement away from dependency toward independence to interdependence, and from passivity to increased activity, is basic to the process of maturing, of becoming a developed human, and this process involves both emotional and cognitive development as well as physical development. And, unless severe physical or emotional restraints are imposed on individuals, they will develop along these lines naturally. There is a natural internal dynamism in human beings toward this kind of growth.

Figure 10-2 attempts to indicate the development of habits, skills, and understandings that allow individuals the freedom to explore and participate in their environment. By mastering and internalizing any skill, individuals no longer have to consciously think about each minute part of the behavior involved in the performance of a skill. Rather, it becomes natural, like breathing or walking, and thus the conscious energies of individuals are freed to explore new areas of their environment, which they gradually assimilate into new skills, new understandings, and new interpretive maps of their environment. As they develop these skills and understandings, they are increasingly able not merely to explore the environment but to interact with it—to develop

FIGURE 10-2
Developing freedom to explore and participate in the human environment.

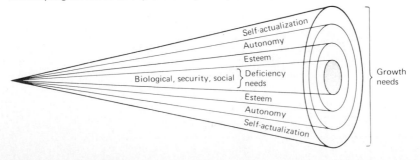

deeper friendships, for example, or to take on part-time jobs, or to solve problems in school assignments.

These basic learnings include social skills, such as learning appropriate manners for different occasions, learning something about sex, age, and authority role-relationships, learning to delay gratification in order to achieve a higher goal, and so forth. Other basic learnings involve physical skills, such as manual dexterity, visual and auditory perceptual differentiation, correct speech habits, athletic skills, and so forth. Besides developing symbolic skills, methodologies for inquiry, and attitudes and values, individuals accumulate a repertory of personal meanings. These are derived from experiences whose intensity left a lasting, and frequently highly emotion-laden, impression. Finally, the emerging self-concept lies at the heart of the developing core of individuals and suffuses all of their accumulated learnings. Together, these elements of the developing core of the person determine the quality and degree of the freedom of individuals to participate in their human environment.

These growth processes can level off after a while, as the result of a variety of circumstances. Everyone is familiar with people who have stopped growing—who simply do not go beyond a certain point either in exploring their universe or in pursuing more intense human experiences. When people stop growing, their experience of their environment levels off, and they settle into a daily routine where things seldom change.

Again, the stress of this platform is on the intrinsic dynamism of human growth. A corollary of this stress is that teachers should appeal to the natural curiosity of students, presenting them with exciting and imaginative learning tasks that will immerse the student in learning activity. Rather than continuously imposing the teacher's own agenda, leaving the student in a passive state while the teacher engages in the activity that the *student* should be performing, this platform emphasizes that the drive to learn and grow is already there in the student. This is not to say that the demands of the logical sequence of learning activities within a specified discipline of knowledge will be ignored. But much more leeway will be given to students to rummage about within the discipline of knowledge, frequently leapfrogging over logical steps to new insights and discoveries. Students can go back and fill in what they have left out; indeed, frequently they will come to recognize this need on their own. The emphasis is, however, on giving the students their head, encouraging them as they experience the excitement of the search or the puzzle. Obviously this leads to another corollary: the necessity of a highly individualized form of instruction, using learning-activity packets, exploratory projects, and expressive activities, and employing a variety of media adapted to different learning styles.

One can go on from this basic platform emphasis to postulate the kind of learning environment that this emphasis would require, including teacher-student relationships, student groups, daily and weekly schedules, grading systems, learning materials, and so on.

BASIC COMPETENCY PLATFORM

1 The purpose of schooling is to ensure a minimal competency in pre-scribed skills and understandings for all children. Enrichment of students' learning beyond these minimum competencies is an important but secondary aim of schooling.

2 Schools can make a great difference in the achievement of these minimum competencies; people who do not achieve them end up as unproductive citizens living on the margins of society.

3 Present and future civic and employment demands point to the absolute necessity of acquiring basic competencies. Mastery of these competencies will assist the person in other areas of personal and social growth.

4 The educator's job is to construct a highly organized environment to promote the gradual mastery of basic competencies in reading, writing, computation, and scientific processes. This implies a careful definition of learning objectives for each major unit of an intentionally sequenced series of learnings, careful assessment of entry-level skills and understandings with built-in correction of start-up deficiencies, careful monitoring of student progress with built-in remediation phases, a requirement of mastery before moving on to the next unit, and a sequential progression to broader and deeper levels of mastery of the competencies as defined by graduation requirements.

5 Almost all students, except a small percentage of more severely handi-capped children, are capable of mastery levels of learning in these minimum competencies, given sufficient time and appropriate instruction.

6 The most significant factor in learning is "time on task." This means that much of class time will be spent on drills and exercises that strengthen the target competency, that additional time will be afforded to those students needing it, and that daily homework will be assigned on the target competency.

7 While one approach to learning a competency may be initially stressed, alternative methodologies will be employed for students experiencing difficulty.

8 Higher-level learnings and cultural enrichment activities will tend to receive less attention, especially in the earlier grades, except for those students who have achieved mastery of the minimum competencies.

9 Classroom discipline will be controlled more by the intense concentra-tion on the learning task than by teachers' imposition of punishments and repetition of rules.

10 All the reward systems of the school should serve to promote academic achievement as the highest priority. Rewards for other desirable behaviors or achievement should hold second place to this priority.

DEMOCRATIC SOCIALIZATION PLATFORM

1 The primary aim of education is to enable the individual to function in society. Assuming a democratic society, the school should promote not only those qualities necessary for survival (employment, getting along with people, managing one's financial affairs, being a responsible family person, etc.) but also those qualities necessary for a healthy democratic society (political involvement that seeks the common good, willingness to displace self-interest for a higher purpose, skills at community building and conflict resolution, an understanding of how the political process works and how to influence public policy, etc.).

2 The school should intentionally arrange itself so that learning takes place primarily in a community context. Students should be taught to collaborate on learning tasks rather than engage in competition against one another. Team projects, peer tutoring, group rewards, and discussion of community problems should have priority even while encouraging the development of individual talents. Individual talents, however, should be prized more for what they contribute to the community than for the exclusive enrichment of the individual.

3 Learning is best nurtured in a community context. Language skills are developed by regular and varied group communication. A sense of history and culture is nurtured by a focus on the group's history and culture. Psychological needs such as self-esteem and assertiveness are best met through active involvement in the community. Acceptance of differences and the development of individuality are negotiated best within a sense of belonging to a community. Values, laws, and social customs are best taught within the context of the community.

4 The educator stands within the learning community and yet holds a special place of authority. The educator facilitates and directs the learning tasks of the younger members of the community but allows the agenda of community dynamics to intrude on the more academic tasks when the need arises.

5 Teachers and students function best when they work in relatively small, relatively self-contained, relatively autonomous learning communities. Hence, those schools with large enrollments should be broken down into manageable learning communities that allow for closer and more continuous contact between a team of teachers and their students.

6 The curriculum should be controlled by a set of schoolwide learning outcomes for each year, but the learning community should have considerable autonomy in the ways it achieves these outcomes. The teams of teachers should be accountable for promoting required learnings but should be allowed to devise the particular learning activities that best respond to the students in their communities.

7 Wherever possible, the learning communities should be involved with the large civic community through parental involvement, by using the civic community as a learning laboratory, by discussing problems in the civic community, and by promoting ideas of community service.

THE SUPERVISOR'S PLATFORM

In stressing the importance of the supervisor's explicating his or her own platform, we realize that it may or may not come out as clearly as the three contained in this chapter. On the other hand, the effort to elucidate one's platform is of primary importance to the supervisor's task. Without sufficient clarity on what one really believes is important in schooling, it will be difficult to assist teachers in clarifying what their educational platforms are. As we will see in subsequent chapters,[4] the process of clinical supervision we propose involves this clarification process. If the teacher is to profit from the interaction with the supervisor and to move clearly and decisively toward sharply focused growth objectives, then the effort at platform clarification, and perhaps at platform amplification, will be one of the supervisor's primary concerns.

What are some practical guidelines, then, that might assist supervisors to draw up their platform? First we will look at some of the key ingredients that should make up an educational platform and then add some that belong specifically to a supervisor's educational platform.

We can identify 10 major ingredients that should be included in any educational platform.[5] Using these as benchmarks, supervisors could identify the key elements of their own platforms and those of teachers they supervise.

1 The aims of education— Here it would help to set down, in order of priority (if possible), the three most important aims of education—not simply education in the abstract, but education for the youngsters in our school system.

2 Major achievements of students this year—Bringing these aims down to more specific application, identify the major achievements of students that one deals with desired by the end of the year. (For example, some might put down mastery of some academic skills up to a certain level; others might put down the acquisition of certain basic principles that would govern behavior; others might put down more personal achievements, such as increased self-awareness or self-confidence, or trust and openness.)

3 The social significance of the student's learning—Here one might find that he or she emphasizes learning for entering the world of work; others might focus more on the utilization of learning for good citizenship; still others might focus on the acquisition of the cultural heritage of our civilization. This element may also draw a response that denies any direct major social significance to the student's learning because of a predisposition to view the individual in a highly individualistic sense.

4 The image of the learner—This element tries to uncover attitudes or assumptions about how one learns. Is the learner an empty vessel into which one pours information? Some may view the learner in a uniform way—as though all learners are basically the same and will respond equally to a uniform

---

[4] See Chapters 16–18.
[5] We have been helped in identifying these ingredients by the categories used by Zvi Lamm in *Conflicting Theories of Instruction,* Berkeley, Calif.: McCutchan, 1976. We have modified these categories and the interpretation Lamm gives them. However, in his provocative treatment, Lamm attempts to expound the logic behind what amounts to three educational platforms. Unfortunately, in our opinion, he has so stereotyped two of them as to render his analysis inapplicable for our purposes.

pedagogy. Some may use "faculty" psychology to explain how students learn. Still others will differentiate among various styles and dispositions for learning that point to a greater emphasis on individualization of learning.

5 The value of the curriculum—This element touches upon attitudes about what the student learns. Some will say that the most important learnings are those most immediately useful in "real" life. Others will say that any kind of learning is intrinsically valuable. Others would qualify that latter position and consider some learnings, such as the humanities or the school subjects to be intrinsically more valuable, because they touch upon those more central areas of our culture. Others would claim that the learning of subjects has value only insofar as it sorts out people of different abilities and interests and channels them in socially productive directions. Some might even claim that the curriculum helps youngsters to understand God better.

6 The image of the teacher—What basically is a teacher? Is a teacher an employee of the state, following the educational policies and practices dictated by the local, state, and federal government? Or is a teacher a professional specialist whom a community employs to exercise his or her expertise on behalf of youngsters? Or is a teacher a spokesperson for tradition, passing on the riches of the culture? Or is a teacher a political engineer, leading youngsters to develop those skills necessary for the reform of their society? This element tries to elicit assumptions about the role of the teacher.

7 The preferred kind of pedagogy—This element should be fairly clear. Will the teacher dominate the learning experience? Some assume that inquiry learning is the best way to teach. Others assume that each discipline lends itself better to some forms of pedagogy. Some would opt for a much more permissive, student-initiated learning enterprise. While there would understandably be some reluctance to focus on *one* pedagogical approach to the exclusion of all others, nonetheless, we usually tend to settle on two or three as the more effective approaches.

8 The primary language of discourse in learning situations—This element frequently concerns the levels and quality of learning involved.[6] Does the language focus on precision of verbal definitions or the precise measurement of phenomena, or does it rather stress imaginative relationships? Frequently the difference between the question "How do you feel about that?" and the question "What do you think about that?" reveals a basic orientation toward the kind and level of learning being emphasized. Frequently a metaphor that is used gives away some underlying attitude, whether it be concerned with exact precision, the moral use of knowledge, or artistic sensibility.[7]

9 The preferred kind of teacher-student relationship—This element involves the quality of interpersonal relationships preferred by the teacher and

[6] Benjamin S. Bloom, *Taxonomy of Educational Objectives: The Classification of Educational Goals, Handbook I: Cognitive Domain,* New York: McKay, 1956.
[7] Dwayne Huebner, "Curriculum Language and Classroom Meanings," in James B. Macdonald and Robert R. Leeper (eds.), *Language and Meaning,* Washington, D.C.: Association for Supervision and Curriculum Development, 1966. pp. 8–26.

student. Some would prefer a very caring kind of relationship in which the "needs of the whole child" are attended to. Others would prefer much more distance, leaving the personal needs of the students for someone else to attend to, stressing more the academic discipline. Still others would be very nondirective, allowing the spontaneous, felt needs of the child to direct the relationship, with the teacher being more of a resource person. Others might prefer a group orientation in which the teacher works primarily to facilitate the work of the group.

10 The preferred kind of school climate—Here, some of the organizational considerations touched upon in the previous chapter would come into play. This element concerns a constellation of factors such as schoolwide and classroom discipline, student pride in the school, faculty morale, the openness of the school community to divergent life-styles, expressive learnings, and individualistic ways of thinking and behaving. Some would opt for order and predictability. Others would prefer a more relaxed climate, perhaps more boisterous but also more creative and spontaneous. This element would be very much related to what is valued in the curriculum and to the social consequences of learning.[8]

It becomes obvious as one tests out one's assumptions under each of the categories listed above that there tends to be an intrinsic logic to them. That is, there tends to be a consistency between assumptions about the nature of the learner and the preferred kind of teacher-student relationship, which in turn relates logically to one's beliefs about the aims of education.[9] As one clarifies one's assumptions, beliefs, and opinions under each of these 10 categories, the platform one uses in one's everyday actions in the school should begin to become apparent. That is to say, we usually make practical decisions about our professional practice as educators based upon convictions, assumptions, and attitudes which are not that clearly or frequently articulated. Nevertheless, they do influence, some would even say dominate, our actions. By bringing these convictions, assumptions, and attitudes out into the open for our own reflection, we can evaluate their internal consistency and cogency. We can also check whether we are satisfied with our platform, or whether, perhaps, we have not taken important factors into consideration. By clarifying the underlying rationale for our actions, we might see a need to grow in specific areas in order to increase our effectiveness as well as to broaden our human capacities.

Two other categories round out the supervisor's platform. That is to say, the above analysis of key elements in a platform has been dealing with an educational platform. This educational platform focuses on what one believes ought to happen in a process of formal education. It could belong to a teacher, a student, an administrator, or a supervisor. The supervisor can elaborate his

---

[8] The material in Chapter 16 very much relates to questions about school climate, although there the focus is primarily on the classroom setting rather than the schoolwide setting.

[9] Again we wish to acknowledge Lamm's *Conflicting Theories of Instruction* as the recent reminder of the logic inherent in our educational platforms.

or her own educational platform, but it becomes complete when the supervisor adds his or her convictions about how the activity of supervising is supposed to help such a platform influence the realities of a school. The two categories that concern supervision are the following: the purpose of supervision and the preferred process of supervision.

11 The purpose or goal of supervision—Some would answer from a neo-scientific orientation. Others would speak from a human relations perspective. Still others would utilize the human resources rationale.

12 The preferred process of supervision—Some would express a preference for the clinical supervision approach.[10] Others would prefer a more eclectic process that responds to the contingencies of the situation.[11]

Again, the point of clarifying one's convictions and unspoken assumptions about the nature of supervision is to open the door for growth, for the sharing of ideas, and for supervisory performance that operates out of a clear sense of direction. Ideally, these last two elements of the supervisor's platform should perhaps be written down at the beginning, before one reads this book, and then at the end, after one has read the book. If the analysis of supervision presented between these covers has an effect, it would show up in the differences between the two platform statements.

APPROACHES TO PLATFORM CLARIFICATION

Many supervisors may find the initial efforts at platform clarification very frustrating. It is not something they do often, and there can be a feeling of awkwardness. Yet everyone has an unexpressed platform. Were a sensitive observer to follow the supervisor around for a day or two on the job, it would be relatively easy to guess that supervisor's belief about how youngsters learn best, about what is important to learn, about good teaching and inferior teaching, and so on. Our actions usually reveal our assumptions and attitudes quite clearly.

Many will find the orderly process of filling out where one stands on the 12 elements of the platform the most convenient approach to take. The categories provide guidance in identifying the essential characteristics of one's platform. One can also check the internal consistency between statements under each category.

Others will prefer a less structured approach, letting their assumptions come out as they are felt and recognized, rather than having to force them into categories with which they are uncomfortable. They will have a more difficult

---

[10] See Chapter 17.

[11] People in this group may identify with many of the sentiments expressed in William Pinar (ed.), *Curriculum Theorizing: The Reconceptualists*, Berkeley, Calif.: McCutchan, 1975. The authors there break new ground using different categories to lend intelligibility to their educational platform.

time expressing their platform, perhaps, but this approach may be far more rewarding for them.

Sometimes it helps to find a quiet place and to write down one's reflections. Normally, these will come out in a jumble, in no particular order of priority. Once we have written down the elements of our platform, we can with further reflection begin to group them in clusters and place them in some order of importance. Almost everyone with any experience in education, however, will feel several times during this exercise the need to qualify and nuance those general statements. "Which teaching strategy I'd use in a given situation depends a lot on a youngster's background. But by and large, I'd choose this approach." "While I'd place my major emphasis on mastery of basic intellectual skills, I still think it's important to spend some time teaching kids good manners." "I almost always prefer to start a lesson with a colorful advance organizer. That usually stirs up the pupils' curiosity. But there are times when I run plain, old-fashioned memory drills."

Others will find the writing exercise too tedious and will seek out a colleague to discuss this whole question. The free flow of shared ideas frequently stimulates the process of clarification. In those instances, having a tape recorder along may help for subsequent transcription of the conversation. Others may find a combination of dialogue and writing the better way. Still others may go to a formal statement of goals that the school or system has in print to begin the process. By studying the goals and *probing the assumptions behind them,* the supervisor may discover areas of disagreement or agreement.

COMPARING PLATFORMS

However one goes about clarifying his or her platform initially, two other steps will prove helpful. After the first tentative statement of the platform, the supervisor should compare his or her platform with those of two or three colleagues, to test out areas of agreement or disagreement. Sometimes this may lead to modification of one's platform. It may also lead to a greater acceptance of diversity of perspectives. It certainly will help supervisors to build teamwork. Knowing the biases behind one another's approach will enable them to work together in areas where they agree or might complement one another.

When the supervisors have discussed their platforms together, they should then compare them with the school's or the system's platform. That may not exist in a written document, but, as in their own cases, it exists implicitly in the operational policies of the school or school system. Frequently, they find some genuine discrepancies between what the goal statements profess and what the school practices. Bringing those discrepancies to light, in itself, would be a service to the school. The purpose of examining against each other the expressed and unexpressed (but operative) platforms of the school, however, is aimed more at a comparison between the school's platform and the supervisor's platform. If they find striking divergences between them, then the supervisors will have to seek some means of reconciling the divergences, or of modifying one or the other to make them more compatible.

The point of this exercise is not to introduce frustration and cynicism but on the contrary to reduce it. It may be that the platform of the school and that of the supervisor are incompatible. In our opinion, the supervisor should leave the school in that case, and go to one that is more compatible. But if the supervisor or supervisory group in a school or school system are to exercise their potential influence in upgrading the quality of education, then they must be generally in agreement with the platform of the school or school system. Where that agreement exists, then supervisors can work with teachers and programs to achieve commonly agreed-upon goals. This does not mean uniformity in its oppressive sense. Rather, the supervisors can mobilize the talent and enthusiasm of the teachers, along with the technical support system of the school to move in an agreed-upon direction.

SUMMARY

In this chapter we have taken up the concept of the educational platform. When three examples of educational platforms were given, it became apparent that a platform is made up of those basic assumptions, beliefs, attitudes, and values that are the underpinnings of one's behavior as an educator.

Some time was spent suggesting ways in which supervisors could draw up their own platform. Ten essential elements to the platform were outlined, with two additional ones added for supervisors. With these as guidelines, supervisors can then begin to draw up their own educational platform. Again, the logic and basic intelligibility that flows from platform clarification to one's supervisory practice was stressed as the point of the whole exercise.

With this as a foundation, we can now move on to other concerns for the supervisor's exercise of educational leadership.

STUDY GUIDE

Recall the concepts, ideas, and meanings associated with each of the following phrases and terms included in this chapter. Can you discuss each of them with a colleague and apply them to the supervisory context of your school? If you cannot, review them in the text and record the page numbers for future reference.

1 Basic competencies platform
2 Democratic socialization platform
3 Educational platform
4 Human growth platform
5 Mastery learning
6 Ten elements of an educational platform

7 Time on task
8 Two elements of a supervisor's platform

EXERCISES

1 Identify the assumptions behind the three platforms proposed in this chapter.
2 In your experience with teachers, pick out two whom you know pretty well and try to write down their platforms according to the 10 categories.
3 Identify an experience of conflict beween a teacher and a supervisor where the conflict was rooted in differing platforms.
4 Write out your platform only for your own eyes. After you have completed it, ask yourself whether it would differ much if you had to show it to your superintendent.

MODELS OF
SUPERVISORY
ADVOCACY

Assuming that teachers and supervisors have clarified their educational platforms, we can now move to one of the more difficult problems in supervision.
This is the problem of advocacy. Often the supervisor is perceived as an
advocate of the bureaucracy or the administration. This perception leads
teachers to label the behavior of the supervisor as "Snoopervision." Sometimes
the supervisor is perceived as an advocate of a program. As computer literacy
or protection from AIDS become a national concern, supervisors (often
carrying responsibility for curriculum development as well) will be called upon
to initiate and monitor the implementation of programs dealing with those
concerns. Moreover, as the "classroom effectiveness" bandwagon gathers
momentum, supervisors will be called upon to advocate the teaching behaviors
that make up that "program."[1] Some supervisors will perceive themselves as
acting in the above ways of advocacy, but many others will think of themselves
as advocates for teacher professional growth or as advocates of student learning.

What frequently blocks communication between teachers and supervisors is
that they are advocating different concerns, or think that they are, or are
perceived as so doing. In any of those cases, messages will not be understood
in the supervisory episode, because of the confusion over who is advocating
what. In this chapter, then, we will propose a general model of supervisory
advocacy and then explore how four types of advocacy follow the logic of that
model. Once again, the purpose of this exercise is to assist both the teacher and
the supervisor in reflecting on their practice.

[1] For a critique of the narrowness of the focus of effectiveness in schooling, cf. Daniel L. Duke,
"What Is the Nature of Educational Excellence and Should We Try to Measure It?" *Phi Delta
Kappan,* vol. 66, pp. 671–674, June 1985. For a broader view of effectiveness that relates teaching
behaviors to a variety of student outcomes, cf. Jane A. Stallings, *Learning to Look: A Handbook
on Classroom Observation and Teacher Models,* Belmont, Calif.: Wordsworth, 1977; Bruce R.
Joyce and Marsha Weil, *Models of Teaching,* Englewood Cliffs, N.J.: Prentice-Hall, 1986.

If a supervisor has worked on her or his educational platform, some of the necessary elements in this model of supervisory advocacy will have been clarified. The supervisor will have reflected on how children learn. Even though such reflection does not result in a thoroughly detailed theory of learning, it provides a framework for thinking about the question. Moreover, the supervisor will have looked at pedagogical strategies in response to the question of what kinds of instructional protocols seem to work well with children. Finally the supervisor will have thought about the repertory of supervisory strategies she or he finds effective. These, as we will see, will provide some of the building blocks for clarifying one's model of supervisory practice.

A MODEL OF SUPERVISORY ADVOCACY

The model has several elements, all of which affect each other. They appear to be necessary to any process of supervisory advocacy.

1 *An advocacy position.* A supervisor needs to have some overall purpose behind her or his supervisory behavior. In many traditional approaches to supervision, that purpose is simply, "the improvement of instruction." In that case, the supervisor would be advocating "improvement of instruction"— whatever that might mean. On the other hand the supervisor might go into a series of supervisory episodes with the purpose of improving a teacher's ability to utilize the computer as an instructional tool. In that case, the supervisor is advocating functional facility with computer-assisted instruction. Supervision for increased teaching effectiveness would then start out with an advocacy of those teaching behaviors called for by the classroom-effectiveness model. So too, supervision to promote effective learning would advocate those teaching behaviors designed to facilitate effective learning.

2 *A theory of learning.* A supervisor would need to have some sense of a theory of learning which would guide the teacher's instructional behaviors. Either that theory will be held by the supervisor in agreement with the teacher or they will hold differing theories. In either case, the supervisor should have some sense of what theory of learning is guiding the teacher's instruction or should be guiding it.

3 *A model of teaching.* A supervisor would need some sense of the model of teaching which stands behind or should stand behind the teacher's actual instructional behavior. In some cases, that behavior might reflect two or three models used in succession or intermingled.

4 *Prior staff development.* A supervisor will in some cases have proposed some in-service workshops on specific instructional strategies targeted to the type of learning being advocated. Even in the case where a supervisor is advocating a vague "improvement of instruction," there may have been one or two in-service days or one or more instructional methods to which he or she might refer.

5 *Supervisory strategy.* The supervisor ought to have a sense of his or her strategy in the supervisory episodes. These strategies should be agreed upon ahead of time between the supervisor and teacher. In some instances, the teacher may be trying something for the first time and so the strategy would be exploratory and discursive. In other instances, the teacher and supervisor might prefer a close analysis of the class according to a fixed sequence of student and teacher behavior. The supervisor needs to decide how much direction will be provided during the postobservation conference. Will the supervisor, for example, adopt the role of cheerleader, interpreter, or socratic inquirer?

6 *Ongoing staff development.* Will the supervisor be able to point the teacher toward seeking specific improvements through an ongoing program, either at the school or sponsored by the local school district, university, or teacher center? Frequently, the primary value of instructional observation is as a stimulus for further development of improved teaching behavior.

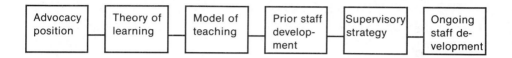

ILLUSTRATING THE MODEL

For the sake of illustration, let us assume that both the school district and the teachers had agreed that there needed to be more attention to the affective learning, contained in the district's statement of educational goals. These affective learnings included the following: self-esteem, teamwork, appreciation of persons of other ethnic, racial, and economic background, good manners, patriotism, and responsible citizenship. Although these goals have cognitive content, they are frequently included under the general label of affective or value education. Supervisors were called upon to work with teachers during the next few years in order to promote these systemwide goals.

Here we see the supervisors called upon to assist teachers in promoting certain learnings. There is an advocacy for these affective learning goals. That advocacy can be carried out, however, in a variety of supervisory approaches. A review of the literature seems to indicate at least three different approaches, which we will label the teacher-responsive approach, the student-responsive approach, and the outcomes-responsive approach. We will add a fourth approach, the bureaucratic-responsive approach, for unfortunately there are supervisors who would use this approach. These four approaches indicate that, besides advocating affective learning, supervisors also advocate basic approaches to achieving such learnings.

The Teacher-Responsive Approach

The teacher-responsive approach would reflect some of the work of Stake, Garman, Walker, and others.[2] Here we see the supervisor initially taking most of

[2] Cf. Thomas J. Sergiovanni, "Landscapes, Mindscapes and Reflective Practice in Supervision," *Journal of Curriculum and Supervision,* vol. 1, pp. 5–17, fall 1985; Noreen B. Garman,

the cues from the teacher. The underlying agenda is to assist the teacher in her or his self-evaluation. The supervisor is a human resource developer, who encourages the teacher to set the agenda and to suggest ways the teacher might like to use the supervisor as a resource. Guided by the model, the responsive approach to supervising affective learning would be reflected in the following diagram:

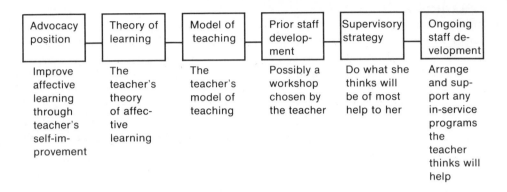

Advocacy position	Theory of learning	Model of teaching	Prior staff develop-ment	Supervisory strategy	Ongoing staff de-velopment
Improve affective learning through teacher's self-im-provement	The teacher's theory of affec-tive learning	The teacher's model of teaching	Possibly a workshop chosen by the teacher	Do what she thinks will be of most help to her	Arrange and sup-port any in-service programs the teacher thinks will help

The teacher-responsive supervisor would look for consistency between the teacher's theory of affective learning and the teacher's model of teaching. In those cases where there was inconsistency, the supervisor would explore with the teacher how she or he could develop a greater consistency. The supervisor would not attempt to impose a point of view on the teacher but would keep encouraging the teacher to clarify what she or he wanted to do. Similarly, the supervisor would look for consistency between the actual teaching behaviors observed in the classroom and the stated intentions of the teacher. Once again the supervisor is seeking to help the teacher actually to do what she or he wants to do. In those cases where the observation and feedback sessions lead in that direction, the supervisor may arrange for some follow-up in-service work by which the teacher would want to strengthen specific teaching strategies. Subsequent observations might focus on the performance of those teaching strategies.

The Student-Responsive Approach

The second approach we call the student-responsive approach. This approach would be based on the works of developmental psychologists like Piaget, Kohlberg, Selman and Fowler, as well as Maslow, Rogers, and Combs.[3] The

"Reflection, The Heart of Clinical Supervision: A Modern Rationale for Professional Practice," in *Readings: Clinical Supervision as Reflection in Action*, Geelong, Victoria, Australia: Deakin University, 1984; Decker Walker, "A Naturalistic Model for Curriculum Development," *School Review*, vol. 80, p. 1, 1971; Robert Stake, *Evaluating the Arts in Education: A Responsive Approach*, Columbus, Ohio: Merrill, 1975; Robert Stake, "A Theoretical Statement of Responsive Evaluation," *Studies in Educational Evaluation*, vol. 2, pp. 19–22, spring 1976.

[3] Robert L. Selman, "A Developmental Approach to Interpersonal and Moral Awareness in Young Children: Some Educational Implications of Levels of Social Perspective Taking," in Thomas C. Hennessy (ed.), *Values and Moral Development*, New York: Paulist Press, 1976. This book provides an excellent overview of several developmentalist perspectives and their educa-

primary focus is on the youngsters in class and on their stages or process of growth. Their growth is seen primarily as an unfolding from within, a gradual movement from one way of viewing various phenomena and responding to them, toward more complex and mature levels of understanding, feeling, and responding. The developmental perspective admits to external influences on the growth of youth, but the focus is on the internal absorption of, and structuring of external stimuli into patterns of meaning and patterns of response. Hence, the teacher does not control the learning of students. The real learning is what students do with the material the teacher presents, how they relate it to past experiences, to the ways they have come to make sense out of their world, to their own growth and survival agenda, to their own affective needs and priorities. The teacher who is sensitive to these developmental patterns in students and recognizes their response to the material of the class as coming out of these internal structures of meaning and feeling can assist the students in their attempts to make sense of the material, to apply it appropriately, to draw relationships and inferences, and to take it into their meaning system.

A good example of educators trying to draw out implications of such development perspectives can be found in the popular 1962 ASCD Yearbook *Perceiving, Behaving and Becoming.*[4] The book presents four essays on the theme of Becoming a Human Person. It then goes on to suggest ways in which the school can promote or facilitate this natural development of children toward becoming a human person.

It is interesting to note, however, that the authors do not prescribe a sequential program for developing any one of the characteristics they list as comprising the human person. Rather they cite anecdotes of what teachers and administrators have done in individual instances which seem to have promoted the youngsters' growth in a given area. More often than not, they seem to suggest a general flexibility of classroom and schoolwide procedures in order to facilitate students' affective growth as students are responding to the material. In other words, these educators propose a high degree of individualization of instruction in which the teacher responds to the students as they attempt to integrate new material into their developing meaning and feeling systems. Hence, there would be many ad hoc interruptions in the regular lesson plan as the teacher responded to an effective learning-in-process on the part of one or more students. At other times, issues would emerge which seemed to touch the whole class, leading to a classwide activity to promote that particular affective learning.

Classroom observation in this approach would probably attend to a more

tional implications. Jean Piaget, *The Science of Education and the Psychology of the Child,* New York: Viking Press, 1970; Lawrence Kohlberg, "Moral and Religious Education and the Public School," in Theodore Sizer (ed.), *Religion and Public Education,* Boston: Houghton Mifflin, 1967; James W. Fowler, *Stages of Faith: The Psychology of Human Development and the Quest for Meaning,* San Francisco: Harper & Row, 1981; essays by Maslow, Rogers, and Combs are found in *Perceiving, Behaving and Becoming: A New Focus for Education,* Arlington, Va.: Association for Supervision and Curriculum Development, 1962.

[4] Maslow, Rogers, and Combs, op. cit.

generalized sensitivity on the part of the teacher to deal with affective learning needs as they arose in the course of a standard lesson.

On the other hand, Piaget and Kohlberg would propose structured learning activities which would bring about a certain cognitive disequilibrium in the students, forcing them to stretch toward more inclusive meaning and value types of reasoning. However, they too would propose a more general environment of peer interaction in the classroom, since those students who were moving toward high stages of reasoning could then challenge the others in an ongoing fashion.[5]

Others like Pinar and Grumet would propose an even greater autonomy to student learning in the affective domain.[6] The teacher and the traditional curriculum would have a diminished role and the students, in their effort to make sense out of their own experience, would occupy center stage. The teacher would guide, facilitate, stimulate, and also present materials for the students to study. But the students would be doing more of the teaching to themselves, with the teachers on the sidelines helping where necessary and giving lots of encouragement. Observing classes following this approach would probably involve charting how consistently teachers let students take charge of their own learning.

The student-responsive approach would appear in the general model as follows:

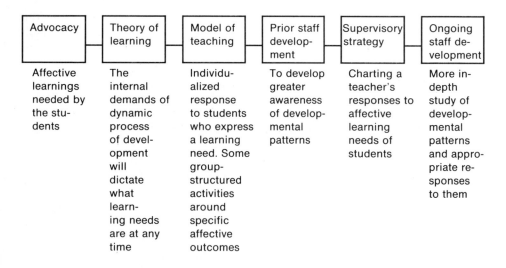

Advocacy	Theory of learning	Model of teaching	Prior staff development	Supervisory strategy	Ongoing staff development
Affective learnings needed by the students	The internal demands of dynamic process of development will dictate what learning needs are at any time	Individualized response to students who express a learning need. Some group-structured activities around specific affective outcomes	To develop greater awareness of developmental patterns	Charting a teacher's responses to affective learning needs of students	More in-depth study of developmental patterns and appropriate responses to them

The Outcomes-Responsive Approach

The third approach is the outcomes-responsive approach. This approach assumes that affective learning outcomes can be spelled out ahead of time, that they can be nurtured in a content-specific, sequenced curriculum by direct teaching, and that

[5] Cf. the introductory essay by Thomas Hennessy in the book he edited, *Values and Moral Development,* op. cit.

[6] Cf. William F. Pinar and Madeleine R. Grumet, *Toward a Poor Curriculum,* Dubuque, Iowa: Kendell-Hunt Publishing Company, 1976; Grumet, "Curriculum as Theatre: Merely Players," *Curriculum Inquiry,* vol. 8, pp. 37–64, September 1978; Pinar and Grumet, "Socratic Caesura and the Theory-Practice Relationship," *Theory into Practice,* vol. 21, 50–54, winter 1982.

their achievement can be evaluated. This approach does not necessarily deny the validity of the developmentalists' theories of growth. Nevertheless, those holding this position would assert that there is much a teacher can do to stimulate and promote in a proactive way the affective growth of students. While individualized attention remains a necessity, learning activities for the whole class can be designed to correspond to the general stage of growth in which one would expect to find most students for any given grade level. While the teacher may not control the students' growth, he or she may decidedly influence it through direct, intentional teaching toward clear outcomes.

This proactive approach is clearly modeled on what we have referred to earlier as effective classroom teaching. There we find a clear theory of learning, a prescriptive model of teaching, and programs of staff development to prepare and develop teachers for greater classroom effectiveness. The difference here is that the supervisor is advocating affective learning instead of the learning of basic skills in reading and math. This approach says that the students can learn through methods of direct instruction, that the instructional methodologies of effective teaching can be used (perhaps supplemented by additional methodologies such as class discussion of controversial issues, expressive exercises, creative exercises, and inclusion of feelings as legitimate responses to the material under study), and that the achievement of outcomes can be evaluated (although not necessarily graded).[7] Probably more than ever, teacher staff development programs will be called for.

Hence, the outcomes-responsive approach can be diagramed according to our basic paradigm as follows:

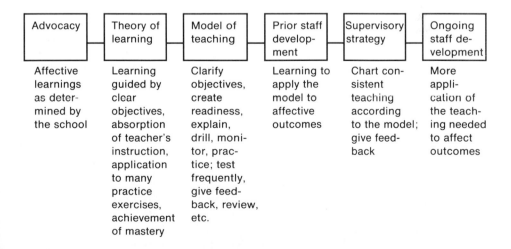

Advocacy	Theory of learning	Model of teaching	Prior staff development	Supervisory strategy	Ongoing staff development
Affective learnings as determined by the school	Learning guided by clear objectives, absorption of teacher's instruction, application to many practice exercises, achievement of mastery	Clarify objectives, create readiness, explain, drill, monitor, practice; test frequently, give feedback, review, etc.	Learning to apply the model to affective outcomes	Chart consistent teaching according to the model; give feedback	More application of the teaching needed to affect outcomes

<hr />

[7] For examples of more direct teaching of affective outcomes, cf. Clive Beck, "Moral Education in the Junior High School," in Kevin Ryan (ed.), *Character Development in Schools and Beyond,* New York: Praeger, in press; Robert J. Starratt, "Moral Development in the High School Classroom," in Ryan, ibid.; Norman A. Sprinthall, "Moral and Psychological Development: A Curriculum for Secondary Schools," in Thomas C. Hennessy (ed.), *Values and Moral Development,* op. cit.

This approach is called outcomes-responsive because it starts with a schoolwide effort. The prior and ongoing staff development programs are not a series of ad hoc in-service sessions but represent a 1- and 2-year commitment on the part of the school to enable all the staff to develop classroom strategies which bring students to achieve those schoolwide affective outcomes.

The Bureaucracy-Responsive Approach

The fourth approach is the bureaucracy-responsive approach. This approach is not based so much on professional considerations as it is on management control and compliance. The school district prescribed that teachers be attentive to districtwide goals of affective learning. Since the machinery of teacher evaluation by supervisors was already in place, that machinery was going to respond to what the district had mandated. Districtwide curriculum supervisors requested reports on how these mandates were being met. Supervisory personnel in the local schools, under pressure to respond to district office superiors, would either ask for teachers to submit reports to them or would spend one or two days visiting classes to gather evidence for their reports. In either case, teachers would be made to understand that the "higher-ups" or "downtown" or "the district office" wanted something for their files so that they in turn could report to the school board and/or state authorities. Besides all the many other items on the district's agenda (reorganizing the special education program, changing the bus routes to correspond to changing population patterns, "reduction in force" efforts due to falling enrollments, the consolidation of two junior high schools) this item on affective learning grew out of a school board meeting when several parent groups brought complaints to the board about ethnic rivalries in the schools, abusive language in school corridors, and the appearance of swastikas among the more standard graffiti on school buildings. The teachers union readily agreed that they too were concerned about these antisocial behaviors. Hence the superintendent's office issued a mandate calling for greater attention to the above-mentioned learning outcomes.

Usually what happens in these cases is that teacher activities already in practice are selected and labeled as evidence of attention to those districtwide learning outcomes. Sometimes the supervisor will be considerate enough to notify the teacher that in a day or so she or he will be coming around to observe their compliance with the mandated attention to those districtwide affective outcomes. At other times, supervisors will not even bother to observe classroom practice, simply recording from recollections of past classroom visits various examples of teachers attending to teamwork, self-esteem, good manners, and groupings of students that reflected ethnic and racial mixes. For good measure, she or he will include anecdotes from corridor supervisors and extracurricular moderators. Notice that the response is to the district office. There is no particular interest in teacher growth. There is no program in place to support the learnings. The evidence gathered is fragmentary and anecdotal, even though it may be presented in such a way as to imply an intentional, schoolwide effort.

A not uncommon practice would include the scheduling of a faculty in-service day on the topic of affective learning. A university professor would be brought in to discuss appropriate learning activities and teaching protocols. That in-service day might figure prominently in the school's report to the central office. Not only will the professor's categories be used for labeling the evidence drawn up that the school is complying with the district mandate, but the professor's comments that research on the effectiveness of school's efforts in this area of affective learning is not conclusive will be used in the concluding paragraph.

The bureaucracy-responsive approach when framed in the elements of the general model would appear as follows:

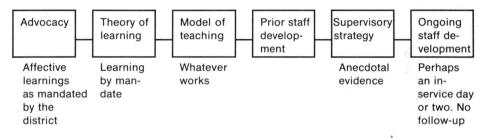

Advocacy	Theory of learning	Model of teaching	Prior staff develop-ment	Supervisory strategy	Ongoing staff de-velopment
Affective learnings as mandated by the district	Learning by man-date	Whatever works		Anecdotal evidence	Perhaps an in-service day or two. No follow-up

This portrayal of the bureaucracy-responsive approach would provide comic relief if it were not so close to reality, in both large city school systems and medium-sized suburban systems. Veteran teachers respond to these kinds of intrusions by supervisors by playing the bureaucratic game. Both teachers and supervisors are protecting themselves and each other by providing evidence of their faithful compliance to district concern. Unfortunately this charade benefits no one.

IMPLICATIONS FOR PRACTICE

The general model offers supervisors a way to reflect on and interpret their normal practice of supervision. When it comes to promoting specific student learnings, supervisors can relate the four approaches to the realities of the schools and classrooms they deal with and thus come to a decision about an approach that best fits their circumstances. Three of the four approaches indicate, however, that improving the quality and extent of those learnings ought to flow from theories of learning and models of teaching which in turn guide staff development programs needed to facilitate teacher improvement. The model calls for a type of supervision that promotes reflection-in-action on the part of both supervisor and teacher.[8] The model links classroom observa-

[8]Cf. Thomas J. Sergiovanni, "Landscapes, Mindscapes and Reflective Practice in Supervision," op. cit.; and Noreen G. Garman, "Reflection, the Heart of Clinical Supervision: A Modern Rationale for Professional Practice," op. cit. The work of Donald Schön, *The Reflective Practitioners: How Professionals Think in Action,* New York: Basic Books, 1983, provides a thorough grounding for this perspective on supervision.

tions to staff development workshops in which teachers can use the perspectives of such workshops as part of their decision-making repertory for classroom practice. The model also offers policy makers a guide for promoting affective learning through a multidimensional effort at the local school level.

SUMMARY

This chapter attempted to generate a paradigm of a supervisory advocacy. Four variations of the paradigm were developed and their use explored. Finally, some research uses of the paradigm were described.

STUDY GUIDE

Recall the concepts, ideas, and meanings associated with each of the following phrases and terms included in this chapter. Can you discuss each of them with a colleague and apply them to the supervisory context of your school? If you cannot, review them in the text and record the page numbers for future reference.

1 Advocacy
2 Teacher-responsive approach
3 Cognitive disequilibrium
4 Outcomes-responsive approach
5 Proactive approach
6 Affective learnings

EXERCISES

1 Interview a supervisor, using the general model contained in this chapter. Can you identify the supervisor's position on all the elements in the model?
2 Interview a teacher. Ask the teacher which of the four advocacy models he or she has experienced in supervisory episodes. Ask the teacher which would be the preferred advocacy model and why.
3 In your local school district, are there policies governing the conduct of supervision which point toward any specific advocacy model? Are supervisors aware of that bias?

CHAPTER 12

CURRICULUM CONCERNS FOR SUPERVISORY LEADERSHIP

The thesis of Part Three of this book is that educational supervision deals with the school not only as an organization but as an organization established for the purposes of education. Educational supervision, therefore, of necessity involves the supervisor in educational theory, in regard to both the general purposes of education and the means to achieve these purposes, the curriculum-instructional program. In this chapter we wish to summarize some of the more important issues supervisors face when, in their interaction with subordinates, they move into the arena of curriculum and instruction.

Curriculum has often been separated from instruction, or pedagogy, for purposes of analysis, research, and evaluation, as well as for professional course work in graduate schools. The supervisor, however, will most often encounter it in its living form, that is, embodied in the behavior of a teacher.[1] Yet what the supervisor encounters in the instructional behavior of the teacher may not be immediately intelligible beyond a surface impression of the teacher's physical actions and interactions with students. Without some frames of reference provided either by the teacher or by his or her own study and experience, the observer may not be able to interpret the significance of the sequence of class activities, or why the teacher chose to introduce the topic in such and such a manner.

---

[1] In his recent book, *Curriculum Renewal,* Alan Glatthorn repeatedly makes the point that the teacher is the one who fashions the curriculum into a usable instructional tool: Alan Glatthorn, *Curriculum Renewal,* Alexandria, Va.: Association for Supervision and Curriculum Development, 1987.

In the previous chapter we saw that the supervisor enters into each supervisory episode as an advocate of the teacher's growth, the student's learning, the program objectives, or the bureaucracy's mandate. In order to understand one's advocacy position, one has to understand the theory of learning and the model of teaching one brings to the supervisory episode. In order to carry out the supervisory process, however, the supervisor needs some conceptual frameworks in order to interpret how the teacher is approaching the curriculum.

One way of attempting to understand curriculum and its influence in what goes on in the classroom is to review the textbook and other materials being used in the class.[2] Another way, which gets one closer to the reality of what one is supposed to be supervising, is to study the teacher's lesson plans, not only for that day, but for the classes that follow. While these two steps are helpful, the observation and analysis of the actual instructional activity lie at the heart of the activity of educational supervision. It is in this instructional activity that the supervisor sees the teacher putting into action the teacher's integration of his or her educational platform with the goals of the school, the goals of this course, the specific objectives of this particular unit or lesson, and his or her knowledge of the ability, interests, and personalities of the students in the class. All these influences are uniquely synthesized, integrated, and molded and then put into action in the teacher's instructional activity. Therefore, one observing that activity somehow has to be very sensitive to the intentions of the teacher to see how the activity of the teacher reflects this complex integration or synthesis. In other words, the supervisor must try to observe how the curriculum or the teacher's perception of it is, in fact, one of the controlling influences in what the teacher *does* in that classroom.

CURRICULUM-INSTRUCTIONAL ACTIVITY

The term curriculum has many definitions, as does the term instruction. For our purposes, we will define *curriculum* as that which the student is supposed to encounter, study, practice, and master—in short the stuff of what the student learns. That can be many things, from a basic skill such as counting numbers, to spelling 100 words correctly, to memorizing the multiplication tables, to understanding the biological explanations of photosynthesis, to playing the piano, to writing verse, to comparing the imagery of two authors. We acknowledge that there is always a hidden or informal curriculum being taught in the classroom as well as elsewhere in the school. But we wish here to restrict curriculum to the formal or overt curriculum.

Instruction we will define as that process by which the student is led to encounter the curriculum to the desired degree of mastery. Not only must the instructional process lead the student to the curriculum, it must so structure

---

[2] A helpful overview of approaches to evaluating curriculum materials can be found in Michael Eraut, Len Goad, and George Smith, "The Analysis of Curriculum Materials," University of Sussex, Occasional Paper 2, Education Area, 1975.

that encounter that the student does not move on to something else before a predetermined level of mastery is achieved. Instruction, then, can be something a teacher does, or it can be built into a programmed textbook or into a computer or a learning packet.

In general, we will speak of curriculum as "what is to be learned" and instruction as "how it is to be taught." One must be aware, however, that these are loose and pragmatic ways of speaking. To say that instruction means how something is to be taught can be misleading. For example, someone could say: "I learned that by hard work, by breaking that problem down myself into the small pieces until I could find where the loose wire was....I taught myself how to do that." In that instance there was no external instructor. In a sense, the person instructed herself. Or perhaps the person had earlier learned a generalizable problem-solving skill that in turn taught her a way of attacking other problems. In that instance, what she learned (the problem-solving skill) taught her in subsequent experiences *how* to learn other things. For our purposes, however, we will use instruction primarily to refer to a process in which a teacher is interacting with a student.

OBSERVING INSTRUCTIONAL ACTIVITY

Now, let us suppose you are having a busy day supervising. You visit the classes of five physics teachers. You discover that each teacher is using quite different methodologies. One teacher has his class divided into small groups and they spend most of the class discussing how best to go about studying the wave versus the particle theories of light. In another, the teacher is showing an animated cartoon that illustrates the different properties of light but concludes by leaving the students in a quandary over which theory of light is correct. In another class, the teacher is relating Newtonian particle physics to individualistic theories of society, and contrasting that with field theory physics and more communal views of society; toward the end of class the students get into a lively discussion of the low level of student morale and the prevailing tendencies of people at the school to "do their own thing." In the fourth class you find the students in the physics laboratory performing an experiment with a ripple tank, carefully following the instructions in their lab books and recording their measurements carefully in their notebooks. There is no class discussion; the teacher merely walks around the lab, occasionally pointing out a faulty measurement notation or telling one student team to stop "goofing off" or he will send them to detention hall. In the fifth class the students have been reading a biography of Isaac Newton and the teacher has assigned teams to prepare a model replication of Newton's laboratory. The class begins with the teacher questioning the students about the antecedent scientific knowledge to which Newton had access that might have shaped much of Newton's approach to his experiments.

You come back to your office at the end of the day with a half hour before you must leave to referee a basketball game in the league quarterfinals.

Tomorrow you are scheduled for individual conferences with all the teachers you have observed today. Besides all the routine aspects of class management such as the lighting, ventilation, noise levels, pupil attentiveness, and so forth, what will you say about the approach the teacher is using, especially as that relates to the curriculum that is supposed to be taught? Granting the observable strengths and weaknesses of each teacher in putting on the instructional performance (self-confidence, good tone of voice, good use of questions, etc.), can you say that one approach was better than another? If you say none of the approaches is necessarily better, do you mean that they are all interchangeable, that it does not really matter which approach one uses? Or does each approach come out of a different idea of what the curriculum is or is supposed to be? Are these approaches mutually exclusive? Is the content learned in one approach totally different from the content learned in another? Or are there some common learnings one finds embedded in each approach? Is it fair, however, to give one departmental exam covering material taught in such divergent ways? How would these students score on a national physics test? Does it make much difference to you if the teacher does not care that much about national test scores? Before you begin to put some order into these bewildering issues, the bell rings and you must dash over to the gym to catch the bus for the basketball tournament.

Let us leave our distraught supervisor and return to our more dispassionate and reflective environment to put some order, sequence, and logic into this task. For example, what were some of the questions that did *not* occur to our frantic supervisor? It might be a good test of our own frames of reference if we were to pause at this point, close the book, and place ourselves in the situation, without the press of time and the basketball game distracting us. Perhaps we could generate 10 other questions of major importance. After we put them down in the haphazard order in which they occur to us, we might order or group them in some sequence, e.g., moving from the more abstract to the more particular, or from those dealing with curriculum to those dealing with student achievement, to those dealing with the teacher's platform, and so on.

OTHER QUESTIONS

An exercise such as the above will yield a variety of results. One salutary effect of going through the exercise and then sharing the results with others is that one quickly recognizes how many potentially useful questions there are. It becomes clear that classroom observation must be preceded by at least one lengthy conference in which the teacher can indicate what his or her intentions for the class are.

Our own first attempt to complete the exercise yielded the following questions. They are by no means exhaustive. We shall see subsequently that the kinds of questions we ask will emerge out of a variety of frames of reference about curriculum. But for the present let us consider the following questions for purposes of illustration.

1 *Methods and instructional effectiveness.* Are any of these five ways the most effective way to teach this? Is there another way that would be demonstrably the *most* effective way to teach that material? Suppose that the students might have had the opportunity to travel to a nearby government research lab doing interplanetary research on light signals? Or might the teacher have invited the director of the lab to come to the school to put on a demonstration lab, using all the latest sophisticated technology involved in spectroscopy?

Does the teacher always or usually use this method? If the teacher uses other methods, what are they? Are they related to specific curricular objectives, or are they used primarily to relieve boredom (which could also be a curriculum objective)?

2 *Instructional activity and curriculum-instructional objectives.* What is the teacher trying to do? Is the teacher trying to teach one thing or several things simultaneously?

What precisely is it that she or he wants to teach? Was that clear to you? Was it clear to the students? Why did the teacher choose this precise activity as the best or at least as a good means to bring the students into a learning encounter with the curricular material? In your judgment, was the means effective? How effective was it? Was it effective for all the students or only for some?

How does what the teacher is doing today flow out of what the class has been doing in previous classes? Is there a sequential order to the course, and if so, how does this part fit into the sequence? How much time does the teacher plan to spend on this matter of theories of light? To what level of mastery does the teacher wish to bring the students? Is the time being spent adequate for this purpose? Is that degree of mastery required to grasp the material coming later? Is there a balance between the time spent on this topic and the time spent on earlier and later topics? Who decides that? Who ought to decide that?

Is the teacher aware of the hidden, or informal, curricula involved in this approach?

3 *Curriculum-instructional units and departmental or school objectives.* How do this class and this course fit in with the departmental or school objectives? Is there a particular focus or emphasis to the objectives that each course is supposed to reinforce? If so, was there evidence of that reinforcement in this class? Why does the department or school support, or at least tolerate, such divergent methods of teaching? Are there specific objectives that are served by these differing approaches? Are these approaches the only methods encouraged in the department or school, or are there others?

4 *Methods and teacher-supervisor platforms.* How does this teaching method or approach fit with the teacher's platform? Are there obvious discrepancies between the observable behavior and the platform? If there are, are there legitimate reasons for the discrepancies? How does the teaching method fit with your (the supervisor's) platform? Are you aware of your comfort or discomfort, pleasure or displeasure over the fit or lack of it? Did these feelings, perhaps unacknowledged during the classroom observation, lead either to perceptions of only weak points of the class or perceptions of only strong points? Do you need to review your observations to weed out at least some of the bias that comes from your own platform?

If you knew nothing about the teacher's platform prior to the observation, could you infer what it was from the instructional activity you observed?

If you knew nothing of the teacher's class plan, could you infer what the primary instructional objectives of this class were?

If you knew nothing of what preceded this class, what could you infer that students already knew about the topic? What could you infer about their possession of skills and understandings necessary for learning the topic of the class?

By comparing your questions with these and those developed by others, you may begin to see some pattern or points of emphasis developing. But where do these questions come from, and why are they important? A little reflection will indicate that many of them come from our concepts or beliefs about the nature of learning, about what a curriculum is supposed to be, about the nature of the academic discipline, and so on. In order for the supervisor to know at least some of the important questions to ask, he or she ought to have some clear ideas about curriculum and how supervisors can affect its improvement or effectiveness in an instructional setting.

SUPERVISORS AND CURRICULUM DEVELOPMENT

Some commentators on supervisory practice complain that "supervision is like a honeycomb without the honey."[3] Supervisors tend to focus on the methods of teaching and not on the content of teaching. Supervision began primarily as inspection by administrators, and only later was it linked with curriculum development. While some curriculum specialists are involved with classroom observation and some supervisors are involved with curriculum development, the roles tend to be split. Curriculum developers tend to spend their time on the design and testing of curriculum materials.[4] Supervisors tend to spend their time on improving instructional methodology and organizational support services for improving instruction.

Because of increased specialization in both roles, especially in large school systems, it would be difficult in practice for the curriculum designer and instructional supervisor to merge their roles into one. There simply are not enough hours in the week to meet the demands of both roles, even if a single person possessed the knowledge and skills needed in each role. Nonetheless, we affirm that supervisors have an important role to play in curriculum development.

One can view curriculum development as taking place outside the

[3] Daniel Tanner and Laurel N. Tanner, *Curriculum Development,* New York: Macmillan, 1975, p. 621.
[4] Cf. Walter Dick, Instructional Design and the Curriculum Development Process," *Educational Leadership,* vol. 44, no. 4, pp. 54–56, 1987.

classroom or inside the classroom. The curriculum specialist normally is freed from teaching responsibilities in order to engage in the research of available curriculum materials and to design units of curriculum for use by classroom teachers. From this perspective curriculum is designed and produced outside the classroom and is subsequently taught in the classroom. From another perspective, however, curriculum is developed inside the classroom as teachers adapt the prepared materials for classroom episodes of teaching. Teachers frequently alter, expand, rearrange, and reinterpret what the curriculum developer outside the classroom has prepared. Through trial and error, intuition, and responsiveness to the immediate circumstances of students, teachers are or can be involved in curriculum development in the classroom.[5]

In working with teachers in classrooms, supervisors can promote this kind of curriculum development. While curriculum development takes place at many levels (state, school system, school building, classroom), the actual curriculum ends up being what the teacher teaches. Taba and others have stressed the importance of teacher involvement in curriculum development.[6] Unfortunately, the information coming from the classroom back up through the levels outside the classroom does not get communicated or attended to that easily. Nonetheless, it is in the laboratory of the classroom that practical curriculum development occurs. By providing encouragement, supporting exploratory modifications of curriculum materials, and asking probing questions about the effects on students, the supervisor can play a part in this form of curriculum development. As we point out later in this chapter, the supervisor, because of his or her key position in the school organization, can also carry information and suggestions back to those responsible for curriculum design.

Even though supervisors frequently have not been trained in the complex technology of curriculum design, they should bring to their work some broad principles of curriculum theory and development as well as a sensitivity to the complementary educational objectives served by various curriculum-instructional systems. The remainder of this chapter highlights some of these broader understandings and principles of curriculum and their implications for supervisory practice.

---

[5] Numerous studies and reports highlight this phenomenon. Cf. Michael Fullen and Alan Pomfret, "Research on Curriculum and Instruction Implementation," *Review of Educational Research,* vol. 47, pp. 335–397, 1977; and F. Michael Connelly and Freema Elbaz, "Conceptual Bases for Curriculum Thought: A Teacher's Perspective," in Arthur W. Foshay (ed.), *Considered Action for Curriculum Improvement,* Alexandria, Va.: Association for Supervision and Curriculum Development, 1980. Glatthorn, op. cit., and Brant argue for the teacher's involvement: Ron Brandt, "When Curriculum Should Be Locally Developed," *Educational Leadership,* vol. 44, no. 4, p. 3, 1987. Fenwick English, on the other hand, would argue for a curriculum that is matched to statewide tests: Fenwick English, "It's Time to Abolish Conventional Curriculum Guides," *Educational Leadership,* vol. 44, no. 4, pp. 50–52, 1987.

[6] Hilda Taba, *Curriculum Development: Theory and Practice,* New York: Harcourt Brace Jovanovich, 1962, pp. 439–440. An excellent updating of basic principles for curriculum development is to be found in Allan A. Glatthorn, *Curriculum Renewal,* Alexandria, Va.: Association for Supervision and Curriculum Development, 1987.

DEVELOPING ALTERNATIVE CURRICULUM AND INSTRUCTIONAL STRATEGIES

One of the more refreshing innovations in teacher training appears in the work of Bruce Joyce and Marsha Weil dealing with models of teaching.[7] They have studied a variety of teaching styles, processes, and interaction schemes and have come up with over 20 alternative models of teaching. Each model has some theoretical underpinnings to it, has a recognizable sequence of activities and a major orientation or a set of educational objectives, requires a consistent type of classroom interaction and a type of support system, and has, finally, general applicability to either specific purposes or many purposes.

Each one of these models also presumes a curriculum. That is, the models of teaching are not concerned exclusively with methodology, but imply a curriculum, at least in a general sense. Frequently, a theory of learning is embedded in the model. In some of the models a theory of groups or of society is also implied. These models are touched upon here to provide the prospective or practicing supervisor with some mental maps or schemata for use with teachers or others involved in the instructional system, rather than to propose any particular model as the best model.

It is our belief that different models are applicable to the demands of different situations. In that sense, using one model or approach may be "better," not in an absolute sense, but in the sense of its being more appropriate to a given set of circumstances. If a teacher engages in instructional activity that remains always the same, there may be circumstances in which that activity is counterproductive for at least some, if not all, of the students. A teacher's repertory of instructional strategies may be larger, consisting of three or four, but even then the teacher may still lack the versatility to respond to given situations that arise in a classroom.

In like manner, a supervisor may be working with a limited number of models in mind. In a given situation where a teacher asks a supervisor for help in tackling a difficult instructional task, this lack of versatility will limit the instructional options that the two of them produce. Moreover, some familiarity with a wide diversity of possible curriculum-instructional approaches will render the supervisor better prepared for the unexpected. When the unexpected occurs, we usually react negatively, because it does not fit our categories, our mental maps. If, for example, we conceive of art education only as discrete encounters with discrete art forms, then we might be upset by an art teacher whose class is involved in "environmental" art projects in which several art forms and media are simultaneously employed. Familiarity with a broad range of curriculum-instructional options enables the supervisor to appreciate truly unique and creative approaches.

Joyce and Weil have grouped various models of teaching according to four basic families. These families represent different orientations toward the learner and reflect different educational objectives.

[7] Bruce Joyce and Marsha Weil, *Models of Teaching,* 3d ed., Englewood Cliffs, N.J.: Prentice-Hall, 1986.

I Information Processing Models

This family of models stresses the development of general intellectual abilities, logical reasoning, methodologies of academic disciplines, concept formation, problem solving, and methods of inquiry. Examples: scientific inquiry models, moral problem-solving models.

II Personal Development Models

This family of models stresses the development of self- and interpersonal awareness, self-understanding and taking responsibility, affectivity, and creativity. Examples: awareness training, reality therapy, nondirective teaching.

III Social Interaction Models

This family of models stresses the development of group dynamics skills; social, political, and legal problem solving; academic inquiry on social issues; and decision-making skills. Examples: role playing, group investigation, simulations of economic decision making.

IV Changing Behavior Models

Based on principles of stimulus control and reinforcement, this family of models stresses changing of visible behaviors that include acquisition of academic skills, social skills, stress reduction, and self-control. Examples: programmed instruction, assertiveness training, operant conditioning and mastery learning.

Joyce and Weil point out that these families are not mutually exclusive. There is some natural overlapping among methods and objectives. Furthermore, activities based on some models can be used to promote or complement learnings targeted more specifically by other models. For example, the stress on developing logical reasoning and concept formation (information-processing family) could be used in group discussion of a social problem (social-interaction family).

Clearly, further study of alternative models would be called for in order for supervisors to be more fully acquainted with the power and the methods inherent in various models. Suffice it here to point out that supervisors can bring to their work with teachers a wealth of curriculum approaches, as suggested by the inventory of teaching models cataloged by Joyce and Weil. Depending on the objectives of any given class, supervisors can explore with the teacher the possibility of increasing his or her effectiveness by developing alternative instructional strategies. Moreoover, the supervisor who is familiar with a wide range of curriculum instructional models will more readily recognize which of various approaches teachers are employing. The hypothetical case above of the supervisor visiting five classes that are all taking a different approach to the study of wave and particle theory should make that point sufficiently.[8]

---

[8] Cf. Susan S. Ellis, "Models of Teaching: A Solution to the Teaching Style/Learning Style Dilemma," *Educational Leadership,* vol. 36, no. 4, pp. 274–277, 1979, for a description of how a school system used Joyce and Weil's work for staff development.

TABLE 12-1
GROWTH AND DEVELOPMENT OF CHILDREN IN THE FIVE MODELS

	Exploratory	Group process	Developmental-cognitive	Programmed	Traditional-fundamental
Reading achievement		N+*		C+†	N+
Math achievement		N+		C+	N+
Nonverbal problem solving	C+		C+		
Questioning	C+				
Independence	C+		C+		
Cooperation with others	C+		C+		
Accepts responsibility for success	C+		C+		
Accepts responsibility for failure				C+	
Absence rate	C+		C+		

*N+ = better than national norms. †C+ = better than control group in the Follow-through Study.
Source: Jane A. Stallings and David Kaskowitz, *Follow-through Classroom Observation Evaluation* 1972–1973, SRI Project URU-7370, Menlo Park, Calif.: Stanford Research Institute, 1974. ERIC Accession no. ED 104 969, in Jane A. Stallings, *Learning to Look: A Handbook on Classroom Observation and Teaching Models,* Belmont, Calif.: Wadsworth, 1977, p. 237.

ADVANTAGES AND DISADVANTAGES OF SELECTED MODELS

In this section we provide a more detailed comparison of five models of teaching typically found in elementary schools. The models, as proposed by Jane Stallings, are exploratory, group process, developmental-cognitive, programmed, and traditional-fundamental.[9] A comparison of the five models appears in Table 12-1. Each of the five models is discussed below.

Exploratory Models

Exploratory models are relatively unstructured, informal, activity-centered, and open. They are based on the belief that students are inherently curious and intrinsically motivated. Learning takes place as a result of explorations in a responsive environment. Learning centers, resource centers, and interest centers are important to this approach. Successful articulation of this model

[9] Jane A. Stallings, *Learning to Look: A Handbook on Classroom Observation and Teacher Models,* Belmont, Calif.: Wadsworth, 1977.

requires that teachers carefully evaluate the social, emotional, and academic development of each student, develop goals and objectives in each of these areas, and plan the environment so that growth is facilitated. According to Stallings:

> The expected outcome of this environmental approach is children who are self-motivated and who not only succeed in their efforts to solve problems but also recognize their own successes—that is, they are self-motivated, self-directing, and self-evaluating. They explore or play the game because it is self-rewarding, not because it pleases the teacher.
>
> Advocates also believe that children learn to solve cognition and social problems through the experience of solving cognitive and social problems.[10]

In this model, children are allowed to experience dissonance and conflict and are encouraged to search for alternative solutions. They are allowed to risk failure and learn from the consequences of actions. Advocates of the exploratory model envisage a citizenry that is independent in judgment, creative in problem solving, and socially responsible.

Group-Process Models

Group-process models rely heavily on group-interaction methods whereby students participate to discuss and resolve issues proposed by the teacher and of importance to them. Coming to grips with one's perception of reality and building a sense of responsibility are typical concerns of educators who use this method. Students deal with such classroom issues as curriculum, discipline, and general governance as well as the more weighty issues that emerge from subject matter under study and from the broader community and societal context.

> Theoretically, children in the group process model could be expected to develop an ability to govern themselves and express their ideas and feelings. They would listen to the ideas of other people and judge the merit of the ideas. Members of the group would generate several solutions to problems, and through discussion foresee consequences of possible actions. Because they learn to listen to each other, the children would develop empathy for others (the ability to put themselves in another's shoes). Because they deal fairly with each other, they would feel self-worth and would gain experience in giving and receiving love.[11]

Group meetings are used on a regular basis as a means for teaching. Often role playing, simulation,and other group-process techniques are used. The group-process model is not sufficiently embedded in a set of curriculum ideas to establish it as an independent approach to teaching. Typically, the model is used as an adjunct to or within the broad framework of another model. The exploratory model and the developmental-cognitive model are natural compan-

[10] Ibid., p. 61.
[11] Ibid., p. 92.

ions for the group-process strategy, though presumably this approach could be incorporated into programmed and traditional-fundamental approaches as a formally distinct teaching option.

Developmental-Cognitive Models

The developmental-cognitive model of teaching, based on the theories of Jean Piaget,[12] assumes that a student's intellectual or logical thinking occurs in stages according to the student's age and experience. Students learn, according to the theory, through involvement in and manipulation of the environment. The teacher's role in developmental-cognitive teaching is to respond to each developmental level by providing appropriate materials and activities. The physical environment is rich with materials. Interest centers are used extensively.

> To implement this model it is essential that the room be arranged into several learning centers and that a wide variety of materials be made available to the children. The materials and equipment can be ordinary, routine items—they need not be purchased. For instance, a teacher might take the children on a scavenger hunt across the school yard. The children would fill their bags with items they found along the way: seeds, gum wrappers, sucker sticks, paper clips, a leaf, a button, safety pins, stones. Back in the classroom, the children could arrange or classify their findings into categories according to color, shape, or whatever. Then they could play "What's My Set?" In this game, the children take turns guessing by what rules the others classified their objects.[13]

Programmed Models

Programmed models of teaching are based on the operant-conditioning theories of Skinner.[14] Basically, behavior is modified because desired behavior is reinforced. Carefully structured educational programs are developed in a manner that permits instructional materials to be sequenced in small steps. It is believed that students can progress through these steps if provided with consistent reinforcement. As they progress, they master the basic skills necessary to achieve grade-level reading and math scores on national tests. The basic skills in reading and math are stressed above all, with other subject-matter areas receiving considerably less attention. Advocates believe that once basic skill levels are up to normal, youngsters will develop better self-concepts and be better able to engage in more complex learning. Essentially the teacher's job is to state beforehand desired goals and outcomes in a form that can be measured; evaluate the students' present level of functioning; provide sequenced learning materials; drill students, providing reinforcement as necessary; keep track of student progress; and repeat the cycle.

[12] Jean Piaget, *The Origins of Intelligence in Children*, New York: International Universities Press, 1952.
[13] Stallings, op. cit., p. 145.
[14] B. F. Skinner, *The Technology of Teaching*, New York: Appleton-Century-Crofts, 1968.

Traditional-Fundamental Models

The traditional-fundamental approach to teaching is perhaps best known. In this model it is believed that students learn best in quiet and orderly classrooms where teachers are in complete control and assume sole responsibility for administering a structured academic program. Most of the instructional time in this model is spent on basic skills. Curriculum is traditional and textbook-oriented. Drill and homework are common.

Table 12-1 compares each of the five models across several dimensions considered to be important to teaching. Based on the studies summarized in this table, programmed and traditional-fundamental approaches to teaching are superior in their ability to teach basic skills but inferior in obtaining other, equally desirable results such as responsibility, cooperation, independence, and problem-solving outcomes.

BLOOM'S TAXONOMY

Bloom's *Taxonomy* provides another useful interpretive map, or conceptual frame of reference, for the supervisor.[15] Within the cognitive domain especially, Bloom's analysis of levels of learning can illuminate the focus of the instructional activity. The six cognitive levels proposed by Bloom and widely used in educational circles are:

1 Knowledge—ability to recall information from memory; knowledge of specific facts, definitions, symbols, formulae, conventions, and steps in a process.

2 Comprehension—understanding. Ability to translate, rephrase, interpret, recognize essentials, extrapolate or recognize implications and limitations.

3 Application—(some call this transfer). Ability to use knowledge and understanding in a novel situation to solve problems.

4 Analysis—breaking a whole into its elements. Analysis of relationships, organizational principles, multiple causation, etc.

5 Synthesis—putting together elements and parts to form a new whole.

6 Evaluation—making judgments in a field using internal evidence or external standards.

With these levels of learning in mind, one can read through a teacher's manual, or a lesson plan, or a curriculum guide and quickly perceive the objectives of learning units or parts of units. Likewise, by observing the questioning patterns of teachers in an instructional setting, one can quickly see whether the teacher is focusing on simple recall or memory of terms or whether he or she is asking for more. All too often, teachers test for memory only and seldom go beyond that to require students to think. On the other hand, supervisors need to caution the inexperienced teacher who expects third graders to handle an abstract analysis of energy

---

[15] Benjamin S. Bloom, *Taxonomy of Educational Objectives: The Classification of Educational Goals, Handbook 1—Cognitive Domain*, New York: McKay, 1956.

transfers in electronics. The ideal instructional objective would be to gear the learning tasks to the levels of cognitive development that students at their age level should have achieved. Most of the learning exercises should allow the student to employ those cognitive structures that have developed at his or her age level with increasing facility, providing enough repetition to solidify the learning and ensure a feeling of competence and enjoyment. The supervisor, on the other hand, should encourage the teacher to stretch the abilities of the students from time to time, to place expectations on their performance that go just a little bit beyond what they can comfortably handle. Thus, in observing the instructional interaction, supervisors should look for clear evidence that teachers are stimulating the students' learning transactions to move to deeper or broader levels of understanding, application, and analysis.

A whole level of learning that is frequently neglected, even in the best of schools, has to do with *evaluation*. Evaluation can be considered to apply to two distinguishable levels of learning or learning experiences. One involves a type of analysis that leads to judgments of value. Such and such a poem is a "good" poem because it combines startling metaphors with appropriate rhythms to create a unified effect on the listener. Such and such a political decision by such and such a president was decidedly contrary to the Constitution, as Supreme Court decisions two generations later showed. In the above two instances, the learning experience culminates in a judgment of value (as opposed to a judgment of fact). Evaluation in this sense predominantly involves rational factors.

Another learning experience one could label "evaluation" has more to do with *appreciation*. Whether the learning involved mastering a piece of music on the piano or completing a complex mathematics problem or reviewing the intricacies of the physical and psychological processes of sight, the learner dwells in, or simply experiences, the pleasure, harmony, mystery, and complexity of what he or she is doing or observing. The learner in this instance experiences the value intrinsic to the learning transaction itself and enjoys it for its own sake. Frequently students dislike the learning tasks of the school because they seldom move into the level or the experience of evaluation. Sometimes learning ought to culminate in genuine enjoyment.

As with earlier perspectives on curriculum, Bloom's levels of learning are not content-specific. The supervisor could apply this analysis, however, to almost any curriculum content, whether it involves language arts, group counseling, or vocational education. The usefulness of Bloom's taxonomy is that it can help the supervisor and the teacher explore ways to lead students beyond simple memorization to a more mature grasp of the learning intended.

THE IMPORTANCE OF LEARNING STYLE

Recent research is uncovering important information about how students learn, what has been labeled *learning styles*. Some students learn best what they hear; others remember best what they see. Still others learn better by hands-on

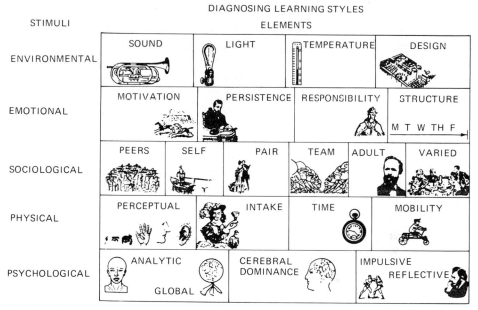

DIAGNOSING LEARNING STYLES

FIGURE 12-1
Learning style variables. (*Presented in R. S. Dunn and K. J. Dunn, "Learning Styles/Teaching Styles: Should They...Can They...Be Matched?"* Educational Leadership, *vol. 36, no. 4, p. 241, 1979.*)

manipulation of materials, while others use a combination of senses for learning.[16] These findings have clear implications for curriculum materials design. Dunn and Dunn have identified several variables that affect learning and can be said to contribute to differences in learning style. These are grouped under four categories: environmental, emotional, sociological, and physical. Figure 12-1 represents 18 variables under these four categories.

Environmental variables suggest that the absence or presence of sounds, bright or subdued light, cooler or warmer rooms, and formal or informal seating will either enhance or detract from learning.

Emotional factors involve the motivation to achieve, the ability to stay with a task, the ability to hold oneself responsible, and the ability to work in structured or unstructured lessons. In general, some students learn best when their independence is recognized, whereas less motivated students require more structure and extrinsic motivation.

Sociological factors cluster around how students respond to people in a learning situation. Some students work best alone, some better in a team, others prefer to work directly with an adult.

[16] Rita S. Dunn and Kenneth J. Dunn, "Learning Styles/Teaching Styles: Should They...Can They...Be Matched?" *Educational Leadership,* vol. 36, no. 4, pp. 238–244, 1979; and Dunn and Dunn, *Teaching Students through Their Individual Learning Styles: A Practical Approach,* Reston, Va.: Reston Publishing Company, a division of Prentice-Hall, 1978.

Physical factors concern elements such as the freedom to move around, the time of day when one's learning energy is high, food intake, and especially which senses are used most comfortably for receiving and processing information.

Fisher and Fisher[17] present a different array of variables on learning styles. Some of their variables coincide with those of Dunn and Dunn. Other variables include whether students normally proceed from the part to the whole or from the whole to the part.

Once again it is clear that the supervisor who is sensitive to curriculum alternatives targeted to different learning styles will be able to recognize these alternatives in action and be able to encourage their use by teachers who are unfamiliar with them.

GENERAL PRINCIPLES OF CURRICULUM AND INSTRUCTION

We have looked at a diversity of curricular-instructional strategies with which supervisors should be familiar. Now, however, we raise the question of whether there are some general principles that should apply to all or almost all units of instructional activity. Research and experience answer affirmatively.[18] We propose the following series of normative principles that should be evident in any instructional setting and that supervisors would do well, gently and persistently, to insist on.

1 Students must be given the opportunity to practice the kind of behavior implied by the learning-teaching objective. In the case of simple memorization of terminology, students should be called on rather often to repeat that terminology precisely and accurately. In the case of the learning objective of application, students must be given the opportunity to make several applications and to return from time to time to other applications to reinforce the learning desired. In all of this first principle, we stress the importance of the activity of the students. Unless they are actively involved in learning, they will not learn except in the most superficial way.

2 The learning experience must give students the opportunity to deal with the content implied by the objective. If the objective is to develop the skill of inductive scientific reasoning, then the learning experience must place students in a genuinely scientific setting where they encounter scientific data that can be analyzed by means of appropriate scientific instruments. Insofar as that learning experience lacks specifically scientific content, then the experience becomes diluted, or thinned out.

[17] B. B. Fisher and L. Fisher, "Styles in Teaching and Learning," *Educational Leadership*, vol. 36, no. 4, pp. 245–254, 1979.

[18] These principles can be found under a variety of labels in the research literature. For example, Tommy M. Tomlinson and Herbert J. Waberg (eds.), *Academic Work and Educational Excellence*, Berkeley, Calif.: McCutchan, 1986; Louis Rubin, "Instructional Strategies," in Herbert J. Wahlberg (ed.), *Improving Educational Standards and Productivity*, Berkeley, Calif.: McCutchan, 1982; U.S. Department of Education, *What Works*, Washington, D.C.: 1986.

3 Students must obtain satisfaction from carrying out the behavior implied by the objective. This principle insists on some sense of successful closure in the learning episode. One of the major problems in nonindividualized instructional settings is that one-third of the class seldom catches up with the rest of the class; they only partially complete their assignments. Their grades usually reflect the penalties imposed and lead to further loss of sense of worth and interest in the learning tasks.

4 The desired learnings or level of performance must be within the range of possibility for the students involved. This principle calls for an awareness on the part of both teachers and supervisors of the development stages and levels of cognitive, moral, and psychosocial growth. Some teachers expect fourth and fifth graders to engage in democratic group decision making. They will severely punish the miscreant who destroys the phony harmony of a simulated town meeting by laughing at the "goody-goody" who is simply trying to imitate the teacher. This is not to say that teachers should not introduce simple concepts of democracy. This principle holds for appropriate expectations of pupils' performance—appropriate to their level of development.

5 There are many particular experiences that can be used to attain the same objectives. Frequently teachers settle on only one or two examples or one or two ways to look at the problem or concept. This principle encourages more concern for diversity of student learning styles, or cultural or ethnic backgrounds. It also encourages the teacher and supervisor constantly to be enlarging their repertory of teaching aids and resources, their bag of tricks, so to speak, in order to provide the student with a new approach to a learning task when another one has failed to bring about the desired results.

6 The same learning experience will usually bring about several outcomes. Not infrequently a student's response to a question will take the teacher completely by surprise. Instead of responding that that was the wrong answer, the teacher should ask the student to clarify how he or she came up with that response. Frequently students come to quite legitimate learning or insights that the teacher had not foreseen as flowing from the assignment. This principle also alludes to the hidden, or indirect, curriculum. Sometimes the teacher unwittingly communicates a value, an attitude, or a reward system that is quite contrary to the objectives of the instructional activity. Supervisors can be especially helpful in pointing this out to teachers.

7 Student learnings will be strengthened, deepened, and broadened if a skill, a concept, relationships, principles, etc., are encountered and used repeatedly in several disciplines or discrete frameworks of learning. This principle points to the importance of a teacher's knowing what other teachers are teaching and have taught to their students. In that way the teacher can draw many comparisons, contrasts, and examples from the student's own experience. Consistent repetition in the use of learning and expressive skills will not only lead to their habitual use but to their refinement and broader scope as well. Not enough attention has been given in the literature on teaching and learning to the importance of repetition and review. The rhetoric of the literature on learning and teaching leads the inexperienced teacher to believe that instructional activity must always move into new material after initial mastery has been achieved. This often results in a wide but shallow coverage of many topics rather than a solid and usable mastery of the learning task. This principle seeks quality, not quantity, in instructional activity.

THE SUPERVISOR AND THE EDUCATIONAL PROGRAM

Sometimes the function of supervision is completely separated from the function of curriculum development. Sometimes the same person is involved in both, such as a building principal or a department chairperson. In either event the supervisor, who normally would focus primarily on the instructional activity of teachers and the use of their instructional materials, of necessity must observe the effectiveness of the curriculum in action. Where one and the same person, such as a department chairperson, is involved with both supervision and curriculum development, the information about the effectiveness of the curriculum on classroom learning comes immediately through the observation of instructional activity.

The department chairperson, observing teachers use the new textbook that the department had chosen that year, not only observes the teachers' adaptation of the textbook but the influence of the textbook on the teachers, on the flow of learning tasks, and on the attention, interest, and attitudes of the students. Through such observation, the supervisor may discover a considerable gap between two major sections of the text, a gap that the students were having difficulty crossing. With this information, and from discussions with the teachers, the chairperson may design a transitional unit to help teachers and students bridge the gap. This would be a clear example of the activity of supervision involved not only with the instructional activity of the teacher but, in a real sense, with the educational program. From this perspective, then, it is appropriate to speak of supervising the curriculum or the educational program.

The distinction between supervision and curriculum development can still remain. The activities relating to both can be assigned to different roles in the school system, if that seems best. Nonetheless, the supervisor can act as one of the main sources of feedback to the curriculum developer. The supervisor observes both the instructional activity of the teacher and the learning activity of the student. From such a vantage point, the supervisor can make some valid inferences about the effectiveness of the curriculum design, its scope, its sequence, its pedagogical appeal, its pace, and its effective marshaling of available learning resources. The supervisor may not be in a position to suggest *another* way of designing the curriculum, but he or she can at least point out what works and what does not.

In some cases, such as that of the department chairperson, this feedback can immediately begin to generate modifications in the sequence, the pace, the clarity or dramatic appeal of the advance organizers, and so on. A department usually is self-enclosed enough that programs can be modified quickly and easily.

In other instances, a supervisor may be working with an age or grade cluster of teachers and students, say grades 1 through 4. It may happen that the sequence of curriculum materials between grades 3 and 4 is causing considerable problems for the youngsters, and therefore problems for the teachers who have run out of alternative strategies to effect the learning encounter. The supervisor can huddle with teachers from all 4 years and try rearranging the learning units, with the end result that the second-grade teacher will not spend twice as much time teaching and reinforcing the learning of a specific spatial concept, the grasp of which is required for the third graders to handle related conceptual material. Or the supervisor and teachers may decide to remove those one or two learning units from the curriculum altogether and place them in the sixth-grade curriculum where the youngsters' cognitive structures will have developed adequately to handle such cognitively complex material.

In other instances, several supervisors from different grade or school levels or from different discipline areas may be in a position to address a curricular problem common to each of their areas of responsibility. By teaming up to attack the problem, they may come up with at least a clear identification of what the problem is (say, lack of software resources to support such a curriculum), where it primarily is (say, in the seventh grade when the inquiry method is introduced), and what needs to be done about it. By taking this kind of action, the supervisors, even though their primary responsibility is not in curriculum development, can effect beneficial changes in the curriculum.

THE CENTRAL ORGANIZATIONAL POSITION OF SUPERVISORS

In systems where different people are responsible for supervision and for curriculum development, such cooperation and mutual support are necessary for both the supervisor and the developer of the curriculum in order to maximize their common objectives—the best opportunities for the most appropriate growth of youngsters. From the human resources perspectives of supervision, which the authors advocate, the supervisor appears in a key position to bring complementary influences to bear on the instructional tasks of the school. The supervisor can be an advocate for the students vis-à-vis the teacher. The supervisor can be an advocate for the teacher vis-à-vis the administration (say, in urging a different class schedule). The supervisor can also be an advocate for the teacher vis-à-vis the curriculum developer *and vice versa*. In other words, the supervisor frequently stands between the instructional activity and the organizational resource staff and administration. The supervisor is, in a sense, the link. He or she sends messages in both directions. While within the organization chart the supervisor may not appear to, he or she occupies what is perhaps the key position in the school system. The supervisor is close enough to the instructional activity of the school and yet sits in on most of the important administrative meetings. Both by the relative prestige attached to various supervisory positions and by the range of contacts within the school system, the supervisor occupies a key position in the organizational network, from which it is possible to marshal and channel all the best resources the system possesses toward more effective instruction. In small systems where the supervisor is also the chief administrator, the concentration of this potential in one person (there being no need for numerous meetings with different bureaucratic layers of support staff) offers the possibility of rapid program change. And, as the literature on instructional leadership has urged for the past 50 years, that kind of administrator ought to spend much more of his or her time doing instructional supervision.

SUMMARY

This chapter has attempted to focus the supervisor's attention on how the curriculum influences the instructional activity under observation. Besides the more general platform of beliefs, theories, and attitudes upon which teachers habitually base their instructional activity, teachers also bring to the instructional setting their knowledge of the subject matter or discipline and their strategies for bringing the student into a genuine encounter with some aspect of it. In the examples cited, we saw how five different teachers approached the teaching of the nature of light. The group inquiry approach, the historical approach, the experimental approach, the conceptual approach through a lecture or film, the analogy approach—all provide access to the reality of light and to theories to explain the physical properties of light. The supervisor needs to be able to move freely into the frame of reference of the teacher and student in order to support the genuine learning and sound instruction that can and does take place within that perspective. The supervisor should be able to rummage about in his or her own repertory of curriculum-instructional strategies to come up with additional suggestions to enrich, enliven, and open up to even further possibilities the teaching and learning that could be occurring within that framework.

Joyce and Weil's inventory of curriculum-instructional models and Stallings's models of teaching can further enlarge the supervisor's repertory. They provide additional maps, or paradigms, to enable the supervisor to interpret the instructional activity being planned or under observation. Bloom's *Taxonomy* reminds the supervisor that any instructional activity can be pointed to various levels of learning. By examining the levels of learning possible within the curriculum-instructional models, the supervisor is equipped for a kind of two-dimensional analysis or interpretation of the teacher's instructional activity. Research on learning styles provides additional insight into the need for alternative instructional strategies.

Regardless of the type of its instructional activity, the following seven principles should apply to every instructional unit:

1 The student must be given the opportunity to practice the kind of behavior implied by the learning-teaching objective.

2 The learning experience must give the student the opportunity to deal with the content implied by the objective.

3 The student must obtain satisfaction from carrying out the behavior implied by the objective.

4 The desired learnings or levels of performance must be within the range of possibility for the students involved.

5 There are many particular experiences that can be used to obtain the same objectives.

6 The same learning experience will usually bring about several outcomes.

7 Student learnings should be reinforced by being used in different settings and disciplines, and by being used repeatedly.

Finally, the role of the supervisor, while remaining distinguished from that of the curriculum developer, was studied in terms of its potential for curriculum revision. It is legitimate to speak of supervising the curriculum. The supervisor, because of his or her central position in the organizational network of the school, can have considerable influence on curriculum reform.

STUDY GUIDE

Recall the concepts, ideas, and meanings associated with each of the following phrases and terms included in this chapter. Can you discuss each of them with a colleague and apply them to the supervisory context of your school? If you cannot, review them in the text and record the page numbers for future reference.

1 Curriculum
2 Exploratory models
3 Four families of teaching models
4 Instructional activity
5 Learning styles
6 Normative instructional principles
7 Supervision and curriculum development
8 Taxonomy of educational objectives

EXERCISES

1 Observe a film of a teacher teaching a class. Does that teaching fit into one of the families of teaching models? Go back and see which of the levels of learning are getting most of the teacher's attention. Go back a third time and see whether the seven instructional principles are being followed.

2 What kinds of other questions are generated by viewing the film? Imagine that you would be meeting with that teacher within an hour for the post-observation conference. Divide up into teams of three and plan your strategy for the conference. Perhaps someone could role-play the teacher.

3 Consider all the classes you attend in your college or graduate program. How would you analyze and describe the instructional activity that goes on in them? Are they effective in the instructional strategies employed?

4 Ask someone who is involved in curriculum design and development where he or she receives most of the feedback on the curriculum's effectiveness. Ask a practicing supervisor how often she or he gets involved in curriculum revision.

13

SUPERVISION AND PROGRAM EVALUATION

Evaluation is a growing concern in education. From the federal and state governments down to local taxpayer groups, one finds an increasing demand for evaluation. Much of this stress on evaluation arises from a desire to find out what is wrong with the schools, why test scores are declining, why schools seem ineffective in controlling violence and vandalism, teenage pregnancies, and drug abuse. Some would stress evaluation as a way of holding schools accountable to taxpayers and funding agencies for the money they spend. Others, such as university researchers, are seeking to increase information about effective programs or teaching strategies. A new wave of books and articles on evaluation is growing in volume as researchers, foundations, and government agencies seek not only to evaluate what goes on in schools but to develop the most effective evaluative tools and procedures for generating useful information.

Many of the evaluations were conducted as a basis for generating new social policies about schools.[1] Other studies such as that by Rutter and associates[2] or by Edmonds[3] championed what appeared to be effective educational practices.

---

[1] See, for instance, the National Commission on Excellence in Education, *A Nation at Risk: The Imperative for Educational Reform,* Washington, D.C.: U.S. Department of Education, 1983; The College Entrance Examination Board, *Academic Preparation for College,* New York: College Entrance Examination Board, 1983; Carnegie Corporation of New York, *Educational Economic Progress: Toward a National Educational Policy,* New York: Carnegie Corporation, 1983; Task Force on Education for Economic Growth, *Action for Excellence: A Comprehensive Plan to Improve Our Nation's Schools,* Denver: Education Commission of the States, 1983.

[2] Michael Rutter et al. *Fifteen Thousand Hours: Secondary Schools and Their Effects on Children,* Cambridge, Mass.: Harvard University Press, 1978.

[3] Ronald R. Edmonds, "Schools Count: New York City's School Improvement Project," *Harvard Graduate School of Education Association Bulletin,* vol. 25, pp. 33–35, 1980.

What is clear is that the money and effort expended on program evaluation over the past twenty years or more has been extraordinary. What is not so clear, especially to the leaders in the field of program evaluation is whether this effort has yielded beneficial results.[4] Nonetheless, the effort at program evaluation and its counterpart, policy analysis, goes on based on the assumption that, if evaluators are conscious of their limitations, more careful about their research design, and more adept at bringing their information to politicians, program managers, and the general public, their program evaluation can have a gradual and cumulative impact on ameliorative, social, and educational policy formation and implementation.[5]

Cronbach and associates propose "ninety-five theses" regarding the limitations of program evaluation. Some of these theses are as follows:

• Evaluation is the handmaiden to gradualism. It is both conservative and committed to change.
• A theory of evaluation must be as much a theory of political interaction as it is a theory of how to determine the facts.
• "Evaluate this program" is often a vague charge because a program or a system frequently has no clear boundaries.
• Results of a program evaluation are so dependent on the setting that replication is only a figure of speech; the evaluator is essentially a historian.[6]

The supervisory process, whether exercised by a superintendent or by a department chairperson, inescapably involves program evaluation. In order to establish precisely what that means, however, several distinctions are needed. First, we should distinguish between evaluation that is exercised as part of a supervisory process and evaluation exercised by other agents or professionals. Second, we should distinguish between the object of evaluation, such as the evaluation of a school system, the evaluation of an individual school taken as a single social entity, the evaluation of an instructional program, the evaluation of a process, the evaluation of a teacher, the evaluation of a student, and so on. Third, we should distinguish between the various audiences for which an evaluation is intended. Fourth, we should distinguish between various types of evaluation procedures and the assumptions behind the procedures employed in an evaluation. Fifth, we should distinguish between the purposes of evaluation. Basically, these distinctions involve the who, what, for whom, how, and why of evaluation. Once we have clarified these distinctions, we should be able to narrow our focus on the more important and essential tasks of program evaluation with which the supervisory process is involved.

---

[4] For a thorough discussion of the recent history of program evaluation and its impact on policy or program improvement, see Lee J. Cronbach and associates, *Toward Reform of Program Evaluation*, San Francisco: Jossey-Bass, 1980, pp. 14–75.

[5] Cf. recommendations of the National Science Board Special Commission on the Social Sciences, *Knowledge into Action: Improving the Nation's Use of the Social Sciences*, Washington, D.C.: National Science Foundation, 1969.

[6] Cronbach et al., op. cit., pp. 2–7.

THE QUESTION OF WHO EVALUATES

Evaluation is carried on by a number of professional agents in the educational universe. At the federal level, where special programs are funded, personnel within the agencies or, more commonly, outside evaluation experts are called upon to evaluate the impact of these programs on the target populations. Head Start, for example, has been evaluated several times in order to determine whether that program was accomplishing its objectives. Evaluation experts from universities, state departments of education, or consulting agencies are frequently called in to use their technical expertise to evaluate special or new programs. State and regional accrediting agencies employ teachers and administrators who visit schools for cyclical reevaluations in order for the schools to retain their accreditation. Research and development centers employ evaluators to assess the impact of new or experimental programs. Foundations usually require a thorough evaluation of programs they fund, by either outside or inside evaluators. Department chairpersons evaluate new teachers. Teachers evaluate students. Supervisors evaluate teachers and programs. Therefore, when discussing evaluation in education, who is doing the evaluation makes a considerable difference to the discussion.

THE QUESTION OF WHAT IS BEING EVALUATED

Many things or many people can be the object of an evaluation. The evaluation of a national program such as Head Start involves broad evaluation technologies and standardized testing of both product and process; a national evaluation of library expenditures involves the appraisal of different data; a local evaluation of a consumer education program would involve the measure of outcomes different from those in a state evaluation of fair hiring procedures for school personnel. A systemwide evaluation of a reading program would differ from teacher X giving a home-grown test to her third-grade pupils. A supervisor's evaluation of a department's testing procedures would differ from a supervisor's evaluation of a beginning teacher. To evaluate students' reading skills involves a search for specific behaviors; to evaluate students' practices of democratic citizenship behaviors would involve a search for quite different kinds of data.

THE QUESTION OF THE AUDIENCE OF THE EVALUATION

An evaluation report can be prepared for different audiences. The evaluation of an experimental program, when prepared for a research community, might be unintelligible to a citizens' oversight committee. A self-study report prepared by a schoolwide, faculty-parent committee would differ from a student's report card. A faculty report on new textbooks prepared for the school board would differ from a psychologist's evaluation of the match between students' stages of cognitive development and a new textbook prepared for a publishing house. Recent research on the politics of evaluation reporting indicates that not only what is evaluated but the way conclusions are drawn from the evaluation depends a lot on the audience for whom the evaluation is prepared.[7] For the supervisor, it makes a difference whether an evaluation of a class is prepared for the superintendent or for the teacher who is seeking instructive information in order to test a new teaching strategy. Sometimes the audience for whom the evaluation is targeted, as well as the evaluators themselves, can seriously disrupt the very activity on which the evaluation is supposed to report.

THE QUESTION OF EVALUATION
PROCEDURES AND TECHNOLOGY

Currently there is a debate over the use of "hard" or "soft" evaluation procedures and technologies.[8] The earlier and more widespread practice of evaluation appears to have employed the hard procedures and technologies, namely, the quantification of what was being evaluated. Such an approach, based upon an analogy with research in the natural sciences, is seen as more "scientific" or more "objective." By quantifying data through testing or through numerical checklists, evaluators have attempted to provide a basis for comparing their data with data reported by others, using the same or similar scientific procedures, and for measuring "input" and "output."

There has been a reaction against this emphasis on quantification, a reaction that has been growing steadily over the past 10 years. Using analogies with methodologies employed in anthropology, aesthetics, literary criticism, and political analysis, the proponents of the "soft" approaches to evaluation argue that they can capture more of the human variables through "naturalistic" or ethnographic or case-study methodologies. Their argument also refers to the scale of evaluation. They claim that the individual school site or an individual classroom ought to be the locus of evaluation rather than a national, statewide, or even systemwide sample. They maintain that the study of large populations tends to depress the unique features of smaller segments and settings. Evaluation studies that are more attentive to individual schools and individual classrooms do in fact point up significant differences between schools and between classrooms in the same school.[9]

The focus on the smaller unit of schooling, whether the individual school or the individual classroom, as the unit where evaluation produces the most sensitive and useful information, receives further substantiation from several

[7] See Ernest R. House (ed.), *School Evaluation: The Politics and Process,* Berkeley, Calif.: McCutchan, 1973; W. James Popham, "The Evaluators Curse," in Ronald S. Brandt (ed.), *Applied Strategies for Curriculum Evaluation,* Washington, D.C.: Association for Supervision Curriculum Development, 1981; and Deborah G. Bonnet, "Five Phases of Purposeful Inquiry," ibid.

[8] For a good summary of this debate see E. G. Guba and Y. S. Lincoln, *Effective Evaluation,* San Francisco: Jossey-Bass, 1981. The essays in Brandt (ed.), op. cit., aptly illustrate various approaches to program evaluation.

[9] See Michael Rutter et al., op. cit, and George Madaus, Peter W. Airasian, and Thomas Kellaghan, *School Effectiveness,* New York: McGraw-Hill, 1980.

studies of change.[10] They conclude that the individual school, with its unique mix of people, practices, and environment, is the unit most suited for and effective in managing successful change. It seems reasonable, then, to argue that evaluation on or within that scale, rather than on a larger scale, would produce the most accurate and useful information.

While supervisory personnel will make some use of quantitative data for evaluation, it appears that much of their involvement in evaluative activity will occur within the "responsive" or "naturalistic" mode and within the smaller scale of the individual school. As the scale of supervisory activity enlarges, the evaluative procedures will probably move toward the more impersonal and quantitative mode. Thus, a program director at the state Department of Education with responsibility to supervise, for example, the state-mandated program for educating sight-impaired children would probably require quantifiable information for annual reports on this program. This does not rule out using additional modes of evaluation, especially where improvements at particular sites are being sought.

THE PURPOSES OF EVALUATION

Finally, the purpose for which evaluation is undertaken will shape the form and process of evaluation. If the purpose of an evaluation is to provide information about the more effective of two or three approaches to the teaching of reading, then it is supposed to lead to the choosing of one over the other(s) for future implementation or continuation. If the purpose of an evaluation is to seek improvements in an existing reading program, then it is supposed to lead to improvements in that program. An evaluation of teaching effectiveness in a department will start out with the objectives of that department and seek to verify whether the students achieve those objectives. An evaluation of the stated objectives of a department will compare those objectives with the objectives of similar departments in other schools, or with objectives laid down by state or professional associations involved with that academic area in order to judge whether they fall within accepted standards and criteria. Some evaluations may involve comparison of two or more schools in order to see which schools produce the highest student scores on national achievement tests or do best according to some other standardized criteria.

---

[10] See John L. Goodlad, *The Dynamics of Educational Change: Toward Responsive Schools,* New York: McGraw-Hill, 1975; Paul Berman and Wilbrey W. McLaughlin, *Federal Programs Supporting Educational Change,* vol. IV: *The Findings in Review,* Santa Monica, Calif.: Rand Corporation, 1975; Daniel A. Neale, William J. Bailey, and Billy E. Ross, *Strategies for School Improvement: Cooperative Planning and Organizational Development,* Boston: Allyn and Bacon, 1981; Gilbert R. Austen, "Exemplary Schools and the Search for Effectiveness," *Educational Leadership,* vol. 37, no. 1, pp. 10–14, 1979; Michael H. Long, "Process and Product in ESL Program Evaluation," *TESOL Quarterly,* vol. 18, no. 3, pp. 409–425; and William E. Bickel, "Evaluation in Residence: New Prospects for District Evaluation Research," *Educational Evaluation and Policy Analysis,* vol. 7, no. 2, pp. 297–306, 1984.

PROGRAM EVALUATION AND THE SUPERVISORY PROCESS

The supervisory process can be exercised on any level, from the supervision of a federal or state program to a districtwide program. It can involve the total educational program of a single school or, within a school, a departmental curriculum or an individual course. Figure 13-1 highlights some of the many levels at which program evaluation takes place. At whatever level supervision is involved with program evaluation, we believe that it is exercised best when the supervisor monitors and participates in the evaluative efforts of those implementing the program. This is to say that the supervisory process ought to be separated from evaluation of the program by an evaluation expert. It is not to say that supervisors do not evaluate. Their evaluation, however, is not as an

FIGURE 13-1
Evaluation of programs according to scale.

Level	Example	Type of evaluation	Purpose
Federal	Head start	Statistical norm referenced test	Report to congress & federal officials
State	Vocational education	Statistical survey	Report to state legislature and state officials
Independent research and development center	Experimental reading programs	Highly sophisticated psychometrics; use of experimental and control groups	Isolation and measurement of program effects
Regional accrediting agency	Cyclical self-evaluation and assessment by visiting team	Self report, observation by visitors, naturalistic evaluation	To judge whether school meeting minimum standards
Local school system	K-12 Modern language program	Norm reference and criterion referenced testing	To judge effectiveness of their program compared to other school systems using different approaches
Single school	Volunteer community-service program	Supervisor reports, agency reports, teacher reports, student reports	To assess impact on improved citizenship attitudes
Single course	Geography	Criterion referenced tests, student inclass responses, supervisor's observation, student interviews, etc.	To improve over all course design, sequence, pacing, use of audio visuals, etc.

outsider but as an insider, working with those who are delivering the instruction or the program.

We believe that the principles that guide the supervisory process when it is engaged in program evaluation are best illustrated at the level of a specific program in a single school, working with teachers who are implementing the program through instructional activity. That could be a third-grade reading program, or a science program in a senior high school. As distinguished from other kinds of evaluation activity, the supervisor's evaluation activity is exercised with and for teachers, for the purpose of program and instructional improvement, and for enhanced student learnings; it is exercised more by soft technology than by hard technology. The who, for whom, how, and why distinctions were made above in order to clarify more precisely how supervision can involve program evaluation and to distinguish supervision from the more formal aspects of program evaluation by nonsupervisory personnel. Figures 13-1 and 13-2 map out those distinctions.

Furthermore, the point of view adopted in this chapter is that supervisory evaluation of program effectiveness is exercised with teachers as they seek practical ways to improve their instruction. That is, evaluation activity is not extrinsic to instruction but is intrinsically involved with instruction itself and with instructional improvement. As will become clear in later parts of this chapter, there is a dynamic relationship between evaluating student learnings, evaluating teachers' activities in stimulating student learnings, and evaluating the effectiveness of the curriculum that the teachers use. Hence our primary focus in this chapter will be the supervisor's monitoring and assisting in teachers' evaluation of their own activities for improved student learnings, for improved instructional planning, and for improved program design. Much of the teacher's evaluation of the program will depend very much on how the teacher evaluates student learnings. The supervisor, by assisting the teacher to ask the right questions when evaluating student learning, will also help the teacher explore ways to improve the program in order to enhance student learnings.

THE ACTIVITY OF EVALUATION

Program and pupil evaluation formerly was thought of primarily as something that happened at the end of the term or the end of the year. At the conclusion of the course, students were evaluated on their progress in attaining the goals of the program by means of a test, a "final exam" of some kind or other. When the course was over, the teacher might have spent some time looking back over the curriculum and specific instructional strategies to see whether or not some units clearly were inappropriate and unsuccessful. In the case of a new course, the teacher and supervisor might compare student achievement with the earlier course. They also would probably ask teachers in whose classes their students subsequently enrolled whether there was any noticeable difference after the new course.

WHO	Administrators	Supervisors	Evaluation Experts
Does what	Decide whether to initiate, continue or terminate programs, based on information received by evaluators Decide whether to alter program, or commit more resources to program, based on information received by supervisors and program implementors	Work on program improvement with implementors (teachers) of the program. Examine effectiveness of small segments of the program implementation. Help program implementors assess multiple effects of program on recipients (students) Explore alternative forms of implementing the program Help program implementors and recipients review the overall impact of the program.	Gather data on a program Assess program effectiveness Compare this program with alternatives Report results to various publics Interpret results to various publics
How	Review reports	Responsive evaluation Participative observation Work with mediating variables Looking for unintended effects Clarifying objectives Posing alternative approaches	Clarifying goals, means, and products Measuring, testing, observing, charting, comparing Clarifying relationships between program design, implementation activities and results on tests and other hard and soft measures
Why	Responsibility and accountability to publics Seeking maximum effectiveness for enhanced student learning	Seeking best fit between program design, learning resource materials, teacher activities and student learning To improve program effectiveness, teacher effectiveness and student learning	To measure what the program accomplishes. To establish relationship between program and results To provide basis for making enlightened decisions about the program

FIGURE 13-2
Role of administrators, supervisors, and evaluation experts in program evaluation.

Michael Scriven, in writing about curriculum revision, calls this type of evaluation *summative evaluation*.[11] It sums up, so to speak, the cumulative impact of the curriculum on learning, or it makes a general assessment of the cumulative learning of the whole curriculum by the student. He distinguishes summative evaluation from *formative evaluation* by positing formative evalu-

[11] Michael Scriven, "The Methodology of Evaluation," in Robert Stake (ed.), AERA, *Monograph Series on Curriculum Evaluation*, no. 1, pp. 39–83, 1967.

ation as an ongoing process within the curriculum-instructional activity sequence. Through formative evaluation of the instructional program the teacher, learner, and curriculum designer can receive rapid feedback on the effectiveness of short-term segments of the program, rather than having to wait until the conclusion of the program for the more summative type of evaluation. Formative evaluation, since it goes on so close in time to the instructional activity and the learning encounter, can have a formative influence on the instructional activity and the learning encounter. In a given situation the teacher can see that use of a particular advance organizer or a demonstration simply is not getting the students' attention or, by questions from the students, that it is well over their heads. This kind of quick feedback will probably lead the teacher to discard that approach on the spot and to try a new tack. Or a student may discover that he or she has not yet mastered the rule on capital letters. The teacher and the student can then set up some exercises to ensure a more adequate grasp of those rules.

Bloom and associates divide evaluation into three types: *diagnostic, formative,* and *summative.*[12] Diagnostic evaluation is closely related to both formative and summative evaluation, but it is distinguished by its purposes. Diagnostic evaluation is used to place a student properly in the level of instruction that best matches his or her entry behaviors and skills with learning objectives of the instructional unit. It is also used to determine the underlying causes or circumstances behind repeated deficiencies in a student's performance that have not responded to ordinary remedial measures.[13] Diagnostic evaluation usually employs some recognized standardized test or battery of tests that will highlight cognitive, affective, physical, psychological, and environmental factors in the student. With such information concerning how well the youngster is functioning in his or her stage of development, more appropriate resources can be made available. Some of the similarities and differences between diagnostic, formative, and summative evaluation as listed by Bloom and associates appear in Figure 13-3.

FORMATIVE EVALUATION

For the moment, we will consider the activity of formative evaluation, for the supervision of evaluation activity would seem more involved in that form of evaluation. A brief overview of formative evaluation of the curriculum points to particular activities of students, other activities of the teacher, and the formative use of testing for both. Depending on the situation, supervisors may or may not participate in the evaluation activities, but they will certainly be expected to monitor in some fashion the effectiveness of these evaluation activities.

---

[12] Benjamin S. Bloom, J. Thomas Hastings, and George F. Madaus, *Handbook on Formative and Summative Evaluation of Student Learning,* New York: McGraw-Hill, 1971, p. 87 et passim.
[13] Ibid., p. 87.

Type of Evaluation

	Diagnostic	Formative	Summative
Function	Placement: Determining the presence or absence of prerequisite skills Determining the student's prior level of mastery Classifying the student according to various characteristics known or thought to be related to alternative modes of instruction Determination of underlying causes of repeated learning difficulties	Feedback to student and teacher on student progress through a unit Location of errors in terms of the structure of a unit so that remedial alternative instruction techniques can be prescribed	Certification or grading of students at the end of a unit, semester, or course
Time	For placement at the outset of a unit, semester, or year's work During instruction when student evidences repeated inability to profit fully from ordinary instruction	During instruction	At the end of a unit, semester, or year's work
Emphasis in evaluation	Cognitive, affective, and psychomotor behaviors Physical, psychological, and environmental factors	Cognitive behaviors	Generally cognitive behaviors; depending on subject matter, sometimes psychomotor; occasionally affective behaviors
Type of instrumentation	Formative and summative instruments for pretests Standardized achievement tests Standardized diagnostic tests Teacher-made instruments Observation and checklists	Specially designed formative instruments	Final or summative examinations

FIGURE 13-3
Similarities and differences between diagnostic, formative, and summative evaluation.

**Student Evaluative Activity: Evaluation of the
Curriculum-as-Learned**

Let us consider an ordinary class setting, say a self-contained classroom with one teacher and 24 students. The class has just concluded a comparison of two poems. Previous classes have dealt with aspects of poetry, such as mood, figures of speech, rhythm, unity, image, and symbol. They have seen a variety of poems and have done some analysis using these critical concepts. The objective of today's class was to have them use these critical concepts to compare two poems and to argue why one poem was a "better" poem than the other. This objective fit into the larger goal of the course that aimed at the students' developing a discriminating taste for superior literary expression.

Toward the end of the class the teacher felt satisfied that most if not all of the students reflected a good grasp of the analytical concepts and had applied them well in arguing for the superiority of one poem over the other. In an attempt to further reinforce the learning and to test out her impressions that the class had pretty well achieved the instructional objectives she said, "Now let's all pause a minute and reflect on what it is we learned today. What new thing struck us? What have we understood with greater clarity? How does what we've done today fit with what went on before? Of what practical use was this whole experience, anyway?"

The following answers came back:

"I learned that it makes a difference when you read a poem out loud. I could *hear* how much superior that first poem was to the other one."

"I learned that you can still like an inferior poem—I mean, yeah, the first poem is a better poem, by all the measures we apply to it, but I like the second poem because it expresses a feeling about being alone that I've had many times. Just because a poem is a mediocre poem doesn't mean it's no good at all."

"I learned that I had to read both poems at least four times before they made any sense to me. It seems that with poetry, kinda like music, you gotta acquire a kind of familiarity with it before it really says anything to you."

"I learned that all this art stuff isn't entirely a matter of feeling, you know, all from inside someone's fantasy. There's something to it, some kind of intelligence. And you can talk about poetry intelligently, instead of simply leaving it to subjective feelings of like or dislike."

"I learned that I have no poetic imagination. I never thought those kinds of thoughts. And I'm wondering how one gets to be a poet—are you born that way, or can you develop it?"

"I'm really having a hard time understanding what makes a poem 'unified.' It's a word that seems to me to mean perfect, or perfection. Like a perfect circle or something. So if a poem has unity, then it must mean that every word, every line is in perfect place. But who could ever decide that? Maybe I need to see examples of *really* unified poems and some that are a little off-center and maybe I'll catch on."

"I learned that it feels good to discover that a lot of people agree with my conclusions. Before the class started, I wasn't sure whether my picking the first poem as better was the right answer, you know. But when other people gave the same reasons as I had, I really felt good, because I figured—yeah, for the first time—that I'm understanding all the stuff we've been doing on poetry."

Suppose you were observing in that class. After the class you and the teacher sat down to review the class. What practical things would the two of you do as a result of those student responses?

The example illustrates a range of student learnings that reflected not only the achievement of the teacher's objectives, but also the many idiosyncratic, ancillary learnings that always occur. The example points to the importance of taking that kind of time to let students reflect on what they have learned. Obviously, the students in that honors poetry class had rather high levels of motivation and of verbal and abstractive abilities. Students in third or fourth grade will come up with simpler responses, to be sure. But getting them into the habit early of evaluating what they are learning will pay enormous dividends as it develops into ongoing reflective habits of mind and a genuine satisfaction over knowing that they are making progress.

Students' evaluation of their appropriation of the curriculum can lead to both cognitive and affective results. On the one hand, by reflecting on their grasp of the learning task, they can clarify what they know. Frequently, the simple recall of the class material or unit will reinforce the grasp of the material. When this reflection is done in a nonthreatening environment, students can also clarify and admit what they have not yet grasped or understood. They can trace back the instructional sequence until they get to the point where the teacher or the textbook lost them. This clarifying of what one does not know will often lead to a desire to learn that, to get at that the first thing in the next class.

On the affective level, students can also be encouraged to review what they learned, not so much for intellectual understanding but simply for enjoyment. The youngster who had to repeat the poems many times was discovering how poems are meant to be enjoyed. This kind of enjoyment is not limited to those subjects within the humanities. A sensitive biology teacher or a physical education teacher can lead students into a kind of repetitive appreciation of what they have learned. Sometimes that leads to genuine wonderment.

In either case, student evaluation of this learning can lead to ownership. Recognizing what they have learned, what it means, how it is related to what they have learned before, how they can use it, what a sense of excitement or enjoyment comes with that mastery of a skill or discovery of a surprising piece of information—all of this leads students to appropriate that learning as theirs. Once appropriated, the learning tends to be effective, which is to say the student owns it and can use it in many ways in the immediate future. Unfortunately, many teachers fail to take the time to encourage this sense of ownership. What they miss by omitting the encouragement of student self-evaluation is the genuine satisfaction of knowing how much actually gets absorbed and how fascinating it is to observe the individual coloring of the learning that was supposed to take place. Moreover, much of the formative evaluation the teacher engages in will not pick up the obvious clues that students put forth in their self-evaluation. A supervisor who helps a teacher to initiate student self-evaluation may have provided a stimulus for instructional and program improvement more effective than several semesters of in-service lectures on the topic.

The Teacher's Formative Evaluation Activity:
Evaluation of the Curriculum-as-Taught

By means of student self-evaluation, brief quizzes, questions right in the middle of instructional activity, by checking homework assignments, and through informal out-of-class conversations, teachers can get an idea of the effectiveness of the curriculum unit as well as their teaching strategies. It will take a multiplicity of feedback mechanisms rather than the single mechanism of an occasional test to provide the formative information. Sometimes a test will be the real problem because it has been poorly constructed.

In any event, the teacher's formative evaluation activity will have several foci. The teacher must try to evaluate how well the student is encountering and mastering the learning task. There may be several reasons why the student is having difficulty. There may be emotionally upsetting conditions at home; a fight in the school yard that morning could have made concentration on schoolwork impossible. But it may be that the pace of the class was too fast, or that the examples used were too strange, or that the student was distracted briefly at the beginning of the class and missed one of the initial steps in the explanation.

If most or all of the class is showing disinterest or confusion, then the teacher has to evaluate what in his or her teaching is lacking. Or is it the learning-unit design in the textbook that is confusing or flat? Sometimes the only way to identify the cause is to ask the students. From time to time, however, the teacher is not all that aware of the deficiency in the textbook or in his or her teaching. Sometimes the problem does not surface for a week or two, when a test shows up a consistent gap in the class's grasp of an essential part of the sequence of learning.

And then there are the teachers who are perpetually unaware of how they smother any student initiative in learning. Low grades are simply their way of punishing what they perceive as the recalcitrance and general laziness of youth. Here, the formative evaluation of the teacher is almost totally ineffective because the source of the problem is ignored.

Supervisors can help teachers address the difficult task of formative evaluation primarily by communicating to the teacher a sense of respect for the teacher's competence to refashion his or her curriculum-instructional plan more effectively. Frequently, teachers think that a textbook is too sacred to be altered one iota. On the contrary, the teacher is in the best position to know what will work with his or her youngsters and should deviate from the textbook when that is called for. The supervisor can work alongside the teacher, exploring alternative strategies, testing out an idea on one or two students before trying it with the whole class, and looking for gaps and blind spots and filling them in so that students can move easily from one thing to another. Once the teacher gains the self-confidence, he or she will be much more likely to carry on such self-corrective activities independently.

In cases where substantial program revision may be called for, the supervisor can enlist the assistance of someone more skilled in curriculum design to work with several teachers. The point is, however, that the teacher ought to be the central person in his kind of formative evaluation, not the supervisor. Frequently the most important activity of the supervisor is convincing the teacher that he or she can do it, and furthermore ought to, and finally, has to do it. Familiarity with a variety of evaluation techniques such as those presented by Bloom and associates[14] will equip the supervisor with a certain repertory of approaches, some of which may be useful to get the teacher started.

In this regard, a formative use of testing can be a key source of feedback data that will unlock the problems besetting both teachers and students. More often than not, quizzes and tests are not carefully reviewed. The grades are entered into the mark book, and the papers are handed back to the students, who look at the grade at the top of the page, give off a whine, a curse, or a gleeful expletive, crumple up the paper, and toss it in the basket.

A careful review of tests and quizzes, however, can be turned into very effective learning. First, there is usually a high level of interest because of the grade involved. By reviewing the quiz or the test, students have a chance to see where they made their mistake, thereby clearing up what could be a lingering problem if not corrected. It also provides the teacher some clues as to why some students failed to achieve the objective of the instruction. Such information often leads to more appropriate remedial exercises. In the exchange of information, the teacher can likewise score all kinds of other useful points, such as reinforcing the main point of the instruction, reviewing previous learnings leading up to the material under consideration, clarifying the level of exactitude or logic or basic English required in the course, pointing out the necessity to ask questions in class when points are unclear, etc.

Students, even the ones who put down most of the correct answers, have an opportunity to review the essentials of the previous class or learning unit. For students whose low performance was due to one key deficiency, the opportunity is there to see the principle or concept or formula or rule as such, that is, as a generalization that applies to many particulars; through the review of the mistake that is underlined before them in glowing red, they can now have the insight that they could not grasp before.

Such review also allows the rhetoricians in the class an opportunity to debate the precise meaning of a word or phrase in the question that they took to mean something other than what the teacher intended. Sometimes a student has a legitimate complaint when the wording of the question allows for two

___

[14] Bloom, Hastings, and Madaus, op. cit.

different readings and therefore for two different responses. The teacher's review of the test can help clear up such problems before some disgruntled youngster goes home to enlist the support of his or her parents who in turn become disgruntled and demand an appointment with the principal.

Again, supervisors can help teachers get far more instructional mileage out of their tests and quizzes. Rather than being something extraneous to instruction, this kind of formative evaluation can become one of the regular tools of instruction. Only in this way can testing be restored to its proper place as an aid to instruction rather than being a specter dominating both instruction and student motivation.

The Supervisor in Formative Evaluation

As should be evident from the above, the role of the supervisor is that of monitoring the type and effectiveness of the formative evaluating activity that goes on in the classroom. By keeping uppermost in mind that this type of evaluation is intended to improve the learning of the student, as well as the instructional effectiveness of the teacher and the curriculum program, the supervisor can help the teacher and student stay on target in their evaluation efforts.

Furthermore, the supervisor should have enough distance from the evaluation activity itself to perceive the values that are brought into play by the type and style of the evaluation procedures employed by the teacher. That is to say, evaluation is a process of assigning value and significance to actions, things, answers, or questions. Behind any evaluation activity there is a whole host of assumptions that have value content. These assumptions usually go untested or unquestioned.

Some assumptions behind some forms of evaluation include the following: that knowing or understanding something means giving this response to that question; that this curriculum design or this text contains a legitimate approach (or the most legitimate, or the only legitimate approach) to this area of human knowledge (for example, modern Latin American history), and therefore a test of the student's knowledge of this approach indicates that he or she knows something true or objective or valid about that area of human knowledge; that using the language of public discourse in evaluation is the best means of measuring what the student has learned (rather than using poetry or music or graphics to measure it); or that teachers and other school officials have the authority and competency to decide the criteria for evaluating and ranking students.

Behind these assumptions, of course, are other assumptions: that learning primarily involves learning what others have discovered (and seldom the way they discovered it), and so evaluation monitors learning on that level; that there is always a causal connection between learning and instruction (rather than learning and the *students'* search, inquiry, practice, trial and error, or logical deduction), and hence evaluation of learning implies an evaluation of instruction; that the proper place for most learning is a classroom, and so evaluation never compares classroom learning (with all its constraints) with learnings in other settings. One could go on and on, describing assumptions behind assumptions. The point of listing these is to encourage supervisors occasionally to create enough distance from the evaluation activity for both the teacher and themselves so that they can perceive the value assumptions that are embedded in their evaluation procedures. If nothing else, such distancing can be a healthy antidote to dogmatism; at best it will encourage flexibility and more holistic approaches to evaluation.

Kunkel and Tucker propose five criteria by which supervisors and other evaluators might evaluate the quality of their evaluation activity.[15] These criteria were developed as part of their perception-based model of evaluation. Even without endorsing the theory of knowledge upon which the model is based, we believe these criteria can be applied to ensure quality evaluation in any evaluation scheme.

Quality 1 *Holism.* The evaluation should avoid distortion of the total reality being evaluated by an undue emphasis on quantification or on only a few variables. Toward this end both statistical and existential forms of inference should be used.

Quality 2 *Helpfulness toward program improvement.* This is really the key to formative evaluation, and what distinguishes it from summative evaluation. The primary purpose of formative evaluation is to assist the one responsible for the curriculum program. It looks to growth, improvement, increased effectiveness, rather than to ranking, judging, categorizing, criticizing.

Quality 3 *Acceptance of hard and soft data.* In order to reduce distortion through methodological rigidity or theoretical bias (e.g., positivism or mechanistic reductionism), the reality being evaluated should be described by both empirical and intuitive methodologies. The qualities of the phenomena as well as the quantitative properties deserve attention.

Quality 4 *Evaluation vulnerability.* The process of evaluation requires dialogue between the evaluator and the evaluated in which the theory and methodology of the evaluator are open to question. Rather than assuming an elitist posture, the evaluator must enter a shared enterprise with the evaluated in which perceptions are discussed and conclusions negotiated. The evaluator has to be as vulnerable as the evaluated.

Quality 5 *Vision of the future.* Since the purpose of the evaluation is the improvement of the program or the behavior being evaluated, the evaluator ought to be able and willing to disclose his view of the future context in which such improved programs or behaviors will function better. In this way, evaluation is seen as dynamic, as creative, and as open to the future, as in fact that essential activity that keeps an action system in a process of self renewal.[16]

These critiera will also be evident in our later treatment of clinical supervision.[17] For the moment, however, we can appreciate the necessity of the supervisor's awareness of the values embedded in any evaluation scheme.

[15] Richard C. Kunkel and Susan A. Tucker, "A Perception-Based Model of Program Evaluation: A Values Oriented Theory," paper presented at AERA Annual Meeting, New York, 1977.
[16] Ibid., pp. 2–4.
[17] See Chapter 17.

In the ongoing process of formative evaluation, it is possible to achieve a more holistic appraisal of teacher, student learning, and program. When one moves into summative evaluation, however, supervisors will have a much more difficult time preventing the exterior imposition of the one exclusive set of values.

SUMMATIVE EVALUATION

In treating summative evaluation, we wish to distinguish between the *activity* of summative evaluation and the *reporting* of the results of summative evaluation. Frequently summative evaluation is spoken of exclusively as the reporting of results. Supervisors ought to monitor not only the reporting of results, but also how the activity of summative evaluation itself is designed and carried out. For example, a teacher may have a very fine method of preparing her students for a final exam, but may have a very one-sided approach to reporting results. Beyond the individual teacher's reporting of results, the supervisor needs to look at the system's use of these reports and the system's reporting procedures to outside agencies.

When dealing with summative evaluation of students, then, supervisors can help teachers realize the significant instructional activity and learning that can take place through summative evaluation. Teachers, for example, can encourage students to engage in a summative-type self-evaluation, aiming for the students' review of what significant things *they* think they have learned in the course. Some teachers will assign a final project of this type. Even in a more structured class review of the course prior to a final exam, the students can deepen much of what they have learned. Frequently the review provides the opportunity for a whole new synthesis of learnings. What was said in the discussion of formative evaluation about going over test results would also apply here: it would be the teacher's last chance to get the point across before the students move on.

When considering the reporting of summative evaluation results, we may wish that the five criteria mentioned earlier could be applied. There are many reasons why summative evaluation usually is far less complete than what the five criteria would require. Summative evaluation has as its primary purpose the reporting of results at the conclusion of a program or of a time span. Among the people reading these reports of summative evaluation are guidance counselors, principals, parents, college admission officers, employers, state licensing officials, and so on. By and large, they are looking for brief reports using recognizable symbols of a quantifiable result. It would be impossible for this reporting system to work with substantially expanded reports that measured up to the five criteria. First, it would put an intolerable burden on teachers to prepare an extensive portfolio on each of their students. The agencies receiving these reports would have to hire additional personnel simply to read and code these reports. Given the political and legal climate surrounding information systems and their use, a more expansive summation of the pupil's achievements would open a Pandora's box of problems. While more holistic summative evaluation reports would be desirable for a variety of purposes, then, the practical difficulties involved would seem to prevent any useful developments in this arena.

When we move into the *reporting* of summative evaluation of the teacher's effectiveness and the effectiveness of the curriculum, we move into a process fraught with problems and misunderstandings. Because of the neoscientific-management influences in education[18] and political and economic issues surrounding schooling, summative evaluation of teachers, instructional strategies, curriculum design, and instructional materials has been used for purposes other than what might be called scientific objectivity.

Recently, schools are being held accountable by local, state, and federal agencies. Teachers, supervisors, building principals, and superintendents are under increasing pressure to give an account of themselves to the taxpayers and legislatures. There is the simplistic assumption that if youngsters are falling behind in scores on standardized tests, then the fault can be laid exclusively on the school's doorstep.

Even if the schools were largely to blame, a conclusion certainly without any clear evidence, the methodologies of reporting and evaluation used in most accountability schemes, and the theory of knowledge upon which they rest, are highly simplistic and value-biased. First, the issue of accountability has become a highly political issue. It is impossible to assume that the evaluation, interpretation, and reporting of school results would remain untainted by political motives. Any claim to scientific objectivity in accountability reports will involve at least as much rhetoric as truth.[19]

Second, the almost total reliance of accountability schemes on test scores or quantifiable aspects of learning rests upon a theory of knowing or learning that comes out of behavioristic psychology. The view of human beings reflected by behavioristic psychology would more than likely be rejected by most citizens as entirely too simplistic or reductionist. Yet measures of learning dictated by this model of humanity are used as the primary source of evidence that the schools are doing—or not doing—what these same citizens are paying taxes for. That the irony in this goes unnoticed or is ignored only points to the muddying of evaluation purposes by political concerns.[20]

Supervisors have recognized competence and expertise within the school system. They should use their authority and join forces with other supervisors and teachers to resist accountability schemes that take such a one-dimensional and biased view of learning and instruction. If supervisors and teachers allow accountability schemes to intrude more and more into the schools, the end result will be a program that leaves teachers and students little or no latitude in the classroom.

---

[18] This is discussed in Chapters 1 and 2, as well as throughout this book.
[19] See Bonnet, op. cit.
[20] See House, op. cit.; Robert E. Stake, "Overview and Critique of Existing Evaluation Practices and Some New Leads for the Future," paper presented at AERA Annual Meeting, San Francisco, 1976; and Kunkel and Tucker, op. cit.

Everything will already have been spelled out in a tightly systematic process leading to the achievement of preestablished behavioral objectives.[21]

Finally, supervisors and teachers (and, where possible, students) will engage in summative evaluation activities at the end of the course. Not only will they review what the final results were in student learnings, but they will review the results of their formative evaluations throughout the course. It is during the summative evaluation activity that one can see again the usefulness of the five criteria of good evaluation. The entire program should be reviewed as to the effectiveness of its scope and sequence. This comprehensive evaluation should also include an assessment of the adequacy of instructional materials such as films, slides, reference books, field trips, etc. Those involved in the evaluation should also question whether the use of time and space was helpful. Was the pace about right? Is there any way to revise the class schedule to allow for longer or shorter periods or for a more flexible schedule for large and small group sessions? Such a general overview should also include a look at the high and low points of the course and some guesses at the probable reasons for both. This comprehensive summation of the course or program will enable the teacher to make those necessary decisions about changes in the program next time around. Here is where the supervisor can be an enormous resource as the two come up with a variety of program changes and test them out for logic and "fit" in the overall program. Such a program evaluation often becomes the starting point for the supervisor's agenda the following year.

SUMMARY

This chapter has taken up the supervisor's role in program evaluation. In order to clarify what that role is and to distinguish it from that of the evaluation expert, we presented an overview of program evaluation, of its different levels and technologies and audiences and purposes. Then the thesis was presented that a supervisor's role in program evaluation is primarily to work alongside the teachers as they engage in the ongoing task of evaluating the impact of the program and their implementation of it on students.

We established the distinctions between formative and summative evaluation. We saw that students can engage in their own self-evaluation process in both formative and summative evaluation. This is a central activity that reveals to the teacher how the student is personally appropriating the learning tasks. We saw how in the teacher's use of tests for both formative and summative purposes valuable learning could be taking place. In other words, we stressed that evaluation can be and ought to be viewed as an intrinsic element in both teaching and learning.

While the supervisor acts in a manner supportive to the teacher's evaluation activities and occasionally becomes involved with the teacher in planning and

---

[21] Ernest R. House, "Beyond Accountability," in Thomas J. Sergiovanni (ed.), *Professional Supervision for Professional Teachers,* Washington, D.C.: Association for Supervisors and Curriculum Development, 1975.

designing evaluation activities, we saw that one essential activity of the supervisor is to keep enough distance from the evaluation activity to perceive the values embedded in the process. Some value assumptions behind rather standard evaluation procedures were highlighted. The five criteria for good evaluation were presented as a means for both teacher and supervisor to check that their evaluation activities were on target.

It is apparent, then, that evaluation is a critical aspect of the supervisor's professional responsibility. Evaluation must be continuous and not simply an end-of-year or end-of-semester assessment. It involves much more than rating the teacher according to the test results of students, and much more than the grading and promotion of students. Rather, the comprehensive evaluation process provides a continuous and responsible basis for decision making throughout the curriculum-instructional program. Only by means of an ongoing evaluation process can the program be improved and adapted to the human needs of students and hence result in more effective student learnings. The neglect of continuous and thorough evaluation on the part of supervisors, teachers, and students can be cited as the single most pervasive cause of stale and irrelevant instructional programs. Continuous and honest appraisal of the quality and effectiveness of the instructional program, on the other hand, can be the necessary catalyst for imaginative curriculum development itself, as well as for improved teaching strategies.

STUDY GUIDE

Recall the concepts, ideas, and meanings associated with each of the following phrases and terms included in this chapter. Can you discuss each of them with a colleague and apply them to the supervisory context of your school? If you cannot, review them in the text and record the page numbers for future reference.

1 Diagnostic evaluation
2 Evaluation activity
3 Evaluating evaluation
4 Evaluation expert
5 Evaluation reporting
6 Formative evaluation
7 Misuses of testing
8 Student self-evaluation
9 Summative evaluation

EXERCISES

1 Inquire at a school you are familiar with about current accountability reports that the state requires. Do you think the taxpayers are receiving adequate information about the effectiveness of that school? Discuss your reactions in class.

2 Write out your own assumptions behind a method of formative student evaluation that makes sense to you.

3 In your formal education, have you been asked to evaluate what you have learned? How might a student encourage that practice with his or her teachers?

4 Discuss the supervisor's role in program evaluation with two practicing supervisors. How do their views differ from those in this chapter?

FOUR

A HUMAN RESOURCES APPROACH TO STAFF DEVELOPMENT, CLINICAL SUPERVISION, AND TEACHER EVALUATION

INTRODUCTION: GROWTH-ORIENTED CLASSROOM SUPERVISION

The state of the art of classroom supervision is perhaps best illustrated by examining prevailing teacher-evaluation strategies. Teacher evaluation has typically meant the rating, grading, and classifying of teachers using some locally standardized instrument as a yardstick. The instrument generally lists traits of teachers assumed to be important, such as "the teacher has a pleasant voice," and certain tasks of teaching considered to be critical, such as "the teacher plans well." The evaluator usually writes in comments as, increasingly, does the teacher.

This evaluation instrument is filled out after a classroom observation of the teacher, often lasting from one-half to one hour. The observation visit is usually preceded by a conference, which varies from a brief encounter to a session where lesson plans, objectives, and teaching strategies are discussed. Sometimes a post-observation conference follows, wherein comments and ratings are discussed and negotiated. Usually, the teacher-evaluation procedure is concluded when both parties sign the instrument. The instrument is then forwarded to the district archives. This teacher evaluation procedure may occur once or twice a year for the tenured teacher and two to four times a year for novices. Many teachers report having been observed in the classroom only a handful of times, and reports of almost never being observed after achieving tenure are common.

In an effort to correct this problem some states have passed laws which require a much more intensive evaluation, often using state-provided standardized instruments. The instruments are comprised of teaching behaviors claimed to be linked to the "teaching effectiveness" research and thus are considered to be "scientific" and "objective." As we shall point out in the next chapter the systems turn out to be neither scientific nor objective and the teaching-effectiveness research upon which they claim to be based is often misrepresented.

At this writing state mandated and standardized evaluation systems exist in Texas, parts of Florida, and Georgia. In Texas, for example, evaluators are trained by the state and certified after such training to ensure that everyone interprets the behaviors listed in the state instrument the same way. Teachers are awarded credits based on the number of behaviors they manage to display during a 45-minute observation. The more behaviors displayed the higher the score. The behaviors are the same regardless of the level of teaching, the subject matter area, and other considerations. Thus a kindergarten teacher, high school physics teacher, a special education teacher teaching students on a one-to-one basis, and a music teacher are all required to display the same behaviors. Since no preconference is required the evaluator typically has no idea what the teacher intends. But no matter, for regardless of intents the same behaviors must be displayed. Since most of the behaviors are based on the "teaching effectiveness" research and that research links direct instruction methods to basic skills acquisition the Texas system implicitly requires teachers to teach in a particular way even when that way may not be appropriate.

Though exceptions exist and progress is being made in many school districts, by and large neither teachers nor administrators and supervisors are satisfied with present procedures. More damaging, many supervisors privately view the procedures as lacking in credibility. What are the likely effects of participating in a system characterized by such doubts? The system takes on a certain artificial or mechanical quality, a routine functioning that becomes an end in itself.

The present state of classroom supervision can be attributed to *faulty ideology* and *faulty technology*. The dominant ideologies in supervision are those associated with human relations and scientific management. The effects of human relations have been to adopt laissez faire approaches that severely downgrade classroom supervision. Presumably, it is considered that teachers are professionals, and if treated nicely, but otherwise left alone, they will respond properly. The classroom is the castle of the teacher as a professional, and classroom supervision is viewed as threatening to, or usurping of, teacher authority. This argument provides an attractive rationalization for many principals and supervisors who have good management skills and some interpersonal facility but are otherwise weak or uncomfortable in dealing with the educational side of the enterprise.

Increasingly, the emphasis in schools has shifted from classroom supervision to general supervision, and this is the scientific-management side of the ideology question. In the scientific-management view it is felt that if one can focus primarily on educational program administration and supervision through developing a materials-intensive curriculum, usually linked to a detailed curriculum syllabus or detailed predetermined objectives, then teachers can be supervised in classrooms by remote control. Teaching behavior becomes more predictable and reliable as teaching objectives and materials become more detailed, structured, and standardized. Thus we can control what teachers do by controlling the objectives they pursue, the materials they use, the curriculum they follow, the assignments and tests they give, and the schedule they follow. Granting that the existence of this kind of materials-intensive program is a means to control classroom practices, nagging questions born of the accountability movement remain. How can supervisors *be* sure that teachers are indeed performing prescribed duties up to standard? What evaluation technology can be used to answer this question? Technologies are associated with ideologies, and the language of scientific management (objectivity, rationality, reliability, precision) has been found by most Americans to be irresistible. The technology of classroom observation and evaluation, as most readers will attest, is shrouded in a sense of scientism not found even in the more legitimate sciences. This phenomenon is contrary to what most educators actually believe—*that teaching is far more an artistic enterprise than a scientific one*. Not willing to admit this publicly, we continue our deception by willy-nilly participation in a doubtful system of supervision and evaluation.

The pressure for accountability is, in our view, legitimate and cannot be ignored. Classroom supervision and evaluation is important and is needed and desired by teachers and the public alike. But the typical response to this pressure—tightening up a set of procedures with ideological and technical shortcomings, doing more of the same but now doing it with more intensity— needs to be reversed. These issues are discussed in Part Four, where more artistic approaches to supervision and evaluation more consistent with the values of human resources supervision and the nature of work in education are suggested. A caveat at this point is significant. Though we are strong advocates of more artistic approaches, we seek not to throw out the proverbial baby with the bath water. Present methods have value if viewed more modestly and intelligently, if applied in a more discriminating fashion, and if supplemented by more artistic approaches. For example, Chapter 15, concerned with classroom and teaching-effectiveness research and models of teaching, adopts a contingency perspective in search of useful insights into teaching. Key to this perspective is that a particular method of teaching or style of classroom organization should be judged by what it can and cannot accomplish. This relative view is recommended over more dogmatic views that seek to establish true and false ideologies in teaching.

GENERAL VERSUS CLINICAL SUPERVISION

Most of the literature on supervision and textbooks on supervision tend to emphasize either (or some combination of) the organizational and behavioral aspects of general supervision or the educational program administration aspects of general supervision. Parts One and Two of this book are also concerned with general supervision. Part One, for example, is concerned with the organizational aspect of general supervision and Part Two with leadership aspects. The strong emphasis one finds in the literature on general supervision is related in part to the decline of interest in classroom supervision by scholars and practitioners.

In the interest of focusing attention anew on classroom supervision, some experts have attempted to distinguish between the two by referring to classroom supervision as clinical and out-of-class supervision as general. Cogan, for example, cites two purposes of clinical supervision in his popular book entitled *Clinical Supervision:* "The first is to develop and explicate a system of in-class supervision that, in competent hands, will prove powerful enough to give supervisors a reasonable hope of accomplishing significant improvements in the teacher's classroom instruction. The second purpose is to help correct the neglect of in-class or clinical supervision and to establish it as a necessary complement to out-of-class ('general') supervision."[1]

In a similar vein Goldhammer refers to clinical supervision as follows:

> First of all, I mean to convey an image of face-to-face relationships between supervisors and teachers. History provides the principal reason for this emphasis, namely, that in many situations presently and during various periods in its development, supervision has been conducted as supervision from a distance, as, for example, supervision of curriculum development or of instructional policies framed by committees of teachers. "Clinical" supervision is meant to imply supervision up close.[2]

General and clinical supervision are, of course, interdependent. Meaningful classroom interventions are built upon healthy organizational climates, facilitated by credible leadership and premised on a reasoned educational program. Though general supervision is an important and necessary component of effective supervision, without clinical supervision it is not sufficient.

THE FOCUS OF CLINICAL SUPERVISION

Clinical supervision refers to face-to-face contact with teachers with the intent of improving instruction and increasing professional growth. In many respects, a one-to-one correspondence exists between improving classroom instruction and increasing professional growth, and for this reason staff development and clinical supervision are inseparable concepts and activities. How does evaluation fit into this picture? Evaluation is a natural part of one's professional life and occurs continuously. Every decision that teachers, administrators, and supervisors make is preceded by evaluation (often implicit) of some sort.

---

[1] Morris L. Cogan, *Clinical Supervision,* Boston: Houghton Mifflin, 1973, p. xi.
[2] Robert Goldhammer, *Clinical Supervision: Special Methods for the Supervision of Teachers,* New York: Holt, 1969, p. 54.

Evaluation is valuing, and valuing is judging. These are natural events in the lives of educational professionals and, of course, are critical aspects of clinical supervision and staff development.

But evaluation can take a number of foci, some of which are more compatible with events, purposes, and characteristics of supervision than others. Evaluation experts, for example, make an important distinction between *formative* evaluation and *summative* evaluation.[3] Teacher-evaluation procedures typically found in school can be classified as summative. Evaluation that emphasizes ongoing growth and development would be considered formative. Consider the following distinctions:

1 Summative evaluation of teachers has a certain finality to it—it is terminal in the sense that it occurs at the conclusion of an educational activity. In evaluating a teacher's performance, summative evaluation suggests a statement of worth. A judgment is made about the quality of one's teaching.

2 Summative evaluation is a legitimate and important activity which if done carefully can play a constructive role in a school's total evaluation strategy.

3 Formative evaluation of teachers is intended to increase the effectiveness of ongoing educational programs and activity. Evaluation information is collected and used to understand, correct, and improve ongoing activity.

4 With respect to teaching, formative evaluation is concerned less with judging and rating the teacher than with providing information which helps improve teacher performance.

5 In the strictest sense formative and summative evaluation cannot be separated, for each contains aspects of the other, but it is useful nevertheless to speak of a formative focus and a summative focus to evaluation.[4]

The focus of clinical supervision should be on formative evaluation. The supervisor is first and foremost interested in improving teaching and increasing teachers' personal development. Does this emphasis conflict with demands that teachers be held accountable for their actions? We think not. A formative evaluation emphasis is entirely consistent with holding teachers accountable, but in a professional, not bureaucratic, sense. Professional accountability is growth-oriented and implies a commitment to consistent improvement. Bureaucratic accountability is not growth-oriented at all but merely seeks to ensure that teachers measure up to some predetermined standard.

From time to time supervisors will indeed be engaged in a more summatively focused evaluation. Though the supervisor's major commitment is to formative evaluation, occasional problems occur and incompetent teachers or teachers whose philosophy and orientation differ markedly from that of the school will

---

[3] Michael Scriven, "The Methodology of Evaluation," in Robert Stake (ed.), *AERA Monograph on Curriculum Evaluation*, no. 1, Chicago: Rand McNally, 1965. See also Benjamin Bloom, Thomas Hastings, and G. F. Madaus, *Handbook on Formative and Summative Evaluation of Student Learning*, New York: McGraw-Hill, 1971.

[4] Thomas J. Sergiovanni, *Handbook for Effective Department Leadership Concepts and Practices in Today's Secondary Schools*, Boston: Allyn and Bacon, 1977, p. 372.

be discovered. As a result, withholding tenure or dismissal of a tenured teacher may well be considered. Personnel actions of this sort are so intertwined with existing local administrative policies and state statutory restrictions and requirements that a totally different mind-set is needed. Such a procedure is best placed in the hands of a line administrative officer of the district. In the case of a principal who assumes both a supervisory and administrative role, the teacher should be informed of the focus and the tone of the evaluation procedure that is to follow. The school attorney would most likely be consulted regarding due process if administrative guidelines on this question are wanting. In Toledo and other school districts the teachers' union is involved in the process, working cooperatively with "management" to ensure due process on the one hand and *warranted* dismissal on the other. Many state education agencies and state school board associations publish pamphlets and other guidelines on this touchy and increasingly legalistic problem. These issues are discussed in the latter part of Chapter 16.

Practically speaking, improving classroom instruction must start with the teacher. Sustained changes in teacher behavior and sustained improvements in classroom functioning occur as a result of teachers who are committed to these changes. That being the case, supervisors are forced to depend upon the willing cooperation of teachers. Indeed, supervisors rarely change teachers but help them to change, a condition more suited to formative evaluation.

BRIGHT PROSPECTS AHEAD

When it comes to clinical supervision and the direct evaluation of classroom teaching, problems are bound to arise. Much is at stake in the process for both supervisors and teachers. At present, and despite exceptions in some school districts, the process is not going well. Supervisors and teachers typically report a lack of confidence in present procedures, and frequently more damage than good seems to be the result. The problem, we believe, is that present supervisory practices are too often based on naive assumptions of what is science and Theory X assumptions about the capacities and motivations of teachers. The result is the widespread emergence of evaluation systems which are rationalistic rather than rational in design and bureaucratic rather than professional in practice. But there is good news ahead. More now is known about effective teaching and helpful supervision than ever before. With a few changes in basic assumptions and with better choices about how to proceed, a professional practice of supervision, designed to be helpful and able to win the confidence of supervisors, teachers, and the public, can emerge.

CHAPTER

THE THEORETICAL BASIS FOR CLINICAL SUPERVISORY PRACTICE

If the theory is wrong the practice is wrong. This is the reality we face in teaching and in clinically oriented supervision—a reality we share with all other professional fields. In the introduction to this book and again in Chapter 2 we pointed out that many teachers and supervisors claim not to practice according to theory. Instead they claim to practice in response to the realities they face and the experiences they accumulate. Despite these claims, it is evident that their practice is theory-based—though the theories they rely on may be implicit. It does not matter whether supervisors and teachers rely on theories that emerge from scholarly speculations and research or rely on intuition and practical experience (or some combination of both) the effect is the same, *theory-based practice*. Since all teaching and supervisory practice is theory-based, the caution "if the theory is wrong the practice is wrong" is a serious one. If we want to understand current practice, come to grips with its shortcomings, and work to improve it, we have to start at the beginning by examining the adequacy of underlying theories, be they implicit or explicit. That is the purpose of this chapter.[1]

---

[1] For a more in-depth analysis of the point of view provided in the chapter see Thomas J. Sergiovanni, "Expanding Conceptions of Inquiry and Practice in Supervision and Evaluation," *Educational Evaluation and Policy Analysis,* vol. 6, no. 3, pp. 355–365, 1984; "Landscapes, Mindscapes and Reflective Practice in Supervision," *Journal of Curriculum and Supervision,* vol. 1, no. 1, pp. 5–17, 1985; "Understanding Reflective Practice," *Journal of Curriculum and Supervision,* vol. 6, no. 4, pp. 355–365, 1986; "The Metaphorical Use of Theories and Models in Supervision: Building a Science," *Journal of Curriculum and Supervision,* vol. 2, no. 3, pp. 221–232, 1987; and "We Need a TRUE Profession!" *Educational Leadership,* vol. 44, no. 8, 1987.

RATIONAL OR RATIONALISTIC THEORIES?

Many supervisors and teachers dream of building a body of knowledge, a method of inquiry, and patterns of practice that will provide the basis for a true profession of teaching and clinically oriented supervision comparable with that of architecture and medicine or perhaps the performing arts professions. We believe that it is possible for supervision and teaching to become established and recognized fields of inquiry and professional practice. Efforts to improve the scientific basis for and professional practice of teaching and supervision aim at the right goal and a doable goal. The question is: Are we going about it the right way? On this count we are more pessimistic. The problem is that presently our theorizing and model building is patterned too closely after the physical sciences. Unfortunately, this patterning is too simplistic to be considered scientific by the standards of that guild. Put another way, the problems we address, our theorizing, how we conduct research, the conclusions we draw from this inquiry, and the building of practice models and prescriptions based on this inquiry are not sufficiently complex or comprehensive to be considered scientific by the established scientific community. Nor do they meet the standards of scientific and professional rigor that characterize the established professions. When we persist nonetheless in traveling this course, the result is the development of rationalistic theories and rationalistic rather than rational practices.

In Chapter 2 we described the rationalistic tradition as follows: "The rationalistic tradition is distinguished by its narrow focus on certain aspects of rationality which...often leads to attitudes and activities that are not rational in a broader perspective."[2] Further, as the philosopher Taylor suggests, rationalistic theories and models are typically implausible given the realities of practice and tend to lead to bad science by being either wordy elaborations of the obvious or by dealing with trivial questions.[3] Stated in our context, rationalistic theories and models do not fit the real world of teaching and supervision. When such models are used anyway, teaching typically suffers, and teachers and supervisors experience frustration, combined with a loss of confidence in what sound theory and research can provide.

Building generic models of teaching and supervisory practice based on the "teaching effectiveness" research is an example of rationalistic rather than rational thinking. This research reveals that the explicit or direct teaching model is an effective way to teach basic reading and computational skills and simple subject matter mastery to elementary school children. Assuming that this method represents "effective teaching" and thus prescribing this teaching as a means by which all learning should take place is hardly a rational approach to model building and to teaching practice. Yet consultants, workshop special-

[2] Terry Winograd and Fernando Flores, *Understanding Computers and Cognition*, Norwood, N.J.: Ablex Publishing Corp., 1986, p. 8.

[3] Charles Taylor, *Philosophy and the Human Sciences Philosophical Papers*, vol. 2, London: Cambridge University Press, 1985.

ists, contributors to widely circulated professional publications, and others have been quite successful in convincing many policy makers and professionals that explicit teaching is indeed the same as effective teaching. This results in the development of rationalistic policies and school practices. One popular example at this writing is the adoption by school districts and in some cases by entire states of teacher-evaluation checklists and other instruments composed of items primarily or exclusively based on this research. This results in uniform use of an instrument that might be appropriate for a limited range of teaching and learning outcomes but is invalid for other teaching and learning outcomes. This reasoning is similar to medical professionals considering a procedure found to be effective for one ailment to be "effective medical practice" and thus prescribing this same procedure for other ailments.

HOW SCIENTISTS AND PROFESSIONALS THINK

In the more established professions and sciences advances have been made in understanding the nature of knowledge which are not sufficiently reflected in mainstream supervisory thought. There is, for example, remark-able agreement that human thinking influences scientific reality. The well-known psychologist McGrath states, "We can never know anything independently of the ways we found it out; empirical knowledge is always contingent on the methods, populations, situations and underlying assumptions involved in the process by which knowledge was acquired."[4] Throughout the social sciences there is wide acceptance of the notion that scientific decisions are human choices and thus what counts as scientific evidence is often little more than an artifact of these choices. Different choices result in different scientific evidence. Gestalt psychologists are fond of demonstrating how human decisions help to create reality. One well-known example they use is the picture of a vase made of two profiles. Is it a vase or two profiles? You can see either but you cannot see both at the same time. You have to decide which reality you are going to see, and it is your decision that creates reality.

The link between human decisions and existing reality is true as well in the physical sciences. The examples most often cited are drawn from the strange behavior of light and matter in quantum mechanics. The principle of complementarity, for example, provides that in some cases complementary concepts whose meanings exclude each other are, nonetheless, different representations of the same thing. With respect to light, particle representations and wave representations are complementary properties of electrons. Whether an electron appears as a particle or as a wave (the nature of scientific reality for that electron) depends upon how it is measured. One method of measurement provides a particle representation and the other a wave representation. Thus the representation of an electron cannot be determined separate from a human

---

[4] Joseph E. McGrath, Joanne Martin, and Richard Kulka, *Judgment Calls in Research,* Beverly Hills, Calif.: Sage, 1982, p. 105.

decision as to how it will be measured. That decision, in a very large sense, *creates* the nature of scientific reality.[5]

The link between scientific evidence and human decision making in supervision and teaching can be illustrated by the "teaching effectiveness" research referred to earlier. The indicators of effectiveness commonly cited in the literature are an artifact of how the researchers decided to define effectiveness. Had they defined effectiveness differently, different indicators would have been discovered. The indicators, therefore, are not independent or objective but a function of human decisions. Imagine what the consequences of redefining effectiveness would be in schools and indeed states that use evaluation instruments based on the original teaching-effectiveness research? Since the instrument behaviors would no longer be "valid," teachers thought to be "winners" might well be "losers" and vice versa. Winning and losing in teacher evaluation is never objective but always an artifact of the evaluation system used.

THE MISMATCH WITH PRACTICE

Not only are rationalistic models of teaching and supervision not scientific, they are mismatched with the realities of practice. For example, rationalistic models emphasize uniform answers to problems, value-free teaching strategies, separation of teaching and evaluation process from context, objectivity, and a uniform-technical language system. Patterns of supervision and teaching practice found in the real world, however, are characterized by a great deal of uncertainty, instability, complexity, and variety. Further, value conflicts and uniqueness are accepted aspects of educational settings. Since the real world of teaching is characterized by unique events, uniform answers to problems are not likely to be very helpful. Since teachers, supervisors, and students bring to the classroom beliefs, assumptions, values, opinions, and preferences, objective and value-free supervisory strategies are not likely to address issues of importance. Since reality in practice does not exist separate from persons involved in the processes of teaching and supervision, knowing cannot be separated from what is known. Since evaluation reality in teaching is linked to the observer and to decisions she or he makes about methods of evaluation, it is not independent or objective but an artifact of this situation. Since supervisory reality is context-bound and situationally determined, the practical language of actual classroom life and actual teaching events will be found more meaningful than the theoretical language or generic language which may be inherent in rating scales and other measurement devices associated with the rationalistic view.

What changes are needed in the ways in which we think about, inquire, and practice if teaching and supervision are to become less rationalistic and more

---

[5] For a popular discussion of this theme see Heinz R. Pagels, *The Cosmic Code: Quantum Physics as the Language of Nature*, New York: Simon and Schuster, 1982. For further applications to supervision see Sergiovanni, op. cit., "Expanding Conceptions of Inquiry and Practice in Supervision and Evaluation."

rational? First our mindscapes of how schools work and how life in classrooms unfolds need to change. Mindscapes help construct our reality. Different realities lead to different supervisory and teaching practices. Teaching, for example, is often thought of as a tightly connected process which resembles the throwing of teaching pitches into a learning outcome zone. There is always the danger that some pitches will miss the zone and thus will be declared balls. Therefore, supervision, within this mindscape, focuses on increasing the likelihood of teaching strikes being thrown. The emphasis is on programming and monitoring the practice of teaching to ensure that the process unfolds in a reliable and predictable manner. The problem with this mindscape is that it does not reflect the realities of practice, provides a limited and unsophisticated view of the nature of teaching and learning, and provides a regressive view of the role of the teacher.

GOOD TEACHERS ARE SURFERS, NOT PITCHERS

In teaching conceived as pitching, having detailed, specific goals and objectives in mind is considered to be critical. But in reality, teachers typically do not think and act in accord with discrete goals and objectives as much as they do in value patterns. For example, in teaching reading teachers are as concerned with the students' ability to synthesize and extend as they are with the mastery of reading fundamentals. They recognize that both goals need to be pursued in a manner which makes the experience of reading a joyful activity. But the three goals are often in competition. Too much emphasis on one can negatively affect each of the other two. The issue for the teacher is how to achieve a balance between and among competing values, and the rationality that is appropriate is not linear or bureaucratic but rationality in pursuit of a pattern of outcomes. Some experts refer to this rationality as *patterned rationality*.[6] Since teachers are concerned with outcomes that produce a sensible pattern, it is difficult to ask them to think specifically in terms of this outcome or that or even several outcomes discretely.

The surfing metaphor is much more descriptive than pitching of how teachers think and act. Teachers ride the wave of the teaching pattern as it unfolds. In riding the wave they use various models of teaching and learning not rationalistically to prescribe practice but rationally to inform intuition and enhance professional judgment. A rational science of supervision and teaching would give more emphasis to developing strategies that reflect a higher concern for values than goals, for patterns than discrete outcomes, and for learning how to ride the pattern of the wave of teaching.

Craft knowledge reveals that when teachers do think about goals and objectives they're just as likely to think about discovering them in the act of teaching as they are in setting them beforehand. Teachers adopt a more

[6] Jean Hills, "The Preparation of Educational Leaders: What's Needed and What's Next?" UCEA Occasional Paper 8303, Columbus, Ohio: University Council for Educational Administration, 1982.

strategic than tactical view of goals and objectives. When surfing they gear their practice toward broad and often changing goals and rely heavily on assessing what it was that was worthwhile after learning encounters have been concluded. They're not so proud or foolish as to declare something worthwhile that is accomplished as not counting simply because it was not anticipated beforehand. This reality is not sufficiently accounted for in rationalistic models of teaching and supervision.

CONFUSING EVALUATION AND MEASUREMENT

An important step toward developing a rational science and practice of supervision and teaching would be to acknowledge the existence of subjectivity rather than try so hard to stamp it out. Accepting the reality that there is no such thing as objective evaluation would put us on a comparable footing with our colleagues in the basic sciences and in other more established fields. As pointed out earlier, evaluation systems are a result of human decisions. Somebody makes a decision to define effectiveness in a certain way. Thus "good teaching" is always an artifact of the evaluation system used. A teacher who follows a model of teaching which fits a particular evaluation would be declared a winner though this same teacher could be a loser under a different system.

Rationalistic thinking is encouraged by the confusion which exists between measurement and evaluation. Much of what passes as evaluation isn't evaluation at all but measurement. Suppose, for example, you are interested in buying blinds for a window in your home. You would first need to know the size of the window. Let's say the window is 22 inches wide by 60 inches long. This set of figures is now your standard. You find some extra blinds in the attic. Using a ruler, you carefully measure the blinds and learn that none "measures up" to your standard. Though you had a role to play in this process it was really the ruler that counted. Someone else using the same ruler would very likely have reached the same conclusion.

Though measurements need to be accurate and some skill is involved in the process the standard against which measurements are weighed and the measuring device are more important than the person doing the measuring. Ideally, measurement should be "personproof" in the sense that each person measuring should reach the same conclusion. Interrater reliability is highly valued. Thus in measurement-oriented evaluation systems the role of the evaluator is *diminished*. Principals and supervisors are *less important* than the instruments and procedures they use. Further, when a measurement-oriented evaluation system is imported to a school or state, principals, supervisors, teachers, and the public forfeit the right to decide for themselves what is good teaching—what is the kind of teaching that makes sense to them given their goals, aspirations, the characteristics of their community, and so forth. Measurement-oriented evaluation systems, therefore, not only frequently result in rationalistic practices; they can threaten one of the fundamental values undergirding schooling in America—the right to choose.

Evaluation, by contrast, is a distinctly human process that involves discernment and making informed judgments. Evaluation is never value-free or context-free. In our example, having decided on the size of blinds needed, all subsequent decisions are a matter of preference, taste, and purpose. What effect do you want to create in the room you are decorating? Do you prefer wooden or metal blinds, a soft or bold look, warm or cool colors? How will the available options fit into the broader decorating scheme of the room? In matters of evaluation "interrater reliability" is not highly valued. Instead the evaluator's judgment given desired effects is what counts. Evaluation is a distinctly human rather than mechanical process.

IMPROVING THE ACCURACY OF EVALUATION

Accuracy and precision are the standard criteria used by the more established disciplines and professions to judge the adequacy of knowledge claims and the applicability of these claims to practice. Accuracy refers to the relevance and importance of problems pursued and resulting findings. Precision refers to the cogency and rigor with which problems are pursued. In the established disciplines and professions accuracy is never sacrificed on behalf of relevance. Medical researchers and physicists, for example, do not pursue trivial questions at the expense of important ones simply because they lend themselves to greater scientific rigor and study. The Nobel laureate Medawar states: "It has been shrewdly observed that an experiment not worth doing is not worth doing well."[7] Emphasizing precision over accuracy follows the reasoning of the fellow who lost his keys in the middle of the block but looked for them at the street corner because the light was better.

Rationalistic decisions are made every time we opt for teaching and supervisory models because they are clearly stated, easy to learn and use, and because the dimensions they tend to are readily observable and measurable with little regard for whether they address what really is important in teaching. A rational approach accepts the fact that it is far better to find an approximate answer to the right question no matter how vague than an exact answer to the wrong question which can always be made precise.[8] Much of the appeal of rationalistic models of teaching and supervision is in their precision regardless of whether they are accurate or not. They look scientific, they are tight, they are easy to use, and too often that's all that seems to matter.

Some evaluation experts might prefer the words "validity" and "reliability" seeking a more focused definition of meaning than having these important psychometric concepts subsumed by the more general concepts of accuracy and precision. Rationalistic thinking and practice is widespread with respect to validity and reliability. Such well-known evaluation experts as Michael Scriven

---

[7] P. B. Medawar, *The Limits of Science*, New York: Harper & Row, 1984, p. 79.
[8] John Tukey as cited in R. Rose, "Disciplined Research and Undisciplined Problems," Carol Weiss (ed.), *Using Social Research in Public Policy Making*, Washington, D.C.: Heath, 1977, p. 23.

and Ernest House, for example, point out that validity is frequently sacrificed for reliability and often reliability substitutes for validity, creating an evaluation error of the first magnitude.[9]

COLORS AND WINKS: THE PHONETICS AND SEMANTICS OF TEACHING

Teaching and supervision can be examined at two levels—the level of observed behavior and the level of meaning and understanding. The level of observed behavior represents the phonetics of teaching and the level of meaning and understanding the semantics. Phonetic teaching is easily observed and lends itself to "scientific" measuring with a great deal of reliability. The semantic side of teaching, on the other hand, because it refers to the deep structure and meanings that people attribute to and derive from teaching behaviors and events, is not so easily possessed.

Take, for example, the common prescriptions for teaching: communicate expectations, monitor to ensure that students comply, solicit frequent responses, provide corrective feedback, and reteach as necessary. Carefully assessing teaching behaviors to ensure that these prescriptions are in evidence leaves unanswered the questions of what this approach to teaching means to students, how this teaching is to be understood by teachers and supervisors, whether the steps fit teaching purposes, and what useful personal meanings different students might derive from the same teaching. Consider how the color yellow is understood differently against fields of white and black. At one level yellow is yellow but at another level yellow against a white field is quite different from yellow against a black field. Considering yellow to be "yellow" regardless of the field emphasizes too much the phonetic aspect of this word rather than the semantic. Consider as well the meaning of winks exchanged by a grandparent or child. How can one tell the wink of affection from that of conspiracy or of deception? A wink is a wink. But then again, a wink is not a wink. Phonetically we can provide a dictionary definition of the word *wink* but semantically winks have different meanings.

Teaching too needs to be understood in light of the circumstances at hand. The common prescriptions for teaching described above may represent good teaching when it is important to direct students toward a common performance goal requiring low-level and noncontroversial skill acquisition. But for more complex learning purposes where students are required to discern and judge, synthesize and extend, create and problem-solve, the same teaching prescriptions are neither meaningful nor effective. From a rational perspective, as teaching intents and circumstances change, teaching steps and behaviors take on different meanings and must be understood and valued differently.

[9] Michael Scriven, "Objectivity and Subjectivity in Educational Research," *Philosophical Redirection of Educational Research,* National Society for the Study of Education, 1972; and Ernest R. House, *The Logic of Evaluative Argument,* Los Angeles: Center for the Study of Evaluation, University of California, 1977.

RATIONALISTIC LEADS TO BUREAUCRATIC

Taken together our rationalistic emphasis on discrete objectives, teaching pitches, simplistic objectivity, precision, measurement, and the phonetics of teaching frame the ways in which we think about teaching and teachers and the process of supervision in the direction of bureaucratic rather than professional work. Bureaucratic evaluation is more concerned with control than with understanding. Bureaucratic teaching is more concerned with following than with creating teaching protocols. Professionals and bureaucrats function differently at work. The work of bureaucrats is programmed for them by the system of which they are a part. They are subordinate to this system. Professionals too are part of a work system. But the work of professionals emerges from an interaction between available professional knowledge and individual client needs. Professional work requires that professionals be *superordinate* to this system. Professionals use the system to make informed decisions which are sensible in light of the situations they face. Teacher-proof teaching and evaluator-proof evaluation represents a retreat from professionalism. In bureaucratic work the purpose of supervision and evaluation is to provide the necessary reinforcement, conditioning, and training to produce predictable behaviors and outcomes which conform to the work system. In professional work the purpose of supervision and evaluation is to increase knowledge and understanding and thus enable the professional to make better practice decisions. Professional knowledge is created in use as professionals practice.

DEVELOPING A RATIONAL THEORY OF PRACTICE

Instead of continuing efforts to develop and use "scientific" theories separate from the realities of practice we believe that a more useful and rational approach is to develop "theories of practice." Consider, for example, the following allegory. Suppose there is a windowless classroom with three doors A, B, and C. Next to each door is a switch. The switch by door A puts on a green light, the switch by door B a red light, and the switch by door C a blue light. Suppose that students, a teacher, and a supervisor enter the room often, each always using the same door, but never the door of others. Students use door A, the teacher uses door B, and the supervisor door C. Each of the parties will firmly believe, and have evidence that substantiates his or her belief, that the room is a specific color. Is it the task of the supervisor in this case to establish the facts as he or she sees them? What is truth and what facts exist in this instance? No matter how carefully the supervisor builds a case, truth and fact cannot be separate from the meanings and realities of each of the participants involved in this allegory, and such is the case as well in the real world of supervision.

A useful and realistic conception of evaluation in teaching cannot be developed separate from a concern for purpose and for beneficiaries. If the purpose of evaluation is to inform and improve teaching practice and the beneficiaries are teachers, students, and supervisors, then we should distinguish between "scientific" theories of measurement and evaluation and theories of practice. Theories of measurement and evaluation are concerned with the discovery of truth, the establishment of fact, and the accurate recording of the world as it is. Frequently such theories seek to advance the science and art of measurement and evaluation, and the prime beneficiaries of such efforts are theorists and analysts, not teachers and students.

Theories of practice, on the other hand, are designed to improve things, to bring about higher standards, to cause individuals to strive for a better life. They have, in other words, purposive and practical qualities. When applied to such fields as supervision and teaching, theories of practice must account as well for the particularistic and phenomenological qualities of human activity. Within theories of practice the semantic side of understanding teaching is considered to be more important than the phonetic side of describing. Determining what the facts are and what teaching behaviors are present is only a first step in a process of interpretation which seeks to identify meanings giving the specifics of the teaching context.

MODES OF INQUIRY

Within a theory of practice a variety of modes exists for analyzing and understanding teaching and supervision. As Garman suggests, modes of inquiry should be viewed as alternate ways of knowing, with no one mode designed to rival others. Instead, modes give attention to and highlight different issues of interest in supervision and evaluation. She proposes five modes as follows:

> *Discovery* has as a goal the inductive search for a well-articulated phenomenon and appropriate questions inherent in the classroom scenario. Both qualitative and quantitative data are appropriate here. The analysis often begins by identifying the teacher's stated intent of the lesson and the signs of consistency or inconsistency as a result of subsequent actions. . . .
>
> *Verification* is a deductive mode that provides for a degree of objectivity (which suggests that others using the same method with the same data can arrive at similar conclusions). When the salient features of the lesson have been discovered, it is imperative that the supervisor verify, usually with quantitative methodology, the extent to which the discovery was justified. Objectivity is also regarded as a general frame of mind that helps the supervisor assume a detached and neutral posture. Hypothesis testing is a feature of this verification mode.
>
> *Explanation* is both inductive and deductive. Its purpose is to explain the verified phenomena through inference derived from the content analysis of stable data. The supervisor and teacher bring their subjective "best estimates" of what is happening from their own reality base. Concept formation is a vital part of the process since this becomes the means for the two to share their construed realities from both worlds. Understanding through language is the basis for explanation.
>
> *Interpretation* is the search for meaning in the events under study. The interpretive mode often provides a way to get to what really matters, to derive mature interpretations

from that which has been verified and explained. Through appropriate methodology one has the sanction to go beyond the literal, encouraged to look for deeper meanings than the inferences derived through explanation. The supervisor understands internally by intuitively referring to his/her experience and externally by searching for symbolic acts which reveal insights about the myths and predispositions of those involved. Through the interpretive mode the supervisor and teacher are able to seek deeper significance beneath the surface content that may appear trivial.

Evaluation is a normative mode which addresses values and judgments about the events under consideration. Evaluative methods are used to determine the effectiveness of a particular action or the worthiness of the meaning. They help the teacher answer such questions as "How well have I performed?" or "Am I doing what I should be doing?" By valuing, the supervisor and teacher come to know the internal and external criteria for setting priorities and making judgments in the evaluation mode.[10]

THE BASIC QUESTIONS

In the remaining sections we wish to emphasize the interpretive aspects of supervision, the search for meaning. This emphasis recognizes that searching for meaning is an exercise of little value without having established as well what is and what ought to be in the evaluation of teaching. We conclude by suggesting some modes of inquiry that need to be developed if a rational theory of practice in supervision and evaluation of teaching is to emerge.

Three major avenues of inquiry are suggested as being important in a theory of supervisory practice. Interpretation is an art that is enhanced by multiple perspectives on reality, and meanings are sufficiently idiosyncratic to require that avenues of inquiry be pursued in partnership by teachers and supervisors. The avenues of inquiry are suggested by three questions.

1 *What is going on in this classroom?* How does this work? Can it be explained and predicted? What laws and rules govern behavior in this context? How can I accurately and vividly describe classroom events?

Thin descriptions of reality are important in presenting an overall map of classroom events. Such a map gives a general orientation of the classroom's breadth and scope, much like a road map provides for a particular region. Thick descriptions of reality are important in identifying and recording aspects of the hidden curriculum, estimates of quality, and indicators of cultural imperatives that provide a more vivid portrayal of classroom life. The maps in a travel atlas, for example, present a general descriptive orientation of a particular region; the accompanying text and photographs describe the mind and pulse of this region. Each is useful to the traveler.

2 *What ought to be going on in this classroom?* What cultural imperatives should determine action? What values should be expressed? What qualities of

[10]Noreen Garman, "A Clinical Approach to Supervision," in T. J. Sergiovanni (ed.), *Supervision of Teaching*, 1982 Yearbook, Association for Supervision and Curriculum Development, Alexandria, Va., 1982, pp. 50–51.

life should be in evidence? What standards should be pursued? What visions of excellence should prevail?

"Ought" dimensions of classroom life can be obtained and verified from empirically established standards (i.e., teacher-effectiveness research) on the one hand and from cultural preferences, values, and beliefs (i.e., conservative or humanistic ideology) on the other. Admittedly, the two sources are more easily separated in word than in action. Symbolic interactionists, for example, would suggest that values are products of interaction among people and are qualities of mind that arise through such interaction on the one hand and through symbolic meanings on the other.

Establishing that a particular level of student achievement can be obtained if teachers follow closely a given set of teaching procedures suggests a standard of fact. Such relationships ought to be rigorously pursued and empirically established as *teaching facts*. Deciding that the particular level of student achievement that might be obtained is valuable and that the trade-offs of what is lost to students and others by obtaining this gain in achievement or by adopting this method of teaching are acceptable, however, does not necessarily follow from teaching facts. Making decisions among alternatives is the establishment of *teaching values*. Strong teaching facts scientifically determined are important prerequisites for establishing teaching values but are not substitutes for these values. The establishment of both teaching facts and teaching values is important in the development of the theory of supervisory practice.

3 *What do events and activities that constitute the "is" and "ought" dimension of classroom life mean to teachers, students, supervisors, and significant others?* What is the cultural content of the classroom? What implicit educational platforms exist? What values are suggested by actual behavior and events? What are the meanings implicit in discrepancies between the espoused and in-use theories?

The discovery of meaning and the creation of meaning await the further development of the art of interpretation in the supervision and evaluation of teaching. The work of Eisner is an important step in this direction.[11]

It may be helpful in illustrating the importance of teaching facts and teaching meanings in evaluation to distinguish between *picturing* and *disclosure*.[12] Picturing models of evaluation try to be as much like the teaching activity and classroom life under study as possible. In contrast disclosure models contain key characteristics of the teaching activity and classroom life under study but move beyond picturing per se to the interpretation of meaning by raising issues and testing propositions about the phenomenon. Picturing and disclosing models will be discussed in greater detail in Chapter 16. In examining the disclosure side of the ledger emphasis is given to going beyond the data in the strictest sense to telling a story represented by the data. The data are enriched in disclosure as a means of communicating more vividly and fully. But

---

[11] Elliot W. Eisner, *The Educational Imagination*, New York: Macmillan, 1979.
[12] Ian Ramsey, *Models and Mystery*, London: Oxford University Press, 1964.

disclosure is not invention, and the story developed is based on the social facts present in teaching. Meaningful disclosure requires accurate picturing.

A TURNAROUND IS POSSIBLE

What will it take for supervision and teaching to evolve into disciplined fields of inquiry and practice? We think a better understanding of rationality is needed. Our present attempts at rationality seem not to hold up when evaluated against the standards of rationality that characterize the physical sciences, the social sciences, or the established professions. All these fields recognize, accept, and work with multiple and often conflicting goals and purposes which resemble value patterns; a mode of inquiry and practice more like surfing than simplistic linear thinking; subjective reality linked to human perceptions and decision; accuracy in pursuing problems regardless of difficulty in method; evaluation as discernment and judgment; and the semantic level of knowledge development and use.

Who should be the guardians of rationality in supervision and teaching? What responsibilities, for example, should basic researchers, synthesizers, model builders, and practicing professionals each have in ensuring rationality? Researchers have a responsibility to become much more school-based and practice-focused as they seek to create new knowledge. But they bring to their inquiry a commitment quite different from the commitment professionals bring to their practice. Though not eschewing relevancy to practice, the researchers' rightful obligation is to the process of inquiry itself and to the development of independent research findings. At another level, the synthesizers of knowledge have a responsibility to be much more realistic, open, and modest as they work to bring order and interrelatedness to existing research findings, concepts, and theoretical generalizations. The articles and books they write need to present a more accurate and modest picture of the available knowledge base. In our discussion of theory in Chapter 2 we pointed out that the greatest threat to rationality in teaching and supervision comes from the "middlemen" who translate knowledge synthesis into models of practice and communicate these models to professionals through workshops, consulting, and the writing of textbooks and articles. At this point in the knowledge chain theoretical and research knowledge has already undergone two independent interpretations (synthesis and model building). Rationality requires that models of practice not be viewed as truths to be applied but as useful frames of reference that can enhance the vision of professionals at work and inform their intuition and judgment as they practice.

In the final analysis the guardians of rationality are those who are engaged in teaching and supervisory practice. They have a right to expect more than rationalistic prescriptions from the knowledge developers and model builders and an obligation to demand more. Will supervision and teaching evolve into disciplined fields of inquiry and practice? That depends on the extent to which teachers and supervisors exert their rights and fulfill their obligations.

We began this discussion with the assertion that "if the theory is wrong the practice is wrong" and we conclude with the same thought. Theory exists in our minds and guides our practice whether we know it or not and whether we admit it or not. This being the case, one cannot discuss practices fairly or rationally without first coming to grips with his or her governing theories. You now know ours. The theoretical discussion in this chapter provides the basis for our discussion of classroom supervision, evaluation of teachers and teaching, and staff development that follows.

SUMMARY

This chapter provides a theoretical basis for understanding clinical supervisory practice. Working from the assumption that if the theory is wrong the practice will be wrong a distinction was made between rational and rationalistic theories. Rationalistic theories were described as being narrowly focused and ill-fitting with the realities of practice. Rational theories, on the other hand, though more difficult to describe and use are nonetheless more comprehensive and useful to teachers because they take into account the realities of practice. In drawing contrasts between the two theories a distinction was made between the phonetics and semantics of teaching, teaching conceived as pitching and surfing, measurement and evaluation, and accuracy and precision. Noting that rationalistic theories lead inevitably to bureaucratic teaching and evaluation an argument was then made for developing a rational theory of practice. Such a theory would be concerned with describing classroom and teaching events as accurately and as objectively as possible, seeking to determine what ought to be good teaching and what is quality in classroom life, the events and activities that comprise actual teaching, and what these transactions mean given the circumstances of teaching being studied.

STUDY GUIDE

Recall the concepts, ideas, and meanings associated with each of the following phrases and terms included in this chapter. Can you discuss each of them with a colleague and apply them to the supervisory context of your school? If you cannot, review them in the text and record the page numbers for future reference.

1 Accuracy
2 Bureaucratic evaluation
3 Evaluation
4 Interpretation
5 Measurement
6 Mindscapes
7 Patterned rationality
8 Phonetics of teaching

 9 Picturing and disclosure
10 Precision
11 Rational theories
12 Rationalistic theories
13 Semantics of teaching
14 Teaching as pitching
15 Teaching as surfing
16 "Teaching effectiveness" research
17 "Theories of practice"
18 Thick and thin descriptions

EXERCISES

1 Gather together evaluation policies, designs, and instruments now being used in your school district and in several neighboring districts. Evaluate the extent to which they are rational and rationalistic by noting whether they are based on a single model of teaching (i.e., teaching-effectiveness research) or several models; emphasize the phonetics of teaching or the semantics; view teaching as "pitching" or "surfing"; emphasize measurement or judgment; and sacrifice accuracy for precision.
2 Develop a strategy or plan that a supervisor might use in working with you as a teacher which would focus on the three basic questions: What is going on in your class? What ought to be going on in your class? What do teaching events and activities mean?

SUPERVISION FOR CLASSROOM EFFECTIVENESS

The purpose of human resources supervision is enhancing the effectiveness of teaching in our schools. Teaching effectiveness is typically defined as bringing about desired student learning. If the objective of a particular classroom lesson or unit is to have every student spell 10 new words correctly, then the teacher who brings all the students to that happy conclusion is said to be effective. Further, the more students learn, the more effective is the teaching. The supervisor's job is to help teachers increase their effectiveness in bringing about increased student learnings. But effective teaching is more complex than this, and other dimensions of effectiveness must be considered. Two such dimensions are the teacher's ability to teach in a way in which learning is viewed by students as meaningful and significant and the teacher's ability to adjust teaching strategies as warranted by changes in the teaching and learning situation.

Adding meaning and significance to the definition elevates teaching and learning from training and conditioning to educational experience. Educational experiences are characterized by intellectualism and emotional involvement that results in student self-sufficiency, learning independence, and a commitment to growth not found in training and conditioning. The ability to adjust one's teaching strategy in light of changes in the teaching situation, the second dimension of teaching effectiveness we add, is a sign of reflective practice in teaching and the hallmark of professionalism.

In this chapter we review research findings on teacher effectiveness and draw implications for supervisory practice. As with our earlier discussion on curriculum, we find that the conclusions from research on effective teaching are not all pointing in the same direction. Frequently the assumption and beliefs of the researchers lead them to focus more on certain aspects of teaching than on others. We will focus here on teaching methodologies and their impact on student learning rather than on the content of what is taught and the adaptation of instructional formats to various content and skill objectives of learning episodes.

There is a burgeoning literature of research on teaching effectiveness.[1] Some school systems have already begun staff development programs to help teachers develop classroom skills that research studies have shown to be related to increased student achievement. Others are talking about and trying supervisory evaluation of teachers according to prescribed effectiveness behaviors in their classroom teaching.[2] Although the last word on teaching effectiveness has not been spoken, supervisors will need to be familiar with the findings of teacher-effectiveness research and will need to explore ways to incorporate effectiveness strategies in their work with teachers.

RESEARCH ON DIRECT-EXPLICIT TEACHING

While the findings may sound very familiar to an experienced teacher or supervisor and appear to the ordinary citizen as good common sense, the research has been able to document that certain teacher behaviors are related to student gains on both criterion- and norm-referenced tests. Among those behaviors frequently cited by research studies are the following:

- Establish classroom rules that allow pupils to attend to personal and procedural needs without having to check with the teacher.
- Communicate expectations of high achievement.
- Start off each class by reviewing homework and by reviewing material covered in the previous few classes.
- Make the objectives of the new instructional episode clear to the students.
- Directly teach the content or skill that will be measured on the test.

[1] C. W. Fisher, N. N. Filby, R. Marliave, L. S. Cahan, M. M. Dishaw, and D. C. Berliner, "Teacher Behaviors, Academic Learning Time and Student Achievement," Final Report of Phase III-B, *Beginning Teacher Evaluation Study Technical Report Series* (Tech. Rev. V-I), San Francisco: Far West Laboratory, 1978.

Cf. *Educational Leadership*, vol. 37, no. 1, 1979, in which 12 essays on teacher effectiveness appear. One of the better collections of research reports on teacher effectiveness is Penelope P. Peterson and Herbert J. Walberg (eds.), *Research on Teaching: Concepts, Findings, and Implications*, Berkeley, Calif.: McCutchan, 1979.

Cf. Tamar Levin with Ruth Long, *Effective Instruction*, Alexandria, Va.: Association for Supervision and Curriculum Development, 1981. The annotated bibliography at the end of this book is first-rate. Three other books that contain very useful information on effective teaching are Don M. Medley, *Teacher Competence and Teacher Effectiveness: A Review of Process-Product Research*, Washington, D.C.: American Association of Colleges for Teacher Education, 1977; N. L. Gage, *The Scientific Basis of the Art of Teaching*, New York: Teachers College Press, 1978; and Doug Russell and Madeline Hunter, *Planning for Effective Instruction*, Los Angeles: University Elementary School, 1980.

[2] David A. Squires, William G. Huitt, and John K. Segars, "Improving Classrooms and Schools: What's Important," *Educational Leadership*, vol. 39, no. 3, pp. 174–179, 1981; and Shirley B. Stow, "Using Effectiveness Research in Teacher Evaluation," *Educational Leadership*, vol. 37, no. 1, pp. 55–58, 1979.

- After teaching the new material, assess student comprehension through questions and practice.
- Provide for uninterrupted successful practice that is now monitored by the teacher moving around the classroom.
- Maintain direct engagement by the student on the academic task. Engaged academic time is a critical variable for student achievement.
- Assign homework to increase student familiarity with material.
- Hold review sessions weekly and monthly.

Before jumping to conclusions about the implications of these research findings for supervisory practice we need to see them in perspective. First of all, most of these studies were concentrating on the teaching of basic skills in reading and arithmetic in the earlier grades of elementary school. Whether these teaching behaviors are appropriate for higher-level learning in reading and mathematics or for learnings in other areas, such as geography or art, is an open question. Indeed, as pointed out in Chapter 14, it is very likely that had effectiveness been defined differently, the same teaching-effectiveness research would have established different teaching behaviors. In this sense the indicators of teaching effectiveness are neither objective nor independent but are directly linked to how researchers define effectiveness. This point raises the question as to whether what is called "teaching effectiveness" research is properly named. A more scientific label for this research would communicate more precisely just what is involved. As a group the behaviors identified in this research describe direct or explicit teaching.[3] The research establishes that this approach to teaching is very effective in enhancing student skill acquisition and simple subject matter mastery in the basic subjects. A more accurate and precise label for this important body of research would be the direct-explicit teaching research since this is the style of teaching described by the identified teaching behaviors.

The research on effective teaching does not account sufficiently for other variables that may affect student achievement. Research on home influences, for example, indicates that family stability, the prior education of parents, juvenile delinquency, alcoholic or drug-addicted parents, family income, and so on can enhance or limit classroom effects.[4] While a teacher following the prescriptions of effective teaching may increase the achievement levels of most students, he or she may be unable to reach some students whose home backgrounds are so chaotic as to cripple their ability to concentrate on academic tasks. Likewise, the success of some teachers in bringing about higher achievement of their students may be enhanced by the stable family

[3] See, for example, Barak V. Rosenshine, "Synthesis of Research on Explicit Teaching," *Educational Leadership,* vol. 43, no. 6, pp. 60–69, 1986.

[4] See Ralph Scott and Herbert J. Walberg, "Schools Alone Are Insufficient," *Educational Leadership,* vol. 37, no. 1, pp. 24–27, 1979; James S. Coleman et al., *Equality of Educational Opportunity,* Washington, D.C.: U.S. Office of Education, National Center for Educational Statistics, 1966; and Christopher Jencks et al., *Inequality: A Reassessment of the Effects of Family and Schooling in America,* New York: Basic Books, 1972.

backgrounds of their students, rich in educational resources. Is it proper to rate one teacher as more effective than another whose students come from far less favorable home environments?

Research on effective schools reveals that there are schoolwide variables that can enhance or limit the impact of a given classroom teacher's efforts to move toward more effective teaching behaviors. While no one school variable of itself may account for school effectiveness, taken together a critical mass of positive school factors can support an individual teacher's effective teaching practices.[5] If all the teachers in the school have high expectations of students, a single teacher's effectiveness will be greater than if he or she is the only one in the school with high expectations. If no one else in the school assigns homework, that teacher's effectiveness will be diminished when he or she initiates the effort to assign homework.

SUMMARY OF RESEARCH ON TEACHING

Herbert Walberg and his associates Diane Schiller and Geneva Haertel became interested in assessing the adequacy of educational research completed in recent years. They conducted a thorough review of research published between 1969 and 1979.[6] Of particular interest was research on teaching and instruction. They sought to demonstrate that during the decade in question the educational research community had accumulated highly useful findings addressed to policy makers and professional practitioners alike. A side benefit of this review was to demonstrate the effects of a variety of approaches to teaching and instruction. Some of the studies tabulated by Walberg and his associates are shown in Table 15-1.

The studies we select from Walberg's summary are grouped into three categories: those that support aspects of structured approaches to teaching, those that compare aspects of structured with unstructured approaches to teaching, and those that support the effects of climate on learning.

Most approaches to teaching characterized as structured are similar in their emphasis on cognitive learning, predetermined objectives, teacher direction, and carefully paced instruction. A personalized system of instruction (PSI), for example, relies on small units of written instruction, student self-pacing, mastery of subject matter at level A before proceeding to level B, and repeated testing. Mastery learning relies on diagnosis of entry-level skills and understandings, on clear objectives and specific learning procedures, on small units of learning, feedback, and flexible learning time. Direct instruction refers to methods of instruction, under tight teacher control, that focus specifically on the content of tests. These are overwhelmingly effective techniques for

---

[5] See Gilbert R. Austin, "Exemplary Schools and the Search for Effectiveness," *Educational Leadership*, vol. 37, no. 1, pp. 10–14, 1979; and Michael Rutter, Barbara Maughan, Peter Mortimer, and Janet Ouston, *Fifteen Thousand Hours: Secondary Schools and Their Effects on Children*, Cambridge, Mass.: Harvard University Press, 1979.

[6] Herbert J. Walberg, Diane Schiller, and Geneva D. Haertel, "The Quiet Revolution in Educational Research," *Phi Delta Kappan*, vol. 61, no. 3, pp. 179–183, 1979.

TABLE 15-1
SELECTED SUMMARY OF RESEARCH ON TEACHING AND LEARNING AS TABULATED BY
WALBERG, SCHILLER, AND HAERTEL

I. Selected research on structured approaches to teaching		
Topics	**No. of results**	**Percent positive**
Behavioral instruction on learning	52	98.1
Personalized system of instruction (PSI) on learning	103	93.2
Mastery learning	30	96.7
Programmed instruction on learning	57	80.7
Advanced organizers on learning	32	37.5
Direct instruction on achievement	4	100.0

II. Selected research comparing more and less structured approaches		
Topics	**No. of results**	**Percent positive**
Lecture favored over discussion on		
Achievement	16	68.8
Retention	7	100.0
Attitudes	8	86.0
Student-centered discussion favored over teacher-centered on		
Achievement	7	57.1
Understanding	6	83.0
Attitude	22	100.0
Factual questions favored over conceptual on achievement	4	100.0
Open or informal education favored over traditionally structured education on		
Achievement	26	54.8
Creativity	12	100.0
Self-concept	17	88.2
Attitude toward school	25	92.0
Curiosity	6	100.0
Self-determination	7	85.7
Independence	19	94.7
Freedom from anxiety	8	37.5
Cooperation	6	100.0

TABLE 15-1 *(Continued)*
SELECTED SUMMARY OF RESEARCH ON TEACHING AND LEARNING AS TABULATED BY
WALBERG, SCHILLER, AND HAERTEL

III. Selected research on climate and teaching		
Topics	No. of results	Percent positive
Motivation and learning	232	97.8
Sociopsychological climate and learning		
Cohesiveness	17	85.7
Satisfaction	17	100.0
Difficulty	16	86.7
Formality	17	64.7
Goal direction	15	73.3
Democracy	14	84.6
Environment	15	85.7
Speed	14	53.8
Diversity	14	30.8
Competition	9	66.7
Friction	17	0.0
Cliqueness	13	8.3
Apathy	15	14.3
Disorganization	17	6.3
Favoritism	13	10.0

Source: Herbert J. Walberg, Diane Schiller, and Geneva D. Haertel, "The Quiet Revolution in Educational Research," *Phi Delta Kappan,* vol. 61, no. 3, pp. 180–181, 1979.

teaching the basic skills in reading and math and for teaching subject matter where achievement is measured by recall.

Notice in the comparisons depicted in the second category of Table 15-1 that lecturing is favored over discussion in achievement and retention of subject matter but that student-centered discussion is favored over teacher-centered discussion for building understanding of subject matter and promoting positive attitudes toward learning. The lower the level of learning (facts, simple recall), the more appropriate are direct methods of instruction.

Informal or more open teaching strategies seem superior to structured approaches in promoting creativity, self-concept enhancement, positive attitudes toward school, curiosity, self-determination, independence, and cooperation.

Teaching approaches, therefore, seem less an issue of which is the best way than of which is the best way for what purpose. Good classrooms and gifted teachers exhibit a variety of teaching approaches, mixing both formal and informal methods as circumstances require. The cautions about how the research on teaching should be interpreted are worth repeating. Teacher-effectiveness researchers and consumers of this research are naturally excited about the discoveries, and in their commitment to improve practice, they often make unrealistic and misleading claims as to what constitutes effective teaching. Typically, teacher-effectiveness research attempts to link certain teacher behaviors and modes of instruction to student outcomes. When the link is established (as in the case of direct instruction being related to higher student achievement in the basic skills), the claim is often made by researchers, and interpreted as such by practitioners, that the instructional methods investigated are generally effective. Not specifying exactly what student outcomes are of issue or what relationships between teacher behaviors and outcomes are suggested can lead to confusion and misrepresentation of the facts.

Medley's comprehensive review of teacher-effectiveness research, which links teaching processes to student outcomes, is an example of proper representation.[7] He is careful to point out that the research he reviews involves correlational studies; thus relationships observed do not prove that certain teacher behaviors *cause* particular student outcomes. These studies show only that a relationship exists. Further, the studies he reviews consist almost entirely of dependent variables defined as pupil performance on reading and mathematics achievement tests in the primary grades. Despite Medley's care in pointing out these limitations, his findings are often assumed to refer to general concepts of teacher effectiveness that apply to all students, for all outcomes, in all settings.

SOME NECESSARY CONDITIONS TO EFFECTIVE SUPERVISION AND EVALUATION

Fundamental to the process of supervision and evaluation is that the supervisor have a firm and informed knowledge of substantive aspects of educational programs and teaching. It is true that certain aspects of teaching are so obviously ascertained that even amateurs can successfully evaluate them. Picking up indicators of warmth, patterns of classroom interaction, differences between on- and off-task behaviors, describing classroom arrangements, and detecting teacher or student boredom do not require that one be well versed in pedagogy, principles of learning, or curriculum development. But discerning the appropriateness of a teaching strategy given a particular set of objectives, commenting on the adequacy of an advance organizer, detecting whether an interest center is functioning properly, understanding how the inquiry method works, judging the adequacy of chosen curriculum materials, and commenting

[7] Medley, op. cit.

on the implications of a particular reinforcement pattern on student long-term motivation require a higher level of sophistication in things educational.

Teacher-effectiveness research can play an important role in increasing our understanding of supervisory issues and in helping to develop supervisory stategies. But the relationships uncovered to date are too complex and too situational to become surrogates for educated judgments. Gage's suggestions that we view teaching as a practical art with a scientific basis may well be worth noting:

> Scientific method can contribute relationships between variables taken two at a time and even, in the form of interactions, three or perhaps four or more at a time. Beyond say, four, the usefulness of what science can give the teacher begins to weaken, because teachers cannot apply, at least not without help and not on the run, the more complex interactions. At this point, the teacher as artist must step in and make clinical, or artistic, judgments about the best ways to teach. In short, the scientific basis for the art of teaching will consist of two-variable relationships and lower-order interactions. The higher-order interactions between four and more variables must be handled by the teacher as artist.[8]

Efforts to bring a scientific basis to teaching are important despite the fact that a one-to-one correspondence does not exist between scientific knowledge and practice. Instead, such knowledge can best serve and inform the decision-making process in supervision and enhance the art of teaching.

MATCHING TEACHING AND EVALUATION STRATEGIES

The following assumptions are essential to developing a balanced perspective in supervision and teacher evaluation.

1 No one teaching method is inherently better than another.

2 Supervisors and teachers need to be sensitive to the conditions under which various approaches to teaching are more and less effective.

3 Evaluation strategies need to take into account the characteristics of the teaching strategy under study in evaluating teaching.

4 Effective evaluation requires that the supervisor be well informed about such educational matters as curriculum, models of teaching, principles of learning, and classroom arrangements.

5 Asking the supervisor to develop a sense of purpose and a vision of future possibilities should not be confused with asking the supervisor to develop a narrow, rigid, dogmatic view of teaching.

6 A choice of teaching approach is *contingent* upon a number of factors found in the teaching situation such as purposes, characteristics of students, availability of materials, space, and time, and needs of teachers.

7 Adopting a variable approach to teaching does not obviate the necessity for *any* chosen approach to contain certain nurturing and human characteristics toward students.

[8]Gage, op. cit., p. 20.

In the following sections, we provide some guidelines in the form of questions that can help supervisors apply a contingency perspective, identify evaluation issues, and plan an evaluation strategy.

• What is the approach to teaching this teacher has in mind?

Let us assume that the teacher plans a role-playing exercise that engages students in a mock trial.

• Is this approach appropriate to the teaching purposes or outcomes sought? Is this approach appropriate to the teaching setting envisaged?

Role playing is a suitable teaching strategy for clarifying student values and addressing attitudinal issues. If the teacher envisions a lesson designed to help students learn the official names and duties of various roles common to jury trials, this method is less appropriate than direct-explicit teaching. Discussions with the teacher as to how students will be evaluated can provide clues to intended purposes. If the teacher has a matching test in mind, then probably role playing is a poor teaching choice. Perhaps the teacher is not sure of intended outcomes but feels that role playing is a good educational encounter anyway. In evaluating students the teacher might have in mind an open-ended essay as to how the student profited from the lesson. Then under these circumstances role playing might well be an excellent choice.

• Given what is known about the particular approach to teaching, how knowledgeable is the teacher about the theoretical aspects of this approach? How successful is the teacher in implementing this approach?

Evaluation strategies and methods need to take into account the purposes of the teacher and the proposed method of teaching. It would not be appropriate to criticize a teacher using direct-explicit teaching for too much teacher talk. Collecting materials used by students to assess their diversity or photographing students every 5 minutes to determine the extent to which they are engaged in a variety of learning settings does not fit this teaching method either. Certainly the supervisor can and should comment on whether direct-explicit teaching fits the purposes intended. But once teacher and supervisor agree that this method makes sense, the evaluation should do justice to the method. The same can be said for more informal or open methods of teaching. Asking all students to measure up to certain standard and predetermined criteria may well be an evaluation technique inappropriate to informal methods of teaching.

• How does this approach fit into the teacher's overall frame of reference or philosophy of teaching? How does this approach fit into the school's overall frame of reference or philosophy of teaching?

One danger in adopting a contingency perspective is that it leads teachers and supervisors to conclude that anything goes. The supervisor need only ask the teacher what the intents are and evaluate accordingly. We do not accept this point of view. Schools and classrooms should operate from a set of principles and a vision of ideals. An educational platform should be developed from this broad view of the desirable and possible. This educational platform should serve as a basis for decision making and as a standard for evaluating the appropriateness of decisions about curriculum matters and broad teaching strategies. Particular teaching strategies selected by the teacher should be evaluated for goodness of fit against this standard.

• Given the array of approaches available to the teacher and acceptable to the school, does the selection of a given approach suggest a balanced repertoire of teaching strategies?

Though it is not reasonable for a school to permit teachers complete autonomy in the selection of teaching strategies, it is reasonable and indeed imperative to expect that teachers incorporate a variety of strategies to accommodate the diverse purposes of education and the array of unique learning styles of students.

TEACHING AS DECISION MAKING

When one adopts the stance that no one teaching method is inherently better than another and that best teaching practice is characterized by successfully matching method to the circumstances at hand, suddenly the process of teaching becomes more complex than is typically portrayed in the literature or sometimes reflected in the evaluation scales of school districts and states. The view of teaching changes from a low-level applied technology to a high-level executive role, and teaching practice changes from faithful application of provided teaching models (i.e., explicit teaching, informal teaching, the "lesson cycle") to the making and carrying out of decisions.

Many experts hold the view that teaching needs to be understood as a process of decision making, but differences exist as to how this decision-making process is to be understood. There is, for example, an academic view of teacher decision making as a rational and explicit process of logical steps in search of optimal solutions and in contrast, a practical view of teacher decision making as a "science of muddling through." Each of these views is examined below.

During the last four decades a highly credible literature on decision making has emerged that has not received the attention it should from those interested in teaching as decision making. The overarching theme of this literature is that decision making is not nearly as rational as previously thought and as often depicted in the traditional literature. This new view of decision making does not emerge from theoretical speculations about decision making or logical treatises about how decision making should unfold but from concrete studies of how decisions are actually made in real life. In other words, the oughts and the is's of decision making are at variance with each other. This new view of decision making is based largely on the work of such organizational theorists and decision-making theorists as the Nobel laureate Herbert A. Simon and such distinguished scholars as James G. March and Charles E. Lindblom. These scholars point out the limits of rational decision theory and provide alternative models and frames for thinking about how decision making actually occurs.

THE LIMITS OF "RATIONAL" DECISION THEORY

Rational decision making is based upon the following assumptions: Problems can be clearly defined and delineated; complete sets of alternatives can be discovered and described as a result of an extensive search; a set of consequences can be attached to each alternative; these consequences can be weighted according to some objective formula in terms of the probabilities of success in solving the problem at hand; this weighting procedure permits cardinal ordering of alternatives; and individuals can process an unlimited amount of information. James G. March and Herbert A. Simon, in their classic 1958 book *Organizations*,[9] point out numerous difficulties with this rational view. They note, for example, that the occasions when decision makers have complete and accurate knowledge of the consequences that follow various alternatives are rare and indeed decision making typically involves high risk and a great deal of uncertainty. Thus judgments, beliefs, prior experiences, and professional and human intuition become increasingly important. They state:

> One can hardly take exception to these requirements in a normative model—a model that tells people how they are to choose. For if the rational man lacked information, he might have chosen differently "if only he had known." At best, he is "subjectively" rational, not "objectively" rational. But the notion of objective rationality assumes there is some objective reality in which the "real" alternatives, the "real" consequences, and the "real" utilities exist. If this is so, it is not even clear why the cases of choice under risk and under uncertainty are admitted as rational. If it is not so, it is not clear why only limitations upon knowledge of consequences are considered, and why limitations upon knowledge of alternatives and utilities are ignored in the model of rationality.[10]

These experts argue that except under routine or simple circumstances most decision makers seek to uncover and select satisfactory rather than optimal alternatives, alternatives that will do the job rather than those that will do the job best. Decision makers, in other words, do not search the haystack looking for the best needle but rather settle for the first needle that will work.

Perhaps the most classic statement of limits on rational decision making can be found in Simon's work *Administrative Behavior: A Study of Decision-Making Processes in Administrative Organization.*[11] Simon notes: "The limits of rationality have been seen to derive from the inability of the human mind to bring to bear upon a single decision all the aspects of value,

[9] James G. March and Herbert A. Simon, *Organizations,* New York: Wiley, 1958.
[10] Ibid., p. 138.
[11] Herbert A. Simon, *Administrative Behavior: A Study of Decision-Making Processes in Administrative Organization,* New York: Macmillan, 1945.

knowledge, and behavior that would be relevant. The pattern of human choice is often more nearly a stimulus-response pattern than a choice among alternatives. Human rationality operates, then, within the limits of a psychological environment."[12]

In describing how decision making takes place in organizations such as schools Michael D. Cohen, James G. March, and Johann P. Olsen use the metaphor "garbage can."[13] Though some might find this label to be a distraction or perhaps frivolous, the label itself is far less important than the underlying ideas it intends to communicate. How does garbage can decision making take place? These researchers observed that three things are deposited in the "can." First are problems which arise from nowhere and everywhere. They may be related to issues of curriculum, discipline, parent interference, competency testing, career ladders, frustrations at work, interpersonal relations, administrative styles, criteria for evaluation, money, or ideology. All these problems are considered to be legitimate and require attention. Next, various solutions are tossed into the can. Solutions are the wants, preferences, and desires of various people within the school. They are answers to particular problems and needs but they are generated separate from the official problems being faced. Solutions tossed into the can by teachers might include getting a duty-free lunch period of at least one hour, a lighter teaching load, parents to help monitor the playground or supervise the lunchroom, the teachers' lounge redecorated, a new textbook series adopted, some help from teacher aides, smaller classes, and more support from the administration in disciplining students. In the minds of teachers, these are desirable outcomes. Bargaining for solutions, however, in the absence of problems is not often viewed as a successful strategy. Administrators, for example, respond to problems not teacher wants. Teachers, therefore, must search for more acceptable and legitimate problems to match up with their desired solutions. Thus declining test scores become a problem and such teacher wants as the need for lower classes, a lighter load, and teacher aides is offered as a solution.

Students are particularly adept at understanding how garbage can decision making works in schools. Consider, for example, a group of junior high school students who would like to have a jukebox or stereo system installed in the school cafeteria (a solution). It would be naive of them to approach the principal with this idea without having some sort of justification (a problem). Thus the students pool their collective wisdom and invent a problem. They note a general disorder in the cafeteria characterized by litter, noise, and horseplay. Seeking to alleviate these problems, they go to the principal and discuss various alternatives that might serve as successful solutions. Together the principal and students stumble on the desired solution, install a jukebox or a stereo system. Their solution is accepted only when it finds an appropriate problem.

[12] Ibid., p. 108.
[13] Michael D. Cohen, James G. March, and Johann P. Olsen, "A Garbage Can Model of Organizational Choice," *Administrative Science Quarterly,* vol. 17, no. 1, pp. 1–25, 1972.

RATIONAL VIEWS OF TEACHING AS DECISION MAKING

In "rational" views of teaching as decision making discrete goals emerge as the lynchpin in a chain of events that is presumed to characterize best practice. Tight alignment is prescribed between these discrete objectives and curriculum, the curriculum and teaching, teaching and testing. Evaluation systems carefully monitor this chain of events to ensure that objectives are set and communicated to students, students are made ready to learn the objectives, teachers teach to the objectives, students are on task with regard to these objectives, in-class assignments and home assignments reflect these objectives, and a testing system exists to measure student progress toward obtaining these objectives. Under this highly rational system supervisors are supposed to use various rating scales, on-task charts, and other data-collection devices to monitor this teaching system.

Throughout the process the importance of discrete objectives looms large. Teacher and supervisor should have in mind specific outcomes, and all other decisions are linked to the accomplishment of these outcomes. Often complete transcripts of verbal teaching interactions are recorded and analyzed to determine the extent to which teachers and students tend to the objectives. Answers to such questions as the following are important in supervision and teaching rationally conceived: Does the transcript of teaching reveal that the teacher provides positive reinforcement when students are tending to the objectives? Do instances exist when students and teachers stray from the objectives? What can be done to get the class back on course? Are students aware of what they are supposed to do? Has the teacher instilled in students the proper mental set to learn the objectives at hand? Are lesson plans specific? Do students know beforehand what it is they are supposed to do? Are materials selected to reflect these objectives? Is this the case also with in-class and out-of-class assignments? For example, is "seat work" aligned with the objectives at hand and does the teacher monitor seat work to ensure that the students are on task?

The facts of the real world of teaching and schooling reveal that professionals do not always think and act in accordance with discrete goals and objectives. When they do, these goals and objectives are likely to be quite general. Instead, teachers respond to certain values and tend to certain patterns of goals and objectives that are often in competition with each other. On the one hand, for example, a teacher may push for "maximum" cognitive learning from students but the teacher cannot push too far for fear that students will become dissatisfied and cause trouble or perhaps even drop out. Further, the teacher is concerned with the psychological and social well-being of students and recognizes that pushing too hard in cognitive matters may incur costs in these important areas. Learning outcomes typically compete with each other. Too much drill and tedious workbook activity in teaching reading may result in students not liking reading and thus reading less in later life. Allowing students too much freedom in choosing reading material may result in omission of important works.

Though rational models of teacher decision making assume that teaching involves a series of interconnected choices in which teachers try simultaneously to maximize several conflicting demands, in the real world of teaching typically no sequential assumptions are made about the relationships among discrete goals, curriculum, teaching, and outcomes. Indeed any of the four can drive the other three. Goals, for example, are often selected as a result of materials available as are materials selected as a result of goals. Teaching styles and preferences determine objectives as often as objectives determine teaching styles and preferences. Outcomes become goals as often as goals become outcomes. The metaphor garbage can decision making indeed does fit teaching on many occasions.

MUDDLING THROUGH AND REFLECTIVE PRACTICE

The organizational theorist Charles E. Lindblom likens the decision-making process to "the science of muddling through."[14] To him decision making is based on successive and limited comparisons of one decision with the next as part of an intuitive process which builds out continually from current situations. It is incremental in nature and is aimed at arriving at decisions based on past experience. A teacher, for example, has in mind various value patterns and goals and various favored teaching strategies but views each as being closely intertwined. That is, by habit or experience the teacher has come to learn that grouping students in a certain way makes sense and works. This teaching strategy is not arrived at by logically matching it to a set of outcomes or subject matter to be taught as if strategy and outcome were independent. Instead, having confidence in what works, the teacher searches the teaching content and various teaching outcome possibilities that fit the strategy. Since teaching means and the outcomes to achieve are not distinct, the means-end analysis of rational decision making is considered to be limited. The test of a good decision about what to teach or how to teach is a simple one. Other teachers too agree that this is the case or other teachers too operate in the same way or other teachers too arrive at the same decision place. Rational decision making and this science of muddling through are compared in Table 15-2.

Similarly, Donald A. Schön, in his important book *The Reflective Practitioner: How Professionals Think and Act,* describes decision making as a process of "managing messes."[15] Instead of relying on a highly theoretical and rational process of decision making, professionals reflect on their practice in terms of their personal experience, previous successes, hopes, preferences, strengths and weaknesses, and desired outcomes. Reflection and action, according to Schön, involves "on-the-spot surfacing, criticizing, restructuring, and testing of

[14] Charles E. Lindblom, "The Science of Muddling Through," *Public Administration Review,* vol. 19, no. 1, pp. 79–88, 1959.
[15] Donald A. Schön, *The Reflective Practitioner: How Professionals Think and Act,* New York: Basic Books, 1983.

TABLE 15-2
RATIONAL AND INTUITIVE APPROACHES TO DECISION MAKING

Rational decision making	Muddling through
1a. Clarification of values or objectives distinct from and usually prerequisite to empirical analysis of alternative policies.	1b. Selection of value goals and empirical analysis of the needed action are not distinct from one another but are closely intertwined.
2a. Policy formulation is therefore approached through means-end analysis: first the ends are isolated, then the means to achieve them are sought.	2b. Since means and ends are not distinct, means-end analysis is often inappropriate or limited.
3a. The test of a "good" policy is that it can be shown to be the most appropriate means to desired ends.	3b. The test of a "good" policy is typically that various analysts find themselves directly agreeing on a policy (without their agreeing that it is the most appropriate means to an agreed objective).

4a. Analysis is comprehensive; every important factor is taken into account.	4b. Analysis is drastically limited:
	    (i) Important possible outcomes are neglected.
	    (ii) Important alternative potential policies are neglected.
	    (iii) Important affected values are neglected.

5a. Theory is often heavily relied upon.	5b. A succession of comparisons greatly reduces or eliminates reliance on theory.

Source: From Charles E. Lindblom, "The Science of Muddling Through," *Public Administration Review,* vol. 19, p. 81, spring 1959.

intuitive understandings of experienced phenomenon; often it takes the form of a reflective conversation with the situation."[16]

There is a certain logic and rationality to the process of muddling through or to decision making construed as a garbage can. In some respects, if these images of decision making are indeed more realistic they are *more* rational than the tidy descriptions of decision making one finds in the traditional literature. As suggested in Chapter 14, what we often assume to be more rational can turn out to be rationalistic and less rational turns out to be very rational. It makes no sense, for example, for supervisors to ignore this reality and assume that decision making unfolds in a way in which it actually does not.

Still, these newer descriptions of decision making often suggest that the theorists who originate them have given up on rationality, order, and purposiveness. This is not the case. Though it is not realistic to view goals as being unduly fixed and operational and to develop stepwise plans and strategies (except in those cases where teaching objectives are simple and noncontrover-

---

[16] Donald A. Schöon, "Leadership as Reflection in Action," in *Leadership and Organizational Culture,* Thomas J. Sergiovanni and John E. Corbally (eds.), Urbana-Champaign: University of Illinois Press, 1984, p. 42.

sial) teachers and supervisors are capable of valuing, agreements as to what is good teaching and what knowledge makes sense are possible, strategic goals can be determined, and teachers and supervisors as part of the school as a whole are capable of goal-seeking behavior.

In Chapter 14 we observed that teaching for complex learning is much like surfing. That is, teachers ride the pattern of the wave of teaching as it unfolds. This reality does not mean that we are unable to assess the value of learning outcomes or to judge the adequacy of teaching decisions made. This complex view of decision making does, however, require supervisors to rely far less on canned images of good teaching and far more on reflection and judgment. The process of reflection and judgment requires that supervision be far more collaborative than is now the case. If we want to assess the adequacy of learning outcomes independent of intents and to understand better the rationale for and nature of decisions that the teacher makes, teachers need to be involved in the process as fuller partners. This theme will be elaborated on in subsequent chapters of Part Four.

TYPOLOGY OF DECISION-MAKING MODES IN TEACHING

To this point several different decision-making modes have been discussed. The mode of decision making that a teacher is likely to find her or himself in depends in part upon the extent to which goals and learning outcomes are readily agreed to and easily identified. That is, in those cases where low agreement exists or where outcomes are difficult to identify or need to be assessed after teaching takes place, certain modes of decision making will be more appropriate than when we have high agreement and easy identification. The extent to which teaching means and methods are well defined and easily identified also determines the mode of decision making likely to occur.

Four modes of decision making in teaching (rational, muddling through, collaborative, and garbage can) are depicted in Figure 15-1. Rational decision-making teaching models are most appropriate when goals and learning outcomes are easily identified and readily agreed to and when appropriate teaching methods are well defined. In those cases where it is difficult to agree on goals and learning outcomes or when they must be assessed *after* teaching takes place, but the teacher has in mind fairly well defined teaching strategies that can be readily identified, decision making is more like the science of muddling through. Here the teacher adopts a contingency perspective and in the process of surfing moves from strategy to strategy as appropriate. Collaborative decision making would be most appropriate in those instances where goals and learning outcomes are easily agreed to and are easily identified, but teaching methods are difficult to identify or are not well defined. In collaborative decision making teacher and students have in mind what it is that needs to be accomplished and work together to decide how these outcomes will be achieved. Teaching strategies characterized by exploration, group work, and independent contracts are likely to be in evidence. And finally, where learning

Goals and Learning Outcomes

		High agreement Easy to identify	Low agreement Difficult to identify
	Well defined Easy to identify	Rational Decision Making Explicit teaching "lesson cycle" Executive plan Objectives oriented	Muddling Through Decision Making Teaching as surfing Strategic goals Contingency plans Outcome oriented
Teaching Strategies	Not well defined Difficult to identify	Collaborative Decision Making Exploratory learning Learning contracts Group work Objectives oriented	Garbage Can Decision Making Experimental learning Discovery Playfulness Outcome oriented

FIGURE 15-1
Typology of decision-making modes in teaching.

outcomes are either difficult to identify or agree to and where teaching means and methods remain vague or uncertain, decision making is likely to resemble the image of garbage can. Teaching and learning activities will take on the character of discovery and experimental research and will be characterized by a certain playfulness. This garbage can mode of teacher decision making often makes teachers and supervisors feel uncomfortable. Yet, it can be a very productive mode and historically has been the one that has yielded dramatic gains in knowledge. Consider, for example, the number of important medicines (or, for that matter, the array of "Scotch" tape products) that have been discovered or stumbled upon because of the accidental matching of problems and solutions.

ROLES OF TEACHING

The roles that teachers assume in teaching are many and vary with the learning conditions faced. Four such roles are described in Table 15-3. The simplest and most direct role is that of manager. As manager the teacher executes fairly specific teaching steps according to well-defined and highly structured protocols. Rational decision making is the mode in teaching. The teacher functions as manager where teaching is conceived as a pipeline. The role of teacher as manager is to manage the flow of information through this line. Objectives are defined rather specifically for the student, motivation is extrinsic, and both the teacher and students are somewhat subordinate to the structured teaching system of which they are a part. Two different teachers assuming this role for the same purpose are likely to teach in the same way. The managerial role is most effective for teaching basic skills and simple subject-matter content.

Executive is the second role of teaching. When in the role of teacher as executive, the teacher uses the available research on teaching and principles of learning to make proper teaching decisions in light of the situation faced but within a fairly set framework for teaching. Rational decision making is the mode in teaching. There is, for example, an executive plan for teaching that is followed, and effective teaching is one which parallels this plan. Within this framework the teacher makes very important decisions about subject-matter content, grouping for and pacing of instruction, student assignments, and other teaching and learning considerations. Objectives are defined for the student but motivation is typically extrinsic. Students are subordinate in the sense that they are not partners in the teaching but objects of the teaching. But teachers are active decision makers who are controlled, who are very much in control provided that they follow the established teaching protocols and the approved executive plan for teaching. This role is most suitable for teaching straightforward subject-matter content and suitable as well for teaching basic skills, though the managerial role would be much more efficient for this purpose.

The remaining two roles, mediator and leader, are associated with higher-level learning and with the development in students of attitudes and commitment to learning as something worthwhile. Decision making is more collaborative and at times resembles the garbage can or the process of muddling through. As mediator the teacher uses interaction or reciprocal teaching strategies which enable students to process new information and new learnings in light of their own personal meanings and experiences and prior learnings. The idea is not to define for the student what the nature or the value of a particular learning experience is but to have the student search for him or herself for this value.

Emphasis is on helping students make sense of learning encounters by constructing new understandings and by linking new to prior learnings. When in the mediating role the teacher helps students interact with information and ideas. Though at times teachers decide the actual learning outcomes of teaching, a balance is sought between teacher-determined and student-determined outcomes. The attempt of this kind of teaching is to move students away from being absorbers of information to being processors, synthesizers, creators, and users of information; from being dependent upon the learning system provided to using the learning system provided. Motivation is frequently intrinsic. The mediating role is very effective for teaching analysis, problem solving, and higher-order skills as well as complex concepts, higher levels of comprehension, and for having students extend what is learned to new applications and new situations.

The role of teacher as leader is probably the most important of the four. The idea here is to instill in students a love for, commitment to, and appreciation of learning that carries them not only through their school years but throughout their lives. Here the teacher models the importance of subject matter and

TABLE 15-3
ROLES OF TEACHING

Roles	Description	Characteristics	Strengths
Teacher as manager	The teacher executes explicit teaching steps according to highly structured protocols associated with direct instruction. The teacher manages student behavior accordingly.	Teaching is conceived as a pipeline. The role of the teacher is to manage the flow of information through the line. Objectives are defined for the student. Motivation is typically extrinsic. Both teacher and students are subordinate to the structured teaching protocols. Reliability in teaching, therefore, is very high.	Very effective for teaching basic skills and effective for teaching simple subject-matter content.
Teacher as executive	The teacher uses research on effective teaching and psychological principles of learning to make proper teaching decisions in light of situations faced but within a set framework which provides decision-making rules. Within this framework, for example, the teacher makes important decisions about subject-matter content, grouping for and pacing of instruction, student assignments, and other instructional features. Decisions are typically made beforehand in the form of an executive plan for teaching. Effective teaching results when this plan is followed.	Teaching is conceived as executive decision making which requires that situations be diagnosed and that established teaching principles be applied correctly. Objectives are typically defined for the student. Motivation is typically extrinsic. Students are subordinate to the system (that is, they are viewed as objects of teaching rather than partners to the teaching). Teachers are active decision makers and are in control, provided that they follow the established teaching protocols.	Very effective for teaching simple subject-matter content and effective for teaching basic skills.

Teacher as mediator	The teacher uses reciprocal and interactive teaching strategies which enable students to process new information and new learnings in light of their own personal meanings and experiences and prior learnings. Emphasis is on helping students make sense of learning encounters by constructing new understandings and by linking new to prior learnings.	Teaching is conceived as a mediating process within which students, with the help of teachers, interact with information and ideas in terms of personal meanings and previous learnings. Though at times teachers decide the actual learning outcomes of teaching, a balance is sought between teacher-determined and student-determined outcomes. The intent is to move away from students as absorbers of information to students as processors, synthesizers, creators, and users of information; from students being dependent upon the learning system provided to students using the learning system provided. Motivation is frequently intrinsic.	Very effective for teaching analysis, problem-solving, and higher-order skills, complex concepts, higher levels of comprehension, and for having students extend what is learned for application to new situations.
Teacher as leader	The teacher models the importance of subject matter and learning intents by the manner and enthusiasm with which teaching is provided. Modeling dimensions include time (teaching reflects a great deal of effort), feeling (the teacher cares deeply about the content, learning outcomes, and students), and focus (teaching reflects a deep understanding of the subject taught: the whys as well as the whats, the structure of knowledge; and a focus on key issues and dimensions of importance).	Teaching is conceived as a sacred activity which reflects a reverence for the importance of knowledge and of learning as ends in themselves. Through modeling students find teaching and learning to be meaningful and significant and respond with higher levels of motivation and commitment.	Very effective for communicating the importance, meaning, and significance of subject matter and learning intents; for promoting learning attitudes and values in students.

learning intents by the manner and enthusiasm with which teaching is provided. Modeling dimensions include time, feeling, and focus. That is, teaching reflects a great deal of effort, the teacher cares deeply about the content, learning outcomes, and students, and teaching reflects a deep understanding of the subject taught. The whys as well as the whats, the structure of knowledge, and key issues and dimensions of importance are emphasized. When this role is successfully implemented teaching is conceived as a sacred activity which reflects a reverence for the importance of knowledge and of learning as ends in themselves. Through modeling students find teaching and learning to be meaningful and significant and respond with higher levels of motivation and commitment. This role is not independent of the other three but serves as a complement. That is, the qualities of leadership that are part of this role can be in evidence as the teacher assumes the role of manager, executive, or mediator. Different roles are associated with different teaching strategies and with different purposes and learning outcomes.

CHOOSING A TEACHING STRATEGY

Recognizing that in the real world of teaching there are many reasons why teachers choose a particular teaching strategy (such as the availability of materials, confidence in the particular method, their own comfort zones, and previous successes) most teachers try, nonetheless, to be fairly deliberate in matching strategy to purpose and desired learning outcome. In his work on developing a "Supervision for Intelligent Teaching," Arthur L. Costa describes four general teaching strategies from which teachers might choose: directive, mediative, generative, and collaborative.[17] Directive strategies help students remember important facts, ideas, and skills. Mediative strategies help develop reasoning, concepts, and problem-solving abilities. Generative strategies help students invent new solutions, insightfulness, and the ability to communicate and extend. And finally, collaborative strategies help students to relate to each other better and to work cooperatively in groups.

The strategies and the goals and objectives for which they seem most appropriate are depicted in Table 15-4. Costa points out that when directive strategies are chosen teachers make virtually all decisions about instruction. They set the goals, decide the methods to be used and the criteria for determining whether teaching has been effective, and are responsible for motivating students. In mediative strategies the general goals are set by teachers but the methods and means are determined by students and students assume responsibility for coming to grips with the criteria that will determine whether their learning has been successful. The source of motivation in mediative learning is more intrinsic. That is, the teacher relies on the meaningfulness and significance of the learning activity itself as the source of motivation for learning. In generative strategies goals are set by both teacher

[17]Art L. Costa, *Supervision for Intelligent Teaching*, Orangevale, Calif.: Search Models Unlimited, 1982.

and student, though the student assumes major responsibility for determining how the goals will be met and how successful completion will be determined. In cooperative strategies goals are set by teacher and student but students as a group assume responsibility for determining how learning will take place and the criteria for success. The source of motivational learning rests with the group and tends to be normative. The Costa framework for supervision and teaching and that of others with similar views is outlined in some detail in the

TABLE 15-4
CHOOSING A TEACHING STRATEGY

When the educational goals are:	And the specific behavioral objectives are to:	The appropriate strategies are:
I. The directive		
1. Information acquisition	*Know about	1. Direct instruction
	*Recall	Drill and practice
	*Understand	Mastery learning
2. Remember	*Memorize	2. Mnemonics
3. Skill development	*Perform	3. Rehearsal command
	*Demonstrate	
II. The mediative		
1. Concept development	*Distinguish among	1. Concept attainment
	*Formulate	2. Concept development
	*Induce	
	*Discover	
	*Conceptualize	
2. Opinion expression	*Express ideas	3. Open-ended discussion
	*Consider other's opinions	Circle of knowledge
	*Articulate	
	*Support ideas with logical evidence	
3. Values awareness	*Become aware of own and other's values	4. Values awareness/clarification
	*Appreciate values of others when different	
4. Problem solving	*Theorize	5. Inquiry/discovery
	*Test ideas	
	*Validate	
	*Develop a strategy for	

TABLE 15-4
CHOOSING A TEACHING STRATEGY *(Continued)*

When the educational goals are:	And the specific behavioral objectives are to:	The appropriate strategies are:
	III. The generative	
1. Creativity	*Create	1. Brainstorming
2. Innovation	*Generate	
3. Fluency	*Innovate	
	*Design	2. Creativity
4. Insightfulness	*Develop insight	3. Lateral thinking
5. Productivity	*Elaborate	4. Mind mapping
	*Illuminate	
6. Metaphorical thinking	*Think metaphorically	5. Synectics
	IV. The collaborative	
1. Cooperation	*Cooperate	1. Cooperative learning
	*Participate in group tasks	
2. Interdependence	*Produce insights, solutions, and products through group efforts	2. Role playing Simulations Pair problem solving
3. Socialization	*Develop social skills	3. Class meetings

From Arthur L. Costa, *Supervision for Intelligent Teaching: A Course Syllabus,* Orangevale, Calif.: Search Models Unlimited, 1982, pp. 134–135.

Association for Supervision and Curriculum Development publication, *Developing Minds: A Resource Book for Teaching Thinking.*[18]

REFLECTIVE PRACTICE IN SUPERVISION AND TEACHING

A reflective practice of supervision and teaching recognizes that no one best way of teaching is inherently better than another. There is no room in reflective practice for a one best way mentality. But still, some approaches to teaching are better than others for certain purposes. What then is the basis for choosing one teaching strategy over another? Academically speaking we have suggested that the choice of teaching strategy should reflect a number of characteristics that define the teaching situation. Different student needs and learning styles, different goals and purposes, different motives, different problems, and different desired outcomes should result in the choice of different strategies. The idea is to match strategy with situation. Though most teachers are committed to practice in this way and indeed do try to engage in this matching, other

[18]Art L. Costa, *Developing Minds: A Resource Book for Teaching Thinking,* Alexandria, Va.: Association for Supervision and Curriculum Development, 1985.

concerns also help determine choice of strategy. These include the teacher's personal preference, needs, previous successes, opinions and pressures from other teachers, likes and dislikes of the supervisor, availability of materials, time, a sense of what will fly with the students, teaching behavior indicators on an evaluation instrument, and other less lofty but nonetheless real concerns. The mix of the two reasons for choosing a particular strategy can come to light as supervisors and teachers work together as colleagues and through conferencing and other techniques within an atmosphere of trust and mutual respect.

Where does this then leave the various models of teaching that are offered to teachers? Even with the best of relationships between supervisor and teacher, how do both come to grips with what makes sense and does not make sense? Should the Hunter lesson cycle, one of the Joyce models, the direct instruction model, informal teaching, or some other model of teaching prevail? Though all the models possess a certain logic and appear scientific when described and arrayed in lists and charts in books such as this, the reality is that rarely does *any* fit exactly as described. In a sense, none of the models of teaching are true, though all can be helpful. They are frames of reference and cognitive maps that can help teachers and supervisors understand better the problems they face and help them make better decisions about how to practice.

An alternative to considering models as being "true" or "false" is to consider relative worth. A model is worthwhile if it helps one understand better the teaching events and situations under study and helps one to make informed decisions about this reality. In considering relative worth it is important to note that no matter how refined a model becomes or how precisely it is translated into practice it cannot enlarge the basic premises upon which it rests. This is the law of conservation of information that is well understood in the more established sciences. In discussing this law, the Nobel laureate Medawar states, "No process of logical reasoning...no mere act of mind...can enlarge the information content of the axioms and premises or observation statements from which it proceeds."[19] Taken literally and applied to all situations the dimensions of any particular model of teaching and supervision provide small premises upon which to base a science of teaching and a practice of supervision.

Models in teaching and supervision are much like windows and walls. As windows they help expand our view of things, resolve issues that we face, provide us with answers, and give us that surer footing we need in order for us to function as researchers and practicing professionals. As walls these same models serve to box us in, to blind us to other views of reality, other understandings, and other alternatives.

In reflective practice supervisors are able to transcend the limitations of windows and walls. They do this by viewing research and practice models metaphorically rather than literally. That is, the models are not conceived as truth designed for application but as thought frames that inform decisions of teachers and supervisors as they practice. This reflective stance is well

---

[19]P. B. Medawar, *The Limits of Science,* New York: Harper & Row, 1984.

supported in the literature. Scheffler, for example, states, "The notion that one can confidently proceed by simple deduction from theory to practical recommendations without regard to related theories, auxiliary assumptions, or possible feedback from recalcitrant cases into the theoretical assumptions themselves, is a mistaken notion."[20] On this point he quotes William James, who stated in 1892:

> You make a great, a very great mistake, if you think that psychology, being the science of the mind's laws is something from which you can deduce definite programmes and schemes and methods of instruction for immediate schoolroom use. Psychology is a science, and teaching is an art; and sciences never generate arts directly out of themselves. An intermediary inventive mind must make the application, by using its originality.[21]

Informed intuition and reflective practice are key concepts in understanding the link between knowledge and use. Neither is directly dependent upon models of teaching and supervision but neither can evolve separately from such models.

When supervisors and teachers view teaching-effectiveness, clinical, and other supervisory models reflectively, they are concerned with conceptual rather than instrumental knowledge.[22] This conceptual knowledge considered as part of a broader array of knowledge (i.e., the teacher's motives and intentions, those of the supervisor, idiosyncrasies that define the teaching and learning context under study) becomes professional knowledge when decisions and actions ensue. Professional knowledge in teaching and supervision, therefore, is not the same as the knowledge of research and practice models but is created in use as teachers teach and supervisors supervise. Professional knowledge is an accumulation of the referentially based decisions that professionals make as they practice.

INDICATORS OF GOOD TEACHING

Given what is known about the complexities of teaching and best practice in supervision for classroom effectiveness, is it possible to describe the indicators of good teaching? The answer would be no if one had in mind a technical list of discrete teaching behaviors. The result would be too rationalistic and bureaucratic to be considered credible. But if one viewed teaching as being somewhat analogous to surfing and worked from a professional conception of teaching practice, then a list such as the following might be developed. Try editing the list or developing one of your own in light of your conception of good teaching and the complexities of the real world we describe. The teacher

- Behaves as a decision maker who takes charge of teaching, reflects on his

[20]Israel Scheffler, *Reason and Teaching*, New York: Bobbs-Merrill, 1973, p. 185.
[21]Ibid.
[22]Mary M. Kennedy, "How Evidence Alters Understanding and Decision," *Educational Evaluation and Policy Analysis*, vol. 6, no. 2, pp. 207–226, 1984.

or her practice, and makes defensible choices in light of intents and the requirements of the situation at hand.

- Demonstrates a keen understanding of his or her subject matter (the whys as well as the whats, the structure of the discipline, the wheat from the chaff).
- Relies on the value and interest of the subject matter and on the presentation of same as the primary means by which "classroom management" is achieved.
- Places greater emphasis on intrinsic rather than extrinsic reasons in "motivating" students. When extrinsic is necessary, can demonstrate the usual tricks of the trade in maintaining order and obtaining compliance (skillful monitoring, pacing of instruction, use of behavior-modification techniques, etc.).
- Demonstrates a sense of purpose and vision which gives teaching meaning and significance.
- Is able to translate this sense of purpose and vision into operational goals and objectives.
- Uses goals and objectives "strategically" to guide planning and teaching.
- Develops "tactical" goals and objectives which are fixed and rigid for some kinds of teaching (training-pitching) but dynamic and evolving for other kinds of teaching (education-surfing).
- Aligns teaching to goals *and* goals to teaching as appropriate.
- Monitors and assesses teaching and learning activities and behaviors, making corrections as needed.
- Evaluates outcomes of teaching and learning behaviors and activities for alignment with stated goals as well as goals which emerge from teaching.
- Evaluates for outcomes and other worthwhile happy events not anticipated prior to and during teaching.
- Knows about and uses available teaching models (direct instruction, teaching for critical thinking, informal teaching, etc.) as resources (to inform intuition and professional judgment) as "tailored" decisions are made in response to the specific teaching and learning context.

As appropriate, students are given assignments that

- Are consistent with teaching intent.
- Provide practice in mastering subject matter.
- Extend the subject matter by requiring application, synthesis, and judgment.
- Are engaging, stimulating, and fun.
- Are reasonable with regard to available time and other constraints.
- Are within the capabilities of students to ensure successful completion while remaining challenging and interesting.
- Require the student to be actively engaged in learning.
- Allow students some choice within a carefully planned array of options.

In interacting with students, the teacher is

- Clear with regard to expectations.
- Sensitive to individual differences.

- Challenging to stimulate student interest and achievement.
- Supportive and respectful of the students' humanness.

Classroom climate is characterized by

- A "businesslike" environment in the sense that teachers and students know why they are in the classroom and work hard.
- A comfortable and easy feeling among students and between teacher and students.
- A free exchange of ideas.
- An exchange of helpful and supportive behaviors.
- A sense of community characterized by a common commitment to work together and a sharing of responsibility for making classroom life productive and meaningful.

SUMMARY

This chapter alerted those with supervisory responsibility to the emergence of impressive research findings on teacher effectiveness. Noting that these findings can be very helpful, we suggested that supervisors be aware of creating a new dogma on teaching methodology that would be applied exclusively and uniformly to all classroom situations at every level of schooling. It was pointed out that approach to teaching should be adapted to the learning objectives being pursued and that such objectives are multiple and varied. They include student achievement in the basic skills, to be sure, but they also include a variety of problem-solving skills, analytical reasoning, metaphorical expression, group skills, creativity, citizenship skills, divergent thinking, and so on.

Teaching was described as a process of decision making. Pointing out that decision-making theory is not very well understood in teaching, the limits of rational theory were then described. Teaching, for example, often resembles more a science of muddling through than a logical and highly deterministic science of application. Viewing teaching and supervision as reflective practice was offered as an alternative. Within this view teaching sometimes resembles rational decision making but at other times resembles muddling through, collaborative, and garbage can decision making. Linking purpose and context to choice of teaching strategy, the managerial, executive, mediating, and leadership roles of teaching were then described. It was pointed out that within reflective practice, models of teaching and supervision are much like windows and walls. As windows they help expand one's view of things and provide frames of reference and inform one's intuition, thus helping the person make better practice decisions. But as walls these same models of teaching can blind and program professional practice. In reflective practice the windows and walls problem can be overcome by viewing models of teaching not as literal truths to be applied but as metaphors to inform. The chapter concluded by providing examples of indicators of good teaching.

STUDY GUIDE

Recall the concepts, ideas, and meanings associated with each of the following phrases and terms included in this chapter. Can you discuss each of them with a colleague and apply them to the supervisory context of your school? If you cannot, review them in the text and record the page numbers for future reference.

1 Contingency perspective
2 Direct-explicit teaching
3 Executive role
4 "Garbage can" decision making
5 Informed intuition
6 Leader role
7 Manager role
8 "Managing messes"
9 Mediator role
10 Metaphorical view
11 Objectives-oriented
12 Outcomes-oriented
13 Professional knowledge
14 Rational decision-making limits
15 Reflective practice
16 Science of muddling through
17 Teaching as decision making
18 "Teaching effectiveness" research
19 Teaching strategies
20 Typology of decision making
21 Windows and walls

EXERCISES

1 Assume a basic economics class is studying a unit on paying taxes. What would be some potential learning outcomes from teaching by direct instruction? What different oucomes would emerge from a class discussion on the fairness of tax loopholes? Are the two methods opposed or complementary? Are they both necessary?
2 List at least three different sets of learning outcomes you have focused on in your teaching. Do they require different teaching methods, styles of classroom management, and performance evaluations?

CLINICAL SUPERVISION AND TEACHER EVALUATION

Typically a distinction is made between general supervision and clinical supervision. General supervision refers to the attention and concern supervisory leaders give to organizational factors such as healthy climate and supportive relationships and the educational leadership and statespersonship responsibilities of supervision. Clinical supervision, by contrast, refers to face-to-face encounters with teachers about teaching, usually in classrooms, with the intent of enhancing professional development and improving teaching and learning. Clinical supervision is also used in a special way to refer to a specific method of supervising teachers using several steps that comprise the clinical cycle. Both of these aspects of clinical supervision are of concern in this chapter. Further, since clinical supervision in all its forms involves making informed judgments about teaching, teacher evaluation is inevitably involved in the process.

TAKING THE MYSTERY OUT OF EVALUATION

The literature on supervision and evaluation is filled with reports highlighting the disdain with which teachers regard evaluation. One expert even refers to the process of supervision as a "cold war" which takes place between supervisors and teachers.[1] There are many reasons why evaluation is often a rocky road. One reason, we believe, is that evaluation has been too narrowly defined in both purpose and method. The second reason is that attempts are often made to hide evaluation by using the term supervision. When we are supervising, it is assumed, we are not evaluating. Evaluation is an integral part

[1] Arthur Blumberg, *Supervisors and Teachers: A Private Cold War,* Berkeley, Calif.: 1967.

of supervision, and this reality cannot be ignored by supervisors and teachers. Indeed attempts to mask evaluation aspects of supervision by not using the term or by denying that evaluation occurs or by declaring that evaluation is reserved only for the annual administrative review of one's teaching will not be convincing. Despite the rhetoric everyone involved knows that evaluation is part of the process of supervision.

Much can be done, however, to shift the focus of attention in supervision from whether evaluation does or does not occur to expanding the meaning of evaluation and understanding its ordinariness. Evaluation is often defined narrowly as a process of calculating the extent to which teachers measure up to preexisting standards of one sort or another. To what extent, for example, is the teacher fulfilling teaching intents or displaying teaching behaviors thought to be desirable and included on a checklist. Broader conceptions of evaluation would include describing what's going on in a classroom, discovering learning outcomes actually achieved, and assessing their worth. In broader conceptions the emphasis is less on measuring aspects of teaching and more on describing and understanding teaching and learning events as well as on identifying the meanings that these events have for different people. In its broadest sense evaluation involves *judgment* more than measurement. Judgments of teaching and learning are less fixed, more personal, and are embedded in a particular context or situation.[2] Of interest in judgmental evaluation are particular teachers and students, specific teaching situations and events, and the actual teaching and learning issues, understandings, and meanings that emerge from teaching. Though measuring teaching against preexisting standards or in light of a checklist of some sort has its place in the process of supervision and evaluation, our present onerous view of evaluation will be greatly lessened if judgmental aspects are emphasized.

It may be helpful to use the word evaluation in its ordinary rather than technical sense. Evaluation is a common and inescapable aspect of most of what we do. Whether we are buying shoes, selecting a vacation spot, redecorating the living room, enjoying a movie, football game, or art show, evaluation is part of the process. In its ordinary sense evaluation means to discern, understand, and appreciate; to judge, value, and decide. These very same natural and ordinary processes are at play in evaluating teaching. As in ordinary life, these processes serve to heighten our understanding and appreciation of teaching and to inform our intuition as we make decisions about teaching. In sum, evaluation is more than measurement; it is a process of understanding and decision making. Broadly conceived, evaluation seeks to answer the following questions:

What is actually going on in this classroom?
What is the teacher and what are students actually doing?
What are the actual learning outcomes?

[2] John Dewey, *Art as Experience,* New York: G. P. Putnam, 1958. See, for example, chapter XIII.

What ought to be going on in this classroom given our overall goals, educational platform, knowledge of how youngsters learn, and understandings of the structure of the subject matter to be taught?

What do these events and activities of teaching and learning mean to teachers, students, and others?

What are the personal meanings that students accumulate regardless of teacher intents?

How do teacher and principal interpretations of teaching reality differ?

What actions should be taken to bring about even greater understanding of teaching and learning and better congruence between our actions and beliefs?

WHY EVALUATE?

What is supervision for? Who is to be served by the process? Why evaluate anyway? How one answers such questions determines how one approaches the tasks of supervision and evaluation and influences the relationships emerging among teachers and between teachers and supervisors. Supervision and evaluation have many purposes. These range from ensuring that minimum standards are being met and that teachers are being faithful to the school's overall purposes and educational platform, to helping teachers grow and develop as persons and professionals.

Purposes can be grouped into three major categories:

1 *Quality control.* Here the supervisor is responsible for monitoring teaching and learning and does so by visiting classrooms, touring the school, talking with people, and visiting with students.

2 *Professional development.* Helping teachers to grow and to develop in their understanding of teaching and classroom life, in improving basic teaching skills, and in expanding their knowledge and use of teaching repertoires is the second purpose of supervision.

3 *Teacher motivation.* Often overlooked, but important nonetheless, is a third purpose of supervision—building and nurturing motivation and commitment to teaching, to the school's overall purposes, and to the school's defining educational platform.

A good supervisory system reflects these multiple purposes. No supervisory system based on a single purpose can succeed over time. A system that focuses only on quality control invites difficulties with teachers and lacks needed expansive qualities. A supervisory system concerned *solely* with providing support and help to teachers (and thus, by omission, neglecting teaching deficiencies and instances where overriding purposes and defining platforms are ignored) is not sufficiently comprehensive. Quality control and teacher improvement are, therefore, basic purposes that should drive any system of supervision and evaluation. A third purpose, often neglected but important in the long run, is that of teacher motivation. Overwhelming evidence exists suggesting that when the climate for evaluation is supportive and trusting, "knowledge of results" is an important ingredient in increasing a person's motivation to work and in building commitment and loyalty to one's job.[3]

PUBLIC AND PRIVATE VIEWS OF TEACHER EVALUATION

Before continuing, take a moment and examine your personal views of teacher evaluation. Assume that you are at a workshop for supervisors and others with responsibility for teacher evaluation. The workshop leader asks you to write three statements, each of which expresses a personal feeling or belief you have about teacher evaluation. First write a *public* statement that you would be willing to share with teachers, board members, and parents; next a *confidential* statement that you would be willing to share only with trusted colleagues; and finally a *private* statement that you would not readily share with others. Chances are that doubt about the credibility of present practices characterizes your confidential and/or private statements. If this is the case, you join many others with responsibility for teacher evaluation. Indeed, these thoughts become major problems when one realizes that the same teacher-evaluation practices that raise doubts of credibility in the minds of many are today being implemented with more intensity and on a wider scale than ever before. Were we to ask teachers to participate in the exercise as well, it is very likely that the majority would have significant doubts about the validity and usefulness of teacher-evaluation systems now in use.

What are the effects of participating in a system characterized by doubts? We have noticed that the system takes on a certain artificial or mechanical quality, a routine function, that becomes an end in itself. In many school districts where the emphasis on evaluation is on determining whether the teacher displays listed teaching behaviors, teachers become conditioned to "showboating" the required behaviors while being observed. When the list of required behaviors is long and when evaluation takes place frequently, this showboating becomes increasingly ritualistic. Little concern is given to whether the required behaviors make sense given the teacher's purpose, particular characteristics of the students, or the subject matter being taught. Further, it seems not to matter what the meanings of these various behaviors are for teacher and students or for that matter whether the behaviors are being displayed when the supervisor is not present. During the post-observation conference very little attention is given to the actual teaching and learning that took place, but instead the focus is on whether this or that behavior was present or not.

SCIENTIFIC AND ARTISTIC ASSUMPTIONS

This section reviews some of the assumptions basic to present teacher-evaluation practices and contrasts these with alternative assumptions and

[3] See, for example, J. R. Hackman, G. Oldham, R. Johnson, and K. Purdy, "A New Strategy for Job Enrichment," *California Management Review*, vol. 17, no. 4, 1975; and J. R. Hackman and G. Oldham, *Work Redesign*, Reading, Mass.: Addison-Wesley, 1980.

practices that we believe hold promise for increasing meaning in the process of teacher evaluation and that seem more compatible with the nature of teaching.

At present the dominant view of teacher evaluation is characterized by a commitment to such technical-rational values as predetermination and the scientific method. As pointed out in Chapter 14, predetermination is evidenced by establishing before a teaching episode specific objectives and competency levels to be exhibitied and by otherwise specifying the rules of the game, or the blueprint for evaluation, before the evaluation takes place. The scientific method is evidenced, for example, by an emphasis on empirical design characteristics in the evaluation process and on a primary concern for precision in measurement. Though "scientific" supervision is offered as being rational, it turns out instead to be rationalistic.

In recent years a number of prominent program-evaluation experts have developed and begun to test alternatives to this technical-rational approach that rely far less on the scientific method and far more on the intuitions, aspirations, and capabilities of those involved at both ends of the evaluation.[4] Theirs is an approach that sees value in discovering as opposed to determining and in describing as opposed to measuring. Though the primary focus of this pioneering work is on program evaluation, its underlying assumption, characteristics, and design features apply to teacher evaluation as well.[5]

In Table 16-1 key assumptions and practices associated with technical-rational approaches to teacher evaluation are contrasted with those associated with more artistic approaches. Though it would be a mistake to choose one of those views exclusively, the nature of reality in teaching practice suggests that the emphasis should be on the artistic assumptions.

Why is it important to describe prevailing assumptions behind teacher-evaluation practices? In Chapter 14 we pointed out that evaluation methods and technologies are associated with ideologies, and the language and values of science (objectivity, rationality, reliability, and precision) have been found to be irresistible to many educators. Present classroom observation and evaluation technology is shrouded with a sense of scientism often not

---

[4] See, for example, Robert E. Stake, *Program Evaluation, Particularly Responsive Evaluation,* paper 5 in Occasional Paper Series, Kalamazoo: Western Michigan University, Evaluation Center, November 1975; Robert E. Stake (ed.), *Evaluating the Arts in Education: A Responsive Approach,* Columbus, Ohio: Merrill, 1975; Elliot W. Eisner, "Emerging Models for Educational Evaluation," *School Review,* vol. 80, no. 4, 1972; Decker Walker, "A Naturalistic Model for Curriculum Development," *School Review,* vol. 80, no. 1, 1971; Michael Scriven, "Goal-Free Evaluation," in Ernest House (ed.), *School Evaluation: The Politics and Process,* Berkeley, Calif.: McCutchan, 1973; George Willis, "Curriculum Criticism and Literary Criticism," *Journal of Curriculum Studies,* vol. 7, no. 1, 1975; and John S. Mann, "Curriculum Criticism," *Teachers College Record,* vol. 71, no. 1, 1969.

[5] See, for example, Elliot Eisner, "The Perceptive Eye: Toward the Reformation of Educational Evaluation," Washington, D.C.: AREA, Division B, Curriculum and Objectives, 1975, invited address; Morris Cogan, *Clinical Supervision,* Boston: Houghton Mifflin, 1973; James Raths, "Teaching without Specific Objectives," *Educational Leadership,* vol. 18, no. 7, 1971; and T. J. Sergiovanni, "Expanding Conceptions of Inquiry and Practice in Supervision and Evaluation," *Educational Evaluation and Policy Analysis,* vol. 6, no. 3, pp. 355–365, 1984.

TABLE 16-1
CONTRASTING TEACHER EVALUATION ASSUMPTIONS

Scientific	Artistic
1. Evaluation can be viewed as a process designed to determine the worth of something—a teacher, teaching episode, or performance.	1. But evaluation is also valuing something. Before one can begin to value something fully, one needs to understand it. Therefore, evaluation is seeking to understand something. What is going on in this classroom and why? What does it mean?
2. The emphasis is often on observing words and behavior and not on intuition and understanding. Indeed, intuition can be considered as something to be controlled because of its impressionistic rather than scientific nature, and understanding is often a luxury that may distract the evaluation process from its true course.	2. But words and behavior are only proxies for understandings and meanings and therefore much is missed by focusing only on the proxies. The evaluation is designed to inform the supervisor's intuition, not to replace it.
3. At times it is appropriate for the evaluator to follow a blueprint and evaluate the teacher according to the specifications called for in the blueprint.	3. But at times the evaluator should develop a representation of events that have taken place—a portrait of the teaching episode. Thus "specifications" not previously determined are included in the evaluation.
4. The blueprint characteristics of the evaluation specify what is of worth and define meanings and understandings. This is an exclusive process.	4. The portrait characteristics of the evaluation assume that multiple and sometimes contradicting understandings and meanings exist. The evaluator's job is to identify and describe them. Portraits of teaching episodes often reveal a hidden curriculum more potent than that intended and the achievement of unanticipated outcomes that may have more value than those intended by the teacher or specified in the lesson planned. This is an inclusive process.
5. Sometimes what is important to the evaluator are the stated intents of the teacher and the predetermined objectives held for the student.	5. Sometimes what is important to the evaluator are the implicit assumptions and guiding platform statements that teachers bring to the classroom, the manner in which these assumptions and platform statements are articulated into classroom activities and practices, and the implications and effects of these activities and practices.
6. When using scientific approaches, the evaluator is primarily concerned with methodology. He or she asks, How can I be sure that I can describe and measure without error the extent to which predetermined objectives are being met by the teacher and that this teacher exhibits predetermined competency levels in teaching?	6. When using artistic approaches, the evaluator is primarily concerned with discovering, describing, and measuring important things that occur. He or she is willing to choose methods suited to important things even though they may be weak or considered by others as subjective or impressionistic.

TABLE 16-1
CONTRASTING TEACHER EVALUATION ASSUMPTIONS *(Continued)*

Scientific	Artistic
7. The evaluator relies heavily on rating scales and other teacher-evaluation instruments. These help him or her to be objective, to treat all teachers the same, and to ensure that the focus of the evaluation is on important events.	7. The evaluator believes that rating scales and other teacher-evaluation instruments often prevent him or her from fully understanding classroom events and prevent the evaluator and teacher from becoming personally involved in the evaluation process. The evaluator prefers to use data from the situation at hand to help define the parameters of the evaluation and to help understand crucial evaluation issues. He or she prefers to use videotape, teacher and student interviews, artifact collections, and evaluation portfolios and considers these as better methods of representation than instruments and rating scales.
8. The evaluation is primarily concerned with estimating the worth of a particular teaching performance and by inference the teacher. The teacher assumes a subordinate role in the process. The evaluator is the expert. Evaluation is something done to teachers by evaluators.	8. The evaluator is primarily interested in increasing understanding and stimulating thought and in extending the experiences of the teacher being evaluated. The teacher assumes a key role in the process. The evaluator and teacher share the expert role and evaluation is something done together.
9. Even when it makes sense to use more scientific approaches to evaluation, artistic aspects cannot be ignored.	9. Even when it makes sense to use more artistic approaches to evaluation, scientific aspects cannot be ignored.

Source: Thomas J. Sergiovanni, "Reforming Teacher Evaluation: Naturalistic Alternatives," *Educational Leadership,* vol. 34, no. 8, 1977.

even found in the more legitimate sciences. The irony in this is that most educators believe that teaching is far more an artistic enterprise than a scientific one. That being the case, it may be that we have adopted methods and technologies of teacher evaluation ill-suited to the nature of the educational enterprise.

In the sections which follow, several strategies for teacher evaluation are described that build upon scientific but are more characteristic of artistic assumptions and more consistent with the nature of teaching and learning practices. Well-known traditional methods have a place in teacher evaluation, but they should play a minor role compared with the alternatives proposed.

CLINICAL SUPERVISION

Earlier we referred to clinical supervision as an activity distinct from general supervision. There is, however, a special meaning associated with the phrase that refers to a cycle or pattern of supervision. This cycle was pioneered by

Robert H. Anderson, Morris Cogan, Robert Goldhammer, and others and is perhaps best known through Cogan's book *Clinical Supervision*.[6]

Emerging from the real world of professional practice this technique evolved from a series of problems faced by supervisors as they worked with teachers and would-be teachers. The essential ingredients of clinical supervision include the establishment of a healthy general supervisory climate, a mutual support system called "colleagueship," and a cycle of supervision comprising conferences, observation of teachers at work, and pattern analysis.

Clinical supervision is based on a number of assumptions that differ from those of traditional rating and evaluating and prescribes a pattern of action that departs substantially from present practice. In clinical supervision it is assumed that the school curriculum is, in reality, what teachers do day by day, that changes in curriculum and in teaching formats require changes in how teachers think about and understand their teaching and how they behave in classrooms; that supervision is a process for which both supervisors and teachers are responsible; that the focus of supervision is on teacher strengths; that given the right conditions teachers are willing and able to improve; that teachers have large reservoirs of talent, often unused; and that teachers derive satisfaction from challenging work. These assumptions are consistent with those associated with Theory Y as discussed in Chapter 7 and are key to the concept of human resources supervision.

Clinical supervision is, therefore, a partnership in inquiry whereby the person assuming the role of supervisor functions more as an individual with experience and insight (or, in the case of equals, with a better vantage point in analyzing another colleague's teaching) than as an expert who determines what is right and wrong. The issue of authority is very important in the process. The clinical supervisor derives her or his authority from being able to collect and provide information desired by the teacher and from being able to help the teacher to use this information in a useful way. This authority is functional, as compared with formal authority derived from one's hierarchical position. As discussed in Chapter 3, functional authority is associated with higher levels of teacher satisfaction and performance.

Following these assumptions, clinical supervision is an in-class support system designed to provide assistance directly to the teacher. In practice, clinical supervision requires a more intense relationship between supervisor and teacher than that found in traditional evaluation, first in the establishment of colleagueship and then in the articulation of colleagueship through the cycle of supervision. The heart of clinical supervision is an intense, continuous, mature relationship between supervisors and teachers with the intent being the improvement of professional practice.

---

[6] Clinical supervision evolved from a series of techniques developed as a result of the pioneering work of Robert Anderson, Morris Cogan, and Robert Goldhammer in the Harvard MAT program of the late fifties and early sixties. Originally conceived as a component of preservice teacher education, the technique has since been developed for in-service use. Morris Cogan, *Clinical Supervision*, New York: Houghton Mifflin, 1973.

The purpose of clinical supervision is to help teachers to modify existing patterns of teaching in ways that make sense to them. Evaluation is, therefore, responsive to the needs and desires of the teacher. It is the teacher who decides the course of a clinical and supervisory cycle, the issues to be discussed, and for what purpose. Obviously, those who serve as clinical supervisors will bring to this interaction a considerable amount of influence; but, ideally, this influence should stem from their being in a position to provide the help and clarification needed by teachers. The supervisor's job, therefore, is to help the teacher select goals to be improved and teaching issues to be illuminated, and to understand better her or his practice. This emphasis on understanding provides the avenue by which more technical assistance can be given to the teacher; thus, clinical supervision involves, as well, the systematic analysis of classroom events.

During the last decade, interest in the development of clinical supervision has been substantial. Representative of this progress is the appearance of the second edition of Robert Goldhammer's classic book *Clinical Supervision: Special Methods for the Supervision of Teachers,* first published in 1969. The second edition was revised by Robert H. Anderson and Robert J. Krajewski.[7] The original version was pioneering, and the revised edition sets a new standard for the state of the art in clinical supervision. The 1986 appearance of *Learning about Teaching through Clinical Supervision,* edited by John Smyth and published by Croom Helm of London attests to widespread international interest in clinical supervision. The good news, as reflected in these books and in developments of other scholars interested in clinical supervision,[8] is a decided shift from emphasis on the steps of clinical supervision themselves to its concepts, assumptions, and basic framework. Increasingly, clinical supervision is viewed as an overall pattern of working with teachers that operationally should take a number of forms and follow a number of paths. Consistency is needed, of course, at the strategy level where assumptions and the overall framework come into play. But diversity is needed in developing operational tactics if clinical supervision is to accommodate itself to the array of needs of supervisors and teachers and to the particular characteristics of teaching situations. Clinical supervision is, therefore, basically a design for working with teachers within which a number of technologies, perspectives, and approaches can be used.

Some excellent "hands-on" books and articles are available that provide specific operational techniques for use within the clinical supervision framework. One we especially recommend is Keith A. Acheson and Meredith Damien Gall's *Techniques in the Clinical Supervision of Teaching.*[9] Many

---

[7] Robert Goldhammer, Robert H. Anderson, and Robert J. Krajewski, *Clinical Supervision: Special Methods for the Supervision of Teachers,* 2d ed., New York: Holt, 1980.

[8] See, for example, Noreen Garman, "A Clinical Approach to Supervision," in Thomas J. Sergiovanni (ed.), *Supervision of Teaching,* 1982 Yearbook, Association for Supervision and Curriculum Development, Arlington, Va.: 1982, pp. 35–52.

[9] Keith A. Acheson and Meredith Damien Gall, *Techniques in the Clinical Supervision of Teaching,* 2d ed., New York: Longmans, 1986.

highly developed observational systems are also available for use in collecting information within the clinical supervision framework. The Galloway, Flanders, Blumberg, Kounin, and Morine systems are some examples. Respectively, they provide techniques and instruments for accurately recording nonverbal behavior in classroom interactions, student-teacher verbal interaction in classrooms, interaction of supervisors and teachers in conference, teacher-classroom management techniques, and a system for observing behaviors teachers find most important. As useful as these hands-on materials may be, as a *group* of techniques available to clinical supervision, they are still underdeveloped. Too much emphasis is given to objectives and systematic collection of *readily observable* data. They tend to emphasize "low-inference" tactics rather than "high-inference." High-inference tactics require that judgments be made and data be interpreted to assess unique meanings given actual persons in situations involved in teaching. Low-inference tactics, by contrast, more precisely define behaviors to be observed and the data-collection strategies to be used. All in all, not enough attention is given to artistic perspectives in clinical supervision, a topic to be pursued later in this chapter. This bias toward the scientific and neglect of the artistic may well reflect the present state of the field, with better balance between the two forthcoming as clinical supervision continues to mature.

THE CYCLE OF CLINICAL SUPERVISION

One cannot provide in a few pages all the techniques and know-how associated with clinical supervision. Competency will come with practice as supervisors team together in learning the skills of clinical supervision. The intent here is to describe the cycle of supervision, to provide some basic principles and concepts underlying clinical supervisory practice, and to suggest some techniques and tools which supervisors might find useful as they begin to develop competencies as clinical supervisors.

Cogan identifies eight phases to the cycle of supervision.[10]

1 *Phase 1 requires establishing the teacher-supervisor relationship.* This first phase is of particular importance, for upon its success rests the whole concept of clinical supervision. Teachers are suspicious of evaluation in general, and the intense sort of supervision prescribed by Cogan can be even more alarming. Further, the success of clinical supervision requires that teachers share with supervisors responsibility for all steps and activities. The supervisor has two tasks in Phase 1: building a relationship based on mutual trust and support, and inducting the teacher into the role of co-supervisor. Cogan believes that both tasks should be well advanced before the supervisor enters the teacher's classroom to observe teaching. Phase 1 establishes the colleagueship relationships deemed critically important by Cogan.

2 *Phase 2 requires intensive planning of lessons and units with the teacher.* In Phase 2 teacher and supervisor plan, together, a lesson, a series of lessons, or a unit. Planning includes estimates of objectives or outcomes, subject-matter concepts,

---

[10] Cogan, op. cit.

teaching strategies, materials to be used, learning contexts, anticipated problems, and provisions for feedback and evaluation.

3 *Phase 3 requires planning of the classroom observation strategy by teacher and supervisor.* Together teacher and supervisor plan and discuss the kind and amount of information to be gathered during the observation period and the methods to be used to gather this information.

4 *Phase 4 requires the supervisor to observe in-class instruction.* Cogan emphasizes that only after careful establishment of the supervisory relationship and the subsequent planning of both the lesson or unit and the observation strategy does the observation take place.

5 *Phase 5 requires careful analysis of the teaching-learning process.* As co-supervisors, teachers, and supervisors analyze the events of the class. They may work separately at first or together from the beginning. Outcomes of the analysis are identification of patterns of teacher behavior that exist over time and critical incidents that occurred that seemed to affect classroom activity, and extensive descriptions of teacher behavior and evidence of that behavior. It is believed that teachers have established persistent patterns of teaching that are evidenced and can be identified as a pattern after several carefully documented observations and analysis.

6 *Phase 6 requires planning the conference strategy.* Supervisors prepare for the conference by setting tentative objectives and planning tentative processes, but in a manner that does not program the course of the conference too much. They plan also the physical settings and arrange for materials, tapes, or other aids. Preferably, the conference should be unhurried and on school time. Cogan notes that it may well be necessary to arrange for coverage of a teacher's classroom responsibilities from time to time.

7 *Phase 7 is the conference.* The conference is an opportunity and setting for teacher and supervisor to exchange information about what was intended in a given lesson or unit and what actually happened. The success of the conference depends upon the extent to which the process of clinical supervision is viewed as formative, focused evaluation intended to help in understanding and improving professional practice.

8 *Phase 8 requires the resumption of planning.* A common outcome of the first seven phases of clinical supervision is agreement on the kinds of changes sought in the teacher's classroom behavior. As this agreement materializes, the eighth phase begins. Teacher and supervisor begin planning the next lesson or unit and the new targets, approaches, and techniques to be attempted.

As one reviews the cycle of clinical supervision, it appears as though the cycle describes that which many supervisors have been doing all along. But a quick review of the assumptions basic to clinical supervision, particularly the concept of co-supervisor, suggests that the resemblance may be superficial. The supervisor works at two levels with teachers during the cycle: helping them to understand and improve their professional practice and helping them to learn more about the skills of classroom analysis needed in supervision. Further, while traditional classroom observation tends to be sporadic and requires little time investment, clinical supervision asks that supervisors give 2 to 3 hours a week to each teacher. Supervisors can better manage their time by involving only part of the faculty at a time—perhaps one-third for 3 months in rotation.

As teachers themselves become competent in clinical supervision and assume increased responsibility for all phases, they should participate in clinical supervision as a form of collegial supervision. No hard-and-fast rules exist that exclude teachers from assuming roles as clinical supervisors. Collegial supervision and clinical supervision are quite compatible.

EDUCATIONAL PLATFORM

In Chapter 14 we pointed out how tempting it often is to view teaching as a rational set of activities, directed to clearly stated and understood objectives. Indeed, one is often led to believe that classroom activity is a logical process of determining objectives, stating them in acceptable form, developing learning experiences, and evaluating the outcomes of these experiences in relation to predetermined objectives. This view assumes that the teaching arena is objective and that teachers come to this arena with a clean slate, free of biases, willing and able to make rational choices.

In reality, however, most supervisors know that teaching is not nearly as objective and explicit as one might think. Indeed, teachers, supervisors, and others bring to the classroom a variety of agendas, some public, many hidden, and probably most unknown, each of which influences the decisions they make. The agendas tend to fall into three major categories: what one believes is possible, what one believes is true, and what one believes is desirable. Together the three are the essential ingredients of one's *education platform.*[11] A platform implies something that supports one's action and by which one justifies or validates one's own actions. An approximate analogy would be that of a political platform. This platform states the basic values, critical policy statements, and key positions of an individual or group. Once known, the political platform can be used to predict responses that a politician or political party is likely to make to questions on various campaign issues. The concept of educational platform, particularly as it affects curriculum and educational program matters, is discussed at length in Chapter 10. Here our attention is on platform as it relates to clinical supervision.

Assumptions, Theories, and Beliefs

The components of one's educational platform are the assumptions, theories, and beliefs one holds for key aspects of effective teaching, such as the purpose of schooling, perceptions of students, what knowledge is of most worth, and the value of certain teaching techniques and pedagogical principles. For purposes of illustration, let us consider each component below, recognizing that operationally they are inseparable.

Assumptions that teachers hold help answer the question "What is possible?" Assumptions are composed of our beliefs, the concepts we take for

---

[11] Decker Walker, "A Naturalistic Model for Curriculum Development," *The School Review,* vol. 80, no. 1, pp. 51–65, 1971.

granted, and the ideas we accept without question about schools, classrooms, students, teaching, learning, and knowledge. Assumptions help the teacher to define what classrooms are actually like and what is possible to accomplish within them. Assumptions are important to the decisions that teachers make, because they set the boundaries for what information will or will not be considered and for other possibilities and actions at the onset of instruction.

Theories we hold help answer the question, "What is true?" Theories are beliefs about relationships between and among assumptions we consider to be true. Theories form the basis for developing teaching strategies and patterns of classroom organizations.

Beliefs about what is desirable in classrooms are derived from assumptions and theories that one holds regarding knowledge, learning, classrooms, and students. What is desirable is expressed in the form of intents, aims, objectives, or purposes.

Consider, for example, a teacher whose educational platform includes the assumptions that "little or no knowledge exists that is essential for everyone to learn" and that "youngsters can be trusted to make important decisions." The two assumptions might well lead to the theory that "students who are allowed to influence classroom decisions will make wise choices and will become more committed learners." That being the case, a corresponding aim for that teacher might be "to involve students in shared decision making," or perhaps "to have students interact with subject matter in a manner that emphasizes its concepts and structure rather than just its information."

Contrast this with a teacher whose educational platform includes the assumption that "the only justifiable evidence of good teaching is student acquisition of subject matter as specified by the teacher" and the assumption that "motivation of students should reflect the realities of the world outside the school, where good behavior and performance are publicly rewarded and poor behavior and performance are publicly punished." The two assumptions might well lead to the theory that "students need to be motivated, on the one hand, and disciplined, on the other, to get the behavior and performance that leads to acquiring the most subject matter in the least amount of time." In this case a corresponding aim might be "to provide rewards and privileges to students who behave and perform to the teacher's expectations and punishment to those who do not."

Educational platforms are powerful determinants of the nature and quality of life in classrooms. For example, imagine the fate of students in the classrooms of people who consider themselves teachers of French or biology and not of students as compared with teachers who view instruction in a more holistic and integrated way. Consider next the fate of the supervisor who wants the first type of teacher to be more sensitive to individual differences of students and to emphasize the joy of learning French or biology as well as mastery of subject matter, but does not take into account the teacher's educational platform. Unless the supervisor is a master at behavior modification and the teacher witless enough to respond passively to stimuli from the supervisor, change in teaching behavior will require some altering of educational platforms.

Known and Unknown Platform Dimensions

In the world of the classroom the components of educational platforms are generally not well known. That is, teachers tend to be unaware of their assumptions, theories, or objectives. Sometimes they adopt components of a platform that seem right, that have the ring of fashionable rhetoric, or that coincide with the expectation of important others, such as teachers whom they admire, or of groups with which they wish to affiliate. Though teachers may overtly adopt aspects of educational platforms in this manner, covertly, or unknowingly, they are often likely to hang onto contradictory assumptions, beliefs, and theories. Publicly they may say (or espouse) one thing and assume that their classroom behavior is governed by this statement, but privately, or even unknowingly, they may believe something else that actually governs their classroom behavior. Indeed, teachers are not aware that often their classroom decisions and behavior contradict their espoused platform.

THEORIES GOVERNING TEACHER BEHAVIOR

It has been suggested that the classroom is an artificial setting where form and function are influenced largely by the stated and implied assumptions, theories, and aims of individual teachers. Together these beliefs form an educational platform that supports teachers' actions and by which they justify or validate their actions. As has been suggested, many aspects of a teacher's platform are unknown or perhaps known but covert. When covert dimensions differ from espoused, the former are likely to constitute the *operational* platform for a given individual.

The clinical supervisor needs to be concerned with two theories that the teacher brings to the classroom—an *espoused theory* and a *theory in use*. As Argyris and Schön suggest:

> When someone is asked how he would behave under certain circumstances, the answer he usually gives is his espoused theory of action for that situation. This is the theory of action to which he gives allegiance, and which, upon request, he communicates to others. However, the theory that actually governs his action is his theory in use. This theory may or may not be compatible with his espoused theory; furthermore, the individual may or may not be aware of the incompatibility of the two theories.[12]

When one's espoused theory matches one's theory in use, they are considered congruent. Congruence exists, for example, for the teacher who believes that self-image development in youngsters is desirable in its own right and is related to student achievement and whose teaching behavior and artifacts of that behavior confirm this espoused theory. Lack of congruence between a person's espoused theory and the theory in use, *when known,*

[12] Chris Argyris and David A. Schön, *Theory in Practice: Increasing Professional Effectiveness,* San Francisco: Jossey-Bass, 1974, p. 7.

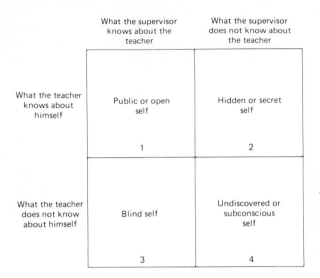

	What the supervisor knows about the teacher	What the supervisor does not know about the teacher
What the teacher knows about himself	Public or open self 1	Hidden or secret self 2
What the teacher does not know about himself	Blind self 3	Undiscovered or subconscious self 4

FIGURE 16-1
Johari Window and educational platform. (*From Thomas J. Sergiovanni,* Handbook for Department Leadership Concepts and Practices in Today's Secondary Schools, *Boston: Allyn and Bacon, 1977.*)

proposes a dilemma to that individual. A second teacher, for example, shares the same espoused theory regarding self-concept, but his or her pattern of questioning, use of negative feedback, use of the bell curve, and insistence on standard requirements may reveal a theory in use incongruent with the espoused theory. The social studies teacher who believes in and teaches a course in American democracy in a "totalitarian" manner represents another example of incongruency between espoused theory and theory in use.

THE JOHARI WINDOW

A useful way of understanding how known and unknown platform dimensions of teachers fit into clinical supervision is by examining the *Johari Window* as it relates to espoused theories and theories in use.[13] This relationship is illustrated in Figure 16-1.

The Johari Window in this case depicts the relationship between two parties, teacher and clinical supervisor. The relationship revolves around aspects of the teacher's educational platform known to self and others, known to self but not others, not known to self but known to others, and not known to self or others. Four cells are depicted in the Johari Window, each representing a different combination of what the teacher knows or does not know about his or her teaching as contrasted with what the supervisor knows and does not know about that teacher's teaching.

In the first cell, *the public or open self,* the teacher's knowledge of his or her teaching behavior and other aspects of his or her professional practices

[13] Joseph Luft, *Of Human Interaction,* New York: National Press Books, 1969. The Johari Window was developed by Joseph Luft and Harry Ingham and gets its name from the first names of its authors.

corresponds with the supervisor's knowledge. This is the area in which communication occurs most effectively and in which the need for the teacher to be defensive, to assume threat, is minimal. The clinical supervisor works to broaden, or enlarge, this cell with the teacher.

In the second cell, *the hidden or secret self,* the teacher knows about aspects of his or her teaching behavior and professional practice that the supervisor does not know. Often the teacher conceals these aspects from the supervisor for fear that the supervisor might use this knowledge to punish, hurt, or exploit the teacher. The second cell suggests how important a supervisory climate characterized by trust and credibility is to the success of clinical supervision. In clinical supervision the teacher is encouraged to reduce the size of this cell.

In the third cell, *the blind self,* the supervisor knows about aspects of the teacher's behavior and professional practice of which the teacher is unaware. This cell, though large initially, is reduced considerably as clinical supervision for a given teacher develops and matures. This is the cell most often neglected by traditional teacher-evaluation methods. Indeed clinical supervision is superior to most other supervising strategies in helping teachers understand dimensions of teaching found in the "blind self."

In the fourth cell, *the undiscovered self,* one finds aspects of teacher behavior and professional practice not known to either teacher or supervisor. The size of this cell is reduced as clinical supervision progresses. Teachers and supervisors discover and understand more and more about their beliefs, capabilities, strengths and weaknesses, and potential.

HELPING TEACHERS CHANGE

Creating a condition for change greatly facilitates the change itself. If, for example, individual teachers are unaware of inconsistencies between their espoused theories and their theories in use, they are not likely to search for alternatives to their present teaching patterns. One way in which search behavior can be evoked is by surfacing dilemmas. Dilemmas surface as a result of teachers learning that their theories in use are not consistent with their espoused theory.

Dilemmas promote an unsettled feeling in a person. Their espoused educational platforms mean a great deal, and what they stand for and believe is linked to their concept of self and sense of well-being. Dilemmas that emerge from inconsistencies between these images and actual behavior are upsetting and need to be resolved. Indeed they are likely to lead to a search for changes either in one's espoused theory or in one's theory in use.[14]

Readiness for change is a critical point in the process of clinical supervision. It is at this point that an appropriate support system needs to be provided. Part of this support system will be psychological and will be geared toward

[14] Leon Festinger, *Theory of Cognitive Dissonance,* Evanston, Ill.: Row, Peterson, 1975; and Milton Rokeach, "A Theory of Organizational Change within Value-Attitude Systems," *Journal of Social Sciences,* vol. 24, no. 21, 1968.

accepting and encouraging the teacher. But part must also be technical and will be geared toward making available teaching and professional practice alternatives to the teacher.

Argyris and Schön point out that congruence is not a virtue in itself. Indeed a "bad" espoused theory matched to a theory in use may be far less desirable, from the supervisor's point of view, than a "good" espoused theory insufficiently matched.[15]

SOME EVIDENCE

To this point in our discussion of developing a theory of clinical supervision we have suggested that:

A teacher's classroom behavior and the artifacts of that behavior are a function of assumptions, theories, and intents the teacher brings to the classroom. Together these compose the teacher's educational platform.

Educational platforms exist at two levels: what teachers say they assume, believe, and intend (their espoused theory) and the assumptions, beliefs, and intents inferred from their behavior and artifacts of their behavior (their theory in use).

Espoused theories are generally known to the teacher.

Theories in use are generally not known to the teacher and must be constructed from observation of teacher behavior and artifacts of that behavior.

Lack of congruence between a teacher's espoused theory and the teacher's theory in use proposes a dilemma to the teacher.

Faced with a dilemma, a teacher becomes uncomfortable, and search behavior is evoked.

Dilemmas are resolved by teachers modifing their theory in use to match their espoused theory. It is possible that espoused theory will be modified to match theory in use, but because of the link between espoused theory and self-esteem, and self-esteem with the esteem received from others, the more common pattern will be the former.

Though a number of studies suggest that indeed teachers are likely to respond as suggested,[16] a number of caveats are in order. McGuire, for example, in reviewing the literature on consistency theory notes that search behavior is only one of several possible reactions to dissonance. Additional examples of dissonance reduction, he notes, are *avoidance,* whereby one represses the matter by putting the inconsistency out of mind; *bolstering,* whereby the inconsistency is

---

[15] Argyris and Schön, op. cit.
[16] Using Flanders's interaction-analysis techniques as a means of collecting information and as a basis for producing verbal feedback, Tuckman, McCall, and Hyman conclude that "behavior and self-perception of experienced, in-service teachers *can* be changed by involving a discrepancy between a teacher's observed behavior and his own self-perception of his behavior, and then making him aware of this discrepancy via verbal feedback." See Bruce W. Tuckman, Kendrick M. McCall, and Ronald T. Hyman, "The Modification of Teacher Behavior: Effects of Dissonance and Feedback," *American Educational Research Journal,* vol. 6, no. 4, pp. 607–619, 1969.

submerged into a larger body of consistencies so as to seem relatively less important; *differentiation*, whereby one sees the situation causing dissonance to be different in a particular case ("I wasn't actually putting down the youngster but just giving her a taste of her own medicine"); *substitution*, whereby one changes the object about which he or she has an opinion rather than the opinion itself ("It is true that I said all school administrators are petty bureaucrats, and they are, but he is a statesman, not a bureaucrat"); and *devaluation*, whereby one downgrades the importance of the inconsistency in question, thus making it more tolerable.[17] The extent to which a teacher faces up to inconsistencies between espoused platform dimensions and those actually in use may well depend, as suggested earlier, upon the quality of climate and setting the supervisor provides—colleagueship, in Cogan's language.[18]

In an extensive review of the literature Fuller and Manning conclude that self-confrontation and discrepancy analysis, though achieving uneven results, is by and large a powerful supervisory technique. In addition they note that "if the person is not too stressed, or closed, or anxious, or distracted, the self-confrontation experience 'takes,' i.e., the person notices some discrepancy. This is either a difference between what he thought he was doing and what he was actually doing (an incongruence discrepancy), or a difference between what he was doing and what he wanted to do (a deficiency discrepancy)."[19] This again highlights the importance of the climate that accompanies the process of clinical supervision. But as Fuller and Manning point out, a supportive climate is a necessary but not sufficient requirement for success: "Change is said not only to require the presence of facilitative conditions such as acceptance and empathy, but also 'confrontation.'... The teacher will not benefit from seeing her video tape alone since there is no confrontation.... Feedback that is not accompanied by some focus has been found to change behavior little, if at all."[20]

Alan Simon developed and field-tested a supervisory strategy that incorporates many of the features of clinical supervision described above.[21] Using videotaping techniques, Simon, as the supervisor, interviewed teachers, asking them to specify aspects of their espoused educational platform as it applies to education in general and to a particular lesson. He then videotaped the teachers actually teaching the

[17] William J. McGuire, "The Current Status of Cognitive Consistency Theories," in Shel Feldman (ed.), *Cognitive Consistency, Motivational Antecedents, and Behavioral Consequents,* New York: Academic, 1966, pp. 10–14.

[18] Cogan, op. cit., p. 67.

[19] Frances F. Fuller and Brad A. Manning, "Self-Confrontation Reviewed: A Conceptualization for Video Playback in Teacher Education," *Review of Educational Research,* vol. 43, p. 487, 1973.

[20] Ibid., p. 493.

[21] Alan Simon, "Videotapes Illustrating Concepts of the Argyris and Schön Model in Instructional Supervisory Situations," doctoral dissertation, Urbana: University of Illinois, Educational Administration and Supervision, 1976. See also Alan Simon, "Analyzing Educational Platforms: A Supervisory Strategy," *Educational Leadership,* vol. 34, no. 8, pp. 580–585, 1977. For a further extension of this work and its application to high school teachers see Michael Hoffman, "Comparing Espoused Platforms and Platforms-in-Use in Clinical Supervision," doctoral dissertation, Urbana: University of Illinois, Educational Administration and Supervision, 1977; and Michael Hoffman and Thomas J. Sergiovanni, "Clinical Supervision: Theory in Practice," *Illinois School Research and Development,* vol. 14, no. 1, pp. 5–12, 1977.

lessons described. The videotape was then reviewed by the supervisor, sometimes with the help of outside experts not familiar with the teachers' espoused platform, and from this analysis a theory in use, as perceived by the supervisor, was constructed. This theory in use was also recorded on videotape. Together, the supervisor and teacher viewed the videotape now containing the teacher-espoused theory, an example of the teacher at work, and the supervisor's perception of the teacher's theory in use. The teacher was then interviewed to determine whether the videotaped espoused platform actually represented his or her thoughts before the lesson, whether the videotaped lesson represented his or her teaching, and whether the supervisor's videotaped rendering of the theory in use was fair and accurate. Overall the teachers verified the accuracy and fairness of the videotapes. Interviewing continued, to determine attitudes toward the process and to obtain perceptions of the effectiveness of the process from the teachers. Judges, listening to the audiotaped interviews, concluded that overall the teachers had positive attitudes toward the process and found it helpful. Further, by rating teacher responses into defensive and open categories, judges concluded that indeed dilemmas had surfaced and that search behavior had been evoked.

Many forms of clinical supervision resemble artistic approaches. Such forms are artistic when they rely on developing a complete representation of a teaching episode and when they use this representation as a basis for making inferences and building understanding of events. Videotaping is the most common method of representation associated with clinical supervision. Clinical supervision uses the data at hand (actually generated from the environment and activities being evaluated) rather than data that fit a preconceived rating form or a set of instrument specifications, and it places the teacher in a key role as generator, interpreter, and analyst of events described.

Sometimes clinical supervisors take too seriously the need to "scientifically" and "objectively" document events. Sometimes they focus too intensely on the stepwise or work-flow aspects of clinical supervision. Sometimes they rely too heavily on predetermined objectives or on specifying detailed blueprints and plans that subsequently determine the direction of the evaluation. But clinical supervision can be geared to discovering and understanding rather than determining, and in that sense it has artistic potential. Additional artistic strategies that can be used either separate from clinical supervision or as a part of clinical supervision are described in the sections that follow. These techniques are powerful means for providing rich descriptions of classroom activity from which theories in use might be inferred.

CONNOISSEURSHIP AND CRITICISM

It is difficult to discuss artistic alternatives to present teacher-evaluation practices without reference to the work of Elliot Eisner.[22] Eisner is concerned

[22] Elliot Eisner, "Applying Educational Connoisseurship and Criticism to Education Settings," Stanford, Calif.: Stanford University, Department of Education, undated, mimeo: see also his "Emerging Models for Educational Evaluation," op. cit., and "The Perceptive Eye: Toward the

with developing in supervisor and teacher the qualities and skills of appreciation, inference, disclosure, and description. He refers to these qualities as the cultivation of educational connoisseurship and criticism. It is through the art of connoisseurship that one is able to appreciate and internalize meanings in classrooms and through the skill of criticism that one is able to share or disclose this meaning to others. Eisner uses references to wine connoisseurship and art criticism as illustrations of these concepts. The art of appreciation is the tool of the connoisseur and the art of disclosure the tool of the critic. Cross uses the example of sports commentators and writers to illustrate the combined application of connoisseurship and criticism.

> Most of us are familiar with some of the techniques employed by commentators in describing and remarking on well-executed plays or potentially victorious strategies. Plays executed with finesse are often seen in stop action, instant replay, slow motion or are recounted in stirring detail on sports pages. One of the major contributions of these commentators is their great knowledge of sports, familiarizing them with possibilities so they know whether a flanker reverse, off tackle run, screen pass or drawplay was used or has potential for gaining yardage in a given situation, or when the bump and run, blitz, or single coverage was used or likely to prevent gain. Knowledge about educational potentials is also necessary. The potentially worthwhile tactics of teaching or those in use—the bump and runs or flanker reverses of schooling—need to be described and conveyed.[23]

The commentator's ability to render play-by-play action in a fashion that permits us to see and feel the game as he or she does depends upon a feel of intimacy with the phenomena under study not permitted by mere attention to game statistics and other objective information and upon a quality of disclosure more vivid than a box score. And in education, the evaluator's ability to describe classroom life in a fashion that permits us to see and feel this environment as he or she does depends upon a similar intimacy with classroom phenomena (educational connoisseurship) and a rendering of this intimacy (educational criticism) well beyond that provided by a brief observation or two accompanied by a series of ratings or a teacher-evaluation checklist. Eisner maintains that educational connoisseurship is to some degree practiced daily by teachers and supervisors:

> The teacher's ability, for example, to judge when children have had enough of art, math, reading or "free time" is a judgment made not by applying a theory of motivation or

Reformation of Educational Evaluation," op. cit. Eisner notes that, unfortunately, to many the word "connoisseurship" has snobbish or elitist connotations, and criticism implies a hacking or negativistic attitude. In his words, "Connoisseurship, as I use the term, relates to any form of expertise in any area of human endeavor and is as germane to the problem involved in purse snatching as it is to the appreciation of fine needle point." And "criticism is conceived of as a generic process aimed at revealing the characteristics and qualities that constitute any human product. Its major aim is to enable individuals to recognize qualities and characteristics of a work or event which might have gone unnoticed and therefore unappreciated." Quoted from "The Perceptive Eye: Toward the Performance of Educational Evaluation," footnote 2.

[23] James Cross, "Applying Editorial Connoisseurship and Criticism to Supervisory Practices," doctoral dissertation, 1977, Urbana: University of Illinois, Educational Administration and Supervision.

attention, but by recognizing the wide range of qualities that the children themselves display to those who have learned to see. Walk down any school corridor and peek through the window; an educational connoisseur can quickly discern important things about life in that classroom. Of course judgments, especially those made through windows from hallways, can be faulty. Yet the point remains. If one knows how to see what one looks at, a great deal of information...can be secured. The teacher who cannot distinguish between the noise of children working and just plain noise has not yet developed a basic level of educational connoisseurship.[24]

Eisner believes that the existing level of connoisseurship found in teachers and supervisors can and should be refined, that perceptions can be enhanced and sharpened, and that understanding can be increased. He further points out that

...connoisseurship when developed to a high degree provides a level of consciousness that makes intellectual clarity possible. Many teachers are confronted daily with prescriptions and demands from individuals outside the teaching profession that are intended to improve the quality of education within the schools. Many of these demands the teachers feel in their gut to be misguided or wrong-headed; the demands somehow fly in the face of what they feel to be possible in a classroom or in the best interests of children.[25]

In this context he notes: "Many teachers, if you ask them, are unable to state why they feel uneasy. They have a difficult time articulating what the flaws are in the often glib prescriptions that issue from state capitols and from major universities. Yet, the uneasiness is not always, but often justified." And further: "Many teachers have developed sufficient connoisseurship to feel that something is awry but have insufficient connoisseurship to provide a more adequate conceptualization of just what it is."[26]

When applied to supervision, educational connoisseurship is a necessary but insufficient art. Classroom understanding needs to be described and communicated, and this aspect of the process, the art of disclosure, is what Eisner refers to as educational criticism. We have much to learn about cultivating the art of connoisseurship and the skills of disclosure. Much will depend upon our ability to regain confidence in ourselves, in our ability to analyze and judge, in our willingness to rely on intuition and perception—all today often considered dubious skills, ones to be discounted in the face of objective and scientific demands for accountability.

MORE THAN DESCRIBING

Unique to artistic approaches to supervision and evaluation is the emphasis on identifying meanings in teaching activity and classroom life rather than *only* describing teaching and classroom events. Many advocates of clinical supervision, for example, recommend that the supervisor develop an accurate and

[24] Eisner, "The Perceptive Eye," p. 9.
[25] Ibid., pp. 10–11.
[26] Ibid., p. 11.

TABLE 16-2
COMPARING PICTURING AND DISCLOSURE MODELS OF TEACHER EVALUATION

Picturing	Disclosure
1. Intent	
To describe the teaching phenomenon under study as exactly as possible. To develop a replica, photo image, or a carbon copy of reality. Agendas and issues are those embedded in the data.	To interpret the teaching phenomenon under study. To illuminate issues, disclose meetings, and raise hypotheses or propositions. Agendas and issues are those which emerge from the data.
2. Analogies	
Legal transcript, video-tape, photo-replica, interaction-analysis, electronic portrait, music or dance score, playscript, historical chronology.	Impressionistic painting, collage, book review, interpretive photo, music, dance or play performance, story.
3. Key Questions	
What exactly happened in this class? How can I describe events objectively?	What issues emerge from the study of this class? How can I represent or illuminate these issues in a meaningful way?
4. Validity Check	
Are events described accurately?	When actual events are observed, do they reasonably lead to the inferences and interpretations?

objective record of teaching. Often videotapes of teaching, exact transcripts of teacher-student talk, or tally sheets of some sort that record data occurrences of interest to the teacher and the supervisor are recommended. Typically, the supervisor is expected to avoid interpretation, leaving the extraction of the meaning behind events to the teacher or, when a particularly good relationship exists between teacher and supervisor, to both parties during the conference phase of a clinical supervision cycle.

When using more artistic approaches to clinical supervision, supervisors try to go beyond description to the interpretation of teaching events. Following Ramsey,[27] John Mann distinguishes between *picturing* and *disclosure* models.[28] Picturing models of evaluation try to be much like the teaching activity and classroom life under study. Disclosure models, on the other hand, contain key characteristics of the teaching activity in classroom life under study but move beyond to interpreting meaning, raising issues, and testing propositions about this phenomenon. Some of these distinctions are suggested in Table 16-2. As you examine the disclosure side of the ledger in Table 16-2 notice the emphasis given to going beyond the data in the strictest sense to telling a story represented by the

[27] Ian Ramsey, *Models and Mystery*, London: Oxford University Press, 1964.
[28] John S. Mann, "Curriculum Criticism," *The Teachers College Record*, vol. 71, no. 1, pp. 27–40, 1967.

data. Consider, for example, the following excerpt from the "disclosure" of a classroom by Robert Donmoyer:

> All these forces combined to produce a profound effect upon the teacher and to profoundly influence her behavior in the classroom. She becomes, as she herself has said, an accountant. Most of her day is spent checking and recording what students have and haven't done. Math, spelling, and language assignments must be checked, and if there are mistakes (and there usually are) they must be rechecked and, sometimes, rechecked again. Then checked assignments must be checked off on each student's math, spelling, or language contract. When each contract is completed, each contract must be checked out. After this is done, the student must take home the work included on this contract and bring back a note signed by his parents indicating they saw the work. This note, of course, must be checked in.
>
> This checking and rechecking and checking out and checking in is all performed with mechanized precision. The teacher's face remains immobile except for an occasional upward turn at the corners of her mouth, the eyes never smile.
>
> The teacher exhibits great economy of movement and gesture. It's almost as if Ms. Hill were a marionette whose strings are too tight, hence her gestures must be tight and close to her body.[29]

Notice that Donmoyer does not provide a detailed description of the number of times the teacher checks this or that, but offers instead the word "accountant" not only to suggest the actual checking of student work but to communicate a meaning that transcends the particular issues of checking and rechecking and instead comments on an important dimension of the climate and quality of life in this particular classroom.

The concepts of picturing and disclosure might be viewed as range parameters within which a supervisor can work. At times picturing events as accurately as possible might make sense and at other times moving toward the disclosure end of the range might be more appropriate. One can catalog approaches to supervision and evaluation used by a particular school or a particular supervisor on such a range scale as a way of identifying the array of possibilities that exist in the school. It should be noted, however, that the more a supervisory and evaluation strategy approaches the disclosure end of this range, the more important is the quality of the relationship between teacher and supervisor to the success in this approach. Disclosure strategies of supervision and evaluation require a particularly strong climate of trust and understanding among those involved in the process of supervision and evaluation. The relatively safer picturing end of this continuum may be appropriate initially, and as the supervisory relationship matures, movement could then progress toward the disclosure end.

SUMMARY OF CONCEPTS BASIC TO ARTISTIC EVALUATION

In summarizing concepts basic to artistic approaches to supervision and evaluation Elliot Eisner identifies the characteristics he considers important:

---

[29] Robert Donmoyer, "School and Society Revisited: An Educational Criticism of Ms. Hall's Fourth-Grade Classroom," as quoted in Eisner, *The Educated Imagination,* op. cit., p. 231.

1 Artistic approaches to supervision require attention to the muted or expressive character of events, not simply to their incidence or literal meaning.

2 Artistic approaches to supervision require high levels of educational connoisseurship, the ability to see what is significant yet subtle.

3 Artistic approaches to supervision appreciate the unique contributions of the teacher to the educational development of the young, as well as those contributions a teacher may have in common with others.

4 Artistic approaches to supervision demand that attention be paid to the process of classroom life and that this process be observed over extended periods of time so that the significance of events can be placed in a temporal context.

5 Artistic approaches to supervision require that rapport be established between supervisor and those supervised so that a dialogue and a sense of trust can be established between the two.

6 Artistic approaches to supervision require an ability to use language in a way that exploits its potential to make public the expressive character of what has been seen.

7 Artistic approaches to supervision require the ability to interpret the meaning of the events occurring to those who experience them and to be able to appreciate their educational import.

8 Artistic approaches to supervision accept the fact that the individual supervisor with his or her strengths, sensitivities, and experience is the major "instrument" through which the educational situation is perceived and its meaning construed.[30]

CRITICISMS OF ARTISTIC APPROACHES

Artistic approaches to supervision and evaluation are often criticized for lacking precision and for being subjective. These criticisms are undeniable, but the alternative, to limit analysis of teaching and supervisory practice to only what is precise and objective, is neither scientific nor helpful and thus is unacceptable. As we suggest in Chapter 14, a helpful and effective system of supervision must give prime attention to data that make sense to teachers. "Brute" data become sensible when interpreted and as meanings are established. But can such a subjective system of supervision be fair? How can we have confidence that the meanings have validity? The key to solving these problems rests in the person who assumes responsibility for establishing meanings. Some protections are offered, for example, if proposed meanings are offered as hypotheses and if accepted meanings are arrived at cooperatively by teacher and supervisor.

The precision issue remains important. Some argue that only data that can be accurately and precisely observed and recorded should be part of the evaluation process. Unfortunately, evaluation issues that can meet this rigorous, albeit artificial, standard are often less important than those that cannot. Limiting the evaluation to issues that lend themselves to precision can lead to a serious measurement error, often referred to as an "error of the third type." In this type of error, statistical confidence limits are correctly set and precise

---

[30] Elliot W. Eisner, "An Artistic Approach to Supervision," in Thomas J. Sergiovanni (ed.), *Supervision of Teaching,* 1982 Yearbook, Alexandria, Va.: Association for Supervision and Curriculum Development, 1982, p. 66.

measurements standards are applied but the *wrong problem* is addressed. As suggested in Chapter 14, this misplaced cogency might best be summed by Tukey's admonition: "Far better an approximate answer to the right question, which is often vague, than an exact answer to the wrong question, which can always be made precise."[31] A more helpful approach in sorting out the extent to which artistic approaches to clinical supervision are useful and the circumstances under which they are useful is to understand their limitations as well as their strengths.

THE EVALUATION PORTFOLIO

Videotaping is a common technique associated with clinical supervision and with the arts of educational connoisseurship and criticism. Indeed, videotaping can provide a useful and readily accessible representation of teaching episodes and classroom activities. But because of the selective nature of lens and screen, this technique can also frame perception and evoke slanted meanings. Further, what the screen shows always represents a choice among possibilities and therefore provides an incomplete picture. And finally, some aspects of classroom life do not lend themselves very well to lens and screen and could be neglected.[32]

Artifacts analysis and/or portfolio development, when used in conjunction with videotaping, can help provide a more complete representation of classroom life and therefore can increase meaning.[33] These approaches, however, can stand apart from videotaping and indeed can stand apart from each other.

Imagine a classroom or school deserted suddenly 20 years ago by its teacher and students and immediately being sealed. Everything there remains exactly as it was at the moment of desertion—desks, chairs, interest centers, work materials, test files, homework assignments, reading center sign-up lists, star reward charts and other "motivational devices," bulletin boards, workbooks, student notebooks, grade books, plan books, library displays, teacher workroom arrangements, student lounge-area arrangements, and so on.

Twenty years later you arrive on the scene as an amateur anthropologist intent on learning about the culture, way of life, and meaning of this class (its goals, values, beliefs, activities, norms, etc.). As you dig through the classroom, what artifacts might you collect and how might you use them to help you learn about life in this school? Suppose, for example, you were interested in discovering what was important to teachers, how teachers viewed their roles in contrast to that of students, what youngsters seemed to be learning and/or enjoying, and how time was spent. In each case what might you collect? What

---

[31] Quoted by R. Rose, "Disciplined Research and Undisciplined Problems," in C. Carol H. Weiss (ed.), *Using Social Research and Public Policy Making,* Lexington, Mass.: Heath, 1977, p. 23.
[32] This discussion follows Sergiovanni, "Reforming Teacher Evaluation," op. cit.
[33] See Patricia Scheyer and Robert Stake, "A Program's Self-Evaluation Portfolio," Urbana: University of Illinois at Urbana-Champaign, Center for Instructional Research and Curriculum Evaluation, undated mimeo, for a discussion and application of this concept for program evaluation.

inferences might you make, for example, if you were to find most of the work of students to be in the form of short-answer responses in workbooks or on ditto sheets, no student work displayed in the class, all student desks containing identical materials, and a teacher test file with most questions geared to the knowledge level of the taxonomy of educational objectives?

Portfolio development represents a teacher-evaluation strategy similar to that of artifacts analysis but with some important differences. The intent of portfolio development is to establish a file or collection of artifacts, records, photo essays, cassettes, and other materials designed to represent some aspect of the classroom program and teaching activities. Though the materials in the portfolio should be loosely collected and therefore suitable for rearrangement from time to time to reflect different aspects of the class, the portfolio should be designed with a sense of purpose. The teacher or teaching team being evaluated is responsible for assembling the portfolio and should do it in a fashion that highlights their perception of key issues and important concerns they wish to represent.

Like the artist who prepares a portfolio of his or her work to reflect a point of view, the teacher prepares a similar representation of his or her work. Together supervisor and teacher use the collected artifacts to identify key issues, to identify the dimensions of the teacher's educational platform, as evidence that targets have been met, and to identify serendipitous but worthwhile outcomes. A portfolio collection could be used, for example, to examine such issues as:

Are classroom activities compatible with the teacher's espoused educational platform and/or that of the school?

Do supervisor and teacher have compatible goals?

Are youngsters engaging in activities that require advanced cognitive thinking or is the emphasis on lower-level learning?

Do youngsters have an opportunity to influence classroom decisions?

Is the classroom program challenging all the students regardless of academic potential or are some youngsters taught too little and others too much?

Are the youngsters assuming passive or active roles in the classroom?

Is the teacher working hard? That is, is there evidence of planning, care in preparation of materials, and reflective and conscientious feedback on students' work, or are shortcuts evident?

Does the teacher understand the subject matter?

What is the nature and character of the hidden curriculum in this class?

Though portfolio development and artifacts analysis share common features, the most notable of which is the collection of artifacts, portfolio development is the responsibility of the teacher. The teacher decides what will be represented by the portfolio and the items to be included in its collection. Together the teacher and supervisor use this representation to identify issues for discussion and analysis.

A CAVEAT ON THE USE OF PORTFOLIOS

The evaluation portfolio is a good idea. But, as is the case with many other good ideas, when portfolio use is uniformly mandated or linked to a bureaucratic and measurement-oriented system of evaluation it becomes both ritualistic and burdensome. Items are collected and filed not because of reasons that make sense to teachers and supervisors but because of the characteristics of the evaluation system. In a worst-case scenario, supervisors wind up using portfolio items as a way to play "gotcha" with teachers and teachers develop padded portfolios to cover all the bases or to logjam the evaluation system. In the Texas state-mandated evaluation system in use at this writing, for example, supervisors may develop a file of memos that "document" instances of "good" and "bad" teaching in correspondence with the required teaching behaviors that appear on the state instrument. This portfolio of memos can then be used to change, for better or for worse, the teacher's score on the observation of teaching record. Such use misinterprets and misrepresents best practice use of the portfolio technique.

In this chapter we have suggested that classroom supervision and teacher evaluation are shrouded with a false sense of scientism. Though present approaches have a place and can be helpful as an exclusive or even primary strategy, they have not been effective, and, indeed, teacher evaluation is characterized by widespread doubt among teachers and supervisors. What is intended to be a rational system turns out to be rationalistic.

The proposed solution is to tighten up existing procedures, to get serious, to increase objectivity—or to otherwise emphasize even more our present technical-rational procedures. What we may not realize, however, is that the defects of technical-rational views are not just in the procedures but are inherent in underlying assumptions. The practices we suggest, those based on artistic assumptions, are emerging and are yet to be refined. Much more work needs to be done by *practicing supervisors* and their university counterparts in developing these ideas.

The primary emphasis in this chapter is on formative evaluation. But supervisors must also concern themselves with summative evaluation. They must check to be sure that teachers are performing at an acceptable level to ensure quality control for the sake of the public and the children. This problem is considered in the next section.

SUMMATIVE EVALUATION OF TEACHERS' PERFORMANCE

Suppose it is part of your job to evaluate teachers' performance and to recommend or decide, based on that evaluation, whether to retain, promote, or grant them tenure. As a person with supervisory responsibilities you have two basic questions to answer:

1 How can I evaluate a teacher responsibly and professionally?
2 How can I evaluate a teacher's performance (with the assumption that it

will inevitably result in some critical judgments) and at the same time retain my role as facilitator of teacher growth?

For many supervisors, the second question poses the real dilemma. If one assumes that the purpose of supervision is to help teachers grow and improve their classroom effectiveness, an objective that requires trust and a collegial relationship, then to evaluate a teacher's performance will undermine that trust and cancel one's ability to facilitate teacher growth. This may be the primary reason why supervisors typically avoid evaluation. This part of a supervisor's job seems to place him or her in an adversarial, judgmental relationship with a teacher. The teacher will feel threatened and thus will not trust the supervisor, and he or she will tend to be defensive, closed, and legalistic in their relationship.

The first question poses serious difficulty as well. Anyone who has experienced the pain of telling a teacher that his or her performance does not measure up and that it would be best to seek employment elsewhere knows how difficult it is to document in a clear and unambiguous analysis the reasons why an unfavorable decision was rendered.

A review of the literature on supervision reveals that this aspect of teacher evaluation receives rather thin treatment. It is more important to talk about the formative aspects of teacher evaluation than the summative aspects. Exploring ways to generate teacher improvement through a shared quest with the teacher ought to be the emphasis for supervisors. We agree wholeheartedly with that emphasis. The uncomfortable reality of performance evaluation, however, will not disappear simply because theoreticians wish it would. Nor will the professional responsibility for someone in the school or school district to evaluate teacher performance disappear simply because it is done badly, or sporadically, or not at all.

SOME PROBLEMS WITH TEACHER EVALUATION
FOR PERSONNEL DECISIONS

When faced with responsibilities to evaluate the performance of teachers to determine if it "measures up," supervisors should beware of possible evaluation "land mines." Many of these land mines concern facile and unsupportable assumptions that can explode if not carefully examined and avoided. Consider the following examples.

Assumption 1. There is a clear set of criteria or standards understood and accepted by all with which a teacher's performance can be evaluated.

Assumption 2. Sporadic, unannounced classroom visits, with no prior conversation and no subsequent discussion, are a legitimate and an acceptable way to assess teacher performance.

Assumption 3. Student achievement of course objectives is the only way to evaluate teacher performance.

Assumption 4. Evaluation of teacher performance should only deal with observable classroom behaviors.

Assumption 5. One or two class visits are all that is required to make judgments about the quality of a teacher's performance to make decisions about retention, tenure, and promotion.

These five assumptions will not measure up to rigorous cross-examination. If a supervisor, acting on these assumptions, were to render a recommendation or a decision not to rehire a teacher or not to grant tenure, the supervisor would encounter legal and professional difficulty. Courts have established very clearly that teachers, even beginning teachers, must be given due process. The essence of due process is that teachers know beforehand the criteria or standards as well as the procedures by which they will be evaluated, and that these procedures and standards have in fact been followed. Beyond due-process concerns, the very criteria and standards and procedures that a school or school system establishes for such evaluation can be challenged, as well as the evidence used to arrive at the unfavorable judgment.

Furthermore, a supervisor cannot employ haphazard procedures in visiting classes. Visits have to be preceded and followed by discussions with the teacher in which the purposes of the visit are established, an analysis of the class activity developed, and specific improvement efforts agreed upon. Some predictable and clearly understood procedures, acted upon over a period of time, have to be followed.

Even when a more detailed process is followed, there are questions both teacher and supervisor must clarify.

1 Is the evaluation seeking to determine whether certain specific teacher skills are practiced at all, are practiced with a certain mastery, or are practiced to a superior degree? In other words, is the evaluation seeking to establish evidence of rock-bottom, minimum competency of the teacher for decisions about retention, or is the evaluation to establish evidence of superior teaching qualities for merit or promotion?

2 What is the time frame of the evaluation? Suppose the first few evaluation sessions reveal several basic deficiencies. Will the teacher have an opportunity to correct those deficiencies before judgment is passed? If so, how much time will the teacher have before a decision will be made?

3 Are there serious differences between the educational platform of the supervisor and that of the teacher? Is the platform of either clearly out of phase with the educational platform of the school? If such differences exist, must they be reconciled? If so, who will arbitrate the reconciliation? If not, on whose platform will the teacher be evaluated?

4 Is the evaluation intended to be exercised in an exclusively summative way, or does it take place in a larger framework of formative evaluation and staff development? In other words, does the evaluation assume a static state, or is teacher growth primarily what is being assessed?

5 What evidence from student achievement and effective response to the teacher will enter into the evaluation?

6 Will observation and evaluation by a third party be used to establish the validity of the conclusions reached by the supervisor? If so, will the teacher being evaluated have any say about who that third party is?

7 If the evaluation is particularly rigorous, can the teacher cite examples of other teachers who received a far less rigorous evaluation? In other words, are there grounds for claiming that one is being singled out, or harassed, perhaps for extraneous reasons (race, age, sex, religion, ethnicity)?

Other equally important questions could be raised about aspects of summative evaluation of teacher performance. The above questions simply point to the general conclusion that a supervisor must think through the process he or she will use very carefully. More than likely, the school or school system will already have developed a plan and a procedure for carrying out performance evaluation. This plan should be reviewed with other supervisors and improved as circumstances may call for. Representatives from faculty groups should also participate in the formation and modification of evaluation policies and procedures where teachers are organized. The union or association should be formally involved. Not only does such involvement make practical sense, it assumes that teachers too have a legitimate stake in and professional concern for maintaining minimum teaching standards.

Dealing with Extremes

Let us consider three situations where evaluation of teacher performance might lead to nonretention of the teacher.

1 Probably the easiest solution to deal with is a teacher who is so ineffective that it would be obvious to almost anyone that he or she should not be in a classroom. As a supervisor, your first visit to the class of this beginning teacher reveals that the teacher physically and verbally bullies the children in class, that children are intimidated, frightened, and angry, that the teacher responds to questions by personal insults and ridicule of the students, and that for most of the class time the teacher sits at the desk saying nothing while the children are simply required to read the textbook and do the exercises at the end of the chapter. Further discussions and visits reveal that this pattern continues, with the teacher refusing to alter his behavior.

By documenting this behavior of the teacher, having another teacher, supervisor, or administrator visit the class to corroborate your reports, and by putting in writing your recommendations for improvement, with the clear statement that his present behavior is unacceptable and must be changed, you can show that you have no alternative but to remove this teacher as soon as possible.

2 As a supervisor your visits to this teacher's classroom reveal a technically competent teacher. This teacher shows some of the behaviors called for in the research on effectiveness for achievement in basic learning skills. But you also find that the teacher holds to very narrow but strong religious convictions, and that she preaches these views to a religiously pluralistic class of students at every opportunity and unambiguously proposes her views as the only acceptable way to salvation. In this instance, you have on your hands a teacher who possesses certain technical teaching skills but whose educational platform is infused with religious values that aggressively deny any validity to other interpretations of ethical behavior. After several conversations with this teacher, you have evidence that she refuses to change her behavior. This involves the delicate issue of religious freedom, but you are convinced that the teacher is violating accepted professional practice in public education and is doing serious harm to some of the students in her class.

In this case, the supervisor should consult with school district officials, and perhaps with legal counsel, about ways to proceed. By following due process, however, and using extreme tactfulness, the supervisor can succeed in having that teacher removed.

3 A more difficult situation for supervisors involves a teacher with tenure whose performance occasionally rises to a level of mediocrity, but whose classes are normally dull and oppressive. Repeated efforts to get him to improve meet with verbal agreement but no improvement in practice. While his colleagues agree that he is an inferior teacher, and parents and students complain, the teacher union will not support efforts to remove him. In this instance, should you spend a lot of time and energy trying to get him to improve or spend even more time and energy trying to get him fired, or should you recommend administrative action whereby he will be transferred out of the classroom into some noninstructional job? A lot will depend on individual circumstances. Most experienced supervisors know of one or more cases like this, and they are a constant source of aggravation. In large public organizations, sometimes there is little one can do to change an incompetent veteran. The mistake was made years ago when he could have been weeded out.

Human Resource Development and Judgments about Performance

Let us assume we are beyond the stage of evaluating performance for job retention decisions. The question facing a human resource development supervisor is nonetheless quite real: How can I make an evaluative judgment on teachers' performance without destroying the trust and collegial relationship by which I exercise my human resources style of supervision? Even though teachers may feel secure in their job, will not critical judgments of their performance lead to resentment, defensiveness, and distance?

The reactions of teachers to negative assessment of their performance will depend on a variety of factors. Some of these factors will be personality variables, such as how teachers and supervisors deal with authority and the tact and sensitivity with which supervisors express themselves. Some of these factors will be process variables, such as whether there is a shared sense of purpose, an agreed-upon focus to evaluation episodes, a use of self-evaluation, a thorough discussion of the impressions of the supervisor after the class visit, the setting of clear growth targets, and so on. Other factors may relate to the overall climate in the school system, such as the feelings of an adversarial relationship between teachers and school board and superintendent, how teacher cutbacks are handled, levels of teacher dissatisfaction with conditions of their workplace, and so on. The latter factors are normally beyond the control of the supervisor.

Much of the resentment and defensiveness of teachers toward being evaluated will be diffused if the evaluation takes place in a clearly understood, mutually agreed-upon plan. Teachers want to know and deserve to know what the ground rules are. They also want to feel that those rules reflect their own thinking about how teachers should be evaluated. They will feel even more comfortable (or less uncomfortable) with performance evaluation if it is placed in a larger framework of formative evaluation and staff development. Hence we propose that the concerns of this chapter be situated within the larger perspectives developed in the next chapter.

One key to successful evaluation is the encouragement of self-evaluation. The evaluation by the supervisor should probably follow an initial attempt by the teacher to assess strengths and weaknesses. Furthermore, the teacher should be encouraged to use this self-evaluation to generate some needed growth targets. The evaluation of the supervisor can then support the teacher's own conclusions and the two of them can work on ways to build on strengths and improve on some weak areas. Self-assessment allows the teacher to set the initial agenda, to retain a sense of dignity because the judgment has been made initially by himself or herself. The supervisor may have some additional points to raise, but all things being equal, should hold off on them initially to work with the teacher on those points that seem significant to him or her.

Facing the Music

Some supervisors have high affiliation needs and hence are very reluctant to deal with anything potentially damaging to their relationships with teachers. Other supervisors have low affiliation needs and are insensitive to the feelings of teachers when expressing their evaluations. Both kinds of supervisors need to recognize that making judgments about the performance of others can be painful, but that it is a necessary part of the enterprise of maintaining and improving the learning environment for students. It is better to get those feelings out in the open, to deal with them in an adult and professional manner, and to get on with the task. Tiptoeing around the sensitivities involved will not make them go away. Making believe that no one is responsible for assessing the quality of instruction is irresponsible. Pointing only to the growth and development side of evaluation and not admitting that teachers also receive grades or performance ratings every year is not facing the realities of the school setting.

These realities can be faced honestly and rationally and can even be the source of improved performance and growth. Summative evaluation of teachers' performance, then, is not intrinsically contrary to human resource development supervision. In fact, the summative and the formative stages of the larger evaluation process can complement each other. If the supervisor and teacher work more and more as a team, then the summative evaluation that emerges can be more and more a team assessment. The following chapter highlights constructive approaches to staff development that can create a positive environment for the difficult task of performance evaluation.

DIFFERENT PURPOSES, DIFFERENT STANDARDS

One theme of this chapter is that different teacher-evaluation purposes require different teacher-evaluation standards and criteria. When the purpose is quality control to ensure that teachers measure up, standards, criteria, expectations, and procedures take one form. When the purpose is professional improvement to help increase teachers' understanding and enhanced teaching practice standards, criteria, expectations, and procedures take on a different form. In evaluation for quality control the process is formal and documented; criteria are explicit and standards are uniform for all teachers; criteria are legally defensible as being central to basic teaching competence; the emphasis is on teachers meeting requirements of minimum acceptability; and responsibility for evaluation is in the hands of administrators and other designated officials. When the purpose of teacher evaluation is professional improvement, the process is informal; criteria are tailored to the needs and capabilities of individual teachers; criteria are considered to be appropriate and useful to teachers before they are included in the evaluation; the emphasis is on helping teachers reach agreed-upon professional development goals; and teachers assume major responsibility for the process by engaging in self-evaluation and collegial evaluation, and by obtaining evaluation information from students.

The outcome of evaluation for quality control is the protection of students and the public from incompetent teaching. Unquestionably this is an important outcome and a highly significant responsibility for principals and other supervisors. The outcome of evaluation for professional improvement is quite different. Rather than ensuring minimum acceptability in teaching, professional improvement guarantees quality teaching and schooling for the students and the public.

The 80/20 Quality Rule

The 80/20 quality rule spells out quite clearly what the balance of emphasis should be as schools, school districts, and states engage in teacher evaluation. *When more than 20 percent of supervisory time and money is expended in evaluation for quality control or less than 80 percent of supervisory time and money is spent in professional improvement, quality schooling suffers.* The 80/20 quality rule provides a framework for those responsible for evaluation of teachers to evaluate whether their efforts are indeed directed toward quality schooling. In making this assessment, one should give less attention to the rhetoric that one hears (that is, to what those responsible for teacher evaluation say their purposes are) but more to the standards and procedures that they use. The standards and procedures associated with each of the two purposes of evaluation are outlined in Table 16-3. If the standards to the left of the table are emphasized, quality control is the purpose of the evaluation regardless of what is said about the purposes. We should be less concerned with what officials claim to be the "espoused theory" of evaluation and more with their "theory in use."

SUMMARY

This chapter was concerned with clinical supervision and teacher evaluation. It was suggested that by and large supervisors and others responsible for teacher evaluation privately view the procedures as lacking in credibility. The technology of present practices was characterized as scientific management and the underlying assumptions as technical-rational. The integrity of these approaches with respect to their application to school settings was questioned. Artistic assumptions and practices were then discussed as alternatives more fitting the nature of teaching and learning practices. Clinical supervision, in the specific sense of a

TABLE 16-3
PURPOSES AND STANDARDS FOR EVALUATION

Purposes	
Quality control (ensuring that teachers meet acceptable levels of performance)	Professional improvement (increasing understanding of teaching and enhancing practice)
Standards	
The process is formal and documented.	The process is informal.
Criteria are explicit, standard, and uniform for all teachers.	Criteria are tailored to needs and capabilities of individual teachers.
Criteria are legally defensible as being central to basic teaching competence.	Criteria are considered appropriate and useful to teachers.
Emphasis is on meeting minimum requirements of acceptability.	Emphasis is on helping teachers reach agreed-upon professional development goals.
Evaluation by administrators and other designated officials counts the most.	Self-evaluation, collegial evaluation, and evaluation information for students count the most.
Outcome	
Protects students and the public from incompetent teaching.	Guarantees quality teaching and schooling for students and the public.

The 80/20 Quality Rule: When more than 20 percent of supervisory time and money is expended in evaluation for quality control *or* less than 80 percent of supervisory time and money is expended in professional improvement, quality schooling suffers.

supervisory cycle associated with Cogan and of adaptations of this process were then presented as fairly well developed techniques with artistic potential. It was argued that clinical supervision can and should take many forms and that more experimentation with different forms is needed. A theoretical framework was offered as a means to understand this process. Basic to the framework was the assumption that teacher behavior is governed by the interplay of two theories: an espoused theory, which represents the teacher's public educational platform and a theory in use, which represents the teacher's actual educational platform. Sometimes the actual platform is unknown to the teacher. Theory in use is inferred from classroom observations, analysis of videotapes, collected artifacts and portfolios, and other techniques. Confronting an individual with a theory in use inconsistent with that person's espoused theory results in the surfacing of dilemmas that she or he seeks to resolve. This process acts as a stimulus to change and a means to generate substantial change issues. Emerging artistic techniques were then presented either as methods by which theories in use might be constructed or as techniques to use independently of clinical supervision. These include concepts of educational connoisseurship and criticism and practices of artifact collecting and portfolio development.

Attention then shifted to the summative evaluation of teachers' performance and the problems that supervisors face when they evaluate for personnel decisions. Noting that different purposes for supervision and evaluation require different standards, the 80/20 quality rule was then proposed.

STUDY GUIDE

Recall the concepts, ideas, and meanings associated with each of the following phrases and terms included in this chapter. Can you discuss each of them with a colleague and apply them to the supervisory context of your school? If you cannot, review them in the text and record the page numbers for future reference.

1 Artistic evaluation
2 Brute data
3 Clinical supervision
4 Clinical supervision cycle
5 Connoisseurship in education
6 Criticism in education
7 Disclosure
8 Educational platform
9 80/20 quality rule
10 Espoused theory
11 Evaluation
12 Evaluation portfolio
13 Evaluation purposes
14 Formative evaluation
15 General supervision

16 Johari Window
17 Measurement
18 Picturing
19 Sense data
20 Summative evaluation
21 Technical-rational values
22 Theory in use

EXERCISES

1 Our contrast of technical-rational assumptions and practices and artistic assumptions and practices deliberately separates the views in an opposing fashion and indeed sets up the technical-rational assumptions as "straw men." Rewrite this section, showing the contrast between technical-rational and artistic assumptions as complementary and supplementary rather than competing, with each set adding power and meaning to the other.
2 Refer to Figure 16-1. Assuming the role of supervisor, identify three teachers in your school. For each, prepare a list of "public or open self" traits of his or her teaching. Compare the lists. Do the same sorts of characteristics appear in the "public self" for all three teachers? Repeat this procedure for the "blind self" quadrant. If you are a teacher, what sorts of characteristics would you write about your teaching in the "hidden or secret self" quadrant?
3 How would you describe concepts of educational connoisseurship and criticism to your superintendent?
4 Ask one or two teachers to prepare a portfolio collection over a span of two weeks or artifacts that highlight a particular issue, such as individualized instruction or whether youngsters are assuming more active roles in the classroom. How might the collection of artifacts and portfolio development be used to supplement more traditional "rating scale" approaches to teacher evaluation?
5 Apply the 80/20 quality rule to your school. To what extent are evaluations for quality control and for professional development emphasized?

CHAPTER 17

SUPERVISION AS STAFF DEVELOPMENT

Only a thin line exists between what we normally consider to be supervision and staff development. In fact supervision well done is a form of staff development and staff development conceived most effectively is part of the school's daily routine emphasis on personal and professional improvement. With this thought in mind it is useful to think of staff development as representing a range of possibilities and emphases. Among these are informal classroom visits, clinical supervision, collegial supervision, quality circles, workshops, field trips, institute days, mentoring relationships, and individual professional development efforts. The power of each of these possibilities to promote professional development and school improvement is enhanced when they are part of the same effort. The best workshops are related to teacher-identified problems and issues that emerge from classroom supervision. And teaching practice improves when linked to problems and issues examined in more formal staff development settings.

TECHNICAL COMPETENCE IN TEACHING

Teaching conceived as the expression of technical competence is the driving force behind most models of supervision and teacher evaluation in use today. It is as well the basis for most staff-development programs. An example of concern for technical competence is focusing on a list of teaching behaviors found to be linked to certain dimensions of teaching effectiveness. When technical competence is overemphasized, such teaching behaviors inevitably find themselves on evaluation checklists and become the basis for developing companion supervisory strategies designed to check for and encourage their use. Completing this picture are workshops and other staff-development efforts designed to teach how to use the behaviors and to provide tips to supervisors as to how they might be assessed.

As a general rule, the particular teaching competency being addressed and its resulting view of teaching determine the kind of supervisory and staff-development practices that are used. Technical teaching competency is indeed important to successful teaching and learning. But the question is, is this the only type of competency of concern to teaching? If the answer is no, what other types of teaching competency should be addressed by supervision and staff development? Further, should other types of teaching competency suggest other and better matched supervisory and staff-development practices?

CLINICAL, PERSONAL, AND CRITICAL TEACHING COMPETENCIES

In a groundbreaking synthesis of a broad range of philosophical, theoretical, and research knowledge on successful teaching practices, Zimpher and Howey describe four major types of teaching competence that they believe can be facilitated by appropriate supervisory and staff-development practices: technical, clinical, personal, and critical.[1] The four are depicted and discussed in Table 17-1. Zimpher and Howey maintain that all four competency types are essential to good teaching and that each should be considered in choosing appropriate supervisory practice and determining appropriate emphasis in staff-development programs. When the emphasis is on clinical competence the teacher functions as a problem solver and expert clinician who frames problems and issues and comes to grips with solutions. The image of teaching as reflective decision making is at the heart of clinical competence. Supervisory and staff-development efforts that enhance inquiry, encourage reflection, build problem-solving skills, and help teachers make more informed decisions about their practice address the clinical competence.

When the emphasis is on personal competence the teacher functions as one able to understand and interpret his or her teaching in a manner that provides for meaning and significance. Supervision and staff development addresses personal competence by helping increase teacher self-awareness, understanding of his or her teaching practice, and interpretive capacities.

Critical competence deals with issues of value and importance in the hidden meanings that underlie teaching practice. Within the critical competence teaching is viewed as an ethical science concerned with worth and purpose. Technical competence, for example, emphasizes doing things right. Critical competence, by contrast, emphasizes what is worth doing and doing right things.

Zimpher and Howey's detailed description of each of the four types of competence can be used by supervisors to evaluate the balance of emphasis

[1] Nancy Z. Zimpher and Kenneth R. Howey, "Adapting Supervisory Practice to Different Orientations of Teaching Competence," *Journal of Curriculum and Supervision*, vol. 2, no. 1, pp. 101–127, 1987.

TABLE 17-1
ZIMPHER AND HOWEY: FRAMEWORK FOR EXAMINING FOUR TYPES OF TEACHING COMPETENCE

	Technical competence	Clinical competence	Personal competence	Critical competence
Conception of the teacher	Determines in advance what is to be learned, how it is to be learned, and criteria by which success is to be measured	Instructional problem solver; clinician frames and solves practical problems; takes reflective action; inquirer	Understanding of self; self-actualized person who uses self as effective and humane instrument	Rational, morally autonomous, socially conscious change agent
Focus of supervision	Mastery of methods of instruction: specific skills (how to ask good questions); how to apply teaching strategies; how to select and organize curriculum content; how to structure the classroom for learning what techniques to use to maintain control	Reflective decision making and action to solve practical problems (what should be done about disruptive behavior) as well as reconsideration of intents and practices to take action to solve practical problems	Increase self-awareness, identity formation, and interpretive capacities, e.g., self-confrontation; values clarification; interpersonal involvement; small-group processes; develop personal style in teaching roles	Reflective decision making and action to form more rational and just schools, critique of stereotypes/ ideology, hidden curriculum, authoritarian/ permissive relationships, equality of access, responsibilities, and forms of repressive social control
Conception of the supervisor	Technical expert/master provides for skill development and efficient/effective use of resources in classroom; translator of research theory into technical rules for application in classrooms	Fosters inquiry regarding the relationship of theory and practice: fosters reflection about the relationship of intents and practice and reconsideration/modification of intent/practice in light of evaluation of their conscience	Expert in interpersonal competence and theories of human development; nondirective participant: warm and supportive learning environment, responsiveness to teacher-defined needs and concerns, wisdom in guiding free exploration of teaching episodes, diagnosing theories-in-use	Collaborator in self-reflective communities of practitioner-theorists committed to examining critically their own/institutional practices and improving them in interests of nationality and social justice; provides challenges and support as do other participants in dialogue

Type of theoretical knowledge	Technical guidelines from explanatory theory; analytic craft knowledge about what constitutes "good" practice	Synthesis of normative, interpretive, and explanatory knowledge to form intellectually and morally defensible practical judgments about what to do in a particular situation	Analytic and interpretive theory to understand and make explicit reasons underlying symbolic interaction essentially those which occur in the class	Critical theory of education; unite philosophical analysis and criticism and causal and interpretive science
Mode of inquiry	Applied science, functional and task analysis, linear problem solving to determine how to accomplish given ends	Practical action research to articulate concerns, plan action, monitor action, and reflect on processes and consequences to improve our teaching practices; rationale building	Phenomenological, ethnographic, hermeneuticanalysis and interpretation; analyze elements of teaching episodes	Collaborative action and reflection to transform the organization and practice of education; group inquiry regarding conditions of communicative interaction and social control
Level of reflectivity	Specific techniques needed to reach stated objectives involve instrumental reasoning; means-end (if, then) relative to efficiency/effectiveness	Practical reasoning and judgment relative to what should be done (best course of action under the circumstances)	Interpretation of intended meaning of verbal and nonverbal symbols and acts; introspection relative to self-awareness/identity	Critical self-reflection; reflexivity and social critique to uncover contradictions/inadequacies and different conceptions of educational practice as values with society
Range of complexity	From: Learning/using specific skills To: Learning/using complex curricular and instructional systems	From: Examining what one is doing in the classroom and making needed changes (inquiry and reflection about one's teaching) To: Action research and practical deliberation among colleagues in school/district to solve common educational concerns	From: Self-awareness and survival concerns To: Using knowledge of adult moral and cognitive development to inform teacher practice	From: Consciousness raising about school practices that are self-defeating in terms of learning and teaching, such as exposing hidden curriculum To: Collaboration of critical inquirers to reconstruct/transform schooling/society

From Nancy L. Zimpher anc Kenneth R. Howey. "Adapting Supervisory Practices to Different Orientations of Teaching," *Journal of Curriculum and Supervision*, vol. 2, no. 2, 1987. This table combines Table 1 and Table 2 from their article. Zimpher and Howey acknowledged the major contribution of Sharon Strom, a doctoral candidate at the University of Minnesota, in the development of Tables 1 and 2.

that characterizes present school practice. Using Table 17-1, readers might, for example, examine teacher-evaluation practices now in use in their schools, the dominant models of supervision that accompany these practices, and the content and structure of staff development programs that have occurred over the past two years. Then using a total of 100 points, assign points to each of the four critical competencies to reflect the emphasis that characterizes current practice. The following grid might be helpful:

	Technical competence	Clinical competence	Personal competence	Critical competence	Total points
Evaluation practices					100
Supervision models					100
Staff development purposes, content, structure					100
Total					300

A best distribution among the four types of teaching competence cannot, of course, be determined separate from the characteristics of the situation at hand. A school with a large proportion of novice teachers might well need more attention to the technical competencies of teaching, and, by contrast, a school with a large proportion of highly accomplished and experienced techers might need more attention to other types of teaching competence. Total the points in each of the competency columns and using 300 points as base, determine the percentage of emphasis across the four competency areas.

STAFF DEVELOPMENT AND IN-SERVICE EDUCATION

Not only is it desirable to provide a balance among the four types of teaching competence but a better balance is needed as well between directive and highly structured professional improvement efforts and those more informal and teacher-directed. Though in-service education of teachers has a long history, present practices have many shortcomings and have not been met with enthusiasm by teachers. Reasons often given are that in-service is often too formal and bureaucratic, characterized by a high degree of administrative planning and scheduling. A successful in-service program becomes one that meets legal requirements and is executed smoothly, efficiently, and according to schedule. Program activities are often selected and developed for uniform dissemination without serious consideration of the purposes of such activities and of the needs of individual teachers. High structure, uniformity, and tight control from above result in a *training* rather than education emphasis. We are not suggesting that such in-service education programs be abandoned, for they have utility. We are proposing, however, that they be emphasized less.

Staff development is not something the school does to the teacher but something the teacher does for himself or herself. Staff development is basically growth-oriented. Traditional in-service, on the other hand, typically assumes a deficiency in the teacher and presupposes a set of appropriate ideas, skills, and methods that need developing. In-service works to reduce the teacher's range of alternatives—indeed to bring about conformity. Staff development does not assume a deficiency in the teacher, but instead assumes a need for people at work to grow and develop on the job. Rather than reduce the range of alternatives, staff development works to increase this range.

Teacher growth is less a function of polishing existing teaching skills or of keeping up with the latest teaching developments and more a function of a teacher's changing as a person—of seeing himself or herself, the school, the curriculum, and students differently. One should not have to make a choice between the two, for both are important. But it is the latter sort of change that is the essence of the staff-development orientation. The former emphasizes keeping teachers up to standard, the latter the continual raising of quality.

In sum, the distinctions we make between an in-service education and staff-development orientation is a *conceptual* one designed to help supervisors gauge their own thinking and monitor their own activities with better balance in the hope that we might be more responsive to teacher needs. The in-service orientation is necessary at times and seems best matched to formal intervention strategies. The staff-development orientation should receive major focus and seems best matched to informal intervention strategies. Though the emphasis of each may differ, both are concerned with remediation and growth.

A DESIGN FOR STAFF DEVELOPMENT

In the section that follows, a design for staff development is presented. This design is composed of five critical components: *intents, substance, competency areas, approach,* and *responsibility.* The design requires staff-development planners to be concerned about program intents and substance and, in turn, to match these with appropriate approaches, competency levels, and responsibility designations. Let us consider each of the components separately.

Intents

Staff-development programs and activities are typically designed around such themes as presenting information of one kind or another, helping teachers understand this information, helping teachers apply this understanding in their teaching, and helping teachers to accept, and be committed to, these new approaches. Presenting information is a *knowledge*-level intent. A program, for example, might be designed to introduce a group of science teachers to the concept and language of inquiry teaching. Promoting understanding is a *comprehension*-level intent. The intent here might be to help teachers to understand how inquiry teaching might affect the way they presently plan and organize instruction. Using inquiry methods effectively in teaching a particular biology unit is an example of an *applications*-level intent. Though each of these levels is necessary, none is sufficient to gain sustained use of inquiry methods by teachers. Teachers may be able to demonstrate such methods on demand but are not likely to use them once out of the spotlight unless they believe in, and are committed to, such methods. Becoming committed to inquiry methods as a useful approach to science teaching is a *value-* and *attitude-integration-* level intent.

Often only knowledge and comprehension levels are legitimately appropriate focuses for staff-development programs. But programs specifically designed to meet intents at these levels are not likely to be sufficient for such higher levels as value and attitude integration. By the same token programs designed for higher-level intents, when only knowledge-level intents are necessary, may well be too elaborate, wasteful, and exhausting for both supervisors and teachers.

Substance

Rubin has identified four critical factors in good teaching, each of which he believes can be improved through appropriate staff-development activities:

> The teacher's sense of purpose
> The teacher's perception of students
> The teacher's knowledge of subject matter
> The teacher's mastery of technique[2]

Sense of purpose and perception of students are part of a teacher's *educational platform* and as such represent values, beliefs, assumptions, and action theories a teacher holds about the nature of knowledge, how students learn, appropriate relationships between students and teachers, and other factors. One's educational platform becomes the basis for decisions one makes about classroom organization and teaching, and, indeed, once a platform is known, key decisions the teacher will make can be predicted with reliability.

A teacher, for example, who considers his or her purpose to be imparting information is likely to rely heavily on teacher talk and formal classroom arrangements. Likewise, a teacher who perceives youngsters as being basically

---

[2] Louis J. Rubin, "The Case for Staff Development," in Thomas J. Sergiovanni (ed.), *Professional Supervision for Professional Teachers,* Washington, D.C.: Association for Supervision and Curriculum Development, 1975.

trustworthy and responsible is likely to share responsibilities for decisions about learning with the class. If a supervisor were interested in reducing teacher talk and/or increasing student responsibility, he or she would have to contend with the critical factor of purpose and perception of teachers. His or her target is the restructuring of educational platforms of teachers.

In describing the importance of knowledge of subject matter, Rubin notes:

> There is a considerable difference between the kind of teaching that goes on when teachers have an intimate acquaintance with the content of the lesson and when the acquaintance is only peripheral. When teachers are genuinely knowledgeable, when they know their subject well enough to discriminate betwen the seminal ideas and the secondary matter, when they can go beyond what is in the textbook, the quality of the pedagogy becomes extraordinarily impressive. For it is only when a teacher has a consummate grasp of, say, arithmetic, physics, or history that their meaning can be turned outward and brought to bear upon the learner's personal experience. Relevancy lies less in the inherent nature of a subject than in its relationship to the child's frame of reference. In the hands of a skilled teacher, poetry can be taught with success and profit to ghetto children.[3]

Though content versus process arguments continue from time to time, both aspects of instruction are necessary for effective teaching. Our observation is that the less the teacher knows about a particular subject the more trivial the teaching and the more defensive the pedagogy. By defensive pedagogy we mean dominance by the teacher and strict adherence to curriculum materials. But one can have a great appreciation for a particular field of study and still not be able to disclose its wonder and excitement effectively. Mastery of technique, classroom organization and management, and other pedagogical skills make up the fourth critical dimension of effective teaching. Each of the critical factors in good teaching can be understood and developed as technical, clinical, personal, or critical teaching competence.

These dimensions are the basis for deciding the substance of staff-development programs. Comprehensive programs are concerned with all four—the teacher's conception of purpose, sensitivity to students, intimacy with subject matter, and basic repertory of teaching techniques.

Competency Areas

What are the major competency *areas* for which teachers should be accountable? It is reasonable to expect that teachers, as is the case with other professionals, *know how* to do their jobs and to keep up with major developments. The areas of knowledge for professional teaching are suggested above— knowledge about purposes, students, subject matter, and techniques. But knowing and understanding are not enough. Teachers are expected to put their knowledge to work—to demonstrate that they *can do* the job. Demonstrating knowledge, however, is a fairly low-level competency. Most teachers are

[3] Ibid., p. 47.

competent enough and clever enough to come up with the right teaching performance when the supervisor is around. The proof of the pudding is whether they *will do* the job of their own free will and on a sustained basis. Finally, professionals are expected to engage in a lifelong commitment to self-improvement. Self-improvement is the *will-grow* competency area. Self-employed professionals (doctors, accountants, etc.) are forced by competition and by visible product evaluation to give major attention to the will-grow dimension. Teachers, as organizational professionals whose "products" are difficult to measure, have not felt this external pressure for continuing professional growth. Increasingly, however, school districts are making the will-grow dimension a contractual obligation, and indeed teachers who are perfectly satisfactory in the know-how, can-do, and will-do competency areas face sanctions (including dismissal) for less than satisfactory commitment to continuing professional growth.

The relationships between competency areas, intents, and substance are shown in Figure 17-1. Let us begin explaining this figure with the know-how competency area. Knowledge- and comprehension-level intents are associated with this competency area, and the teacher is expected to know and understand purposes, students, subject matter, and techniques. In the can-do area, teachers apply this knowledge of substance to their classrooms. The will-do area, however, requires not only ability to apply this knowledge but also an identity and commitment to the application. Staff-development programs aimed at the will-do dimension must have value and attitude integration as well as application intents. Will-grow is equally dependent upon value- and attitude-integration intents. It follows, then, that supervisors who are interested in working with teachers in the will-do and will-grow competency areas and who choose programs and strategies suited only to knowledge and comprehension (they invite an expert from the state university to speak to teachers about inquiry teaching) are not likely to be successful.

FIGURE 17-1
Building a design for staff development.

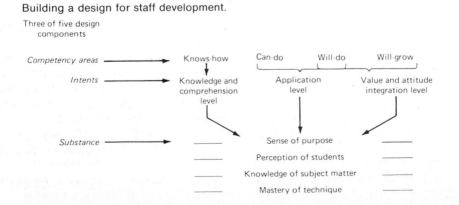

Approach and Responsibility

We have now discussed three of five design components for staff development: intents, substance, and competence areas. Two more remain: the strategy, or *approach,* to staff development and the locus of major *responsibility.* Approaches can be grouped into three general categories: traditional, informal, and intermediate. Traditional approaches are generally more formal and structured and are designed to meet specific and uniform objectives. Informal approaches, on the other hand, are very low in structure and rely on discovery and exploration techniques. Often objectives are not predetermined but are discovered or assessed after the fact. Intermediate approaches are moderately structured with a predetermined agenda that permits a great deal of flexibility. Let us consider each approach briefly.

Traditional Approaches and Administrative Responsibility Traditional approaches to staff development are well known to supervisors and administrators and need little elaboration. They seem best suited when a staff-development problem can be defined as a deficit in knowledge of some kind. Traditional approaches are typically accompanied by clear objectives and rely on conventional, though well-executed, instruction. Teachers generally assume passive roles and are exposed to logically structured programs or activities. Techniques most often used are lecture, illustrated lecture, demonstration, and observation, often followed by guided discussion activities.

Traditional approaches seem well suited to routine information updating of the latest books, techniques, principles, and ideas relating to one's work. It is assumed not that a particular group is considering adopting something new, but that the group is only learning more about it. As intents change from learning to understanding, to applying, to integrating new things into one's repertoire of behavior, approaches will need to change if staff development is to be effective. If one were to generalize about intents of staff development programs typically found in schools, the widespread use of traditional approaches to the virtual exclusion of other approaches would lead one to conclude that educators have an insatiable appetite for knowledge but are not interested in doing very much with this knowledge.

The locus of responsibility for traditional approaches to staff development is with the administration as it executes its personnel administration functions. Though traditional approaches have a place and should remain administrative responsibilities, alone they represent a minimum commitment to staff development.

Informal Approaches and Teacher Responsibility Perhaps the most innovative and provocative approaches to staff development are those that rely on exploration and discovery by teachers. It is assumed that by providing teachers with a rich environment loaded with teaching materials, media, books, and devices, and that with generous encouragement and support from principals and supervisors, teachers will interact with this environment and with each other through exploration and discovery. Exploration and discovery can help many teachers to find themselves, to unleash their creativity, to learn more about their own capabilities as people and teachers, and at the same time to pick up new teaching ideas, activities, and methods.

Thelen notes that in the most useful staff-development programs "one finds intensity of personal involvement, immediate consequences for classroom practice, stimulation and ego support by meaningful associates in the situation and initiating by teacher rather than outside."[4] Informal approaches seem best able to meet these critieria, and because of their enormous potential, such approaches should play an important role in school district staff-development planning.

Major responsibility for informal approaches rests with teachers. Such efforts can take a variety of forms. Two teachers sharing ideas, a team or family of teachers working and planning together, teacher involvement in an in-building resource center, and participation in district or area teacher centers are examples. Informal staff-development approaches should be encouraged and supported. Indeed, the benefits derived from approaches are a good reason for supervisors and administrators to advocate patterns of instruction that encourage teachers to plan and work together. Team teaching, schools within the school, and family grouping are examples of arrangements that naturally stimulate informal staff-development activities.

Teacher centers deserve special attention in that they represent fledgling, but promising, attempts to elevate and legitimize the role of teacher in accepting some of the responsibility for staff development. In describing such centers Kathleen Devaney notes:

> There is a notion of *teachers centers* which is essentially an image of a place—small, welcoming, hand-built—where teachers come voluntarily to make things for classrooms, to exchange ideas, and to learn in a format of one-shot or short-series workshops rather than semester-long courses based on lectures and texts. Because this place is non-institutional neutral ground, teachers can let down their hair, drop competitiveness and defensiveness, and thus find starting points for self-improvement and professional growth.[5]

Some centers indeed fit the "non-institutional neutral ground" pattern, but no hard and fast rules regarding location exist. A teacher center can be developed and operated in a surplus classroom or perhaps in an overlooked or poorly used basement location of a particular school. The center could be limited to only teachers of that school or perhaps expanded to serve district or area teachers. The closing of schools in many districts throughout the country lends itself to the establishment of a district or area teacher center in abandoned

---

[4] Herbert Thelen, "A Cultural Approach to In-Service Education," in Louis Rubin (ed.), *Improving In-Service Education,* Boston: Allyn and Bacon, 1971, pp. 72–73.
[5] Kathleen Devaney, "What's a Teacher Center For?" *Educational Leadership,* vol. 33, no. 6, p. 413, 1976. This issue of *Educational Leadership* was guest-edited by Vincent Rogers, and its theme is teacher centers.

school buildings. Indeed, some centers are located in storefronts and ware-houses. Regardless of scale or location, some common aspects exist, the most notable being that the locus of responsibility for planning and operation is with teachers. Further commonalities are suggested by Devaney:

> The common purpose which stands out as a bond linking widely dissimilar teachers centers is the aim to help teachers enliven, individualize, personalize, enrich, elaborate, reorganize, or re-conceptualize the curriculum within their own classrooms. Study of scores of teachers center program offerings and calendars demonstrates center leaders' belief that help to teachers in the area of curriculum is the most teacher-responsive service they can offer. These centers teach teachers how to use manipulative, real-world, exploratory, frequently individualized curriculum materials and how to gradually reorganize classroom space and time to accommodate greater student activity and interaction. They engage teachers in adapting packaged curriculum materials, making their own materials, or building classroom apparatus, and often they involve teachers in some new study—often math or science—or craft so as to reacquaint them with the experience of being active, problem-solving learners themselves.[6]

Changes of lasting quality in schools depend heavily on grass-roots process-es. Further, it seems clear that teachers look to other teachers as important models for change. In two separate studies with similar themes both Haller and Keenan[7] asked teachers to identify to whom they go for help when they run into curriculum problems and to whom they could go for ideas and insights about teaching and learning. The Canadian and American teachers who responded to these questions were further asked which sources of new ideas were most creditable. Choosing from such categories as principal, supervisor, central office staff, professor, research journals, and so on, the overwhelming choice in response to each question was *other teachers*. Teachers go to other teachers for help and for sources of new ideas, and they believe in each other—potent reasons why supervisors need to provide support for informal staff-development approaches.

Intermediate Approaches and Supervisory Responsibility   The cornerstone of a comprehensive staff-development program for any school or district is a *supervisory* system of staff development. Traditional approaches with admin-istrative responsibility and informal approaches with teacher responsibility should be viewed as supplements to this primary thrust. Informal approaches are low-keyed, classroom-focused, teacher-oriented, and particularistic. Tra-ditional approaches, on the other hand, are high-keyed, more formal, system- or school-oriented, and universal.

A supervisory system of staff development assumes an intermediate position whereby the supervisor enters into a relationship with teachers on an equal

---

[6] Ibid., p. 414.

[7] Emil J. Haller, *Strategies for Change*, Toronto: Ontario Institute for Studies in Education, Department of Educational Administration, 1968; and Charles Keenan, "Channels for Change: A Survey of Teachers in Chicago Elementary Schools," doctoral dissertation, Urbana: University of Illinois, Department of Educational Administration, 1974.

footing and assumes an active role along with teachers. The teachers' capacities, needs, and interests are paramount, but sufficient planning and structure is introduced to bridge the gap between these interests and school program and instruction needs.

Intermediate staff-development approaches usually have the following characteristics:

1 The teacher is actively involved in contributing data, information, or feelings, solving a problem, or conducting an analysis.

2 The supervisor shares in the contributing, solving, and conducting activities above as a colleague of the teacher.

3 In colleagueship the supervisor and teachers work together as professional associates bound together by a common purpose. The common purpose is improvement of instruction through the professional development of teacher and supervisor.[8] Neither the teacher's autonomy as a professional nor the supervisor's responsibilities as a professional are compromised in the process since the relationship is based not on authority but on a commitment to professional improvement.

4 Staff-development activities generally require study of an actual situation or a real problem and use live data, either from self-analysis or from observations of others.

5 Feedback is provided, by the supervisor, by other teachers, or as a result of joint analysis, which permits teachers to compare observations with intents and beliefs, and personal reactions with those of others.

6 The emphasis is on direct improvement of teaching and learning in the classroom.

For the remainder of this chapter the focus will be on this intermediate approach to staff development in which supervisors play such an important part.

CHARACTERISTICS OF EFFECTIVE STAFF-DEVELOPMENT PROGRAMS

By way of summary, excerpts from a study of staff-development programs conducted under the auspices of the Florida State Department of Education are provided. The study suggests a number of clear patterns of effectiveness consistent with the recommendations provided above:

> School-based programs in which *teachers participate as helpers to each other and planners of in-service activities* tend to have greater success...than do programs...conducted by college or other outside personnel without the assistance of teachers.
>
> In-service education programs that have *differentiated training experiences for*

---

[8] Our definition of colleagueship follows Morris Cogan, *Clinical Supervision*, Boston: Houghton Mifflin, 1973, chap. 5. By contrast, the relationship between supervisor and teacher in traditional approaches is more clearly superordinate-subordinate, and in informal approaches the supervisor is more of a helper, facilitator, or passive supporter. In the intermediate approach the supervisor is neither dominating nor passive but is involved, side by side, with the teacher as a colleague.

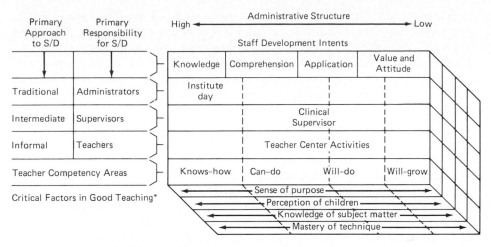

*Note that each of the critical factors in good teaching can be understood and developed as technical, clinical, personal or critical teaching competence.

FIGURE 17-2
Design for staff development.

different teachers (that is, "individualized") are more likely to accomplish their objectives than are programs that have common activities for all participants.

In-service education programs that *place the teacher in an active role (constructing and generating materials, ideas, and behavior)* are more likely to accomplish their objectives than are programs that place the teacher in a receptive role....

In-service education programs in which *teachers share and provide mutual assistance* to each other are more likely to accomplish their objectives than are programs in which each teacher does separate work.

Teachers are more likely to benefit from in-service programs in which they can *choose goals and activities for themselves,* as contrasted with programs in which the goals and activities are preplanned. [Italics added][9]

Notice the importance given to teacher involvement in planning, differentiated experiences for different teachers, active roles, using ideas, materials, and behavior found in the actual teaching situation, teachers working with and helping other teachers, and teacher goals.

MAPPING STAFF-DEVELOPMENT STRATEGIES

In this section the five critical components of staff development are arranged into a conceptual design to help in planning and decision making. This design for staff development is illustrated in Figure 17-2.

[9] Roy A. Edelfelt and Margo Johnson, *Rethinking In-Service Education,* Washington, D.C.: National Education Association, 1975, pp. 18–19, as quoted in Devaney, op. cit., p. 416. The original report is Gordon Lawrence, *Patterns of Effective In-Service Education,* Tallahassee, Fla.: State Department of Education, 1974.

Before we begin to discuss this design, refer back to Figure 17-1 and note the relationship between three of the five design components. Here we suggested that staff-development intents at the knowledge and comprehension levels were suited to increasing teachers' knowledge; intents at the applications level, their can-do and to a lesser extent their will-do competence area; and intents at the value and integration level, their will-grow competence area. The content, substance, or "subject matter" of intents could be concerned with one or a combination of four aspects of effectiveness in teaching: purposes, perceptions of students, knowledge of subject matter, and technique. In Figure 17-2 two additional critical components, approach and responsibility, are included, and all five are illustrated in a fashion to help monitor existing staff-development programs or make decisions about new programs.

Let us consider the box in Figure 17-2 first. Notice that the box consists of four layers, each corresponding to aspects of teacher effectiveness. For illustrative purposes let us refer only to the bottom layer, mastery of technique, and specifically to the technique of inquiry teaching. Staff-development intents are shown across the top of the box and teacher-competency areas across the bottom of the box. If we are interested only in knowing about inquiry teaching, then we are concerned with knowledge-level intents and the know-how competency area. If we are interested in committed adoption and use of inquiry teaching, then we are concerned with value- and attitude-integration intents and will-do–will-grow competency areas.

The programs we develop for the latter intents should be different from those for the former. To the left of the box appear the approach and responsibility components of staff development. Traditional, intermediate, and informal approaches correspond to administrator, supervisor, and teacher responsibilities. The box area directly to the right of each approach-responsibility designation suggests which intents and competency areas are likely to be effectively served by that approach. Traditional approaches seem best suited to knowledge-comprehension intents. Intermediate approaches seem best suited to comprehension, application, and value- and attitude-integration intents. Similarly, informal approaches point toward applications intents though these seem most potent for value- and attitude-integration intents.

What approaches to staff development should be used for our inquiry-method example? Who should assume major responsibility for this approach? The answer depends on the kind of purposes or intents sought. If one were interested only in knowledge and comprehension, then an administrator-directed-institute day might be best. Clinical supervision might be a strategy if inquiry teaching were seen as important to the school and the intent were committed implementation of this technique by teachers. Though informal approaches are typically more potent than others, staff-development agendas in this approach belong to teachers, and they may not choose to pursue inquiry teaching. If they did, then the approach might well be the most effective for achieving committed implementation of this technique by teachers. An additional drawback of informal approaches is that they are often not effective at the knowledge level. It seems best therefore to view staff development in a more comprehensive fashion.

INFORMING REFLECTIVE PRACTICE

In most schools and school districts the technical teaching competence commands the major share of staff-development attention and resources. The emphasis is on learning the facts, rules, and procedures and applying them to a presumably nonproblematic, relatively uniform, and stable teaching situation. Often these technical teaching skills are considered to be generic and thus universally applied to all situations, and sometimes this is indeed the case. At one level of abstraction, for example, it is true that positive reinforcement is positive reinforcement, wait time is wait time, on task is on task, and monitoring is monitoring regardless of the teaching and learning context. Supervision and staff development that responds to this focus seeks to train teachers in the appropriate techniques and to provide coaching directed to detecting and correcting errors as the techniques are applied.

In addition to professional knowledge construed as technical facts, rules, and techniques, Schön proposes two other understandings: professional knowledge in the form of "thinking like a teacher" and professional knowledge as "reflection-in-action."[10] In thinking like a teacher one not only masters the appropriate facts and techniques but learns form of inquiry "by which competent practitioners reason their way, in problematic instances, to clear connections between general knowledge and particular cases."[11] In knowledge of this sort it is presumed that a right way exists to match every situation and the emphasis is on how one analyzes situations and makes the decision as to what is the appropriate right way to apply. There is a link between this way of knowing and professional knowledge construed in a technical sense. But the emphasis in thinking like a teacher is on learning how to decide when to use what. Supervision and staff development that emphasizes thinking like a teacher relies less on training and more on coaching, apprenticing, and other forms of mentoring.

In earlier chapters we pointed out that one problem with overemphasizing technical aspects of supervision that may be suitable for specific problems, stable environments, and deterministic teaching is that the real world is for the most part ambiguous, complex, and fluid. Teachers, for example, are often unsure of what their goals and objectives are, sometimes discover goals and objectives while they are teaching, and invariably pursue multiple goals and objectives that from time to time even conflict with each other. In the real world of teaching plans rarely unfold as planned. Circumstances are typically not quite like that anticipated. Student reactions are difficult to predict. Subject matter, content, and concepts connect themselves in ways not anticipated, and so on. Teaching, then, is somewhat like surfing and teachers ride the pattern of

[10] Donald A. Schön, *Educating the Reflective Practitioner*, San Francisco: Jossey-Bass, 1987.
[11] Ibid., p. 39.

the wave of teaching as it unfolds. Teachers, therefore, need to learn to make new sense of uncertain unique and conflicting situations that they face in their practice. To do this, Schön suggests that professional knowledge be construed as reflection-in-action. From this stance one does not assume that existing professional knowledge fits every case or that every problem has a right answer. Instead teachers will need to "learn a kind of reflection-in-action that goes beyond stable rules—not only by devising new methods of reasoning ...but also by constructing and testing new categories of understanding, strategies of action, and new ways of framing problems."[12]

When professional knowledge is understood as reflection-in-action, staff development and supervision are drawn together. The context for reflection-in-action is the teacher's practice and this practice takes place in the classroom, not in the school auditorium, during institute day, the cafeteria as setting for an after-school workshop. Staff development designed to inform reflective practice, therefore, will need to be largely classroom-based. In this sense, staff development, supervision, mentoring, and coaching should not be viewed as separate and distinct roles but as dimensions of the role of supervisor as he or she works to enhance the technical, clinical, personal, and critical competencies of teaching and to promote professional knowledge in its technical sense in the form of thinking like a teacher and in the form of reflective practice.

SUMMARY

This chapter was concerned with supervision as a form of staff development. It was pointed out that only a thin line exists between supervision and staff development and in the ideal the two are brought together as a single process in the school's daily routine emphasis on personal and professional involvement. Noting that major emphasis in staff development is given to technical competency in teaching, three other types of teaching competence were described: clinical, personal, and critical. A conceptual distinction was then made between the traditional in-service education orientation and a staff-development orientation. The former tends to focus on deficiencies in teachers and on bringing them up to some standard while the latter tends to focus on a professional growth and on raising the quality of performance.

A design for staff development consisting of five critical components was then presented. The components were intents, substance, competency areas, approach, and responsibility. The relationships and interdependencies between and among intents were discussed. With respect to approach and responsibility three approaches to staff development with corresponding responsibility designations were described. The chapter concluded by noting that the technical teaching competency commands the major share of staff development, attention, and resources. Recognizing the importance of addressing this competency level, it was noted that more often than not the actual context of teaching is too complex to assume that staff development directed to enhancing

[12] Ibid.

technical competence and training people to apply teaching skills is sufficient. Following Schön, two other views of professional knowledge were discussed: thinking like a teacher and reflection-in-action. When staff development works to enhance one's ability to think like a teacher the emphasis is on learning the tacit rules which enable one to select appropriate teaching repertoires that match given situations. But often situations are uncertain or conflicting or unfamiliar and thus searching for the right established repertoire does not work well. When this is the case, staff development designed to enhance the teacher's ability to reflect-in-action was recommended. Here the emphasis is on helping teachers to go beyond the application of teaching skills and the matching of established repertoires to situations to creating professional teaching knowledge in use to devising new methods of reasoning to constructing and testing new understandings and strategies. It was noted that staff development which seeks to enhance and inform reflective practice cannot be conceived as something done on an institute day or in a workshop but must take place in the classroom as professional practice unfolds. When this is the case, staff development and supervision are brought together as one process.

STUDY GUIDE

Recall the concepts, ideas, and meanings associated with each of the following phrases and terms included in this chapter. Can you discuss each of them with a colleague and apply them to the supervisory context of your school? If you cannot, review them in the text and record the page numbers for future reference.

1 Administrative approaches to staff development
2 Clinical teaching competence
3 Competency areas
4 Critical teaching competence
5 Design for staff development
6 Informal approaches to staff development
7 "In-service" orientation
8 Intermediate approaches to staff development
9 Personal teaching competence
10 "Staff development" orientation
11 Technical teaching competence

EXERCISES

1 Develop a 10-item attitude questionnaire assessing teacher feelings about staff development in your school. Use the questionnaire to collect teacher impressions and views and to prepare a state-of-the-art report on staff development in your school.
2 Prepare a short talk (10 minutes) to be given before a citizen's advisory committee or school board entitled "Staff Development: Important in the Eighties—Critical in the Nineties."

3 Using the design summarized in Figure 17-2, select a topic for staff development. Work this topic through the design, reaching staff-development decisions about approach—responsibility, types of intents, and competency areas.

4 Interview a staff-development specialist and a specialist in classroom supervision about competencies they believe to be most important as they work to enhance teaching. Using Table 17-1 as a guide, evaluate their responses, determining the extent to which they emphasize each of the four types of teaching competence.

18

A CONTINGENCY APPROACH TO SUPERVISION AND STAFF DEVELOPMENT

In Chapter 15 we discussed the importance of taking a reflective practice stance in deciding on what constitutes best teaching practice in any given situation. Thinking reflectively was offered as a rational and professional alternative to the rationalistic and bureaucratic view that a "one best way" to teach can be determined as being appropriate to all teaching. Thinking reflectively about supervision and teaching, we argued, requires that a contingency practice perspective replace the one best way view. This chapter extends the concept of reflective practice and contingency by discussing the matching of supervisory styles and models to particular characteristics of teachers and to particular purposes. As these important situational characteristics change so, we will argue, should how we supervise and how we think about staff development. We propose a number of options for supervision and provide implications for determining the suitability of each for given situations. But first, let's review the concept of reflective practice.

REFLECTIVE PRACTICE IN SUPERVISION

Ordinary and reflective practice in supervision are different. Ordinary practice is characterized by a uniform system of supervision based on a single conception of "good" teaching and a narrow view of educational program. By contrast, reflective practice is characterized by the view that appropriate teaching strategies and tactics depend on the goals and objectives being pursued and the desired curriculum context for learning. Reflective teachers select from an array of teaching repertoires strategies suitable to intentions and context. Teaching strategies range from highly directive, teacher-controlled, and narrowly focused to very indirect, student-centered, and widely focused. How we supervise should reflect differences in teaching formats. As contrasted with ordinary supervision, reflective practice forces us to consider the establishment of a *differentiated system of supervision* that provides teachers with an array of options from which they may choose and provides supervisors with different supervisory techniques matched to various options. Supervisory options are reflective responses to differences in teacher personality, needs, professional development levels, and learning styles.[1]

A differentiated system of supervision should function within and be consistent with an overarching framework. This framework would be comprised of the school's purposes, education and management platforms, and other defining dimensions of the school's culture, all of which should be reflected in supervision and teaching. In differentiated supervision not anything goes. For example, in schools where active learning is prized this characteristic should be present in the vast majority of teaching strategies observed. In schools committed to the concept of shared leadership, selected supervisory strategies should be characterized by high teacher involvement. Other values comprising the school's overarching framework would be reflected similarly as options are selected and implemented.

CLINICAL SUPERVISION AS AN OPTION

The concept of clinical supervision was presented in some detail in Chapter 16. Clinical supervision was presented as a partnership in inquiry shared by teacher and supervisor designed to help teachers to modify existing patterns of teaching in ways that make sense to them. Clinical supervision is not for everyone nor is it a strategy that can sustain itself over a long period of time. The process is demanding in the time it requires from both teacher and supervisor. There is a danger that continuous use of this approach can result in a certain ritualism as each of the steps are followed. Clinical supervision may be too much supervision for some teachers. That is, not all teachers will need such an intensive look at their teaching. And finally, teachers' needs and dispositions at work as well as learning styles vary. Clinical supervision may be suitable for some teachers but not for others when these concerns are taken into consideration.

COOPERATIVE PROFESSIONAL DEVELOPMENT

Cooperative professional development is the phrase Allan Glatthorn uses for describing a collegial process within which teachers agree to work together for

---

[1] The discussion of differentiated supervision presented in this chapter follows very closely the view of Allan A. Glatthorn, *Differentiated Supervision,* Alexandria, Va.: Association for Supervision and Curriculum Development, 1984; and the discussion of options for supervision that appears in T. J. Sergiovanni, *The Principalship: A Reflective Practice,* Boston: Allyn and Bacon, 1987, pp. 190–232.

their own professional growth and development.[2] He prefers this term over peer supervision or collegial supervision, fearing that these labels might suggest teachers are supervising one another in a management sense. Cooperative professional development is a nonevaluative strategy for teachers to help one another as equals and professional colleagues. Glatthorn defines this approach as a "moderately formalized process by which two or more teachers agreed to work together for their own professional growth, usually by observing each other's classroom, giving each other feedback about the observation, and discussing shared professional concerns."[3]

Cooperative professional development can take many different forms. In some schools teachers might be organized into teams of three. In forming such teams teachers would have an opportunity to indicate with whom they might like to work. Often at least one member of the team is selected by the principal or the supervisor but there are no hard and fast rules for selecting teams. Once formed the teams may choose to work together in a number of ways ranging from clinical supervision to less intensive and more informal processes. They may, for example, simply agree to observe each other's classes providing help according to the desires of the teacher being observed. The teachers then might confer, giving one another informal feedback and otherwise discussing issues of teaching that they consider to be important. An approach relying on Hunter's teaching steps and elements of lesson design might be used on another occasion. In this case the emphasis on teaching might be narrowly focused on specific issues identified by the teacher. On still another occasion the emphasis might be quite unfocused in order to provide a general feel or rendition of teaching. Teachers might, for example, use the four types of teaching competence (technical, clinical, personal, critical) discussed in Chapter 17 and summarized in Table 17-1 as a framework for deciding strategies and intentions. All that is needed is for team members to meet beforehand to decide "the rules and issues" for the observation to take place and for any subsequent conversations or conferences.

It is a good idea for cooperative professional development to extend beyond classroom observation. It should provide a setting where teachers can informally discuss problems they are facing, share ideas, help one another in preparing lessons, exchange tips, and provide other support to one another. Some suggestions for prinicpals seeking to implement cooperative professional development are provided in Table 18-1.

INDIVIDUALIZED PROFESSIONAL DEVELOPMENT

Another option suggested by Glatthorn in establishing a differentiated system of supervision is individual professional development.[4] Here teachers working alone assume responsibility for their own professional development. They develop a yearly plan comprised of targets or goals derived from an assessment of their own

[2] Glatthorn, op. cit.
[3] Ibid., p. 39.
[4] Glatthorn uses the term "self-directed development."

TABLE 18-1
GUIDELINES FOR IMPLEMENTING COOPERATIVE PROFESSIONAL DEVELOPMENT

1. Teachers should have a voice in deciding with whom they work.

2. Principals should retain final responsibility for putting together CPD teams.

3. The structure for CPD supervision should be formal enough for the teams to keep records of how and in what ways time has been used and to provide a general *nonevaluative* description of CPD activities. This record should be submitted annually to the principal.

4. The principal should provide the necessary resources and administrative support enabling CPD teams to function during the normal range of the school day. The principal might, for example, volunteer to cover classes as needed, or to arrange for substitutes as needed, or to provide for innovative schedule adjustments enabling team members to work together readily.

5. If information generated within the team about teaching and learning might be considered even mildly evaluative, it should stay with the team and not be shared with the principal.

6. Under no circumstances should the principal seek evaluation data from one teacher about another.

7. Each teacher should be expected to keep a professional growth log which demonstrates that she or he is reflecting on practice and growing professionally as a result of CPD activities.

8. The principal should meet with the CPD team at least once a year for purposes of general assessment and for sharing of impressions and information about the CPD process.

9. The principal should meet individually at least once a year with each CPD team member to discuss her or his professional growth log and to provide any encouragement and assistance that may be required.

10. Generally, new teams should be formed every second or third year.

From Thomas J. Sergiovanni, *The Principalship: A Reflective Practice Perspective,* Boston: Allyn and Bacon, 1987, p. 198.

needs. This plan is then shared with the supervisor, principal, or other designated individual. Teachers are allowed a great deal of leeway in developing the plan but supervisors should ensure that the plan and selected targets are both realistic and attainable. At the end of a specified period, normally a year, the supervisor and teacher meet to discuss the teacher's progress in meeting professional development targets. Teachers are expected to provide some form of "evidence" (such as time logs, reflective practice diaries, schedules, photos, tapes, samples of students' work, and other artifacts) illustrating progress toward goals. This conference then leads to the generation of new targets for subsequent individual professional development cycles.

A number of problems are associated with approaches to supervision that rely heavily on target setting. Supervisors, for example, sometimes rigidly adhere to prespecified targets and sometimes impose targets on teachers. Rigidly applying a target setting system unduly focuses the evaluation and limits teachers to the events originally anticipated or stated. When this happens, teaching energies and concerns are directed to a prestated target and other areas of importance not targeted can be neglected. Target setting is meant to help and facilitate, not to hinder, the self-improvement process.

Individual professional development approaches to supervision are ideal for teachers who prefer to work alone or who, because of scheduling or other difficulties, are unable to work with other teachers. This supervisory option is efficient in use of time, less costly, and less demanding in its reliance on others than is the case with other options. For these reasons individual professional development is a feasible and practical approach to supervision. This approach is ideally suited to competent and self-directed teachers. Some guidelines for implementing individual professional development are provided in Table 18-2.

INFORMAL SUPERVISION

Included in every differentiated system of supervision should be a provision for informal supervision. Informal supervision is a casual encounter by supervisors with teachers at work and is characterized by frequent but brief and informal observations of teachers. Typically no appointments are made and visits are not announced. Successful informal supervision requires that certain expecta-

---

TABLE 18-2
GUIDELINES FOR IMPLEMENTING INDIVIDUAL PROFESSIONAL DEVELOPMENT

---

1. *Target setting.* Based on last year's observations, conferences, summary reports, CS episodes, or other means of personal assessment, teachers develop targets or goals that they would like to reach in improving their teaching. Targets should be few, rarely exceeding five or six and preferably limited to two or three. Estimated time frames should be provided for each target, which are then shared with the supervisor, along with an informal plan providing suggested activities for teacher engagement.

2. *Target-setting review.* After reviewing each target and estimated time frame, the principal provides the teacher with a written reaction. Further, a conference is scheduled to discuss targets and plans.

3. *Target-setting conference.* Meeting to discuss targets, time frames, and reactions, the teacher and principal revise targets if appropriate. It may be a good idea for the principal to provide a written summary of the conference to the teacher. Teacher and principal might well prepare this written summary together.

4. *Appraisal process.* Appraisal begins at the conclusion of the target-setting conference and continues in accordance with the agreed-upon time frame. The specific nature of the appraisal process depends on each of the targets and could include formal and informal classroom observations, an analysis of classroom artifacts, videotaping, student evaluation, interaction analysis, and other information. The teacher is responsible for collecting appraisal information and arranges this material in a portfolio for subsequent discussion with, and review by, the principal.

5. *Summary appraisal.* The principal visits with the teacher to review the appraisal portfolio. As part of this process, the principal comments on each target, and together the teacher and principal plan for the next cycle of IPD.

From Thomas J. Sergiovanni, *The Principalship: A Reflective Practice Perspective*, Boston: Allyn and Bacon, 1987, pp. 199–200.

tions be accepted by teachers. This approach, for example, assumes that principals and supervisors are indeed first and foremost lead or principal-teachers and thus have a right and responsibility to be a part of all the teaching that takes place in the school. They are instructional partners to every teacher in every classroom for every teaching and learning situation. When informal supervision is properly in place principals and supervisors are viewed as relatively common fixtures in classrooms, coming and going as part of the natural flow of the school's daily work.

The general management literature refers to informal supervision as management by wandering around (MBWA). This practice is found to be common among leaders of highly successful business firms and is discussed at great length in the writings of such business authorites as Deal and Kennedy, Peters and Waterman, and Peters and Austin.[5]

Informal supervision should not be considered as an option for teachers. Glatthorn, for example, believes that a differentiated system of supervision should require all teachers to participate in informal supervision.[6] In addition to informal supervision they would be involved in one additional approach such as clinical supervision, professional development, or independent professional development. In selecting additional options principals and supervisors should try to accommodate teacher preferences but should retain final responsibility for deciding the appropriateness of a selected option and indeed should reserve the right to veto the teacher's choice.

DIFFERENTIATED SUPERVISION AND THE CONTINGENCY VIEW

A contingency view of supervision is based on the premise that teachers are different and that matching supervisory options to these differences is important. In recent years developmental theorists such as Glickman[7] and Costa[8] have made considerable progress in suggesting how this matching might be done. These experts examine such dimensions as levels of professional maturity and cognitive complexity and suggest that as levels vary among teachers so should supervisory approaches and styles. Another group of theorists, such as Dunn and Dunn,[9] and Kolb, Rubin, and McIntyre,[10] have

[5] Terence E. Deal and Alan A. Kennedy, *Corporate Culture*, Reading, Mass.: Addison-Wesley, 1982; Thomas J. Peters and Robert H. Waterman, *In Search of Excellence*, New York: Harper & Row, 1982; Tom Peters and Nancy Austin, *A Passion for Excellence*, New York: Random House, 1982.

[6] Ibid., p. 59. Glatthorn prefers the term "administrative monitoring" to describe this form of supervision.

[7] Carl D. Glickman, *Supervision and Instruction: A Developmental Approach*, Boston: Allyn and Bacon, 1985.

[8] Art L. Costa, *Supervision for Intelligent Teaching: A Course Syllabus*, Orangevale, Calif.: Search Models Unlimited, 1982.

[9] R. S. Dunn and K. J. Dunn, "Learning Styles Teaching Styles: Should They...Can They...Be Matched?" *Educational Leadership*, vol. 36, no. 4, 1979.

[10] David A. Kolb, Irwin M. Rubin, and James M. McIntyre, *Organization Psychology: An Effective Approach to Organizational Behavior*, 4th ed., Englewood Cliffs, N.J.: Prentice-Hall.

been interested in the concept of learning styles and how, as these styles vary, opportunities for learning, problem solving, and personal growth should also vary. Accounting for motives of teachers provides still a third dimension to the matching of individual teachers with supervisory options. Social motives theories such as McClelland's find that as such important work motives as the need for achievement, power, and affiliation vary among workers the work conditions and setting they find motivating vary as well.[11] Matching supervisory options to individual needs, therefore, has great potential for increasing the motivation and commitment of teachers at work. The section that follows *explores* these important individual dimensions and *suggests* compatible supervisory options.[12] We are not under the illusion that tight and concise matching is possible but believe, nonetheless, that more informed decisions can be made by considering that possibility.

COGNITIVE COMPLEXITY LEVELS OF TEACHERS

Important to developmental theorists is the concept of cognitive complexity. More specifically, these theorists are concerned with levels of cognitive growth for teachers as embodied in the cognitive complexity they exhibit in their teaching practice. Lower levels of growth are characterized by simple and concrete thinking and practice whereas higher levels of growth are characterized by more complex and abstract thinking and practice. An important finding from the research on teaching is that teachers with higher levels of cognitive complexity provide a greater range of teaching environments to students and that their practice is characterized by a wider variety of teaching strategies and methods.[13] Further, students of teachers with higher levels of cognitive complexity tend to achieve more than students of teachers with lower levels.[14]

Cognitive complexity is concerned with both the *structure* and *content* of a teacher's thoughts with particular emphasis on the structure.[15] Two teachers may share the same beliefs about the value of informal teaching but they may differ markedly in the complexity with which they view these beliefs. The content of these beliefs is similar but the structure is different. The first teacher views informal teaching as universally applicable rather than as one of many strategies. The second teacher, on the other hand, views informal teaching as a strategy more appropriate for some teaching and learning settings but less appropriate for others. Though both teachers share common beliefs about informal teaching they differ in the structure with which these beliefs are held. The second teacher's thinking is characterized by higher levels of cognitive

---

[11] See, for example, David C. McClelland, J. W. Atkinson, R. A. Clark, and E. L. Lowell, *The Achievement Motive*, New York: Appleton-Century-Croft, 1953; McClelland and D. Burnham, "Power Is the Great Motivator," *Harvard Business Review*, vol. 54, no. 2, pp. 110–111, 1976.

[12] This section follows closely T. J. Sergiovanni, op. cit., pp. 210–225.

[13] David E. Hunt and Bruce R. Joyce, "Teacher Trainee Personality and Initial Teaching Style," *American Educational Research Journal*, vol. 4, no. 3, pp. 253–255, 1967.

[14] O. J. Harvey, "System Structure, Flexibility and Creativity," in Harvey (ed.), *Experience, Structure, and Adaptability*, New York: Springer, 1966.

[15] Ibid.

complexity than is the first. Teachers with higher levels of cognitive complexity, for example, are able to give attention to a number of different concepts relating to a particular issue and to see interconnections among these concepts. They are able to be more reflective in their practice, to understand better the subtleties of teaching, and to make more complex decisions about teaching.

Supervisory strategies that account for levels of cognitive complexity actually enhance this complexity. Cognitive complexity increases as teachers are exposed to more stimulating teaching environments.[16] Examples would be teachers who have greater opportunities to interact with their supervisors and other teachers about teaching, have greater opportunities for obtaining feedback about their teaching and thus for reflecting on their practice, have greater opportunities for experimenting in a supportive environment, and have greater opportunities for assuming more responsibility for the outcomes of their teaching. The differentiated system of supervision that provides informal supervision combined with other options can provide these benefits. When teachers are provided with an intellectually stimulating, challenging, and supporting supervisory environment levels of cognitive complexity increase with subsequent improvements in teaching and learning.[17]

SUPERVISORY STYLES AND COGNITIVE COMPLEXITY

Within any supervisory option supervisors may choose to provide leadership and help in a number of different ways. These behavioral choices represent styles of supervision. The developmental theorist Glickman refers to three major supervisory styles as directive, collaborative, and nondirective.[18] Costa, referring to the same styles, prefers the labels directing, mediating, and counseling.[19]

Styles are different from options in that different styles can be used when working with different teachers though all the teachers may be involved in supervision using the same option. For example, when working with three different teachers within individual professional development it might make sense to use a directive approach with one, a collaborative with the second, and a nondirective approach with the third. The directive would emphasize a great deal of structure and more frequent interaction with the teacher; the collaborative would emphasize shared responsibility, joint decision making, and colleagueship; and the nondirective would emphasize facilitating the teacher's plans and efforts and providing necessary support. Levels of directiveness in supervisory style and corresponding teacher role are illustrated in Figure 18-1.

The matching of teacher concerns, levels of responsibility, maturity, cognitive complexity, supervisory options, and supervisory styles is illustrated in Figure 18-2. This figure suggests an alignment between concerns of teachers and levels of responsibility and maturity and levels of cognitive complexity.

---

[16] N. A. Sprinthall and L. Thies-Sprinthall, "Career Development of Teachers: A Cognitive Perspective," *Encyclopedia of Educational Research*, 5th ed., New York: Free Press, 1982.
[17] Harvey, op. cit.
[18] Glickman, op. cit.
[19] Costa, op. cit.

Teachers primarily concerned with the problems, needs, and learning characteristics of students, who are autonomous with respect to accepting responsibility, and who are growing in levels of maturity are likely to display moderate or medium levels of cognitive complexity. Cognitive complexity is, therefore, an important construct. The intersection line brings together these dimensions of teacher development and indicates the recommended supervisory style and supervisory option.

Teachers located at or near point 1 on the intersection line would probably benefit best from directive supervision regardless of the supervisory option being used. Informal supervision characterized by frequent and direct contact with the supervisor is recommended as the most suitable option. Cooperative professional development and independent professional development would be appropriate as supplements. Should cooperative professional development be chosen (for example, teaming the teacher with another teacher who might be located at point 3 on the intersection line) the supervisor will need to be involved to be sure that this teacher is getting the direction and help most needed.

The collaborative supervisory style would be most appropriate for teachers at intersection point 2. On this occasion both teacher and supervisor tackle problems together, plan activities and events, and make decisions cooperatively. Individual professional development is highly recommended as an option.

Teachers with more professional concerns that bring together student concerns with broader issues affecting quality schooling and who reflect higher levels of cognitive complexity in their practice will be found at or near point 3 on the intersection line. These mature professionals are more willing and able to assume full responsibility for their own self-evaluation and improvement. When this is the case, supervision is more appropriately nondirective. Cooperative professional development is ideally suited to teachers at point 3. Here, groups of teachers work together as mature colleagues. Individual professional development may be selected by some teachers who might prefer to work alone. Informal supervision would remain an important part of a comprehensive supervisory system in the school and thus should be used as well with teachers at or near point 3. For these highly motivated and competent teachers the purpose of informal supervision is one of providing needed recognition and support.

Peaks and dips appear periodically on the intersection line of Figure 18-2. Peaks represent occasions when teachers might require more intense and prolonged help in the classroom perhaps because they face a special problem or challenge. Dips represent trouble spots that might be identified by either the teacher or the supervisor. On these occasions clinical supervision can be an effective and appropriate option.

LEARNING STYLES OF TEACHERS

Two additional situational characteristics that should be considered in a contingency view of supervision are learning styles of teachers and the particular motivational needs that they bring to work. Teachers, like students,

	More directive style	**More collaborative style**
Direction	High ←	
Behavior	The supervisor recalls and analyzes the data, proposes alternative strategies, and chooses one to implement.	The supervisor presents the data, invites the teacher to consider alternatives, suggests alternatives. Together they choose alternatives. The initiating supervisor presents the data, invites the teacher to analyze the data, proposes alternatives, and selects those to implement.
Example	Supervisor: "One reason why the class was shouting out answers is that you did not lay out the ground rules as to how they should respond. Also, your classroom was arranged so that they could interact more with you than with each other. You should arrange your class in a circle so they could see each other. Also, you must start the lesson by stating that you want them to take turns and listen to each other's ideas. In the future, I'd like you to begin each lesson by setting some ground rules for how they should interact. Then you should plan to spend a few minutes at the end of the lesson evaluating how well they followed those rules. When we meet next Tuesday, I'd like you to share with me just how you intend to structure the lesson and the classroom that day."	Supervisor: "I noted today that several students were not taking turns as you hoped they would. Why is that, do you think?" Teacher: "I don't know. It's always a few kids who interrupt. They just don't seem to know how to listen to each other and wait. I scold them when they do it but they just keep right on." Supervisor: "Would it help, do you think, to lay down some ground rules at the beginning of the lesson?" Teacher: "It might. What do you suggest?" Supervisor: "I think you might tell them what you expect them to do. Take turns, listen to each other, raise their hands." Teacher: "You'd think they'd know that by now. You mean I should be more specific about my expectancies." Supervisor: "Yes. Perhaps, when the lesson is finished, you might take some time to evaluate how well they followed those rules." Teacher: "I can do that. That way the students will evaluate their own behavior rather than making me do it." Supervisor: "Do you think the way you have the classroom arranged is conducive to total group listening and sharing?"

FIGURE 18-1
Levels and examples of directiveness in supervisory style. (*From Art Costa,* Supervision for Intelligent Teaching, *Orangevale, Calif., Search Models Unlimited, 1982, p. 114.*)

More non-directive style

→ Low

The supervisor invites the teacher to share the data, to analyze the data, to propose alternatives for himself or herself.

The teacher initiates by recalling data, analyzing, and prescribing. The teacher invites the supervisor to perform a role.

Supervisor: "How do you feel the lesson went today?"

Teacher: "Pretty well. However, I'm disappointed that so many students are still not taking turns. Did I make my directions clear, do you think?"

Supervisor: "I understood them."

Teacher: "I wonder if I changed the arrangement of the classroom, would that help, do you think?"

Supervisor: "When students sit in a circle, that is the position in which most students can see most other students. They can read each other's body language and facial expressions."

Teacher: "Mmm. That's what I'm trying to get them to do; to listen to one another. Next time, I think I'll try that. Is there anything else I could do to get them to take charge of their own behavior?"

Supervisor: "Having students evaluate themselves, you mean?"

Teacher: "Yes. When the discussion is over, I could take some time to have them discuss how well they listened to each other and took turns."

Teacher: "Today I noticed that there are still some students who are not taking turns and listening to each other. I've got to do something to help them take charge of their own behavior and to be courteous to each other."

Supervisor: "Like what?"

Teacher: "Well, I've gotten them into a circle where they can face each other, I've tried to model these behaviors in my own interaction, and I've talked privately with those students who have the problem. I guess I'm just going to have to lay down some ground rules for good discussion."

Supervisor: "Have you talked this over with the class?"

Teacher: "No, I haven't. Maybe if we'd have a whole class discussion to develop some criteria for good discussions, they could follow their own rules better than mine."

Supervisor: "That's possible."

Teacher: "Could you come into my classroom Tuesday morning during our class meeting? I'd like you to observe the students and me to see if they are setting their own ground rules and whether I'm helping them become more self-directed. Look for those students who are not taking turns and tell me if I could do anything more to help them learn to listen to each other."

Supervisor: "OK."

FIGURE 18-1 *(Continued)*

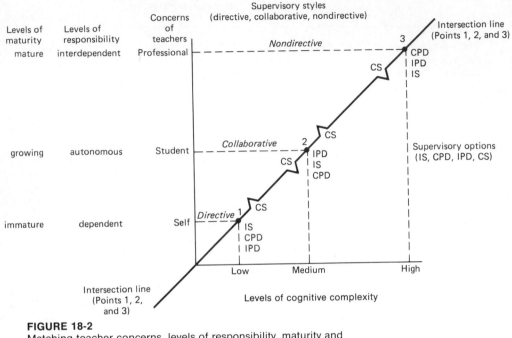

FIGURE 18-2
Matching teacher concerns, levels of responsibility, maturity and complexity, supervisory options, and supervisory styles. (*Adapted from Thomas J. Sergiovanni,* The Principalship: A Reflective Practice Perspective, *Boston: Allyn and Bacon, 1967, p. 213.*)

are unique in their learning styles and in the ways in which they solve problems. A reflective supervisory program would take note of these differences and seek to accommodate them in assigning teachers to supervisory options and in providing appropriate supervisory styles within options. David A. Kolb, Irwin M. Rubin, and James M. McIntyre provide a model of learning that conceives of adult learning and problem solving as one process.[20] The model is intended to increase understanding of how adults generate from their experience the concepts, rules, and principles that guide their behavior in new situations and how they modify these concepts to improve their effectiveness in learning at work. Within the model, learning and problem solving is viewed as a four-stage cycle beginning with concrete experiences and progressing in turn through observation and reflection, the formulation of concepts and generalizations, to experimenting with what is learned in a new setting. This model represents an ideal conception of learning.

Kolb and his colleagues identify four different learning modes each corresponding to one of the stages of this learning cycle: concrete experience (CE), reflective observation (RO), abstract conceptualization (AC), and active ex-

[20] Kolb, Rubin, and McIntyre, op. cit.

perimentation (AE). They believe that learners "must be able to involve themselves fully, openly and without bias in new experiences (CE); they must be able to reflect on and observe these experiences from many perspectives (RO); they must be able to create conceptions that integrate their observations into logically sound theories (AC); and they must be able to use these theories to make decisions and solve problems (AE)."[21]

Despite the logic of this progression it is very likely that different people have slightly different learning cycles. Some teachers feel more comfortable with and are more confident with some of the stages of the cycle than others. Simply put, some teachers learn best when dealing concretely with something and may have difficulty responding to this same thing when presented abstractly. Others are confused by starting with concrete matters, preferring instead to read about something—to become cognitively oriented before experiencing it firsthand. Others might prefer to observe new learning possibilities in action first and then to reflect on what is observed before developing a conceptual map or having concrete experience. Still other teachers are quick to jump in and experiment with new ideas and practices, using a process of muddling through as they then move to more reflective, abstract, or concrete understandings. What is clear is that learning best takes place when all of the four learning modes are tended to. What is not clear is the order in which different individuals progress through the learning cycle. Some learn best starting with a concrete experience, others learn best starting with a more abstract approach, and so on. Typically one's actual learning style represents a blending of modes. For practical purposes it is more useful to think of a person as being oriented toward a particular learning mode than as being typed or labeled more rigidly. Patterns are intended to reveal relative emphases on one or another learning mode and to suggest strengths and weaknesses.

TEACHER LEARNING STYLES AND SUPERVISORY OPTIONS

Learning styles can be useful in helping to decide which particular supervisory option is most suitable for a given teacher. But the real value is less in deciding the option itself and more in suggesting ways in which supervisors and others can work most effectively with teachers within options. Following are some recommendations for matching supervisory option with teacher learning style. They are based on our interpretation of the literature and on our clinical experience as supervisors.

Cooperative professional development is the recommended choice for teachers oriented toward concrete experience for it gives them opportunities to interact with other teachers about their work. Concrete-experience teachers are less interested in "bookish" interpretations of practice and more interested in knowing about and experiencing "what works" in the classroom next door. They often like the opportunity to try out a new idea or teaching practice much

---

[21] Ibid.

as does an apprentice by working side by side with another teacher. Sometimes their concern for what is immediate prevents them from "seeing the forest because of the trees." Sometimes they adopt practices by mimicking them and thus not understanding them fully. As a result they may have difficulty in extending their practice, in applying newly learned practices to new situations, and in modifying practices as situations change.

Concrete-experience teachers typically like to interact with each other and thus are not likely to prefer options that require them to work alone. Thus they are not likely to be comfortable with individual professional development. Should this be the choice anyway, concrete-experience teachers will need a fair amount of close supervision and a reasonable amount of directiveness. In cooperative professional development settings it makes sense to team concrete-experience teachers with those who have strengths in abstract conceptualization or reflective observation. Both types of teachers will profit by this combination.

High-reflective-observation teachers are very likely to respond favorably to either cooperative professional development or individual professional development. In each case, however, the teacher is likely to be passive, preferring to observe and make sense of what is going on rather than taking a more active role. If assigned to individual professional development and left alone the reflective observer will often not make much progress. If this must be the choice it might be a good idea for supervisors to insist on the development of an explicit contract detailing the action outcomes of supervisions. Targets and goals should be action-oriented and should specify the teaching behaviors or classroom changes being sought. Care should be taken to ensure that targets have been met and the supervisory contract has been fulfilled.

A better choice for the reflective observer would be assignment to cooperative professional development teams, but care should be taken to provide that other team members are reasonably action-oriented and can provide the teacher with the kinds of practical assistance that will be needed to get on with the work of self-improvement. In exchange the reflective observing teacher can provide others with the kind of reflection that will help them to view their teaching with greater depth and meaning.

Abstract-conceptualization-oriented teachers resemble reflective-observation teachers in many ways but are more action-oriented and better able to focus on problems of practice and the theoretical ideas associated with these problems. They like reading about theoretical ideas, issues of practice, and reports of research regarding teaching and learning, and discussing these issues and ideas in depth. They like to "see the data" and are frequently good at making sense of these data. Sometimes in their enthusiasm for abstract concerns they have less energy available for getting on with the day-by-day implementation of ideas. They are good planners, however, and when assigned to individual professional development will often get the highest marks for preparing the most elaborate and reasoned set of target-setting documents. This supervisory option works well for them if time is taken to ensure that action deadlines are set and that teachers follow these deadlines with evidence of practical accomplishments of their objectives and targets.

Teachers oriented toward abstract conceptualization often profit from cooperative professional development and can contribute to it. But sometimes they can be distracting to group efforts because of their tendency to emphasize theoretical issues. To abstract conceptualizers the theoretical is a delight in its own right and well worth discussing regardless of implications for practice. In using the cooperative professional development option, therefore, care should be taken to form a team that includes more action-oriented teachers to provide the necessary balance.

Individual professional development is the most likely choice for teachers oriented toward active experimenting. These teachers are doers and as such are interested in getting on with their work. They like to set objectives and enjoy focusing on tasks. They are willing to take risks and are not afraid to modify their practice. Individual professional development provides these teachers with an opportunity to grow and develop at their own rates. They need help, however, in sticking with a course of action, in tempering their experiments, and in reflecting on their practice to ensure that it is reasonably stable and sensible. Active experimenters tend not to prefer cooperative professional development and if assigned to this option can often be a hindrance to other teachers. Other teachers assigned to the same option are likely to view the active experimenter as being a maverick of sorts. As with teachers oriented toward each of the other three learning styles an appropriate supervisory strategy is one that leads with the teacher's strengths and provides the necessary help, and sometimes discipline, to ensure that the less favored learning modes are tended to as well. If Kolb, Rubin, and McIntyre are right, sustained learning will not take place unless all of the four dimensions of the learning cycle are experienced.

ACCOUNTING FOR MOTIVES OF TEACHERS

Differences in reactions of teachers to the same supervisory option or style are in part natural reflections of the motives they bring to their work. Motives are the thoughts and feelings that cause teachers to act and to react in certain ways. In this sense, motives are sources of motivation for people. Motivational theories are often grouped into two major categories—active and internal. Active theories assume that teachers bring to their work certain needs that are translated into goals and desires. According to active theories teachers are motivated to work in exchange for achieving desired goals. Active theories of motivation were discussed in Chapter 5.

Internal theories, by contrast, assume that teachers are already motivated to work and that the motives accounting for this motivation are related to more complex personality characteristics than to desired goals. According to internal theorists, carrot and stick aproaches to motivation are likely to be less effective than understanding underlying motives and creating conditions allowing these motives to be expressed. Thus motives and aroused motivation are considered to be different. Motives are construed as underlying personality characteristics. They resemble energy valves that are related to motivation. When the valves are closed, a teacher's energy remains in a state of potential and behavior is not motivated. Aroused motivation results from opening the motive valve and is reflected in a release of energy in the form of motivated behavior. Key motives differ for different individuals. When teachers find themselves in work settings that correspond to their underlying motives, the motive valve is opened and the potential for motivation is greatly enhanced.

ACHIEVEMENT, POWER, AND AFFILIATION

Three motives have been identified as having particular importance to the world of teachers at work: achievement, power influence, and affiliation. David C. McClelland found that the three motives are present in all people but not to the same degree.[22] Some teachers are influenced greatly by the need for affiliation, only moderately by the need for power influence, and only modestly by the need for achievement. Other teachers might be very high on the need for achievement and comparatively low on the needs for affiliation and power and influence. The first group of teachers are likely to think more about social interaction, friendships, and human relationships at work and in controlling others at work than in job objectives and how well they can accomplish various teaching tasks. In contrast, the second group would probably be much more concerned with work issues and progress in achieving objectives than in interacting with and controlling others.

The achievement motive is associated with teachers wanting to take personal responsibility for their own success or failure; liking working situations where goals are clear and reasonably obtainable though challenging; preferring frequent and concrete feedback allowing them to gauge their success and failure rates in a continuous fashion. High-achievement-motivated teachers are task-oriented, prefer short-range specific targets to more ambiguous and long-range targets, like to be on top of things, and seek personal responsibility for their actions. They find it difficult to delegate responsibility and to share authority with others. It is often difficult for them to emphasize human relationships and social interaction behaviors for their own sake. High-need-for-achievement teachers are likely to be committed to building achievement-oriented classrooms with visible and detailed standards. They seek and accept responsibility for their own work behaviors and growth and gladly accept moderate risks in an effort to achieve personal success.

Supervisory options that encourage individual initiative, target setting, and charting of accomplishments are favored by high-achievement-oriented teachers. Individual professional development, for example, is ideally suited to them but they are likely to respond less favorably to cooperative professional development. They respond well to informal supervision if the feedback they

[22] David C. McClelland, *The Achieving Society*, Princeton, N.J.: Van Nostrand, 1961.

desire is provided. Continuing with the valve metaphor, when the supervisory situation is properly matched the achievement-motive valve is opened and motivation results.

The affiliation motive is associated with people who have a high concern for warm and friendly relationships and for social interaction. Teachers for whom this need is important enjoy working with other teachers in group settings, find teaching and other assignments that require them to work alone, learn alone, or problem solve alone to be less satisfactory. They depend heavily on other teachers for much of their work satisfaction and enjoy interacting with others about work. Affiliation-oriented teachers suffer more from isolation and experience more loneliness than do their achievement and power-influence counterparts. They need and seek opportunities to interact with other adults. Should they find this opportunity within the supervisory situation their affiliation-motive valve is opened and they respond with motivated behavior.

Individual professional development and other supervisory options that leave them to their own devices are not likely to be viewed favorably by high-affiliation teachers. On the other hand, cooperative professional development elicits a very positive response. Affiliation teachers can feel uncomfortable when involved in informal supervision unless the supervisor makes a point of providing *supportive* feedback after every classroom visit.

High-need-for-power-and-influence teachers are interested in influencing other people. They like group contacts and social interaction supervisory settings but view these less as opportunities for satisfying social interaction needs and more as opportunities that will enable them to exercise leadership. When provided with supervisory situations of this type the power-influence motive valve is opened and motivative behavior results.

High-power-influence teachers like to assume supervisory roles and will respond very positively to collegial supervision. Since they like to be in charge and enjoy assuming leadership roles they often resent competition in these areas from other teachers and from supervisors. An important strategy is to harness the motivational potential of high-power-influence teachers by delegating responsibility to them and in other ways sharing leadership roles and functions.

During the early stages of social motives research it was thought that the achievement motive was associated with increased performance at work and successful accomplishment of goals and that the other two motives actually interfered with the accomplishment of work. More recent research, however, suggests that none of the three emerges as being superior. Teachers with high needs for affiliation and teachers with high needs for power and influence can be every bit as productive and effective as teachers with high needs for achievement. Key to motivation is not the most pressing motive of a particular teacher but whether a person's work circumstances allow for expression of the motive—the opening of the motive-energy valve, so to speak.

PRESCRIPTIONS OR FRAMES OF MIND?

When contingency approaches to supervision, teaching, and staff development are described they often "read" differently than is actually the case. The idea of matching A with B has a certain logical ring of sure footing and certainty that in the real world of schooling simply cannot be claimed. It would be unfortunate indeed to view our speculations and recommendations as prescriptions to be literally applied. A more practical and reasoned strategy is to view the contingency relationships discussed as frames of mind that can help supervisors reflect on their practice, take into account more complex dimensions, form better hunches, and make more informed professional decisions. Contingency theory cannot take the professional guesswork out of practice but it can make guessing easier.

SUMMARY

In this chapter a contingency approach to supervision and staff development was proposed. Key to the concept of contingency is that one best way to teach or supervise does not exist. Instead teaching and supervisory strategies should be matched to the characteristics of a situation at hand. Following the work of Allan Glatthorn a differentiated system of supervision was proposed. This system included four options: clinical supervision, cooperative professional development whereby teachers work together as collegial teams; individualized professional development, which involves target setting; and informal supervision. Informal supervision was described as a casual encounter by supervisors with teachers at work and is characterized by frequent but brief informal observations with teachers. Cognitive complexity level of teachers was then discussed as one situational characteristic that could be used to help decide which of the forms of supervision might make most sense. Cognitive complexity was also discussed in the context of choosing a supervisory style. Other situational characteristics discussed included learning styles of teachers and social motives. Four learning styles were discussed: concrete experience, abstract conceptualization, reflective observation, and active experimenter. In each case, recommendations were made for taking into consideration teachers' style patterns when selecting an appropriate supervisory option. The needs for achievement, power influence, and affiliation were the motives that were considered. Again in keeping with the contingency theme recommendations were made for matching teacher motive patterns with supervisory options.

It was pointed out that when contingency approaches to supervision are described they often "read" differently than is actually the case and they have an attractive ring of logicalness that unfortunately does not match the real world. For this reason the discussions and recommendations made in this chapter should not be viewed as prescriptions to be literally applied but as frames of mind that can help supervisors reflect on their practice and make better guesses as to what best fits with what.

STUDY GUIDE

Recall the concepts, ideas, and meanings associated with each of the following phrases and terms included in this chapter. Can you discuss each of them with a colleague and apply them to the supervisory context of your school? If you cannot, review them in the text and record the page numbers for future reference.

1 Achievement
2 Active theories of motivation
3 Affiliation
4 Clinical supervision
5 Cognitive complexity
6 Collaborative style
7 Contingency view
8 Cooperative professional development
9 Developmental theory
10 Differentiated supervision
11 Directive style
12 Individualized professional development
13 Informal supervision
14 Internal theories of motivation
15 Learning styles
16 Motives
17 Overarching framework
18 Peer supervision
19 Power

EXERCISES

1 With which of the four supervisory options discussed do you feel most comfortable? If you were a teacher, for example, which one would suit you the best? Which one do you feel most comfortable with as a supervisor?
2 Study Figure 18-2. Are you able to explain each of the concepts and relationships depicted? Explain supervisory styles, supervisory options, levels of maturity, levels of responsibility, and concerns of teachers. How do they all fit together?
3 Select a teacher you know well as a prospective person for supervision. Show how Figure 18-2 helps you to decide what might be best for this person. Remember to use the figure as a "frame of mind" and not as a "prescription" dispenser.

CHAPTER 19

HUMAN RESOURCES SUPERVISION: AN ACTIVE VOICE IN SCHOOL REFORM

Currently the public schools, and to an extent the nonpublic schools, are caught up in a spirit of reform and renewal stimulated by numerous national reports purporting to catalog the failings of the schools. This spirit of reform has led the majority of states to pass new legislation and adopt new policies which seek to overcome the schools' perceived failures.[1] These new policies represent assumptions about the purpose of schooling and the definition of excellence in schooling that are clearly political and economic, rather than educational.[2]

In an effort to reform the teaching profession, states have mandated various schemes of teacher evaluation. These schemes are occupying the energies of supervisory personnel throughout school systems, leaving them little time for the kind of human resources supervision proposed in this book.[3] Although the new teacher-evaluation practices have positive features, they also reflect serious shortcomings.

POSITIVE CHARACTERISTICS OF CURRENT TEACHER-EVALUATION PRACTICES

Teacher evaluation has moved beyond the simplistic practices of using cookbook checklists to rate teachers. The current practice of teacher evalua-

---

[1] National Governors' Association Center for Policy Research and Analysis, *Time for Results: The Governors' 1991 Report on Education,* Washington, D.C.: Center for Policy Research and Analysis, National Governors' Association, 1986.

[2] "Better schools mean better jobs. Unless states face these questions, Americans won't keep our high standard of living. To meet stiff competition from workers in the rest of the world, we must educate ourselves and our children as never before." Ibid., p. 2.

[3] For descriptions of teacher-evaluation schemes in various states, cf. the April 1987 issue of *Educational Leadership,* vol. 44, no. 7, passim.

tion is much more carefully planned and carried out. Among its more positive features are the following:

- Teacher evaluation is focused on teacher improvement, not on gathering data to fire or demote teachers.
- Teacher-evaluation criteria are based on findings from research on effective classrooms, which link teacher behaviors to student outcomes.[4]
- Safeguards are built into present teacher-evaluation schemes: in-house committees of teachers agree to the procedures ahead of time; more than one visit to a teacher's class is required; observers are trained in more clinical techniques of observation and feedback; there is more flexibility in defining and applying quantitative rankings; variety is built into the types of evaluation procedures employed, etc.
- Teacher evaluation is tied into specific staff-development programs aimed at nurturing more effective classroom behaviors.
- Teacher evaluation is constantly related to schoolwide goals and specific student learnings.

NEGATIVE CHARACTERISTICS OF CURRENT TEACHER-EVALUATION PRACTICES

While the present schemes have advanced the field of teacher evaluation significantly, they are still flawed at their core. Among the most serious flaws are the following:

- The present emphasis on teacher evaluation is based upon a supposed link between the failure of American business to maintain dominance over foreign competition and school practices which are supposed to be responsible for declining tests scores of youngsters. The logic here is faulty. Shouldn't someone first do an assessment of American business practices and the mistakes made there, before blaming schools and schoolchildren for what adults in the business sector have done?
- Proposing economic productivity as the only or even the primary reason for schooling reflects an inappropriately narrow conception of schooling. While concern to prepare youngsters for the world of work is one of many appropriate concerns, the school-effectiveness research and teacher-evaluation schemes based on it ignore other educational concerns such as citizenship education, the fostering of respect for people from different cultural traditions, initiative and creativity, community building, expressive learnings, and quality of life issues.
- The definition of effectiveness in the present literature presents a closed educational system where there are only preordained outcomes to which everyone must be matched in uniform ways.[5]

---

[4] A good example of this kind of linkage can be found in *Effective Schooling Practices and Teacher Evaluation: Beyond Ceremonial Congratulations*, rev. ed., Eugene, Ore.: Center for Educational Policy and Management, College of Education, University of Oregon, 1983.

[5] Cf. Daniel L. Duke, "What Is the Nature of Educational Excellence and Should We Try to Measure It?" *Phi Delta Kappan*, vol. 66, pp.671–674, June 1985.

• The recently mandated approaches to teacher evaluation take the initiative away from the teacher as a professional; they tend to strip away the professional character of the practice of teaching, reducing it to a set of 28 (more or less) behaviors.[6]

• The new policies do not take sufficient account of the lessons which research into policy implementation teaches, namely, that implementation at the local level takes place within a context of local politics. The rationality of the policies of teacher evaluation may not be at all recognizable during implementation at the local level when the full force of local personalities and the organizational politics of the local school system come into play.[7]

• The recent teacher-evaluation schemes are too mechanistic, based as they are on the conception of learning presented in the effectiveness literature, namely, that learning is primarily a matter of learning discrete isolated units of material, which through drill and practice can be mastered. Learning, even in the basic skills, is a much more complex matter, involving patterns, relationships, a fluid motion that is constantly rearranging what appear to be bits and pieces but are much more like a wave or a viscous pond in motion.

SUPERVISION WITHIN THE CONTEXT OF SCHOOL REFORM

In one sense, "reform" has been an ongoing reality for educators. Hardly a decade goes by without a new concern or issue arising either from within the educational community or from the wider civic community. These concerns lead to calls for reform. Frequently, supervisors are requested or required to monitor or direct the implementation of such reforms. In the present case, supervisory personnel, especially principals and assistant principals are being required under the rhetoric of "instructional leadership" to implement a system of teacher evaluation based on models of what is labeled "effective classroom instruction."

As this book has consistently emphasized, however, these policies and mandates do not automatically usher in the targeted outcomes. Those policies are taken by each school system and by each individual school, interpreted by the local administrators and teachers, adapted to the local organizational dynamics (authority relationships, informal group traditions and rituals, resource allocation, role relationships, program priorities, political antagonisms, subgroup fiefdoms, etc.), translated into and by the local school culture, and eventually implemented. The end result may or may not resemble what the policy intended. Supervisors, as players in the local drama, can only do what the local context will allow, even though they may have a missionary-like commitment to the reform policies. Hence, as this book has emphasized,

---

[6] David Holdzkom, "Appraising Teacher Performances in North Carolina," *Educational Leadership,* vol. 44, no. 7, p. 41, April 1987.
    [7] Cf. Allan Odden, "When Votes and Dollars Mingle: A First Analysis of State Reforms," *Politics of Education Bulletin,* vol. 13, no. 12, pp. 3–8, summer 1986.

supervisory effectiveness will depend more on the supervisors' facility in working with the complex realities (culture, power structure, communication dynamics, intergroup rivalries, etc.) of the local context than on the logic and reasonableness of the reform policies.

Thus, supervisors can play a critical role in the current reform effort. They can promote those beneficial elements of the "classroom effectiveness" models, while protecting both teachers and students from a mindless conformity to the more simplistic assumptions and features of those models. As was suggested in various chapters of this book, supervisors not only can promote a reflective practice that ranges over the broader human meanings teachers deal with every day, they ought to. There are times when that necessity becomes, as it were, a moral as well as a professional obligation.

Insofar as the present teacher-evaluation programs stress formative evaluation, rather than judgmental, primitive, summative evaluations, supervisors embracing a human resource development perspective can utilize them to promote the development of teachers. Insofar as the present teacher-evaluation programs are tied to flexible staff-development programs, supervisors espousing human resource development can capitalize on the timeliness and funding behind these programs. Insofar as the present teacher-evaluation programs have created new protocols for observing and analyzing classroom instruction that go beyond the superficial checklists of old, human resource development supervisors can use and adapt them as helpful tools in the reflective practice they are promoting. In all these ways supervisors can use the present climate of reform to promote improved instruction in school. But supervisors need also to remember that there are other issues and questions which the present teacher-evaluation programs do not address.

A LARGER VIEW OF SUPERVISION

One of the disadvantages of supervisory specialization is that it is easy to lose a unified perspective on supervision as a comprehensive process. Some supervisors deal with discrete areas of the curriculum such as science or language arts across the whole school district. Other supervisors occupy positions within individual schools, such as assistant principal for instruction or department chairperson. Some are in charge of beginning teachers; others are in charge of recommending teachers for promotion. Such divisions of supervisory tasks can fragment the view of supervision as one process that touches multiple facets of the schooling enterprise.

Supervision as a process involves multiple activities. It begins with the decision to hire a teacher and proceeds with support efforts for beginning teachers wherein individual strengths are identified and growth targets set. The process complements the supervision of individual teachers with both departmental concerns and schoolwide staff-development concerns. Finally, the supervisory process can marshal all these individual and group efforts toward larger program and schoolwide improvements.

FOCUS ON DEVELOPMENT

Human resource supervision assumes a dynamic environment. Unlike supervisory practices, which focus on control and fitting people into prepackaged job specifications, human resources supervision is aimed at the human and professional growth of the people in the school. Hence the relationship between supervisor and staff is primarily proactive, seeking improvement, development and increased effectiveness based on a shared perception of individual strengths, talents, and interests. In this process supervisors deal with the human and professional needs of the staff from three perspectives. One perspective involves the individual, his or her unique personality and talents, and the seeking of ways to promote a fuller expression of personal strengths in the individual's work. A second perspective involves the supervisor with groups of the staff, where common staff-development concerns are addressed. A third perspective involves program improvement, where supervisor and staff seek ways to increase the school's overall effectiveness.

Frequently these three aspects of the supervisory process are in dynamic interdependence. Figures 19-1, 19-2, and 19-3 illustrate how the three perspectives can function in isolation or in dynamic interaction. Work with individual teachers on increasing their effectiveness in the classroom often relates to achieving program goals more effectively. As individual teachers improve, the program improves and student learning improves. Likewise, a teaching team or department's efforts to improve their program by the use of new resources, such as more sophisticated audiovisual materials, computers, or simulation games, inevitably involves teachers in learning new skills and mastering new methods of teaching. What began as program development merges into staff development. So, too, staff-development workshops that begin by focusing on skill development often lead to program considerations whereby the program gets modified to better accommodate the exercise of these new skills. Thus staff development frequently leads to program development.

FIGURE 19-1
Staff-development orientation.

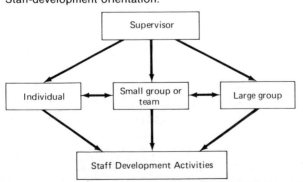

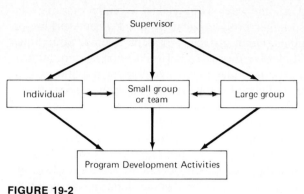

FIGURE 19-2
Program-development orientation.

From this outlook, therefore, we can see that supervision takes place in a dynamic environment. Work with individuals flows frequently into and out of work with groups; work on staff development flows frequently into and out of work on program development. The size of the group keeps shifting from a subgroup in a department to the whole department and then back again to work with individuals. The focus likewise shifts dynamically, moving from clarification of program goals to concentration on specific classroom skills and activities that will promote these goals and then back to program modifications for increased program effectiveness.

A SENSE OF DIRECTION

The supervisor, therefore, must have a larger perspective than improving individual performance. Ultimately the improvement and growth of individual

FIGURE 19-3
Interaction of program and staff development.

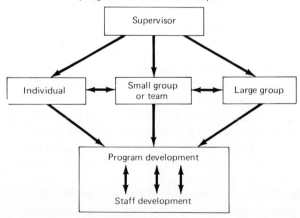

teachers must contribute to and in some way be directed by overall program goals. Supervisors need to keep those larger program goals in mind when working on staff development with individuals, small groups, and departments. Sometimes staff-development activities will involve more general skills such as communication or conflict-resolution skills. At other times staff-development activities will be directly related to acquiring skills needed for increased program effectiveness, such as learning how to manage computer-assisted simulation games or how to introduce students into role-playing exercises. Sometimes a supervisor will be working on an overall staff-development program for the whole faculty and simultaneously be working with individual teachers on more basic growth targets. Through all these multifaceted activities, the supervisor should have a sense of the larger direction to the activities, namely, that the whole department or whole school faculty is moving toward greater program or schoolwide effectiveness. This movement will take place slowly, perhaps over a 3- to 5-year time frame. But it is within this larger sense of direction that most or all of the individual efforts of the supervisor take on significance.

A supervisory process that assumes and promotes this dynamic interaction between staff and program development requires coordination on a school- or districtwide level. When the long-range plans are spelled out, supervisors will need to further refine these into intermediate plans for 1 year to 6 months. Given the dynamic environment assumed above, such planning will obviously include discussions with teachers.

Supervisors should subsequently meet to reflect on how their plans are working out in practice, to pick up creative ideas from one another, and to continue to coordinate their efforts in the immediate future. As a result of these regular meetings, supervisors will be able to advise the top administrators of the school or school district about common organizational dysfunctions, program resource needs, and staff needs that require their attention. This coordination effort will also enable supervisors to work more closely with curriculum specialists in the district whose job it is to facilitate curriculum development. In this way, supervisors help to set the agenda for school reform.

HUMAN RESOURCES SUPERVISION: SUMMING UP

We have tried to show how human resources supervision differs from, and goes beyond, other forms of supervision. We believe that there is sufficient—not extensive enough yet, but still sufficient—evidence from the field of organization and management research to validate this claim.

We believe that when human resources supervision is self-consciously exercised within an organizational setting, it can simultaneously increase the effectiveness of the people involved and their job satisfaction and human growth. The application of this form of supervision to schools leads to some obvious conclusions, which we have touched upon.

At the same time that we developed the rationale for this style of supervision, we were attempting to expose the reader to the dynamics of organizational life. The supervisor functions within that matrix of organizational and bureaucratic activity. If the supervisor knows how the organization works, then he or she can use the potential of the organization for educational purposes, rather than be victimized by unintended, perhaps, but actually dysfunctional aspects of the organization.

Because they are so often at a middle level in the organization, supervisors have access to top-level decision makers as well as to the instructional scene. Because supervisors can interpret the different levels to one another, serve as advocates of now one level, now the other, and tap and coordinate the very considerable resources of the organization as well, they can actually keep the organization on course.

The organization—the school or the school system—was set up to serve a purpose, to provide for the formal education of children. Those at the top are frequently distracted by financial or political concerns from that primary goal. Those individual teachers in the classroom are so close to their own activities that it is difficult for them to see other aspects of the school organization as deserving of equal attention. The supervisor is usually in the best position, then, to help the organization function the way it was intended to. And therefore it is essential, absolutely essential, that supervisors understand how organizations in general and schools in particular function. Without such understanding, they, and all the participants in the school organization will end up floundering their way through crisis after crisis without knowing why things are always turning out so badly.

Every bureaucracy began, as Weber noted,[8] with a charismatic vision or an inspiration. The resulting organization or bureaucracy was a way of enfleshing that vision, making it operative, functional. Organization or bureaucracy ensured an orderly continuation of the vision and intentions of its founders throughout following generations.

Public schools as well as private schools were founded on such visions and inspirations. Some would call these inspirations myths, not in the sense of wild fancies or improbable superstitions, but rather in the sense of beliefs in a possibility that could not be empirically verified at the time, perhaps could never be empirically verified. We have argued that, besides understanding how organizations function and utilizing those managerial skills that will make the organization responsive to human beings, supervisors need to reestablish or clarify what that myth or that vision is for themselves. We have called it a platform because it is a term that is more manageable for our more empirical sensibilities.

Whatever one wants to call it, the organization does not function well when its participants lose sight of the basic purpose of the organization. One of the essential tasks of a human resources supervisor will be to encourage the formulation and/or review of these basic purposes as they are personally appropriated by the staff. In that way, many arguments over ancillary purposes

[8] S. N. Eisenstadt, *Max Weber: On Charisma and Institution Building*, Chicago: University of Chicago Press, 1968.

can be put in their proper perspective and the major focus of people's energies can be kept on the educational purposes of the school.

Finally, human resources supervision acts on very basic beliefs about human nature. We think that these beliefs about human beings are most consistent with our most cherished political and religious beliefs as well as with the expressed purposes of the schools. We know from our own experience as well as from research findings that acting on those beliefs more often than not enables men and women to work together effectively.

These three characteristics of human resources supervision should be highlighted: it is founded on beliefs about human nature that center on human beings as active, responsible, and growing persons; it is exercised with a conscious understanding of organizational dynamics; and its logic and intelligibility are rooted in an educational vision and platform that is both personal and yet legitimated within educational tradition. These three characteristics of human resources supervision give it a power and a direction that we believe enable it to accomplish the upgrading of the quality of education in a local school or school system. And no matter at what higher level of government, plans, laws, projects, and policies are made for the improvement of education, the proof of the pudding will always be found at the local level. If it does not happen there, it does not happen.

Hence, those concerned with the formulation and enactment of public policy should recognize the need for qualifed and committed educators at the local level. The local-level educators, moreover, need to appreciate the issues at stake in the deliberations of state and federal legislators. They will need to be more active in making their voices heard, as well as to listen carefully to the points of view being argued before the legislatures.

We close with this word. Supervision, in our opinion, is entering a phase bright with promise but also one in which supervisors will have to stay alert to the political arena as never before. It can be the best of times or the worst of times—but it will be an exciting time, a time for making history.

A FINAL SALUTE

In closing, we salute those exercising supervisory responsibility in schools. Theirs is a difficult profession, demanding skills, sensitivity, intelligence, and leadership. Upon their shoulders, and the shoulders of their teacher colleagues, rest the brightest hopes of our romance with wisdom through education. This book is a modest attempt to inform their practice. It is an easy thing to write a book, however. It is a great thing to contribute to the development of human beings and human intelligence. Despite the difficulties besetting education today and the work of supervisors in particular, that is a work worth giving one's life to.

INDEX